KING

KING

A LIFE

JONATHAN EIG

**SIMON &
SCHUSTER**

London · New York · Sydney · Toronto · New Delhi

First published in the United States by Farrar, Straus and Giroux, 2023

First published in Great Britain by Simon & Schuster UK Ltd, 2023

1 3 5 7 9 10 8 6 4 2

Simon & Schuster UK Ltd
1st Floor
222 Gray's Inn Road
London WC1X 8HB

www.simonandschuster.co.uk
www.simonandschuster.com.au
www.simonandschuster.co.in

Simon & Schuster Australia, Sydney
Simon & Schuster India, New Delhi

A CIP catalogue record for this book
is available from the British Library

Hardback ISBN: 978-1-4711-8100-9
Trade Paperback ISBN: 978-1-4711-8101-6
eBook ISBN: 978-1-4711-8102-3

Designed by Patrice Sheridan

Printed and Bound in the UK using 100% Renewable
Electricity at CPI Group (UK) Ltd

MIX
Paper | Supporting
responsible forestry
FSC® C171272

FOR JEFFERY

They said to one another,
Behold, this dreamer cometh . . .
Let us slay him . . .
And we shall see what will become of his dreams.

—Genesis 37:19–21 (King James Version)

Contents

PART III

KING

Prologue

On December 5, 1955, a young Black man became one of America's founding fathers. He was twenty-six years old and knew the role he was taking carried a potential death penalty. The place was Montgomery, Alabama, former capital of Alabama's slave trade.

On this day—four generations since the Civil War ended slavery—Montgomery remained a fortress of white supremacy. It was a bastion of the Ku Klux Klan, whose members had endorsed and participated in Alabama's 360 lynchings since Reconstruction.

A nervous crowd of five thousand gathered, filling a big Baptist church and spilling onto the streets. Angry and frightened, they were bracing to challenge an America where Black people were at risk of murder for a casual glance, where the legacy and reality of racial subordination pervaded the land, as proven from lunch counters to oak trees.

As the young Black man prepared to speak, his purpose remained unclear to the protesters, and to him. Would he urge them to stand down, as others had done, or stand up and resist?

His voice lacked the fire of a call to arms: "We are here this evening for serious business."

Until it didn't:

"We are not wrong in what we are doing!"

"If we are wrong, the Supreme Court of this nation is wrong!"

"If we are wrong, the Constitution of the United States is wrong!"

"If we are wrong, God Almighty is wrong!"

For most of the five thousand, it was the first time they had heard the voice of Martin Luther King Jr.

＊

Before King, the promises contained in the Declaration of Independence and the U.S. Constitution had been hollow. King and the other leaders of the twentieth-century civil rights movement, along with millions of ordinary protesters, demanded that America live up to its stated ideals. They fought without muskets, without money, and without political power. They built their revolution on Christian love, on nonviolence, and on faith in humankind.

This book tells the story of the man who, in a career that spanned a mere thirteen years, brought the nation closer than it had ever been to reckoning with the reality of having treated people as property and secondary citizens. That he failed to fully achieve his goal should not diminish his heroism any more than the failure of the original founding fathers diminishes theirs.

To help readers better understand King's struggle, this book seeks to recover the real man from the gray mist of hagiography. In the process of canonizing King, we've defanged him, replacing his complicated politics and philosophy with catchphrases that suit one ideology or another. We've heard the recording of his "I Have a Dream" speech so many times we don't really hear it anymore; we no longer register its cry for America to recognize the "unspeakable horrors of police brutality" or its petition for economic reparations. We don't appreciate that King was making demands, not wishes. "In a sense, we've come to our nation's capital to cash a check," he said that summer day in 1963 as he stood at the foot of Abraham Lincoln's statue. We've mistaken King's nonviolence for passivity. We've forgotten that his approach was more aggressive than anything the country had seen—that he used peaceful protest as a lever to force those in power to give up many of the privileges they'd hoarded. We've failed to recall that King was one of the most brutally divisive figures in American history—attacked not only by segregationists in the South but also by his own government, by more militant Black activists, and by white northern liberals. He was deliberately mischaracterized in his lifetime, and he remains so today.

King was a man, not a saint, not a symbol. He chewed his fingernails. He shouted at the TV during quiz shows. He hid his cigarettes from his children. He had a little white dog named Topsy. He bore a scar on his chest where, in 1958, surgeons extricated an ivory-handled letter opener lodged beside his aorta. He had skin so sensitive he couldn't use a razor. He slept poorly but napped well. He ran chronically late for meetings. As an adolescent, he twice attempted suicide, although perhaps halfheartedly. As an adult, he was hospitalized repeatedly for what he called exhaustion and others described as depression. He possessed a wicked sense of humor, improved by the knowledge that certain jokes were funnier coming from a Baptist minister. He depended on his wife, Coretta, in ways few people understood at the time. He also cheated on her, continually, even when he knew the FBI was tapping his phones and bugging his hotel rooms, trying to destroy his marriage and reputation. He maintained one intimate relationship for so long that friends referred to the woman as his second wife.

He was a man who announced at an early age that God had called him to act. He lived his life accordingly. And he was willing to die.

———— ⚫ ————

Martin Luther King Jr. has been the subject of excellent biographies and exhaustive scholarship, but even now the literature remains incomplete. This book is based on thousands of recently released FBI documents and tens of thousands of other new items—including personal letters, business records, White House telephone recordings, oral histories, unaired television footage, and unpublished biographies and autobiographies of people close to King. This is the first biography to make use of thousands of pages of materials that belonged to the man who served as the SCLC's official historian, L. D. Reddick, as well as the first to benefit from the discovery of audiotapes recorded by Coretta King in the months after her husband's death, and an unpublished memoir written by King's father. This book is also built on hundreds of interviews with people who knew King, including family members and close friends, many of them willing to speak more openly than ever thanks to the passage of time.

The book represents an attempt to observe King's life as it was lived—and through that life to better understand his times and our own.

The portrait that emerges here may trouble some people. But those closest to King saw his flaws all along and understood that his power grew from his ability to grapple with contradiction, to wrestle with doubt just as his biblical heroes did. "Great men . . . have not been boasters and buffoons," wrote Emerson, "but perceivers of the terror of life, and have manned themselves to face it."

King faced it, and challenged his followers to face it, too. He asked his supporters to love Birmingham lawman Theophilus Eugene "Bull" Connor, FBI director J. Edgar Hoover, and others who enforced the laws and customs of white supremacy. King understood that President Lyndon B. Johnson could be one of his greatest allies and one of his most dangerous enemies. He pushed white liberals to confront their own racist behaviors, even as it cost him their support. King felt despair. He felt misunderstood. But when pressure against him grew and he might have backed down, he stepped up, time after time, despite the obvious risk. He warned that materialism undermined our moral values, that nationalism threatened to crush all hope of universal brotherhood, that militarism bred cynicism and distrust. He saw a moral rot at the core of American life and worried that racism had blinded many of us to it.

He called himself "a victim of deferred dreams, of blasted hope."

He also insisted that "we must never lose infinite hope."

He never did.

PART I

1

The Kings of Stockbridge

TAKE THIS BUCKET of milk to the neighbors, Delia King told her son Michael one day.

Delia and her husband, Jim King, lived with their growing brood of children in a tiny wooden sharecroppers' shack in Stockbridge, Georgia, about twenty miles southeast of Atlanta. The shack and the land around it belonged to a white man. The white man kept most of the money from the crops, but it was the King family, one generation removed from slavery, that cleared the soil stone by stone, planted and picked the cotton, and went hungry when the scorching sun rendered the earth no more fertile than a rutted road. Yet when Delia heard that her neighbor had a sick cow that wouldn't give milk, she acted without hesitation.

"She was a very devout Christian," recalled Michael, who would go on to change his name to Martin Luther King Sr. "I remember, as a small boy, my mother was a woman who shared what she had with others," he said in a newly discovered set of audiotaped interviews he made for an unpublished autobiography.

Michael was about twelve years old when his mother sent him on his mission that bright summer day around 1910. As he carried his bucket, he paused in front of a sawmill where he watched burly men and oxen at work, hauling timber. A voice snapped him to attention. It was the white mill owner: "Say, boy, run get a bucket of water for my men from down at the stream."

Apologizing, Michael told the mill owner he was on an errand. He needed to go. The mill owner grabbed Michael by his shirt and kicked over his bucket of milk. As Michael bent to pick up the bucket, the white man's boot connected with the boy's ear. He tumbled. He tried to rise, but a fist smashed his face. Blood poured from his mouth. Everything went hazy.

Michael got up, ran home, and spotted his mother in the yard, washing clothes in an iron tub set over a fire. Delia scanned her son's blood-crusted face and torn shirt.

"Who did this to you, Michael?" she asked, voice low and tight.

The boy didn't answer.

"*Michael!*" Delia screamed. "*Who did this?*"

Delia marched to the mill, squeezing her son's wrist as she tugged him along. She found the owner.

"Did you do this to my child?" She locked eyes with the man.

"Woman! You lost your mind? Get the hell outta here before I—"

Delia screamed: "Did you do this to my child?"

"Yeah..."

She lowered her shoulder and rammed the mill owner in his chest, knocking him into the side of a shed. She forced him to the ground and hammered at his face with hands and arms hardened by a lifetime of manual labor. When one of the mill workers tried to pull her away, Delia punched him, too. The others backed off.

"You can kill me! But if you put a hand on a child of mine, you'll answer."

Delia balled her fists, ready for more, but the mill owner wanted none of it.

Back home, Delia cleaned her son's face. She warned him not to tell his father what had happened. A Black woman might get away with beating a white man, but a Black *man* would likely pay with his life.

Soon, though, Jim King heard about the mill owner's attack on his son. As Delia had feared, Jim grabbed a rifle and went to the mill bent on revenge. The owner wasn't there. That night, a mob of white men on horseback rode to the Kings' shack. Jim King knew the law offered no protection, so he did the only thing he could think of to save himself and his family: he ran. He took off into the woods and stayed away through the summer and into the fall.

Delia became sick. The cotton crop suffered, and the vegetables got picked too late. The family struggled to survive the winter.

Months later, Michael heard from a friend that the mill owner was no longer angry. Things could go back to normal, the friend said. Jim King came home, but normal was not an option. "I'm gonna blow one of these crackers' heads off," he told his son. Jim drank heavily and argued forcefully with Delia. When he left the house, he went alone, and took his rifle. He tried to shoot something his family could eat, but he was often too drunk to *see* a rabbit, much less hit one.

"I just wondered what was normal for us," Michael recalled, "and how long we could expect it to last."

Michael King's parents were born in the so-called Reconstruction years immediately following the Civil War. Men and women recently released from slavery purchased land, started churches, and built communities. They voted, too, electing more than two thousand Black public officials, including a governor in Louisiana, ten Black members of the U.S. House of Representatives, and two U.S. senators. The historian Eric Foner described Reconstruction as "a radical experiment in interracial democracy," during which formerly enslaved laborers became free laborers.

But the experiment failed. As W. E. B. Du Bois wrote, "The slave went free; stood a brief moment in the sun; then moved back again toward slavery."

The white backlash to Black people's gains was immediate—and vicious.

The U.S. government permitted white elected officials in the South to address the so-called Negro problem as they liked. Racial animosity metastasized. A system of land rental, known as sharecropping, forced Black farmers into a relationship with white landowners that was deeply exploitative. Factory owners and financiers in the North went along, for the most part, silenced by the profits generated by cheap labor. White officials in the South concluded that Black people were not only inferior, and therefore unfit to be treated as equal citizens, but also a threat to their physical safety. Southern lawmakers passed codes to establish systems of peonage not far removed from slavery. By the start of the twentieth century, every state in the South had laws designed to divide the races and subordinate Black people. The segregation rules—commonly known as Jim Crow laws—mandated separation of the races: in schools, trains, theaters, churches, hotels, hospitals, barbershops, restrooms, orphanages, prisons, funeral homes, cemeteries, and elsewhere. Jim Crow laws prohibited Black and white people from playing checkers, dominos, and card games together in their own homes. Marriage between races was forbidden, too. For many in the white community, the greatest fear of all was miscegenation, which would blur the line they had worked so hard to create and enforce. For others, the greatest fear was a reordering of power.

Supporters viewed the Jim Crow laws as a system of controls, like dams and dikes, designed to preserve the natural order as they perceived it. In 1896, the U.S. Supreme Court gave legal sanction to segregation in *Plessy v. Ferguson*, creating a standard of "separate but equal" that was anything but equal.

Atlanta became the unofficial capital of the booming, divided South. It was in Atlanta, in 1895, that the Black educator Booker T. Washington proposed his famous compromise, saying Black people would at least for the upcoming future accept separation of the races if the white community, in return, took responsibility for improving the skills and social conditions of Black people. But Washington's critics feared that such a compromise would leave Black people permanently subservient. Georgia, as W. E. B. Du Bois wrote in 1903, became "the centre of the Negro problem,—the centre of those nine million men who are America's dark heritage from slavery and the slave-trade."

Jim King—born the year before the abolition of chattel slavery—personified the crushing frustrations of Black life in the South. He never learned to read or write. He never voted. He never owned property. Instead, he lived in a perpetual state of debt to the white men for whom he farmed. He grew lean, edgy, and angry. America hadn't given Jim King much, and then, bit by bit, it took away what little he had managed to accumulate, leaving frustration, travail, and rage. That's how his son Michael described it. The

American dream, built on promises written into the nation's founding documents, lost all meaning. Jim King drank until he had "a look of very quiet but very serious fire in his eyes," wrote his son, until he no longer cared, "not about living, not about pain, not about his anger or anything else."

Delia, ten years younger than her husband, held the family together. Born Delia Linsey in Ellenwood, Georgia, she, too, had grown up on a white-owned farm. Her father, Jim Long, had been used in slavery to sire children, to build up the owner's supply of enslaved laborers and boost the owner's return on investment in human property. Enslaved women were the victims of these forced sexual encounters. Delia's mother, Jane Linsey, born in 1853, gave birth to her first child at the age of sixteen and went on to have four more, without marrying. By 1880, the federal census reported that Jane was twenty-seven, the mother of five, single, not widowed or divorced, with no occupation other than "keeping home." Jim Long appears on the next page of the census, living nearby at the age of thirty-six, married to a woman named Francis, with ten more children.

Delia Linsey married Jim King in Henry County on August 20, 1895. On the marriage license, Delia's maiden name was spelled Lindsey. Five years later, the Kings were living in Ellenwood, where Jim worked as a day laborer and Delia took care of their daughter Woodie and their son Michael. Another son, Lucius, died at some point during infancy. In addition to farming, Jim King worked part-time at a rock quarry until an accident in the quarry took one of his fingers and made further work there impossible. By 1910, the Kings were farming cotton in Stockbridge and raising seven children.

Federal census reports show that Delia King didn't know how to read or write in 1900 or 1910. But by 1920, at age forty-five, she had learned, most likely by reading the Bible. When she wasn't giving birth, feeding children, cooking for her family, sewing, washing, planting vegetables, or picking cotton, Delia cleaned and ironed clothes for white families. When it rained, the roof leaked. When ice-cold wind blew through the cracks in the flimsy walls, the family crowded around the fireplace, Michael recalled, "while our backs shivered." They had no running water and no indoor toilet. "But Mama was at peace with herself," Michael wrote, "because of her abiding faith." No matter what misfortune befell her, Delia King would never "close her eyes so tight in sorrow or rage that she did not see God's hand reaching out to her."

Every Sunday, Delia and the children walked to church, carrying their shoes so as not to wear them out. They alternated between Methodist and Baptist churches. Jim King did not attend either one. "He didn't care anything about church," Michael recalled. "He wouldn't go to church . . . My daddy would work all week and at the end of the week he would get drunk and then scrap with my mother . . . I got to where I hated Saturdays and Sundays for what my father was going to do and how he was going to act up." But as long as Delia and the children were in church, they were safe from Jim King's anger.

Black Baptists outnumbered white Baptists in Georgia. Black culture and Black political activism rose from the pews and pulpits of the Black church. For many, religion offered release from the pain of ordinary life. Black Baptist preachers frequently imparted the radical message that *all* people were free and equal under God's laws, that the rules and regulations handed down by white men were wrong, that the racial hierarchies invented by men to justify slavery were false and craven, that the savagery of the Ku Klux Klan and the segregation laws of the South were abominations in the eyes of God, and that God would never love one group of people more than another based on the color of their skin. Prayers and hymns eased Delia King's suffering. They offered hope that her children and grandchildren might live to see a better day. Faith in God also helped create a sense of community. Hog-killing time, for example, brought a festive sense of community and a living reminder of the spirit of Jesus's love. As Michael King would recall years later, those who owned animals big enough to slaughter shared meat with those in need, knowing they would be repaid in kind one day. "That kind of sharing was to me Christianity in action," he said.

Martin Luther King Jr., Delia's grandson, would often remark on the role Christianity played in the lives of the enslaved and indentured. The land they farmed was not their own. The crops they planted and sowed were not their own. Their bodies were not entirely their own. But their souls, he said, would *never* belong to a plantation owner, a landlord, a hooded Klansman, a prison warden, a sheriff, a senator, or anybody else; their souls would always be free.

"So many things stood there to discourage them," Martin Luther King Jr. said, "but the old preacher would come up with his broken language. He would look out to them and said, 'Friends, you ain't no nigger. You ain't no slave, but you God's chillun.'"

They were not educated, King said, "but they knew God." They knew that the God they worshipped would not punish some of his children and exalt others. "And, so," he continued, "although they knew that some days they had to go out into the field in their bare feet, that didn't stop them. And they could sing in their broken language:

> I got shoes, you got shoes,
> All of God's chillun got shoes.
> When I get to heaven gonna put on my shoes
> And just walk all over God's heaven."

Much of the King family's history can't be traced back before the Civil War. Owners prevented the enslaved from learning to read and write. Births and deaths often went unrecorded. Tax collectors and census takers treated Black people as property, their names not worth noting. In the first census after the Civil War, taken in 1870, Jim King appears to be recorded as a five-year-old named James Branham of Eatonton, Georgia, in Putnam County. Jim's age and the ages of his parents—listed as Nathan and Malinda Branham—match the ages of King's ancestors, suggesting perhaps that the family chose to drop the Branham name, which was a vestige of enslavement, and become Kings in freedom.

Tax records show that Jim and Delia King worked on a farm owned by a white man named William B. Martin, on land in Stockbridge partially occupied today by a Walmart Supercenter.

Michael King, father of Martin Luther King Jr., was born in 1897, the second child of Jim and Delia. "My mother was way over on the Indian side, and my father was a mixture of Negro, Irish, and Indian," he once said. "I never knew where my father was born or who his parents were." Jim and Delia eventually had ten children. They heated water for bathing and cooking on a "two-eyed kitchen stove" and made their underclothes from flour sacks, as Michael later recalled. The demands of farmwork, combined with impoverished schools, meant the children went to school "two or three months a year in poorly equipped rural, one-room schools manned by semi-literate teachers only slightly better prepared than the children entrusted to them," he wrote. No amount of labor would make tenant farming profitable for the Kings.

After Delia's attack on the mill owner and Jim's flight from the white mob, the family never again felt secure, Michael recalled. Jim King's drinking destabilized everything. "He forgot things he was supposed to do," his son wrote, "broke up tools when he got mad, and stayed away from the little shack we had moved into. He'd be gone for days at a time. When he came back he'd be yelling and ordering everybody around with threats." One day he came home "full of whiskey," his eyes half shut, jaw slackened. As the children watched, Jim slapped Delia in the face.

"Don't you hit my mama," Michael said as he wrestled his father to the floor in his mother's defense.

"I'll kill you," the father screamed at his son. "I'll do it, damn you . . . !"

Michael took the threat seriously and fled to the woods. But he didn't disappear for long, and he didn't turn to alcohol or violence. He turned to God.

"I needed help," he wrote, "and at least I knew that."

He prayed and went home.

Soon after, while everyone slept, Michael King slipped past his brothers and sisters, snuck out of the house, and headed down the road. He walked barefoot, his shoes slung over his shoulder on a string. The year was 1912. He was fourteen years old and bound for Atlanta.

2

Martin Luther

MICHAEL KING LIED about his age and landed a job shoveling coal for a railroad company in Atlanta. He slept on a pallet in a toolshed in the railyard. He was big for his years, and rugged, too. He could read but couldn't write. He impressed his bosses and earned promotion to the dangerous job of fireman, firing coal for steam engines.

"Pretty soon they thought of me as a young bull who could make steam and be a good nigger, too," he said, the latter meaning that he knew how to show obedience.

But Michael King wanted to preach. He shuttled between Atlanta and Stockbridge. While he helped with chores on the family farm, he practiced delivering eulogies for dead chickens, praising each for a life well lived and "assuring survivors and the congregation that its soul was safe in the bosom of the Almighty." By December 1917, he had made up his mind that the Christian ministry would be his life's work. He had once heard a Methodist bishop talk to his parishioners "as if they were dogs," he recalled, and he "wanted no part of that kind of tyranny." In the Baptist church, he said, "I found the most freedom and the greatest potential for growth and service."

On September 12, 1918, when he was twenty years old, he registered for the draft, describing himself as a farmer still working for a white landowner in Stockbridge. But he was a man in transition. By 1920, he had settled in Atlanta and begun working steadily as a preacher. Soon, he was renting a comfortable room in a boardinghouse and driving a used Model T Ford purchased for him by his mother following the sale of a cow. He found work

at several churches, reciting Bible verses from memory and improvising sermons based on those he'd heard at Floyd Chapel Baptist Church in Stockbridge. In the early twentieth century, Georgia was home to 334,000 Black
Baptists, more than any other state. Black churches needed preachers—even
young, inexperienced, unschooled preachers such as the Reverend Michael
King.

More than 90 percent of America's ten million people of African
ancestry—Negroes, as polite people called them at the time—lived in the
South in the first decades of the century, usually in segregated communities.
They were obstructed from voting and placed in inferior schools. Their sewer
service, their garbage pickup, their recreational facilities, their law enforcement operations, and their health-care facilities were inferior to those found
in white communities. Between 1885 and 1930, more than four thousand
Black people were lynched as part of the enforcement of racial segregation
and subordination. But a growing number of southern Black people, urged
on by teachers and preachers, refused to accept second-class status without
a struggle. Literacy rates rose rapidly among the children and grandchildren
of enslaved people. Young men and women with ambition left the South to
escape the blatant and often violent discrimination. Their ranks included
Michael King's older sister, Woodie, who moved to Detroit, as well as the
young A. Philip Randolph, who left Florida for New York, where he worked
by day, took classes by night, and, in 1925, organized the Brotherhood of
Sleeping Car Porters, the nation's first predominantly Black labor union.

Others with ambition, like Michael King, remained in the South but
moved from small towns to big cities, where they, too, discovered power in
numbers. As Atlanta grew and diversified, the movement for racial justice
gained force. Atlanta University, a school for Black students, had an integrated faculty that included W. E. B. Du Bois, the first Black man to earn
a doctorate from Harvard. Du Bois proposed a strategy of "ceaseless agitation," using education, litigation, lobbying, and physical resistance to win
rights.

Michael King recalled the preachers back in Stockbridge "carrying a
coat-pocket full of pencils they didn't know how to use," trying to hide their

illiteracy. Burning with ambition, he registered for classes at the Bryant Preparatory School, a private Baptist institution established to educate children not served by public schools, as well as adults. When told he would have to join the fifth grade, based on his reading and writing abilities, the broad-shouldered, barrel-chested King humbled himself and squeezed into his seat in the classroom.

King glimpsed a bright future in Atlanta, and he meant to be part of it. Atlanta was also at the heart of an increasingly well-organized national campaign of resistance to segregation. The National Association for the Advancement of Colored People (NAACP), founded in 1909 and focused on using litigation to attack the Jim Crow regime, had a strong branch in Atlanta. Its leaders included John Hope, president of Atlanta University; Harry Pace, an executive at the Standard Life Insurance Company; Benjamin J. Davis, editor of *The Atlanta Independent*; and Adam Daniel Williams, pastor of the Ebenezer Baptist Church.

Williams, known as A.D., was a short, stocky man, his back and shoulders thickened from years of manual labor in his native Greene County, Georgia, eighty miles east of Atlanta. His parents had been enslaved—owned by a white man named William Nelson Williams. A.D.'s father, Willis Williams, had been a preacher *and* an enslaved person. A.D., born around 1860, had lost his right thumb in a sawmill accident. Determined to work with his mind rather than his body, he left Greene County, moved to Atlanta, and enrolled at Atlanta Baptist College, which would later become Morehouse College. In 1894, when he took over Ebenezer Baptist Church, the church had thirteen members and a burdensome mortgage. But Williams's sermons and his wife's music inspired a following, and the church grew. A. D. Williams became one of the most popular and influential Black Baptist preachers in the South. He was a country preacher adapting fast to the city. One Sunday, when he overheard a few schoolteachers snickering about his poor grammar, he pulled one of the teachers aside and reminded her of a time, not long ago, when the church had been raising its building fund. "I have give a hundred dollars," he told the teacher, "while the man with the good speech have give nothin'!"

For Williams, theology and social action were like voices in the choir, better together than apart. When the city proposed a bond issue for schools that included no money for construction of a public high school for Black students, he used the pulpit to organize a protest. When he tired of seeing racial slurs printed in one of the city's white-owned newspapers, *The Atlanta Georgian*, he and other preachers encouraged their followers to boycott the paper's advertisers. In 1920, Williams persuaded the NAACP to hold its national convention in Atlanta, the first time the meeting had taken place in the South.

Reverend Williams and his wife, Jennie Celeste Williams, had three children but only one who survived infancy: a daughter named Alberta. She was short, solidly built, and self-conscious about her looks. But she possessed a hundred-watt smile, a sweet shyness, and a sharp mind. In the interviews he recorded for his unpublished autobiography, Martin Luther King Sr. said he heard about Alberta before seeing or meeting her. He was attending services at Ebenezer when a preacher filling in for Reverend Williams made mention of the reverend's only daughter. "As he talked about this only daughter, I was quite impressed," he said. "I had never seen or talked with her. I had said to some of the boys around there, that's going to be my wife." Ambition, not attraction, seemed to drive him.

"She would not even spit on you," one of King's friends said.

"You watch what I tell you," he answered. "She's going to be my wife."

While it was true that he was a good-looking young man and the owner of a Model T in respectable condition, the rest of his romantic résumé was thin. His finances were shaky, his wardrobe shabby, and his reading, writing, and speech ragged. He admitted that, yes, the preacher's daughter might be out of his league. But Michael King had confidence and drive. As he traveled around Georgia to preach, congregations sometimes paid him with bushels of potatoes or farm animals, which he traded for gasoline or secondhand shoes. His preaching, he said, "was rooted in the emotional appeal that country Baptists understood better than anybody in the world." But he was careful not to let emotional appeal lead him to "early entanglements" with country women. He didn't want to wind up back on the farm.

Back in Stockbridge, Michael King's young friends had often teased him for smelling like a barn after his morning chores. He had shot back at them, "I may *smell* like a mule, but I sure don't think like one!" He maintained the same stubbornness now in his determination to capture the attention of Alberta Williams. He walked slowly along Auburn Avenue every day, waiting to catch her eye. One evening, to his delight, she appeared on the front porch of her home and smiled, supplying all the encouragement he needed. Day after day he went to see her. He marveled at the fact that she "spoke so well, so clearly, and she put so many words together so well in one sentence." He struggled to keep up. He told her, in his own description of the dialogue, "Well, I'se preachin' in two places . . . Ain't been here but a short while."

But he had plans.

"Why, Reverend King," said the woman who ran the boardinghouse where Michael lived, as she watched him leaving in his best white shirt and with his shoes shined to a high polish, "you must be fixin' to court some nice young lady."

"No ma'am," he said. "I'm fixin' to get married."

At first, Jennie Williams objected to Michael King's request for permission to marry Alberta. But A. D. Williams defended the young man, saying, "Wife, this King has nothing. He has no money, no church, nothing. But my thought is, wife, that all he hasn't, in time he will have and more. Because he is a man of integrity and honesty."

Even so, Williams insisted that the young man wooing his daughter would have to wait and prove his worth. "It's going to be different here in a few years, King," he said. Black people were speaking up and acting out in bold new ways. Marcus Garvey's "Back to Africa" movement won countless thousands of supporters. America was changing, "whether the white man can handle it or not," said Reverend Williams to Reverend King. "There may be a lot of difficult times, and I hope you're a young man ready to deal with it."

Michael King waited more than six years for his chance to marry Alberta

Christine Williams. He joined parishioners for picnics, tea parties, and boat rides, until everyone at the church knew him and knew his intentions. He called Alberta his "bunch of goodness," because she brightened everything and everyone around her. Eventually, he shortened it to the nickname by which he would call her the rest of her life: Bunch.

Alberta studied at Spelman College, while Michael enrolled at Morehouse. Both schools had been built on land donated by John D. Rockefeller, the white oil magnate and philanthropist, and established to improve educational opportunities for Black people, Spelman for women and Morehouse for men. Morehouse professors were among the most respected Black men and women in town. Graduates joined a club that would define them and shape much of the rest of their lives. At first, Michael King failed his Morehouse entrance exam. Undeterred, he marched into the office of Dr. John Hope, the college president, and pleaded for a chance to prove himself. Dr. Hope granted King admission to the school without making him retake the test. He failed freshman English twice, finally passing the class in summer school, with a D for his grade. He failed other classes, too. But one lesson stuck, he said: Morehouse men didn't quit.

Michael King told Alberta that he could see their future. He would get his college degree and become the minister of a big church. They would marry, buy a brick house on Atlanta's Bishops Row, and start a family. Jim Crow be damned, he said. He and Bunch would live the American dream.

The courtship continued even when Alberta moved to Virginia for eighteen months to pursue a teaching certificate. She urged Michael to continue his education and tutored him in some of the subjects he'd missed as a child. She was the more educated of the two, and she had the deeper background in the church. At times, however, Alberta couldn't believe Michael found her attractive. She would one day tell her family that she felt as if professional aspiration more than amorous feelings had fueled his romantic pursuit. Michael's friends teased him about the same thing, saying he was marrying for status, lining himself up to join one of Atlanta's more prominent Black families and to lead Ebenezer Baptist Church.

When the wedding invitations finally went out, Michael King was identified in handsome calligraphy as Reverend Michael Luther King, marking the earliest known use of a middle name that was almost certainly not given at birth. The wedding took place on Thanksgiving Day, November 25, 1926, in Ebenezer's sanctuary. The newlyweds lived in a second-story bedroom in the Williamses' home on Auburn Avenue. It was a square, Queen Anne–style house, built in 1895 for a family of German immigrants, set back almost forty feet from the street, perched on a small hill, surrounded by elm and sycamore trees. A covered porch wrapped around two sides. Sunlight beamed through big second-story windows.

At the start of the new year, 1927, Reverend King became the associate pastor of Ebenezer Baptist Church, working alongside his father-in-law. On September 11, Alberta gave birth to a daughter, Willie Christine King. They called her Christine, or Chris.

A second child arrived sixteen months later, at around noon on January 15, 1929. Alberta delivered the baby at home, in the master bedroom, while Michael waited outside in the hallway. Alberta's second pregnancy had been difficult, the labor requiring heavy sedation. When the baby finally emerged, a mournful silence filled the room. The boy lay motionless, seemingly lifeless. Finally, a slap on the child's bottom brought a cry, relief, and celebration.

"I hear that I was a burden to you in the period before I was born," the boy would tease his mother in later years. "Was I worth it?"

Alberta King would smile and tell her son that, yes, of course he was worth it.

They named him Michael King, no middle name, no initial, no "Junior." They called him Little Mike.

In 1930, when a government census-taker visited the King household, he recorded "Marvin L. King" as the head of the household. His one-year-old son was recorded as "Marvin L. King Jr." After a few years, the elder Michael King began listing his name in church programs as "M. L. King." He later told one of his grandchildren that the decision to change his first name from Michael to Martin, and to make Martin Luther King his full name, was clinched during a 1934 trip to Germany, where King learned more about the sixteenth-century German friar Martin Luther, who purportedly nailed his ninety-five theses to the door of the Wittenberg Castle Church in an act that split Western Christianity and led to the Protestant Reformation.

"He really related to Martin Luther," said Isaac Newton Farris Jr., King's grandson. "He had that same fighting spirit in him."

The switch would prove brilliant. "Martin Luther" gave the King name distinction. It served as a kind of honorific. It linked the King men to a fearless religious reformer who held fast to his beliefs despite excommunication and threats of death. As Martin Luther King Jr. would say years later, "Both father and I have fought all our lives for reform, and perhaps we've earned our right to the name." Luther, like the Kings, was often bedeviled by uncertainty, but he knew that his faith was stronger than his doubt. The name also connected the twentieth-century Kings to one of Martin Luther's key theological and personal insights: that a Christian is *simul justus et peccator*— both righteous *and* sinful.

Martin Luther King Jr.'s name would one day grace a national holiday, a national monument, and a thousand streets. But at home, as a boy, he was Little Mike or, more often, M.L.

3

Sweet Auburn

MARTIN LUTHER KING Jr. had the good luck to be born and raised on Auburn Avenue in Atlanta.

Sweet Auburn, as area residents called it, was a magical place, partially buffered from the racist rituals and rules that applied across most of the South. The Black Atlantans who lived there declared their pride in big bold letters on painted wooden signs: GATE CITY BARBER SHOP, DESOTO SHAVING PARLOR, ZIG-ZAG BILLIARD PARLOR, HOLLOWAY'S JEWELRY. One writer called it "the richest Negro street in the world."

Sweet Auburn had its origins in violence. In 1906, a series of exaggerated newspaper reports had described assaults by Black men on white women in Atlanta. Violence erupted throughout the city, leaving at least a dozen dead and hundreds injured, most of the victims Black. In the aftermath of the violence, many Black small-business owners relocated from the central business district to the safer enclave of Auburn Avenue. At the same time, many white business owners on Auburn Avenue fled. Depressed real estate prices made it possible for the Reverend A. D. Williams to build his church on the corner of Jackson Street and Auburn Avenue.

Georgia's deeply furrowed racism made Sweet Auburn's relative prosperity and independence more precious. In 1926, the white businessman and civic leader Ivan Allen Sr. launched a campaign that attracted 679 factories, sales offices, and warehouses to the city in a span of four years. Allen boasted of Atlanta's climate, its schools, and its "intelligent, adaptable, Anglo-Saxon workforce," making clear, as the writer Gary Pomerantz put it, "that neither

immigrants nor blacks would stand in the way of prosperity." On Sweet Auburn, where Black people owned banks and bookstores, insurance companies and funeral homes, nightclubs and newspapers, freedom felt like both a
gift and a provocation. The possibilities were both frightening and thrilling.
Black children who earned good grades in school also earned the chance to
study in nearby colleges with Black professors who had been educated in the
North and had bold new ideas about what they and their students could do
with their lives. The *Atlanta Daily World*, the nation's first successful daily
newspaper produced by and for Black people, listed the achievements of its
readers and encouraged them to set even loftier goals. On Sundays, Black
preachers, including A. D. Williams and Martin Luther King Sr., offered
soaring sermons to fill worshippers with the hope that one day all of America
would be as sweet as Sweet Auburn, if not sweeter.

One morning in the spring of 1931, while getting ready for church, Williams collapsed and died. The sound of his fall "shook the house," recalled
Christine King, who was three years old at the time. At first, Martin Luther King Sr. didn't want to take over for his father-in-law at Ebenezer, as he
recalled in interviews. Ebenezer had financial trouble and a declining membership, and King had developed a strong following at another church, one
he didn't name. But Alberta didn't want to leave the church "where she had
worshiped since birth," said King, who agreed to follow his wife's wishes.
The church welcomed its new pastor with an elegant banquet that included
a four-course meal served by uniformed waiters. The tables were arranged
with spring flowers, green and yellow candles, and bowls filled with green
and yellow mints. It didn't take long for Reverend King to win over the members of the church and for attendance to begin to climb.

W. E. B. Du Bois described the job of a Black preacher as "a leader, a
politician, an orator, 'boss,' an intriguer, an idealist." King thus enjoyed a
position of prestige in the community. As a member of the church's first family, young M.L. enjoyed a position of prestige, too, and he was expected to
live up to his princely status. He usually did: he was a friendly, kind, and
obedient child.

The King family continued to live in the Williams home on Auburn

Avenue. On the block where M.L. grew up, the heads of households were business owners, porters, laborers, and servants. A small grocery store sat across the street from the King home. When he was three years old, M.L. made friends with a white boy whose father owned the store. "We always felt free to play our childhood games together," M.L. wrote years later in a college essay. "He did not live in our community, but he was usually around every day until about 6:00 . . . At the age of six we both entered school— separate schools of course." Even then, in late afternoons and on weekends, M.L. sought out his friend. He later struggled to understand why their friendship faded. That's when the white boy told M.L. that it wasn't just the start of school that had caused the separation; it was the color of M.L.'s skin. The boy was no longer permitted to play with Black children.

Shocked, M.L. asked his parents to explain one evening as they sat at the family's dinner table. "For the first time I was made aware of the existence of a race problem," he wrote. "I had never been conscious of it before."

Alberta King consoled her son. "You're as good as anyone," she said.

M.L. described this as a formative experience. He would remember and recount it several times over the rest of his life. He revised a few of the details with repetition, but the aching pain of lost friendship compounded by his new knowledge of racism never changed. When his mother told M.L. he was as good as anyone, she implied that there were others who didn't think so and raised an issue that would shape her son's life, as it would shape the lives of many others. Why am I defined and categorized? Why am I judged?

"I was greatly shocked," he wrote, "and from that moment on I was determined to hate every white person."

His story was hardly unusual. "Every black child in the South has an experience of racism that shafts his soul," wrote James Farmer, the civil rights activist, who was nine years older than Martin Luther King Jr. and had his own such story. "For the lucky, it is like a bolt of lightning, striking one to his knees. For the others, a gradual dying, a sliver of meanness working its way to the heart." As W. E. B. Du Bois's biographer David Levering Lewis has written, the truth of such stories may lie as much in their moral validity as in their factual accuracy. When he told the story of his shattered boyhood friendship, Martin Luther King Jr. never mentioned the white boy's name or said what became of him. That wasn't his point. His point was to show that children were not born racist. He also sought to describe how skin colors had been accorded unequal values in American society, how those values shaped the lives of Black and white Americans, how those values in turn shaped the nation, and how his dawning awareness forged his inner strength just as his father's had been forged and had compelled him to escape from Stockbridge.

M.L.'s determination to hate every white person faded quickly, but his determination to fight racism never diminished.

"You just wait and see," the six-year-old M.L. told his family, "I'm going to get me some *big* words."

M.L. heard his father preach big words from the pulpit—big words such as "sanctify," "grace," "forgiveness," and "benevolence." He heard big words lofted to heaven by his mother's choir and big words read from the Bible and burned into his memory, words that forged his identity, and placed him in relationship with God. He worked to master an impressive vocabulary. The right words, he once said, were like his grandmother's biscuits—so good he felt he had to "run around the community and share them." Big words baked inside him from an early age and fueled an outsize sense of ambition.

He loved books before he could read, took comfort in their solidity, in their promise of conversations to come, and surrounded himself with them the way other children surrounded themselves with stuffed animals and blankets, although he did not specify which books from childhood shaped his extraordinary mind. He memorized long passages from the Bible. He learned hymns and, with his mother on piano, sang for church groups and conventions. He adored attention, competing not only with his siblings but also with his father, who stood and preached every Sunday before rapturous audiences. When his parents were away from home, their father's church secretary, Lillian Watkins, babysat the King children. One of their favorite games was "church," and M.L. always did the preaching.

When he was only four, M.L. snuck into Yonge Street Elementary School with his sister, Christine, passing himself off as her classmate. M.L.'s mother permitted her son to attempt this act of deception, and M.L. got away with it for several months, nabbed only when a teacher heard him boasting about his upcoming birthday and a cake with "five big candles on it." When he enrolled legitimately at the all-Black school in 1935, he won promotion to the second grade after half a year.

M.L. was sixteen months younger than his sister and eighteen months older than his brother, Alfred Daniel, whom everyone called A.D. The siblings were so close in age that birth order mattered little. They were peers, playmates, and rivals, their interactions shaped by personality more than age. Christine had a bedroom on the first floor of their house, while M.L. and A.D. shared a messy room on the second floor, next to their parents' bedroom. The King children revealed their personalities when they played games such as Monopoly, as one neighborhood friend recalled. A.D. cheated; Christine approached with caution that limited her success; and M.L. studied the rules, rejected invitations to join in his brother's duplicity, and moved aggressively to dominate the board and bankrupt his rivals.

In addition to his good fortune to have grown up on Auburn Avenue, M.L. was fortunate to have grown up in a loving household with educated parents in a stable marriage.

Young M.L. knew he was loved, and not only by his parents but also by his maternal grandmother, Jennie Williams, who lived with the family and was known as "Mama" to the children. No matter how busy they got, the King children were expected home for dinner. Alberta and Jennie did the cooking in the kitchen at the back of the home's first floor. Though their workspace was small, they produced great quantities of food, always more than enough to feed the family, as guests were frequent. The Kings took great pleasure in fried chicken, chitterlings, macaroni and cheese, glazed ham, smothered pork chops, corn on the cob, black-eyed peas, collard greens, cakes, pies, cobblers, and bread pudding. For a family not long removed from poverty, every meal was a celebration, and a reminder of God's blessings. The Kings even had their own backyard garden.

"My father always had my mother and me to prepare extra dinner,"

Alberta Williams said in recalling how her own childhood shaped those of her children. "He never came home from the ministers' union without bringing two or three preachers or more, and they would sit around the table and they would have the best time, they were telling jokes and just talking . . . M.L. Jr. was very much like that, because he always had somebody around even when he was a little boy, they used to keep my house so full of children sometimes it seemed like they were running a nursery or a playground or something."

Several times a year, Daddy King, as Martin Sr. liked to be called, took his children back to Stockbridge to show them how different his life had been not so many years ago. He stopped his car and picked pokeweed—a common poisonous plant that made for good eating only after it was boiled several times to remove the toxins. He took the family to Floyd Chapel Baptist Church, where he had learned to preach. Unfortunately, the children never got to meet his mother, Delia, who had died of cancer in 1924 at the age of forty-nine. "Hatred makes nothin' but more hatred, Michael," she told her temperamental son before she died. "Don't do it." His father, Jim, lived in Atlanta in his later years and did get to see his grandchildren. He died in 1933 at age sixty-eight.

To show off their powers of memorization and to impress the out-of-town ministers and educators who joined the family for meals, the King children recited Bible verses. Daddy King sat at the head of the table, Alberta at the other end, the children between them. M.L. showed a talent for memorization, especially when it came to songs. "He was very interested, I think from the very beginning, in music," Alberta said. "And of course he would very easily follow the choirs along as they sang, and during the next week we would hear him singing around home." When it was time to clean up, the children were expected to wash the dishes. M.L. sometimes hid in the bathroom to avoid the chores, but his siblings never let him get away with it.

Daddy King was a powerful, feared presence. He had a muscular frame, a booming bass voice, and, as he admitted, a red-hot temper. He was also attentive, consistently on hand for his children's music recitals and oratorical performances. As the son of an abusive alcoholic, Daddy King ran the household the way he wished his daddy had—with sober discipline. "My prayer," he said once, "was always: Lord, grant that my children will not have to come the way I did."

When his children misbehaved, Daddy King thrashed them with a belt, a rod, or a stick. Sometimes he ordered the children to spank or whip one another. Was he trying to demonstrate that he didn't enjoy handing out the beatings? Was he punishing two children at once by making one the dispenser of pain and the other the recipient? Louis E. Lomax, a friend of M.L., said men like Daddy King were "so strong and hard driving" that they tended to "confuse their own desires with God's will," and, as a result, their children lived with unbearable pressure and unrealistic expectations. Whatever Daddy King's motivation, it became clear that his middle child preferred absorbing punishment to delivering it, especially if ordered to hit his sister. When M.L. was spanked, he would never let his father see him cry. But neither would the son confront his father or fight back.

Years later, Martin Luther King Jr.'s closest friends and associates would speculate about the effect of those beatings. "I think Martin was a much more fearful man than he appeared," said Bayard Rustin, a civil rights activist and pacifist who was one of King's closest advisers. King had no trouble confronting racist white sheriffs, Rustin said, but he could not bear conflict with older civil rights leaders such as Roy Wilkins or Whitney Young, or even, sometimes, with the members of his own organization. "Now I think all this sprang from the fact that his father had so brutalized him as a kid," Rustin said. He longed for his father's approval, and yet he also yearned to assert himself and explore his great talents. The conflict would shape his life.

Despite his objection to his father's method of punishment, young M.L. had not yet embraced a philosophy of nonviolence. Once, when A.D. was pestering Christine, M.L. grew so angry he picked up a telephone—when telephones were big and heavy—and brought it crashing down on his brother's head. "You've killed him!" Christine screamed before A.D. revived with a splash of water.

M.L. grew up during the Great Depression, at a time when about two-thirds of Atlanta's Black population survived on paltry public relief payments.

Nationwide, 90 percent Black families endured poverty at some point during the Depression (compared with less than 50 percent of all white families). Hunger, homelessness, and a frightening sense of helplessness crept across the country. Droughts worsened the crisis. Racism worsened it even more. The Depression offered a painful reminder that Black Americans had not achieved anything approaching equality since the Civil War. Half of all Black Americans remained illiterate as of 1915, and three quarters lived as impoverished sharecroppers or tenants. The number of Black craftsmen had actually declined since slavery had ended. New Deal programs designed to help people in poverty were limited in their effect because they were often run in the South by white officials uninterested in Black people or unwilling to help them.

Not far from Auburn Avenue, M.L. saw ramshackle shanties, overcrowded boardinghouses, and children wearing clothes far shabbier than his own. "I was much too young to remember the beginning of this depression," M.L. wrote not long after the Depression's end, "but I do recall how I questioned my parent [sic] about the numerous people standing in bread lines when I was about five years of age." Alberta King said of her children, "We tried to instill within them such qualities as love, kindness, and to have a great concern for other people, and this I feel followed him and followed the others on through life."

During the Depression, a new generation of politicians supported the government's role in relieving human suffering. Lyndon Baines Johnson, the son of a Texas farmer and politician, won election to Congress in 1937 and began pursuing federal funds for projects that would improve living conditions for his poor, rural constituents. Racial justice was not yet high on the federal agenda, but the ground was being plowed and seeded, and new ideas soon would sprout.

Even in difficult economic times, Reverend King's church salary allowed the family to have a house and an automobile, debt free. The children had a dog named Mickey. Young M.L. had his own bicycle. He and his siblings received allowances. They dressed smartly. Their privilege, however, came with a cost: the children were watched wherever they went and expected to behave. For M.L., Ebenezer Baptist Church was a second home. M.L.'s personality was not only expressed but forged by religion. In church, as in the home, his mother and father played offsetting roles. His father delivered booming sermons filled with prophetic fury. His mother offered joyful, hand-clapping hymns. It was Alberta King, as one of M.L.'s friends said, who showed her son the "sweetness in religion" and in life. It was Alberta King, said another friend, who was a pacifist by nature and taught her son "you don't have to fight, particularly when you are secure in spiritual ways."

In late April 1936, when M.L. was seven, an evangelist from Detroit came to Atlanta for a revival at Ebenezer, preaching and leading a chorus every night for two weeks. "Bring some unsaved person with you," said the notice in the *Atlanta Daily World*. M.L. referred to this event, in his later application to Crozer Theological Seminary in Pennsylvania, as the occasion in which he was baptized and joined the church. The Reverend H. H. Coleman led the revival, aimed at saving souls, including those of children. He had listeners shouting with joy.

"Men must get hungry for religion," Coleman preached in one of his sermons at Ebenezer. "They must thirst for the water of life. Jesus will give us a well of water—a supply that will never cease to exist. We carry the well with us everywhere we go, and we can drink when we get ready."

M.L.'s version of these events is a bit off (he remembered being five, not seven years old), but he did say in his Crozer application that he joined the church on May 1, 1936, and was baptized two days later. Baptists generally practice "believers' baptisms" after accepting Jesus as their savior, but such ceremonies usually involve older children. The traveling evangelist may have asked, after his sermon, if any of the boys or girls wanted to accept Jesus and "join the church." Christine, M.L.'s older sister, volunteered first. "I decided that I would not let her get ahead of me," M.L. recalled, "so I was next. I had never given this matter a thought, and even at the time of my baptism I was unaware of what was taking place." Given that he had grown up in a fundamentalist Black church, M.L. may have felt, simply, that he was doing what was expected of him. "From this it seems quite clear I joined the church not out of dynamic conviction," he said, "but out of a childhood desire to keep up with my sister."

The King children were competitive. Their home had a big backyard and an empty field nearby that offered space for football games, foot races, and rock-hurling contests, in which boys tested their arm strength as well as their talents for dodging incoming projectiles. M.L. was a small child who compensated for his size with hustle, strategy, and guts. On the basketball court, he shot too much for his teammates' tastes. On the football field, he torpedoed ball carriers. "If you were running after him" on the football field, his friend Emmett Proctor said, "and you started gaining on him, he'd fall down in front of you. Right in front of you. And you'd fall right over him and wind up skinning yourself, and he'd be up and gone."

The rough play occasionally led to fistfights. "Let's go to the grass," M.L. would say, showing that he was practical even in his aggression, selecting a field of battle that would cushion the inevitable falls. He was twice struck by cars while riding his bicycle, yet he complained only about the damage to his bike.

What made a boy who was shorter and slighter than most of his peers think he could go to the grass and win? What made him think he could score a victory of self-assertion by not crying out when his father strapped him? What made him so confident around adults and, later, around beautiful women? What made a child born in a deeply, violently racist society grow up to think he could change it? His attitude derived at least in part from the status that came with being the son of a prominent minister and growing up sheltered from at least some of the hardship others faced. Of course, growing up under a prominent, demanding, and sometimes violent father may have also contributed to young M.L.'s feelings of insecurity and tendency to depression.

Though M.L. didn't know he would follow his father into the ministry, the Black Baptist church shaped him in fundamental ways. His name shaped him, too. "The boys would tease him," M.L.'s friend June Dobbs Butts recalled. "'I thought you was Mike and now you Martin,' they'd say." Gradually, throughout childhood, he transitioned from Mike to M.L. But though his father had officially changed his name, no one called the younger King Martin yet. "I think that name change pulled him even more into the ministry," she said.

Martin Luther King Jr. grew up believing in a God of redemption, a God of judgment, a God of grace and miracles, a personal God who believed that Black people mattered no matter what racist white people and government regulations said. He grew up in an urban church that blended prayer with calls to action. He grew up understanding that racism was not merely wrong but evil, corrosive of the soul. He grew up hearing shouted sermons and soaring songs that moved audiences to tears and ecstasy, sermons and songs that called for freedom on earth as well as in heaven.

In "An Autobiography of Religious Development," written when he was twenty-one, King called his father a "real father," saying Daddy King took care of his family while living within his financial means. His mother, he said, was "behind the scenes setting forth those motherly cares." As a child, he spent all day Sunday at Ebenezer and several nights a week at the church. The church taught him morals and ideals, he wrote. These ideals, he said, "have been real and precious to me, and even in moments of theological doubt I could never turn away from them. Even though I have never had an abrupt conversion experience, religion has been real to me and knitted to life. In fact, the two cannot be separated; religion for me is life."

In the 1930s, three out of every four Black workers in the South toiled as domestics or farmhands. But young M. L. King saw Black people everywhere asserting themselves in bold new ways. In Atlanta, the owner of an Auburn Avenue gas station, John Harden, took over the city's leading Black baseball team, the Atlanta Black Crackers, and briefly made it a winner in the late 1930s. In Germany, Jesse Owens won gold and glory for the United States in the 1936 Olympics. Joe Louis captured boxing's heavyweight crown the following year. In 1939, Marian Anderson sang before a crowd of seventy-five thousand at the Lincoln Memorial in Washington, D.C. Never mind that the Black Crackers could not test their skills against white professional baseball teams. Never mind that Jesse Owens returned to the United States as a second-class citizen with few opportunities to reap the rewards for his fame. Never mind that Joe Louis was ordered by his white managers never to boast about defeating white opponents and never to be seen in the company of white women. Never mind that Marian Anderson couldn't spend the night in many of the capital's best hotels or dine in its finest restaurants after her groundbreaking performance. M. L. King Jr. would find opportunities that Owens, Louis, and Anderson hadn't had, in part because those people and countless others, including his parents, had cut a path for him.

"Children are less likely to learn from abstract teachings," the psychologist Kenneth Clark once said, "than from the concrete realities of their daily experiences."

Sweet Auburn insulated M.L. from many of the bitter experiences faced by young Black Americans. Away from Auburn Avenue, however, M.L. became more alert to the cold truth of racism. He recognized that he could not swim in any of the city's public pools or play in any of its parks. In a 1961 interview, he said he could recall seeing Black people physically attacked by members of the Ku Klux Klan on the streets of Atlanta, although he offered no details.

When he was eight years old, King read the *Atlanta Daily World* every Sunday, according to a letter he wrote to the newspaper's editor seeking membership in the newspaper's Junior Circle, a letter that also appears to mark the first time he saw his written words published.

At about the same time, he took a job as a delivery boy for *The Atlanta Journal*, a white-owned newspaper. One day, when he was collecting payments from subscribers, a white customer refused to pay. "The man said he didn't owe what M.L. asked for," Daddy King recalled. "M.L. said that was what his book called for. The man then called him a little nigger. Little M.L. said, 'I'm not a nigger,' and stopped delivering that man a paper. He then lost his paper route."

The incident may have marked M.L.'s first overt protest of racism. Daddy King recognized the similarity between M.L.'s newspaper delivery story and some of his own experiences dealing with racism in Stockbridge. "I can see how it went from me to him," he said, referring both to racism and the urge to fight it.

Once, a white police officer stopped M.L.'s father for running a stop sign and addressed him as "boy."

"That's a *boy* there," Daddy King said, pointing to his eldest son in the car's passenger seat. "I'm *Reverend* King."

On another occasion, a white woman slapped M.L. in the face, mistakenly identifying him as "that nigger that stepped on my foot." Once again, M.L. said, he felt torn between the words of his mother, who taught him he was loved and special and as good as anyone else, and the evidence put forth by much of white society that told him, "You are less than, you are not equal to."

On yet another occasion, M.L. went shopping with his father for shoes at Rich's, a popular department store in downtown Atlanta. The white clerk in the shoe department asked the father and son not to sit in the area reserved for white customers.

"We're comfortable in these seats," Reverend King said.

"Well, you can't sit there," the clerk said angrily.

"If I can't sit here with my boy," King said, "I just won't buy any shoes." And he didn't.

As they returned to their car, Reverend King said he could tell that his son was filled with "the questions, the confusions." He explained to M.L. that white people used their power in the South to subjugate Black people, but that didn't mean they had to accept it. "I was going to be fighting against it in some way or other as long as there was breath in me," Daddy King wrote. "I wanted him to understand *that*."

Meanwhile, Alberta King took another approach. She traced her son's footprint on newspaper, cut out the pattern, and took it to the store to buy him shoes that would fit. "It wasn't that she was compromising," her grand-daughter Alveda King recalled. "Her solutions were just different."

Reverend King discouraged his children from taking jobs with white families, fearing they would learn to tolerate servitude and condescension. He urged them to avoid Atlanta's buses, which operated on a first-come, first-served basis, with white passengers taking the front seats and Black passengers filling in from the rear. He also taught his children that protest in response to injustice was a duty. When Atlantans went to the polls to vote on whether to repeal Prohibition laws in 1935, white supporters of the laws sought the support of Black Baptist preachers. King and three other minis-ters issued a statement saying that while they surely hoped to preserve the government's ban on alcohol sales, they regretted that their "white friends" were only interested in seeing Black people vote when it suited white people's interests. "If our white ministers are really interested in our voting," King and the others wrote, "let them courageously join us to fight for our elemen-tal rights."

Several years later, Reverend King served as chairman of a committee demanding that Atlanta boost the pay of Black public-school teachers. At the time, the average salary for Black teachers was about 60 percent that of white teachers, and the NAACP had made equalization of teacher salaries one of its goals.

Evil things should be fought, Reverend King said. "To serve God in truth is to serve one's fellow man," he wrote. "For 'in as much as ye have done it unto of the least of these, ye have done it unto me,' as Jesus admonishes us. That is why I felt impelled to attend all the civic and political meetings called to help blacks improve their status." He preached the same message to his congregation and to the growing number of Black citizens who turned out for public meetings on social and political issues. The power of that mes-sage gave King and other ministers newfound clout at city hall, and it would inspire the next generation of Black activists to take bigger steps and bigger risks.

As his son M.L. recalled, Daddy King taught that "there was a sense of somebodiness within us that always kept us moving toward the sense of dignity and self-respect that any human being should have."

———◆———

At least once, however, Daddy King sent a mixed message.

On December 15, 1939, when Hollywood stars converged on Atlanta for the premiere of one of the most eagerly anticipated films of all time, *Gone with the Wind*, King offered to send the Ebenezer Baptist Church choir to perform at a celebratory costume ball. The wealthy white women in attendance were dressed in hoop skirts and pantalets. The men wore tight trousers and grew mustaches. Black men and women were not invited to attend the party, but "300 or more colored ushers" and "200 colored chauffeurs" were hired to serve the white guests, according to the *Atlanta Daily World*. Members of the Ebenezer choir, led by Alberta King, embraced the spirit of the event by dressing in slave costumes, their heads wrapped in cloths.

Gone with the Wind, starring Clark Gable and Vivien Leigh, was based on Margaret Mitchell's Pulitzer Prize–winning novel, published in 1936. The book was already a sensation. The movie's arrival offered Americans a welcome distraction after a year of largely dismal news. Germany had invaded Poland. Unemployment rates soared. *Gone with the Wind* was especially welcomed by white Atlantans for its celebration of antebellum southern life and customs. While the city had been striving for years to promote itself as a modern, progressive place, the book had generated too much attention and too much money to be ignored; it had sold more than two million copies by the time the movie premiered. *Gone with the Wind* would shape America's impression of both Atlanta and the Civil War for years to come. The book captured the South's last moment of glory, according to one white critic, before "a social-economic regime of great beauty crashed to its ruin amid the thunder of war."

By the time of the movie's release, Atlanta mayor William B. Hartsfield and the city's white leaders were locked in full embrace of the film. American Airlines offered Clark Gable his own DC-3, with the movie's title stenciled across its side, for the flight from Los Angeles to Atlanta. A band struck up "Dixie" as Gable and his wife, the actress Carole Lombard, stepped from the plane and into a Packard convertible. Hundreds of thousands of people, Black and white, lined the streets of Atlanta to gaze at the stars.

As Daddy King surely knew, Black activists had a long history of protesting racism in Hollywood. Many community leaders in Atlanta encouraged Black men and women to sit out the festivities, seeing no reason in this case to romanticize slavery. I. P. Reynolds, writing in the *Atlanta Daily World*, complained that *Gone with the Wind* not only celebrated racist views but also perpetuated them. In advance of the big premiere, Reynolds complained, Atlanta police were tidying up the city by raiding bars and, in essence, arresting Black men for being Black.

Reverend King's decision to bring the Ebenezer choir to the premiere rankled many of his peers. "Reverend King was beseeched not to let his wonderful choir go," said June Dobbs Butts, whose father, John Wesley Dobbs, known as "the Mayor of Auburn Avenue," had been among the critics. The event was not only segregated, Dobbs and others complained, but also sinful. Why, Dobbs wondered, would a Baptist choir appear at a function where people would be dancing and drinking alcohol? But Daddy King argued that it was only a movie, and not an entirely inaccurate one. Butts said she had the impression that Reverend King enjoyed gaining access to and winning the approval of Atlanta's white leaders. Like many leaders in the Black southern church, Butts added, Reverend King led with a combination of protest and accommodation.

At the ball, hundreds of white celebrants gazed upon a facade representing the fictional plantation Tara. Confederate flags fluttered in the breeze as Ebenezer's choir sang spirituals, including "Get on Board Little Children":

> The fare is cheap
> And all can go
> The rich and poor are there

No second class aboard the train
No difference in the fare
Get on board, little children

Martin Luther King Jr., dressed as a young slave, sat in the choir's first row, singing along.

4

"Black America Still Wears Chains"

DADDY KING REMAINED a plainspoken preacher, bursting with ideas and passion. He studied country preachers and copied them, trying out not only their styles but sometimes their precise words. He ambled up and down the aisles as he delivered his sermons. He called out in a booming voice and waited for parishioners to echo him, the voices volleying back and forth. He liked to begin his sermons slowly and calmly and to carry his parishioners on cresting waves. He sang short phrases from spirituals and hymns—"ditties," he called them—as his fervor grew. And, like the slave preachers and free Black preachers of generations past, he spoke of justice in heaven and on earth.

Daddy King was more than a preacher. He preached emphatically about sin, but when parishioners got into scrapes with the law, they knew they could count on their pastor to bail them out of jail. Reverend King also made sure the church provided food for the hungry, clothes for the poor, and day care for the children of working men and women.

The sharecropper's son had no intention of returning to poverty, and neither would he allow his church to struggle. When congregants gave donations, he listed their names in the church ledger, knowing that no one would want to have his or her name left out. He bragged about the economic and political power of his flock, about the number of loans they could write, the number of homes they could own, the number of votes they could deliver. He encouraged congregants to patronize one another's businesses. The United States was enduring an economic nightmare. By 1932, half of all Black men and women nationwide were out of work. In rural Georgia, government relief money flowed to white landowners while Black tenant farmers faced eviction. Even on Auburn Avenue, shops closed and homes fell into disrepair. Reverend King promised Ebenezer's members they would get through the hard times by having faith in God and in one another.

Though Reverend King would get most of the credit for expanding the church's membership, his wife played a vital role, too. Alberta King had grown up in Ebenezer. She knew every family in the congregation. She visited the sick and counseled the weary, sometimes alone, sometimes with her husband. Alberta served as the church's unofficial executive director. She kept the schedules. She organized meetings. When a church member's phone rang at eleven at night or six in the morning, they knew it was probably Alberta King, who seemed to never need sleep. One interviewer described her as "almost imperturbable, rarely registering any facial expression."

As Ebenezer's music director, Alberta King led three choirs. She was not a classically trained musician, but she sang and played piano well, and her choirs sang loudly and beautifully. She oversaw the purchase of an impressive new Wurlitzer organ in 1940, replacing an old pump organ, and initiated a series of annual musical events. Alberta King got little recognition for her contributions, in part because preachers' wives were expected to silently support their spouses. But Alberta came to the silence naturally, too, preferring not to raise her voice or call attention to herself. She led the choirs from the shelter of her keyboard, seldom out front, never stomping, never shouting. Indeed, she was, as June Dobbs Butts put it, "the most obsequious, quiet woman I've ever seen in my life."

If Alberta King's children were shaped in reaction to their father's high expectations and frequent sternness, they were shaped, too, by their mother's comforting, unconditional love. Alberta maintained a calm and soothing tone even when she had reason to be angry. She corrected the children's grammar at the kitchen table. By providing singing lessons, she helped M.L.

discover the power of his voice. She persuaded her husband to stop whipping the children and to let her handle the punishment. Alberta also bought M.L. his sharp clothes, so he could be "draped," as the style was known at the time, in a brown tweed suit, baggy around the legs and tight at the ankle, for his sixth-grade graduation ceremony.

"He loved that suit," his sister recalled. "He wore it everywhere he could." He wore it so much that his friends started calling him "Tweed," a nickname for a snazzy dresser that would stick with him for years.

While her husband was stern, Alberta was warm, with a "lovely, dry sense of humor," as one of her grandchildren said. Alberta once recalled the time she was driving through the country with her husband, trying to find a small church where Reverend King had been invited to preach, and pulled over to ask an old Black man for directions. "Let's see, now," the old man said. "To get to that church, you go down this road about two miles, then turn right . . . No, that's not right. What you do is, you turn around and go up the crossroads, then turn left and . . . No, that's not right, either. Let's see . . ." He scratched his head. "You know, I reckon I don't know *where* that church is." As the Kings thanked him for his time and drove away, they heard someone shouting. They turned and saw the old man running down the road after their car. They stopped and waited for him. "I just wanted to tell you . . . ," he said, panting. "I just saw my brother, and I asked him . . . and he don't know where that church is either."

Reverend King recognized his wife's gifts, especially her ability to connect emotionally with their children. "Bunch was very gifted with children," he said, using her nickname. "She raised all of ours with great love and respect for their feelings." She and M.L. could make small talk for hours. "She knew each of her children as well as she knew herself. M.L. came along with sensitivities only she could investigate and soothe."

M.L.'s strong convictions, his fearlessness, and his ambition came from his father, Daddy King boasted. The child's kindness, he said, came from his mother. "She never did have hate in her heart, for anybody, ever. But I did. She was the kind who did not hate. She was a great person, a *great* person."

M.L. grew up with an extraordinary amount of female attention—his wishes catered to by his mother, Alberta; his sister, Christine; his maternal grandmother, Jennie Celeste Williams; and Jennie's younger sister, Ida Worthen, who also lived with the family for a time and loved reading to the children from the encyclopedia. But he also grew up at a time when women—even educated, ambitious women such as his mother—were expected to confine their ambitions largely to the home.

M.L. felt especially close to his grandmother. Jennie Williams was the daughter of a carpenter and one of thirteen children. At almost every phase of her life she had defied orthodoxy. At fifteen, she had enrolled at Spelman Seminary. She had waited until she was twenty-six to marry, which was four years older than the median age for women of her time. L. D. Reddick, King's earliest biographer and a close outside observer of the King family, called Jennie Williams a "woman of health and spirits" who "radiated cheerfulness."

"She was very dear to us, but especially to me," M.L. wrote.

One day, when M.L. and A.D. were running around the house, A.D. slid down the wooden banister and collided with his grandmother near the foot of the stairs, knocking her unconscious. M.L. panicked, believing his hijinks had killed his grandmother. He ran upstairs and jumped from a tall window overlooking the house's front steps and fell about twelve feet. He suffered no serious injury.

On Sunday, May 18, 1941, as she prepared to give a lecture at Mt. Olive Baptist Church in Atlanta, Jennie Williams suffered a heart attack and died at age sixty-six. Young M.L. wasn't home when the news reached his family. Disobeying his father's order, he had gone to watch an Elks Lodge parade.

When he returned home and heard about his grandmother's death, M.L. once again climbed the stairs and jumped out the window. Once again, he escaped serious injury, but he cried for days and couldn't sleep at night. "He believed Mama's death was God's way of punishing him for having disobeyed our father," Christine recalled. "It took M.L. months to come to terms with Mama's loss. After this experience, more than one person observed that he seemed to have grown more mature."

—————— • ——————

The Great Depression hurt Atlanta's Black community, including Sweet Auburn. Financial institutions labeled the neighborhood risky, cutting off much of the capital that might have flowed in for improvement. Morris Brown College moved out, and many professionals followed. By 1939, only 13 percent of the homes on the Kings' block were owner occupied, and 67 percent were "in need of major repairs or unfit for use," according to a government survey. Families that could afford it moved away. Though many of them returned on Sundays for church, the neighborhood would never be the same.

Reverend King rose in prominence and prestige even as the neighborhood slipped. Shortly after the death of Jennie Williams, King moved his family to a yellow-brick house that sat high on a terrace at 193 Boulevard, still a short walk to the church. Reverend King finally had the brick house he'd promised Bunch. The move came as renovations were completed on Ebenezer Baptist Church, with pews replacing benches. By 1941, the church had more than 2,500 members, making it a powerful force in Atlanta's Black community, and Reverend King a figure of influence and admiration throughout the city. In the 1940 government census, he reported his annual salary as $2,500 (about $47,500 today).

The new home on Boulevard came with a housekeeper, Georgia Lewis, who had worked for the house's previous owners. The Kings decided to keep her on, perhaps because she was a member of Ebenezer church. Children in the neighborhood knew the housekeeper as unsmiling and unfriendly. "Don't you touch that cake," she would tell them when they entered her kitchen. "Keep your hands behind your back." But she warmed under her new employers. The Kings treated her like family, and she took pride in knowing she played an important role in caring for her minister's children. M.L., Christine, and A.D. had cheese, eggs, and bacon for breakfast. When they came home from school, they would walk up the sloped driveway, around to the back door, and enter through the kitchen, where "Mother Lewis," as the children called her, would have their favorite snack waiting: white bread slathered in butter and sprinkled with sugar. "Have some cake," she would say when the children brought their friends.

In 1940, Franklin D. Roosevelt won an unprecedented third term as president. Black voters supported Roosevelt and the Democratic Party in growing numbers, despite the party's acceptance of Jim Crow. Roosevelt's economic policies gave hope to impoverished Black families, and his appointees to the Supreme Court proved receptive to many of the NAACP's legal strategies. In his annual message to Congress in January 1941, Roosevelt made his case for more concrete support of America's allies in the war abroad, saying the fight was not to save Europe but to save the four freedoms that people everywhere had a right to possess: freedom of speech, freedom of religion, freedom from want, and freedom from fear. Activists pointed out that many Black people in America were routinely denied those freedoms.

Reverend King fought for social change, but he also urged his followers to be patient. He had the ear of Atlanta's white politicians and didn't care to lose it, even when he was rudely treated. When, for example, King and other members of the NAACP's Committee for Negro Policemen met with Mayor Hartsfield to push the city to hire Black police officers, the mayor replied: "We'll get colored policemen in Atlanta just as soon as we get colored deacons in the white First Baptist Church." King would continue to support Hartsfield. He also struck a conciliatory tone in 1941 when he presided over a meeting of the joint committee of "white and colored" ministerial councils, as *The Atlanta Constitution* put it, saying in his opening remarks: "The racial condition . . . will never be settled right until a more friendly contact is made among the ministers of both races."

But others were angry, unafraid, and ready to act. Scattered sit-ins occurred around the country in the 1930s, the action inspired in part by union organizers who had seized factories to fight for better working conditions. Communist organizers in America took up the fight for racial justice. Labor unions followed. In January 1941, before the United States joined the fight in World War II, A. Philip Randolph of the Brotherhood of Sleeping Car Porters called for a march on Washington to demand the right of Black people "to work and fight for our country." After a series of negotiations, Roosevelt signed Executive Order 8802, barring racial discrimination in defense industries, and Randolph agreed to call off the march. Other protests went on, however, and they were often met with violent reactions. As rallies, sit-ins, and boycotts continued, Roosevelt promised to address one of the protesters' biggest complaints: that men and women—including Black soldiers—

were routinely denied the vote through the imposition of poll taxes, literacy tests, and other forms of disenfranchisement. In 1940, less than 3 percent of Black people in the South were registered to vote, and southern politicians blocked attempts to expand voting rights.

At the same time, the Federal Bureau of Investigation (FBI) under J. Edgar Hoover conducted surveillance on hundreds of Black organizers, writers, artists, lawyers, and organizations. The FBI's investigation produced a classified report, *Survey of Racial Conditions in the United States*, code-named RACON, which warned that Black people and their organizations were involved in conduct that might subvert American interests. In the FBI's appraisal, this subversive behavior was not a response to centuries of injustice; it was the work of the Communist Party, which sought to destroy the United States by inciting racial conflict.

During World War II, Black newspapers called attention to a glaring hypocrisy: Black Americans helped win democracy abroad but not at home. On January 3, 1942, *The Pittsburgh Courier* published a story about Doris "Dorie" Miller, a Black sailor who rescued fellow sailors aboard the USS *West Virginia* during the attack on Pearl Harbor, then manned a .50-caliber machine gun and fired on Japanese planes. After the navy refused to officially honor Miller, the *Courier* launched what it called the "Double V" campaign, the first *V* for victory over America's enemies in the war, the second *V* for victory over enemies of justice within the United States. All over the country, Double V posters and signs appeared in the windows of Black-owned shops.

A few months later, the accomplished Black tenor Roland Hayes was jailed in Rome, Georgia, seventy miles from Atlanta, when a shoe-store clerk asked Hayes's wife to move from her seat near the window to one in the back of the store. When Hayes complained that he and his wife had done nothing wrong, a police officer "gave me all he had on the jaw," Hayes said, and then handcuffed and arrested him. Two weeks later, in his Sunday sermon at Ebenezer, Reverend King addressed the attack on Hayes. Perhaps it would help if more well-known Black men and women were beaten up, Reverend King said, so that the world might be alerted to their plight.

The war shot rocket fuel into the economy, but not everyone shared equally in the prosperity. When the fighting was over, Black people's lives remained segregated, their work often poorly paid, their educations far from equal to those of white people. When Black soldiers returned home from the war, Jim Crow laws and second-class housing options greeted them. Lynching continued. The mere sight of a Black man in uniform at times provoked violence. Black veterans were encouraged to apply for GI Bill benefits, but many banks wouldn't let them step in the lobby, much less borrow money, and many colleges wouldn't consider their applications for enrollment. Black families continued to migrate from south to north, but countless neighborhoods remained off-limits. At the same time, urban white families relocated to suburbs and established residential patterns that would undermine efforts to integrate schools for generations to come.

At Yonge Street Elementary School, M. L. King was exposed to more social activists, including the school's principal, Cora B. Finley, who had a bachelor's degree from Spelman and a master's from Atlanta University. She was the founder of the nation's first Negro Parent-Teachers Association.

After Yonge Street, beginning in the fall of 1936, M.L. attended David T. Howard Colored Elementary School, where NAACP officials sometimes addressed the students. After sixth grade, he enrolled at the Laboratory High School of Atlanta University, an all-Black private school with a racially integrated faculty. He took the bus every day to the Lab School. When budget cuts forced the Lab School to close, M.L. went back to public school, at Booker T. Washington High School, the city's only public high school for Black students. The closure of the Lab School compelled him to skip another grade, making him a thirteen-year-old tenth grader.

M.L. was a good student, but skipping grades had disadvantages. His math skills were solid, but his grammar and spelling lagged. His sister tried to help him catch up, and in these years M.L. found himself closer to his sister than his brother. An obstreperous child, A.D. picked fights, played pranks, and showed little fear of his father's fury. M.L. and Christine were more studious. Brother and sister competed to learn and use fancy vocabulary, "like 'concatenation,'" Christine recalled. When A.D. was sent to a boarding school in North Carolina, M.L. and Christine grew closer still. He accompanied his sister to dances and joined her on double dates. At parties, M.L., without being asked, would take on the role of chaperone, interrupting when he saw a boy trying to dance too closely with a girl.

He grew more rebellious as a teenager, and, like many young men, he made his father one of the primary targets, telling Daddy King he had no intention of becoming a minister. In one Sunday-school session he shocked his class by announcing he did not believe in the bodily resurrection of Jesus. His earliest career goal was to be a firefighter. Later, he told his parents he might become a doctor or lawyer—something more "intellectually respectable" than a preacher. The emotionalism of the Black church troubled him, "the shouting and the stamping," he said. "I didn't understand it, and it embarrassed me."

When he was fifteen, M.L. entered a statewide public speaking contest for Black high school students sponsored by the Elks Club. On April 17, 1944, he traveled about 140 miles by bus to Dublin, Georgia, accompanied by one of his teachers, Sarah Grace Bradley, and another student from his high school.

His roots in the church had equipped him well for oratory. He had grown up listening to Baptist preachers, and he had no fear of standing on a stage and speaking to a crowd, thanks in part to his long hours of practice as a soloist with his mother's choir.

"Negroes were first brought to America in 1620 when England legalized slavery both in England and the colonies and America," he said as he opened the speech. "The institution grew and thrived . . . on the backs of these Black men. The empire of King Cotton was built, and the southland maintained a status of life and hospitality distinctly its own and not anywhere else."

He cited the promise of the Emancipation Proclamation and its pledge of freedom before moving on to address race relations. "Black America still wears chains," he said. "The finest Negro is at the mercy of the meanest white man." He concluded with the kind of passion that might have animated one of his father's sermons and featured elements he would make famous years later: the use of metaphor, the tone of moral authority, the fast flow of concrete language, and a conclusion that insisted optimistically on change. It was an oration that, in a way, provided a blueprint for "I Have a Dream," the most celebrated speech he would ever give, in that it cited the Declaration of Independence, the Emancipation Proclamation, and the Bible to condemn segregation. "My heart throbs anew," he said in conclusion, "in the hope that, inspired by the example of Lincoln, imbued with the spirit of Christ, they will cast down the last barrier to perfect freedom. And I with my brother of Blackest hue possessing all my rightful heritage and holding my head erect, may stand before the Saxon, a Negro and yet a man!"

Years later, King would brag of having won the contest, but in truth he was neither the winner nor one of the two runners-up. The judges gave first prize to Euris Smith, the daughter of a Pullman porter from Savannah. If King felt disappointed, he never said so.

There was one more reason why M.L. might have been inclined not to complain about the results: he had copied a significant portion of his address, including most of his concluding paragraph, from a speech by Henry F. Coleman called "The Philosophy of the Race Problem (From a Negro's Standpoint)." Coleman, the son of formerly enslaved parents and a junior at Cornell College in Iowa, had won a statewide intercollegiate speaking contest in 1910. His speech had been reprinted in a 1928 book called *Fifty Orations That Have Won Prizes in Speaking Contests*, a book that may have been in King's school library or recommended to him by a teacher.

On the long ride home from Dublin, the bus was empty enough at first that Black passengers could sit where they liked. But when the bus stopped in Macon, about eighty miles from Atlanta, the white bus driver ordered King and his classmate to give up their seats to oncoming white passengers. "We didn't move quickly enough to suit him," M.L. recalled. The bus driver began cursing, calling them "niggers" and "Black sons of bitches."

For the next eighty miles, M.L. stood.

"That night will never leave my memory," he said. "It was the angriest I have ever been in my life."

The optimism of his speech's conclusion had been crushed.

"Suddenly," he said, "I realized you don't count, you're nobody."

5

The Open Curtain

RACISM HAD GROUND down his paternal grandfather, but M. L. King Jr. saw prejudice and discrimination as evils to confront, not curse. Justice, in his youthful view, was like love: denial only made the desire for it grow.

"He came through it all really unscarred," a childhood friend of King's said with wonder. "He never went around fighting with himself, like we all did." King seemed to love people and bore no hidden desire to hate white people, one Black writer observed.

In the spring of 1944, at the end of his junior year of high school, King took a test to gain early admission to Morehouse College. Though he continued to insist that he did not intend to follow his father into the ministry, he very much resembled his father in his "single-minded determination, faith and forthrightness," said his sister, Christine. M.L. knew his father would approve of his decision to attend Morehouse, and the young man had already been indoctrinated in the school's culture. Morehouse faculty members and administrators lectured regularly at Atlanta's Black schools, and high school students often visited the college to attend sporting events and theatrical performances.

Though he had not yet been admitted to the college, King was nevertheless eligible in the summer following his junior year to go north with a group of Morehouse students to work on a tobacco farm in Simsbury, Connecticut. Farmers in Connecticut had long made it a practice to import seasonal workers from the South, especially with World War II removing many local men from the workforce. The white-owned Cullman Brothers tobacco company struck a deal with Morehouse, providing students with summer jobs that would help them pay their tuition. If the students lasted the whole summer, Cullman paid their round-trip train fare.

For many of the students, including King, tobacco farming in Connecticut for the summer offered a chance to slip the strictures of segregation. King knew the rules of Jim Crow as well as he knew the rooms in his house. He knew precisely where he could not eat, where he could not use the restrooms, where he could not sit on a bus or train, where he could not work, where he could not go to school, where he could not safely walk at night, and where he could not shop. But those rules did not apply, for the most part, in Connecticut.

On the train from Atlanta, King sat in the curtained-off section reserved for Black passengers. "The first time that I was seated behind a curtain in a dining car," he later wrote, "I felt as if the curtain had been dropped on my selfhood." Once the train reached Washington, D.C., the curtain parted and he could sit wherever he liked.

In his letters home, he sounded happy and confident, pleased to be finding his wings. In one of his first letters, he marveled that, in Connecticut, "Negroes and whites go to the same church." In the same letter, he said he had taken on the job of religious leader, giving Sunday sermons for more than a hundred boys, suggesting he was perhaps more open to a career in the ministry than he admitted. He noted, too, that he had secured a job in the kitchen so that he would eat better than other students. He closed the letter by asking his mother to check on the results of his Morehouse exam.

The students woke at six each morning, went to work at seven, and continued until at least five in the afternoon, picking the big, broad tobacco leaves, hanging them in barns, and packing them for shipping. Early in the season, when the plants were small and low to the ground, the young men slid on their bottoms from stalk to stalk as they harvested the leaves. As the plants grew taller, the pickers moved to their knees and, by summer's end, to their feet. Some students complained about the grueling labor, but King described the work in a letter home as "very easy." Emmett Proctor, a friend from Atlanta and King's picking partner that summer, said the two boys settled into a leisurely pace, shooting the breeze, sometimes even napping in the fields. "Tweedie and I were voted the laziest tobacco workers on the farm," Proctor bragged, referring to King by his fashion-inspired nickname. Most of the supervisors were white men—Polish immigrants, usually—with years of experience. By now, King had a growing sense of his purpose in life, and his exposure to farmwork perhaps reinforced his conviction that he was meant to use his mind rather than his hands.

King filled his letters home with assurances that he was attending church services in town, leading more services on the farm, and even singing in a choir that would perform on the radio. "Tell everyone I said hello," he wrote to his father, "and I am still thinking of the church and reading my bible. I am not doing any thing that I would not [be] doing [in] front of you."

When they finished work on Fridays the Morehouse students might walk or take the train to Hartford, where they could shop, eat in restaurants, or see movies without fear of being denied service. "Yesterday we didn't work," King wrote to his mother on June 18, 1944, "so we went to Hardford [sic] we had a really nice time there. I never thought that a person of my race could eat anywhere." He also described attending an integrated church, probably for the first time.

On August 5, the president of Morehouse, Dr. Benjamin Mays, visited the tobacco farm. The son of a sharecropper, he stood tall and slender, his posture perfect, his silver hair carefully cut and seeming to illuminate his dark, handsome face. Mays had risen impressively through the church and academy, and held a doctorate from the University of Chicago. Morehouse was the most prestigious all-Black, all-male college in the United States, but it had been struggling since the 1929 Wall Street crash. Mays had earned the nickname "Buck Bennie" for his efforts to repair the school's finances. He insisted students pay their tuition promptly, and he helped them find jobs. But he had done more than shore up the school's budget. He boosted the school's academic reputation, too. Before Morehouse, Mays had served as the dean of the Howard University School of Religion, where he worked with two of the most influential African American preachers of the early twentieth century, Mordecai Johnson and Howard Thurman. At Howard, these preachers had created a laboratory where the theologian Walter Rauschenbusch's social gospel (that religious belief *must* be put in action to correct society's flaws) and Mahatma Gandhi's views on nonviolent resistance would be applied in fighting racial injustice. At Morehouse, Mays set out to empower his students, to produce young men charged with changing the world. To be a Morehouse man, he made clear, was to be a part of a special order and to bear a special responsibility.

In his letter home, King mentioned that, in honor of the president's visit, the students had scraped together money from their savings and made an impressive donation of $135 (equivalent to about $2,000 in 2022) to Morehouse.

When summer ended, King was free to sit anywhere on the train until he reached Washington, D.C., and then he returned to one of the curtained sections reserved for Black passengers.

"It was a bitter feeling going back to segregation," he said.

———— • ————

Segregation militated against and dishonored democracy. But, at the same time, glimmers of hope appeared. Black voter registration in the South, though still heavily contested, was on the rise. In 1944, the same year King went to Connecticut, the Swedish economist Gunnar Myrdal published *An American Dilemma: The Negro Problem and American Democracy.* The book was the most detailed examination of American racism ever compiled by a white man, based on research performed before the United States entered World War II. Nearly 1,500 pages long, the book described what Black Americans knew but couldn't quantify: the disparities between the races in infant mortality, employment, education, and political representation. Though Negroes made up 10 percent of the American population, Myrdal wrote, they "do not by far have anything approaching a tenth of the things worth having in America." The Negro people, in Myrdal's view, were being treated like aliens in their own country. This fundamental unfairness permeated every aspect of American democracy, creating a tragic gap between what it was and what it was supposed to be. Everyone knew it. The only question was how long a nation could go on failing to live up to its own moral code.

Yet Myrdal saw cause for optimism. The recent work of social scientists had undercut the notion of biological Black inferiority. Like an earthquake, World War II had shaken and destabilized the nation's racial system. After Black men had fought and died to save democracy and freedom, the hypocrisy of their treatment became more difficult for some white people to ignore, especially as Black people organized to do something about it. The key to the organizers' success, Myrdal said, would be finding allies among those newly awoken white Americans. "The American Negro problem is a problem in the heart of the American," he wrote. "It is there that the interracial tension has its focus. It is there that the decisive struggle goes on."

But Myrdal suffered a serious blind spot, as he later acknowledged: he largely ignored the structural inequality in the American North and West, failing to anticipate that many liberal white people would find it easy to criticize the South but difficult to accept change in their own communities. King would major in sociology at Morehouse, and he would go on to call out the hypocrisy of northern whites who explained away their own discriminatory systems of housing, education, employment, and law enforcement.

Nevertheless, M.L. "seemed changed," as his mother said, after his trip north. King said himself that he felt more determined than ever to begin "playing a part in breaking down legal barriers to Negro rights." Still, he maintained doubts about whether he wished to do it from the pulpit.

In September, having passed his admissions exam, he enrolled at Morehouse, where he was three years younger than most freshmen, a gap not disguised by his tweed jackets, deep voice, and capacious vocabulary. At a slender five-foot-six, he stood several inches shorter than his father and only a touch taller than his sister. "We called him 'Runt,'" said Samuel McKinney, a classmate.

In his first days on campus, King and other freshmen were required to wear maroon caps to make it easier for upperclassmen to identify and harass them. The upperclassmen insisted on being addressed as "Mister" by the lowly freshmen. Any freshman who failed to accurately recite the Morehouse hymn might be thrown in a shower with his clothes on or have a stripe shaved down the middle of his head, a fate that King appears to have avoided.

His transition was probably eased by the strong sense of community at Morehouse. Enrollment at the college averaged 350 students during the war years and slipped to a low of 272 in 1943–44. It helped, too, that most of the students came from Atlanta, and that King already knew his way around.

He lived at home, not on campus. Most of the time, his confidence carried him. Though he could blend in with a crowd, as one of his fellow students recalled, it was his sly sense of humor and a genuine desire to get to know people that earned him popularity. He sang with the Morehouse Glee Club and the Atlanta University–Morehouse–Spelman Chorus. He signed on as a member of the YMCA and the NAACP. He chose not to join a fraternity (although he did become a member of Alpha Phi Alpha years later), and he seldom attended dances. Once, he asked his mother's permission to attend a dance. When Alberta told him to ask his father, M.L. gave up. "Well, we just won't go," he said, "because I'd just as soon go before the Supreme Court as go before him."

Early in his first semester, King needed a haircut. He heard that Walter McCall, a fellow freshman, offered ten-cent trims. But after his haircut, King told McCall he didn't have any money on him, and promised to pay later. The young men argued until the argument turned into a fight. Though McCall was twenty-one years old, an army veteran, and bigger than King, they wrestled to a draw. Whether King ever paid for the haircut remains unclear. Either way, the men became dear and lasting friends.

McCall had grown up poor. He owned one suit and wore it every day. He must have envied King's relative wealth, just as King must have envied McCall's worldliness. McCall enjoyed home-cooked meals from Alberta King's kitchen, and King enjoyed being goaded by McCall to engage in more adult behavior, such as throwing dance parties and playing cards, behavior that the younger King knew his Baptist preacher father would not condone.

Despite his wide-brimmed hats and two-toned shoes, the younger King remained quiet, careful not to call too much attention to himself. His grades were good, not great, and testing revealed that he read at only an eighth-grade level, perhaps a result of those skipped grades as well as the inferiority of Atlanta's Black public schools. King chose to major in sociology. His adviser was a sociology professor named Walter Chivers, who had conducted research on lynchings in the South and who taught students that money lay at the root of racism. The Black church, as James H. Cone writes, forged King's intellectual views more strongly than anything. But teachers such as Chivers reinforced the notion that racism shaped the nation's political and economic systems and fueled King's interest in democratic socialism. King confirmed Chivers's lessons between sessions at Morehouse when he sought odd jobs to help cover some of his college costs. Given his family connections, he might have easily found work with a Black-owned business, but, against his father's wishes, King took a job one summer unloading trains and trucks for the Atlanta Railway Express Company. He quit when a white foreman called him "nigger," and he understood that not everyone could afford to quit when they suffered such insults. He took other jobs not only for money, he said years later, but also to meet some of the poorly paid men who faced a lifetime of economic struggle, the people Chivers talked about, "to learn their plight and to feel their feelings."

He and Walter McCall often spoke of how best to work for racial equality, and at that moment in their lives they agreed that a career in law made most sense. "We used to sit up, oh, way into the morning discussing the social issues of the day," McCall said. King's comparatively privileged upbringing supplied him with confidence in many respects, but it also left him with lifelong guilt—a guilt that might have compelled his urge to be a reformer. Of course, he was also driven by social and political conditions in America, by racism, by heroes such as Benjamin Mays and A. Philip Randolph, by his parents and grandparents, and now by his Morehouse education.

Every Tuesday in Sale Hall, Mays addressed the student body from a low platform that jutted out almost to where the students in the first row could touch it. Attendance was mandatory. Mays was a gifted speaker. He rocked back and forth, as if to hypnotize his audience, while he lectured on religion, personal decorum, and political engagement, chiding students for their general inability to focus on "anything larger than a hamburger." The sessions were lessons on leadership and social ethics. Mays knew that only about 2 percent of Black men and women completed college, that the students arrayed before him were among the lucky, the elite, the most promising, and he urged them to consider the responsibilities that accompanied their privilege. He laced his lectures with calls for religious faith rooted in action, informed by Rauschenbusch's social gospel. "The Negro is on a special errand from God," Mays once wrote. That errand made the quest for justice a central part of the Black church. Mays told students they had the power to fight racism in ways that God would show them in good time. He made clear he would be deeply disappointed if his students failed to achieve distinction and do something to solve the world's problems. "However learned the Morehouse man may become," read a pamphlet at the time, "his destiny is tied up, and inevitably so, with the great mass of people who do the ordinary work of the world and need their souls lifted by contact and fellowship with the more privileged among us." Mays would send a small army of Black activists into the world, giving his young charges the hope, confidence, and connections to attack injustice at a time when the fear of reprisals deterred many others.

If Mays paid special attention to King, it may have been because King was one of the youngest students on campus, or because the college president enjoyed King's probing questions, or because King's father was a community leader. Later, Mays would say he sensed the young student's ambition and rebelliousness. King explored socialism and communism in college, but he developed no great attachment to any alternative economic system. "Whatever the system was," Mays said, "he would wage war against it."

From the moment he arrived at Morehouse, King understood that his great passions—scholarship, religion, public speaking, and the pursuit of racial justice—could coalesce, even if he wasn't sure how. He knew it because he saw how they came together in Mays. He also knew it because his professors challenged him to think critically and see old issues, including religion, in new ways. "During my student days at Morehouse," King recalled, "I read Thoreau's essay 'Civil Disobedience' for the first time. Fascinated by the idea of refusing to cooperate with an evil system, I was so deeply moved that I reread the work several times. This was my first intellectual contact with the theory of nonviolent resistance."

King said little at the time, as best we can tell, about his musical and artistic discoveries, about his thoughts on Ella Fitzgerald's hit single "Into Each Life Some Rain Must Fall" or the boxing heroics of Joe Louis. As far as his letters and sermons tell, he had little to say about World War II or Franklin Roosevelt. Even in later years, he made little mention of extracurricular reading, art, or popular culture. When he recalled his college years, he focused, understandably, on race and philosophy. Morehouse was a hothouse for the growing Black activist movement, where students grew more confident and more determined to see how quickly and how dramatically they could change society.

During his second year at Morehouse, "King came to the conclusion that he should be a minister," McCall said. The decision stemmed from his growing comprehension of the role a preacher could play in the community, as well as the influence of his father.

In 1946, King wrote a letter to the editor of *The Atlanta Constitution*— one of the first instances in which he took a public stand in the struggle for equality. The letter, which may have been written in response to the shotgun murder of two Black couples in Walton County, Georgia, read in part:

> We want and are entitled to the basic rights and opportunities of American citizens: The right to earn a living at work for which we are fitted by training and ability; equal opportunities in education, health, recreation, and similar public services; the right to vote; equality before the law . . .

> M. L. KING, JR.
> Morehouse College.

Two months after his eighteenth birthday, King made his debut as a journalist, covering Youth Day at Ebenezer church for the *Atlanta Daily World*. He also submitted an essay to the school newspaper, *The Maroon Tiger*, that ran under the headline "The Purpose of Education." In the *Tiger* essay, he stressed the importance of character and moral development for students, warning that educated men without morals might be the most dangerous men of all. He cited the example of Herman Eugene Talmadge, the Georgia governor who won reelection after declaring the perpetuation of white supremacy the only campaign issue that mattered. "We must remember that intelligence is not enough," wrote King. "Intelligence plus character—that is the goal of true education . . . If we are not careful, our colleges will produce a group of close-minded, unscientific, illogical propagandists, consumed with immoral acts. Be careful, 'brethren!' Be careful, teachers!"

King was impressed with Morehouse teachers like George D. Kelsey, who possessed a PhD from Yale and taught religion and philosophy. Kelsey gave King his only A at Morehouse. More important, Kelsey helped King see that Black pastors could be emotional, intellectual, and political all at the same time. Kelsey and Mays embodied that message. Kenneth L. Smith and Ira G. Zepp Jr., authors of a pioneering study on King's intellectual development, wrote that it was the experience with Kelsey and Mays that persuaded King to choose the Christian ministry as a career instead of law or medicine. King came to believe, Smith and Zepp wrote, that serving God was also the way he could best serve society.

King learned to put the emotionalism of the church in context. "All week long," he said, "at his job, traveling, shopping, eating, in almost everything he does, the Negro represses his emotions; puts up with discrimination; sees himself segregated and shunted into inferior housing, schools, jobs; closes his ears to the names he is called. On Sunday, when he goes to church, all these emotions burst forth. He shouts 'Amen.' He sings and stamps his feet, partly from joy at his freedom in his own church, partly from the sorrow of his experiences. For many Negroes, religion has probably provided a safety valve against insanity or rebellion. But there's a danger in this emotionalism, too. It can become as empty a form as any other. I often say to my people that if we . . . had as much religion in our hearts and souls as we have in our legs and feet, we could change the world."

In an exam in one of Kelsey's classes, King showed a keen understanding of the Bible and its historical context, writing words that would one day apply to himself: "It is obvious that prophets address themselves to the conditions existing in their time. Prophecy is a moral, not a magical thing."

In the summer of 1947—the season in which Jackie Robinson integrated big-league baseball with the Brooklyn Dodgers—King returned to Simsbury, Connecticut, for another season of tobacco farming. He continued preaching to his fellow farmers. But he was more confident than the last time he'd traveled north—and perhaps wilder, too. One night, he and some of his friends were stopped by police. Were they stopped simply because they were Black? Had they been drinking? Speeding? It's not clear. It's not even clear if they were issued a citation. But the encounter was serious enough that King decided to call home and tell his parents before they found out about it from someone else. Perhaps hoping to soften the blow, he began the conversation by saying he had finally made up his mind to follow his father into the ministry, something he had not firmly declared until that moment.

Daddy King, taking no chances, quickly scheduled a date for his son to deliver his first sermon at Ebenezer.

Years later, the younger King's friends would tease him, suggesting he was not called to the ministry by God so much as chased there by police. While admitting his calling was not "miraculous or supernatural," as he put it, King offered a practical explanation, saying he recognized the central importance of the church in Black life, understood the power of the preacher, and glimpsed a future in which his talents might serve God and humanity. At eighteen, he imagined a career as a "rational" minister, one who dedicated his life to God and justice and new ideas—and, perhaps, one who had his office on a college campus.

Preaching to his peers in Connecticut also may have had a greater impact than M.L. himself recognized. "Right in there," Daddy King said, referring to his son's second summer on the farm, "he found himself as a preacher." In interviews conducted for his unpublished autobiography, Daddy King says several times that he wanted his boys to choose careers other than the ministry, careers in which they would be generously paid, such as business or law. In fact, he returns repeatedly in the interviews to the theme of financial stability, saying he tried at one point to purchase the land his family farmed in Stockbridge, and saying at another point that he was proud to use his political connections to help his daughter get a job. "I thought I could help them choose what they wanted to be," he said. "Just a parent, anxious, but I didn't know. I wanted one to be a business major . . . This didn't work."

When M.L. called him from Connecticut to say he had made up his mind to preach, his father asked: "Now, are you sure of it . . . ? You're not going to make a whole lot of money."

"I know that," M.L. said. "I'm not looking for money. I'm looking to serve."

As the young King put it years later: "I came to see that God had placed a responsibility on my shoulders, and the more I tried to escape it the more frustrated I would become."

Benjamin Mays explained it another way: "King became a minister because he had to be one."

6

"A Sense of Responsibility"

"Can't hold 'em!" Martin Luther King Sr. shouted on the day of his son's first sermon at Ebenezer. It was the fall of 1947.

They were in the cramped, low-ceilinged church basement. But the basement couldn't contain the growing crowd.

"Can't hold 'em!"

Daddy King ushered everyone upstairs. Soon the main chapel was filled to capacity, a rare occurrence at Ebenezer, as even Daddy King admitted. "Never before had we seen so many people in that auditorium," he recalled years later. "My son was a drawing card."

Ebenezer Baptist Church was made of red brick. It looked like it had been constructed in the image of Reverend King: solid, strong, and humble, three stories tall, but with no spire reaching for the sky. It squatted on a city corner in a manner that suggested it wasn't going anywhere. Though A. D. Williams had built the church, it was the Reverend Martin Luther King Sr. and his wife, Alberta, who, beginning in 1914, had kept the pews filled ever since, he with his shouted sermons, she with her sweet, soulful music, promising a better tomorrow.

Now it was their son's turn. As their slender second child stepped to the pulpit, sunlight streamed through stained-glass windows, reflecting off the gold-painted pipes of the organ. M.L. had been rehearsing for years, standing before mirrors and checking the expression on his face, the manner in which his open hands sliced at the air, the thrust of his chest, the tilt of his head. He and his friend Larry Williams had traveled the city listening to

Black ministers, sampling phrases, comparing, and imitating. Williams, an Ebenezer member, was four years older than King. They had heard preachers even more emotional than Daddy King, men who whooped, moaned, and hollered until their voices gave out and sweat soaked their shirts. They had heard preachers whose sermons progressed from spoken to chanted to sung. They had heard preachers who read their sermons slowly and carefully, and others who improvised on favorite themes. They had heard Benjamin Mays many times, of course, as he delivered his smooth and sophisticated speeches. They had visited Wheat Street Baptist Church, a block away from Ebenezer, to hear William Holmes Borders apply the lessons of Moses and the slaves of Egypt to the lives of African Americans.

King and Williams had also studied the Reverend Harry Emerson Fosdick, the most celebrated preacher of his day, who reached millions with his nationwide radio broadcast. In the early 1930s, John D. Rockefeller built the Riverside Church in New York City as a base for Fosdick, who preached to more than two thousand people there on Sundays. Fosdick, a white man, was referred to as a pulpit psychologist. He chose not to wallow in talk of sin and punishment; instead, he spoke of hope, of the promise of the future, of God's purpose for all men. He used his wide appeal, as he put it, "to harness the great dynamics of the Gospel to contemporary tasks," much the way Benjamin Mays did.

Martin Luther King Jr. fused these elements to make his own style. He flashed evidence of his education as a sign of hope and pride. He made the pain of poor Black people his own. Although he was young and slender, his deep voice thundered even more emphatically than his father's from the pulpit. There was strength and warmth in it. He hit hard on the first syllables of his words and stretched his vowels. He started slowly and built speed. Even as he accelerated, as his voice crescendoed, as he swept his audience to greater heights, he remained in complete control. His promise was unmistakable.

The Kings' housekeeper, Georgia Lewis, shouted her approval as the boy she'd helped to raise began to speak. M.L.'s friend June Dobbs listened attentively, even nervously, because she knew how much this moment meant to him. She was glad that M.L. chose not to imitate his father. He didn't shout. He didn't stroll through the aisles as he spoke but used his hands, dramatically, to build energy behind his words. He made no attempt to hide his impressive vocabulary. He both challenged and embraced his audience. "He was a good thinker, and he had a touch, a way of putting it that went straight to your heart," she said. "Had he been just like his father, a little bit ostentatious, a little bit ready to argue . . . it would have gone flat. His emphasis was: don't just stick with the Bible, but think about how it can make you a better person. And he was sincere. He never changed from that."

The young preacher connected quickly to his audience, Dobbs said, and when he finished, the congregation rose in celebration.

—— · ——

Later, Larry Williams said King had borrowed his first Ebenezer sermon from a Fosdick sermon called "Life Is What We Make It." King changed one word of his sermon's title, calling his version "Life Is What *You* Make It."

Williams didn't say how much his friend borrowed, but if King stuck to the points Fosdick made, he would have told his congregation that life was theirs to shape. Life is what you make it by focusing on the things you like, the things you choose to do with your time. If you live in the city, you might like the city of culture; you might like the city of sweet, quiet family life; or you might like the city of crime. Life is what you make it by the way you handle trouble. When malice or misfortune finds you, do you hold it so close to your eyes that you can't see anything else? When someone judges you cruelly, do you curse them and fight? Do you quit? If Beethoven had listened to his critics and abandoned his music, how much beauty would be missing from the world? Life is what we make it by how we do our work. The hardest work in the world is the best work if we do it with dedication and passion for the cause. Learn to like the best things. Learn to handle life's difficulties with kindness and courage. Learn to do good work well, with the goal of improving the world. Do all those things, proving that life is what you make it, and you will enter the spirit of Christ.

Most, if not all, of the audience didn't know or didn't care whether King borrowed from another sermon. Many young preachers learned by trying out others' words. When he'd lifted a speech in high school, King had done it from the most obvious source possible: a book of prizewinning student speeches. Now he'd borrowed from one of the nation's most popular radio preachers. In later years, when he was confronted on his sourcing, he would speak forthrightly and unashamedly about his influences. King wasn't concerned with plagiarism; his goal was to move audiences. With that in mind, perhaps he thought it made sense to rely on texts that had already proved popular and sound. In fact, for years to come, King would continue using Fosdick's sermons, as well as the works of other well-known preachers. As the scholar Keith D. Miller wrote, King grew up in the tradition of preachers who presumed that "words are shared assets, not personal belongings." King was a voracious reader with a splendid memory. Everything he read became material for his own use. Like a talented jazz musician who integrates patterns and borrows phrases from classical music, pop, and opera, as well as from other jazz musicians, he possessed enough style and skill to make the finished product feel unique.

Daddy King never mentioned whether he recognized the influence of Fosdick on his son's first Ebenezer sermon. Nothing would cloud the satisfaction he felt at seeing M.L. ascend to his pulpit. He went home that night, got on his knees, and thanked God—though he did not tell his son how proud he felt.

———— · ————

King earned B's and C's in his senior year at Morehouse. He grew a mustache that he kept neatly trimmed. He was not so handsome as to take anyone's breath away, but he had a dazzling smile that inflated his cheekbones and altered the entire shape of his face, almost illuminating it. His low-key charm made men and women seek his company. He continued to dress more sharply than most of his classmates, and he carried himself with steadily growing confidence. Morehouse had something to do with that. The college did more than partially shield students from Jim Crow America. It urged them to think of themselves as special, as destined for greatness. King put it succinctly when he described Morehouse by saying, "I noticed that nobody there was afraid."

He dated beautiful women from prominent Atlanta families. Among his girlfriends were Mattiwilda Dobbs, the future opera singer and the sister of his friend June; and Juanita Sellers, a Spelman student, friend of Christine King, and daughter of one of the city's most successful Black morticians. He wooed them with poetry. He offered tributes to their beauty and boasted of the Rubicons he would cross for their affections, sometimes offering lines from Edgar Allan Poe, delivered in that deep voice, with those hammered first syllables and vibratory vowels:

On desperate seas, long wont to roam,
Thy hyacinth hair, thy classic face,
Thy Naiad airs have brought me home
To the glory that was Greece.
And the grandeur that was Rome.

King dated many women. He and Larry Williams referred to themselves in jest as "Robinson and Stevens, the Wreckers," after an Atlanta wrecking company. When a friend asked why, King smiled: "We wreck girls," he said.

The closest he came to a steady girlfriend in Atlanta was Juanita Sellers. After Spelman, Sellers studied at Columbia University and taught college English in Savannah, Tallahassee, and Princess Anne, Maryland, before taking over her family's funeral home in Atlanta. Daddy King approved of Sellers, too, perhaps because marriage to a local girl from a prominent family might keep his son at home in Atlanta.

Reverend King still held a powerful grip on M.L., but the elder King seemed to grow less fearsome as his son matured. Not long after M.L.'s trial sermon, for example, father and son argued over M.L.'s decision to join an organization called the Intercollegiate Council and Forum, an interracial group that discussed bridging the divide between the races and alternated its monthly meetings between Emory University, an all-white school, and the Atlanta University colleges, which were entirely Black. Daddy King told his son not to trust the organization's white leaders. "You don't need to risk any betrayals from them, and that's mainly what you'll get," he said. Though M.L. had long resented the way some white people had treated him, he told his father that maintaining such resentment "would be too easy." He wasn't ready to give up on white people, he said. The men went back and forth until Daddy King admitted he'd "run out of arguments."

The young men and women of M. L. King's generation could afford to take more risks than their parents had. They saw the NAACP and A. Philip Randolph make gains. They saw Jackie Robinson integrate major league baseball. They saw President Harry Truman establish a commission to study civil rights and saw the commission publish a report stating that the government had a duty not only to prevent discrimination but also to guarantee equal rights for all citizens.

All of this coincided with M. L. King's senior year at Morehouse. He still lived at home. And though he still expressed doubts about his father's style of preaching, he served as an assistant pastor at Ebenezer. Since his formal ordination on February 25, 1948, he no longer spoke of other career options. The only question was whether he would stay on as assistant to his father or strike out on his own. M.L. faced frustrations working in the family business. When Daddy King learned that his son had attended a dance with some of his Morehouse classmates, for example, the senior pastor reminded his assistant pastor that Baptists frowned on dancing. The following Sunday, Daddy King made M.L. stand before the congregation and apologize.

They clashed yet again when M.L. announced that he had decided that after completing his bachelor's degree at Morehouse he would continue his education in the North, at Crozer Theological Seminary, a predominantly white, nondenominational school in Chester, Pennsylvania. It was small, with only about forty students. Crozer was often called "the little University of Chicago Divinity School," as the scholars Kenneth L. Smith and Ira G. Zepp Jr. have noted, because it taught the kind of American religious liberalism that had emerged in reaction to the rigid orthodoxy of much of the nineteenth-century Protestant establishment. The faculty at Crozer embraced biblical criticism and reckoned with Darwin's theory of evolution, preparing students, as Smith and Zepp wrote, to engage with the "modern mind" and "the spirit of the age."

Daddy King didn't believe that his nineteen-year-old son needed a seminary education. He relented, though, and wrote a letter of recommendation to Crozer, calling his son "very conscientious" and possessed of a "very pleasing personality." Benjamin Mays was less glowing in a letter he wrote on behalf of King and his friend Walter McCall, saying the men were "not brilliant students, but they both have good minds." Morehouse's dean, Brailsford R. Brazeal, wrote in his letter of recommendation that King had been held back by "a comparatively weak high school background," and assured officials at Crozer that the undergraduate's middle-of-the-pack 2.48 grade point average was not the truest measure of his intelligence.

Speaking for himself, King wrote in his application: "My call to the ministry was quite different from most explinations [sic] I've heard. This dicision [sic] came about in the summer of 1944 when I felt an inescapable urge to serve society. In short, I felt a sense of responsibility which I could not escape."

—— · ——

"If you can do one single thing towards a just, durable, and creative peace, you will have fulfilled your major obligation to the world," said Dr. Kenneth I. Brown, president of Denison University, as he addressed King and 112 other Morehouse graduates in June 1948.

King was one of three students to receive an oratorical prize at graduation. The *Atlanta Daily World*'s report on the graduation would appear to mark the first publication of the full name "Martin Luther King Jr."

King worked that summer with June Dobbs on a research project for Ira De Augustine Reid, a sociology professor who had recently left Morehouse to become the first Black tenured faculty member at Haverford College, a Quaker school outside Philadelphia. Reid asked King and Dobbs to conduct interviews with Black Baptist ministers for a comprehensive survey he planned to publish. The highlight of the summer, "for both M.L. and myself," said Dobbs, was listening to a sermon by the Reverend Vernon Johns at

Gammon Theological Seminary in Atlanta. Johns was a radical minister who treated racism as a social evil held in God's contempt. On the day Dobbs and King heard him, Johns reflected on the question posed by the German zoologist and atheist Ernst Haeckel—Is the universe friendly?—and concluded that the life of Jesus Christ compels us to answer in the affirmative.

Dobbs, who would go on to become a sex researcher and therapist, had a way of making people comfortable, helping them express feelings that might otherwise have remained submerged. M.L. told her that Daddy King was a frequent womanizer. Dobbs had already heard the rumors. M.L. said he was worried that he would someday wind up like his father, unable to resist the temptation of adultery. The subject arose every day M.L. and Dobbs were together that summer. "It obsessed him," she said. The subject arose as often as it did in part because young King and Dobbs were talking to ministers who were Daddy King's peers, men who whispered about Daddy King's reputation as an adulterer. "There was a great deal of gossip about Reverend King," Dobbs recalled.

M.L. and Dobbs would look for a shady spot to eat lunch or cool off between interviews, and they would talk about their frustrations and dreams. Dobbs recognized that, in many ways, M.L. worshipped his father. Daddy King was a powerful figure who had escaped poverty, overcome his own father's violence, and emerged as a man of God and a leader in the battle for the rights of Black people. His life story offered a path forward for his son, but, as Dobbs saw it, M.L. was determined to do more than follow his father.

That summer at a Black Baptist convention in Jackson, Georgia, M.L. challenged the views of church leaders, including his father, who declared dancing a sin. M.L. argued that the act of dancing was not a sin unless the dancer's thoughts were sinful, according to a letter to the editor in the *Atlanta Daily World* written by a young woman who heard M.L. speak at the convention.

M.L. grew angry at his father's moral failures, Dobbs said. At the same time, he understood that women were drawn to men in positions of authority. Already, he told Dobbs, women at Ebenezer were "throwing themselves at him." He vowed to resist. M.L. told Dobbs he wanted to marry a woman like her, someone smart and strong, someone who could be his equal, and that he intended to be a faithful husband.

Dobbs doubted him.

Still, she said years later, "My heart went out to him because . . . he tried to be honest about it."

7

The Seminarian

Before leaving Atlanta in the fall of 1948, King registered for the draft, recording his height at five-foot-seven-and-a-half and his weight at about 150 pounds. The Selective Service System noted that he had a scar on the back of his left hand.

On his way to Crozer, he stopped in New York City to visit his sister, Christine, who was studying for a master's degree in education at Columbia University. At Crozer, he moved into Room 52 on the second floor of the school's main building, referred to as Old Main. He had a six-by-eight-foot room with a twin bed, a dresser, a desk, a table lamp, and a chair. His window overlooked the center of campus and its thick grove of maple trees. The campus covered more than two dozen acres of fertile countryside in the quiet town of Chester, twelve miles from Philadelphia. Old Main had once been a military hospital. A wounded Confederate soldier had once occupied M.L.'s room.

At nineteen, King was younger than most of his classmates. Years later, he would describe his life's mission in the grandest terms—to discover a method for the elimination of social evils. At this point, he imagined a career in the pulpit or perhaps in a teaching position at a university, not as a civil rights activist. His focus was on spiritual development. At Crozer, he said, the quest truly began.

He'd been away from home before, but never for so long, never with so much freedom, and never in such an integrated setting. White maids cleaned his room, and white cooks prepared his food. White teachers judged him against white students, some of them a decade older, some of them married with children, others World War II veterans. Dormitory room doors had no locks. King expressed guilt at times, wondering why his friends back in Atlanta couldn't enjoy such wonders. Prior to his arrival, the school had had only two Black students. But in King's class, ten of the sixteen students were Black, their admissions part of an attempt to offset declining enrollment.

Crozer was so small that no one escaped scrutiny. King introduced himself as Mike, although he wrote his name on papers and in correspondence as M.L. Eager to make a good impression, he studied harder than ever, dressed extra sharply, and tried not to laugh too loudly, not to dispense too many gratuitous compliments, and not to call attention to himself by arriving late to class. But he still stood out for his intelligence and sociability. Even then, said his classmate James Beshai, King talked of leading his people in the fight for racial justice, although he envisioned doing so mostly from the pulpit. "He once asked if I considered myself white or Black," said Beshai, who was born in Egypt and had fair skin. "I told him in Egypt that question was never raised, that they talked about whether you were Christian or Muslim." As a Christian, Beshai told King, he grew up feeling like a minority. But years later, Beshai would reflect on whether he'd been completely honest or completely aware of his feelings at the time. He would wonder why he preferred the companionship of white students at Crozer. He would reflect on the universality of racism, of the deep scars of slavery. King was already grappling with such issues at Crozer, but Beshai was not. "He was a very honest man and a modest person," Beshai said, "and he was already searching for the brotherhood of man and equality, which is also the Christian method. It's the search for truth."

In his first semester at Crozer, in the fall of 1948, King took a class called Introduction to the Old Testament, taught by James B. Pritchard, who challenged students with his historical-critical take on the Bible, saying many of its stories were not to be taken as reliable history. Pritchard had found that Black students from the Deep South were particularly literal about their approach to the Bible, and he strived to shake them of their old ideas, as Patrick Parr wrote in *The Seminarian,* his important book on King's Crozer years. That approach appealed to King, who had long bristled at his father's fundamentalism. Yet for all his enthusiasm and determination, when in his first semester he was assigned by Pritchard to write a paper about the prophet Jeremiah, King fell back on a bad habit: he plagiarized—and this time in an academic setting where the consequences might have been severe.

"Religion, in a sense, through men like Jeremiah, provides for its own advancement, and carries with it the promise of progress and renewed power," he wrote. The line came from a 1932 book titled *The Rebel Prophet*, by T. Crouther Gordon. Elsewhere in the same paper he copied all but one word of a passage from *Prophecy and Religion*, first published in 1922 by the renowned Old Testament scholar John Skinner.

With only nine students in the class, Pritchard should have had ample time to scrutinize his students' papers. He might have noticed that King's writing was far smoother in some passages than others. But he didn't. He later hired King to babysit his children, paying him thirty-five cents an hour and giving the young student one of his first and most intimate views of white middle-class home life.

King also took a class called Preaching Ministry of the Church, the first of ten courses he would take with Robert Keighton, a scholar of British literature, a theater lover, and a liberal Protestant. Keighton encouraged his students to preach like Harry Emerson Fosdick, who had already inspired King, teaching them to apply grace and sophistication rather than sweaty exhortations. Keighton stressed the three *p*'s of oratory: proving, painting, and persuading. He taught structure, too. The "ladder sermon" built one argument atop another. The "jewel sermon" considered one idea from multiple perspectives. The "skyrocket sermon" began with a bang followed by a cascade of smaller ideas.

Many students struggled to meet the professor's expectations, but King earned a B-plus in his first class with Keighton. In a handwritten outline for the course, King showed eagerness to embrace the teacher's approach, although he made it clear that sophistication was not enough and that he, like Fosdick, hoped to use sermons to fight for the cause of social justice. "I think that preaching should grow out of experiences of the people,"

King wrote. "Therefore, I as a minister must know the problems of the people that I am pastoring." Often, an educated minister leaves people "lost in the fog of theological abstractions." Above all, King said, the preaching ministry was a dual process. "On the one hand I must attempt to change the soul of the individuals so that their societies may be changed. On the other hand I must attempt to change the societies so that the individual soul will have a change." Mentioning the problems of unemployment and poverty, he added: "I am a profound advocator of the social gospel."

King navigated Crozer, in part, by managing what W. E. B. Du Bois called "double-consciousness," or an ability to look at oneself through the eyes of another. King said he hesitated to eat watermelon because he didn't wish to feed white stereotypes. White people who knew him at Crozer would sometimes recall him as humorless and soft-spoken, but that was because King chose not to reveal himself, as he explained:

> I was well aware of the typical white stereotype of the Negro—that he is always late, that he's loud and always laughing, that he's dirty and messy—and for a while I was terribly conscious of trying to avoid identification with it. If I was a minute late to class, I was almost morbidly conscious of it and sure that everyone else noticed it. Rather than be thought of as always laughing, I'm afraid I was grimly serious for a time. I had a tendency to overdress, to keep my room spotless, my shoes perfectly shined and my clothes immaculately pressed.

When he was among his Black friends, he opened up. He ate his favorite southern foods in massive quantities and often with his hands, laughing, saying the ham and chops and collard greens were too delicious to let utensils interfere with their consumption. "He could eat more than any little man you ever saw in your life," said the Reverend J. Pius Barbour, who invited King to dine frequently at his home in Chester. King also attended services at Barbour's church. Barbour would become one of King's major pastoral influences. Born in 1894 in Galveston, Texas, Barbour had studied at Morehouse and Crozer—the same path King was following—and gone on to lead a church in Montgomery, Alabama, in the 1920s. In Chester, even as he preached to an all-Black congregation, Barbour served as a kind of diplomat to the white community, writing a regular column for the *Chester Times*.

King admired the older preacher's rhyming, rhythmic phrases, and he doodled similar phrases of his own in his notebooks. He absorbed the lessons of white professors who encouraged him to preach with calm, cool intellect, but he never forgot the audiences to whom he'd one day be preaching, and he never forgot that the Gospel could be used for social change. King told Barbour the revolution would have to be a nonviolent one if the minority were to have a chance of success. "Just a matter of arithmetic," he said.

King's genius in later years would be his ability to deliver messages that inspired Black and white listeners alike, messages that made racial justice sound like an imperative for all, messages that crossed lines of theology and geography, that suggested both sides needed to act if the racial divide were ever to be erased without violence. He knew from his childhood in Atlanta and from the stories told by his parents and grandparents that America was the product of Black and white culture, the product of the conflict and mixture of different people. Crozer helped him find the right words and the right tone so that he could one day explain his diagnosis clearly and passionately to audiences of every race.

"I guess it must have been a gift from God," his mother once said of her son's talent. "I don't think anybody taught him. Can you be taught to preach? I didn't think you could."

Yet Crozer helped. At Crozer, King read Plato, Aristotle, Rousseau, Hobbes, Bentham, Mill, Nietzsche, and, during the Christmas holidays of 1949, Marx. King had already written and spoken of his doubts about the fairness of capitalism and the gap it created between the rich and poor. He had problems with communism, too, primarily because of its secular and materialistic foundation. "This I could never accept," he wrote, "for as a Christian I believe that there is a creative personal power in the universe who is the ground and essence of all reality—a power that can not be explained in materialistic terms." History, he concluded, was guided by the spirit, not by matter.

He experienced a crisis of confidence, he said, while reading Nietzsche, who described Christianity's call for universal love as a sign of weakness. King wondered for a time if Christ's instruction "Love your enemies" (Luke 6:27) really had enough power to resolve conflicts among nations or racial groups.

He continued to show particular interest in the social gospel of Walter Rauschenbusch, who argued that the "Kingdom of God" required not only personal salvation but social justice, too. King admired Rauschenbusch's call to action and related to his sense of optimism. It is "quite easy," he wrote, "for me to think of the universe as basically friendly."

———— · ————

King believed that human personality reflected the spirit of God. But the negative corollary to that belief meant that racism, which degraded personality and denigrated human life, had to be evil. Even in the North, he experienced that evil. A white student pulled a gun on King after accusing him of performing a prank that involved messing up the white student's room. King earned respect and popularity on campus for his calm response to the incident and his refusal to file a complaint against the white student.

On June 11, 1950, King and Walter McCall attended a Sunday-evening church service. When it was over, they drove to Mary's Café, a tavern in nearby Maple Shade, New Jersey, accompanied by McCall's girlfriend and her roommate. By the time they arrived, it was after midnight. They asked for two bottles of beer and four glasses. But the bartender, a German immigrant, refused to serve them, saying it was against the law to sell packaged liquor on Sunday or on any day after 10:00 p.m. McCall asked for draft beer instead, but the bartender still refused. When McCall asked for ginger ale, the bartender grew angry. He drew a .45, stepped outside, fired in the air, and then returned to the bar and cursed McCall and the others. King's group fled to a nearby police station, where they made a report. Later, King and McCall filed charges against the bartender for violating New Jersey's antidiscrimination laws, among the first in the nation, alleging that they'd been denied service because they were Black. The local chapter of the NAACP agreed to represent them, saying the case would be part of a larger drive against public places that refused service to Black customers. In a front-page story, *The Philadelphia Tribune* named King as one of the complainants, referring to him as Michael.

The bartender went to court on a weapons-possession charge the same day that King's brother, A.D., had planned to get married in Atlanta. On the morning of the wedding, M.L., still in Pennsylvania, called and asked his brother to postpone the ceremony. A.D. was angry. His father had always made him feel inferior to his brother. Once again, he was being asked to defer to M.L., and yet he agreed. The bartender was found guilty and fined $50. King and McCall dropped the discrimination case when some of the customers in the tavern refused to testify before a grand jury.

Years later, King would compare his encounter with the bartender to sit-ins that swept across the South, when Black students demanded service at whites-only lunch counters and restaurants. He also strongly suggested that he and his friends had chosen Mary's Café to test the state's integration laws.

"They refused to serve us," King said. "It was a painful experience because we decided to sit in."

McCall described it as King's "first civil rights struggle." It also marked one of his earliest lessons in the limits of northern liberalism.

8

"Madly, Madly in Love"

KING DATED HIS first and only white girlfriend at Crozer. Her name was Amelia Elizabeth Moitz.

Betty, as everyone called her, was two years older than King. She and her family lived on campus. Betty's father was an electrician; her mother was the school's cook and dietician, having taken over the position from her own mother. Betty had one more connection to Crozer: before dating King, she had been the steady girlfriend of a professor there, Kenneth Lee "Snuffy" Smith, a white Baptist from Virginia. When King met Betty in the Crozer kitchen, he almost certainly knew that Betty had been dating Smith; romantic liaisons on such a small campus were almost impossible to hide. But Betty took a quick liking to King—his elegant wardrobe, his soothing smile, his warm laugh, his confidence—and she soon dropped the professor.

At first, some of King's friends thought his interest in Betty Moitz grew from the novelty and boldness of dating a white woman. "King was extremely fond of her," said his friend Marcus Wood. "But he was also rather proud of the fact that he was able to socialize openly with a white girl."

King continued dating other young women, including several in Atlanta.

Returning home in the summer of 1949, King showed how serious he had become about his future career. He preached almost every Sunday, sometimes twice in a day, at Ebenezer and other churches. One Sunday morning, a young man from Alabama dropped by Ebenezer, eager to listen to the sharp new preacher he'd been hearing so much about. This young Alabaman, Ralph David Abernathy, was also preparing for a career in the ministry.

Abernathy burned with envy as he listened to M. L. King Jr. The young man had a big congregation in a big city, but he was not merely the beneficiary of nepotism; he was gifted. "Already he was a scholar," Abernathy recalled, "and while he didn't holler as loud as some of the more famous preachers I had heard, he could holler loud enough when he wanted to." The men shook hands after the service.

A few days later, Abernathy attended a choir concert on the Spelman College campus. He was supposed to have a date, but the young woman had canceled at the last moment, saying she had a bad cold. Abernathy went to the concert alone. But when he arrived at the venue and scanned the crowd, he spotted his date on the arm of the man whose sermon he had recently admired: Ebenezer's M. L. King.

"Well, hello, Mr. Abernathy," King said, waving with his free hand.

"Good evening, Mr. King," Abernathy said.

The girl on King's arm ducked her head but did not release her grip.

"I just want to tell you again how much I enjoyed your sermon," Abernathy said.

"Thank you," King answered. "It's kind of you to say so."

King worked hard in his second and third years at Crozer and impressed professors with his ambition. He became a more resolute student and leader. He developed, as Patrick Parr wrote in *The Seminarian*, a "desire to give himself to a greater cause—a cause he hoped God would help him see." In a 1950 evaluation, George W. Davis, who taught King for 30 of his 110 course hours, wrote:

1. Exceptional intellectual ability—discriminating mind;
2. Very personable;

3. Makes good impression in public speaking and discussion. Good speaking voice;
4. A man of high character;
5. Should make an excellent minister or teacher. He has the mind for the latter.

King's beliefs became more nuanced as he studied the works of Reinhold Niebuhr, in classes taught by Smith. Niebuhr argued that man's sinfulness would inevitably interfere with attempts to form a more just society. Christian love alone would not change the world, not so long as political and economic systems created vast inequalities among God's children. Nations and privileged groups within those nations would preserve the status quo, by force if necessary. In his 1932 book, *Moral Man and Immoral Society*, Niebuhr wrote that an oppressed minority group with no chance of amassing the power to challenge its oppressors might do well to adopt a strategy of nonviolence, as Gandhi did in India. "The emancipation of the Negro race in America probably waits upon the adequate development of this kind of social and political strategy," Niebuhr wrote. "It is hopeless for the Negro to expect complete emancipation from the menial social and economic position into which the white man has forced him . . . It is equally hopeless to attempt emancipation through violent rebellion."

King earned A's in his philosophy classes and C's in public speaking, in part because some of his white professors, it seems, were not enthralled with the Black Baptist style.

He learned to accept contradiction. He studied with distinguished scholars who said the Bible could only be understood by considering the historical context in which it was written, by stripping away the colorful legends. But on Sundays he went to Black churches and preached to worshippers for whom Moses was as real and relevant as Abraham Lincoln. Exodus was not only understandable to his church audiences; it was underway. King never let his scholarship get in the way of his message. He was finding a voice, a voice that combined what he had learned from his father and his fellow Black preachers as well as from his professors, a voice full of passion and sophistication, a voice that would appeal to audiences across racial and economic lines, and a voice that would one day be essential to the success of the civil rights movement.

He honed his delivery. He had a gift for making his speech both rhythmic and melodic, but it was a gift improved by practice. One Crozer classmate recalled hearing King, his deep, rich, trembling voice echoing from his small dorm room in Old Main, as he recited the famous passage from Amos 5:24: "But let judgment run down like waters, and righteousness as a mighty stream."

On November 19, 1950, a Sunday, King traveled from Chester to attend a lecture by Mordecai Johnson, a Morehouse graduate and the president of Howard University, at Philadelphia's First Unitarian Church. Johnson, who had just returned from a trip to India, lectured on Gandhi. "His message was so profound," King wrote years later, "that I left the meeting and bought a half dozen books on Gandhi's life and works." The books helped King overcome some of the doubts raised from his reading of Nietzsche. Gandhi showed King that "the love ethic of Jesus . . . was a potent instrument for social and collective transformation. It was in this Gandhian emphasis on love and nonviolence that I discovered the method for social reform that I had been seeking for so many months."

Using a Greek word from the New Testament that theologians often employed, King referred to that loving spirit as *agape*, a love that offered understanding and goodwill to all, a force that made no distinction between friends and enemies, that encouraged love of everyone because God loved everyone. *Agape*, he said, offered the kind of power to fuel a nonviolent movement for justice.

"When we love on the *agape* level," he wrote years later, "we love men not because we like them . . . but because God loves them."

It was a message true to Hebrew prophets, true to the idea that God's grand design required the participation and struggle of God's people, true to the idea that unearned suffering was redemptive. The mighty stream of righteousness represented a movement—one strong enough to wear away the stones of injustice.

———— • ————

As King's studies continued, so did his romance with Betty Moitz. The couple made little effort to hide their relationship during King's second year on campus. The sweethearts sat together on park benches, held hands, and took drives in Betty's car. M.L. told Betty about his plans to return to the South and fight for justice for his people, something they both knew would be impossible with a white spouse. "I listened," Betty recalled in an interview decades later, "and he'd just talk and talk."

When Christine King visited her brother at Crozer, she did not meet or hear about Betty. Decades later, when Christine did learn about Betty, she said her brother had been more worried about their mother's reaction to the relationship than their father's. M.L. had defied his father every time he had sipped alcohol, smoked a cigarette, shot a game of pool, attended a dance, or suggested he might grow up to be something other than a preacher—but defying his mother was another matter. It was Alberta to whom he turned for advice, Alberta with whom he could gab for hours on the phone, Alberta with whom he shared laughs, and Alberta whose approval he craved when the issues were the most personal.

Once Christine had gone, Betty no longer hid. She tagged along as M.L. played table tennis and shot pool with classmates.

"We were madly, madly in love," she recalled, "the way young people can fall in love."

King asked his friends what they thought might happen if he and Betty were to marry. He would almost certainly not be able to lead a church in the South. If he had to remain in the North, would he be happy there? Ambitious young ministers of King's generation understood that a good early marriage could help one's career. It offered proof of maturity and commitment for congregations in search of new leaders. In fact, King told a friend he hoped to be married within a year of graduation from Crozer, although he did not say to whom.

"He wanted to marry her," said James Beshai, King's classmate, "but his father told him it would create obstacles for him."

One day King brought Betty to the home of his mentor, the Reverend J. Pius Barbour. He asked Barbour, for the sake of argument, why he and Betty shouldn't be married right then and there, with Barbour officiating. Barbour argued that society would never accept an interracial marriage, even if Pennsylvania law allowed it, and that King's decision would wreck his career regardless of whether he lived in the North or the South. King argued that perhaps love was more important than society's prejudiced views or one man's career ambitions.

As she listened, Betty understood how little support King would receive from family and friends if they were to wed.

Eventually, King ended the relationship.

"She liked me and I found myself liking her," he explained years later to one writer. "But finally I had to tell her resolutely that my plans for the future did not include marriage to a white woman."

Betty left Chester before the end of King's final year at Crozer. King dated other women. On the morning of his graduation, he phoned Barbour to say that several women were planning to attend the graduation ceremony, each one expecting to be introduced to King's parents as his fiancée. King asked Barbour to sit with them in the hopes that others would think they were members of Barbour's congregation. Still, Barbour said, King was deeply saddened by his breakup with Betty Moitz. Barbour described him as "a man of a broken heart," adding: "He never recovered."

Harry Belafonte, who became King's close friend years later, seconds the point. King never stopped thinking about Betty Moitz, never stopped talking about her, especially with Belafonte, who had married a white woman. King marveled at the way society had accepted Belafonte's marriage, although he surely knew that standards were different for a Baptist preacher in the South than they were for a celebrated entertainer who spent most of his time in New York and Hollywood and who enjoyed popularity with Black and white audiences.

But those were rational thoughts, and King's feelings were emotional. Betty Moitz, according to Belafonte, had been King's "true love."

Betty went on to become an interior decorator and an antique dealer. She married in 1955 and had three children.

"I wouldn't say he was broken-hearted," she recalled decades later. "I would say he was probably more angry that he would have feelings for someone and he couldn't go ahead and do what he wanted to do because of the race situation."

9

The Match

KING EARNED A bachelor of arts degree in divinity from Crozer and graduated as valedictorian, winning a $1,200 scholarship for graduate study. His parents rewarded him with a car, a green Chevrolet with Powerglide, the new two-speed automatic transmission that allowed for quick, smooth acceleration without the use of a clutch.

But if Martin Sr. and Alberta King had hoped to see their son driving the Chevy around Atlanta, smoothly accelerating from home to church, and perhaps soon hauling grandchildren in the back seat, they were disappointed. In the fall of 1951, King took the car from Atlanta to Boston, where he enrolled at Boston University in pursuit of a doctorate.

Daddy King hadn't been happy with his son's decision to go to seminary. He had more reason to complain now that his son seemed intent on an academic career. M.L. knew better than to argue with his father. "Oh, yes," he would say vaguely when listening to something he didn't want to hear and didn't wish to debate. He knew by now that he didn't need to persuade his father to get his way. If there were any doubt that M.L. had his mind on a career beyond the pulpit, he confirmed it in his application to Boston University. "For a number of years I have been desirous of teaching in a college or a school of religion," he wrote. "It is my candid opinion that the teaching of theology should be as scientific, as thorough, and as realistic as any other discipline. In a word, scholarship is my goal."

Boston University was a historically Methodist school, with a predominantly white faculty and student body. Daddy King, despite reservations about his son's decision, agreed to pay all of M.L.'s graduate school expenses not covered by his scholarship. Perhaps he was relieved that M.L. had chosen Boston University and not the University of Edinburgh in Scotland, which had been among his top choices, and which might have set his life and career on a dramatically different path.

King chose BU, in large part, for the chance to study with Edgar S. Brightman, known for his philosophical understanding of the idea of a personal God, not an impersonal deity lacking human characteristics. "In the broadest sense," Brightman wrote, "personalism is the belief that conscious personality is both the supreme value and the supreme reality in the universe." To personalists, God is seen as a loving parent, God's children as subjects of compassion. The universe is made up of persons, and all personalities are made in the image of God. The influence of personalism would support King's future indictments of segregation and discrimination, "because personhood," wrote the scholars Kenneth L. Smith and Ira G. Zepp Jr., "implies freedom and responsibility."

Before he left for Boston in the fall of 1951, the Kings had hoped that M.L. might propose marriage to Juanita Sellers. Mama and Daddy King liked Juanita. She was one of Christine King's best friends. She was practically family. According to June Dobbs Butts, M.L. did propose to Juanita that summer. At age twenty-two, he felt ready to start a family. But Juanita wanted assurance that they would live in Atlanta when M.L. finished his studies, and M.L. would not guarantee it. He had his eyes on a job in academia, but he also knew that he might work as a preacher in a small town before he settled into a university job. "He said God talked with him," Butts recalled, and God told him to get his degree, find a mate, and "go to the first church that calls," even if turned out to be in the fictional small town "Chitlin' Switch, Georgia." But Juanita "wasn't good with that," and talk of marriage ended, according to Butts, who said she heard of the conversation from Juanita immediately after the proposal had taken place.

In Boston, where he began to introduce himself as Martin, he didn't take long to find new romances. His approach to women at times resembled a competitive sport, according to Dorothy Cotton, the civil rights activist who would later become close to King. He would "try to make sure he could win the girlfriend of the tallest . . . handsomest guy on the campus," Cotton said. "And that became a bit of a habit, I feel."

One day while he was eating lunch at a Sharaf's Cafeteria, he spotted a fair-skinned African American woman, seated alone. King got up from his seat and approached her.

"You're not eating your beets," he said.

The young woman looked up and said she hated beets.

King said he felt the same way and asked if he could join her for lunch. Her name was LaVerne Weston, and she was a Texas native who studied at the New England Conservatory of Music. She and King bonded over the cafeteria's failure to offer an alternative to beets with the chicken platter. LaVerne admired King's natty wardrobe and warm personality. He talked a lot and bragged a bit, but he asked good questions, and he listened, too. She could tell he was smart. She could tell he came from a good family. It was obvious that he was flirting, but LaVerne wasn't interested. King was too short for her taste.

"I'm going to kill Jim Crow," King told her.

Amused, LaVerne didn't ask how he planned to get it done.

King addressed the subject of marriage right up front. He told LaVerne he wanted to marry a woman who would treat him like his mother did, rubbing liniment on his chest when he was sick and tending to his every need. That was not the picture of wedded bliss that LaVerne, an aspiring opera singer, had in mind. Nevertheless, she was charmed. When they finished their food, leaving the beets behind, he offered to take her home.

"And he had a car!" she recalled. "Black kids did not have cars in those days . . . I had never in my life got in a car with a strange person. I said, 'Oh, my goodness!' But I did, I got in his car." He did not try to kiss her, but he said he hoped they would meet again soon.

LaVerne did see him again soon, and often. On Sundays after church, she and her friends ate at Western Lunchbox, a tiny soul food restaurant, and she would run into King and his friends there.

After his first semester at BU, King and one of his friends from Morehouse, Philip Lenud, a student at the Crane Theological School, affiliated with Tufts University, rented an apartment at 397 Massachusetts Avenue, a South End rowhouse. The place was piled high with books. Morehouse pennants hung on the wall above the sofa. Lenud, an Alabama native, did most of the cooking; King washed dishes. King made frequent phone calls home, reversing the charges. The apartment became a hub for young intellectuals and artists. King hosted a weekly potluck supper for a group he called the Dialectical Society or, sometimes, the Philosophical Club. The men smoked pipes. Graduate students read their papers aloud. Spirited discussions followed. They recorded the minutes and reviewed them at subsequent meetings. At first the meetings were attended exclusively by Black men, but they diversified over time, accepting women and the occasional white person. King was more than comfortable in taking a leadership role. With the Philosophical Club, peers saw King already as a leader and a charismatic figure, urbane, sociable, and pleased to be at the center of attention.

"Martin was the guru," said Sybil Haydel Morial, who grew up in New Orleans, attended Boston University, and went to parties as well as casual gatherings at King's apartment. She would become an educator, an activist, and wife to the first Black mayor of New Orleans, Ernest N. "Dutch" Morial. "He was the leader of it," she said of King. "He was so even-tempered and so self-possessed and so humble . . . And he had a car!"

Boston was not free from racism by any stretch. The Red Sox would not integrate their team until 1959, although Sam Jethroe integrated the Boston Braves in 1950, before that team moved to Milwaukee. Public schools remained segregated in practice. But it was far better than the South, Sybil Morial said. Boston had art and theater and integrated colleges. From September 21 to September 23, 1951, the Boston Garden hosted an all-star jazz concert with the Duke Ellington Orchestra, Sarah Vaughan, and the Nat King Cole Trio, whose recording of "Too Young" had topped the charts that summer. The Boston Celtics, with Chuck Cooper, had one of the first racially integrated teams in the National Basketball Association. Boston also had a seemingly endless array of ambitious young Black men and women from prosperous families. King attended services at Twelfth Baptist Church, a congregation that had been founded by free people of color in 1840, served as a stop on the Underground Railroad, and had a long history of organized protest.

"It was thrilling because everything was open," Morial said. "Those of us from the South loved the freedom of the North." The young men and women often discussed whether to remain in the North, or "Freedomland," as Morial called it. At first, Morial said, most of her acquaintances in Boston vowed to stay in the North, but their views shifted as they began to miss home and began to see signs that cultural and political reform might be possible in the South. Even in Boston, King felt pulled to return to the South, in part because Boston's Black community was "spiritually located in the South," as the scholar Lewis V. Baldwin writes. "I am going back where I am needed," King said in Boston.

One day, King told a friend from Atlanta, Mary Powell, that he'd been having little luck in dating of late. Mary said she knew two women Martin might like: one of them was LaVerne Weston, whom King had already met over lunch at Sharaf's Cafeteria; the other was a conservatory classmate of Weston's named Coretta Scott. Years later, King said he was so excited by Powell's description of Coretta Scott that he couldn't wait for a formal introduction. "I said, 'You better give me the telephone number' . . . I decided that I would introduce myself." He phoned her within two hours of receiving her number, on a Thursday night in February 1952. As usual, he flashed confidence. "I am like Napoleon; I'm at my Waterloo and I'm on my knees," he said. Coretta took that to mean he had reached the end of the line when it came to dating. He was desperate to find a woman he could love and marry.

"He was a typical man," she said. "Smoothness. Jive. Some of it I had never heard in my life."

She enjoyed the jive, as she later admitted, but at first she didn't want to let him think it was working. She pointed out in that initial phone call that he was getting awfully carried away about a woman he had never met.

King replied that he didn't need to meet her to know. Coretta's voice was so lovely, her intelligence so evident, her reputation so sterling, that he was certain he had found his match. Coretta laughed and agreed to meet him for lunch the next day. King said he would pick her up in his Chevy. The ride from Boston University to the New England Conservatory usually took ten minutes, but this time, he promised, borne by enthusiasm, he would make it in seven.

He arrived right on time. Coretta stood in the rain, clutching an umbrella and wearing a topcoat and scarf over a light blue suit. She got in the car, and King drove them to Sharaf's on Massachusetts Avenue for lunch. Even in the car she could see he was short—and not particularly handsome, by her initial assessment. He had a large head with unusually small ears, a wide nose, and a forehead so high that his hair seemed to be receding. But the more he talked, the better he looked.

"You have some *great* hair," he said, admiring Coretta's bangs. She smiled.

They discussed the merits of capitalism versus communism. He explained that he intended to devote himself to the fight for racial justice. Coretta, having attended the progressive and integrated Antioch College in Yellow Springs, Ohio, thought she would have the edge on this well-bred young man when it came to passion for social reform. She was pleasantly surprised to find that he seemed determined to fight racial discrimination, even if he was not yet sure how to do it. They batted ideas back and forth across the lunch table. At one of Coretta's comments, King's eyes widened. "Oh, you can think, too," he said. Though she didn't say it aloud, Coretta thought: Of course I can.

By the end of lunch, King informed his date that she possessed all four of the traits he sought in a wife: "intelligence, character, beauty, and personality." Would she agree to see him again?

His passion and authenticity worked like sunshine, melting away her concerns about his height and his "typical" jive. He "just radiated so much charm," she said. He carried himself as if "he knew where he was going and he was going to get there," she said. But, at the same time, she wondered if his commitment to social justice was as strong as her own "because he had come from a middle-class background and had not known conditions as I had."

— · —

King had just turned twenty-three. Coretta was almost two years older, and her earnest, solitary nature made her seem even more mature. She was the second of three children born to Obadiah and Bernice McMurry Scott in Perry County, Alabama, where Black people outnumbered whites by about three to one, but white voters outnumbered Black voters by thirty to one. Most of the Black men and women worked low-paying jobs as share-croppers, tenant farmers, housekeepers, and manual laborers. But there were exceptions. The town of Marion had a Black-owned funeral parlor and a Black-owned grocery and general store. The Scotts farmed three hundred acres outside town. They named their second girl, Coretta, after her grand-mother, Cora Scott, and Cora's sister Etta.

Coretta Scott's family had found a way to get ahead against stagger-ing odds, acquiring and maintaining land. Coretta's paternal grandfather had twenty-five children from two marriages. Her father, Obie, as every-one called him, was a lean, handsome man, and a snappy dresser. He never smoked or drank. Though he dropped out of school after sixth grade, Obie Scott had a gift for math and used his skills to manage household finances as well as numerous business operations. He owned his own truck and used it to haul lumber. He saved enough money to open his own sawmill, only to see it burned to the ground two weeks later in what he and his family be-lieved to be an act of arson. Undaunted, he went back to work. He ran a small barbering business, drove a taxi, built a new house for his family, and ran a farm where he grew vegetables, raised hogs, and kept up to four thousand chickens at a time.

Coretta's mother, Bernice, tall and powerfully built, was the daughter of a slave. She had only a fourth-grade education, but she was a careful reader of newspapers and magazines and unafraid of speaking her mind. "She ain't nothin' but breath and britches," Bernice would say of a woman possessed of low intellect. A liar was someone, according to Bernice, "who ain't talking about what they talking about." In the 1920s, she became the first Black woman in her community to drive a car and, later, a school bus.

Like her mother, Coretta was physically and emotionally strong. "She was a hardy youngster, with a symmetrical face, flawless olive brown complexion, pug nose, thin lips, and long, thick, wavy hair," her older sister Edythe recalled. Corrie, as friends called her, kept that long, wavy hair in pigtails. She toted bags of feed and boxes of food that were too heavy for Edythe. She fished, caught crawfish barehanded, wrestled with boys, and whacked hornets' nests with sticks. She could be aloof at times, but she was fearless.

When she was little, her home had no running water or electricity. But the Scotts did have a Victrola on which they played the music of Bessie Smith, the Empress of the Blues, who sang boldly and defiantly about what she wanted, what she needed, and what she refused to tolerate, especially where men were concerned. "I got the world in a jug, the stopper's in my hand," she sang in "Down Hearted Blues." "I'm gonna hold it until you men come under my command."

Coretta walked five miles to attend the Crossroads School, a one-room schoolhouse with outdoor toilets, built with money donated by Julius Rosenwald, one of the founders of Sears, Roebuck and Co. White children in the area went to school for nine months a year, but Black children went only for seven, as Coretta recalled. "And every day I watched the white children being transported by bus to *their* school," she said. "This was one thing that stands out in my mind: the injustice of having to walk this distance in the cold and in the rain, especially, and yet the white children were being carried to school every day in the buses."

After sixth grade, Coretta's educational options improved. In the 1860s, the American Missionary Association, in partnership with local residents, founded a school in Marion for Black children and named it after Abraham Lincoln. The faculty at the Lincoln School included seven Black and seven white teachers. Coretta learned to play violin, piano, and trumpet. Her teachers encouraged her to pursue music as a career. She found dignity in the places where she could isolate herself from white society, she said: at school, church, and on the farms owned by her parents and aunts and uncles. "This factor," she said, "perhaps more than anything else, helped to instill in us racial pride, self-respect, and dignity which inevitably gave us the proper self-image."

Coretta grew up seeing the best and worst of Black American life. She saw Black children and white children lined up at different ends of the drugstore counter to be served ice cream, with the white children always served first. She noticed that her parents taught her to address adults as "Mister" and "Missus," but white people—even white children—called her parents Obie and Bernice. "This kind of humiliation, constantly, does something to you," Coretta said. "It does create a kind of attitude of distrust and suspicion."

When she was fifteen, her parents' home burned down. Coretta suspected the fire had been set by white men who were angered by her father's business success. Law enforcement never investigated, saying the Scotts lived outside town limits, but Coretta believed there was another explanation, saying "really no one cared about what happened to Black people."

In addition to her sister Edythe, Coretta had a younger brother named Obadiah. (A second sister had died in infancy from pneumonia.) Edythe attended Antioch College in Yellow Springs, Ohio, and Coretta followed her there. Founded in 1852, Antioch admitted students of all races as early as the 1860s. Horace Mann, an abolitionist and social reformer, was once the president of the college.

Coretta enrolled at Antioch in 1945 and discovered that her high school education, while better than that of many Black Alabamans, had been inferior to that of most white students. "So that meant I had to spend a lot of time catching up," she said. She majored in elementary education, minored in voice, roomed with two white women, and for two years dated Walter Rybeck, a Jewish student from Wheeling, West Virginia. Rybeck, a pianist, traveled by bus throughout the South with Corrie, as everyone in school called her, accompanying her performances in Black churches. They enjoyed long walks and bird-watching. Early in the relationship, Walter brought Corrie home to West Virginia to meet his parents. "We went to the Twelfth Street Grill for dinner," Rybeck recalled. "The manager looked at us and said, 'Of course *she*,' pointing to Corrie, 'will have to eat in the kitchen.' My dad said that was unacceptable, and we left."

Rybeck had a wealthy aunt who arranged for Coretta to audition at the Juilliard School of Music in Manhattan. On her trip to New York, Rybeck's aunt Edna, who was ninety years old at the time, hired a limousine to show Coretta around the city, making stops at Grant's Tomb and several museums. That night, Aunt Edna phoned Rybeck to say she was disappointed by Coretta's lack of interest in the arts. She couldn't understand why the young woman spent so little time in the museums. Coretta phoned Rybeck that same night. She said she had felt badly that Aunt Edna had to wait in the car, given her age, so she had dispatched with the museums as quickly as she could, staying just long enough to report back to Aunt Edna on one or two things she had seen. "She was just a princess of a girl," Rybeck said. "Everybody liked Corrie."

To pay for college, Coretta bused tables at the Antioch dining halls and worked as a camp counselor at Karamu House, an artists' retreat in Cleveland. She also joined the campus chapter of the NAACP, a race relations committee, and a civil liberties committee. She challenged a rule that prevented Black students from student-teaching in local schools. Rybeck recalled that she also joined in a protest when a barbershop in Yellow Springs refused to cut Black people's hair. In 1948, she supported Henry Wallace for president and attended the Progressive Party's national convention as a student delegate. Wallace had broken with President Truman and campaigned for president with a platform focused mostly on foreign policy, including conciliation with the Soviet Union, though it also called for an end to Jim Crow.

That same year, 1948, Coretta published an article headlined "Why I Came to College" in *Opportunity: Journal of Negro Life*, an Urban League publication, in which she supplied an indication of her ambition as well as her passionate feelings about civil rights activism. She began: "As far back as I can remember, I wanted to go to college. My parents are Negroes, respectable but poor . . . I found early in life that being respectable did not necessarily bring respect—not in my home town." The only Black people in town who earned any esteem, she observed, were her teachers, who were college graduates. "They had greater freedom of movement; they went on trips; they visited cities; they knew more about the world. They had greater economic security." If a college education could do that, she wrote, she knew she needed one.

Coretta chose Antioch because her sister did, she wrote, although she felt some anxiety about whether she would fit in among northerners. But, by the time of her third year, she was happy with her decision. "It seems to me now that every Negro student in the South ought to try to get some of his education in the North if at all possible . . . For a southerner . . . it seems to me important to find out that there really are some white people working for racial equality and to be able to work with them. I've learned something from them; they've learned something from me."

After Antioch, Coretta sought to pursue a graduate degree in music, but Juilliard and New York City intimidated her. Instead, she enrolled at the New England Conservatory in Boston, where she studied voice. Her studies were funded in part with a so-called Jim Crow Scholarship from the state of Alabama, which denied entry to Black students at most of its tax-supported colleges and universities. In providing the scholarships and sending students out of state, Alabama sought to avoid legal challenges to its system of segregated education. Many of those ambitious students, once educated, would return to Alabama determined to reform the system that had paid for their education.

Coretta Scott was in her second semester of study in Boston and soon to turn twenty-five when she met Martin Luther King Jr. In the 1950s, women typically married in their early twenties, but Coretta appeared to be in no hurry. "I looked ahead at the ground I could cover," she said. "I saw myself as a concert singer, paving the way for other Blacks." At first, she was uninterested in dating a minister, and especially a Baptist minister. Coretta grew up in the African Methodist Episcopal Zion Church. She was taught that the Baptists were too emotional. In fact, much of organized religion struck her as too emotional. She seldom attended church in Boston, saying, "I can worship in my room."

As Scott and King began going out together, Coretta noticed that her date was often recognized upon entering a room, that he enjoyed his reputation as "the most eligible young Black man in the Boston area at that time," as she put it. Coretta did her best to act as if she didn't mind.

Despite his confidence, despite his pretensions, including his use of Shakespearean sonnets in his romantic approaches, Coretta sensed that, deep down, Martin was humble. He hated to hurt anyone's feelings. He expressed guilt at having been born into a relatively privileged family. He loved people, loved parties, loved conversation. He was a good dancer. It was easy to see why he enjoyed the company of women and why they enjoyed his company, too. King teased Coretta about his knack for attracting women, but he would always laugh and assure her that she was the only girl who mattered, that he was serious and dedicated and deeply in love with her. He knew what kind of woman he wanted to marry, she said, and "he was always trying to convince me I was it."

At the same time, King worried that Coretta might have a difficult time returning to the South after her years at Antioch and the New England Conservatory. He was attracted by her intelligence and her ambition, yet those qualities had the potential to complicate their relationship. King wondered if Coretta would have difficulty adapting to the role of the pastor's wife, especially if he took a job in a small southern town. He also confessed to Coretta that his parents wanted him to marry a woman in Atlanta. (Coretta didn't name the woman in her memoir or in the interviews conducted in its preparation, but she was almost certainly referring to Juanita Sellers.) While King told Coretta about his Atlanta relationship, it's not clear if he admitted that he was seeing other women in Boston, too.

"I thought he was a very nice young man," said Jeanne Martin Brayboy, a South Carolina native and a graduate music major at Boston University. She dated King in 1952, at the same time he was seeing Coretta. King bragged to Jeanne that he would start his career as a preacher and then, someday, perhaps become the president of Morehouse College. "Benny Mays can't live always," he joked.

Coretta was a farmer's daughter, a self-described tomboy. She owned a nice coat and a few good dresses, but she cared little about impressing people with her clothes. She combed her hair and put on makeup in the morning, and then she was done for the day. She was not the type to freshen up and retrace her lipstick—until Martin suggested that she pay more attention to her appearance. "Perhaps you'd like to go to the ladies' room and comb your hair," he would say. "You look so pretty with lipstick on." Later, Coretta said, she realized that this was Martin's way of grooming her for the role of the minister's wife.

10

The Dynamic Force

CORETTA HAD NO fear of marriage. She did not shudder at the idea of becoming a housewife and deriving her status and sense of purpose, at least in part, from her connection to a man. The more pressing question was whether she wanted to become a minister's wife, and a southern minister's wife to boot. "Of course he asked me . . . if I could be a good preacher's wife," she recalled, "and I didn't answer. I thought time would tell."

She considered herself a deliberate person who preferred not to act impulsively. Now she pondered and prayed over the question for months. On the one hand, yes, she would likely have to sacrifice her ambitions. On the other hand, if she wanted to fight for racial justice and serve her community, she might find opportunities stemming from her would-be husband's work. Then there was the matter of Martin's parents. What if Daddy King opposed their marriage? Would Martin stand up to him? Would he go back to Juanita Sellers?

Coretta had no interest in competing. She took herself seriously, and she wanted Martin to take her seriously, too. "I had a kind of warmth, but it was not something I expressed very freely," she said in recalling her early days with her future husband. "I was reserved, I guess. I was reserved in my expression of praise . . . When I would hear him speak, I would tell him how much I enjoyed it, if I did, and most times I did. Almost always. And then I would comment on certain aspects of the sermon that I liked . . . He appreciated it."

Though she felt certain Martin respected her intelligence, she worried nonetheless that her identity would be subsumed if they married. For months, she tried to hold her feelings in check, afraid of falling too deeply in love only to discover that Martin would appease his parents and marry Juanita or someone else. A dream helped her resolve her feelings. She dreamed she was in a room with Martin, Martin's father, and Juanita Sellers. In the dream, Martin's father smiled at Coretta, "and somehow I knew he approved of me," she wrote. "It seemed a miraculous kind of thing."

But it was only a dream. That summer of 1952, King returned to Atlanta and Coretta stayed in Boston to continue her studies. It was the same summer that Malcolm Little, who'd changed his name to Malcolm X and joined the Nation of Islam while serving time in a Massachusetts prison, won his release; soon he'd be running a Boston mosque for the group, which advocated for Black separatism. Bookstores carried Ralph Ellison's new novel, *Invisible Man*. The U.S. Supreme Court announced it would hear oral arguments in the case that would become *Brown v. Board of Education*, the NAACP's challenge to separate-but-equal laws in public education. When Martin suggested that Coretta come to Atlanta that summer to meet his family, she declined. King became upset, writing in a letter that if she didn't want to come to Atlanta, perhaps she should "just forget everything."

In July, King wrote to Coretta again. It is one of the only love letters made public by Coretta, although her personal secretary later said Coretta kept a blue Samsonite suitcase full of letters under her bed. In this missive, he said he had gotten over his anger:

> Your letter was sweet and refreshing to my heart, which had well-nigh grown cold toward you. Of course I have become convinced in the last few days that my love for you is based on such a solid foundation that the stormy winds of anger can not blow it asunder.

King went on to discuss Edward Bellamy's late-nineteenth-century utopian novel, *Looking Backward: 2000–1887,* a book that Coretta had given him, one that forecast a society in which equality and widespread prosperity arrived without violent revolution. Capitalism may be on its deathbed,

King wrote in the letter, but social systems often managed to survive for long stretches while in such conditions.

Finally, he returned to personal matters and wrote that he hoped Coretta would visit Atlanta. "It hurt me very much to know that you believe that I would invite you to Atlanta and then mistreat you . . . Oh well I guess all of us have a little of the unappreciative attitude in us." He said that if she still chose not to visit Atlanta, he wouldn't mention it but would nevertheless assume that she had no confidence in him. "I hope we won't have to break up about this trip," he wrote. He signed off saying, "Be sweet and remember that daddy still loves you." He signed the letter "Martin," not "Mike," or "M.L.," and followed with a postscript, saying he hoped she could read his poor handwriting.

Coretta did ultimately travel to Atlanta in August.

The visit did not go well.

King was still dating other women, including Juanita Sellers, and he had not told his parents that he was considering marrying Coretta. Daddy King made clear he did not consider Coretta a good match for his son. He deemed it inappropriate for a Baptist minister to marry a young woman planning a career as a concert singer. He may have considered her unsophisticated, too, despite her education, simply because Coretta was an Alabama farm girl.

Martin picked up Coretta from the train station, and then he picked up his mother from the beauty parlor. They chatted awkwardly in the car on the way to the house. Alberta, in Coretta's view, was "hard to know." Of Daddy King, she said: "He was a big man, bigger than I expected. One could feel his strength of character as well as his physical power." He, too, seemed distant, she said.

Later that summer, on her way back to Boston from Alabama, Coretta stopped in Atlanta again. She was visiting the Kings' home on a Sunday night when Martin said he had to go see some elderly members of the parish. But when he failed to return, Coretta suspected that he had gone to see Juanita. "The next morning I woke up and I was just so unhappy, and I just felt like crying," she said, "because I knew I had been mistreated. I could hardly speak to him."

When they got back to Boston, Martin confessed that he had been with Juanita, but he promised that he had only gone to her home to tell her that their relationship would soon be over. Regarding Martin's dalliances with other women, Coretta said, "He would always tell me, eventually . . . He had a very strong moral conscience and he could not do wrong and not feel guilty. He would feel guilt that would just eat him up."

Four months later, King's parents came to Boston, and Coretta got another chance to demonstrate that she and Martin were in love. The conversation took place in Martin's apartment.

"Coretta, do you take my son seriously?" Daddy King asked.

She misunderstood the question. She thought Daddy King was referring to a joke Martin had just made.

"No," she answered.

"I'm glad to hear you say that," Daddy King said, going on to say M.L. had been involved with beautiful girls from fine families, that he had a habit of introducing his parents to young women and then losing interest. Some of these young women, Daddy King said, had "a lot to offer."

Coretta grew irritated. "I have something to offer, too," she said.

Daddy King went on, saying there was a wonderful girl back in Atlanta waiting for Martin, a girl the whole family loved.

"Unless you know my son better than I do," Daddy King said, "I would advise you not to take him too seriously."

Coretta didn't answer. Coretta wondered why Martin wasn't rising to her defense.

"Not a word, just like a little child," she recalled.

Martin left the room. Later, Coretta learned that he had gone into the next room and announced to his mother that he intended to marry Coretta. But, at that moment, he had not impressed Coretta with his courage or commitment.

When he drove her home that night, King criticized Coretta. "He was so displeased with me," she recalled. He told her that Juanita had a much more radiant personality.

Two days later, however, Daddy King came around and endorsed the marriage. "I agree to it," he told his son, "because I respect your opinion and your choice."

As Coretta and Martin began planning their wedding, Coretta switched her major from performance to musical education, acknowledging that her husband's career would come first and she would not likely sing profession-ally. "I went to school, I would say, with a mission," she recalled. "I felt that if I got the training, developed my personality and my talents to the fullest possible extent, I would be able to make a good contribution to society." But, as a minister's wife and a mother, Coretta would be expected to play a more traditional role. Martin was "very definite," Coretta said, that he wanted his wife waiting for him every day when he came home from work. Years later, Martin Luther King Jr. would write that "when a mother has to work she does violence to motherhood by depriving her children of her loving guid-ance and protection."

Coretta called it "the most important decision I would make." She had already faced her fiancé's attraction to other women. Now she faced the pri-macy of his professional ambitions, too.

Why did she choose him? Coretta answered the question often in in-terviews and in her writing. He was ambitious, intelligent, and exciting. He oozed charm. He shared her passion for the pursuit of justice. She hinted at something elemental, too, referring to him repeatedly as manly, or all man, or a he-man. Coretta's closest confidante, her sister, asked directly why Coretta would marry a southern preacher and why she would sacrifice her music career. "I suppose it's because Martin reminds me so much of our fa-ther," Coretta said. Speaking of Martin and her father, she told one reporter in 1965, "They are industrious and religious men. Their interests are very similar, and it is remarkable how alike they are in drive and personality."

Harry Belafonte, who knew the couple well, said he felt there was "noth-ing transcendent" between Martin and Coretta. Martin emitted warmth, made friends easily, and laughed lustily. Despite her rural origins, Coretta was more refined, with no patience for salty humor. "Coretta Scott was a proper bourgeois prospect," Belafonte said, "with light skin, straight hair, and social ambitions . . . Her manner was stately and stern." With her looks, her education, and her demeanor, she would impress the deacons at any church in which Martin might choose to start his career. "He wound up with Coretta," Belafonte said, "because it satisfied the community." But that wasn't all. At that point in their lives, Coretta had more experience than Martin as an activist. Martin, Belafonte said, "stepped into her space."

King knew Coretta was more than a beauty or a good potential "first lady" of a church. "She was a quintessential African-American woman," as the poet Maya Angelou later said, "born in the small-town repressive South, born of flesh and destined to become iron, born—born a cornflower and destined to become a steel magnolia."

11

Plagiarism and Poetry

HE CALLED HER Corrie or Coretta. She called him Martin.

They married on Thursday, June 18, 1953, at Coretta's family home near Marion, Alabama. Temperatures were in the nineties all day, with no rain in sight. The front page of *The Marion Times-Standard* that day noted that the first cotton bloom of the year had been delivered to the newspaper office by Clayton Sanders, "Negro tenant on the J.C. Moore place."

Martin, along with his friends and family, arrived by caravan from Atlanta. Coretta fretted over what the Atlantans would think of her family's six-room house and the dirt road leading to it. With help from her sister and mother, she prepared a "country-style dinner." The women picked vines and flowers from the nearby woods to decorate a wedding arch in the backyard. Martin wore black tuxedo pants and a white dinner jacket. Coretta wore a pale blue gown that she'd purchased in Boston, with matching gloves and shoes. As an accent, she added a strand of pearls that had been a gift from the groom. Martin's sister, Christine, designed a veil with a crown made from flowers for Coretta. In their wedding photos, Coretta, in heels, nearly matched Martin's height.

Coretta wanted a small, informal ceremony. Though the guest list grew to more than three hundred, she stuck firmly to other decisions. She refused to choose a pattern for china or silver, deeming such extravagances frivolous. More impressively, and in another sign of independence, she informed Daddy King that she would omit from her vows the promise to obey her husband. Before the ceremony, the elder Reverend King sat with the couple on the porch in front of the Scott family's store, which was right next to the

Scott family's home. Daddy King gave the couple his standard pre-wedding advice: "Coretta, I wouldn't marry M.L. if I could help it," he said. "M.L., I wouldn't marry Coretta if I could help it. Now, I preach because I can't help myself. And when you get married you should think of it as something you *have* to do."

She and Martin assured Daddy King they felt precisely that way: they *needed* each other.

After the wedding and dinner, Martin and Coretta drove to Marion. Since no hotels in the city would accommodate them, they spent the first night of their marriage in the guest bedroom of a funeral parlor. The next day they made the 220-mile drive to Atlanta, where another wedding reception awaited, giving Martin's friends—and former girlfriends—a chance to meet the bride. More than 350 guests greeted them at the King home.

"They were very concerned about who Martin Luther King was marrying," Coretta recalled. "Everybody liked him and they had a special feeling toward him so they were concerned about who this girl was, especially since it wasn't an Atlanta girl." She wore the same ice-blue dress for the occasion.

The next day they went to church, where Martin preached. On Monday, Coretta started a summer job at a Black-owned bank in Atlanta. They lived that summer with Daddy and Mother King, as Coretta took to calling them.

They were already too busy for a honeymoon.

The newlyweds returned to Boston in the fall and rented a four-room apartment for $35 a month at 396 Northampton Street, near the New England Conservatory. While Coretta took a heavy slate of classes, Martin began to research his doctoral dissertation. Since he was home more than Coretta, Martin tried to perform some of the housework. He cooked occasionally, although most of his recipes did not extend much beyond adding heat, salt, and pepper to meat. His specialties included pork chops, fried chicken, pigs' feet, pigs' snouts, and pigs' ears. He was a city boy who ate like a country boy, as Coretta put it. He sometimes washed clothes in the big tub they kept in the kitchen, but Coretta lamented that the clothes tended to come out merely wetter, not cleaner. Still, he performed the chores without complaint. At the same time, Martin informed Coretta that he expected to be treated like the head of the family. He would follow the comment with a laugh, saying he knew that marriage was a partnership. But that didn't mean it was a partnership between equals in his view, according to Coretta.

In the 1950s, American marriage rates were at an all-time high. Women were marrying at younger ages than earlier in the twentieth century. The media portrayed women—white women, mostly—as happy homemakers, suggesting they were helping America win the Cold War by taking care of their families. From 1940 to 1960, before the advent of the birth-control pill, the number of American families with three children doubled and the number with four children quadrupled, in part because the growing U.S. middle class could afford to raise more children. Coretta and other women found their career ambitions checked not only by their husbands' expectations but also by shifting cultural standards. When Martin told Coretta he wanted eight children, it was clear he did not wish to stay home raising them. Coretta wrote:

> Martin had, all through his life, an ambivalent attitude toward the role of women. On the one hand, he believed that women are just as intelligent and capable as men and that they should hold positions of authority and influence. But when it came to his own situation, he thought in terms of his wife being a homemaker and a mother for his children. He was very definite that he would expect whomever he married to be home waiting for him ... At the same time, Martin, even in those days, would say, "I don't want a wife I can't communicate with." From the beginning, he would encourage me to be active outside of the home, and would be very pleased when I had ideas of my own or even when I could fill in for him. Yet it was the female role he was most anxious for me to play.

For the most part, Coretta resigned herself to playing the role her husband desired. "That was an adjustment I had to make," she said, "and I believe I made it very well."

At Boston University, King listened to addresses by the African American minister, theologian, and mystic Howard Thurman, who served as dean of the school's Marsh Chapel from 1953 to 1965. King found lasting inspiration in Thurman's beliefs on integration, community, and the interrelatedness of all life. "There is but one refuge that one man has anywhere on this planet," wrote Thurman. "And that is in another man's heart."

In the fall of 1953, King watched Jackie Robinson and the Brooklyn Dodgers play the New York Yankees in the World Series on a television at Thurman's house. Thurman spoke often of his 1935 trip to India and his meeting with Gandhi, who reportedly told Thurman, "It may be through the Negroes that the unadulterated message of nonviolence will be delivered to the world." One can only wonder if Thurman and King, as they watched the World Series, reflected on the connections between Gandhi and Robinson. If any Black public figure in America embodied the principles of Gandhi, it was the Dodgers' second baseman, a proud, hypercompetitive athlete who had vowed to endure the racist insults of white fans and opposing ballplayers and had done so without appearing meek.

For his doctoral dissertation, King compared the conceptions of God presented by two theologians: Paul Tillich and Henry Nelson Wieman. King criticized both Tillich and Wieman for their distance from personalism. Tillich ascribed personality only to beings, not to God, while Wieman described God in relatively depersonalized terms, as an "integrating process." King rejected both ideas, saying human fellowship with God could only occur when both parties to the relationship possessed understanding and respect. Ascribing a human personality to God, King argued, in no way implied a limitation of God's power.

Personalism stresses that every human being shares the image of God. In the view of King and other personalists, every act of injustice toward a person is thus an insult to God. Unlike more abstract theologies, personalism connected to people's everyday lives and, to King, felt consonant with the action-based preaching of his father and grandfather.

King's dissertation attracted little attention until 1990, when scholars at Stanford University announced that substantial portions had been plagiarized. In his first draft, King copied most of the introduction verbatim from a book called *The Theology of Paul Tillich*. His problems seem to have been rooted in his use of note cards to organize information he gathered from books. In many cases, he copied verbatim from his source onto his note cards without creating a citation. He was especially weak when it came to citing secondary sources. He might read an author's interpretation of a Tillich quote and then transcribe the quote and the interpretation onto a note card without taking note of the secondary source.

King's approach to his dissertation, as the scholar David J. Garrow writes, may have been primarily a reflection of an awkward stage in life. He was a young dandy working to become a scholar, as his leadership of the Philosophical Club suggests. But he was only twenty-two years old when he entered the doctoral program. "Was the King of Crozer and BU actually a rather immature and insecure young man?" asks Garrow. "Was he a talented young preacher with no particular aptitude for scholarly creativity?"

King's indiscretions, regardless of their cause, should have been caught. His advisers should have noticed King's heavy reliance on a Boston University dissertation written three years earlier by a student named Jack Boozer. While acknowledging Boozer's "very fine" dissertation in his introduction, King cited it only a few times while copying more than fifty sentences and relying heavily on its structure. Boozer and King had the same dissertation adviser, L. Harold DeWolf, yet DeWolf made few comments on King's first draft while praising the writer's "convincing mastery of the works immediately involved."

Despite his plagiarism, and despite his fundamental disagreements with them, King learned lasting theological lessons from Tillich and Wieman. In his seminal work, *The Courage to Be*, Tillich wrote that the courage to be requires acceptance of anxiety—the anxiety that comes with guilt, condemnation, and death. That courage means staying connected to God when one loses faith. "But doubt is not the opposite of faith," Tillich wrote, "it is one element of faith." That philosophy would help King find strength in the face of fear, in moments of exhaustion, and, perhaps most poignantly, as he became consumed with the certainty of his own premature death.

King's plagiarism was part of the process by which he found his own voice, according to Clayborne Carson, the former director of the King Papers Project at Stanford University, where the plagiarism was discovered. King developed a style of writing and speaking that impressed white audiences without sacrificing the emotion that made him so effective in moving Black congregations. King, in other words, took enough from Tillich to adapt the theologian's work to his own purpose and own audiences. In a 1967 sermon, King said people didn't need complicated philosophy or theology. He compared Tillich's notion of God as "Being-Itself" to the way that ordinary people had always worshipped, thinking of God as a "lily of the valley . . . a bright and morning star."

That kind of belief, King said, leads to the simplest conclusion of all, when a man or woman says of God: "He's my everything."

12

Gideon's Army

In November 1953, King, twenty-four years old, began to make career plans. He had nearly completed his coursework at Boston University and continued writing his dissertation. Churches in New York, Michigan, Massachusetts, Tennessee, and Alabama expressed interest in hiring him as a pastor, thanks in part to his father's reputation among preachers, M.L.'s own growing reputation, and his strong academic record. Eager to return south, he pursued positions at First Baptist Church in Chattanooga, Tennessee, and Dexter Avenue Baptist Church in Montgomery, Alabama. He made plans to visit them and preach "test sermons" during his break from school in January.

Of course, he also had a standing offer to join his father at Ebenezer Baptist in Atlanta. His brother, A.D., after marrying at age nineteen and starting a family, had already joined the church as an assistant pastor. Now Daddy King had visions of a dynasty. He even sweetened the deal. Knowing that his son remained interested in an academic career, the elder King spoke to Benjamin Mays about letting M.L. teach part-time at Morehouse.

Daddy King warned his son about taking the Montgomery job, saying the congregation was snooty and difficult to please. The church had been led previously by the brilliant, bombastic, and abrasive Reverend Vernon Napoleon Johns, who had both riveted and rattled his parishioners with his furious calls to social action. People said Johns was ahead of his time, but in truth he was determined to *change* his time. Johns made his congregation uncomfortable. He brought collard greens and cabbage from his own garden, shaking off the dirt, selling the vegetables after church to remind people they could grow their own food to break free from white merchants who didn't respect them. He also neglected mundane church matters. When the church's leaders finally fired him and began the search for a new minister, they approached King, as well as King's friend Walter McCall and his former Morehouse classmate Samuel McKinney.

Coretta preferred to remain in the North, but the choice was Martin's to make, she said, and Martin felt a sense of duty. "The South, after all, was our home," he wrote. "Despite its shortcomings, we loved it as home, and had a real desire to do something about the problems we felt so keenly as youngsters."

Moving to the Deep South required bravery. McKinney decided not to pursue the Dexter pulpit because Montgomery scared him. "I asked God if he would follow me into the South," McKinney recalled with a chuckle, "but He said He'd only follow me to Cincinnati."

At that moment, the NAACP led the nationwide fight for racial equity, with Roy Wilkins at the head of the organization, Clarence Mitchell Jr. running lobbying efforts in Washington, D.C., and Thurgood Marshall pressing the organization's challenge to public school segregation with *Brown v. Board of Education*. A. Philip Randolph, head of the Brotherhood of Sleeping Car Porters, served as a kind of dean among activists. Black newspaper editors added their increasingly loud and strong voices. New NAACP branches opened all over the country after World War II, often led by Black veterans and Pullman porters. Many white Americans, repulsed by the Holocaust, became more attuned to issues of racism. As the United States fought the Cold War with the Soviet Union, seeking to gain political and military influence around the world, American leaders sought to present themselves as the champions of global freedom. But the country's treatment of its Black population undercut that position. When the finance minister of Ghana visited the United States and tried to order orange juice at a Howard Johnson's restaurant in Delaware, he was told that Black customers were not welcome. "Racial discrimination in the United States remains a source of constant embarrassment to this Government in the day-to-day conduct of its foreign relations," wrote Dean

Acheson, the secretary of state in the Truman administration, as part of a brief filed in *Brown v. Board of Education*, "and it jeopardizes the effective maintenance of our moral leadership of the free and democratic nations of the world."

Rather than waiting for the government to put action behind the words, Black men and women joined the struggle.

"You just let 'em know," a Black South Carolina farmer told a journalist in 1953, "that we Negroes down here are like Gideon's army . . . fit to fight."

There were more encouraging signs. The Tuskegee Institute announced that it would no longer publish its annual statistics on lynching. Acts of lynching occurred so seldom, the institute reported, that statistics no longer revealed much about the state of race relations. Bombings and threats of violence continued to terrorize Black people, especially in the South, but the experts at Tuskegee believed they would learn more by evaluating employment, income, education, and political participation.

Two days before King's trial sermon in Montgomery, the local Black newspaper, the *Alabama Tribune*, reported that a U.S. Senate subcommittee had urged bus lines in the nation's capital to hire Black drivers; Baptist ministers in Birmingham had pressed Alabama's governor to begin making plans in anticipation of a possible Supreme Court order to integrate schools; and Georgia's governor, Herman Eugene Talmadge, announced that if a school desegregation order did come from the court, he would use state police and militia to make sure it was not obeyed. The local Black newspaper did not report on King's arrival in Montgomery or on his audition for the job at Dexter Avenue Baptist.

Montgomery was less than a third the size of Atlanta, though growing fast. Among the city's 120,000 residents in 1955, about 63 percent were white and 37 percent were Black. The city had nine hotels, two radio stations, and seven movie theaters, including two for Black patrons. Black men in the city were most likely to work in service jobs, as waiters, cooks, and shoe shiners, and Black women were overwhelmingly likely to perform household labor for white families. The median annual income for Black people was $970, compared with $1,730 for white people.

Cotton and slavery had long dominated the city's economy. In the decades preceding the Civil War, Montgomery's slave market had emerged as one of the biggest and most important in the country. When southern states seceded from the Union, they elected Jefferson Davis president of the Confederacy and made Montgomery its first capital. Montgomery earned the nickname "Cradle of the Confederacy."

Alabama, which became a state in 1819, came to the slavery business relatively late. But it didn't take long for slave owners from Georgia and elsewhere, with backing from New York financiers, to force indigenous Americans off the land and expand their cotton kingdom. In 1820, about 42,000 enslaved Black people resided in Alabama. Forty years later, that number had multiplied by more than ten, to about 435,000, or about half of the state's total population.

Many of those enslaved men, women, and children were bought and sold in downtown Montgomery, marched through the city's streets, made to stand on auction blocks, shackled, inspected, and traded for cash or animals. More than half of all enslaved families were broken up. "Babies wuz snatched from dere mother's breas' an' sold to speculators," Delia Garlic, an enslaved Montgomery woman, recalled in an oral history transcribed phonetically by the interviewer. "Chilluns wuz separated from sisters an' brothers an' never saw each other ag'in. Course dey cry; you think dey not cry when dey wuz sold lak cattle?"

In the years after the Civil War, all over the South, former slave owners grew enraged and tried to maintain the uneven balance of power by forcing Black men and women into new forms of subordination. In 1901, white delegates in Alabama drafted a new constitution that locked in the second-class status of Black people, prohibited interracial marriage, and mandated segregated schools. In Montgomery, city ordinances required separate lines for Black and white citizens buying theater and amusement park tickets. City laws forbade Black and white people from playing pool or dominos together. The law also insisted on segregated streetcars, bathrooms, movie theaters, and hospitals. The rules were often contorted, though. Black people could shop in department stores, but they couldn't try on clothes. Black women who cared for white children were permitted to sit in the front of a bus when they rode with the white children of their employers, but not when they rode alone.

"Treading the tight-rope of Jim Crow from birth to death, from almost our first knowledge of life to our last conscious thought . . . is a major mental acrobatic feat," wrote Rosa Parks, then an NAACP secretary and a seamstress in Montgomery, in a notebook she kept in the 1950s. "It takes a noble soul to plumb this line. There is always a line of some kind—color line, hanging rope, tight rope. To me, it seems that we are puppets on string in the white man's hands . . . and we perform to their satisfaction or suffer the consequence if we get out of line."

These lines defined life in Montgomery when Martin Luther King Jr. arrived in January 1954 for his tryout at Dexter Avenue Baptist Church. The church, once home to a white congregation, was located two blocks from the first White House of the Confederacy, as Jefferson Davis's former home was known.

On the same weekend that King planned to preach at Dexter, the church's former pastor, Vernon Johns, had been invited to preach at another Montgomery church, First Baptist, which was led by the Reverend Ralph David Abernathy. Johns wasn't upset that a young preacher from Atlanta was auditioning for his former job. In fact, he viewed it as fortuitous. Johns, who happened to be passing through Atlanta on his way to Montgomery, phoned the Kings at home and asked if young Martin might give him a ride.

Later, King would write about making the drive alone, on a clear wintry day, the radio playing one of his favorite operas, Donizetti's *Lucia di Lammermoor*. It was the scene he would use to open his first book, *Stride Toward Freedom*, in which he sought to portray himself as a solitary figure, a worldly man at the outset of an important journey. In truth, the weather was gray and drizzly, and he had Vernon Johns beside him in the front seat.

At about four in the afternoon, Ralph Abernathy looked out the window of his house and saw a car rolling up the driveway. He knew that Johns liked to hitchhike, so he was pleased to see that the preacher had found a driver willing to take him all the way to the house. When the driver got out of the car, Abernathy recognized Martin Luther King Jr., the charming young preacher who had stolen his date in Atlanta years ago.

Abernathy invited them both to stay for dinner. King said he had promised to dine with one of the deacons at the Dexter Avenue church, but after he caught a whiff of the food Juanita Abernathy was preparing in the kitchen, he vacillated.

"That certainly does smell good," Johns said.

"It certainly does," King agreed.

Johns warned, perhaps in jest, that the deacon's wife preparing dinner for King that evening cooked like a white woman. King would likely be served cheese and crackers with a salad. Meanwhile, Juanita Abernathy brought out turnip greens, hot rolls, and steak smothered in onions. King threw up his hands in surrender. He wasn't going anywhere.

"I immediately fell in love with him," Abernathy said.

Juanita and Ralph Abernathy had been married less than two years. They were native Alabamans, and they were among the young, educated Black people in Montgomery most eager for change. Juanita had grown up in the same county as Coretta Scott, and had come from hardworking parents who had saved enough to send her to college. Ralph Abernathy was twenty-six years old, one of twelve children, the youngest of seven boys. He grew up on his parents' five-hundred-acre farm in Linden, Alabama. Short, round-faced, and easygoing, Abernathy made friends quickly and laughed warmly. Like Johns, who had become his mentor, Abernathy knew how to deliver a compelling sermon in a colloquial style. He connected with his audience in a manner that felt entirely unpracticed. People trusted him, which helps explain why he took leadership positions in the army; at his fraternity, Kappa Alpha Psi; and in campus protests during his student years at Alabama State College. "My husband always said, 'You've gotta be anchored in the Lord, else they will scare you to death,'" Juanita said. Nothing ever scared Ralph Abernathy, she said. Juanita carried with her some of the same faith-fueled fearlessness. Every day she had heard her father repeat the words from a hymn: "Father, I stretch my hands to Thee, no other help I know. If Thou draw Thyself from me, Lord, whither shall I go?"

As they ate, Juanita and the three men talked about Montgomery. They compared the Dexter and First Baptist congregations, saying both of them were refined to the point of stuffiness but that Dexter was the stuffier of the two. Abernathy and Johns liked to make fun of the high-class parishioners, saying they were more interested in hearing about Plato and Socrates than Jesus. They told the story of the time Johns interrupted the wedding ceremony of a prominent physician's daughter to announce that the church would have watermelon for sale at the reception, his way of reminding the doctor not to take himself too seriously. But the sense of complacency that settled in, especially among members of the Black middle class, irritated Johns. They talked about how activism in the Black community could push the federal government into service in the fight for justice. They talked about mobilizing churches in the campaign.

The worshipers at Dexter Avenue Baptist Church may not have been ready for Johns's aggressive brand of race-based preaching, but King and the Abernathys found it inspiring. "There was not a docile or scared bone in him," Juanita Abernathy said of Johns.

The Abernathys liked King from the moment he sat down, having chosen good food and conversation over the chance to impress one of Dexter's deacons. If they had any concern that he might be a stodgy intellectual, that concern vanished as King laughed and dug into his food with gusto. And they were glad to hear him say he planned to marshal foot soldiers in the war against segregation.

"How long do you think it will be before we can make a move?" Ralph Abernathy asked.

King may have been thinking about his personal life as much as social and political affairs when he answered. He may have been thinking about starting a family, finishing his dissertation, and establishing his leadership with a new congregation. Or he may simply have been thinking about the slow rate of social and political change he'd seen in the first twenty-four years of his life, in the North and South.

"Not for a long time," he said. "At least several years."

He was wrong. Montgomery would soon erupt in protest, and King and Abernathy would help lead it.

King's trial sermon proved a hit. He was every bit as smart as Vernon Johns, every bit as eloquent, every bit as passionate, but smoother, and without the former preacher's hot temper.

"When I discovered King," said Robert D. Nesbitt Sr., chairman of the church pulpit committee, "he was twenty-five. That was one of the gripes that the church tried to have about him. They said, 'We can't follow that little boy.' But after they heard him preach two or three times, they were ready to do anything he wanted." He was offered the job at a salary of $4,200 a year (equivalent to about $43,000 in 2022), enough to make him the highest-paid Black minister in Montgomery. On April 14, 1954, he wrote to the chairman of the church's search committee, saying he would take the position so long as Dexter renovated the parsonage, agreed to pay for his travel between Montgomery and Boston while he worked to complete his dissertation, and committed to salary increases as the church made progress under its new leader.

Daddy King wasn't pleased. Coretta was ambivalent. "I will make myself happy in Montgomery," she told her husband. "You perfect your preaching . . . and I will learn to be a good minister's wife." But it would seem she had not entirely given up hope of having her own career. In the spring of 1954, Coretta traveled to Chicago to attend a national conference of music educators.

Her husband, meanwhile, had been saying for years that he intended to fight Jim Crow, that he would finish his studies and go to work in the South, where segregation was quicksand to so many. But before he could get there, the rules of engagement changed. On May 17, while King was still in Boston, the U.S. Supreme Court, reaching a unanimous decision in *Brown v. Board*, struck down school segregation as unconstitutional. Separate educational facilities, Chief Justice Earl Warren wrote, "are inherently unequal."

Jim Crow had been issued a death sentence, although it remained far from the grave.

Hope, hatred, and fear reverberated from the decision. Benjamin Mays said the Supreme Court had "given America an opportunity to achieve greatness in the area of moral and spiritual things just as it has already achieved greatness in military and industrial might and in material possessions." Some white southerners called the day of the court's decision "Black Monday." Robert "Tut" Patterson and others in Sunflower County, Mississippi, launched a resistance movement—the Citizens' Councils, also called White Citizens' Councils—to fight integration and further intimidate Black people. Led by prominent white businessmen, professionals, and government officials, Citizens' Councils formed throughout the South, and particularly in places where Black people were in the majority, as a somewhat more aboveboard version of the Ku Klux Klan. Southern white newspaper columnists insisted that outsiders would never change the South—and by "outsiders" they meant not only the NAACP but also the federal government.

U.S. senator James O. Eastland, a Mississippi Democrat, said that the South would neither abide nor obey orders to integrate. As chairman of the Senate Judiciary Committee's subcommittee on civil rights, Eastland knew that his words would embolden southern officials in their resistance. "Education cannot thrive in a climate such as would result from mixture of the races in the public schools," Eastland said. Several governors in the South vowed to abolish public schools entirely rather than integrate them. King believed the harsh reaction could have been avoided. Dwight D. Eisenhower, then in his first term as president, was virtually silent on *Brown*, and that silence may have encouraged southern resistance, King said.

Brown v. Board would prove to be the capstone of one of the most successful campaigns of social reform ever undertaken through litigation. While many southern officials tried to ignore or evade the decision, the ruling had at least one clear and relatively immediate effect: it caused a shift in white public opinion, a shift seen clearly in the white northern media, which expanded coverage of the story of segregation. Major northern newspapers had no southern news bureaus. "To get publicity is of the highest strategic importance to the Negro people," Gunnar Myrdal had written in *The American Dilemma*. Now, a decade after the book's publication, publicity would arrive, and a new activist would emerge as the most visible and powerful Black man in America.

13

"A Precipitating Factor"

ON THE DAY of the Supreme Court's ruling in *Brown v. Board,* a reporter for *The Montgomery Advertiser* visited all-white Lanier High School and asked students what they thought about school integration.

"The South isn't ready for it," one student said.

"They aren't as civilized as we are," said another student, referring to Black students.

"Next thing you know," said yet another Lanier student, "they'll be riding with us on the buses and everything."

Three months later, in August 1954, Martin and Coretta packed their belongings in their green Chevrolet, leaving Boston for Montgomery, soon to become the crucible for the civil rights movement. After saying he wanted a job that would place him on the front lines of the fight against segregation, the Reverend Martin Luther King Jr. had been granted his wish.

The city seemed designed, in every way, to reinforce separation of the races. Martin and Coretta moved to a little wood-frame parsonage at 309 South Jackson Street in the West End neighborhood of Montgomery, "the Negro section of town where we would be living without choice," as King put it. Their neighbors were working-class men and women—sanitation workers, plumbers, truck drivers, and maids. A block away from the parsonage sat the Ben Moore Hotel, the only hotel in the city that welcomed Black guests. A few other small businesses survived in the shadow of the hotel or near

Alabama State College, but for the most part Montgomery's Black neighborhoods bore little resemblance to Sweet Auburn in Atlanta and even less
resemblance to the lavishly wealthy white neighborhoods of Montgomery.

Montgomery's Black neighborhoods were small, humble, and removed
from the center of commerce. Most Black Montgomery residents relied on
white Montgomery residents for their income and traveled by bus to their
jobs in white neighborhoods. Those who worked in downtown Montgomery
faced WHITES ONLY signs at drinking fountains, restrooms, and restaurants.
They carried their lunches to work and ate sitting on the sidewalk or in stuffy
back rooms.

Martin and Coretta lived for three weeks with a widowed member of
the church, Sallie Madison, at 1136 East Grove Street, while repairs were
made on the parsonage. By the time the Kings moved in, the cozy little box
of a house had new sinks, new wall-to-wall carpeting, new wallpaper, a new
washing machine, new electrical outlets, and new light switches in every
room. Dexter Avenue Baptist Church was a fifteen-minute walk away.

Daddy King and Alberta King drove to Montgomery for their son's
official installation. Daddy King delivered a sermon while Alberta led the
forty-person choir she had brought with her from Ebenezer. Before the service, M.L. took a taxi to the College Hill Barber Shop. The youngest barber in
the shop, Nelson Malden, watched him get out of the cab. Malden, a freshman
at Alabama State, checked the time and saw he had only about fifteen minutes
before his next class started. He looked at the well-dressed man walking toward the shop and made a quick assessment: the man's hair was already short.
Malden decided to give him a quick cut before hurrying to class.

King was a compact man with a lean, boyish face. His mustache was
flawlessly trimmed, his clothing finely tailored, verging on flashy. Anyone
could see this was a man who would not tolerate mediocrity, certainly not
in a haircut.

Malden worked fast but carefully. When the barber finished, King checked
the mirror and offered his appraisal: "Pretty good."

Pretty good? That stung.

Haircuts cost $1.75. King gave Malden $2.00—and waited for change.

King returned two weeks later for another trim.

"That must've been a *pretty* good haircut you got last time you were here?" Malden teased.

"You're all right," King said. But still he didn't tip.

Malden liked King. He learned that the young preacher played pool once or twice a week at a pool hall around the corner from the shop. King played well, he heard, but never for money. Malden noticed that King dressed fastidiously on days off from work. He wore expensive shoes and fine fedoras. Though King was a small man, his well-tailored suits in combination with his short neck and thick shoulders gave him the appearance of vigor. Sometimes the pastor stopped by the barbershop just to have a soda, chat with customers, and encourage men in the shop to visit his church on Sunday. What struck Malden most was King's intelligence. "I felt my brains improve just from touching his head," the barber joked.

But after seven or eight haircuts, Malden decided to ask King why he didn't tip.

"Barber," he said, "do you read your Bible?"

Malden said he did.

"The Bible says you should give ten percent of your earnings to the church. Do you give ten percent?"

Malden said he worked part-time and barely had enough money to live.

King was not impressed. "Well," he said, "I'm the pastor of Dexter Avenue Baptist Church, and I can't afford to tip you, either."

Though he was only twenty-five years old, King carried himself with the gravity of an older man, especially with his congregation, which included college professors and business leaders. He moved fast to establish his authority. He spent days writing and memorizing his sermons, rehearsing before a full-length mirror in his home.

On his first Sunday in the pulpit as pastor, September 5, 1954, he presented the church with a detailed set of recommendations, which he printed and distributed:

> When a minister is called to the pastorate of a church, the main presupposition is that he is vested with a degree of authority. The source of this authority is twofold. First of all, his authority originates with

God. Inherent in the call itself is the presupposition that God directed that such a call be made . . . Secondly, the pastor's authority
stems from the people themselves. Implied in the call is the unconditional willingness of the people to accept the pastor's leadership.
This means that the leadership never ascends from the pew to the
pulpit, but it invariably descends from the pulpit to the pew.

While that doesn't mean the pastor should be followed blindly or treated as
infallible, King continued, it does mean that he should be "respected and
accepted as the central figure" in the church. He followed with thirty-four
suggestions for how Dexter Avenue Baptist should function, including recommendations for new clubs and committees. He announced that church
members would be assigned to one of twelve clubs, based on the month each
person was born. The so-called birthday clubs would foster new friendships
and raise money. He said he expected each birthday club to donate at least
$100 a year to the church.

In his first few months in Montgomery, King focused on finishing his
doctoral dissertation and getting to know his congregation. He stood outside
the church after Sunday services, smiling, shaking hands, and making small
talk. But he could not ignore the world beyond. On September 2, three days
before King's inaugural sermon at Dexter, twenty-three Black children had
tried to enroll at the all-white William R. Harrison School in the southern
section of Montgomery, in a test of the recent Supreme Court ruling. The
students had been turned away, and the adult who had led them received
death threats.

King mixed calls to action with prayer in his sermons, but the response
at Dexter was far different from the response he had learned to expect at Ebenezer. "Nobody ever said anything in response to the sermons at Dexter,"
he recalled. "It was just a tradition at Dexter not to say 'amen' at church." But
he knew they were reacting positively. "The people don't have to open their
mouths, but . . . you can tell."

Less than two weeks after King's first sermon, seven Black women from
Montgomery had appeared before the city's Parks and Recreation Board to

complain about the "shameful and deplorable one-sidedness" of the city's segregated recreational facilities. Montgomery had eight parks for white people and only two for Black people—with no swimming pools for the Black population. The all-white Parks and Recreation Board voted unanimously to study the petition.

In 1950, only 813 of Montgomery's 40,000 Black residents had been registered to vote. Five years later, that number had more than doubled. Black voters still accounted for only about 7.5 percent of voters citywide, but their growing number made them a force local politicians had to take more seriously. The city had opened its first Black high school in 1946 and a second one soon after. In 1951, St. Jude's opened as the city's first hospital for Black people. In December 1953, the city's minor league baseball team, the Grays, announced plans to integrate.

"Montgomery is fast taking the lead as Alabama's most enlightened city," wrote a Black newspaper editor in 1953.

America was getting louder, faster, and freer in the 1950s. In Memphis, a white nineteen-year-old musician attracted attention for a recording of a song called "That's All Right (Mama)," first recorded by the Black songwriter Arthur Crudup in 1946. The version recorded by the white teenager, Elvis Presley, didn't sound quite like Black music or white music. Nor did it sound quite like pop, blues, or country. Black and white musicians seldom performed together at the time of Presley's emergence in 1954, but Black audiences became more likely to listen to white musicians, and white audiences became more likely to listen to black musicians, thanks to radio. Within a year, the Black artists Chuck Berry and Little Richard would have huge crossover hits that defined this new musical style called rock and roll, a raw, sonic expression of the quest for freedom. As Presley sang in one of his early hits, things were getting "all shook up."

Many historians would describe the 1950s as a time of tranquility, a time of prosperity, a time when the gap between the Left and Right narrowed and Americans, for the most part, agreed that they were fortunate to live in the greatest and most powerful nation on earth. But such descriptions overlooked many who did not feel so fortunate. Once those who were overlooked began to express their discontent, once they began to yearn for more, the picture-perfect image of America in the 1950s showed cracks. Where would the fight for real freedom spread next? It would spread almost everywhere, including Montgomery.

"Montgomery was an easygoing town; it could even have been described as a peaceful town," King said. "But the peace was achieved at a cost of human servitude."

When the city gave in to the demands of the Black community and hired four Black police officers, for example, the police chief felt compelled to placate angry white citizens by telling them the new officers were "just niggers doing a nigger's job." For those in power, maintaining the status quo meant maintaining the American way.

At the time of King's arrival, three Black citizens led the fight against racial injustice in Montgomery: Rufus Lewis, E. D. Nixon, and Jo Ann Robinson. Lewis, a graduate of Fisk University in Nashville, had moved to Montgomery in 1935 to become the coach of the Alabama State football team. He married Jewel Clayton, whose parents owned the biggest Black funeral home in town. Coach Lewis, as everyone called him, inherited the mortuary and became one of the city's leading Black businessmen. In the early 1950s, he opened a nightclub at the corner of Myles and Charlotte Streets and called it the Citizens' Club. Lewis turned away customers if they couldn't prove they were registered voters. But he didn't snub them for long. "Only a few days would elapse," he recalled, "before I contacted them and began to make arrangements for them to be registered."

While Lewis exerted influence in the middle-class neighborhood around Alabama State, E. D. Nixon spoke for the community's poorer Black people, especially on the city's west side. One white journalist in town called him the "mayor of the Black underbelly of Montgomery." Nixon was an imposing figure: more than six feet tall, with a square jaw and cinderblock shoulders and arms. He had little formal education, a fact that quickly became clear when he spoke, but his determination made up for any lack of erudition. Born in 1899, he worked as a sleeping car porter, a job that introduced him to A. Philip Randolph, the militant labor organizer, whom Nixon would come to idolize. Nixon led the local branch of the NAACP and went on to become president of the statewide organization. Though forced out of that job because the national leaders wanted someone more sophisticated, he didn't let the snub keep him from his work as an organizer in Montgomery. Nixon, along with the NAACP's branch secretary, Rosa Parks, was the best qualified to lead a movement that resonated beyond Montgomery.

Lewis and Nixon led, in part, because they didn't have white employers who could have fired them for politicking. The same could not be said for Jo Ann Robinson, a soft-spoken professor of English at Alabama State, a school funded and controlled by the government for the education of Black students. Robinson led the Women's Political Council, a group that had formed when the local chapter of the League of Women Voters had denied entry to Black women. Her own story about riding segregated buses was so upsetting that Robinson refused for years to talk about it, except to say it fueled her determination to fight.

Buses in the South were rolling theaters of degradation, with daily dramas acted out for all to see. Jim Crow laws kept Black and white people apart in schools, shops, and restaurants, yet shared buses were all but unavoidable for Black and white working-class people. In Montgomery, each city bus contained thirty-six seats. The first ten seats—two benches facing each other at the front, followed by a single row of forward-facing seats—were reserved for white passengers, even if there were no white passengers aboard and even if Black passengers in the rear had to stand. With those ten seats reserved for white passengers and ten in the back for Black passengers, that left sixteen seats in the middle that shifted as people boarded the bus. Accordingly, bus drivers had the power to order Black passengers out of the middle seats to make way for white passengers.

White bus drivers often required Black passengers to pay their fares at the front of the bus and then step off and reenter by the rear door; that way, the Black passengers wouldn't have to pass down the aisle and disturb white passengers. Sometimes, bus drivers took off before those Black passengers could reach the rear door. Bus drivers routinely passed up Black passengers, especially on cold, rainy days. Drivers refused to make change for Black passengers. They dropped transfer slips rather than handing them to Black passengers, making them bend to pick them up as the bus lurched forward.

Almost every Black person in Montgomery had a horror story. Of all the nightmares of living under segregation in Montgomery, riding the buses was perhaps the most vivid and widely shared. "Hurting feet, tired bodies, empty stomachs often tempted them to sit down," Jo Ann Robinson wrote. "Names like 'black nigger,' 'black bitches,' 'heifers,' 'whores,' and so on, brought them to their feet again."

Segregation had long been recognized as a means of oppression. From 1900 to 1907, Black people had boycotted segregated municipal transportation in at least twenty-seven cities, including Montgomery, winning significant but short-lived concessions. In recent years, Robinson and the Women's Political Council had pressed the city and National City Lines, the Chicago-based company that operated the buses, to change the seating rules. In 1954, Mayor William A. "Tacky" Gayle Jr. and bus company officials agreed to meet one of the group's demands: bus drivers would be instructed to stop at every corner in Black neighborhoods, same as they did in white neighborhoods. But the officials insisted that the buses would remain segregated.

Frustration mounted. Robinson and others knew the city had options. In Mobile, Alabama, and other cities throughout the South, white passengers were seated from front to back and Black passengers from back to front. The dividing line fluctuated, and no seats were saved. If there were no white riders, Black passengers could legally occupy all the seats. Given that the bus systems in Mobile and Montgomery were both operated by National City Lines under the same state laws, Robinson wondered why the Montgomery buses did not follow the same rules as those in Mobile.

Four days after the Supreme Court's decision in *Brown v. Board*, Robinson wrote a letter of warning to Gayle. Black people accounted for about three-fourths of all bus passengers in Montgomery, she said. If they were to boycott, they could put the bus company out of business.

The city's Black activists had considered a boycott in the past, particularly after the recent arrest of a Black teenager named Claudette Colvin. But the activists weren't sure if Colvin, at age fifteen, could handle the pressure.

Fred Gray, the Black attorney who represented Colvin, told Jo Ann Robinson not to worry. He was confident another arrest would soon follow—one that would provide an even stronger basis for a challenge.

As a college student, Gray had sometimes taken eight bus rides a day as he'd traveled from home to school and to his job delivering newspapers. He had seen the way white bus drivers treated Black passengers. He also knew the story of Viola White, a Black woman who worked at nearby Maxwell Air Force Base who had been beaten, arrested, and convicted for refusing to give up her bus seat in 1944. When White had appealed her conviction, she couldn't get her case on the court calendar. Meanwhile, in retaliation, her daughter was seized and raped by a police officer. Gray got so angry he scratched his plans to become a schoolteacher and decided to become a lawyer, following the advice of E. D. Nixon.

"I made a commitment," Gray said, "not only that I was going to become a lawyer, but I was going to come back to Alabama, take the Alabama bar exam, pass it, and destroy everything segregated I could find."

In 1955, Gray was one of only two Black attorneys in Montgomery, and he was the only one intent on fighting segregation. In his first year out of Western Reserve University School of Law in Cleveland (now Case Western), he did not have many paying clients. He continued to deliver newspapers while waiting for business to improve, and he enjoyed leisurely lunches with one of his allies in the growing movement for racial justice in Montgomery, Rosa Parks, a local seamstress. Parks and Gray had met through the NAACP, where Parks was a longtime activist, working on voter rights and complaints of police brutality, among other things. Parks was a petite woman, gentle and serene, but, as Rufus Lewis put it, "her appearance and what was within her was two different things." Inside, she burned with determination and pride. She was delighted that Gray had chosen to practice law in Montgomery. On her lunch breaks, she told the attorney about her numerous encounters with bus drivers and, in particular, about the time a driver had yanked her by the arm and put her off the bus for refusing to reenter through the back door after she'd paid her fare. She said she would know what to do if another bus driver gave her a hard time. She would remain

calm. She would politely but firmly refuse to give up her seat for a white passenger. And if police arrested her, she would not fight back.

"It takes the right type of person to be able to do that," Gray said, looking
carefully at Parks.

Gray may have thought he was helping to prepare Parks, but Parks
seemed to be preparing Gray, too.

King rose each morning at five-thirty to work on his doctoral dissertation
for three hours before switching over to church-related work. Each night, he
said, he spent three additional hours on the dissertation, sometimes falling
asleep with a book on his chest. Coretta typed the dissertation for him.

At the end of his first year at Dexter Avenue, he reported to the congregation that he had preached forty-six sermons at Dexter and seven at other
churches, presented thirteen lectures, attended thirty-six community meetings and ten conventions, made eighty-seven pastoral visits and forty-nine
sick visits, conducted twelve baptisms, performed five marriages, and presided over five funerals. Within months of his arrival, as King developed
a reputation as a fine preacher, the word spread across much of the state of
Alabama. Empty seats on Sundays became scarce. Before long, his church
had to set up chairs in the aisles to accommodate the crowds. He had already
transformed his "silk-stocking" church into a focal point of Black pride. He
had already become, as his first biographer, L. D. Reddick, put it, "a bourgeois leader of the masses."

"Pastor King's preaching had a freshness," recalled Thelma Austin Rice,
one of his congregants. "With most ministers you did not have to follow
them attentively because their words and phrases were well known . . . Dr.
King had an assuredness about what he believed. It was so strong until it
might have come through with a tinge of arrogance . . . He had convictions
and nothing could sway him."

King dressed his sermons in luxury, quoting from Hebrew prophets
as well as the Greek philosophers. He roared but never shouted. He made
his passion and dignity felt with the vibrato in his voice, with the rhythms

of his phrases, with the urgency in his messages. Beyond the pulpit, King charmed the Black people of Montgomery. He was never too busy to stop and chat. He remembered names. He touched people's arms and shoulders when he spoke. He listened. He smiled. He laughed. It was a deep, warm, irresistible laugh that burbled up from his chest like water from a fountain. His favorite way to begin a sentence in conversation was with a long, affirming, welcoming "Yessss."

As he began his career, King operated under the assumption, encouraged by his father, that he would one day return to Atlanta as pastor of Ebenezer Baptist Church. His father often reminded him to hold tight to his spiritual values. In a letter dated December 2, 1954, Daddy King wrote: "Every way I turned people are congradulating [sic] me for you. You see young man you are becoming very popular. As I told you you must be much in prayer. Persons like yourself are the ones the devil turns all of his forces aloose to destroy."

Years later, when members of Dexter Avenue church compiled a book full of memories, they gushed. "Everybody loved him," said Robert D. Nesbitt Jr., whose father was a longtime Dexter deacon. "He made people feel at ease. Above all he was genuine." The church members who contributed to the book seldom spoke of Coretta in their tributes. Of the thirty-four essays, only one contains an anecdote in which Coretta King plays a starring role. Because Dexter was a large church, Coretta didn't feel compelled to assert herself too aggressively. "I didn't have the feeling going then that I had to be in some important position . . . ," she said, "so I had a chance to gradually . . . become adjusted to the congregation."

In his annual report to the congregation, King also neglected to mention Coretta. But surely by then, everyone at Dexter Avenue knew that the pastor's wife was pregnant and due to deliver in November.

King was not directly involved in the struggle over bus segregation yet, but, as *The Huntsville Mirror* wrote in the summer of 1955, he had launched an "intensive campaign in the church for NAACP memberships and voters" and was "participating in everything for the betterment of the community." On June 19, 1955, he spoke to a meeting of Alabama NAACP leaders, saying

Jim Crow was nearly dead, but the fight was not done. "There is no time to pause and be complacent," he said. "We must pay for our freedom, develop courageous leaders, and not be afraid to take a stand for our freedom."

Reverend King became Reverend Doctor King in June 1955, when Boston University awarded him his PhD. Jim Crow etiquette at the time required Black people to address white people as "Mr." and "Mrs." but allowed white people of all ages to refer to Black adults by their first names, which is one reason that King began asking white officials in Montgomery to call him "Dr. King" and why members of his congregation exulted in their pastor's new honorific.

Weeks after getting his degree, Dr. King flew to New Orleans to explore a job opportunity at Dillard University, one of the South's top historically Black colleges. A. W. Dent, Dillard's president, was a Morehouse alumnus and a contemporary of Daddy King's. He asked the younger King to consider becoming dean of the new Lawless Memorial University Chapel, a position that would permit him to preach, teach, and study. It was also a job that would afford him a comfortable lifestyle in a major southern city.

Dent wanted King for the job. But, with the chapel still under construction, the school was not quite ready to hire. No offer would be extended until the start of the next school year, he told King.

Remaining in Montgomery, King engaged with the issues that mattered in his community, including the issue of fear. White people for centuries had used fear to repress Black people, and overcoming fear would take time and unity. "It was always there," said Dorothy Calhoun, one of King's congregants. "Black children were never intentionally taught fear, but it was there. No Black person in those days could tell you the first time he or she became conscious of his or her fear, but it was always present."

When the Reverend George Lee, a grocery owner and NAACP officer in Belzoni, Mississippi, tried to vote in 1955, he was immediately shot and killed. No one was arrested. But it was another act of violence in Mississippi that helped Americans beyond the South to better understand the terror faced by Black southerners. On August 28, 1955, fourteen-year-old Emmett Till was brutally beaten, shot in the head, bound with barbed wire to a seventy-five-pound cotton-gin fan, and dumped into the Tallahatchie River—all because a white woman claimed that Emmett had whistled at her. The accused killers were acquitted, but Emmett Till's mother insisted on an open casket for her son's funeral, boldly displaying what white racists had done to her child, and *Jet* magazine published photos of the boy's mutilated corpse. Newspapers worldwide covered Emmett Till's murder. In Germany one of the headlines read: "The Life of a Negro Isn't Worth a Whistle."

More northern newspapers sent reporters to the South after the Till murder. A few of the media companies even sent Black reporters, including Ted Poston of the *New York Post* and Carl Rowan of *The Minneapolis Morning Tribune*.

"Long repressed feelings of resentment" had begun to stir, King wrote, and the "fear and apathy which had for so long cast a shadow on the life of the Negro community were gradually fading before a new spirit of courage and self-respect."

On November 17, 1955, Coretta gave birth to a girl. The Kings named her Yolanda Denise and called her Yoki for short.

Ten days later, Dexter Avenue Baptist Church hosted a speech by T. R. M. Howard, president of the Mississippi-based Regional Council of Negro Leadership. Howard told the "Mississippi Shame Story," describing the outrage sweeping the country over the murder of Emmett Till. In the audience that night was Rosa Parks. Five days after Howard's speech, Parks finished work in downtown Montgomery and boarded the Cleveland Avenue bus to head home.

In years to come, Parks would describe her bus ride countless times. Historians would mark the date—Thursday, December 1, 1955—as the day the mid-twentieth-century civil rights movement was born. Gradually, her story would become a part of American mythology, the story of a humble seamstress with tired feet who refused to give up her seat and launched a revolution. But before she became famous, Parks gave an account of her arrest to Willie M. Lee, a researcher from Fisk University's Department of Race Relations. The interview took place in Parks's home on February 5, 1956, sixty-seven days after her arrest for violating Montgomery's segregated public transit rules. Only recently discovered, it appears to be her earliest interview on the subject. According to a typed transcript, she said:

> Well, there really isn't too much to tell. First I started not to ride the bus because I wasn't feeling well, however, after leaving the drug store and getting some medicine, a bus came along which was almost empty, so I took it rather than a cab. After the bus had gone a couple of blocks, it became full, then these white people got on. I only noticed them though, when the motorman said, "Alright, let me have those seats!" The two persons across from me moved and the man sitting with me . . . The motorman then said, "Didn't you hear me? I said, let me have those seats!" I then told him that I was not going to move because I got on first and paid the same fare, and I didn't think it was right for me to have to stand so someone else who got on later could sit down. I made up my mind that I was not going to move even if there were seats in back. I was tired of being humiliated. The bus driver then went on for another block to the circle downtown.

The circle in downtown Montgomery was once the center of the city's slave trade.

Parks continued:

> There he stopped and called the police. When they came, they asked me why I didn't move back, and I told them the same thing I told the motorman. Then they talked to the driver secretly, however, I did hear one say "NAACP," and "Are you sure you want to press charges." The driver said that he did, and that he would come down after his next trip. The policemen were reluctant, but they had no choice.

When we got to the jail and the charges were made, I was photo-graphed and finger-printed. I then started to one of the fountains to get some water, but was told that I could not drink from the fountain, so a policeman got the water in a glass for me. After this, I called my husband and told him I was in jail and that my bond would be $100. He and my mother were horrified, after explaining why I was there, they sort of calmed down a bit, and I finally got home.

Parks's courage went beyond her confrontation with the bus driver. She also had to face her husband, who was, she wrote, very angry with her for refusing to give up the seat and accused her of having a "goat head."

In later years, Parks would make small changes in the story, saying the bus was crowded when she got on, adding that only one row of seats had vacancies—the row immediately behind those seats reserved for whites. In later accounts she also omitted the police officer's mention of her connection to the NAACP. Parks didn't seek conflict, but she certainly wasn't the meek character that some would make her out to be. Her early description of the incident suggests that Parks had Fred Gray's advice and the law on her mind. She sat in the section of the bus where she was most likely to face an order to move: in the first row that Black passengers were asked to vacate as buses filled with white passengers. While she didn't say in the 1956 interview that she wanted to be arrested, she knew it would be a possibility.

Fred Gray was out of town at the time of Parks's arrest. When he returned, he spoke to Parks, E. D. Nixon, and, finally, late at night, Jo Ann Robinson. Robinson said she wanted to boycott the buses on Monday morning, December 5.

"Are you ready?" Gray asked.

Robinson said she and two of her students would go to Alabama State College in the early hours of the morning, when no one was around, and use the mimeograph machines to copy leaflets. The students and members of the Women's Political Council would distribute thousands of flyers door to door over the weekend. Robinson would also call a meeting of the city's Black preachers and ask them to urge members of their congregations to stay off the buses on Monday.

They needed the support of Nixon, the influential elder statesman of civil rights in Montgomery, who had access to the white media. But putting Nixon in charge might discourage Rufus Lewis from getting involved, Gray said. If Robinson took the lead, she would probably be fired from her job at the state-funded college. They needed someone who could get Nixon and Lewis to work together, appeal to Black people from all parts of the city, present a respectable image to the press, and handle negotiations well. Robinson and Gray discussed selecting a preacher for the job. But which one?

"Well, Fred," Robinson said, "my pastor hasn't been here long. But one thing he can do, he can move people with his words."

14

"My Soul Is Free"

Martin Luther King Jr. was the third person E. D. Nixon phoned to line up support for a bus boycott in Montgomery. Could he add King's name to the list of supporters?

"Brother Nixon," King said, "let me think about it."

Soon, the phone rang again. This time it was an excited Ralph Abernathy. The men had become close friends since King's arrival in Montgomery. The people were riled, Abernathy said, and ready to go to war against Jim Crow. If King had been hesitant to respond to Nixon's call to action, he couldn't say no to Abernathy. The men started making phone calls and planning a meeting of ministers and civic leaders for that evening at King's church.

Meanwhile, Jo Ann Robinson and her team began distributing leaflets:

Another Negro woman has been arrested and thrown into jail because she refused to get up out of her seat on the bus for a white person to sit down . . . This has to be stopped. Negroes have rights, too, for if Negroes did not ride the buses they would not operate . . . If we do not do something to stop these arrests, they will continue. The next time it may be you, or your daughter, or mother. This woman's case will come up Monday. We are, therefore, asking every Negro to stay off the buses Monday in protest of the arrest and trial. Don't ride buses to work, to town, to school, or anywhere on Monday. You can afford to stay out of school one day if you have no other way to go except by bus. You can also afford to stay out of town for one day.

If you work, take a cab, or walk. But please, children and grown-ups, don't ride the bus at all on Monday. Please stay off all buses Monday.

Early Friday evening, about seventy Black leaders met in the basement of Dexter Avenue to discuss strategy. The Reverend L. Roy Bennett, head of a local alliance of ministers, ran the meeting and rambled on for more than thirty minutes, to the frustration of others. Eventually, the leaders agreed to endorse the boycott and schedule a community meeting for Monday night, after Parks's trial and after they had a chance to see if people stayed off the buses. A new leaflet was written to add information about the Monday-night meeting. Juanita Abernathy typed this one. Her husband and King worked the mimeograph machine at Dexter deep into the night. On Saturday night, the two preachers handed out leaflets at nightclubs.

News of Parks's arrest meant little to the white community. The white-owned *Montgomery Advertiser* printed a five-paragraph story on the bottom of page A9, with the headline "Negro Arrested Here for 'Overlooking' Bus Segregation." But when E. D. Nixon tipped off the reporter Joe Azbell to the looming boycott, the *Advertiser* followed up two days later with a front-page story. The article included a response to the protest from J. H. Bagley, manager of the bus company: "The Montgomery City Lines is sorry if anyone expects us to be exempt from any state or city law. We are sorry that the colored people blames [*sic*] us for any state or city ordinance."

The newspaper story said the proposed boycott was similar to a strategy employed by the White Citizens' Council, which refused to patronize businesses that served Black customers or failed to strictly enforce Jim Crow laws. The comparison troubled King at first. Was it wrong to cause problems for the bus company to solve problems for Black riders? Was it the Christian thing to do? He reflected on Thoreau's *Civil Disobedience* and decided that the practical effect of the boycott was to stop participating in an "evil system." To accept evil without challenging it, King concluded, would be to condone it.

If the mimeographed flyers had missed anyone, the Sunday *Advertiser* story filled the gaps. By Monday morning, December 5, almost every Black man, woman, and child in Montgomery knew they were supposed to stay off the buses. Handmade signs appeared at bus stops. One of them read:

Remember we are
Fighting For a cause
Do Not Ride A
Bus Today

Police removed the signs.

King was too anxious to sleep. By five-thirty Monday morning, he and Coretta were dressed. Half an hour later, Martin was in the kitchen getting a cup of coffee when Coretta spotted the first bus of the day rumbling down Jackson Street.

"Martin, Martin, come quickly!" she called.

King put down his coffee and hustled to the living room window.

The yellow bus, usually filled with Black domestic workers, was completely empty.

Fifteen minutes later, another bus passed. Empty. The next bus, fifteen minutes later, had two passengers, both white.

"I jumped in my car," King wrote, "and for almost an hour I cruised down every major street and examined every passing bus. During this hour, at the peak of the morning traffic, I saw no more than eight Negro passengers riding the buses. By this time I was jubilant. Instead of the 60 percent cooperation we had hoped for, it was becoming apparent that we had reached almost 100 percent. A miracle had taken place."

People took taxis. They shared cars. Most of all, they walked. Police cars followed the buses, checking to see if Black "goon squads" were intimidating would-be passengers. But no goon squads were needed. Black people waved and cheered and stuck out their tongues at the empty buses. A daylong celebration commenced. When a minister stopped to give a ride to a woman who had walked a long way, he asked if she felt tired. "Well, my body may be a bit tired," she said, "but for many years now my soul has been tired. Now my soul is resting. So I don't mind if my body is tired, because my soul is free."

"And as I watched them," King later wrote, "I knew that there is nothing more majestic than the determined courage of individuals willing to suffer and sacrifice for their freedom and dignity."

———— • ————

At 9:00 a.m. that same day, Fred Gray represented Rosa Parks in city court. Originally, Parks had been charged with violating the city's segregation order. But the prosecutor, Eugene Loe, had a problem. Under the city's ordinance, Parks could have been forced to give up her seat only if another seat had been available. Loe dropped the charge and replaced it with a charge based on state law—one that gave bus drivers unlimited power to enforce mandated segregation. It took the judge, John B. Scott, barely five minutes to declare Parks guilty and fine her $10.

Gray filed notice of his intention to appeal, and E. D. Nixon left the courtroom to post the bond. In the hallway of the courthouse, Nixon was stunned to find hundreds of people gathered in support of Parks. They filled the corridor and the stairwell, and spilled onto the street.

Nixon, Abernathy, and another preacher, the Reverend Edgar N. French of the Hilliard Chapel AME Zion Church, discussed whether it was wise to let Reverend Bennett continue to lead the boycott meetings, given his erratic performance at the last gathering. The men hit on an idea: If they formed a new organization, they could choose a new leader and push Bennett aside. Ralph Abernathy recommended his friend Martin Luther King Jr. to lead the new organization.

A larger group of community leaders met at 3:00 p.m. Monday to make plans for that evening's mass meeting at Holt Street Baptist Church. King, arriving late, witnessed the formation of the new organization, which Abernathy named the Montgomery Improvement Association.

"In that meetin' . . . ," E. D. Nixon recalled, "everybody was still—all the ministers was still afraid." They talked about trying to organize a boycott without white people discovering their involvement. "Well, I was sittin' there boiling over, so mad I didn't know what to do."

Nixon stood up and cursed. "How you gonna have a mass meeting, gonna boycott a city bus line without the white folks knowing it?" He said he would lead the movement himself, but it wouldn't succeed without the respectability of the church. "You ought to make up your mind right now that you're gon' either admit you are a grown man or concede to the fact that you are a bunch of scared boys."

It was King who responded, according to Nixon, "that he wasn't no coward, that nobody called him a coward."

That's when he became the president of the Montgomery Improvement Association, selected not only for his courage, according to Rufus Lewis, but also for his broad appeal. King hadn't been in town long enough to have made enemies. King, Lewis said, "was a neutral man, a good man."

Once the question of leadership had been settled, the men and women discussed how to make sure people stayed off the buses as the boycott continued. They also agreed on a list of relatively modest demands:

1. Negro bus passengers should be seated from back to front, whites from front to rear. There should be no signs or lines of separation, and no one should ever be asked by a driver to give up his or her seat. The riders would remain separated, but they would do so without orders from the bus driver.

2. Negroes would be accorded the same courtesy as white passengers with no name-calling or insulting treatment such as being forced to board from the rear door.

3. Negro bus drivers would be hired to drive on predominantly Negro routes.

It was after six o'clock when they finished. In less than an hour, King would have to address the crowd at the Holt Street church. He rushed home and told Coretta about his busy day. He said he felt he had had no choice but to accept his leadership position.

"You know that whatever you do," Coretta said, "you have my backing."

The streets outside grew dark. King went to his study and closed the door. Usually, he spent fifteen hours writing and rehearsing a sermon. Now he had twenty minutes to prepare for what he would later call the "most de-cisive" speech of his life. Newspapers around the country had begun to cover the confrontation. An Associated Press news story said every available Mont-gomery police officer had been "alerted for duty" in case the protests turned violent. King would have to be bold enough to encourage the people to suffer for their freedom, moderate enough to keep their fervor under control, and optimistic enough to make everyone believe they could succeed. He needed to embolden without embittering. "Could the militant and the moderate be combined in a single speech?" he wondered. It was a question he would ask in various forms for the rest of his life.

Panic struck. He fell into "a state of anxiety," he said, and "wasted five minutes of the original twenty."

He prayed away the panic, asking God to guide him. He settled his mind and jotted a few notes on what he might say.

Coretta, who had to stay home with their newborn baby, asked Martin to make sure someone recorded the speech so she could hear it later.

Abernathy's car pulled up in front of the house, and King got in. But before they could reach Holt Street Baptist Church, the site of the meeting, they were stopped by traffic. Parked cars lined both sides of the street. Police cruisers circled. It took King a moment to realize the traffic and the crowds were for him. He and Abernathy abandoned their car and walked in the cool, crisp air.

Thousands of people had reached the church before King, with more on the way. Many had come directly from work. They filled every seat in the sanctuary. They filled the aisles and doorways. They filled the balcony and the basement. They filled the backyard of the church and the surrounding streets for three blocks. Workers hurried to set up outdoor loudspeakers for the overflow audience. *The Montgomery Advertiser* estimated that five thou-sand people turned out for the meeting, most of them in the streets. The church itself was so crowded that it took King fifteen minutes to get from the door to the pulpit.

"By now my doubts concerning the continued success of our venture were dispelled," he wrote. "The question of calling off the protest was now academic. The enthusiasm of these thousands of people swept everything along like an onrushing tidal wave."

At about seven-thirty, after the voices inside and outside the church joined to sing "Onward Christian Soldiers," the speeches began. Joe Azbell, the white reporter from the *Advertiser*, wrote that he had never seen a crowd so full of energy: "They were on fire . . . on fire for Jesus . . . on fire for freedom. There was a spirit there that no one could ever capture again in a movie or anything else because it was so powerful."

King, without notes or manuscript, stepped to the microphone. He was small against the backdrop of the church and the crush of the crowd, but he was perfectly composed. He began slowly and without flourish. This crowd had gathered, he said, first of all, because they were all American citizens, American citizens resolute in their insistence on acquiring the rights to which they were entitled. They were patriots, lovers of democracy, and their actions would prove that democracy was the greatest form of government on earth.

"But we are here in a specific sense because of the bus situation in Montgomery," he said.

The crowd called out and urged him. Most members of the audience didn't know him, but they offered their voices in a chorus of praise, repeating "Yes" and "That's right."

He did not quote philosophers this time. He spoke plainly of the crippling fear that had long gripped the community. He described the week's events and connected those events to the long and momentous history of his people's suffering. Then, after praising Rosa Parks and detailing her arrest, he said: "And you know, my friends, there comes a time when people get tired of being trampled over by the iron feet of oppression."

The crowd thundered its approval. "I was in the street. I couldn't get close to the church," said Willodean Malden, who was fourteen years old at the time. "You could hear the voice of Martin Luther King all over the neighborhood. I'd never heard of Martin Luther King. It was just a shocking experience to hear someone relate to the people like that and hear the reaction. The words just made so much sense . . . You didn't know why, but you felt something *different*."

On this night, King found a new voice. He discovered or sensed that his purpose was not to instruct or educate; his purpose was to prophesize. With a booming voice and strident words, he marked the path for himself and for a movement. He reminded the people that their advantage was in their moral superiority. They would not burn crosses or pull white people from their homes. They would protest peacefully, as their Christian faith instructed. They meant to reform American democracy, not overthrow it.

He called out in his deep, throbbing voice, and the people responded, the noise of the crowd rolling and pounding in waves that shook the building as he built to a climax:

And we are not wrong. . . If we are wrong, the Supreme Court of this nation is wrong. If we are wrong, the Constitution of the United States is wrong. If we are wrong, God Almighty is wrong. If we are wrong, Jesus of Nazareth was merely a utopian dreamer that never came down to earth. If we are wrong, justice is a lie. Love has no meaning. And we are determined here in Montgomery to work and fight until justice runs down like water and righteousness like a mighty stream.

They would show their opponents love, yet love alone would not free his people, he said. The people would have to demand freedom: Follow me, King said, and we will use the power of love to make America our Promised Land, and when history books tell the story they will tell of people with "fleecy locks and black complexion" who rose to fight oppression and launched a revolution that changed the world.

Inside and outside the church, people whooped and shouted and sang. They reached out to touch King.

"The fear left," Abernathy said later, "the fear that had shackled us across the years all left suddenly when we were in that church together."

"It was like a revival starting," said Donie Jones, a forty-seven-year-old mother of six who cooked and cleaned for white families at Maxwell Air Force Base. "That's what it was like . . . You had to hold people to keep them from gettin' to him. Reverend King was a God-sent man."

"That first speech stimulated the people more than anything has ever stimulated them as long as I've been here," Rufus Lewis said. "And from then on, he was the shining light, with information, inspiration, and courage. He had as much courage as any man I've ever seen."

Later, King would call December 5, 1955, "the day of days."

It was the day, at the age of twenty-six, that King found his voice, preaching a mixture of political agitation and gospel, making the radical seem reasonable, perhaps inevitable. The world would change. All men would be free. Their time had come. He promised.

15

"We Ain't Rabbit No More"

WHEN KING REFLECTED on his performance that night at Holt Street Baptist Church, he offered a simple explanation for his success: "Open your mouth and God will speak for you."

He had climbed a mountain with his performance, he wrote. But he was back on lower ground the next day, with work to do. He would use the metaphor often to describe his life's work and sometimes to describe his moods, his "courage to be" followed by anxiety, his hope followed by fear of letting people down.

On Tuesday, at Fred Gray's law office, King talked to reporters, telling them the protesters were not demanding desegregation, merely the same first-come, first-served seating used in Mobile, as well as more courteous treatment by drivers. A compromise would not be difficult to reach, he said. Two days later, Montgomery Improvement Association (MIA) leaders met with city officials and bus company executives in negotiations brokered by white members of the Alabama Council on Human Relations. King expressed surprise that the city would not agree to a compromise, given the modest demands. But city officials and bus company officials pushed back. Jack Crenshaw, the bus company's attorney, blamed the poor treatment of passengers on a handful of rude drivers. Crenshaw told the protesters their demands would be impossible to meet under state and local laws. That response may have "inadvertently radicalized King and the MIA," the Harvard law professor Randall Kennedy writes, compelling them to demand more than they had originally sought.

King and others in the meeting—including Ralph Abernathy and Jo Ann Robinson—realized they might have to prepare for a longer boycott. They organized another mass meeting and passed around sign-up sheets, asking for volunteers to drive the bus boycotters to and from work. At a time when many Black people in the community were still without home telephones, the flyers and mass meetings would prove essential.

The Montgomery Advertiser took an optimistic view, pointing out that, while "there is some animosity and much that cannot be squared with the Christian ethic . . . , nowhere else in the country are the relations between different breeds and creeds so gentle, easy, and benign" as in Montgomery. The paper also praised King for being reasonable and seeking a fix for the buses while not demanding an end to segregation. The next week, when MIA and city officials met again, King agreed to drop the request for the immediate hiring of Black bus drivers. The city still wouldn't budge. "What they are after is the destruction of our social fabric," said the mayor, Tacky Gayle.

When Gayle called on a white pastor to speak, the pastor lectured King, saying ministers should abstain from political acts. King became angry. "I can see no conflict between our devotion to Jesus Christ and our present action," he responded. "In fact I see a necessary relationship. If one is truly devoted to the religion of Jesus he will seek to rid the Earth of social evils. The Gospel is social as well as personal."

With the city and the boycotters at a stalemate, Gayle did what every politician did when he hoped to see an issue die a slow death: he appointed a committee. Hope for a resolution faded when the mayor quietly added to the committee one of the leaders of the city's White Citizens' Council.

King and other leaders forged plans for a long campaign. More volunteer carpool drivers signed on to help. Black taxi drivers pledged to continue to carry passengers for ten cents each, the price of bus fare. The city fought back. Police charged Black cab drivers with breaking the law by not applying their regular fares, and white cab drivers were charged for violating segregation laws by carrying Black passengers. It had become clear to both sides that they were fighting about more than bus seats now.

Emory O. Jackson, a Black journalist for the *Birmingham World*, reported from Montgomery:

History has a way of re-making itself in localized present-day events. The birth of the Christ child was opposed by a king nearly 2,000 years ago. The birth of a new dignity for a segment of the population in Montgomery is opposed today by the ruling hand. The Montgomery story and the Bethlehem story are centuries apart but close enough to tie in with humanity. The Rev. Martin Luther King Jr., a Baptist Minister, [is] helping to give the protest the spiritual direction, the sense of mission, the idealism which it needs . . . Attend one of the informational mass meetings and you come away with a feeling that the leaders know what they want, how to go after it, and the price they will have to pay to get it.

Jo Ann Robinson, E. D. Nixon, Rufus Lewis, and others had been building networks for years, laying the foundation for this moment. Now the mass meetings, built around King's enthralling oratory, united Montgomery's Black community, despite the obvious risk of retaliation. The MIA's leaders vowed they would carry on their protest as long as necessary. Negroes weren't afraid to walk, King said. "Negroes were born walking," he said. "We were raised walking . . . Walking is nothing new . . . walking never hurts us." They would walk and fight, he promised, until they took "the heart out of Dixie."

They walked until they wore out their shoes. They also organized a massive and sophisticated carpool operation. The MIA raised money to pay drivers, purchase gas, and buy auto insurance. Georgia Gilmore and Inez Ricks formed clubs that competed to see which group could sell more baked goods in support of the boycotters. Rufus Lewis let the transportation committee use his place, the Citizens' Club, as the carpool's command center. Walking to and from work became a daily display of pride, an expression of freedom. The carpools reminded the protesters of their communal strength. Well-to-do members of King's church seldom rode the buses. But they owned cars, which meant they could take bus riders to and from work and be part of the campaign. Black professionals made their office phones and secretaries available to serve as dispatchers. At every opportunity, King reminded his followers of the moral beauty of their protest. Their fight, he said, was not only for fairness. It was for the future. It was for redemption. It was to make America a better and more loving country for all people. It was for God.

Police and other city officials harassed and disrupted the protest. When gas stations in Montgomery refused to sell to the carpoolers, King drove one day to Tuskegee, about forty miles away, to see if he could arrange to buy fuel there. Samuel DeWitt Proctor, a Crozer alumnus and president of Virginia Union University, rode with King because, as Proctor said, "you never knew what might happen to a Black radical man on the highway in those days." An Alabama state trooper followed them the entire way, "about a yard behind" the old Pontiac wagon King drove. "We were both frightened, perspiring profusely, and silent," Proctor said.

King's sudden rise seemed remarkable but not surprising to Proctor, who was eight years older than his friend and had a doctorate from Boston University. Proctor knew other Black ministers with talent and courage, he said, but they didn't have Vernon Johns and Daddy King to clear a path or Rosa Parks to light the way or the national news media to amplify their words. King, with his radical social message absorbed from the Old Testament prophets and his insistence on the power of love as exemplified by Jesus, had turned out to be the right man at the right time. When King and Proctor reached Tuskegee city limits, the trooper stopped following them. After King finished meeting with Black gas station owners and started toward home, the trooper tailed them back to Montgomery.

King became more than a spokesman; he became a leader. He stated the boycott's goal, helped strategize its methods, and came to the forefront in discussions with city officials. He united the community by sharing the stories of the men and women who were walking for freedom. Though the boycott was designed to be disruptive, he stressed that this was a Christian movement, one centered on principles of peace and love, one that sought to heal. Mass meetings kept the movement strong. Church services provided the inspiration and the template for meetings. There were hymns and spirituals as well as speeches: "What a Friend We Have in Jesus"; "Leaning on the Everlasting Arms"; "Lord, I Want to Be a Christian"; "O, Freedom"; "Go Down, Moses." "And everyone would go home," Coretta said, "feeling good and inspired and ready to go back the next morning to a long day of hard work."

King had not sought a position of leadership. "I tried to discourage him from taking the lead," his mother, Alberta, said. "I asked him, didn't he think it would be a wiser thing to let some of the older preachers or some of the older people who had worked with the NAACP and some other organizations like that lead this? I didn't want him to lead it. I told him I felt, because he was young, they might not accept him, and, because he was new in the city, they might not accept him."

But her concerns passed. Step by step, the movement gained power, and her son became, as she put it, "so greatly involved."

On a cold, gray Tuesday afternoon, January 24, 1956, a domestic worker named Dealy Cooksey walked home from work. It had been fifty days since she had ridden a bus.

"I'm tired," Cooksey said.

A researcher from Fisk University walked alongside the middle-aged Black woman, asking questions and taking notes. Cooksey told the researcher she worked in the home of a wealthy white woman. Most days, the white woman picked her up and drove her to work. But sometimes she had to walk. The researcher wondered if Cooksey had ever discussed the bus boycott with her white employer. Oh, yes, Cooksey replied, and she went on to recount one of the conversations.

"Dealy, why don't you ride the bus?" her employer had asked. "That Reverend King is just making a fool out of you people."

"Don't you say nothing 'bout Reverend King," Cooksey shot back. "That's us man, and I declare he's a fine one. He went to school and he made something out of his self, and now he's trying to help us. Y'all white folks done kept us blind long enough. We got our eyes open and now we sure ain't gonna let you close 'em back. I don't mean to be sassy, but when you talk about Reverend King, I gets mad. Y'all white folks work us to death and don't pay nothing."

"But, Dealy, I pay you," her employer said.

"What do you pay, just tell me? I'm shame to tell folks what I work for."

"Dealy," said the employer, "I didn't mean to make you mad, I was just talking."

"Well, talk about Sellers and old no-good Gayle," she said, referring to the police commissioner, Clyde Sellers, and the mayor, Tacky Gayle. "I walked to work the first day and I can walk now. If you don't want to bring me, I ain't begging, and I sure ain't getting back on the bus, and don't you never say nothing about Reverend King. I ain't gonna get back on the bus til Reverend King say so, and he says we ain't going back til they treat us right."

The interviewer asked Cooksey how long she thought the boycott would last.

"I don't care if they don't ever start back," she said. "We got these white folks where we want 'em, and there ain't nothing they can do but try to scare us. But we ain't rabbit no more, we done turned 'coon. My daddy used to tell me about 'coon hunting. If he's in a tree and you shake him down, he'll kill three dogs, and if he's in the water, he'll drown every dog that's come in the water. It's just as many of us as the white folks, and they better watch out what they do."

Cooksey's remarks illustrated the truth of something King said: that undeserved suffering was redemptive. He reminded those who suffered of their moral superiority to those who oppressed them, and the Black community's growing sense of righteousness created a problem for the white power structure. Weeks earlier, the city and bus company could have settled the bus dispute with a compromise, letting Black passengers fill seats from back to front and promising to hire a few Black drivers. But King's followers no longer sought compromise; they sought equality. The bus company had lost most of its riders. White owners of downtown businesses had lost sales. King's followers had leverage, and they knew it.

"What you're seeing here is probably the closest approach to a classless society that has ever been created in any community in America," said J. E. Pierce, an economics professor at Alabama State, in a 1956 interview. "The whites have forced the Montgomery people to recognize one thing—that they are colored first and then domestics, doctors' wives, scholars or lawyers second . . . Through their unity, their carpools, their determination to share alike, they have found each other—as colored people."

In a letter to the editor of the *Advertiser*, a white librarian named Juliette Morgan said the bus boycotters followed in the footsteps of Thoreau and Gandhi. Another white woman wrote to the newspaper in support of the boycott but used only her initials. She was interviewed later by the team from Fisk and identified herself as Mrs. Earl R. Johnson. Ever since the *Brown v. Board* decision, Mrs. Johnson said, white southerners had grown nervous. "A woman in my church said the other night that we might as well realize the Nigras are not going to stop this time . . . and no amount of clubs or guns or whips will stop them," she said.

Still, city officials held firm. They spread rumors about King, saying he was lining his own pockets with money raised for the boycott. They whispered that outside agitators, possibly communists, were the real forces behind the campaign. The FBI's office in Mobile began forwarding information about King and the boycotts to their boss in Washington, FBI director J. Edgar Hoover. The White Citizens' Council, vowing to maintain white supremacy, attracted legions of new members, including Clyde Sellers, the police commissioner. "The bus boycott made us," one council member told a reporter. "Before the niggers stopped riding the buses, we had only eight hundred members. Now we got 13,000 to 14,000 in Montgomery alone." Candidates for local office proclaimed their dedication to segregation as if it were the only issue that mattered. "Elect Billy Tucker," read one campaign ad. "He is Not Soliciting the Colored Vote."

On the same day that Dealy Cooksey walked to work and explained her courage to her employer, the local newspaper carried quotes from Tacky Gayle vowing he would no longer be pushed around by radical rabble-rousers intent on ruining the "fine relationship" between the Black and white citizens of Montgomery. Negotiations were over. The white people of Montgomery,

Gayle said, "do not care whether a Negro ever rides a bus again if it means that the social fabric of our community is to be destroyed."

Gayle not only called off negotiations but also ordered police officers to begin a campaign of harassment and intimidation, dispersing groups of Black passengers as they waited for rides, tailing Black drivers, and issuing citations for minor or nonexistent traffic violations. Drivers feared they would lose their insurance or their licenses over the tickets. On one Friday night, police arrested forty Black men for public drunkenness. During a public meeting in a church, police walked the streets outside, ticketing seventy-eight cars for parking violations.

Two days after Gayle called off negotiations, King himself became the target. Driving home from church, King stopped at a carpool station to pick up passengers. Two policemen on motorcycles pulled him over and told him he was under arrest for traveling at a speed of thirty miles an hour in a twenty-five-mile-an-hour zone. A patrol car arrived. Two policemen searched King before putting him in the back seat of their car. As the car cruised away from downtown Montgomery, King felt panic. They turned on to a street he'd never seen. Where were they taking him? He worried he might be lynched. "I found myself trembling within and without," he said. "Silently, I asked God to give me the strength to endure whatever came."

He felt relief at the sight of the Montgomery city jail.

It was his first time behind bars.

They put him in a segregated cell, where men lay on wooden slats and torn mattresses. A toilet sat in the corner, unenclosed. King's thoughts turned to others. Regardless of what the men in this jail had done, he said, they didn't deserve these conditions. Everyone recognized the young preacher. They gathered around and told King, one at a time, why they were in jail and asked if he could help them gain freedom.

"Fellows," he said, "before I can assist any of you in getting out, I've got to get my own self out." They laughed.

Soon, Ralph Abernathy arrived to pay bond and secure his friend's release. King would go to jail twenty-nine times in the years ahead, often by plan, but he would never get used to it. Isolation frightened him, not only because he was a person who took comfort in companionship but also because he had become a symbol of Black pride, and he knew his very existence stirred resentment and might incite retaliation. When it could be arranged, Abernathy would try to get arrested along with King. Abernathy's acts of civil disobedience were acts of love, too; he knew his friend, for all his public bravery, experienced trauma every time he faced a cell. They both knew what white racists might do when there were no witnesses.

Ordinarily, King was a sound sleeper, in bed around ten at night and up around five or six in the morning. "He sleeps well, dreams a great deal but does not snore," wrote L. D. Reddick in the first draft of his 1959 book, *Crusader Without Violence*, based on extensive interviews with his subject. Now King slept only four hours most nights.

"Our house was always full of people and the telephone was constantly ringing and so was the doorbell," Coretta recalled. Reporters, church deacons, college professors, and protesters showed up at all hours, often unannounced. "I remember the first three months or so, every time I'd start to bathe the baby, the doorbell would ring and then the telephone would ring. So I'd . . . wrap the baby up in the blanket, and I'd pick up the telephone and then answer it and say, just a minute, and answer the doorbell." For Coretta, these were thrilling times, but they were tinged with sadness. She heard the racist taunts when she answered the phone. She sat in on planning meetings at her home and listened to her husband's interviews with reporters. But she also had a baby to care for. "I could not be there all the time when the action was taking place," she said.

The death threats and harassing phone calls were constant. When workers at the post office received a letter addressed simply to "Nigger Preacher," they routed it to King's mailbox.

Two days after his jail stint, King attended a meeting about the boycott. He got home around midnight and slipped into bed. Before he could fall asleep, the phone rang.

"Nigger, we are tired of you and your mess now," came an angry voice.

"And if you're not out of town in three days we're going to blow your brains out and blow up your house."

King hung up, as he later recalled, and walked the floors of his parsonage. What was happening to him? What was he supposed to do? Was he prepared to die? Giving up on sleep, he went to the kitchen and made coffee.

That, he said, is when God spoke to him.

"Rationality left me," he said. "Almost out of nowhere I heard a voice that morning saying to me: Preach the Gospel, stand up for the truth, stand up for righteousness."

From that moment on, King said, he possessed no fear. He would not back down. He would die if he had to, he said, but he would not turn back, and neither would the people of Montgomery.

In years to come, journalists, historians, and biographers would speculate about what made King special, about what gave him the courage and vision to lead. Some observers have stressed the competitive nature of King's relationship with his father. Others have focused on cultural factors, noting the guilt he felt about his middle-class upbringing and pointing out that he arrived in Montgomery when liberation battles were erupting in Africa and Asia and when radio and television made it possible for a brilliant young preacher to be seen and heard in millions of homes. But the Reverend James Lawson, one of King's contemporaries, has argued that those interpretations miss an obvious and powerful explanation—that of King's calling from God. "That was my case, that was King's case," Lawson said. "It's not . . . boasting . . . it's the deep-down-inside awareness that connects your life up with the life force of the universe, the God who created the heavens and the earth, to quote the Hebrew poets. So, anyone who has that kind of a calling, that's something that profoundly alters their way of thinking and behavior."

In an unpublished manuscript, L. D. Reddick wrote that King was "a little sensitive" about his "Vision in the Kitchen," as it became known. In Reddick's account of the vision, which he based on interviews with King's secretary, Maude Ballou, and her husband, Leonard, Reddick describes the incident less dramatically. "He was a little sleepy while sitting in the kitchen and had been perplexed by pressures and threats. So while dozing a little he heard a voice consoling him not to worry. After that, he 'left it in the hands of the Lord.'"

According to Reddick, King gave a sermon on June 9, 1957, in which he described a second vision, one that the preacher appears never to have mentioned in his published works or sermons. It came after a difficult day in court, when King had been called to testify as a witness against a man accused of bombing churches and homes. The attorney for the defense had tried to humiliate King, calling him a "nigger preacher," and asking if it was true that King had once "got down on his knees and proposed marriage to a white woman." When he learned the accused bomber had been found not guilty, King "was amazed and depressed. There seemed to be no justice. Afterward . . . he went over to his office and threw himself across his desk," Reddick wrote. "Here, again, he says he heard a voice tell him not to worry and that all would be well in the end."

King was a product of the Black church. He learned the values of love and sacrifice and humility from the church, and he learned to live those values. His visions served to intensify what was already an intense personal relationship with Jesus Christ. One part of that relationship was his understanding that Christian social action, suffering, and martyrdom were connected. King repeated the story of the message from God years later in one of his most personal sermons. The first twenty-five years of his life had been relatively calm, "very happy," he said. He grew up in the church, in a family of preachers, and yet he had never had a deeply personal experience with God.

But now, as he thought about his wife and daughter, both sleeping peacefully, and the idea that they might be taken from him, he reached a point, he said, where he "couldn't take it any longer."

That's when he prayed aloud.

"Lord, I am down here trying to do what's right... But, Lord, I confess that I'm weak now... And I can't let the people see me like this."

An inner voice replied: "Martin Luther, stand up for righteousness... And, lo, I will be with you until the end of the world."

16

A Warning

THE WEATHER IN Montgomery on the evening of January 30, 1956, was cool and mostly clear. At the little house on South Jackson Street, Coretta sat in her living room, chatting with Mary Lucy Williams, a schoolteacher and church member. Yoki slept in her crib in the back of the house. Martin was gone, attending a meeting at Abernathy's church.

Church leaders, concerned about Coretta's safety, had asked Mary Williams to visit the Kings. Ordinarily, Williams said, she would have invited Coretta and Yoki to her home, but her little house had neither central heating nor proper insulation, and she didn't want the baby to be cold. The women got along nicely as they shared stories about their rural childhoods. Suddenly, at about a quarter after nine, Coretta and Mary heard footsteps, a thud that sounded like a brick landing on the porch, and then a giant explosion that shattered glass from four front windows and filled the living room with smoke.

The explosion split one of the pillars on the porch, ripped the mailbox from the wall, and left a four-inch-by-two-inch hole in the porch. No one was hurt. Yoki, somehow, slept through it. Someone called Abernathy's church, urging Martin to get home at once. Police sirens screamed. Hundreds of Black neighbors surrounded the house, many of them carrying weapons. Coretta calmly cradled the baby.

When King arrived, he spoke to Coretta first, retreating with her to the rear of the house. After that, he addressed the crowd on the street. Police told reporters the explosion had probably been caused by a homemade bomb or half a stick of dynamite.

After touring the inside of the tiny house, the mayor, the police commissioner, and the fire chief stood beside King on the porch. King was younger, shorter, and slighter than the white men who surrounded him. He wore a suit, a tie, and an overcoat, and held his hat in his hand. "I do not agree with you in your beliefs," Clyde Sellers, the police commissioner, told King privately, "but I will do everything within my power to defend you against such acts as this." He didn't mention the possibility that his officers, in arresting King days earlier on a highly questionable charge, might have *encouraged* acts such as this. Nor did he mention that his police department almost certainly contained members of the KKK and the White Citizens' Council. But the big crowd assembled outside King's home was angry, and Sellers hoped King would soothe them. Once again, he faced a decisive moment, and, once again, he stepped forward.

King's voice boomed from his damaged front porch:

We believe in law and order. Don't get panicky. Don't do anything panicky at all. Don't get your weapons. He who lives by the sword shall perish by the sword. Remember that is what God said. We are not advocating violence. We want to love our enemies. I want you to love our enemies. Be good to them. Love them and let them know you love them. I did not start this boycott. I was asked by you to serve as your spokesman. I want it to be known the length and breadth of this land that if I am stopped this movement will not stop. If I am stopped, our work will not stop. For what we are doing is right, what we are doing is just. And God is with us.

A shout came from the street: "God bless you, brother King!"

Rufus Lewis later said that every Black person in Montgomery reacted as if his own home had been bombed, and, like King, they were not going to be intimidated.

If anyone in Montgomery wanted to kill Reverend King, one man said, "they waited too late, because Martin Luther King is in all of us now, and in order to kill Martin Luther King, you'll have to kill every Black in the city of Montgomery."

The night of the bombing, Daddy King drove to Montgomery from Atlanta. Obie Scott came from Marion. They wanted their children to leave.

"Coretta, I came to get you and the baby," her father said.

"Well, Dad," she said, "I can't go. I want to stay here with Martin because I feel this is where I belong."

They didn't sleep that night. At breakfast, Martin thanked Coretta. "I don't know what I would've done without you," he said. "You've been a real soldier."

"I realized then," Coretta said in an interview ten years later, "how much it meant to him for me to continue to be strong and give him support, not only in terms of words but actually feeling this way and being this way."

Later, Coretta told her sister that her faith became more real for her after the bombing. Her prayers took on more meaning. "Lord, I've done all that I can do, believing that we are right. Now I leave it up to you," she prayed. She expressed no fear of death. "If I die," she said, "and if my husband should die for His cause in trying to bring about His kingdom on earth, then what a noble way to die." Coretta seemed to have realized that Martin, for all his strength and courage, remained a passionate person who needed support and love, perhaps more now than ever. "He functioned better with a wife and children," she said, "because he needed the warmth we gave him."

But Coretta gave him more than warmth. He had been attracted from the beginning by her intellect and her inclination to activism. Daddy King may have wanted M.L. to move back home, and Obie Scott may have wanted to take Coretta and Yoki back to Marion, but Martin never considered leaving or sending Coretta out of harm's way. As Martin Luther King Jr. found his life moving in new and unexpected directions, into leadership of a burgeoning protest movement and into heightened danger, he relied more than ever on his wife.

"During the bus boycott I was tested by fire," Coretta would recall years later, "and I came to understand that I was not a breakable figurine."

The day after the blast at King's house, dynamite exploded at the home of E. D. Nixon. The day after that, Fred Gray filed suit in federal court on behalf of a group of black women seeking an end to segregated bus seating and police harassment of the carpools. Gray remembered the case of Viola White, whose appeal was never heard, and he didn't want to rely on the Rosa Parks case alone in his legal attack on segregation. On the advice of the NAACP and the progressive white lawyer Clifford Durr, Gray filed a class-action suit on behalf of four women who had faced discrimination on city buses—Aurelia Browder, Claudette Colvin, Susie McDonald, and Mary Louise Smith. The case would be known as *Browder v. Gayle*.

Compromise with the city, once seemingly within reach, no longer represented an option. Volunteers set up a security detail at King's house. King and Abernathy purchased handguns, although they were denied permits for their weapons. King, who had not yet advocated nonviolence as a philosophy, asked Alabama's governor, James E. Folsom, to provide protection for the boycotters or, at least, to reconsider his gun permit. Folsom refused.

Less than two weeks later, on February 10, more than eleven thousand white people—"the largest political crowd in the recent history of the state," according to the *Advertiser*—gathered in Montgomery to hear from U.S. senator James O. Eastland, the ardent segregationist who was known as the "Voice of the White South."

Gayle and Sellers also spoke, declaring they would never accept integration. "If any Negro wants desegregation," Sellers said, "then let him go where there is desegregation. And let me say what I have said before: I will not sell my southern birthright for any number of Negro votes."

The local White Citizens' Council organized the meeting and circulated a leaflet that began: "When in the course of human events it becomes necessary to abolish the Negro race, proper methods should be used. Among these are guns, bows and arrows, sling shots and knives."

If boycotters were not frightened, there was more to come. A Montgomery judge called a grand jury to investigate racial unrest, summoning more than two hundred Black men and women to testify about the boycott's leadership. Rumors swirled that criminal charges would soon be filed for violating a statute prohibiting boycotts without just cause. Fred Gray was arrested and charged with filing unauthorized litigation. He was also informed that his draft eligibility had been changed. A minister as well as a lawyer, he had been deferred from military service; but now he was classified 1-A, making it much more likely he would be called to military service. Thurgood Marshall of the NAACP sent word he would defend Gray.

"In the last three weeks," wrote Joe Azbell in the *Advertiser*, "more whites have used the word 'nigger' than ever before in their lives." Negroes who once felt kindness toward white people "have damned the whole white race as monsters." Montgomery, he wrote, seemed on the verge of a "full scale racial war."

In Mobile, Alabama, FBI agents clipped newspaper articles on the bombing of King's home but did not open an investigation. The national news media showed more interest than the FBI did. Newspapers from the North sent reporters to Montgomery to cover the growing conflict. Black and white newspapers ran the boycott story on their front pages. King was usually the first person out-of-town reporters sought to interview, especially after the bombing of his home.

King and his colleagues embraced the press, and the northern journalists reciprocated with overwhelmingly favorable coverage. King, with his northern education and charm, made the reporters feel welcome and appreciated. National news coverage further angered segregationists, who accused Black people of bombing their own homes to gain attention. The coverage also emboldened protesters, as King reminded them that they had captivated the eyes and ears of the world. "Whether we want to be or not, we are caught in a great moment in history," he said at one mass meeting. "It is bigger than Montgomery ... The vast majority of the people of the world are colored." Until recently, he continued, most of them had been controlled and oppressed by empires of the West. "Today many are free . . . And the rest are on the road . . . We are a part of that great movement . . . We want to see everybody free."

The longer the boycott continued, the more attention King received beyond Montgomery. L. Harold DeWolf, King's adviser at Boston University, on sabbatical and performing missionary work in Southern Rhodesia (now called Zimbabwe), wrote to his former student to say he was proud and praying for him: "Little did any of us know . . . you would so quickly be tried and so gravely, with the eyes of the nation and even the world upon you . . . Even here, in Central Africa . . . your example has sent a quiver of pride and renewed faith through the lives of many Africans."

King replied: "Prayer has been used very effectively in our movement." Despite evidence of "man's inhumanity to man," he wrote, "I am convinced that God lives." Those who stand with God, he continued, "stand in the glow of the world's bright tomorrows."

At times, King seemed weary. In one letter, he declined a speaking engagement by saying his doctor had urged him to slow down because of "the strain under which I am working." Walter McCall, King's friend from Morehouse and Crozer, wrote to King on February 1, 1956, saying he was pleased to have heard directly from King about how he was "getting on." McCall expressed concern for his friend's well-being, slipping frequently into capital letters as he wrote: "DO NOT BACK DOWN, DO NOT SWERVE. KEEP THE COURAGE. KEEP THE PATIENCE. THE task must be met head on."

On February 21, a state grand jury in Montgomery returned indictments against King and other boycott leaders for conspiring to hinder a lawful business. When the grand jury was done, it had indicted 115 people, including two dozen ministers, the biggest group of people ever indicted in Montgomery County on a single charge. Arrests would soon follow.

King was at Fisk University in Nashville when he got the news. Coretta and Yoki were in Atlanta. Concerned that the indictments might shatter the bus boycott, King flew to Atlanta with plans to leave at once for Montgomery.

But Daddy King, afraid for his son's life, urged his son to remain in Atlanta. He convened a meeting of friends, including Benjamin Mays, to make the case. King stood up to them, in what the Black journalist Louis E. Lomax called "the moment of umbilical severance." Said King: "It would be the height of cowardice for me to stay away. I would rather be in jail for ten years than desert my people."

In Lomax's view, King almost certainly would have quit his job at Dexter Avenue church for a college job after a few years had he not been thrust into a position of leadership. But now he had made a commitment to the movement.

Montgomery officials had hoped to squash the rebellion by indicting protesters, but the move backfired. An indictment became a badge of honor. Upon his return to Montgomery, King went to the county jail to be booked, photographed, bonded, and released. Rosa Parks, E. D. Nixon, and Jo Ann Robinson joined him in a show of unity. Rufus Lewis volunteered for arrest even though he hadn't been indicted. The crowd outside swelled with pride. "Well, here comes my preacher," one observer said as a car approached.

The police mug shot of King was a picture of defiance. It showed a young man with his eyebrows arched, his jaw firm, sport coat buttoned, tie knotted tight, dress shirt crisp, a plaque with the number 7089 hung around his neck.

———— • ————

Activists all over America sensed that King was making history in Montgomery, and they pitched in with advice and assistance. Lillian Smith, a white novelist from Georgia, wrote to King on March 10, 1956, expressing her admiration for the preacher's work. Smith was the author of an anti-lynching novel called *Strange Fruit* and a board member of the Fellowship of Reconciliation (FOR), an international pacifist organization that drew on Gandhi's philosophy of peaceful resistance. FOR's leading voice was A. J. Muste, a minister who called for the conscious violation of unjust government laws and actions and who encouraged his followers to go to jail for their beliefs. Such sacrifice, Muste said, was necessary to stir the public's conscience. Smith hoped King would follow this simple strategy in Montgomery. "You can't be an expert in nonviolence; it's like being a saint or an artist: each person grows his own skill and expertness," she wrote. But if King *were* to look for help, Smith recommended Howard Thurman of Boston University and Bayard Rustin of the War Resisters' League.

King already knew them both. Rustin, in fact, had visited King in Montgomery shortly before Smith's letter arrived. Rustin was tall, handsome, and brilliant. At the age of forty-five, he had already been a part of some of the century's most important protests. He had worked with FOR and A. Philip Randolph's Brotherhood of Sleeping Car Porters. The fact that he was gay was an open secret among civil rights activists. The fact that he had been a member of the Young Communist League was no secret at all.

When Rustin arrived in Montgomery, he was pleased to discover that he had already met Coretta, having lectured long ago to her class at the Lincoln School in Marion. Years later, Ralph Abernathy would say Coretta played a key role in deciding to welcome Rustin as an adviser.

Rustin took an immediate liking to King, as most people did, but Rustin was dismayed to learn that King had armed guards at his home and a pistol in his living room. Almost immediately, the men engaged in a "very long, philosophical discussion of nonviolence," as Rustin recalled. King relished his talks with Rustin, who seemed to know all the key figures in the civil rights movement. Soon after Rustin's visit, King disposed of his gun and ordered the men guarding his home to do so without weapons.

"The experience in Montgomery did more to clarify my thinking on the question of nonviolence than all of the books that I had read," King wrote a few years later. "Living through the actual experience of the protest, nonviolence became more than a method to which I gave intellectual assent; it became a commitment to a way of life."

Not everyone bought it. "The man is a genuine intellectual," Grover C. Hall, the editor in chief of the *Advertiser*, said of King. "But that constant Gandhi business of his, that love-those-who-hate-you routine is the biggest bunch of nonsense I've ever run into."

Rustin recognized King's gifts and understood that the young preacher had an opportunity—even a responsibility, perhaps—to take the Montgomery movement national. But it would happen only if the bus boycott succeeded. To give it a chance, Rustin agreed to remain out of sight. Rustin lived as openly and honestly as a gay man could at that time. Most people who knew him knew of his sexual orientation and his arrest in 1953 on charges of lewd vagrancy. He and King both knew that his reputation might do damage to the Montgomery movement if the press reported on it. Rustin decided to work from Birmingham, ninety miles away, so that he might be less visible.

Working from Birmingham, and later from New York, Rustin ghost-wrote magazine articles for King. He composed a song to be sung at mass meetings, the chorus of which went: "We shall all stand together." He wrote to colleagues in the North asking them to raise money, noting that the marchers were wearing out their shoes and spending more on groceries because they were shopping at more expensive local stores rather than those they had previously reached by bus. He proposed "Victory Without Violence" as a motto for the movement. He launched essay and poster contests for students. But, perhaps most important, he spoke to King, Abernathy, and others about how to infuse their struggle with the spirit of "Gandhi-like methods." He wrote in one letter to fellow activists during his first visit to Montgomery, "I am convinced that perhaps one of the really major results of Montgomery will be a revolution in the Negro church." Black churches, Rustin wrote, could become the engine for a powerful social action movement.

As King invoked Gandhi with greater frequency, the national media seized on that element of the story. The protesters' adherence to pacifism added moral clarity. The city of Montgomery added even more clarity by making King the first defendant charged with boycotting without just cause. The grand jury indictment made little attempt to hide its bias: "We are committed to segregation by custom and law," it read, "and we intend to maintain it."

The headline the next day in the *Baltimore Afro-American* declared: "'Not Worried' Says Alabama's Gandhi."

The NAACP volunteered to send its general counsel, Robert Carter, part of a team of lawyers assembled by Thurgood Marshall, to help with

King's defense. But Judge Eugene W. Carter would not allow it. The judge was an ardent segregationist who had once proposed that his church bar all Negroes except the janitors. On March 22, Judge Carter found King guilty and ordered him to pay a $500 fine, plus $500 in court costs. King appealed and went free on a $1,000 bond. More than three hundred people cheered as he left court.

"We will continue to protest in the same spirit of nonviolence and passive resistance, using the weapon of love," King said. "Let us not lose faith in democracy." When a reporter asked King if he was afraid, he said: "No, I'm not . . . This is a great issue that we are confronted with and the consequences for my personal life are not particularly important."

Activists led workshops on avoiding conflict with white antagonists. If cursed, do not curse back, they taught. If struck, do not retaliate. If fired upon, do not return fire. One need not like one's white neighbor, the instructors taught, but one must *love* him. "What Dr. King delivered to Blacks there, far more important than whether they got to ride on the bus, was the absence of fear," Rustin said.

Less than a week after Rustin's appearance in Montgomery, another top FOR official, Glenn E. Smiley, arrived. A native Texan and a white Methodist minister, Smiley was moved by his meeting with King and impressed with the impact of the boycott. "Strange—whites are getting scared stiff and Negroes are calm as cucumbers," Smiley wrote. Like Rustin, Smiley saw King as someone who might lead a national campaign for equal rights. "I believe that God has called Martin Luther King to lead a great movement here in the South," Smiley wrote in a letter to a friend. "But why does God lay such a burden on one so young, so inexperienced, so good? King can be a Negro Gandhi, or he can . . . swing from a lynch mob's tree."

Ella Josephine Baker, a former high-ranking NAACP executive and an experienced organizer, wrote King and invited him to New York to help launch a group called In Friendship, designed to aid the victims of racial terrorism in the South. Though the NAACP supported the Montgomery bus lawsuits, tension grew between King and Roy Wilkins, the NAACP's leader. Wilkins had been working for the NAACP since 1930, when King was still in diapers. "The Negro has to be a superb diplomat and a great strategist," he once said. "He has to parlay what actual power he has along with the good will of the white majority. He has to devise and pursue those philosophies and activities which will least alienate the white majority opinion. And that doesn't mean that the Negro has to indulge in bootlicking. But he must gain the sympathy of the large majority of the American public. He must also seek to make an identification with the American tradition."

That approach struck King and others as too cautious. In one letter to Wilkins, King complained that the NAACP seemed to be using the Montgomery protests to raise money for itself. Wilkins replied that the NAACP was making significant contributions to the boycott and intended to continue doing so as legal fees mounted. Without the NAACP, the Montgomery bus boycott might have ended in failure, a fact King didn't appreciate, NAACP officials said. While King acknowledged the importance of the NAACP and the courts in fighting segregation, he argued that "the law needs help." A bus boycott was more dramatic and more stirring than a court filing and had the potential to awaken "the great decent majority" whose consciences had fallen asleep. King sought to shift the struggle from a legal one to a moral one, making the case that segregation reflected not only a failure of democratic policies and principles but also a failure to live up to Judeo-Christian values.

King learned leadership in the church, where the preacher's power was seldom challenged. As Rustin saw it, that left King "very uncomfortable with people that he felt were his equals." It left him especially uncomfortable with women in positions of power. Though most members of Black Baptist churches were women, church leaders were almost all men, and sexist assumptions about leadership permeated King's organization, limiting the roles of women such as Coretta King and Rosa Parks.

Despite his weaknesses, King remained a gravitational force, pulling in reporters, financial donors, and young volunteers.

"You don't know me, Mr. Belafonte, but my name is Martin Luther King Jr.," King said over the phone one day in the spring of 1956, cold-calling the famous singer and actor.

"Oh, I know you," Belafonte said. "Everybody knows you."

Belafonte and other celebrities, including Sammy Davis Jr., were eager to use their fame and wealth to help King's cause. "He seemed a little bit anxious . . . ," Belafonte recalled, "because he didn't know where he was headed . . . he didn't know how to approach me, or a lot of people he was approaching at that time, with his mission, because his mission was not that clear."

Eleanor Roosevelt sent a telegram to King saying she was "much interested in what you are doing in Montgomery" and asked him to visit her at her New York apartment. Letters of support came from ordinary Americans, too, often accompanied by cash or checks. A woman from Idaho sent two pairs of shoes—"some of my better ones," she wrote—for the Montgomery women who might have worn out their own from all the walking.

Years later, Abernathy said that he and King had no intention of turning the Montgomery fight into a national one, but three important factors compelled them to think bigger. First, they hadn't been lynched, "a fact that never ceased to impress us." Second, supporters from around the country kept showing up in Montgomery to help. Third, they found themselves to be the star and co-star of a worldwide news story. King was something new, something exciting, possibly dangerous.

Louis Lomax wrote:

It was as if Martin had been chiseled out of the black mountain to make an eternal liar out of white people. White people argued that Negroes were stupid; there was Martin with his Ph.D. in his midtwenties. White people alleged that Negroes were lazy, unable to organize and accomplish an objective; Martin not only was hardworking, but he pulled together an organization that put thousands of people to walking for justice . . . White people stereotyped Negroes as men of violence, yet Martin mounted the only nonviolent social revolution in Western history. Most of all, Martin's public speeches combined the wisdom of Socrates, the eloquence of Demosthenes, and the thunder of Isaiah. One could not have created a Black man who could have better filled the nation's television screens.

Black families gathering around the television sets didn't see many of their own. They saw a handful of Black actors, and usually in demeaning roles. Even many white southerners found the young preacher difficult to dismiss. "King has been working on the guilty conscience of the South," said a liberal white Baptist minister in Raleigh, North Carolina. "If he can bring us to contrition, this is our hope."

King, Abernathy, and the others soon discovered that many pieces were in place for a nationwide church-based campaign that took on issues beyond public transit. Almost every city in the South had at least a handful of rebellious young ministers, and those ministers had the potential to lead others in the fight for integration, human rights, and better education. King began traveling around the country, speaking and raising money for the Montgomery Improvement Association.

Coretta got involved, too. In the fall of 1956, she went to Chicago to sing at Olivet Baptist Church and to speak about the Montgomery movement. "Unfortunately, her voice lacked tonal luster as well as resonance," wrote *The Chicago Defender*, "nor did it seem sufficiently projected to carry easily on the scale or line . . . She too is modest and seemingly devoid of any outward flare for personality display." In the months ahead, she would perform more concerts in cities across the country, always including a spoken piece on the nonviolent movement for integration as well as spirituals and classical compositions by Schubert and Verdi. A reporter for *The Pittsburgh Courier*, in a kinder review, said Coretta King's performance conveyed the spirit of the Montgomery movement as well as the "warmth, sincerity and a dedication of a young housewife."

At a concert in New York, Coretta explained to the audience how the people of Montgomery felt. "Segregated and humiliated on the buses," she said, "we were not even left alone to walk in dignity. We have been arrested; our homes have been bombed . . . But we continue to walk with dignity. We refuse to retaliate. We refuse to hate . . . Our only weapon is love."

But it was Coretta's husband who received most of the attention, of course. *Jet*, the nation's most popular magazine among Black people, put King on its cover and called him "Alabama's Modern Moses."

In April, when King reunited with his mentor J. Pius Barbour, the older man was struck by the change in his protégé. "He has grown twenty years in about five," Barbour said. "He is almost to a fault exceedingly retiring; he wanders around in a daze asking himself: Why had God seen fit to catapult me into such a situation?"

The bus boycott caused collateral damage. Five months after her fateful bus ride, Rosa Parks lost her department-store job. Her husband, a barber at Maxwell Air Force Base, lost his position soon afterward. In April, the U.S. Supreme Court affirmed a federal appellate court ruling that struck down segregated seating on buses in Columbia, South Carolina. But when National City Lines announced that it would no longer enforce segregation on its buses, Montgomery mayor Tacky Gayle had other ideas. He warned that bus drivers failing to enforce the segregation laws would be arrested. On June 1, 1956, Alabama's attorney general, John Patterson, arguing that the NAACP was organizing and supporting illegal boycotts, obtained a state court order banning NAACP activities in Alabama and fining the group $100,000, forcing closure of its state offices. It would take the NAACP eight years to void the sanctions.

Four days later, the protesters and attorney Fred Gray notched their first big legal win when a federal district court ruled on behalf of the plaintiffs in *Browder v. Gayle*. Enforced segregation of Black and white bus passengers, the court decided, violated the U.S. Constitution, especially the Equal Protection Clause of the Fourteenth Amendment. But city buses remained segregated while lawyers appealed the ruling to the Supreme Court. Meanwhile, more bomb blasts rocked the city. Gayle and other segregationists once more accused the boycotters of detonating the bombs, this time to boost fundraising. In October, city lawyers asked a judge to halt the MIA's carpool system, saying King's organization was running a transportation system without a license.

"Oh, my God," King told Rustin. "I don't know how much longer we can keep going. The people are getting tired."

Given that Judge Carter was once again presiding, the court probably would have shut down the MIA's carpool system. But on November 13, the U.S. Supreme Court issued its decision in *Browder*, affirming the lower court and thereby outlawing segregation on intrastate transportation. State officials in Alabama asked the Supreme Court to hear the case and make clear where it stood on segregation. The court refused, granting simply that the lower court's ruling was affirmed. But the message was clear. *The New York Times* wrote that the court had "placed a headstone at the grave of Plessy v. Ferguson."

"The universe is on the side of justice," King said.

Years later, Thurgood Marshall would say that the NAACP deserved more credit for its role in ending Montgomery's system of segregated busing, telling one interviewer that he perceived King and the boycotters as a sideshow. It was true that the city of Montgomery had proved mostly impervious to protest and economic pressure, and that litigation had won the day. But the biggest development in Montgomery was the creation of a new state of mind, a new sense of power, coalesced around King, who described the Montgomery movement as "our twelve months of glorious dignity."

The night of the Supreme Court's decision, about forty carloads of hooded and cloaked Ku Klux Klan members drove through Montgomery's Black neighborhoods, aiming spotlights into people's homes and honking horns. But the people did not cower. They turned on their porch lights, stood outside, and waved to the Klansmen, King said, "as though they were watching a circus parade."

A month later, when the Supreme Court refused to reconsider its decision, the city of Montgomery finally accepted defeat. After 381 days, the bus boycott was over, and so was the national illusion that Black Americans were willing to abide by the nation's crushing racial order.

National news reporters were not accustomed to covering racial protests that ended in victory. But the legal battle for justice had turned with *Brown v. Board of Education*. Now, with the bus boycott, the psychological battle had turned, too. The Montgomery experience gave African Americans a new leader and a new strategy for social protest. America's long-oppressed Black people would no longer wait for justice; they would fight for it. Eleanor Roosevelt called it "one of the most remarkable achievements of people fighting for their rights . . . without bloodshed . . . that we have ever witnessed in this country." Harry Emerson Fosdick, the minister and orator who had inspired King for years, said Montgomery had become "one of the most significant places in the world."

Early in the morning on December 21, Ralph Abernathy and Glenn Smiley met King at his house. While the men sipped their coffee, newspaper reporters, photographers, and television camera operators gathered on the sidewalk. At about seven, a bus drew near, headlights on, seats mostly empty. The men stepped outside in their coats and hats and walked to the bus stop at the corner of Key Street and South Jackson Street. King, Abernathy, and Smiley got on the bus. King, boarding first, paid their fares in dimes.

"Is this the reverend?" the white bus driver asked.

"That's right," King said.

The men took seats in front. Cameras flashed. The bus rolled on. When they got off the bus downtown, more reporters and photographers waited. King declared it "a mighty good ride."

PART II

17

Alabama's Moses

Two DAYS AFTER the end of the bus boycott and two days before Christmas 1956, someone fired a shotgun at Martin Luther King Jr.'s home. No one was hurt. On Christmas Eve, five white men leaped from a car and beat a fifteen-year-old Black girl as she stood at a bus stop in Montgomery. Snipers fired shots on at least two city buses, injuring a pregnant Black woman in one of the attacks. Jo Ann Robinson had acid poured on the hood of her car by two police officers and a brick thrown through the window of her home by unknown assailants. Ninety miles away, in Birmingham, fifteen sticks of dynamite exploded under the home of Fred Shuttlesworth, an activist who had pledged to follow Montgomery's example and lead a bus boycott in his city. Somehow, Shuttlesworth escaped the house unhurt.

Anyone in a position of leadership in the Montgomery bus boycott had already wrestled with the issue of mortality. But Martin Luther King Sr. was not prepared to see his son continue to risk his life. When he got news of the latest attack, Daddy King once again rushed from Atlanta to Montgomery. In an interview with a newspaper reporter, the elder King said the past year had been the toughest of his life, no small statement for a man who had been raised in a series of sharecroppers' shacks. "Maybe we'd like to be a proud parent," he said, "but this thing is more serious than many people could realize. We are suffering and our son is suffering more than any of us."

After compelling his son to get on his knees and pray, Daddy King once again begged him to return to Atlanta, join him at Ebenezer, and focus on preaching. M.L. cried tears of anger and frustration as he argued with his father, according to Bayard Rustin, who was visiting King's parsonage at the time and recounted the story decades later.

Rustin was fascinated by the father-son push and pull, the ways M.L. both feared and measured himself against Daddy King, the way Daddy King, even now, tried to bully his son, and the way M.L. still sought to establish his independence without angering his father. Years later, the Black psychologist Kenneth Clark, who knew the King family personally, would become convinced that Martin Luther King Jr.'s approach to nonviolent resistance and love of one's enemies grew in part from his desire for "self-protection" from his father. The King children seldom won arguments with Daddy King. The fear of confrontation would turn the youngest of the King children, A.D., into a heavy drinker (like his grandfather Jim King) and render sister Christine "meek and submissive," as M.L. once said. Only Coretta had the courage to argue with her father-in-law. M.L., meanwhile, had learned to avoid fights by ending conversations inconclusively. In this case, he told his father he would pray and then he would do what he had to do.

On January 10, 1957, King, Rustin, Abernathy, and others traveled to Atlanta to meet with southern Black ministers to begin a series of discussions that would lead to the creation of a new, regional, church-powered organization dedicated to fighting segregation. The idea for the organization had grown out of an earlier meeting in New York among three radical and experienced activists: Rustin, Ella Baker, and a wealthy white New York businessman named Stanley Levison. They believed King's success in Montgomery might spawn a broader movement in the South, led by Black Baptist preachers. Baker and Rustin were expert organizers, and Levison had money and political savvy. The left-wing movement that had once united communists, socialists, trade union activists, church leaders, and others had faded with the Cold War, leaving activists to look for a new way to attack the racial caste system. These older activists thought King might spearhead a mass movement of direct action, but they believed he would need organizational help. They liked the idea of a movement led by ministers, in part because it would help refute accusations of communist influence. Also, Black ministers didn't depend on white people for their paychecks. They were less likely to be intimidated.

Because the bus boycott had successfully brought together disparate elements of the community, King and Abernathy wanted to focus on transportation issues. At first, the organization was to be called the Southern Leadership Conference on Transportation and Nonviolent Integration. Later, it would become the Southern Christian Leadership Conference.

The initial meeting was interrupted, however, when Juanita Abernathy called from Montgomery to tell her husband that dynamite blasts had hit their church and the Abernathy home. She and the children had escaped injury. King and Abernathy rushed home. Coretta filled in for her husband, along with the Reverend Fred Shuttlesworth of Birmingham, as the first meeting of the new organization continued. Meanwhile, King learned of more explosions in Montgomery, four at churches and two at residences. At the home of a sympathetic white minister, twelve sticks of dynamite had failed to explode.

Dynamite was not hard to find in Alabama. Iron ore mines stretched for thirty-three miles, from Trussville to Bessemer. The mines used so much dynamite that no one noticed when an armload of sticks disappeared. Hardware stores sold the stuff, too, no questions asked, mostly to farmers, who used explosives to remove tree stumps or make trenches. The bombs blowing up churches and homes were as crude as the men making them, and often thrown on the run, which explains why the devices often failed or caused limited damage. But even when the bombs failed to kill, they never failed to terrorize. No one knew when the next bomb would explode, and even the bombers did not know how big the blast would be.

When he got back to Montgomery, King discovered that Tacky Gayle had discontinued all bus service, citing risk to the public yet knowing that he was taking away the very thing Montgomery's marchers had fought for and won. Anonymous handbills appeared in Black neighborhoods, seeking to divide the community and undercut King's support. One of the handbills read:

LOOK OUT!
Liver Lip Luther
Getting Us In More Trouble

Every Day . . .
We Get Shot At While
He Hides . . .
Run Him Out of Town!

On Monday night, January 14, King spoke at a rally and found the community in "low spirits." This time, he could not rouse them. In fact, as he
later admitted, his own spirits had darkened. As he spoke, he said, he found
himself gripped by feelings he could not control. "Lord, I hope no one will
have to die as a result of our struggle for freedom in Montgomery," he told
the audience. "Certainly I don't want to die. But if anyone has to die, let it be
me." When members of the audience shouted their disapproval, King froze,
unable to speak, unable to move. One reporter at the scene wrote that King
had "collapsed at the rostrum." By King's own description, it sounded as if
he might have suffered an anxiety attack. He was helped from the pulpit and
eased into a chair.

Two weeks later, a bomb made from twelve sticks of dynamite was
found on the porch of King's house, unexploded, its fuse smoldering. More
bombs detonated across the city. Amazingly, no one died. Eventually, white
businessmen, concerned that the attacks were hindering commerce, urged
city officials to stop the violence. Police responded by arresting seven white
men. Though all-white juries would eventually acquit the accused men, and
though much of the white community rallied in support of the alleged ter-
rorists, a noteworthy precedent had been set: white people had been arrested
and tried for crimes against Black people. The wave of bomb blasts ended,
and the buses rolled again.

King's spirits rose. He described the arrests and the resumption of bus
service as signs of "the basic goodwill of man for man and a portent of peace
in the desegregated society to come." But justice was not running down like
water through Montgomery, because white residents and city officials kept
constructing new dams. Black Americans had always understood the power
of segregation, but they were only now beginning to fully comprehend its
intransigence, the way it wove through hearts, minds, laws, and economic

systems, and how difficult it would be to remove, as the historian J. Mills Thornton III wrote. Many white people in the South feared dealing with people of color as equals and found it easier to treat them as deadly enemies. They resented the call for equal rights, and nothing, it seemed, would erase their anger. Ulrich B. Phillips, the Georgia-born historian, described southerners as "a people with a common resolve indomitably maintained—that [the South] shall be and remain a white man's country."

King offered hints that he might not stay too much longer in such a dangerous environment. His life was chaotic. He spent little time with his daughter. He purchased a high-fidelity record player for Coretta as a Christmas present, but they seldom found a chance to listen to music. "At this point," he wrote to his Boston University adviser, L. Harold DeWolf, "I am not sure of what area of the ministry I would like to settle down in. I have a great deal of satisfaction in the pastorate, and have almost come to the point of feeling that I can best render my service in this area, however, I can never quite get the idea out of my mind that I should do some teaching." If DeWolf were to recommend him for a teaching job, King said, he would give it "the greatest consideration."

But, rapidly, the struggle for racial justice drew him in more deeply. On February 10, on national television, he declared the arrival of a new American Negro, "a person with a new sense of dignity and destiny with a new self-respect." The new American Negro possessed courage, he said. The new American Negro refused to pay lip service to the white man. The new American Negro "says in no uncertain terms that he doesn't like the way he's being treated" and intends to do something about it. King's calm tone and conservative attire may have disguised the boldness of his words: "I think it's better to be aggressive at this point," he said. "It seems to me that it is both historically and sociologically true that privileged classes do not give up their privileges voluntarily. And they do not give them up without strong resistance."

The interviewer asked if strong resistance would generate more white retaliation.

"Well," King said, "I think that is a necessary phase of the transition."

Four days later, at a meeting in New Orleans, King and dozens of other min-isters officially launched the Southern Christian Leadership Conference (SCLC), with King as president and Abernathy as treasurer. "To Redeem the Soul of America" became the group's motto, embracing Christianity and non-violence, and borrowing a phrase that Benjamin Mays often quoted from Walter Rauschenbusch. The church offered stability and independence. By working through the churches, by infusing meetings with prayer and song, by reaching out to pastors and their big, loyal followings, the organization's founders hoped to lead a widespread social movement. Churches would provide meeting places. Ministers would command respect and mobilize support. Perhaps most important, leadership would be almost entirely Black.

In Rustin's experience, two unfortunate things happened when inter-racial organizations formed: white communists joined, and Black lead-ers lost control. In the SCLC, white supporters would remain behind the scenes. The SCLC would stress Christian love even as it fought aggressively for equality. It would strive not to defeat white oppressors but to bring rec-onciliation. In short, the SCLC would try to repeat the Montgomery mira-cle across the South. It remained to be seen how the organization would be structured, how it would raise money, and whether it would work in coopera-tion with the NAACP. For starters, King told reporters the new organization would organize a massive pilgrimage of Black Americans to Washington if the president did not speak out forcefully against southern segregation. "This will not be a political march," he said. "It will be rooted in deep spiritual faith."

On February 18, 1957, *Time* magazine put King's image on its cover and de-clared that the young preacher from Montgomery had "risen from nowhere to become one of the nation's remarkable leaders of men." The magazine portrayed King as the perfect activist for a country turned conservative and caught up in a Cold War. He was nonpolitical, nonpartisan, and "no radical,"

Time assured its predominantly white readership. Here was a man building a reform movement on the most American of pillars: the Bible, the Declaration of Independence, the American dream. King not only inspired Black southerners to imagine new possibilities but also inspired southern white Christians to open their minds, the magazine said. "I know of very few white southern ministers who aren't troubled [about segregation] and don't have admiration for King," one white Baptist minister told the magazine. "They've become tortured souls."

Time's reporter was charmed by his subject, writing: "Personally humble, articulate, and of high education attainment, Martin Luther King Jr. is, in fact, what many a Negro—and, were it not for his color, many a white— would like to be."

King was invited to appear on the TV show *Meet the Press*. A long profile was published in *The New York Times Magazine*. In March 1957, he and Coretta joined the diplomat Ralph Bunche, the New York congressman Adam Clayton Powell Jr., A. Philip Randolph, Roy Wilkins, and others on a trip to Ghana for a celebration of the African nation's independence.

"You're Dr. King," said Vice President Richard Nixon when the men met in Accra. "I recognized you from your picture on the cover of *Time*."

After Ghana, Coretta and Martin traveled to Nigeria, Rome, Geneva, London, and Paris. Martin purchased a postcard for Rosa Parks in Rome and mailed it from London. In Paris, he and Coretta ate fried chicken at one of Europe's only soul-food restaurants, Chez Haynes, founded by Leroy "Roughhouse" Haynes, a Morehouse grad and an army veteran. Charles Diggs, a congressman from Detroit, and Ollie Stewart, the Paris-based correspondent of the *Baltimore Afro-American*, joined them for the meal. Everywhere he went, King was greeted like a man of importance, as if he were Black America's ambassador, or perhaps even its president.

Returning to the United States, he spoke at the Cathedral of St. John the Divine in New York. Soon after that, he became the youngest person ever to win the NAACP's Spingarn Medal, an annual award presented to the person making the greatest contribution in the field of race relations. Morehouse College gave him an honorary degree, with Benjamin Mays declaring

King "wiser at twenty-eight than most men at sixty; more courageous in a righteous struggle than most men can ever be; living a faith that most men preach about and never experience."

Planning for the pilgrimage to Washington continued, despite a cool reaction from NAACP leader Roy Wilkins, who expressed concern about how the SCLC's emergence might affect support for the NAACP's southern branches. Wilkins contended that protests such as the one in Montgomery might work in solving local disputes, but the NAACP's legal challenges would prove most effective in ushering nationwide change. In the end, Wilkins agreed to help plan what became known as the Prayer Pilgrimage for Freedom, advertised as a show of unity, a protest against legal attacks on the NAACP in the South, and a demonstration of support for new civil rights legislation.

The Prayer Pilgrimage was scheduled for May 17, 1957, coinciding with the third anniversary of the Supreme Court's decision in *Brown v. Board of Education*. A. Philip Randolph urged King to focus his speech on voting rights, arguing that local battles to end segregation would never be enough. He wanted King to think more tactically and build support in the North. "Martin, in a sense, had a deeper affection and respect for A. Philip Randolph than he had for his own father," Bayard Rustin said.

The speech would be King's first truly national address. Rustin helped him write it. But the men disagreed on a key phrase. "Give us the ballot!" King wrote. Rustin thought it sounded weak. Black people don't want to be *given* anything by white people, he said.

King tried it Rustin's way: "We demand the ballot!" he said in rehearsal.

But it didn't feel right. He tried it again his way, delivering the words slowly, almost singing them, like a hymn. "Give . . . us . . . the . . . ballot." Rustin grew disgusted.

"Well, it just rolls better for me," King said.

He stood atop the stairs of the Lincoln Memorial, wearing a clergyman's robe over his suit and tie, facing the biggest audience of his life, estimated at somewhere between fifteen thousand and twenty-seven thousand. His voice rang like a deep bell; one felt it as one heard it:

> Give us the ballot and we will no longer have to worry the federal government about our basic rights. Give us the ballot, and we will no longer plead to the federal government for passage of an anti-lynching law; we will by the power of our vote write the law on the statute books of the South and bring an end to the dastardly acts of the hooded perpetrators of violence. Give us the ballot, and we will transform the salient misdeeds of bloodthirsty mobs into the calculated good deeds of orderly citizens. Give us the ballot . . . and we will quietly and nonviolently, without rancor or bitterness, implement the Supreme Court's decision [in *Brown v. Board of Education*] of May seventeenth, 1954.

Rustin was impressed but also puzzled. There was nothing extraordinary in the text of the speech, and yet King had moved his listeners to rapture— Black *and* white listeners. Years later, scholars would analyze the elements of King's speeches and conclude that he employed many of the same skills as the finest professional singers. He controlled his tempo, picking up speed in a way that made his audience feel as if they were moving with him, as if they wanted to sing along. He used harmonics, varying his pitch, to make his speech melodic and never monotonous. And he controlled his rhythm masterfully, pausing when he wanted his audience to contemplate his words and repeating phrases without pause when he wanted listeners to *feel* those same words.

On this day in Washington, King stood out as the youngest and most energetic speaker. He expressed better than anyone the feverish impatience that had been building among Black Americans since his birth. He understood and explained how they had come to this moment. First, men like his father had had to leave their sharecroppers' shacks to see an expanded set of possibilities. Then they began to gain literacy and economic independence. Then came *Brown v. Board of Education*, which appeared, King said, like an exit sign on a long, dark road, showing the path to a better place. Finally, the

American Negro saw dark-skinned people in Africa and Asia struggling for and gaining freedom. The determination of Negro Americans to overcome oppression, King said, came from the same yearning for freedom felt by oppressed people everywhere, always.

He spoke with no trace of fear or doubt. He even managed to upbraid much of his audience without being punished for it, stinging northern liberals, challenging the superficiality of their efforts, and complaining that they were "so bent on seeing all sides" that they often took no side at all. Give us the ballot, he said, and all would be forgiven, all would be made right, the soul of the nation would be redeemed.

King had earned his place, with the Prayer Pilgrimage, "as the number one leader of sixteen million Negroes in the United States," wrote the editor of the *New York Amsterdam News*, New York's biggest Black newspaper. "At this point . . . the people will follow him anywhere."

After his speech, King went to dinner at the Washington, D.C., home of a young white man named J. Blanton Belk. A year earlier, Belk and a friend had driven to Montgomery hoping to meet the young minister they'd been reading about in the paper. King had invited Belk and his friend to dinner that afternoon in 1956, and they had lingered for four hours over Coretta's fried chicken and lemon meringue pie. Eager to return the hospitality, Belk invited King and his guests to have dinner at a posh home on Embassy Row that he had borrowed from a friend. Gathered around the table were Daddy King, his brother Joel, A.D. King, Ralph Abernathy, and others.

Belk, a southerner whose family owned a chain of department stores, would go on to found Up with People, an interracial youth group that worked to unite cultures through song, a group that he hoped would carry forth the spirit of Martin Luther King Jr.'s quest for the beloved community. When King asked Belk what he had thought of his speech that day, Belk said he had been moved by the sincerity in King's tone as much as by his words. The sound of King's voice expressed "the total commitment of the man to what he believed," Belk said. He told King that he thought southern white people, if they had listened without prejudice, would have sensed his honesty and good intentions. King thanked him for the compliment and asked Belk to bring the two Black cooks out of the kitchen to join the group for a prayer before dinner.

"We had a miraculous day today," King said, "and I'm going to ask my father to make the blessing."

A month later, on June 18, 1957, the U.S. House of Representatives passed what would eventually become the Civil Rights Act of 1957, the first significant legislation to address the rights of Black Americans since 1875. It created the Civil Rights Division in the U.S. Justice Department and authorized the U.S. attorney general to seek federal court injunctions to protect voting rights.

American Negroes, King told the graduating class at Kentucky State College that month, were "traveling toward the promised land of social integration, of freedom and justice."

King reminded audiences that he was a religious leader, not an essayist or politician, and he seldom hesitated to chastise those who, in his mind, failed to live up to high moral and ethical standards. In April 1956, he published an article in *Liberation* magazine (ghostwritten by Rustin) that attacked so-called liberal whites, including the Mississippi novelist William Faulkner, who had urged Negroes to slow down their revolution or else risk a violent response. "It is hardly a moral act," read the article, "to encourage others patiently to accept injustice which he himself does not endure . . . We southern Negroes believe that it is essential to defend the right to equality now. From this position we will not and cannot retreat."

King's fervor lit a flame in many of those who heard him. Jesse Jackson, who was fifteen years old at the time of the 1957 Lincoln Memorial speech and would go on to become a minister, activist, and presidential candidate, said King's emergence offered concrete hope that racism could be fought and beaten. Before King, there seemed to be two options: "You could go into a deep dark hole," Jackson said, or "you could adjust—adjust to be the best pool player, adjust to be the best singer, the best barber." Now King offered a realistic third option, Jackson said: "You could resist."

Gradually, King accepted his position of leadership. He began to look more like a leader, too. His chest and shoulders thickened. He toned down his wardrobe, abandoning patterned suits and ties. If photographs from the period offer a reliable indicator, he smiled less.

"The Montgomery bus boycott caused him to recognize that he was called as a prophet, as a kind of Moses," said the Reverend James Lawson, King's friend and fellow activist. "He wasn't arrogant about it, but he accepted that decision and tried to live it and understand it." He despaired over it, too, Lawson said, over the pressures and responsibilities of carrying such a burden, and asking others to carry the burden, too. But the despair never outweighed the sense of responsibility he felt in answering God's call.

"Frankly, I worry about him," Coretta said shortly after the bus boycott's end. "I try to protect as much as I can so he can rest, but there is little I can do." One way to protect her husband, said Coretta, who was expecting their second child in October, was not to complain about feeling left out of the action, and not to make him feel guilty about spending little time at home. Martin was no longer juggling a family and a congregation; now he was juggling a family, a congregation, a new contract to write a book about his experiences in Montgomery, speaking engagements around the country, and a position of leadership in a blossoming nationwide movement for justice.

King also took on a monthly column in *Ebony* magazine called "Advice for Living," which ran from August 1957 to December 1958. The column offered him the chance to serve as minister to a large and diverse audience, answering readers' letters and using Christian values and calm reassurance to guide the troubled through difficult times. He expressed opposition to the death penalty; he urged one angry reader to reconsider his notion of what it meant to be a strong Black man and to embrace nonviolence; he warned Black men and women not to give in to a sense of "inferiority and self-hatred" that white racism had imposed on American society; he defended interracial marriage; he called birth control "rationally and morally justifiable"; he urged a Black man who didn't like Jews to get over his bigotry; he expressed moral opposition to gambling and premarital sex; and he advised a woman with an unfaithful husband to seek counseling but also to consider whether her nagging or inattentiveness had contributed to her husband's desire to have an affair. In what appears to have been King's only known writing on the subject of homosexuality, he told a boy that his feelings of attraction to other boys were "culturally acquired," not innate. King did not condemn the young man's homosexual feelings, but he did say they presented a "problem," one that might be overcome with the help of a psychiatrist.

Coretta helped him compose his answers at times. She might have felt the urge to write a letter of her own, about a frustrated, highly educated woman left at home to raise the children while her busy husband traveled and worked almost constantly. Yet she expressed only pride in the role she played in her husband's life. "I have considered my own role very important from the beginning. I have believed that I had a contribution to make to the cause . . . Being able to relieve him of many of the responsibilities of the home and church made my presence very useful. I felt a sense of being needed and a security in our relationship which gave me understanding and allowed me to be the kind of wife a man in my husband's position needs."

When Martin went out of town, members of the church looked to Coretta for leadership. Her husband's fame generated invitations for Coretta to sing at fundraising events in Montgomery, Mobile, Chicago, Philadelphia, and New York. At the New York concert, she shared a stage with Duke Ellington and Harry Belafonte, two of the world's most famous musicians. It was not the same as having her own career, but, as the biographer L. D. Reddick put it, "she was happy that she had been able to realize that much of her dream."

Others shared Coretta's concern for King's psychological state. The pressure and lofty expectations "caused him some real pain," one Montgomery Improvement Association colleague said. King seemed tired, troubled, and full of doubt at times, friends said. The heat of battle had united the Black community in Montgomery, but only for a time. Opinions were divided on what to do next. Feelings had been hurt. E. D. Nixon thought he deserved more credit for launching the bus boycott, and Rosa Parks complained about being denied a paying job with the Montgomery Improvement Association. One minister complained that the group's main function since the boycott had been to promote King. Former supporters questioned his decisions and gossiped about his frequent travel and media appearances, asking whether "he was taking too many bows and enjoying them," wrote Reddick in *Crusader Without Violence*. "He felt deserted and alone. He told some of his close friends that perhaps he had outlived his usefulness in Montgomery and should leave."

Gossip swirled about his personal life, too. The nation's most popular Black newspaper, *The Pittsburgh Courier*, issued a less-than-subtle warning when it wrote that a "prominent minister in the Deep South, a man who has been making headlines recently in his fight for civil rights, had better watch his step." The article said a detective hired by the White Citizens' Council hoped to catch this prominent minister in a hotel room with a woman other than his wife.

King was no ascetic. He showed little interest in money, but he smoked and drank and shot pool. While it's not clear when he first cheated on his wife, rumors about King's romantic affairs had begun to circulate.

In the fall of 1957, a young Hollywood director named Jeffrey Hayden visited Montgomery, eager to produce a movie about King and the bus boycott. The Montgomery Improvement Association voted to approve the project, but Hayden, who would go on to direct episodes of *Leave It to Beaver* and *The Andy Griffith Show*, never made the Montgomery movie. Nevertheless, Hollywood's interest in King offered another indication of his growing fame.

But fame did not necessarily translate to power, and King had no luck compelling President Eisenhower to stand up for Black students attempting to integrate Central High School in Little Rock, Arkansas, in the fall of 1957. Another celebrated Black man did have an impact, however. When nine students from Little Rock were barred from Central High School, the jazz musician Louis Armstrong, one of America's most beloved and least controversial Black entertainers, made a rare political pronouncement: "It's getting almost so bad a colored man hasn't got a country." Armstrong called Eisenhower "two-faced," and had harsher words for Arkansas governor Orval Faubus.

Though he wasn't happy about it, Eisenhower did, eventually, send federal troops to Little Rock to enforce the integration order. Armstrong's unexpectedly sharp remarks, according to *The Chicago Defender*, had the "explosive effect of an H-bomb." The trumpeter's words also offered a reminder, as the cultural critic Gerald Early has written, that King's fame had been made possible "because of the cultural power, the cultural charisma of the Negro." The Black community had relatively little political power, but it had Jackie Robinson, Duke Ellington, Lena Horne, Eartha Kitt, Richard Wright, Chuck Berry, Harry Belafonte, James Baldwin, and Louis Armstrong, among others, who gained popularity among Black and white audiences and transformed American culture. And now it had a telegenic young preacher, declaring that racism was both unpatriotic and a sin against God, and building a following of his own.

By October 1957, as he marked his third anniversary as pastor of Dexter Avenue church, King noted in his annual report that he had been in the pulpit only thirty Sundays in the past fifty-two weeks. He confessed his frustration, telling the congregation he worried that he had so many things to do that he had failed to do anything well. At one point he apologized for preaching the same sermon, "Loving Your Enemies," for the third time in three years. He told his audience that "each of us is something of a schizophrenic personality. We're split up and divided against ourselves. There is something of a civil war going on within all our lives . . . With the best of us there is some evil, and within the worst of us there is some good."

In a letter to J. Pius Barbour, King wrote: "Frankly, I'm worried to death. A man who hits his peak at twenty-seven has a tough job ahead. People will be expecting me to pull rabbits out of my hat for the rest of my life."

Late in the afternoon on October 7, 1957, a Black seventeen-year-old named Mark Gilmore walked through Montgomery's Oak Park on his way to work. Oak Park was the jewel of Montgomery, more than forty acres of meandering paths, pristine lawns, and burbling streams, with a wading pool, six tennis courts, a Ferris wheel, picnic areas, playground equipment, and a zoo in which visitors could gaze upon an alligator, two lions, two bears, and thirty-four monkeys. Every year it attracted hundreds of thousands of visitors, whites only. An out-of-town reporter called it "better than Central Park" in New York City.

Occasionally, a Black person might walk quickly through Oak Park, going to or from work or school. Police usually ignored it. But that casual approach to law enforcement had changed since the bus boycott. The boycott's success had antagonized many white people, including police officers, which might explain why an officer stopped Mark Gilmore and asked what he was doing in a whites-only park. Gilmore either argued or tried to explain, depending on whose version of the story is to be believed. He was beaten, arrested, and charged with disorderly conduct. When the case went to trial, Judge Eugene Loe said he had often dismissed such charges in the past, but he was no longer inclined toward leniency now that Negroes in the city seemed intent on "making Montgomery a national recognition point." He fined Gilmore $50. Fred Gray, Gilmore's lawyer, promised to appeal the decision.

All over the South, Black people complained, justifiably, about being denied access to public parks. A 1954 survey reported that the South offered 180 state parks for white people and only 12 for Black people. Cities were no better than states. In Atlanta, where Black people comprised more than a third of the population, they had access to only 3 of the city's 132 parks, 8 of the 96 tennis courts, and none of the 5 golf courses. The parks reserved for Black people across the South were almost always smaller, were less well kept, and contained fewer recreational facilities.

Before the bus boycott, Black community leaders in Montgomery had complained about the inadequate number and condition of their recreational facilities. Oak Park, located at the city's center and easily accessible from several Black neighborhoods, reminded them daily of their second-class status; the park was so close, so beautiful, and yet so far out of reach.

Gilmore's arrest presented a possible next step for the Montgomery Improvement Association. Dozens of Montgomery residents, including King and Abernathy, petitioned the city to integrate its parks, beginning with the biggest and most beautiful one. "The denial of Oak Park's facilities to Negroes does not accord with fundamental and inherent principles of justice and equality," the petition said. When the city refused, Fred Gray filed a lawsuit in U.S. District Court. But this time the city did not wait for a protest movement to take shape. They viewed integration as a dangerous, highly contagious disease, and they felt they had no choice but to close every one of the city's public parks lest that disease spread. Grass and weeds soon swallowed Oak Park. Workers filled its waterways with dirt. The city sold its zoo animals. The fences around the park, one newspaper editorial said, would serve as a warning to Montgomery's Black citizens: this is what happens when you make demands.

The bus boycott had played well on television, with images of working men and women walking or jamming into cars, but the park protest didn't. Here, and in countless disputes in countless cities north and south, the establishment used its power to maintain segregation and inequality, building highways, for example, that destroyed, relocated, and isolated Black communities, funneling those communities at times into public housing developments that became clusters of poverty. When opposition arose, government agencies tied the critics up and drained their resources with costly legal maneuvers. In Montgomery, parks remained closed for more than six years. When Oak Park finally reopened in 1965, a chain-link fence remained around most of its perimeter. The only opening was on the east side, the side that fronted a predominantly white neighborhood. Black Montgomery residents would have to go out of their way and pass through white neighborhoods to gain access. Even then, the swimming pools remained closed, for fear of interracial contact.

The segregationists were not finished. Libraries removed tables to prevent Black people from sitting beside white people. More than three years after the Supreme Court's ruling in *Brown v. Board*, not one public school in Montgomery had integrated. Alabama officials promised they would shut down public schools entirely rather than integrate, and Montgomery's boarded-up, fenced-in city parks suggested they weren't bluffing. An Alabama Ku Klux

Klan leader promised "bloodshed" if King pushed for school integration. The white enemies of integration claimed they were the ones being oppressed. Negroes had a right to seek better lives, they said, but not if it disturbed white tranquility. Not if it shifted the balance of power. Not if it affected property values. Not if it forced change so quickly as to make people uncomfortable. Change would come slowly, they claimed, if everyone remained patient and calm.

The white segregationists said they couldn't understand why King remained so intent on upsetting the status quo. "Our maid has worked for us twenty years, but she would quit tomorrow if her preacher told her to," said Clyde Bear, a middle-aged white man who owned the Bear Lumber Company in Montgomery. "They are all like that . . . They are ignorant and they obey."

Despite their feelings of inherent superiority, white people had suddenly developed fear, as Clyde Bear recognized: "The niggers have a powerful weapon in economic sanctions," he said, "and if it works with buses, we don't know when it will spread to other businesses."

18

"I'm Glad You Didn't Sneeze"

THE KINGS HAD floodlights installed on the front of the parsonage to discourage bombers and impair the view of snipers.

"I had no abnormal fears," Coretta told *Ebony* magazine in 1959 for an article called "The Woman Behind Martin Luther King Jr.," explaining in her usual thoughtful way why she only briefly considered taking the baby and leaving Montgomery. "My fears were rational. I tried to face up to the reality of the situation . . . But when I came to grips with this problem, the possibility of death was considered as being a part of the sacrifice we might have to make for the struggle. I came to feel, as Martin felt, that . . . nothing could stop the cause. Since then I haven't stayed awake worrying about it. I've been able to sleep most nights, and Martin has, too."

God and Coretta helped King manage his own fears. Coretta, he said, "was always stronger than I was through the struggle, so I didn't have the problem of having a wife who was afraid and trying to run from the situation."

King estimated that he traveled 780,000 miles and delivered 208 speeches in 1957. His mileage estimate was almost certainly too high, but it sounded about right to Coretta.

"As a matter of fact," she said, "I hardly saw him."

On October 23, 1957, Coretta gave birth to a son: Martin Luther King III. She worried about the burdens of the name, but her husband felt strongly about the choice, and Coretta went along. They called him Marty. For Coretta, it marked another in a series of compromises. She spoke about how she made the adjustment from being a career-oriented college woman to being a wife and then to being a minister's wife and, finally, to being the wife of a nationally celebrated minister and protest leader. "It hasn't been easy," she told the interviewer from *Ebony*.

In an interview about a decade later, she spoke with more candor. It wasn't simply that she yearned to be a part of the movement, she said. It wasn't simply that she sacrificed for the greater good. There was something else, something she wasn't sure her female interviewer could understand. "Having a man around to tell you that you look nice when you went out . . . you look forward to that," she said. "And one thing I want to say is that he made me feel like a real woman . . . He was small in stature, but he had a big voice and he was the kind of man that you could really respect and look up to." Martin believed it was the man's job to make money and the woman's job to take care of her man and their children, she said. It wasn't easy for him to accept her career ambitions, but he listened to her, and, eventually, it seemed to her he came around.

"But I started having babies before I was able to take a job," Coretta said. Even then, she did not feel neglected. "Because he paid attention."

Not long after Marty's birth, a photographer captured the King family in a moment of wholesomeness: Coretta, the new mother, sat on the living room sofa holding their son, while Martin, dressed in a white short-sleeved shirt and dark tie, sat on the floor and smiled at Yoki, who stood closest to the camera, shaking her hips as she showed her prowess with the toy prized by almost every American child in 1958: a hula hoop. They were the picture of the new Black professional class, the group driving King's movement. After World War II, Black Americans made progress. They got more education and better jobs. They moved into better homes, spurred in part by the booming economy and in part by the struggle for civil rights. The people's energy and ambition surged. Black colleges and small Black-owned businesses couldn't hold them all. They were ready to pour out across American society, if only American society would have them. King, born at the right time and in the right place, bursting with confidence and zeal, recognized an opportunity and a possible solution. The time had come for the Black men and women of his generation to press their claim, to show their strength, and to fight for their full and proper place in American society.

⸺ ⸱ ⸺

On January 12, 1958, King gave a lecture called "What Is Man?" at Orchestra Hall in Chicago. It was a speech he'd been working on and practicing since his days in seminary, one of his Fosdick adaptations. King argued that man was created to be in relationship with God, and that our divine relationship should compel us to live better lives, to shape the universe for the better, to love even our enemies as if they were our brothers and sisters. The speech was powerful, but the most remarkable thing about it may have been its effect on one person in the audience. Weeks later, Elijah Muhammad, leader of the Nation of Islam, wrote one of his withering attacks on Christianity in his newspaper column, one that may have been a rebuttal to King's Chicago speech. "The white race and their poison Bible (their slave-making Christianity) have poisoned the very hearts of my people against themselves and their God," Muhammad wrote. Christians had used their faith to justify slavery and pacify the enslaved, he said. Christian ministers had long preached that Black people were not people at all. They had gotten away with it long enough, he said: "The Bible says 'Do unto others as you would like others to do unto you.' This mistreatment of our people by the Caucasian race will be given back to them in full. A taste of it is now going on."

Despite his quarrel with King's theology, Muhammad sent King an invitation to speak to the Nation of Islam's followers in Chicago in March or April. King replied that he was too busy. He signed off: "You have my prayers and best wishes in all of your work."

King's secretary, Maude Ballou, wrote memos to help her boss keep up with work when he was on the road. She summarized incoming mail, identified the church members whose pleas for counseling seemed most pressing, and, in one instance, informed him when the key to the office Coke machine had gone missing. She greeted him as "Dear Martin" in the memos and signed off, sometimes, as "Maude, President, Your Fan Club."

Ballou's memos, while no doubt helpful to King, reveal the scattered nature of his work and help to show why the Montgomery Improvement Association remained divided and directionless and why the Southern Christian Leadership Conference had not yet established a clear mission. King, like a lot of Baptist preachers, was good at preaching but not organizing, said Ella Baker, who was hired to temporarily run the SCLC's Atlanta headquarters. Though she had the qualifications to run the entire organization, Baker knew that the group would never put a woman in charge. John Lewis wrote: "Ella had all the qualities of a successful leader . . . But she was a woman, a woman born at the wrong time." Nevertheless, she persisted in her work and helped recruit the Baltimore pastor John Lee Tilley to serve as executive director. The SCLC launched the Crusade for Citizenship, determined to double Black voter registration within two years, but rallies fizzled for lack of publicity and grassroots support. "Martin wasn't well trained, wasn't seasoned for what he got pulled into," Baker told the historian David J. Garrow.

King also wasn't seasoned to accept women in positions of authority. He grew up in a church that forbade women clergy. He grew up seeing that decisions came from one place—the top. Even though his mother had a better education than his father, and even though his mother had the longer history and the stronger connections within the Ebenezer community, her husband called the shots. In Baker's eyes, that's why King didn't identify strongly enough with the people he led, that's why he struggled with collective decision making, and that's why he overlooked the contributions of women.

"These were young Baptist preachers," Andrew Young said, referring to the men leading the SCLC. "Ella Baker was a determined woman and she reminded them of the strong Mommas they were trying to break free of."

Rustin and Levison had to prevail upon King to hire Baker as executive director, even temporarily, and she never got the financial or administrative support she needed to succeed in the job. Coretta Scott King later wrote that she felt Baker was mistreated because of her gender.

—————————

On June 23, King, A. Philip Randolph, Roy Wilkins, and Lester B. Granger of the National Urban League met with President Eisenhower to press for stronger civil rights laws. Many of the nation's journalists perceived Eisenhower as a benign bureaucrat, detached and ineffectual, especially since his heart attack in 1955 and subsequent hospitalization in 1956. In 1958, his approval ratings slipped below 50 percent for the first time. King was among the disapproving. If Eisenhower had come out strongly in support of civil rights sooner, King said, "much of the tension in the South . . . could have been avoided." Eisenhower had taken a circumspect approach since *Brown v. Board of Education*, and he did the same in his Oval Office meeting with King and the others, saying he would not comment on their proposals but would "be glad to consider them." Two days after the meeting, Rocco Siciliano, an assistant to the president, summed up the outcome with brutal honesty in his follow-up memo to Eisenhower, writing: "The Negro leaders were more than enthusiastic about their reception . . . I am convinced that this meeting was an unqualified success—even if success in this area is built on sand."

With the SCLC and MIA getting little done, Martin and Coretta had time for a vacation to Acapulco, Mexico, and King had time to work on his book about the Montgomery bus boycott, which he would call *Stride Toward Freedom*. One day while writing in a cluttered hotel room in Atlanta, King gave an interview to James Baldwin, the Harlem-born author who had emerged as one of the nation's most vital writers on race. The stepson of a Baptist minister and a child prodigy who once seemed destined for his own career in the pulpit, Baldwin described King as "not like any preacher I had met before. For one thing, to state it baldly, I liked him . . . King is immediately and tremendously winning, there is really no other word for it . . . I wanted to ask him how it felt to be standing where he stood, how he bore it, what complex of miracles had prepared him for it. But such questions can scarcely be asked, they can scarcely be answered." Baldwin found in King no trace of self-importance, no "hideous piety," no chauvinism, no tendency to say one thing to whites and another to Blacks.

The next Sunday, King was back in Montgomery, and Baldwin dropped by Dexter Avenue Baptist Church to hear him preach. The writer felt something there he had never felt before in a church: a sense that the parishioners had made King the symbol of their struggle, and, though hesitant, King had accepted their call. Their struggles had become one. Wrote Baldwin: "The joy which filled this church, therefore, was the joy achieved by people who have ceased to delude themselves about an intolerable situation, who have found their prayers for a leader miraculously answered, and who now know that they can change their situation, if they will."

———— · ————

Despite his extraordinary speaking skills, King struggled as a writer. To help complete his book, he called on a team of friends and allies, including Stanley Levison, Bayard Rustin, L. D. Reddick, and Harris Wofford, a young activist from New York who had been the first white man to graduate from Howard University Law School. Levison became not only King's most important ghostwriter but also a key adviser and his closest white friend.

Levison, forty-six years old, was a Jewish lawyer and businessman from New York and an active sponsor of the group called In Friendship, which offered financial help to southern Black causes. His parents were Yiddish-speaking Russian immigrants. His father had managed a children's clothing store in Queens, New York. At Far Rockaway High School, Levison had been voted "wittiest boy." After college and law school, he'd gone on to make money in real estate. He owned a car dealership in New Jersey and lived in Manhattan. But his résumé was not the perfect picture of capitalism that it seemed. Before meeting King, Levison had served as one of the top financiers for the Communist Party USA. He had been under federal surveillance since 1952. Undercover informants told the FBI that Levison had established businesses to earn or launder money for the Communist Party. As Levison's role in Communist affairs reportedly grew, the FBI increased its scrutiny, going so far as to wiretap his home phone and bug his Chicago hotel room in 1954. By 1955, Levison's role in Communist Party finances had diminished. It was Bayard Rustin who introduced Levison to King.

"Stan, as a strategist, was the single most influential force in Dr. King's life," Harry Belafonte said. "The more he expressed himself and helped Dr. King, the more Dr. King began to see honor in him, and became wholly reliant on much that he said and did."

In 1956, King had made an unforgettable impression on Levison upon their first meeting. Driving around Baltimore, someone had joked about the possibility that King would be arrested upon his return to Montgomery, saying the arrest would only help the cause. Coretta had become upset, saying that going to jail in the South was nothing to joke about for Black people. The mood in the tightly packed car grew tense, Levison recalled, until Dr. King finally spoke: "And he said, 'If anybody had asked me a year ago to head this movement, I tell you very honestly, that I would have run a mile to get away from it. I had no intention of being involved in this way . . . As I became involved and as people began to derive inspiration from their involvement, I realized that the choice leaves your own hands. The people expect you to give them leadership. You see them growing as they move into action, and you know you no longer have a choice.'"

Levison was impressed, he later recalled. "He didn't seem to be the type to be a mass leader. There was nothing flamboyant, nothing even charismatic about him . . . He looked like a typical scholarly kind of person, very thoughtful, quiet, and shy—very shy. The shyness was accented, I felt, with white people. And even in his relations with me in the early period, there was not always a relaxed attitude . . . There was a certain politeness, a certain arm's-length approach, and you could feel the absence of relaxation . . . It was as if Dr. King's southern background, largely with the Black community, had its effect on him as far as thinking comfortably and easily in the company of white people."

But the intimacy and comfort grew. Early in their relationship, Levison told King about his past ties to the Communist Party and said he would understand if the young preacher wanted to keep his distance. But he assured King of his motives, writing in one letter that his business skills had been acquired in a "commercial jungle" that he found "abhorrent." Now he sought to use those skills for "socially constructive ends." Over the years, when King offered to pay Levison for his work, Levison strongly refused to accept compensation. King often phoned Levison after midnight. The men would talk politics for hours, openly, honestly, bluntly, idealistically. Levison's moral fervor was such that King refused to believe his friend's agnosticism. "You don't know it, Stan," King said, "but you believe in God."

Levison surely believed in King, at least, and he believed in him enough

to be honest. On April 1, 1958, after reading the final chapter of King's boycott book, he wrote a four-page letter that might have crushed the soul of
another author. It began:

Dear Martin:

Your last chapter has much of the power, force, and straight
forwardness of your speeches from which so much of it is
derived. However, though it has a basic kind of organization it is
repetitive and lacks a clear, beginning, middle and end, type of
organization ... The result is a somewhat bewildering profusion of
ideas which submerge some of the main points and rob them of the
emphasis they deserve.

Levison's biggest complaint focused on the section in the book about
"Negro self-improvement." Rather than urging Negroes to "hold up the
mirror" and consider how they might improve their own character, Levison
said, King should focus on urging them to join the fight for equality. "If it is
true that the conditions are principally caused by segregation," he wrote, "to
argue that extensive change is possible within segregation seems contradic-
tory." Levison also urged King to avoid hints of moral superiority in describing the troubles of the Black community. "Few people understand the rate
of illegitimacy, broken homes, irresponsibility toward children is a product
of more than economically depressed conditions," he said. "It is a result of
hundreds of years of slavery in which the family unit was brutally ripped
apart in slave deals. Without full treatment the material lacks the intimate
human understanding it must contain." In a speech or sermon, it might be
acceptable to gloss over such history, he said, but not in a book.

Even with help, King fell back on an old habit as a writer: he lifted sections of the book from *Basic Christian Ethics* by Paul Ramsey and *Agape and
Eros* by Anders Nygren, books he had been assigned to read at Crozer. The
plagiarism would go undiscovered for years. Meanwhile, *Stride Toward Freedom* won glowing reviews in the press. *The New York Times* called the book

"a document of far-reaching importance for present and future chroniclings of the struggle for civil rights in this country." The review continued: "Dr. King, who is not yet 30, emerges as an effective leader. A compelling and even heroic figure."

Those who met King in the late 1950s were struck by his modesty, but he never hesitated to step into the spotlight, recognizing his personal power to inspire. In addition to the book, King starred in a comic book. Published by the Fellowship of Reconciliation, and used to teach classes on nonviolent protest, the comic was initially called *The Montgomery Story*. But as King's fame grew, the title was changed to *Martin Luther King and the Montgomery Story*. The cover featured a painting of King cast in a beam of light and overlooking images of a bus, a car, and the dome of the Alabama state capitol. (The uncredited artist was identified years later as Sy Barry, best known for the comic strip *The Phantom*.) The comic proved extraordinarily popular, not only with children but also with older people who had limited reading skills.

With his comic book, his adult book, his constant travel, his radio and television appearances, his *Ebony* advice column, and his access to people in power, King became America's most famous activist. Yet he remained a Black man in a world in which "races trample over races," as he said in an address to three thousand delegates at the National Conference on Christian Education.

On the morning of September 3, 1958, he and Coretta went to court in Montgomery to support Ralph Abernathy, who was testifying in the trial of a man accused of assaulting Abernathy. The assailant believed that his wife had been having an affair with Abernathy. When King was denied entry, he protested, telling a guard that the attorney Fred Gray could explain why he was there. "Boy, if you don't get the hell away from here," the officer said, "you will need a lawyer yourself!"

Before King could answer, two guards seized him and shoved him down the stairs and around the corner to the police station. They warned Coretta not to protest: "Gal, you just nod your head, we'll take you, too, just nod your head." A newspaper photographer captured the moment of the book-ing: King's right arm twisted behind his back by a uniformed officer, his suit jacket pulled back and down from his right shoulder as his body folds over the counter of the police station. From under his fedora, King stares at an officer behind the counter. Coretta, wearing a short-sleeved dress and eyeglasses, her mouth open, stands close by and watches. The police, King later said, "tried to break my arm, they grabbed my collar and choked me, and when they got me to the cell, they kicked me." King was charged with loitering and released on a $100 bond.

The next day, Judge Eugene Loe found King guilty and ordered him to pay a fine of $14 or serve fourteen days in jail. King told the judge the "impelling voice of conscience" prevented him from paying an unjust fine. He preferred jail. But he soon learned his fine had been paid by the police commissioner, Clyde Sellers, who said he was determined not to let King get away with this "publicity stunt intended to further his self-assumed role as a martyr."

Abernathy's run-in with an angry husband prompted one of Daddy King's longtime associates, J. Raymond Henderson, to write a letter of warning to the young preacher he knew as M.L. "You are a 'marked man,'" Henderson wrote. "All sorts of subtle attempts will be made to discredit you . . . One of the most damning influences is that of women . . . Enemies are not above using them to a man's detriment . . . You must be vigilant indeed."

Two weeks later, King traveled to New York to promote *Stride Toward Freedom* and to speak at a rally in Harlem. On September 19, more than six thousand people assembled outside the Hotel Theresa to hear a series of speakers, including King, Jackie Robinson, and A. Philip Randolph. *The New York Times* focused its coverage of the rally on remarks made by New York governor Averell Harriman on issues of school integration, but the Black press took a different view; Black reporters identified King as the rally's main speaker and identified both integration and police brutality as his key themes.

The next day, King was signing books at Blumstein's department store in Harlem when a Black woman in a stylish suit and sequined cat's-eye glasses approached. About forty people waited for King's autograph, but the woman pushed past them to the table where King sat.

"Are you Martin Luther King?" she asked.

"Yes," he said, without looking up from the book he was signing.

The woman reached into her handbag, grabbed a seven-inch letter opener by its ivory handle, and plunged the steel blade into King's chest. King felt no pain. He stayed in his chair and gazed calmly down at the handle protruding from his chest.

The attacker was later identified as Izola Ware Curry, a forty-two-year-old with a history of mental illness. She told police she didn't know King and held no grudge against him. Her account of the stabbing, police said, was incoherent. While people in the store grabbed Curry, and some began to beat her, King didn't move. Still in the chair, he was lifted from the store and taken to Harlem Hospital. As word of the attack spread, more than fifty people came to the hospital to offer blood. A big crowd kept a vigil in front of the hospital.

"Long live King!" one Black man on the street shouted. "And I don't mean the British one."

Others gossiped about whether King's attacker might have been hired by Arkansas governor Orval Faubus.

Harriman arrived while King still had the knife in his chest. "He seemed to be the least concerned person in the hospital," Harriman said.

"I'm going to be all right," King told his visitor. "Don't worry."

Surgeons later said the blade had cut but not completely severed King's aorta. If anyone in the store had tried to remove the letter opener, King would have died instantly. Even a sudden movement, such as a sneeze, might have killed him, they told reporters. A. Philip Randolph, Harry Belafonte, Roy Wilkins, and others waited at the hospital as a team of four doctors removed part of one of King's ribs and a portion of his sternum to reach the blade and remove it. The doctors, who needed two and a half hours, left a cross-shaped scar over the patient's heart that would remind him every day of his vulnerability.

Later, King would joke privately that he had been fortunate: "That was probably the fifth stabbing they had that night at that hospital," he said. "If you're gonna get stabbed, get stabbed in Harlem."

Coretta arrived early the next morning. "My husband was what psy-

chologists might call a guilt-ridden man," she wrote years later in recalling
the time Martin spent recovering from the attack. He used his time in bed,
she said, "to rethink his philosophy and his goals, and assess his personal
qualifications, his attitudes and beliefs." He worried over his "awesome responsibilities," she said, yet he could not escape the idea that his task was
unfinished. He had done little to dent southern segregation. If anything, as
Coretta said, attitudes were hardening among white southerners. A "long,
long struggle" lay ahead, Coretta said, and she and Martin "felt that we were
being prepared for a much larger work."

Two weeks later, dressed in yellow silk pajamas, a blue bathrobe, and
brown slippers, King spoke to reporters from the second floor of the hospital, joined by Coretta, Alberta King, and Ralph Abernathy. King said he
considered it a possibility that Izola Curry had been hired by the enemies of
integration to attack him. In the days after the stabbing, at least one white
supremacist group had taken up a collection to pay Curry's legal fees. "I have
no knowledge that this woman was sent by the South," King said. "It is a
possibility, however. Even if she is unbalanced, an unbalanced person can
be used by balanced people." King urged that Curry receive rehabilitation,
not punishment, so she could rejoin society "as a constructive member." She
was later deemed unfit to stand trial and committed to a psychiatric hospital.

King received about 1,800 cards, letters, and telegrams. The theologian
Howard Thurman visited the hospital and urged the patient to "rest his body
and mind with healing detachment." A. Philip Randolph came to see King
often during the hospitalization, helping to cement a relationship of mutual
warmth and admiration. In a letter of thanks to Randolph sent weeks after
the stabbing, King wrote: "From the moment you came in my room on that
dreadful Saturday afternoon to the moment I left New York City you proved
to be a real source of consolation to me . . . You are truly the Dean of Negro
leaders. If I had to choose the 10 greatest persons in America today, I would
certainly include you on my list."

One three-page letter from a thirty-seven-year-old white woman from
Pleasantville, New York, concluded: "I am so glad you didn't sneeze." Almost
ten years later, King would build the final speech of his life around that line,

although he would add dramatic power to the anecdote by attributing the letter to a ninth-grade student at White Plains High School. "I, too, am happy that I didn't sneeze," he would say. He would repeat the refrain to celebrate all the joys, struggles, and triumphs he would have missed had he made an abrupt move that day in Blumstein's department store. Thoughts of death had long preoccupied him. Now he saw that nonviolent movements grew stronger when they came under attack. Violent assaults on the determinedly nonviolent aroused sympathy and attracted support for the cause. It was a lesson that would shape the last ten years of his life.

"I am now convinced," King told reporters from the hospital, "that if the Negro holds fast to the spirit of nonviolence, our struggle and example will challenge and help redeem not only America but the world."

19

The Pilgrimage

KING'S PACE OF work slowed, even after he recovered from the stabbing. The work of the Southern Christian Leadership Conference and the Montgomery Improvement Association sputtered. The civil rights struggle continued across the South, but sometimes it was difficult to tell whether the struggle itself or the white retaliation against it possessed the greater force.

On January 1, 1959, King received a handwritten letter from a woman who warned that her husband had been hired to kill the preacher. "I ask my husband not to do it," wrote the woman, who claimed to be Black, "but he said the world would be better of [sic] when you are in hell where you belong with the rest of the swine, that you was a disgrace to our race."

Bombings, assaults, and police harassment continued throughout the South. Paul Tillich, the evangelist Billy Graham, and other leading religious figures spoke out against the violence. Four out of five southern ministers said they supported school integration, according to a 1958 survey by *Pulpit Digest*, but the survey was conducted anonymously and did not always reflect what the ministers were ready to say publicly. Racism persisted, largely unaddressed and unchecked among whites.

James Baldwin, who traveled through the American South for the first time in 1957 and interviewed King, wrote: "What it comes to, finally, is that the nation has spent a large part of its time and energy looking away from one of the principal facts of its life. This failure to look reality in the face diminishes a nation as it diminishes a person." Those who love America and claim to love freedom, Baldwin wrote, need to take a "hard look" at themselves. "If we are not capable of this examination, we may yet become one of the most distinguished and monumental failures in the history of nations."

King expressed similar thoughts. He and Coretta were preparing for a trip to India, a six-week journey that would include stops in London, Paris, and Zurich before India, and Beirut, Jerusalem, and Cairo on the way home. A Quaker pacifist group called the American Friends Service Committee sponsored the excursion, hoping King might learn more about Gandhi and gain a perspective on how nonviolent tactics could help America avoid the monumental failure Baldwin described. King had considered a tour of Russia, too, but he feared that segregationists would use his visit to smear him as a communist.

Americans faced a serious challenge, King said in a speech before the India trip. "To become the instruments of a great idea is a privilege that history gives only occasionally," he said. The nonviolent movement might become the kind of great idea that saves the world, that spreads peace and brotherhood far beyond Montgomery, that shows an alternative to war, that proves the power of democracy, that helps prevent the destruction of a planet threatened by nuclear weapons. The Soviet Union had launched a beach-ball-sized satellite called Sputnik four months earlier, heightening fears, as *The New York Times* put it, that the Soviets and the United States were like "two scorpions in a bottle," with little hope of escape or self-defense. Increasingly, King was becoming convinced that nonviolent tactics—"Christianity in action"—offered a way out. He echoed Gandhi, who spoke of satyagraha, the uncompromising insistence on truth, a doctrine that mixed politics and religion. The "colored people" of the earth, the poor and oppressed, King said, would lead the way, meeting violent force with *soul* force, exerting the influence of love, wearing down hatred.

"I hope this is possible," he said.

The next day, he departed, accompanied not only by Coretta but also by L. D. Reddick. Reddick had a PhD in history from the University of Chicago. As a Black man, as a former resident of Atlanta, and as an inveterate note-taker (with exceptionally messy handwriting), he was almost ideally qualified to document King's career. His notes on this trip included his concern that Martin and Coretta had overpacked. The plane rumbled as it rose into New York City's moonlit winter sky, Reddick observed. The stewardesses served warm meals to the first-class passengers and cold cuts to everyone else, including the Kings.

"Well," Martin joked to Coretta at the sight of the meager offerings, "we're still second-class citizens."

As the city's lights faded from view, Martin took off his size-nine shoes, stretched out on an empty seat, and put his head on Coretta's lap. She covered him with a blanket, and he fell asleep.

After two days in London in which Martin and Coretta seldom left the hotel, they flew to Paris, where the novelist Richard Wright greeted them as they stepped off their plane. Wright was fifty-one years old, bespectacled, his hair graying on the sides, "looking like a chubby college professor," Reddick wrote in his notes on the meeting. Fifteen years earlier, Wright had been hailed by critics as Black America's most eloquent spokesman, a role now assigned to the young man he met at the airport.

Wright took Reddick and the Kings to their hotel, and then to a café. He guided them on a brief shopping trip in which Coretta purchased perfume. From there, it was back to Wright's apartment on rue Monsieur le Prince, where Reddick and Coretta mostly listened as King and Wright spoke about politics and race.

Before the Kings departed, Wright summoned his sixteen-year-old daughter, who had been studying for school in the back of the apartment. Wright asked King to show his daughter the red scar on his chest from where he had been stabbed.

King unbuttoned his shirt.

"This is what happens to people in the States who speak up for their rights," Wright said.

— · —

"To other countries I may go as a tourist," King said upon arrival in New Delhi on February 10, 1959, "but to India I come as a pilgrim."

Martin and Coretta were greeted with garlands at the airport, shuttled to their hotel, and questioned by about two dozen reporters. Did King believe that nonviolent protest might be effective in Africa? King said yes. Was it true that southern states in the United States outlawed interracial marriage? He confirmed it. Did his concept of nonviolence include vegetarianism? No, it did not. What did he think of Paul Robeson, the American singer and outspoken supporter of the Soviet Union? King said he had no comment.

India's urban poverty startled him. Nowhere in the United States had he seen such large numbers of people sleeping in the streets, in doorways, under bridges, all their possessions in tote, their emaciated bodies wrapped in newspaper. The American visitors were told not to give money to beggars, but Martin dismissed that advice.

On their first evening in New Delhi, Martin, Coretta, and Reddick dined with India's prime minister, Jawaharlal Nehru, who wore a rose in the lapel of his coat. Nehru and the Kings discussed caste and race. They compared the plight of American Negroes to Indian untouchables. Nehru said the Indian government made prejudice against the untouchables a crime, spent millions of rupees annually to create housing and jobs, and required colleges and universities to give preferential status to untouchables.

"But isn't that discrimination?" Reddick asked.

"Well, it may be," Nehru said. "But this is our way of atoning for the centuries of injustices we have inflicted on these people."

Years later, King would cite his conversation with Nehru as his inspiration for proposing a "broad-based and gigantic" plan to make reparations for the long-running mistreatment of America's disadvantaged citizens, one that would eventually bring "the basic psychological and motivational transformation of the Negro," not to mention the transformation of American democracy. Without going deeply into detail of how such a program would work, he would compare it to the GI Bill, which compensated soldiers for the time and opportunity lost while fighting for their country. No amount of money could ever compensate for the exploitation and humiliation Black people suffered, King said, but a price could be placed, at the very least, on unpaid wages. It would help the poor. It would help America repent for sins of the past. It would help heal a divided nation.

The Kings, along with Reddick, traveled across India. Martin lectured. Coretta sang spirituals. They visited Buddhist and Hindu temples. They met with activists seeking to alleviate poverty, redistribute wealth, and eliminate the caste system. The Kings complained of fatigue at times. Their guide and trip organizer, James E. Bristol of the American Friends Service Committee, noted that the Kings were exhausted even before their trip, "drained terribly nervously and emotionally as a result of the past few years, and the way Martin must drive himself in the States." They seemed unhappy with the rigor of their travel schedule. "What they both want to do is to get to their room and rest as much as possible—and Martin certainly so often wants to be left alone," Bristol wrote.

Nevertheless, the Kings maintained a relentless pace. "We had hundreds of invitations that the limited time did not allow us to accept," King wrote. "We were looked upon as brothers with the color of our skins as something of an asset. But the strongest bond of fraternity was the common cause of minority and colonial peoples in America, Africa and Asia struggling to throw off racialism and imperialism." In meeting Gandhi's son, grandsons, and other relatives, King said he came away more convinced than ever "that non-violent resistance is the most potent weapon available to oppressed people in their struggle for freedom." The vast poverty and hunger of India struck him, too, as did the persistence of the caste system. He learned of and praised the so-called Bhoodan movement, also known as the Bloodless Revolution, a land-reform program that attempted to persuade property owners to turn over a percentage of their property to those without land.

Reddick was intrigued by King. He wrote soon after the trip, "Unlike his Indian models, MLK has not worked at self-purification. Generally he accepts himself and finds no tendency so outrageous that he must wrestle with it. On the contrary, he seems to find himself to be pleasant and winsome . . . He does not seem capable of dramatic self-criticism." After a long day of fascinating encounters, King tended to reflect not on what he'd learned but on the frustrations and challenges he faced back home, wrote Reddick, adding, "Many nights he talked me to sleep on trains."

On March 9, the night before his departure, King, sounding tired, gave a live radio address to the nation. Gandhi had proved that the laws of morality were as inescapable as the laws of gravity, he said. He compared Gandhi to Lincoln, who was shot "for committing the crime of wanting to heal the wounds of a divided nation." He quoted Lincoln's secretary of war, Edwin Stanton, who stood by the dead body of the great leader and said, "Now he belongs to the ages." Gandhi belonged to the ages, too, King said. He added: "And if this age is to survive, it must follow the way of love and nonviolence that he so nobly illustrated in his life . . . Today, we no longer have a choice between violence and nonviolence; it is either nonviolence or nonexistence."

Martin and Coretta's circuitous route home took them through Greece, Lebanon, and Egypt. They visited Jericho and eastern Jerusalem, which were then under the control of Jordan.

On Easter Sunday, back in Montgomery, King told his congregation about strolling along "those little narrow streets" in the Holy City of Jerusalem, passing through the Damascus Gate, following the Stations of the Cross, and seeing the ancient walls of Jericho, the Jordan River, and the Cave of the Patriarchs in Hebron. Then he arrived at the Church of the Holy Sepulchre. "And it's here . . . that you find the point where Jesus was crucified . . . There was a captivating quality there," he said, "there was something that overwhelmed me, and before I knew it, I was on my knees praying . . . And before I knew it, I was weeping. This was a great world-shaking, transfiguring experience."

He was so shaken he left Coretta and walked alone back to his hotel. Jesus didn't *have* to go to the cross, he thought. "Nobody could ever demand that he sacrifice his life in a way like this . . . He could have . . . gone back on to Galilee, forgotten about the whole thing, and everything would have been all right," King told his listeners. But Jesus felt a sense of obedience to what King called "unenforceable obligations." Like Socrates and like King's namesake, Martin Luther, Jesus felt compelled to follow the path of the truth no matter where it led. The cross stands as a reminder of the way Jesus lived, not merely the way he died, King said. The cross calls us to action. The cross expresses a commitment to the faith that God would go to any length to "restore a broken community." The cross promises that the whole world will one day be free and "segregation will one day die ... And this is the hope that can keep us going and keep us from getting frustrated as we walk along the way of life."

Ella Baker, focusing her work on Black voter registration in the South, waited anxiously for King's return. The SCLC needed him, she said, but he was never around. The organization was broke. Staffers hadn't been paid for two weeks. Legislators across the South proposed new segregation laws, and Black people suffered new violent assaults, while the SCLC largely failed to respond.

Baker was fifty-five years old, with a deep, resonant voice, dark brown skin, and a commanding presence that expanded with the size of her audience. Growing up in North Carolina, she had heard her formerly enslaved grandmother tell the story of being whipped by a white man for refusing to agree to an arranged marriage. Baker graduated as valedictorian from Shaw University, a Black college in Raleigh, North Carolina. She moved to Harlem and worked for the Depression-era Works Progress Administration, the NAACP, and the Urban League. She had enough experience to offer advice without hesitation, and to know that Baptist preachers were not good at taking advice, especially from women. Baker suggested King stop making so many speeches and spend more time leading the SCLC. King seemed hurt by her criticism, according to Reddick, who once again had a place in the room. King said he was an artist who should not be denied "his means of expression." He added that "he liked to preach and felt that he should do it."

King understood that he was a performer, in an important sense, and that performance was more easily defined than leadership. He stood before a crowd, as he did at the Holt Street church in Montgomery at the outset of the bus boycott, and became something larger than himself. His artistry galvanized audiences and compelled them to action. But his artistry wasn't the problem, according to Reddick. King's real problem was his inability to say no. To anyone. About anything. While traveling in India, Reddick had suggested that King give up his church and devote himself full-time to the civil rights crusade. "I know he will never do this," Reddick wrote. "He will continue to be a crusader in a gray flannel suit."

King agreed to cut the staff of the SCLC and to fire its executive director, John Lee Tilley, replacing him with Baker, who would be the acting director until a permanent replacement could be found. But Baker still lacked the power to build the organization the way she wanted to. She grew more frustrated. "The personality that had to be played up was Dr. King," she complained. In most other organizations, the executive director served as spokesperson and leader, but not the SCLC. "They couldn't tolerate having an old lady," Baker said. "It was too much for the masculine and ministerial ego to have permitted that."

Even as the SCLC struggled, the force of the Montgomery movement rippled across the South. Five years after *Brown v. Board* and two years after the watered-down Civil Rights Act of 1957, citizens demanded more. Why were there virtually no integrated public schools in Alabama, Georgia, Mississippi, and South Carolina? Why, as more than half of all Black Americans lived outside the Deep South for the first time in American history, did discrimination seem to be traveling with them? Rebellions are born from hope as much as anger, and Black Americans had finally seen signs of hope. Yet much anger remained, too.

On the night of April 25, a Black man named Mack Charles Parker was kidnapped from jail and lynched by a white mob in Poplarville, Mississippi, his body found ten days later in the Pearl River. *The Chicago Defender* said that white vigilantes carried out crimes such as this one in a desperate attempt to push back the forces of integration. But the Black-owned newspaper predicted it would have the opposite effect: "It will galvanize public sentiment against Dixie's flaming racism." About a week after Parker's murder, a Black female student at Florida A&M University in Tallahassee was abducted and raped. Four young white men admitted to the crime. Yet only when students at the Black university announced a campaign of "passive resistance," including a boycott of classes and mass prayer meetings, were charges filed in the case.

King built his movement around the idea that racism was both un-American and ungodly. He aimed to save souls and democracy with lessons from the Bible. That approach helped him build a broad coalition, but it would present a problem as the movement matured and his focus turned beyond the South. "The tragic truth," he said, "is that discrimination in employment is not only dominant throughout the South, but is shamefully widespread in the North, particularly in great urban communities which often pride themselves as liberal and progressive centers in government and economics." King raised these issues at a Washington, D.C., conference of religious leaders in May 1959, one in which he argued that the government had an obligation to take action. But what if America didn't rise to the cause of justice for all? If the repression of the minority continued, unanswered, what would happen to that hungry anger that King had set loose?

What if King promised the American dream, only to find it further deferred, the promise of equal justice an empty one? Would his Christian, nonviolent movement be enough? Already, in the North, new, more militant voices had emerged—Elijah Muhammad and his passionate lieutenant Malcolm X, most notably. In North Carolina, a local NAACP leader formed an armed guard and exchanged gunfire with the KKK and local police. These developments and others raised the question of whether King's nonviolent movement would carry the day or whether people, ever more frustrated, would explode.

20

Leaving Montgomery

EARLY ONE MORNING in the fall of 1959, a *Jet* magazine reporter visited King at his Montgomery parsonage. King wore pajamas and a robe. The reporter was at work on a story that would carry the headline "Why Rev. M. L. King Is Leaving Montgomery." But what seemed to interest the reporter most was not King's pending move to Atlanta as much as the activist's unsettled state of mind. King told the reporter:

> When an airplane takes off, its motors are accelerated to the peak of effort. But it can't fly all the way from say Miami to Chicago at such a high pitch. That would be too much for both the plane and its passengers. It has to shift to cruising speed. I have been under extreme tension for four years because of my multiple duties. The time has long since come for me to shift gears.

At thirty, King was no longer slender and youthful in appearance. His thick neck topped broad, heavy shoulders and a solid frame. Onstage, he possessed the force of a volcano, but at home and in private, he could be somnolent. When he wasn't speaking, his round face and soft features presented a sense of serenity that he often failed to enjoy. The bus boycott had changed his life, putting him in demand and in danger. His father continued to urge him to cut back on his activism and focus on preaching. His son, Daddy King said, had been "scarred by the struggle in very serious ways." M.L. had received high-paying job offers that would have relieved much of the stress,

but he wouldn't consider any of them, saying he couldn't disappoint his followers by succumbing to "the lure of money."

Instead, he made plans to move his family to Atlanta, where he would
serve as co-pastor at Ebenezer, second in command to his father, and devote more of his time and energy to the Southern Christian Leadership
Conference.

"What I have been doing," he told the journalist from *Jet*, who could
see the scar from King's stab wound under his pajama top, "is giving, giving, giving and not stopping to retreat and meditate like I should . . . If the
situation is not changed, I will be a physical and psychological wreck. I have
to reorganize my personality and reorient my life." King bemoaned the toll
his travel had taken on his family. "Daddy, when are you gonna play with
us?" four-year-old Yoki asked him after one long business trip. "You haven't
played with us in a long, l-o-n-g time. All you do is work!"

Even in his pajamas, settled back in a chair, King "painted a word-
picture of 'tension,'" as the reporter put it. He worried that he might be
judged a failure for leaving Montgomery with so much unfinished work,
with the city's buses integrated but its schools, parks, and playgrounds still
as segregated as ever. "I have a sort of nagging conscience that someone
will interpret my leaving Montgomery as a retreat from the civil rights
struggle," he said. "Actually, I will be involved in it on a larger scale. I can't
stop now. History has thrust something upon me from which I cannot turn
away."

King, who kept a tidy desk, did not type. He usually wrote sermons and
notes by hand, in cursive, and dictated letters to secretaries. To frame his
farewell sermon to Dexter on Sunday morning, November 29, 1959, he wrote
out a series of note cards. His public farewell reflected one of the things
Coretta said about her husband: that he was a guilt-ridden man. "For almost
four years now," he jotted in his tight cursive handwriting, "I have been attempting to do as one man what five men should be doing." He went on to list
the demands on his time, including the church, the Montgomery Improvement Association, public speaking, correspondence, and "the general strain
of being known." Family did not make the list. "So I must do something to
reorient my life if I am to be of any useful service."

He wept as he delivered the news.

One white-owned Alabama newspaper, meanwhile, celebrated King's announced departure with an editorial headlined "Alabama's Gain, Georgia's Loss."

Two weeks later, leaders of the SCLC met in Birmingham—the "toughest city in the South" for Negroes living under Jim Crow, as the journalist Emory O. Jackson called it—to lay out the organization's plans for the year ahead. The SCLC would continue to work to boost voter registration, King said, but it would also lead acts of nonviolent protest across the country as part of its push for a "speedier breakdown of segregation."

In a mass meeting the day after the SCLC gathering, King compared his people to the Israelite slaves who had escaped Pharaoh's Egypt. Some Israelites feared the journey to freedom and wanted to turn back; others wanted to be released from bondage but only so long as they didn't have to make any personal sacrifices; while others still—the creative minority, as he called them—were prepared to struggle and suffer to reach the Promised Land. King's job, as Bayard Rustin put it, was to convince his followers to join the creative minority, to make them feel "they could be bigger and stronger and more courageous and more loving than they thought they could be." Yet it wasn't clear he had a strategy and a strong enough organization to do it. The philosophy of nonviolence had inspired many and earned attention in the media, but it had not swept up the masses. King's movement had succeeded in Montgomery in large part because its roots were in the church. Building a nationwide movement, however, required a kind of grassroots organizing that had so far eluded him and the SCLC.

Though King was still a young man, a new wave of activists had come up behind him, inspired by King as well by professors at Black colleges and universities. In 1958, in Wichita, Kansas, the activists Carol Parks-Hahn and Ron Walters had tested lunch-counter segregation. They and their friends sat at the counter every day at the popular Dockum Drug Store, ordering sodas and being refused service. After a month, the owner agreed to serve them. Shortly after King's decision to move to Atlanta, on February 1, 1960, four students from the Agricultural and Technical College of North Carolina attempted something similar in Greensboro, North Carolina. They walked into a Woolworth's, purchased a few items, and sat down at the lunch counter, where they knew Black customers were not welcome. The students—Ezell Blair Jr., Franklin McCain, Joseph McNeil, and David Richmond—all were freshmen. Two of them had just read the comic-book account of the Montgomery bus boycotts, but the protesters had done no planning in advance of their Woolworth's protest. They possessed no clear goals. All they had was a sense of injustice and a desire to act on it.

When Blair ordered coffee, the waitress refused to serve him. The students stayed at the counter until the store closed. The next morning, when the store reopened, the four young men returned, joined by about twenty more students who had heard by word of mouth about the demonstration. The action spread like wind-borne seeds—to lunch counters across North Carolina, South Carolina, Virginia, Florida, and Tennessee. In Nashville, students had begun planning a protest long before the Greensboro sit-in, and now *they* were eager to join the uprising, too. On February 13, more than one hundred young people walked out of a downtown Nashville church and simultaneously took their places at nearby lunch counters. With no national organization backing them, with no national leader speaking for them, with no overarching set of demands, a new grassroots movement began, aimed at one of the most glaring symbols of segregation, the humble lunch counter. Even the name of the campaign was humble: it came to be called "the sit-in movement."

The sit-in movement was a reaction, in part, to the disappointing pace of school desegregation. Five years after *Brown v. Board of Education*, less than 6 percent of Black children in the South were enrolled in integrated schools. By the middle of March, forty-eight southern cities had been hit with protests over an assortment of issues concerning segregation—a wave of nonviolent resistance, *Time* magazine reported, "the likes of which the United States has never seen." Like the Montgomery bus boycott, the sit-ins stressed nonviolent protest. A little more than a year earlier, Stanley Levison had complained in a letter to King that efforts to launch a nationwide movement had been impeded by the "relative apathy of youth and labor." Now the apathy vanished.

"There was a deep appreciation and awareness of the Montgomery bus boycott," said the Reverend James Lawson, who organized the sit-ins in Nashville. King had shown the students that they gained a tactical edge through nonviolent confrontation, Lawson said, especially when the authorities reacted with violence and the media told the story. Some reporters described it as passive resistance, but there was nothing passive about it, as Lawson saw it; it was a subtle way of wedging power away from a group that had no intention of giving it up. "That's why the SCLC was organized," Lawson said. "The NAACP was not interested in adding a direct-action department to exploit this."

In many small southern towns, where there were no Black colleges and no Black media, protests fizzled. "We got arrested a bunch of times, so that was basically how it went," said Robert Avery, who was a teenage protester in Gadsden, Alabama. "We couldn't get any publicity. Even the local newspaper wouldn't write about what we were doing."

While many southern white reporters viewed the student protesters cynically, and white business leaders and politicians dismissed the young upstarts, King embraced them. As in Montgomery, he didn't start the uprising, and yet, again, he found himself thrust into a position of leadership, improvising all the way. On February 16, he traveled to Durham and spoke to a packed crowd of more than 1,200, including students from more than a dozen colleges in North Carolina, South Carolina, and Virginia, telling them they had the moral advantage over their opponents. "Let us not fear going to jail," he said. "We must say we are willing to fill up the jailhouses of the South." He also cautioned: "Our ultimate aim is not to humiliate the white man but to win his understanding."

"Fill up the jailhouses" would become a call to action, one that would inspire a new wave of activists, most of them younger than King. They included John Lewis, James Bevel, Diane Nash, Marion Barry, C. T. Vivian, and Bernard Lafayette Jr. Lafayette, part of the Nashville sit-in movement, was struck by the way King's voice made the preacher seem physically larger than he was. He was also struck by one thing King told the student protest-ers: "I came not to bring inspiration but to *gain* inspiration."

For John Lewis, who had grown up in Alabama and followed King since Montgomery, the famed minister's arrival in Nashville made a last-ing impression. "We believed in Martin Luther King Jr.," Lewis said. King and Lawson both, he said, "taught us how to stand up, to be bold, and to be brave."

King's return to Atlanta made sense for the SCLC. It would give the or-ganization greater national reach. And, with his father leading Ebenezer, the younger King would have fewer responsibilities connected to church. But the arrangement also created emotional complications for King, who confided his feelings to James Lawson. Daddy King and Martin Luther King Jr. were engaged in a constant "wrestling match," Lawson said. The younger King was a star. Visitors would travel great distances to hear him preach. But the congregation belonged to his father. The younger King also had to be conscious of local politics. Daddy King had long-standing relationships with white political and business leaders in Atlanta. The SCLC would sel-dom launch protests in Atlanta, Lawson said, to the frustration of some, "be-cause it would be a slap in the face" to Daddy King and other older church leaders.

That wasn't King's only problem. Soon after his return to Atlanta, two Georgia sheriff's deputies arrived at his Ebenezer church office and served King with an arrest warrant from Alabama. He was charged with two counts of perjury—a felony—for falsely swearing to the accuracy of his Alabama state tax returns for 1956 and 1958. King insisted that he had always scru-pulously accounted for his earnings and paid the taxes he owed. Alabama had already come after him once, and he had agreed to pay the amount the state had said he owed, explaining that it was easier to pay than to fight a rigged system. Now Alabama threatened him again. It was unusual for a state to prosecute a citizen who had already accepted and paid the state's assessment of unpaid taxes, and it was even more unusual for the state to file felony charges in such a case. King labeled the effort an attempt "to harass me because of the stand I have taken in the civil rights struggle."

Even so, the tax charge hit King hard. He had always taken care to avoid any impression that he was profiting from his position of leadership. He rented his modest home and drove a used Pontiac. He took an annual salary of $1 for running the SCLC. Ebenezer paid him $4,000 a year, plus a $2,000 stipend for "pastoral care." He donated most of his speaking fees and book royalties. But now it wouldn't matter. The tax charges had the potential to destroy his reputation. He feared he would never get a fair trial. He told Coretta that, for the rest of his life, "people will believe that I took money that didn't belong to me." Coretta said she had never seen him so upset. King paced his study and prayed. He canceled a trip to Chicago, ashamed of facing anyone, and then changed his mind. "I called the airport and made another reservation and went on to Chicago," he said, as if declaring victory in his inner battle.

The actual battle remained to be fought. His friends—including Harry Belafonte, Bayard Rustin, and Stanley Levison—formed the Committee to Defend Martin Luther King. Nat King Cole served as the organization's treasurer, and Eleanor Roosevelt actively participated. But even those efforts worried King. Wouldn't the money raised for his defense be better spent on the SCLC and the sit-in movement?

As usual, he found strength in words. He wrote several long magazine articles in which he attempted to justify his life's work and frame a vision for the future. In a long essay for *The Christian Century*—part of the magazine's series titled "How My Mind Has Changed"—King wrote that he had been a "thoroughgoing liberal" through much of his early life, "absolutely convinced of the natural goodness of man and the natural power of human reason." But since then he had gained a greater appreciation of the depths of sin and the "glaring reality of collective evil." His liberalism, he had come to realize, had been too sentimental, too idealistic. Humans rationalized their sins, and without the "purifying power" of faith in God, he said, they would continue to do so. In recent months, King wrote, he had become more convinced than ever in the reality of a personal God. "Perhaps the suffering,

frustration and agonizing moments which I have had to undergo occasionally as a result of my involvement in a difficult struggle have drawn me closer
to God," he wrote. "Whatever the cause, God has been profoundly real to me
in recent months . . . Therefore I am not yet discouraged about the future . . .
In a dark, confused world the spirit of God may yet reign supreme."

He also used the essay to describe his growing understanding of the
connections between economic injustice and racial injustice. Finally, he explained the evolution of his thoughts on militarism. Once, he had thought
that war, horrible as it is, might be a necessary alternative to a surrender to
totalitarianism. But he had gradually concluded that war, given the power
of modern weapons, could never be justified. At the time, the Cold War was
viewed as a Manichaean struggle, one that all but shut down debate about
America's use of force. King was one of the few widely known American
leaders at the time to address the moral costs of war. The church, he wrote,
"cannot remain silent while mankind faces the threat of being plunged into
the abyss of nuclear annihilation."

After King submitted his article, the magazine's editor asked him to reflect on whether personal perils had affected his thinking. In his response,
which arrived too late for publication, he wrote that he didn't want anyone to
think he was seeking sympathy, but that the dangers associated with his work
indeed had changed him. Suffering had the power to bring people closer to
Jesus, in King's view. People who were willing to suffer rather than inflict
suffering on others could set the example, he said, changing relationships
between individuals, communities, racial groups, and nations. He echoed
the words of Jesus in Matthew 11:28–30:

I have learned now that the Master's burden is light precisely when we
take his yoke upon us. My personal trials have also taught me the value
of unmerited suffering. As my suffering mounted I soon realized that
there were two ways I can respond to my situation: either to react with
bitterness or seek to transform the suffering into a creative force. I decided to follow the latter course . . . I have lived these last few years with
the conviction that unearned suffering is redemptive . . . The suffering

and agonizing moments through which I have passed over the last few years have also drawn me closer to God.

———•———

Martin and Coretta rented a house at 563 Johnson Avenue in Atlanta, not far from Ebenezer and the SCLC's headquarters. It was a two-story brick house, much like the others on the middle-class block, with burglar bars on the first-floor windows. They paid $110 a month. King still liked to dress sharply, and he stayed in fine hotels when he traveled to the North, but he had no interest in buying a house, and he cautioned Coretta not to decorate their new place extravagantly. The living room had flowered wallpaper. On the wall between the dining room and kitchen, the Kings hung a calendar with a depiction of Archibald M. Willard's iconic painting of the Revolutionary War, *The Spirit of '76*. King insisted that Yoki and Marty would attend public school, even though Atlanta's schools remained segregated and even though Coretta worried their children would receive an inferior education. Private schools, King told his wife, "caused the children in the schools to feel they were better than the other children, that it set up a kind of class consciousness and also sometimes it kept the children from really feeling an identification with all people."

As he settled in Atlanta, King traded in his Pontiac and bought two used cars: a five-year-old Ford station wagon with 19,869 miles on the odometer, and a three-year-old Chevrolet with 43,934 miles on it. King began putting heavy mileage on the Chevy as he traveled to sit-ins around the South, including a protest initiated by Alabama State students in Montgomery, one that led police to storm the campus with shotguns, rifles, and tear gas, threatening to arrest the entire student body. As the sit-ins spread, King appeared on TV's *Meet the Press* and praised the students. "I think the sit-ins serve to dramatize the indignities and the injustice which Negro people are facing all over the nation," he said.

Though King was a hero to the students, Ella Baker urged him to let the students operate independently of the SCLC. King agreed, even as he continued to speak at student meetings. Recognizing that many Black college students were unprepared to lead local protests, Baker organized a gathering of about two hundred students from around the region, beginning April 15, 1960, at Shaw University in Raleigh. She borrowed $800 from the SCLC to rent meeting rooms and sent a note signed by her and King to all the big protest groups, inviting them to attend, even though it was not an SCLC event. The goal, she wrote, was to share experience and set goals. Though "Adult Freedom Fighters" would be in attendance to offer guidance, she wrote, the conference would be centered on youth. Even so, King's presence probably contributed to the strong turnout, as the historian Clayborne Carson notes. King, at thirty-one, was a decade older than most of the students. While he urged them to organize, he did not push them to join the SCLC. He also encouraged them to use their economic power to press for change and to train their volunteers to serve time in jail rather than pay fines. He talked to them about the meaning of nonviolence and offered practical advice, saying, for example, that each group should have one spokesman and that spokesmen should never speak in "bitter terms."

During the meeting, the students voted to create their own organization, the Student Nonviolent Coordinating Committee (SNCC, pronounced "snick"), with King and James Lawson serving as advisers, not leaders. One of the students at the meeting, Julian Bond, said his peers had the feeling Lawson was challenging King "for leadership of this group of young people." King made no distinct impression that day, Bond said, "except that this was Martin Luther King." It was Lawson who captured the imagination of the students in Raleigh, Bond and others said. Raised in the North, Lawson had chosen to go to prison rather than serve in the Korean War. He had spent three years as a missionary in India, where he studied Gandhi's nonviolent tactics. Lawson, who had been expelled from the Vanderbilt School of Theology for his role in the sit-in actions, appealed to the students in part because he remained an outsider, one who insisted that the student protests were rooted in moral and spiritual issues more than legal or political ones.

The Montgomery bus boycott had thrilled Lawson, and now the sit-in movement possessed some of the same spontaneity and militancy. But how,

Lawson wondered, would the students maintain that kind of energy? "I recognized if there was going to be a second campaign that showed the efficacy of nonviolence," he said, "I would have to do it, something I had never done before." Like King, Lawson used the Bible to unite and inspire. "When I told the story of Exodus and Moses and the slaves being emancipated, I used that story . . . as one of the earliest examples of the nonviolent struggle," Lawson said. "I said that . . . if you look between the lines, you know that Moses and Joshua had to do a certain amount of organizing, getting people ready to leave Egypt."

The students at Shaw and elsewhere energized and nationalized the movement. The Nashville student group, inspired by Lawson and led by Marion Barry, John Lewis, and Diane Nash, among others, provided essential leadership. The students began to leave their college campuses. Soon they would fan out across the South, going door to door trying to get Black people to attempt to register to vote. Ella Baker advised the young activists and helped connect them to older activists, but she also warned the students not to be manipulated or dominated by the movement's established leaders. "This inclination toward group-centered leadership," she said, "rather than toward a leader-centered group pattern of organization, was refreshing indeed to those of the older group who bear the scars of the battle, the frustrations and the disillusionment that come when the prophetic leader turns out to have heavy feet of clay."

Soon after, Roy Wilkins pushed back against King. The NAACP leader complained in an April 27 letter that King and his allies had been bashing the nation's oldest civil rights organization for its conservative tactics. "We seek the same goals and we have the same enemies . . . At the same time we feel aggrieved over this unwarranted attack."

It was no wonder that reporters said King looked like a much older man. Coretta, too, grew weary. "The pressure of all this dulls you," she said. "Or perhaps you grow better prepared for anything. When some men came one night and burned a cross on the lawn, Martin was away and the children were asleep. But when I went outside and looked, I wasn't afraid. It just seemed like a piece of wood burning to me."

King accepted the personal sacrifice required, he said, even if he felt exhausted at times:

At times I think I'm a pretty unprepared symbol. But people cannot devote themselves to a great cause without finding someone who becomes the personification of the cause. People cannot become devoted to Christianity until they find Christ, to democracy until they find Lincoln and Jefferson and Roosevelt, to Communism until they find Marx and Lenin and Stalin. I know that this is a righteous cause and that by being connected with it I am connected with a transcendent value of right.

But nothing could have prepared King for the role of "full-fledged martyr," as *Time* magazine described him. Each week brought hundreds of letters, phone calls, and visitors to his home or office, announced and unannounced. Edward Kosner, then a reporter for the *New York Post*, recalled phoning King's home at three in the morning to get his response to a story. "The phone rang five or six times, and then a sleepy but recognizable voice answered," Kosner said. "I popped my question, and then King replied, 'I would say comma . . .'" Not only did King dictate a crisp, clear quote, but he supplied the punctuation, too.

With every quote for a newspaper reporter, every letter, every sermon, and every speech, he attracted attention and followers, planting seeds that would grow at times and in places he could have never imagined. On July 29, 1960, for example, King spoke to a crowd of about two thousand people at Calvary Baptist Church in Oklahoma City. A twenty-seven-year-old man named James Meredith happened to be in Oklahoma that day, having stopped for the night on a drive from California to his home in Mississippi. Meredith had followed news of King while serving in the air force, and he was thrilled at the chance to hear the minister speak. "It was the most impressive thing I had ever experienced, because the place was really crowded. I couldn't get close to the building," Meredith said in an interview sixty years later. "But to see the excitement of the people was something I had never witnessed before . . . I mean, he was a phenomenon." Meredith said he felt like he'd been fighting white supremacy since he was four years old. He didn't care for King's philosophy of nonviolence, but that was only a matter of tactics, in his mind, and not enough to diminish his admiration. King, he said, "was the greatest example of what I wanted to be . . . He was the greatest inspiration . . . You see, he *had* the people!"

"The Negro wants his freedom," King said that night in Oklahoma City, "and he wants his freedom now. The Negro has come to re-evaluate himself and has come to feel that he is somebody."

That was exactly it, said Meredith, who got home to Mississippi and wrote King a series of letters, describing the ways in which he agreed and disagreed with the preacher. "I thought he needed my advice," Meredith said.

King didn't respond, but their paths would cross again.

On May 4, Martin and Coretta hosted the white writer Lillian Smith for dinner. After the meal, King offered to drive Smith to Emory University Hospital, where the sixty-two-year-old novelist was undergoing treatment for cancer.

"As we sat talking before Miss Smith got out, I noticed a police car cruising by," King recalled in an interview a year later. "When we started back the police stopped us, suspicious, I guess, at seeing a white woman leave a car filled with Negroes." The officer issued a citation for driving with an Alabama driver's license when he should have, by that time, acquired a Georgia license.

Later the same month, King returned to Montgomery to stand trial in his income-tax case. In 1956, he had reported income of $9,150. The state, which had reportedly never prosecuted anyone for perjury on a tax return, claimed King's true income had been $16,162. Testimony showed, however, that King had been reimbursed for roughly $7,000 in travel expenses, which accounted for the difference between his actual income and the income figure alleged by the state. King produced detailed diaries and receipts to prove it.

After three hours and forty-five minutes of deliberations, the all-white jury returned a verdict of not guilty, to King's visible relief.

Another legal problem arose at the same time when Montgomery police commissioner L. B. Sullivan filed a libel suit in county court against Ralph Abernathy, three other ministers, and *The New York Times*. The suit came in response to a full-page ad printed in the *Times* to solicit funds for King's legal defense in the tax case. The ad had accused Alabama officials of terrorizing peaceful protesters, but it had included false and exaggerated statements about the actions of police and government officials, which the plaintiffs said had damaged their reputations. The case would go on to become a landmark of First Amendment law, but for now, as King's associates faced the possibility of years in court and crippling fines, it was just another source of stress.

Adam Clayton Powell Jr., the powerful Black congressman from New York, created yet another challenge when he attacked King in the press, calling him a "captive of socialist interests," as *The Pittsburgh Courier* put it, for his close ties to advisers Levison and Rustin. King, Rustin, and A. Philip Randolph were planning to picket the upcoming Democratic and Republican national conventions. Powell opposed the protests, and he leveled a private threat: call off the pickets, or he would publicly allege that King and Rustin were lovers.

It wasn't true, Rustin said, but King worried the allegation would damage his reputation.

"I decided that the best thing to do under these pressures, since I knew Dr. King was distressed," Rustin explained, "was to say, 'Well, I resign.'" Rustin was disappointed, however, when King accepted his resignation from the SCLC. It was a sign of King's greatest flaw as a leader, an ironic flaw for a protest leader, Rustin said: he hated conflict.

The sit-in movement spread to Atlanta. In early March 1960, Black students had been denied service at a lunch counter at Rich's department store, the same store where Daddy King had faced insult when he had tried to take young M.L. to buy shoes. Two weeks later, students picketed the downtown store. The protests quieted over the summer but resumed in the fall and spread to stores and lunch counters around the city. The leaders—including Julian Bond, Roslyn Pope, Marian Wright, and Lonnie King (no relation)— urged King to join them.

At first, King seemed reluctant to challenge white officials in his home-town. He and his family were sewn into the city's fabric. King's sister, Christine, was engaged to marry Isaac Farris, an army veteran and linotypist at the *Atlanta Daily News*. King and his brother, A.D., now pastoring a church in Newnan, Georgia, would perform the ceremony. M.L.'s old girlfriend Juanita Sellers, now married, would serve as a bridesmaid. Coretta, pregnant with her third child, would serve as matron of honor. There was only one snag. Christine had purchased her wedding dress from Rich's. She didn't want to violate the boycott, but the dress had already been paid for and altered, so she asked a Black friend who worked at the store to pick it up for her.

Atlanta's mayor, William B. Hartsfield, was the same mayor who had presided over the city's gala for the premiere of *Gone with the Wind*, when ten-year-old Martin Luther King Jr. had dressed in slave rags and sung with his church choir. Hartsfield considered himself progressive. "We're a city too busy to hate," he said. "Atlanta does not cling to the past. People who swear on the old southern traditions don't know what the hell they are." When Hartsfield talked about getting tough on rabble rousers, he wasn't talking about the Black protesters. "What happened in Little Rock won't happen here," he said. "When racists come in *this* town, they know they're going to get their heads knocked together."

Ivan Allen Jr., president of the Atlanta Chamber of Commerce, bragged: "Racial peace will make it possible for Atlanta to continue the fantastic growth of the past twenty years."

King, like his father, felt inclined to accept the officials' proclamations as honest. "I am optimistic," he said, "and I base it on Atlanta itself . . . Here we have all the forces on both sides, but the forces of defiance are not as strong as those who realize it's futile to stand on the beaches of history and try to hold back the tide." King walked a fine line in Atlanta. The established Black leadership, which included his father, did not welcome Martin Jr.'s participation.

The elders had access to the white power structure and "they didn't want that undermined," as Charles Black, one of the student organizers, put it. Young student activists viewed King warily, too. "But Martin was a great conciliator, a great listener," said Black. "He could find the middle ground so no one was angry."

King was indeed a great conciliator. But his success came from his willingness to back up words with action. He proved it again at 11:00 a.m. on October 19 in Atlanta, as he joined students in a sit-in at the snack bar at Rich's. From the snack bar, they went by elevator to the sixth-floor Magnolia Room, the store's most elegant restaurant. When they refused to leave, King and fifty-one others were arrested.

King understood the powerful message his imprisonment sent and the media coverage it would draw, and he therefore refused to pay his $500 bond and refused the food he was served by his jailers. King, Bernard Lee, and Lonnie King shared a cell, sang songs, and played checkers. Charges were quickly dropped and the prisoners released, but King remained behind bars. Officials in DeKalb County said he had violated the terms of his probation for the traffic violation he'd received earlier in the year while driving with Lillian Smith. "It was such a minor case," as King later said, that he didn't realize his lawyer had entered a guilty plea.

Judge Oscar Mitchell found King guilty of violating his parole and sentenced him to four months of hard labor in Georgia's public-works camp. King's lawyer complained that his client should be released on bond while he appealed his probation violation, but the judge said no. Every Black man and woman in Georgia knew what hard labor in a prison work camp meant. It meant chain gangs. It meant hot, dusty work on remote roads where bodies easily and permanently disappeared. It happened often enough to inspire a folk song, "Another Man Done Gone." Coretta wept as she and Martin met briefly in a holding cell. Five months pregnant, she worried Martin would still be in custody when the baby was born.

"You have to be strong for me," he said. "I think we must prepare ourselves for the fact that I am going to have to serve this time."

At about four in the morning the next day, two white officers with flashlights roused King in his cell. They snapped handcuffs on his wrists, clasped chains to his legs, and clamped the chains to a hook on the floorboard of the police car.

They drove more than six hours along dark, empty roads, the white lawmen talking to each other but never to King. When he complained his handcuffs were too tight, the troopers made them tighter.

"It was a long ride," King said. "I didn't know where they were taking me."

21

"Kennedy to the Rescue!"

KING REACHED THE Reidsville penitentiary, two hundred miles from Atlanta, early in the morning. The prison was a squat concrete terror that, except for the looming guard towers, resembled a giant warehouse. King was stripped of his belongings, told to put on an inmate's uniform, and locked in a narrow cell, alone.

The date was October 25, 1960, two weeks before Americans would choose a new president in a close contest between Republican vice president Richard Nixon and Democratic senator John F. Kennedy. Cold War politics, not civil rights, had dominated the candidates' messages and the mainstream media's campaign coverage. At home, most white Americans enjoyed an age of unprecedented affluence. The economy surged and income inequality shrank. The suburbs sprawled, the growth fueled by the twin engines of middle-class prosperity and the resettlement of white people from cities to suburbs. Three out of five Americans owned their own homes, and they decked out those homes with the latest electronic gear, including dishwashers, record players, televisions, washing machines, blenders, and refrigerators, much of it made in American factories. The race between Nixon and Kennedy remained too close to call in the final weeks of the campaign, which meant the candidates approached Black voters cautiously, eager to win their support in the North without angering white voters in the South.

King had met Kennedy twice and had come away unimpressed by the Massachusetts senator. "I did not feel at that time that there was much difference between Kennedy and Nixon," he later recalled. If the conversations had gone differently, King and Kennedy might have discovered much in common. Though King was twelve years younger than Kennedy, they both had powerful, domineering fathers. Both men were handsome, charming, ambitious, and intellectually curious. But they had not developed a strong rapport, and Kennedy had not acted on King's advice to clarify his commitment to Black voters. Nixon and King, on the other hand, had spoken often and had a solid relationship.

Two weeks earlier, the *Atlanta Daily World* had reported that enthusiasm for the Republican ticket had been "running high" among Black Baptist ministers in Atlanta. The Party of Lincoln still enjoyed the loyalty of many Black voters in the South. Daddy King, M.L., and A.D. had all attended a meeting at which "it was shown conclusively" that Atlanta's leading Black preachers favored Nixon and his running mate, Henry Cabot Lodge Jr. The article didn't mention specifically whether M.L. or A.D. had endorsed the Republicans, but it did report that Daddy King "expressed approval of Nixon and Lodge."

In a letter written the same week, Stanley Levison reminded King of the importance of nonpartisanship. "A long view must be taken," Levison wrote, "which sees that no matter what immediate advantages can be gained by having you speak for one party now, what is lost is a rare leader whose selflessness has been long established and highly prized by the people."

But King's incarceration posed a challenge to both candidates. Should they risk taking a stand? Advisers to Nixon, including Jackie Robinson, urged the Republican candidate to phone the jailed civil rights leader or to say something to the news media in his defense. Robinson had tears in his eyes after he met with Nixon and failed to persuade him to act. "Nixon doesn't deserve to win," the retired baseball legend said.

Meanwhile, before learning King was in jail, the Kennedy campaign had asked Frank D. Reeves, a campaign adviser on civil rights, to explore the possibility of getting the civil rights leader involved in Kennedy's campaign. Reeves had met King at the Fulton County Jail. "He said . . . he was much concerned about his wife, so that anything we might do to reassure her that he was all right he would certainly appreciate," Reeves recalled in a 1967 interview. Back in New York, Reeves met with Senator Kennedy, Harris Wofford, and JFK's brother Robert, who was serving as his campaign manager. "The . . . first suggestion I made was that the senator himself would send a telegram to Coretta, Mrs. King, indicating his concern and asking if there was anything he might do," Reeves said. Instead, Kennedy called her.

Coretta was getting ready to leave the house to meet Daddy King at their lawyer's office when her phone rang, John Kennedy on the line. Kennedy expressed his concern. He said he knew this was difficult for her. He said he was aware that she was expecting a child. He instructed her to get in touch if she or Martin needed his help. Coretta thanked him. The call lasted no more than ninety seconds.

When Coretta told Daddy King about the call, he announced instantly that he was switching his vote from Nixon to Kennedy, and that he intended to make no secret of it.

Reporters showed little interest in Kennedy's call to Coretta. The story merited a two-inch item on page 22 of *The New York Times*. A few days later, Georgia's governor, S. Ernest Vandiver, criticized Kennedy for meddling, for making "a phone call to the house of the foremost racial agitator in the country." But while criticizing the presidential candidate in public, Vandiver didn't mention that he, too, had received a private phone call about King from Kennedy.

A former World War II bomber pilot, Vandiver had run for office in 1958 on the pledge he would maintain segregated schools. When Martin Luther King Jr. had announced his move from Montgomery to Atlanta, Vandiver had declared him "not welcome in Georgia." Yet he had been the more moderate of two candidates in his run for his office, and he had sought to separate himself from the most radical segregationists. Vandiver had also endorsed his fellow Democrat for president. Now Kennedy had put the governor in a tight spot.

"He asked the assistance of the governor's office in seeking the release of Martin Luther King," Vandiver said in a 1967 interview that was not released until a historian disclosed it thirty years later. "He, of course, was very much interested and worried for fear that any activity that we might engage in might become public," Vandiver continued. "I assured him that this was a personal conversation between candidate Kennedy and I, and that nobody other than my wife was aware of the telephone call. We then determined that we would do what we could to use the governor's office to secure the release of Martin Luther King."

Vandiver asked his brother-in-law to call a friend of Oscar Mitchell, the judge who had sentenced King. "Of course," Vandiver said, "it would have been, I think, political suicide, with the temper of the times as it was, for it to have been publicized ... However, with my interest in seeing that Kennedy was elected president, I was willing to take that chance."

Robert Kennedy followed up with a phone call to Mitchell, though by then the judge had already made up his mind to free King. After eight days of incarceration, King was released on a $2,000 bond.

"I think I received a new understanding of the meaning of suffering," King wrote in a letter to L. Harold DeWolf, "and I came away more convinced than ever that unearned suffering is redemptive."

While several of the men close to Kennedy would claim credit for helping to free King, white southerners like Vandiver shunned attention until years later, when they grew comfortable enough to talk about or, in some cases, exaggerate the work they did in the 1960s. The story of King's release attracted little attention in the white press, as Vandiver had hoped. But the Black press celebrated the call to Coretta: "Kennedy to the Rescue!" read the headline in *The Philadelphia Tribune*. The civil rights advisers Harris Wofford and Sargent Shriver, along with the Black journalist Louis Martin, rushed to print a pamphlet for distribution in Black churches in an under-the-radar campaign to remind Black voters that Kennedy, not Nixon, had cared enough to act, that Kennedy, not Nixon, had helped to liberate the nation's leading Black activist. They printed fifty thousand copies of the pamphlet—"the blue bomb," as Wofford called it, for the cheap blue paper on which it was printed—and local Black organizations went on to print and distribute many more.

King, meanwhile, issued a statement that came close to an endorsement, saying he was "deeply grateful to Senator Kennedy for the genuine concern he expressed . . . [He] exhibited moral courage of a high order."

In one of the closest elections in American history, Kennedy won by about 100,000 votes. Many political observers said Kennedy owed his election to the Black electorate, as about 70 percent of the Black vote went his way.

Nixon blamed voter fraud. He blamed the press. He blamed the Eisenhower administration for failing to help King. And he blamed Black voters whose minds had been changed, as he put it, by "a couple of phone calls."

King appreciated Kennedy's willingness to take a risk and act on principle, knowing he might lose more votes in the South than he would gain in the North. Nixon, King said years later, missed an opportunity to take an early stand on civil rights. "So this is why I really considered him a moral coward and one who was really unwilling to take a courageous step and take a risk," he said. "And I am convinced that because of that he lost the election."

King and others expected Kennedy to remember his debt to the Black voters. Yet there was one Black voter who had not cast a ballot: Georgia officials said Martin Luther King Jr. hadn't lived in Atlanta long enough to gain eligibility to vote, and Alabama officials said he was too late to pay the $1.50 poll tax required to file an absentee ballot in Montgomery.

King's role in the election cemented his status as "the best-known leader of Negro opinion in the United States," as the influential *Atlanta Constitution* columnist and editor Ralph McGill called him. King's enemies were to blame for his growing influence, McGill wrote. By arresting him on weak charges, by sentencing him to four months in prison, and by handcuffing him and transporting him to Reidsville under cover of dark, King's opponents were advertising their prejudiced practices and beliefs to the world. "Across a span of three years," McGill wrote, "Dr. King's extremist opposition has succeeded in making him an international symbol of a persecuted man."

Though King felt deeply rooted in the customs and values of the South and focused much of his energy on the transformation of southern society, his Christian optimism compelled him to call out injustice everywhere— including the North, where his audiences included his largest financial supporters and strongest political backers. King had seen the phenomenon of northern racism during his student years in Connecticut, Pennsylvania, and Massachusetts. Though northerners claimed to be more sympathetic, their behavior all too often revealed the lie. White people in the North, same as in the South, justified segregation by saying Black people couldn't handle integration, that they would drag down white schools and neighborhoods, that they were not yet qualified for better jobs and higher pay. In a New York speech, King told members of the National Urban League:

> They are never honest enough to admit that the academic and cultural lags in the Negro community are themselves the result of segregation and discrimination. There is a pressing need for a liberalism in the North which is truly liberal, a liberalism that firmly believes in integration in its own community as well as in the deep South. There is need for the type of liberal who not only rises up with righteous indignation when a Negro is lynched in Mississippi, but will be equally incensed when a Negro is denied the right to live in his neighborhood, or join his professional association, or secure a top position in his business. This is no day to pay mere lip service to integration, we must pay life service to it.

On January 30, 1961, while Martin was in Chicago for a speech, Coretta gave birth to her third child. They named him Dexter, in honor of the Montgomery church in which Martin had begun his career. Yoki was six. Marty was three. Yoki and Marty were old enough now to know their father was someone special—that he appeared on television and radio, that he traveled often for work, and, also, that he went to jail.

"Why did Daddy go to jail?" Yoki had asked after her father's arrest in Atlanta.

"Did Daddy go to jail on an airplane?" asked Marty, who knew his father spent a lot of time on airplanes and who told his mother that he intended to be a pilot when he grew up so he could fly his father anywhere he wanted to go.

"Yes," Coretta said, trying to make it sound like an honor. "Your daddy is a brave and kind man. He went to jail to help people. Some people don't have enough to eat, nor do they have comfortable homes in which to live, or enough clothing to wear. Daddy went to jail to make it possible for all people to have these things. Don't worry, your daddy will be coming back."

Their father always came back, and he showered his children with attention when he got home. He sat them atop the refrigerator and let them leap into his arms. He tossed balls with them in the yard. Inevitably, though, he left home again before long. He couldn't do his job from an office, and he didn't want to. Audiences energized him. He loved meeting new people. After the election, he traveled to Nigeria as a guest of the government to celebrate its independence from Great Britain. In New York, he appeared in a nationally televised debate on the merits and strategy of integration with James J. Kilpatrick, conservative editor of *The Richmond News Leader* and a strong opponent of court-ordered desegregation. King's busy schedule of travel also afforded him opportunities to spend time with women other than Coretta.

"Well . . . of course when a man travels, like you and I do," he told fellow activist James Farmer, "there are bound to be women, and there have been a lot of women."

Four years earlier, on October 5, 1956, King had spoken at Mt. Olivet Baptist Church in Petersburg, Virginia, for the twenty-first annual convention of the Virginia NAACP. He'd been invited by the Reverend Wyatt Tee Walker. In the audience that night was Dorothy Cotton, a twenty-six-year-old native of Goldsboro, North Carolina, recently married and relocated to Petersburg, where she had joined Walker's church and participated in a campaign to integrate the city's libraries. Before King's speech, Cotton stepped to the lectern to recite a poem.

That evening, King was a guest at the home of Reverend Walker and his wife, Theresa Ann. Dorothy Cotton and other members of the local Parish Club served a chicken dinner.

"When we were walking around the table with these big platters of food, I could hear these flirtatious comments that Martin was making, and that was okay, because we were all by that time giggling and acting silly," Cotton recalled later. She was short and slender, with wide-set eyes and big cheeks that ballooned when she smiled. That night, she smiled when King complimented her on the poem she'd recited in church and on the beauty of her legs.

In the same interview, when asked to describe King as a person, Cotton replied: "Who he was as a person is a silly playboy. Yes, he was, he really was." That a married male clergy leader would flirt so brazenly at a church function—and with a married woman—said a great deal about attitudes toward women among preachers. Cotton said she left the dinner that night with King. "We ended up singing and having a great time," she said. A powerful emotion stirred her, she said, something more than a physical attraction. "I felt kind of a connection even then when we were serving the dinner," she said. "From that day on I felt like I discovered a brother I had never had."

Her father, Claude Daniel Foreman, was a tobacco and cotton farmer who didn't make it past the third grade in school. Her mother gave birth to four children in four years and died in her fifth pregnancy. Dorothy recalled her childhood sadly, including the day she walked alone from school to the doctor's office, had her tonsils removed, walked home, and went to bed, all alone. "I recall nothing nurturing in my home environment," she said. "The beatings from my father's belt . . . or a switch were very often the order of the day."

Yet Cotton, a year younger than King, possessed a joyful nature that defied her life's hardships. Theresa Ann Walker called her "a bubbly, nice lady." Laughter and song, Cotton once said, kept her from internalizing her pain. Her sunny personality warmed everyone in her orbit, even the man who beat her. "Dorothy can be washing the dishes," her father said, "and while she's drying a plate she stops midway, holding up the plate until she finishes the song. Then goes on to finish drying the plate."

King visited Petersburg four times from 1956 to 1960. After his 1960 visit, he asked Wyatt Tee Walker to move to Atlanta and become executive director of the Southern Christian Leadership Conference. Walker accepted the job and brought along two associates—Jim Wood and Dorothy Cotton. Dorothy's husband, George Cotton, drove her to Atlanta, stayed a few days, and returned to Virginia. Cotton rented a room in the home of King's new secretary, Dora McDonald, planning to stay about six months in Atlanta while working as Walker's administrative assistant. But she never left. "The movement became my life," she said, "and my husband wasn't too interested in it. I wasn't ending my marriage, but we grew apart and the visits eventually stopped." In time they would divorce.

Cotton became one of the most influential women in the SCLC's male-dominated hierarchy. Her greatest value, one SCLC leader said, was in moderating disputes and soothing the big egos that made up the movement. Almost everyone liked her. Cotton and King, meanwhile, would become more than friends, more than colleagues. And, though she would never publicly reveal her secret, Cotton would tell friends that she and King were as close and devoted as husband and wife.

"He loved his wife," Cotton said in one interview, "but he also, he loved some other folks, too."

Others in King's inner circle knew of the relationship but kept it secret. Cotton, Juanita Abernathy said years later, "did everything but call herself Martin's woman."

"We observe today not a victory of party but a celebration of freedom," John F. Kennedy said in opening his inauguration address, promising to dedicate his presidency to the cause of liberty, saying he hoped that all nations would join in freedom to "explore the stars, conquer the deserts, eradicate disease." He made no mention, however, of race other than stating his commitment to human rights "at home and around the world."

At the start of 1961, King had no clear plan for the year ahead. He was not invited to Kennedy's inauguration. The new president's team decided that civil rights would not be an important part of the administration's first-year agenda, in part because the new president didn't want to alienate the southern whites who had helped him win office. There were no Black members of the Senate at the time, and there were only half a dozen Black members of the House of Representatives. Kennedy saw little to be gained in pressing for major legislative reform or taking extensive executive action on civil rights. Meanwhile, the integration of the schools in the American South wasn't happening. Some white officials had chosen to close schools rather than integrate them. In other cases, white parents had withdrawn their children when Black students had arrived, often sending them to new or expanded all-white private schools as an alternative.

Walker had taken charge of the SCLC, promising to help the organization lead or at least ride the wave of direct-action protests that were being orchestrated mostly by students. Ella Baker had urged the SCLC to develop adult education classes, which would boost voter registration efforts, and she had traveled to Highlander Folk School in Tennessee, a training center for progressive activists, to see how its citizenship education programs worked. With Highlander facing closure as a result of legal harassment, Baker and others urged the SCLC to take over the school's training program and expand it to recruit and educate volunteers throughout the South. Walker and King supported the idea. Dorothy Cotton began recruiting students. Septima P. Clark, the school's program coordinator, directed the training. Cotton and Clark had experience as community organizers, especially when it came to working beyond the structure of the church, where women were more apt to participate than men. They planned to train 240 instructors and help them start classes across the South, teaching literacy and promoting voter registration.

Though the plan to use the Highlander Folk School's program had come from women and would be operated largely by women, the SCLC chose a man to run the new project: a young Black minister named Andrew Young, who had been leading the youth ministry for the National Council of Churches in New York.

Young, like King, came from a respected family. But Young was the son of a dentist, not a preacher. Young's parents had tried to protect him from the pain of southern racism. They had also kept him away from jazz and blues, no easy thing to do in their hometown of New Orleans, in the hopes of raising a sophisticate. The Youngs belonged to a Congregational church, which emphasized civic responsibility and mission work. Following in his father's footsteps, Young attended Howard University and took the premed courses necessary for a career in dentistry. But he chose the ministry, a move that struck his father as a step down in respectability. In leading his first parish in Thomasville, Georgia, Young lived for the first time among poor Black families. He was twenty-eight years old when he joined the SCLC, but he possessed an older man's levelheadedness. He would become a tactician who relished negotiating with white opponents, a moderate who sometimes angered his more fervent associates, and an adviser King could trust. But Young shared King's view about the role of women in the movement, telling one interviewer: "Women can maintain and strengthen, but the protest role, the role of shaping the world, the creative role in a social and political sense, I think is the man's."

King maintained his hectic pace, delivering as many as five speeches a day, raising money for the SCLC. Letters poured into his office asking for help finding jobs, paying off debts, dealing with landlords, helping with homework. A man from Hamlet, North Carolina, asked King to help him find "a nice young lady . . . around 25 or 34 years old and I don't care if she have been married . . . and make sure the girl has a High School education."

At times it seemed that he sought to make the nation his congregation. Even as he grew more political, more powerful, and more respected, he drew his authority from the Bible and relished every opportunity to speak from a pulpit. "In the quiet recesses of my heart," he said, "I am fundamentally a clergyman, a Baptist preacher." His mission, he said, was not simply to change the laws and values of America but to redeem the nation's soul. King's concept of leadership came from the church, from the examples set by his father and grandfather and countless other preachers and biblical prophets who had shaped his heart and mind. He believed that if he spoke the

Word of God, people would listen and be moved to change. For his Black audiences, especially, he hoped the Word of God would inspire confidence that their cause was righteous, that their faith would be rewarded, however unlikely it seemed at the time.

In the fall of 1960, he preached a sermon called "The Seeking God," in which he said many people lose their way like sheep, "just nibbling sweet grass," as they follow the lure of transitory pleasure. The social drinker becomes an alcoholic, he warned. The curiosity seeker becomes a drug addict. The married man who enjoys the flattery of a woman becomes a cheating spouse. But God is our "Cosmic Shepard [sic]," searching for us and guiding us back to the flock, he said. In the spring of 1961, in a sermon he gave many times, one called "Loving Your Enemies," King urged his congregation to remember that Jesus's command to love one's enemies is not pious utopianism; it's practical and realistic and essential to bringing change, especially for Black people of the South:

> Put us in jail, and we will go in with humble smiles on our faces, still loving you. Bomb our homes and threaten our children, and we will still love you . . . But be assured that we will wear you down by our capacity to suffer. And one day we will win our freedom, but not only will we win freedom for ourselves, we will so appeal to your heart and conscience that we will win you in the process. And our victory will be a double victory. This seems to me the only answer and the only way to make our nation a new nation and our world a new world. Love is the absolute power.

A Gallup survey at the start of 1961 asked southerners: Do you think the day will ever come in the South when whites and Negroes will be going to the same schools, eating in the same restaurants, and generally sharing the same public accommodations? Yes, said 78 percent of the respondents, compared with 45 percent four years earlier. But, as Gallup pointed out, expecting it to happen wasn't the same as liking it.

A week after Kennedy's inauguration, Frank Sinatra organized a tribute to King at Carnegie Hall. Harry Belafonte, among others, had been recruiting celebrities to support the civil rights movement. The lineup at Carnegie Hall also included Mahalia Jackson, Sammy Davis Jr., Tony Bennett, Count Basie, and Dean Martin. The event raised more than $50,000 for the SCLC (the equivalent of about $450,000 today).

In an internal memo marked "confidential," SCLC officials discussed how to present King to the public to make the best use of his fame: "Devout, reverent but not pious," the memo said. "Humble, determined, modest but not retiring. Dedicated but not fanatic. Courageous, aggressive but not intimidating."

King was the nation's best-known civil rights leader, but he was far from the only one, which meant the SCLC faced challenges in fundraising as well as in the fight for attention from the media, the Kennedy administration, and the public. In the early part of 1961, James Farmer became the new national director of the Congress of Racial Equality (CORE) and began to take the kind of bold action that had eluded King and the SCLC. Farmer decided to send Black and white bus riders into the South to test the real-world impact of the 1960 Supreme Court decision in *Boynton v. Virginia*, which had declared segregation in interstate bus and rail stations unconstitutional. They would call the excursions "Freedom Rides."

In 1947, another group of activists had launched their own freedom rides, called the Journey of Reconciliation. But the Journey of Reconciliation had been limited to mid-southern states. This new trip would be more dangerous. The first Greyhound bus headed south from Washington, D.C., in May, with plans to arrive in New Orleans on May 17, 1960, the sixth anniversary of *Brown v. Board of Education*. The planners hoped for a conflict that would generate national news coverage and pressure the federal government to get involved.

Conflict came quickly. As the riders neared Anniston, Alabama, a white mob attacked passengers with long lengths of pipe and set fire to the bus. In Birmingham, angry white men waited at the bus station, cradling clubs and pipes. There were no law enforcement officers in sight, despite the fact that city hall was two blocks away. "From reports of our policemen," said

Birmingham police commissioner Theophilus Eugene "Bull" Connor, "it seems that both sides were from out of town—the ones who got whipped and the ones who did the whipping." More than a dozen people were hospitalized, but no one was immediately arrested in either attack. Pictures of the bloodied riders appeared in newspapers and on televisions around the world.

Robert F. Kennedy, the newly appointed U.S. attorney general, phoned King, asking him to use his influence to stop the rides until after the president's upcoming meeting with Soviet premier Nikita Khrushchev. The attorney general feared that news of attacks on protesters in the South would embarrass his brother. It's not clear whether King could have stopped the Freedom Rides, but he nevertheless told Robert Kennedy that the protest could be ended with a federal order banning segregated bus travel; unless that was forthcoming, the buses would roll, he said. And they did.

They rolled on to Montgomery, where, on the morning of May 20, the passengers encountered a mob of three hundred white men armed with bricks, bats, and bottles. The members of the mob attacked, swinging their weapons, hitting not only the riders but reporters and photographers, too. John Seigenthaler, an aide to Robert Kennedy at the U.S. Department of Justice, had been sent to attempt to ease the tension. A pipe-wielding Klansman attacked Seigenthaler from behind when he tried to help a girl being chased by the mob. Seigenthaler's limp body lay in the street for twenty-five minutes before he was taken to a hospital.

"First they started beating members of the press," said John Lewis, one of the passengers on the bus. "If you had a pad, a pencil, pen, you were beaten . . . left lying in the streets. Then they turned on the Freedom Riders . . . My seatmate was a young, white student named Jim Zwerg. We were cut off from the others. He was hit in the head. I was hit in the head with the Coca Cola crate." When Zwerg collapsed, three white men held him up so a white woman could kick him in the groin and punch him in the face "until she was too tired to swing again," according to *The Montgomery Advertiser*. "I was taken to a doctor's office," Lewis said, "where a patch was put on my head. Jim Zwerg was taken to a local hospital. He was so badly, so severely hurt."

Reporters toting portable television news cameras—a new technology—filmed the attacks and beamed the story around the world. Forty million American homes had television sets—exceeding the number of homes that received a daily newspaper for the first time.

King, who had been out of town for a speaking engagement, hurried to Montgomery and spoke to reporters. He also stayed in touch with Robert Kennedy, who sent federal marshals to protect the bus riders after Governor John Patterson refused to ensure their safety. "I guess he called me every day," King said later of Robert Kennedy, "sometimes two or three times a day when we were in Montgomery on freedom rides."

More than a thousand people filled Ralph Abernathy's church the night of May 21, 1961, in support of the Freedom Riders, with supporters of SNCC, CORE, and the SCLC coming together. They sang hymns and listened to a series of speakers while outside the church an angry mob of white men swarmed, throwing bottles and bricks at houses. The mob overturned a car and set it afire. People inside the church worried that the church might be set aflame, too. "Dr. King was very upset, panicky you might say," recalled Burke Marshall of the Justice Department, who listened in on some of King's calls with Kennedy. But when he got off the phone, King leaned forward calmly, rested his arms on the lectern, and spoke soothingly to the gathering:

> Troops are on the way into Montgomery right now and will be here very soon. They have requested that all of us stay in here for the time being . . . We must be sure that we adhere absolutely to non-violence. Now, it's very easy for us to get angry and bitter and even violent in a moment like this, but I think this is the testing point. Now, we had to go out a few minutes ago and counsel with some of our own people who were getting to the point of returning violence. And we don't want to do that. We *can't* do that. We have won the moral victory.

They sheltered all night in the church. King gave phone interviews to out-of-town reporters and remained in frequent contact with Robert Kennedy. Children slept in a basement meeting room. Adults stretched out on pews. In his remarks, King urged the audience to acknowledge the role of government in the fight for justice, and to insist on action from elected officials. "The law may not be able to make a man love me, but it can keep him from lynching me," he said. "The fact is that habits, if not the hearts of men, have been, and are being changed every day by federal action." There would be voter registration drives ahead, he said, as well as protests to push the integration of public parks, schools, lunch counters, and more. The Freedom Riders showed the way, and the way was nonviolent.

Thousands of white people rioted and raged. A few of the agitators charged into the church. Others threw firebombs through the windows. The explosives were quickly extinguished. Robert Kennedy sent four hundred federal marshals to protect those in the church. The next day he sent two hundred more.

"We were expecting the church to be burned down," said Bernard Lafayette Jr., one of the Freedom Riders. When King eventually walked his people out, through the mob, Lafayette expected a slaughter, even with the marshals present. But he followed anyway. "I don't know why the mob didn't attack," he said. The quiet, orderly way they marched seemed to have a hypnotic effect on the angry white crowd. "We got through that night, but it was because of the leadership of Martin Luther King."

Robert Kennedy urged the Freedom Riders to suspend their journey, but they refused, departing a few days later for Jackson, Mississippi, escorted as far as the Alabama border by troops and reconnaissance aircraft.

"All the kids knew that death was a real possibility," said Diane Nash, the twenty-two-year-old student leader, who had already been jailed twice.

King chose not to join them, disappointing some of the riders.

"Several of us wanted Dr. King to travel with us to Jackson," John Lewis said.

"The cause of human decency and black liberation demands that you physically ride the buses with our gallant freedom riders," wrote Robert Williams, an NAACP chapter president from North Carolina, in a telegram to King. "No sincere leader asks his followers to make sacrifices that he himself will not endure."

King had reasons for caution. For one, he feared that an arrest would violate the terms of his probation for his old charge of driving without a proper Georgia license. But that failed to silence his critics.

In Jackson, police arrested all twenty-seven riders as they tried to enter the whites-only cafeteria and restrooms. The arrests and attacks on the buses were designed to thwart a growing social movement, but they had the opposite effect. The men and women who were arrested turned their jail cells into "universities of nonviolence," as James Lawson put it, teaching fellow inmates about Gandhi. The Freedom Rides helped CORE expand its membership and influence. They helped nationalize the movement for civil rights, as whites, clergy, and academics from the North joined the demonstrations and intensified their commitment to the cause.

King had helped jump-start the student movement. Yet it remained to be seen whether that younger generation would leave him behind. His decision not to ride the buses frustrated many younger supporters. "They questioned his reticence about participating in the Freedom Rides," Ella Baker said. "They questioned that very sharply, and I gather there were sharp confrontations with him to the point that, for the first time, some saw anger on his part."

Young Black people had launched "nothing less than a moral revolution," James Baldwin wrote, and that had created a gap between the revolutionaries and the official leadership. "It is because of this gap that King finds himself in such a difficult position. The pressures on him are tremendous, and they come from above and below." But King remained the key figure in the fight for racial justice, according to Baldwin, in no small part because the media continued to put him at the center of the action even when others, including Lawson and Farmer, had done more in recent days to shape the course of events. "He has succeeded, in a way no negro before him has managed to do, to carry the battle into the individual heart and make its resolution the province of the individual will," Baldwin wrote. "He has made it a matter, on both sides of the racial fence, of self-examination; and has incurred therefore the grave responsibility of continuing to lead in the path he has encouraged so many people to follow. How he will do this I do not know."

22

The New Emancipation Proclamation

ONE DAY IN the summer of 1961, King and his colleagues were driving along Highway 278 from Atlanta to Charleston, South Carolina. When they reached the small town of Warrenton, Georgia, more than a hundred miles outside Atlanta, they spotted a teenage boy with a folding table set up by the side of the road.

Tyrone Brooks, age fifteen, had heard that his hero, Martin Luther King Jr., would be passing through his town. Tyrone had filled brown bags with sandwiches and cookies for King and his colleagues. He had cups of cold lemonade waiting for them, too.

King stopped his car. He thanked Tyrone and asked the teen if he wanted to join the youth division of the movement. Tyrone said he had already started picketing his local board of education and was eager to do more. King got back on the road, leaving Tyrone inspired and in awe.

"He was so short," Tyrone said. "I thought he was going to be six-five."

"What happens to a man who becomes owned by a cause?" the journalist Mike Wallace had asked King in a televised interview a few months earlier. "What happens to you as you become the symbol of the segregation struggle? As a man?"

"It has its advantages and disadvantages," King answered coolly. "When you are aware that you are a symbol, it causes you to search your soul constantly, to go through this job of self-analysis, to see if you live up to all of the high and noble principles . . . You do lose some of your individual life, your private life."

Coretta put it differently: "He pays less attention to himself," she told a magazine writer. "There was a time when he was quite concerned about his personal appearance. Today I have to remind him he needs a new suit. Our trip to India in 1959 to study Gandhi's independence movement made a deep impression on him. He became even more committed to nonviolence and much less interested in material things. At times he has even talked seriously about whether or not he should own anything that's not absolutely necessary for the rest of the family."

Said Daddy King: "He is more serious, more dedicated and more fearless; he has lost the sense of protection of his own life . . . And he's more deeply religious . . . He has a faith in people, even those who have persecuted him, that's unbelievable."

The younger King, in an interview with a reporter from *Redbook* magazine, explained in more detail how five years as an activist and public figure had changed him:

First, of course, there is something very satisfying in what has happened to me. I have a strong feeling that I'm involved in a great movement and that I'm part of a struggle I know is right. Just being part of it is a tremendous satisfaction. And I'm sure I've become more serious. I don't think I've lost my sense of humor, but I know I've let many opportunities go by without using it . . . And I know that my religion has come to mean more to me than ever before. I have come to believe more and more in a personal God—not a process, but a person, a creative power with infinite love who answers prayers.

Coretta and the children didn't see Martin as much as they would have liked. The SCLC remained heavily dependent on King to raise money by making speeches, and the ongoing student-led protests compelled him to travel in hopes of generating more publicity and putting more pressure on the federal government. That left Coretta home alone with the children for long periods and forced her, she said, to embrace the roles of both mother and father. She abandoned attempts at establishing a routine for the children, letting them ignore bedtimes when their father came home. Their lives were less stressful in Atlanta than they had been in Montgomery, Coretta said, yet she wondered how the tension affected the children. "Yolanda, the eldest, who is nearly six," she said, "is a sensitive child, but she doesn't express many of the things she feels. We both think she's felt some insecurity, but I don't think it's serious. She does have trouble getting to sleep at night. Whenever Martin has the time, he's down on the floor with the children, full of humor and boyishness. But he doesn't have the time often enough."

King told the same interviewer he had no intention of stepping back from his responsibilities as a leader of the movement, but he looked forward to the moment, "someday," when he could devote more time to the "cultural, intellectual, and aesthetic ideas" he had "been pulled away from by this struggle."

His father didn't sound so sure that such a moment would ever come: "What he has done, he has done under a sense of compulsion," Martin Luther King Sr. said. "He didn't choose this role and he can't reject it."

When leaders become symbols, they often grow power-hungry or self-absorbed. They spend so much time talking to journalists, raising money, and making political deals that they get left behind by the revolutions they launched. But even as King let the Freedom Ride buses roll without him, he listened to and learned from the students. "I marveled at his patience," James Lawson said, "at his ability to sit still in a board meeting or a staff meeting and hear everything that went on . . . He had a wisdom and a calm." King tried not to alienate anyone who might be an ally, young or old, radical or conservative. "Yes, he pushed back," Lawson said, especially when it came to defending nonviolence as the key to his strategy, "but he tried to push back gently and lovingly."

On June 5, 1961, King called on President Kennedy to "issue a formal executive order declaring all forms of racial segregation illegal." He called it a second Emancipation Proclamation. "Just as Abraham Lincoln had the vision to see almost one hundred years ago that this nation could not exist half slave and half free," he said, "the present administration must have the insight to see that today the nation cannot exist half segregated and half integrated."

Meanwhile, the Freedom Rides pushed on through summer. New waves of volunteers, including religious leaders of various denominations, arrived from all over the country to join the campaign. Young people everywhere talked about and copied the sit-ins. The movement spread school by school, city by city, with imagination overpowering fear, action replacing inertia. By the fall, the Interstate Commerce Commission issued an order banning segregation in interstate bus terminals. Though segregation of that kind had already been deemed unconstitutional by the Supreme Court, the federal government's commitment to enforcing the law marked progress. Three major railroad companies serving the South ended segregation on their trains and in their terminals. Each victory sent expectations climbing higher. The Freedom Rides inspired a new group of determined activists to fan out across the South. Young Black and white people, men and women, Christians and Jews, northerners and southerners put their lives on the line because they sensed something important happening.

Nine months into his presidency, John F. Kennedy had not yet met with King. King's friend Harris Wofford had been pressing the White House for months to address the oversight, and, finally, a meeting was set for October 16, 1961. The botched Bay of Pigs invasion and the Cold War more generally had occupied much of Kennedy's attention, but King tried to get the president focused on civil rights and to make good on his promises to Black voters. King met first with Robert Kennedy, and then ate lunch at the White House with the president and the First Lady, Jacqueline Kennedy. King reminded Kennedy of his idea for a second Emancipation Proclamation, one declaring all segregation illegal under the terms of the Fourteenth Amendment. Kennedy said he would consider it. "Kennedy felt uncomfortable with

King," Wofford recalled, and King felt Kennedy lacked the courage to act on his beliefs around civil rights. Kennedy had the necessary political skill, King said, but it wasn't clear if he had the passion.

For Thanksgiving, the gospel singer Mahalia Jackson and her pianist Mildred Falls joined the Kings for dinner. Alberta and Coretta cooked. Juanita Abernathy and her children came, too, although Ralph was out of town on SCLC work. They ate roasted turkey, baked ham, greens, corn bread, and sweet potatoes, with pie and ice cream and coffee for dessert. "Here was a family in which people were thankful for the small things as well as the great," Mahalia wrote later.

Martin excused himself from the Thanksgiving table to take phone calls in his study. The callers were updating him on a growing protest movement in Albany, Georgia.

Earlier that fall, two young Black SNCC field workers—Charles Sherrod and Cordell Reagon—had started a voter registration campaign in Albany. It was a town of fifty-five thousand people, about 40 percent of them Black, closer to Tallahassee than Atlanta. Before the Civil War, cotton had dominated the economy and enslaved people outnumbered free people by a wide margin. There were still patches of cotton, clusters of cattle, and long rows of pecan trees, but by 1961 the economy relied on the Turner Air Force Base and the U.S. Marine Depot of Supplies. As in Atlanta, city leaders in Albany liked to brag about the fine relations between the races, pointing out that the flag at city hall had recently hung at half-mast to mark the death of a popular Black barber. They also boasted that the KKK and White Citizens' Councils had little presence in town. Notably, however, local white people seldom celebrated their most famous native: the singer Ray Charles, born in Albany on September 23, 1930.

Sherrod and Reagon had arrived in Albany filled with hope. Albany had parking meters and sidewalks. It had a newspaper. It had a Black middle class. It had a Black doctor and a Black lawyer. It had a Black college, Albany State College, where Sherrod and Reagon began recruiting. They were soon joined by Charles Jones, a lunch-counter protester and student organizer from Charlotte.

The young men set up an office in a run-down building, where plaster fell from the walls and the mimeograph machine worked intermittently, and began registering voters and listening to complaints about local issues. Dr. William G. Anderson had a medical office above a liquor store in the Black section of Albany, a neighborhood referred to by the locals as Harlem. He noticed Sherrod and Reagon doing their work. "They were rebuffed, they were intimidated, they were harassed," Anderson said. In October, when he heard that the young men were organizing a demonstration, the doctor and his wife, Norma, joined them. The movement quickly grew. Black preachers opened their churches for meetings. A new organization was born, called the Albany Movement, with Anderson as its president. Members of the Albany Movement, joined by members of SNCC, organized sit-ins at Albany's bus station, which had not been integrated, despite the Kennedy administration's recent order. The protesters were promptly arrested. More protesters arrived from Atlanta. They were arrested, too. Marches on city hall followed. By December 15, about five hundred people had been jailed.

"We will not stand for these trouble-makers coming into our city for the sole purpose of disturbing the peace and quiet of the city of Albany," said Laurie Pritchett, the police chief.

Anderson had met King when the famous preacher was a teenager in Atlanta. Anderson knew Ralph Abernathy, too, the men having been classmates at Alabama State. As the tension escalated in Albany, Anderson phoned King and Abernathy, seeking help.

King arrived by car, with a police escort, on December 15. Speaking to a packed crowd of protesters, he called segregation "the Negro's burden and America's shame." He added: "The state of the world today does not afford us the luxury of an anemic democracy." By that time, more than seven hundred protesters had been arrested in Albany, and the Black community had made more demands. In addition to the bus station, they called for integration of libraries, stores, and restaurants. They wanted an end to police brutality. They wanted jobs, including government jobs. They wanted Black jurors on cases involving Black defendants. And they wanted their fellow protesters out of jail. Now the dissidents in Albany were engaged in one of the broadest challenges to legalized segregation the South had ever seen.

"This was a mass movement," Anderson said. "We were taking on a whole city. This was the first non-violent *mass* movement."

Not every activist welcomed King's involvement. James Forman, executive secretary of SNCC, argued against the invitation, saying the protest was already getting plenty of media attention. He feared the people of Albany might back off and let King do the fighting for them. In the long term, Forman felt that too much reliance on King's electrifying leadership might undercut the establishment of a grassroots movement, both in Albany and across the country. But Anderson and other local leaders wanted King, and Forman dropped the argument when it was clear he would not prevail.

By Sunday afternoon, December 17, when Mayor Asa D. Kelley had failed to respond to the protesters' demands, about 250 people prepared to march from Shiloh Church to Albany's city hall. It was a cold, gray, drizzly Sunday. King, dressed in a brown suit, led the procession, along with Abernathy and Anderson. The protesters walked two by two down the center of Jackson Street, past stores decorated for Christmas and past holiday shoppers, many of whom had traveled from surrounding small towns, "where segregation sentiment is even stronger than in this city of 53,000," wrote one reporter covering the protest. A force of about 120 police officers, dressed in yellow raincoats, separated the marchers from the white passersby.

The marchers sang:

> *We shall overcome*
> *We shall overcome*
> *We shall overcome some day*
> *Oh, deep in my heart*
> *I do believe*
> *We shall overcome some day*

As the protesters neared city hall, a contingent of police officers came toward them from the opposite direction, led by Chief Pritchett, his black leather jacket beaded with raindrops. The protesters and police came to-gether at Oglethorpe Street, near the Trailways Bus Terminal. Pritchett stopped the marchers and asked King if he had a parade permit.

"We are simply going to pray at City Hall," King said.

Pritchett, a former tackle at Auburn University, stood six feet tall and weighed 250 pounds. He looked, one of his officers said, "like his head, neck, and shoulders were all one piece." For months, Pritchett had been study-ing the behavior of civil rights activists, talking to police officers in Little Rock, Birmingham, and Montgomery, as he prepared for these protests. "I researched Dr. King," Pritchett recalled years later. "I read about his early days in Montgomery, his methods there. I read that he was a great follower of Gandhi." Pritchett showed his officers films on mob control, urging them to meet nonviolent protest with nonviolent police action. He vowed to fire any officer who raised his baton above his waist. The city had two police dogs, but Pritchett didn't employ them on the day of the march. As long as no vio-lence occurred, the police chief said, he felt confident the federal government would stay out of Albany and the protest would fizzle.

Confronting the marchers, Pritchett raised a megaphone and announced that if they didn't leave, they would all be arrested.

King, Abernathy, and Anderson began marching again. The people followed.

The police herded the crowd to an alley alongside the city jail, blocking their exit with a police car. Those arrested included 162 adults and 104 juve-niles. Bonds were set at $200 cash for each person.

"They have no respect for humans," King said as he stood in the alley. "They have no respect for justice."

Soon, police officers separated King, Abernathy, and Anderson from the group and took them to Sumter County Jail in Americus, forty miles from Albany. The guards called King "boy."

"If convicted I will refuse to pay the fine," he told a reporter who met him at the jail. "I expect to spend Christmas in jail. I hope thousands will join me."

When the same reporter tried to interview Anderson, the sheriff inter-rupted, saying he thought there had already been "enough personal glory for the nigger."

King's announcement that he intended to remain in jail attracted more young activists, journalists, and clergy to Albany. Rabbi Allen Secher, leading a congregation in New Jersey at the time, said he was drawn to Georgia by King's powerful message. "I'll tell you what prepared King to be a leader. It was his *kishkes*," the rabbi said, using the Yiddish word for "guts." "He wasn't one hundred percent perfect . . . But what we knew from the depths of his being was that he was what religion was supposed to be. He might have had *some* of the training, but he had *all* of the soul."

On Monday, city officials and protesters agreed to a truce, and King was released. Albany officials promised to desegregate their train and bus stations, to release most of the jailed protesters, and to hear other complaints at future meetings of the city commission. The Albany Movement leaders, in return, promised to suspend the protests. Journalists, including some in the Black press, labeled King a failure because he had won little more than promises and suggested that he'd been outmaneuvered by the police chief and the mayor.

The truce quickly shattered. In January, a white bus driver poked his finger in the face of an eighteen-year-old Black woman and asked why she was sitting in a front seat. "I paid my damn twenty cents," said the woman, Ola Mae Quarterman, "and I can sit where I want." A bus boycott followed. When the city commission rejected a set of demands, more protests and more arrests followed. A Black café operator, Walter Harris, was shot to death by a police officer who claimed that Harris had resisted arrest and attacked him with a knife.

By the summer of 1962, more than 1,200 people had been arrested in Albany. Pritchett continued to earn praise in the white northern press for his polite-but-firm tactics. *The Washington Post* reported that "the vigor of the Negro demonstrations was waning." Police officials from around the South visited Albany to study Pritchett's approach. "This small city . . . is setting an example by showing how [integration] efforts outside the law can be frustrated," wrote a reporter from Birmingham, Alabama.

King was too busy to devote his full attention to Albany. He traveled through-out the South on what he called his People-to-People Tour, supporting local sit-ins and promoting voter registration. He worked on a book of sermons. He wrote a regular column for the *New York Amsterdam News*. He developed plans to create a new tax-exempt organization called the Gandhi Society for Human Rights, with New York lawyer Clarence B. Jones in charge. He expanded the SCLC, hiring student activists James Bevel and Bernard Lee as field secretaries. Bevel was a Mississippian, an ordained minister. He was creative, courageous, and reckless. Arguing with Bevel, as his colleague Bernard Lafayette Jr. once put it, was like arguing with a brilliant mule. Bernard Lee, a Virginian and an air force veteran, was just as bold and just as brave as Bevel, but he was also affable, funny, and easy to be around. The organization also added Fred C. Bennette to work on voter registration, and Stan Levison brought on Hunter Pitts "Jack" O'Dell to work on a direct-mail fundraising campaign, conceived by Levison, that would prove to be the organization's biggest and most reliable source of income.

Meanwhile, King traveled to Washington to meet with Robert Kennedy and to discuss voter registration in the South. He also taught his first and only college class, a philosophy seminar, at Morehouse.

"I had the sense it was something that was thrown together, partly be-cause King needed money," said Charles Black, who was one of the eight students in King's class, along with the activist Julian Bond. King knew the philosophers—Kant, Plato, Aristotle, and others—and appeared comfort-able in the classroom. "He said, 'yeah' a lot. It was a different kind of vibe from King the orator," recalled Black. The students sat in a semicircle. King addressed them as "mister" and "miss."

In the early part of 1962, meanwhile, Hoover learned that Levison had written a recent speech for King calling for solidarity between the labor and civil rights movements. To the FBI director, it suggested that Levison sought to align King's message with Communist Party interests.

Hoover's memos on communist influence were "very, very persuasive," as John Seigenthaler recalled, even if they omitted mention of the FBI's under-cover sources. Hoover made the case, as David J. Garrow writes, that "some-

one with Levison's secret . . . record of invaluable service to the CPUSA
might very well not have turned up at Martin Luther King's elbow by hap-
penstance." Even if Levison seemed to be moving away from the Communist
Party, Hoover suspected he was doing so in order to more effectively plant
the seeds of communism within the civil rights movement. King listened to
Kennedy's aides and thanked them for the warning about Levison. But, as
he told Harris Wofford, Levison had been a loyal friend and trusted adviser
for five years, and the bureau's allegations were vague at best. Later, King
received a warning that Jack O'Dell, one of the new SCLC employees, also
had a long record of communist ties.

On March 6, 1962, the FBI's domestic intelligence division formally
proposed a telephone wiretap and microphone surveillance device for Levison's office. Robert Kennedy authorized the move. With no court approval
needed, the office microphone was installed in mid-March. A wiretap on
Levison's phone began four days later. Agents began filing memos to headquarters on Levison's conversations with King, and J. Edgar Hoover began
passing along reports to Kennedy. The phone calls proved that Levison was
a key adviser to King, but they failed to prove that Levison had any ongoing involvement in communist matters. Even so, when Levison was heard
recommending O'Dell for a promotion, the move made the FBI more suspicious than ever.

The suspicion was unrelated to anything King said or did; it began, almost
entirely, with the FBI's presumption that the presence of former Communist
Party activists within the SCLC made King a threat to national security. For
J. Edgar Hoover, the investigation of King quickly became personal.

On May 17, King formalized his request for a new Emancipation Proclamation, presenting the president with a sixty-five-page manifesto that opened
with a glorious preamble that drew on the words of Frederick Douglass,
Abraham Lincoln, Woody Guthrie, and even John Kennedy:

> We know that freedom is, indeed, a most precious thing. We know that
> "this land is our land, from California to the New York Island; from the

Redwood forests to the Gulfstream waters," we know that this land exists for all Americans, white and Negro. However, we also know that to millions of Negroes throughout these United States, freedom is not yet a "living reality."

We believe the time has come for Presidential leadership to be vigorously exerted to remove, once and for all time, the festering cancer of segregation and discrimination from American society.

For most white Americans, the perception and meaning of the Civil War had not changed since *Gone with the Wind*. They resisted the notion that the war had been caused by slavery, and they treated both the North and South as noble American combatants. Black people were, at best, parenthetical figures in American history books, including books on the Civil War. King's manifesto attempted to change the narrative. "The struggle for freedom, Mr. President," he wrote, "of which the Civil War was but a bloody chapter, continues throughout our land today. The courage and heroism of Negro citizens at Montgomery, Little Rock, New Orleans, Prince Edward County, and Jackson, Mississippi, is only a further effort to affirm the democratic heritage so painfully won, in part, upon the grassy battlefields of Antietam, Lookout Mountain, and Gettysburg."

The states of the old Confederacy may continue to reject integration, to reject the fulfillment of the promise of American democracy, but they don't have to get the final word, King said. Kennedy had the power to end their rebellion—by demanding passage of strong civil rights legislation that would speed the integration of schools and guarantee the right to vote.

But Kennedy did not embrace King's recommendation. To King, it seemed like the president was more worried at that moment about rising steel prices.

On July 10, King and Abernathy returned to Albany to face trial for their December arrests. When the judge sentenced the men to each pay a $178 fine or spend forty-five days in jail, they chose jail, hoping once again that their imprisonment would call attention to the cause. Quickly, King wrote a letter from jail and released it to Black newspapers, alleging that officials in Albany and elsewhere sought to bankrupt the civil rights movement with bail and court costs. "The time has now come," he wrote, "when we must practice civil disobedience in a true sense or delay our freedom thrust for long years."

Before newspapers could publish the letter, though, King and Abernathy were freed, their fines paid by a "mysterious benefactor." King said he was "very unhappy about the subtle and conniving tactics" that led to the release. Albany's white leaders, seeking to deny King his prison soapbox, had arranged and paid for King's freedom. Their strategy worked. Younger activists complained that King had been outsmarted. They deemed him too conservative, too passive, more thinker than doer. James Bevel recalled asking him once, at about that time, "Dr. King, what do you cats, as non-violent leaders, propose to do?" When King said he didn't know, Bevel recalled, "it became obvious to me that he had never really studied strategy and tactics of nonviolence . . . His nonviolence was philosophical, but never practically applied."

In meetings, King acknowledged that his responsibilities—as a leader, as a minister, as a family man—made him more conservative than some student activists would have liked. King said he welcomed their criticism, that he appreciated the importance of being pushed by "creative antagonists." Sit-ins and protests continued in Albany, meanwhile, as did negotiations. During one march, onlookers hurled rocks at police and slashed convertible tops. The day after the outburst, King, dressed in a short-sleeved shirt, visited Dick's Cue Room, a pool hall in Albany's Harlem neighborhood. He flashed no sign of discomfort in a place where cigar and cigarette smoke stained the walls and cheap beer soaked the floor as he implored young people to remain peaceful. "Nothing can hurt us more than this kind of performance," he said. To avoid further conflict, he called for "a day of penance" and a pause in the demonstrations.

On July 27, King, Abernathy, and others were arrested yet again after they knelt in prayer outside city hall and refused to leave when ordered by police. This time, they remained in jail. On August 5, Coretta visited him, and brought Yoki, Marty, and Dexter along. The children, she said, had not seen their father in a month. Coretta reminded them that their father hadn't done anything wrong, that he had gone to jail to help people. Permitted to leave his cell, King met his family at a shoeshine stand in front of the jail. Coretta wore a white pleated dress and a pearl necklace. Yoki, almost seven years old, wore a sunsuit. Martin, age four, and Dexter, eighteen months, wore plaid shorts and white shirts.

Only Yoki cried. She had seen commercials on television for the Funtown amusement park in Atlanta, had been singing the jingle, and had been asking her mother to take her. Coretta had told her the people who had built Funtown "were not nice Christian people" and had decided to exclude Black people from their park. "But it won't be long before you can go," she said, "because this is what your daddy is doing every day, you see, he's trying to make it possible for you to go to Funtown or any other place that you would want to go."

Now Yoki told her mother that she hoped her father would stay in jail "until he fixes it so I can go to Funtown."

King endured two weeks of incarceration. Upon his release, on August 10, he called off a series of planned protests, saying he hoped city officials would agree to "good-faith" negotiations. But after nearly a year of civil disobedience in Albany, activists had little to show for their efforts. The city remained deeply segregated. Few new voters had been registered. The Kennedy administration had taken no action to enforce federal laws despite clear violations. "We killed them with kindness," one Albany city official bragged. In truth, Pritchett suppressed protest with massive arrests, but he avoided recrimination by managing to be less of a bully than the media had expected.

"The mistake I made there," King said of Albany, "was to protest against segregation generally rather than against a single and distinct facet of it. Our protest was so vague that we got nothing, and the people were left very depressed." Years later, however, William Anderson would dispute the idea that the movement in Albany had failed. King's work proved that Black community members would respond to the appeal of nonviolence. At the same time, white people learned that Black people were not content and would not accept second-class citizenship. Slowly, in fits and starts, white people in Albany began to accord more respect and more opportunities to Black people. "The change started at the top and worked its way down," said Anderson.

"Even in the short term, things got better," said Chris Vail, a white Albany police officer. "You got the feeling in the community there wasn't this invisible wall. The feeling was, 'Hey, we can really talk to you.'"

But that's not how it looked at the time, not to the media, and not to King.

Historians would say years later that King learned from Albany, and that he would take those lessons into his next campaign. But it was more complicated than that. The NAACP attacked the legal underpinnings of segregation, and SNCC organized at the local level, while the SCLC and other groups educated and registered voters. But the movement's progress from Montgomery to Albany and onward was not a coordinated plan or even a cresting wave. The civil rights movement emerged and evolved as expectations grew. Black people in the South saw the possibility of meaningful change. World War II had transformed the economy. Family members who migrated north wrote letters home describing life outside the Jim Crow South. Martin Luther King spoke prophetically of a world without prejudice and hate. It was enough to make even a battered people believe in better days.

When conflict did arise, as in Montgomery and Albany, two important things happened. First, Black communities came together. In Montgomery, the poor and middle class, the followers of E. D. Nixon and Rufus Lewis, united in one cause. In Albany, when Black bystanders threw rocks at police, King may have been dismayed by the violence, but he was encouraged to see that the fight for integration touched people who were not part of his church-based network. And while these crises unified the Black community, a second important thing happened: a split developed in the white political establishment. Not all white leaders proved intransigent. Not all white business owners opposed integration. Not all white politicians acted in lockstep to defend segregation. The wall of opposition showed cracks. And an increasing number of white religious leaders from the North got involved. In the fall of 1962, King sent a personal letter to Rabbi Israel Dresner of Temple Sha'arey Shalom in Springfield, New Jersey, who had been arrested in 1961 during the Freedom Rides and had gone to jail again during protests in Albany.

At least publicly, King expressed confidence that the movement would succeed. "A non-violent campaign toward social change is at least a year long effort and in the deep South, probably longer," King wrote to the rabbi. "Albany is now in its ninth month. We have amassed a nationwide protest, and the world knows through Albany, exactly what the Negro's situation is in the South and the nature of their grievances. During the next few months we will begin working toward reconciliation." He spoke hopefully of the upcoming 1964 presidential election, when moderate white people with the privacy of the voting booth would have an "opportunity to establish a community of Justice."

In September, the SCLC held its annual convention in Birmingham, where the Reverend Fred Shuttlesworth had been leading integration efforts. Shuttlesworth was Birmingham's Martin Luther King Jr., with less education and more rage. His organization, the Alabama Christian Movement for Human Rights, had been founded when the state banned the NAACP, and now it was doing what the Montgomery Improvement Association had tried and failed to do in recent years: it was putting relentless pressure on city officials to end segregation. Shuttlesworth was an inspiring leader for Birmingham's Black residents and an infuriating antagonist to the city's commissioner of public safety, Bull Connor. From 1957 through the end of 1962, seventeen bombs had exploded in Black churches and at the homes of civil rights leaders in Birmingham, with no arrests. In the early months of 1962, students had started a boycott of white Birmingham merchants who refused to serve or hire Black people. King promised Shuttlesworth and others that the people of Birmingham would see more of him in the year ahead.

King also used the occasion of the convention to express support for James Meredith, the young air force veteran who had heard King speak in Oklahoma City two years earlier and who was now attempting to become the first Black student at the University of Mississippi.

On Friday morning, September 28, during the convention's final session, a tall, powerfully built white man rose from a seat in the sixth row and climbed to the stage while King was speaking. The man punched King twice in the face.

"Dr. King dropped his hands like that of a newborn baby," said Septima Clark, who was sitting in the front row of the audience.

"Don't touch him, don't touch him," King said as others subdued the attacker, later identified as Roy James, a member of the American Nazi Party. "We have to pray for him."

Rosa Parks ran to a nearby store to get aspirin and a bottle of Coca-Cola. Someone called the police. Meanwhile, King left the stage and found a quiet place to talk to his attacker. He told the man he would not press charges. He didn't blame Roy James, he told the crowd when he returned to the stage; he blamed the "evil forces" in society that tried to divide God's children. King not only declined to press charges but also invited James to return to his seat and listen to the rest of the program. Reporters did not say whether James accepted the invitation.

The scene made a strong impression on Clark. She was one of the field soldiers, telling young people that if they wanted to march, if they wanted to fight Jim Crow, they had to promise to do it nonviolently. She had heard and she had taught King's lessons, but, still, she had maintained doubts about the effectiveness of nonviolence.

"Well," she said, "when I saw him throwing his hands down when somebody hit him . . . I really felt that he meant it."

King's reaction proved more than his commitment to nonviolence; it also proved that he had reckoned with and come to terms with the possibility of early death. He told one reporter: "Every man should have something he'd die for. A man who won't die for *something* is not fit to live."

Still, Coretta chided her husband. It's one thing to turn the other cheek and decline to press charges, but, she asked, did Martin really have to let his attacker return to his seat?

"Suppose he had a knife or gun?" she asked later over the kitchen table.

"Well," King calmly answered, "if he had, he would have used it before then."

23

Temptation and Surveillance

IN NOVEMBER 1962, King spent nine consecutive days in Atlanta, but only two nights at home.

Often, he would work all day, go home for dinner with Coretta and the children, stay for sixty or ninety minutes, and then leave to go swimming at the YMCA. After his swim, King spent most nights "with Bennett" or "across town," according to his schedule, which was typed by his secretary, Dora McDonald. "Bennett" referred to Fred Bennette, King's aide, who rented an apartment at 3006 Delmar Lane NW that King used to meet women, according to the FBI. "Across town" referred to the same place. King occasionally spent nights at the home of Ralph Abernathy, but those arrivals were unplanned. He would show up late at Abernathy's house, sometimes unannounced, and talk to Ralph while Juanita cooked him a steak. When he fell asleep on the sofa, Juanita would call Coretta to say Martin wasn't coming home.

But when McDonald wrote that King was staying "across town," she knew it wasn't with Abernathy. She also knew it was not a good idea to put her boss's precise location on his itinerary.

Often, King got by on four and a half hours of sleep. In the months following Albany, he felt "depressed." He was going through "an agonizing reappraisal" and wondering how aggressive a role he should play in the civil rights movement, according to Andrew Young, who had taken on greater responsibilities with the SCLC. When faced with stress, Young said, King "plunged into social activities that seemed, on the surface, to have nothing to do with the immediate crisis he was facing."

As a preacher, King understood the importance of living up to the moral standards he preached to his followers. But, as Ralph Abernathy wrote, he "had a particularly difficult time" with sexual temptation. He was a relatively privileged man who had grown up in a time and in a culture in which adulterous activity was commonplace. He knew his father's reputation. He also knew, Abernathy wrote, that with his good looks and charm, he "attracted women, even when he didn't intend to, and attracted them in droves." Abernathy continued:

> Part of his appeal was his predominant role in the black community and part of it was personal . . . Martin Luther King was the most important black man in America . . . That fact alone endowed him with an aura of power and greatness that women found very appealing . . . But he also had a personal charm . . . He was always gracious and courteous to women, whether they were attractive to him or not . . . He was warm and friendly. He could make them laugh. He was good company . . . These qualities made him even more attractive in close proximity than he was at a distance. Then, too, Martin's own love of women was apparent in ways that could not be easily pinpointed—but which women clearly sensed even from afar. I remember on more than one occasion sitting on a stage and having Martin turn to me to say, "Do you see that woman giving me the eye, the one in the red dress?" I wouldn't be able to pick her out at such a distance, but already she had somehow conveyed to him her attraction and he in turn had responded to it. Later I would see them talking together, as if they had known one another forever. I was always a little bewildered at how strongly and unerringly this mutual attraction operated.

King knew that exposure of his affairs would have devastating consequences. At one point, Abernathy warned him that he thought reporters might have noticed King's close relationship with a woman who had been active in the movement and traveled with its leaders—no doubt a reference to Dorothy Cotton. Abernathy advised his friend to "cool it down," but King refused. "Ralph," he said, "what you say might be right, but I don't care . . . I have no intention of cutting off this relationship."

Abernathy offered no deep analysis of his friend's risky behavior, except to say King carried an enormous burden in his work, "and he felt he couldn't do so without this source of strength." The psychologist Kenneth Clark, a friend and adviser to King, said everyone close to King knew of his weakness for women. "Martin really believed in love," Clark said, perhaps jokingly. Clark observed that women propositioned King frequently, and King couldn't bear to turn them down. "Baptist ministers," Clark added, "had to service their congregations."

Levison points out that King and John F. Kennedy had something in common in this regard. "Both had powerful fathers who were men of notorious sexual prowess," Levison told the historian Arthur M. Schlesinger Jr. "Perhaps both were unconsciously driven to prove they were as much men as their fathers."

If King agonized over his lack of restraint, he cloaked his agony in priestly garments, saying in one sermon, for example, that the North and South of man's soul were engaged in an ongoing "civil war." Like Dr. Jekyll and Mr. Hyde, he said, we have private selves that we try to ignore or at least shield from the public; we live one sort of life by day and another by night:

> There is a privacy about all of us that we are ashamed of, that we forever seek to hide . . . And so it boils down that we are sinners in need of God's redemptive power. We know truth, and yet we lie. We know how to be just, and yet we are unjust. We know how to live our lives on the plane of love, and yet we hate, or we are unfaithful to those we should be faithful to . . . Every man experiences it. And that is why the saint always recognizes that he's a sinner, and the worst sinner in the world is the man who feels that he isn't a sinner . . . I don't know about you, but when I look at myself hard enough and deep enough and go on back from my public self to my private self, I don't feel like crying out with the Pharisee, "I thank Thee, God, that

I'm not like other men." But I find myself saying, "Lord, be merciful unto me, a sinner."

In this sermon, King made no mention of repentance. He made no mention of the necessity for the sinner to quit sinning. Instead, he spoke of grace, saying Christ offered grace to the individual who sins. Christ also offers grace, he said, for America's sin of racism.

King had tried to persuade Abernathy to move from Montgomery to Atlanta in 1960, but at first Abernathy refused. The men spoke almost daily by phone, as King yearned for his friend's companionship. "My husband was trustworthy," Juanita Abernathy said. "He was not deceitful. Whatever you saw, that was what you got." King needed that reliability as his life grew increasingly complicated and stressful. Coretta, of course, offered comfort to King, but not in the same way Abernathy did. Soon, Daddy King applied pressure, telling Abernathy he was needed in Atlanta. Still, Abernathy resisted. Raised in rural Alabama, he found Montgomery big enough for his tastes. He may have sensed, as L. D. Reddick wrote in an unpublished biography of the preacher, that in Atlanta he would never escape King's shadow. Juanita opposed the move, too. Eventually, though, Abernathy accepted a position as pastor at West Hunter Street Baptist Church in Atlanta, a church of lesser prominence than King's Ebenezer. It might not have been the best move for his career or for his family, Abernathy said, but he also had to consider what his decision meant "to Martin and the movement."

King and Abernathy were as close as brothers. With other people, even close associates, King could be aloof. He was an attentive listener and, of course, a great talker, but the back-and-forth of easy conversation often eluded him. With Abernathy, King felt relaxed, happy, and loved.

"I tried to provide him with a friendship that every leader needs," Abernathy said. "That is, I was with him whether he was right or wrong."

King could say anything to Abernathy. He knew that no matter how much chaos swirled around him within the SCLC, no matter how much gossip circulated about his personal life, no matter how much criticism rained down on him from the media, from politicians, or from other activists, Abernathy would be at his side. "Abernathy was always making sure nobody got in Martin's way and nobody wasted Martin's time," the Reverend C. T. Vivian said. "He was always making certain that all of us heard Martin . . . making sure Martin's orders got carried out."

King and Abernathy liked the same food. They laughed at the same jokes. They wore the same brand of shoes (Stacy Adams). After 1964 they even shared the same scent, both favoring the popular Aramis cologne. They teased each other knowingly but never cruelly. The men possessed roughly the same height and build, and sported roughly identical mustaches.

"Ralph, you look like a bulldog," King would say as Abernathy began putting on weight. He called his friend "Chops."

"Martin, you're a moneyed Negro," Abernathy would fire back, suggesting King was highfalutin and out of touch. In Montgomery, Abernathy had referred to King's church as "the light and bright and almost white" Dexter Avenue Baptist.

On Tuesday nights in Atlanta, if they were both in town, King and Abernathy would take their children to swim at the YMCA. Each fall, the men escorted the kids to the Southeastern Fair to see the farm animals and ride the roller coaster. The Kings and Abernathys shared family dinners. Martin and Juanita did most of the talking, while Ralph and Coretta were more apt to listen. Martin played Candy Land and Monopoly with the children, never letting them win. When he left a pack of cigarettes unattended—he usually smoked Kents or L&Ms—the children would hide them or destroy them. "I never heard Uncle Martin yell or scream," said Juandalynn Abernathy, the oldest daughter of Ralph and Juanita. "He was just a wonderful, jovial person." But he didn't like having his cigarettes swiped, and he took to hiding them.

The children put on Christmas plays for their parents, with Yoki directing the other children and Coretta capturing the performances on a movie camera. When Yoki got a pet turtle (named Agamemnon), Juandalynn insisted on having one, too. The Kings had a white dog named Topsy, named after the mischievous child from *Uncle Tom's Cabin*. The Abernathys had a cocker spaniel named Brownie. Both families had pet birds.

Coretta became pregnant again in the summer of 1962. By now, she said, she knew that "much of Martin's time was taken up with the movement," and knew that her role as a parent carried the extra responsibility of making up for her husband's absence and ensuring the children felt secure and loved. It also meant helping the children cope with the fear that there were people out there who wanted to hurt their father or throw him in jail.

"I mean, he always spent holidays with the family," she said, "no matter where he was . . . we could always look forward to that . . . and they always looked forward to that special time when they could have daddy all to themselves."

Dexter King, when he reflected on his childhood, would remember his father coming to breakfast in his slippers and a "burgundy-colored satin-like robe." Dexter understood that if his father had on his robe, he wasn't going anywhere right away. The child would remember his father chewing on stalks of green onions before dinner, "lost in thought." And he would remember the "kissing game," in which the children would jump one at a time off the refrigerator and into their father's arms. "Where's your kissing spot?" he would say as he caught them. Yoki's kissing spot was a corner of her mouth. Marty's was on his forehead. Dexter's was the temple. He divided his time equally among the children, Dexter wrote, "what little time he had left."

In articles about the Kings, writers often described Coretta as the woman who stayed home to make her husband's work possible. Coretta, however, saw herself as a coworker, one who discussed strategy and filled in at meetings and public events when her husband was unavailable. She expressed satisfaction that she still managed to pursue her passion for singing and used her talents in fundraising concerts. She also understood that her husband could not have accomplished what he did without her unheralded contributions. "Just being the person that he can come home to and trying to give him consolation when he needs it most, I think is pretty important— and maybe most important," she said.

The women in the movement knew how much Coretta endured and how hard she worked in and outside the home. "Coretta was the smartest woman in the world to me," said Edwina Smith Moss, an SCLC secretary. "She was not only intellectually smart, but she had an inner sense that a lot of people would call common sense, driven by justice and fairness . . . We used to call her 'The Miracle' . . . For her to stay as strong as she did, she really was a miraculous woman."

On Sunday, November 18, 1962, King preached at Riverside Church in New York. After the service, a *New York Times* reporter asked King if he agreed with a report by the historian and activist Howard Zinn that Negroes demonstrating in Albany, Georgia, had distrusted the FBI. The FBI was such a powerful and widely admired American law enforcement operation that criticism of the agency made news. King said he strongly agreed with Zinn's conclusion. "One of the greatest problems we face with the FBI in the South is that the agents are white southerners who have been influenced by the mores of the community," King told the reporter. "To maintain their status, they have to be friendly with the local police and people who are promoting segregation. Every time I saw FBI men in Albany, they were with the local police force . . . If an FBI man agrees with segregation, he can't honestly and objectively investigate."

King had good reason to complain. The FBI's leaders all were white, as were almost all its agents. The agents assigned to Albany all were white. "The FBI men, ever lurking around the Albany Movement scene, made no secret of their unfriendliness to reporters, hostility to Negroes, and, to us, most ominous of all, friendliness to the local police," wrote Pat Watters, a white reporter for *The Atlanta Journal*. "Report after report of violation of civil rights and of violence went to them from the movement, never to be heard about again." For Watters, it came as a shock. The hostility of southern whites, condoned by police and abetted by the federal government, felt alien and un-American. Watters was only beginning to understand, he wrote, that Black people in the South lived with "the dread fact that the police are not on your side or the law's." How they endured and rose above that fear and threat amazed the young journalist. Black Americans, of course, knew all along that FBI agents working in the South were not on their side. "Where were they living? They were living with the sheriff," James Baldwin said in a 1970 interview. "What were they doing on Sunday? Playing baseball with the sheriff and his men . . . Do you think I don't know what's going on?"

In the big picture, the FBI was more focused on exploring King's ties to alleged communists than on protecting him or any other civil rights leaders from violent threats. In the even bigger picture, as King had been pointing out for years, America's system of justice denied Black people equal access to protection under the law. Black men accused of raping white women in the 1960s, King said, faced the likelihood of conviction and even electrocution, while white men accused of raping Black women were seldom even arrested.

In August 1962, Hoover had sent a letter to the U.S. attorney general, Robert Kennedy, that said members of the American Nazi Party were headed to Albany to demonstrate against King and the SCLC, but nothing in the memo indicates King was warned. Roy James, the same Nazi who assaulted King in Birmingham, stalked him months later in Chicago.

J. Edgar Hoover was always sensitive to criticism. When the FBI director heard about King's comments, he asked Berl I. Bernhard, staff director of the U.S. Commission on Civil Rights, to talk to King and explain that not all the agents in the South were southerners. King didn't buy it. "I still think the Bureau's in bed with all of the southern police chiefs, and we're not getting adequate investigations," King told Bernhard.

High-ranking FBI officials decided that the bureau's assistant director, Cartha Dekle "Deke" DeLoach, should contact King and arrange a meeting to discuss the minister's complaints. DeLoach phoned King twice on November 30. He left two messages, but he said that King didn't return his calls. "It would appear obvious," DeLoach wrote in a memo, "that Rev. King does not desire to be told the true facts. He obviously used deceit, lies and treachery as propaganda to further his own causes." In another memo, Hoover called King's failure to return the calls "an instance of his insincerity," and added that "no further attempts are being undertaken by this Bureau to contact him."

Two days after King's critical remarks about the FBI, Robert Kennedy authorized the bureau to expand its surveillance of Levison, putting a tap on Levison's home phone to go with the one already installed at his office. More wiretaps were soon to follow, as the FBI began to treat King himself as a threat.

24

"The Stuff Is Just in 'Em"

AT THE AGE of five and a half, Martin Luther King III was denied admission to the Lovett School, a private Episcopal school in Atlanta.

His was the first application submitted on behalf of a Black student, according to the letter sent to the Kings from the school's headmaster, the Reverend James R. McDowell. The admissions committee of the board of trustees, McDowell wrote, decided it was "not advisable" at that time to accept a Black student.

Martin and Coretta issued a statement to the press in response, saying they had not applied to Lovett to test its integration policies or to prove a point, but simply to secure for their son "the best possible secondary education." One member of the school's board of trustees resigned in protest, but the school remained segregated for three more years. Marty, meanwhile, enrolled at an all-Black public school.

"It only proves again," King told one reporter, "that the church is often an active participant in perpetuating segregation."

Eleven days later, on March 28, 1963, Coretta gave birth to her fourth child, Bernice Albertine King, named after Coretta's mother. They called her "Bunny." Martin would see little of his wife and children in the weeks to come.

Around the country, civil rights protests grew more intense and the backlash more violent. In Petersburg, Virginia, police dogs mauled peaceful protesters. In Greenwood, Mississippi, police, firefighters, and a police dog scattered demonstrators who had gathered to demand the right to vote. The idealism of the sit-ins and Freedom Rides became difficult to sustain in the face of so much brutality. In Los Angeles, activists announced plans to protest the Academy Awards and racism in the movie industry. They warned there would be trouble if police tried to stop the protesters. "If they rough us up," said the protest leader Caleb Peterson, "there'll be violence. This is no Martin Luther King movement."

King felt the pressure building in Black communities and recognized that his pacifist strategy left many frustrated. He sent a telegram to Robert Kennedy, the U.S. attorney general, declaring that it was unclear how much longer protesters would remain restrained in the face of "repeated mayhem and attempted murder." The telegram arrived in Washington as King prepared to confront segregation in Birmingham, a city considered by many to be the nation's most determinedly and viciously segregated. Some called it "Bombingham."

Birmingham had a population of 340,000, about 40 percent Black. For Blacks and whites alike, the city lagged. Only about a third of the adult population had completed high school, and less than 7 percent of adults held college degrees. The median family income for residents of the city was $1,200 less than the national average. Black families had it even worse. They earned about half as much as white families. Black people were far less likely than white people to have completed high school or college. Lawmakers went to great lengths to make sure no cracks appeared in the wall of segregation. For example, if a restaurant wished to serve Black and white customers, the owner needed to build "a solid partition extending from the floor upward to a distance of seven feet or higher" and maintain separate entrances from the street, a requirement so costly and impractical as to make it almost impossible to satisfy. Less than 10 percent of eligible Black voters had managed to register, which allowed segregationists to retain control of city government. If the government failed to maintain segregation, the KKK could be counted on to serve as a last line of defense. When upwardly mobile Black families moved into the middle-class neighborhood of College Hills, they were met with so many bombs that the neighborhood came to be called Dynamite Hill. In 1956, three white men attacked the popular Black singer

Nat King Cole in the middle of a concert at the Birmingham Municipal Auditorium. The following year, a Black handyman named Judge Aaron was abducted by white men and castrated. Aaron's abductors poured turpentine on the wound as they further tortured their victim. In 1962, when a federal court ordered Birmingham to integrate its recreational facilities, the city instead opted to close its parks, playgrounds, pools, and golf courses. If the courts ever ordered the integration of schools, officials said, they would close those, too.

The challenge was great and the stakes high for King in Birmingham. Malcolm X had called the Albany Movement a low point in the civil rights struggle, more proof of nonviolent protest's pointlessness. "You show me a black man who isn't an extremist," he said, "and I'll show you one who needs psychiatric attention!"

King may have been too moderate for Malcolm X's taste, but the Black journalist Lerone Bennett Jr. and others still believed that the SCLC leader's ability to appeal to the masses gave him a greater kind of power than any Black activist before him. "From birth to death, the Negro is handled, distorted and violated by the symbols of white power," Bennett wrote. "As he grows up, he makes a tentative adjustment to white power. At puberty, if he survives and if he remains outside prisons or insane asylums, he makes a separate peace—a peace of accommodation or protest. The price of this peace is high, fantastically high. The price, quite simply, is social emasculation." But the new protesters, led by King, had perhaps found another way, Bennett said. They had found a style of revolt that didn't seem like a revolt as much as a messianic call to usher in a better world. Bennett wrote, "Martin Luther King, Jr., and the sit-in students . . . solved the technical problems by clothing a resistance movement in the comforting garb of love and forgiveness."

Was it enough? At the outset of 1963, even King sounded unsure. In an essay published in *The Nation*, he expressed frustration that civil rights no longer stood atop the nation's list of domestic policy priorities. "The American people," he wrote, "have not abandoned the quest for equal rights; rather, they have been persuaded to accept token victories as indicative of genuine and satisfactory progress." President Kennedy had appointed Black men to a few positions in his administration; a handful of cities, including Atlanta, had made concessions on segregation in public establishments; and Kennedy had proposed measures to expand voter registration. Yet schools and housing remained heavily segregated, in the North and South, King noted, and Black unemployment stood at double the rate of white unemployment.

With the nation's Black population shifting to the North, King said in an interview with *Look* magazine, the issue of legal segregation would soon be less pressing than the issue of discrimination in housing and employment, "which creates a *de facto* segregation," sorting Black people into low-paying jobs and poverty-stricken neighborhoods. He didn't mention Birmingham, even though he was on the brink of launching a major campaign there, perhaps because he remained hesitant, worried that the absence of a large Black student population would leave him with a shortage of foot soldiers. But Fred Shuttlesworth kept up the pressure, and that, more than anything, said James Lawson, "made Martin decide it was time to go into Birmingham."

On January 14, 1963, George C. Wallace became Alabama's governor, promising those who elected him that he would enforce "segregation now . . . segregation tomorrow . . . segregation forever."

King and the SCLC postponed the Birmingham protests while waiting for the outcome of the city's mayoral election, which went to a runoff scheduled for April 2. Though both candidates were staunch segregationists, King and the other planners of the campaign assumed they would have an easier time negotiating with the more moderate candidate, Albert Boutwell, rather than Theophilus Eugene "Bull" Connor, the notorious public safety commissioner. Boutwell defeated Connor in the runoff, but Connor refused to give up his old job. With the city in transition from a three-man commission to a nine-man council of governance, Connor and other commissioners insisted on remaining in office until their terms expired in 1965, leaving Connor in charge of law enforcement. It would eventually require the Alabama Supreme Court to force Connor out of office. In the meantime, the city functioned with two governing bodies.

"I'm just a good old country boy," Connor had said back in 1931, when he was beginning to gain public attention as a minor league baseball radio broadcaster, covering the Birmingham Barons of the Southern Association. Connor was born in 1897 in Selma, the son of a railroad dispatcher and a housewife. When his mother died, Connor moved in with an aunt and uncle on their farm in North Birmingham, where planting and plowing took priority over school. He might have followed his aunt and uncle into farming if he had not discovered a knack for describing minor league ball games based on the minimal account of events received over the telegraph machine when the home team was on the road. He sat in a studio, telegraph clacking, taking a transmitted report of a fly-out to right field, for example, and turning it into a story, inventing the looks on players' faces between pitches, the joyful dash of a child in pursuit of a foul ball, the sweat and spit and sultry summer breeze. Another up-and-coming politician, Ronald Reagan, got his start the same way, combining nostalgia and fantasy to build rapport with an audience.

As a young man, Connor was slender. Even when he got older and grew thick-bodied and bulldog-faced, he was not physically imposing. His nickname derived from his gruff voice, which made him easily recognizable on the radio, as well as from his ability to "shoot the bull" in conversation. A reporter at the time of his emergence as a local celebrity described Connor as "absolutely genuine, totally unaffected, and lovable even at first meeting." Before long, Connor leveraged his radio popularity to launch a political career. Like many office seekers at the time, he assured white voters that he would defend their right to live in a segregated society, but he was hardly more extreme or more vocal than other white Alabama politicians. As commissioner for public safety, he made race a priority, which meant using the police force to control and discipline the Black community. At that point, his nickname took on a new meaning: Connor assured voters he would be stubborn as a bull in preserving the city's system of racial stratification.

Early in his political career, Connor proved his commitment to law and order with well-publicized raids on prostitutes and gamblers. In 1938, his officers interrupted the founding convention of the Southern Conference for Human Welfare, attended by Eleanor Roosevelt, and forced Black and white delegates to sit on opposite sides of the auditorium. Ten years later, he ordered the arrest of U.S. senator Glen Taylor of Idaho for entering a meeting of the Southern Negro Youth Congress through a door police had marked "colored." In the 1940s, Connor had overseen the installation of "race boards," movable panels that divided Black and white bus passengers. In 1948 at the Democratic National Convention in Philadelphia, he waved a Confederate battle flag as he led the so-called Dixiecrat delegation in a walkout to protest the party's civil rights platform. Such moves boosted Connor's popularity among white voters—the only ones who mattered to him in Birmingham.

Connor was not the only reason the SCLC labeled Birmingham "the South's toughest city." As the city's steel industry grew, white workers of Anglo-Saxon heritage took a hostile view toward the Black, Italian, and Irish men who competed for jobs. Unionists were among the many Birmingham residents who joined the Klan and the White Citizens' Councils.

Years later, Wyatt Tee Walker would say he and the SCLC crafted a plan for Birmingham called Project C, for "confrontation," counting on a hostile reception. But SCLC records suggest that Walker didn't come up with that name until after the campaign. In fact, at least initially, King sought to *avoid* confrontation with Bull Connor. King knew, as he made clear in *The Nation*, that racism was not merely a southern problem, and he didn't want to make it easy for people to blame discrimination on a few outspoken segregationists. He understood that some northern white people justified their own racist practices by telling themselves they weren't as bad as Bull Connor and his ilk. Southern bigots described Black people as genetically inferior, he wrote, while northern segregationists argued that Black people were victims of the culture of poverty who needed better work habits and stronger family values. The results were no less harmful in the North, but they were more visible in places such as Birmingham. A year earlier, when Black students had organized a series of selective-buying campaigns against white merchants, the city of Birmingham had responded by withdrawing support for a surplus-food program that benefited many in the Black community. When a group of merchants agreed to desegregate, Bull Connor and other city officials harassed them, sending city inspectors who cited the businesses for things such as unsafe stairs and inadequate fireproofing.

King hoped to do in Birmingham what he had done in Montgomery: he aimed to hit the city's economic power structure, force concessions from politicians, unite the Black community, and use the news media to compel others across the country to join the struggle. In Albany, it had been a mistake to pressure the local political leaders, because those leaders didn't have to answer to Black voters. In Birmingham, they would shift their strategy. King recognized his role as a dramatist. Television was the new American stage, and King put on a show with good guys and bad guys.

Reporters who followed King found him aloof, too dignified to give them the kind of stroking they had come to expect from important sources. But that also made him seem genuine. In Birmingham, King would communicate not only with the media but also with President Kennedy and civil rights leaders. James Bevel, Dorothy Cotton, and Andrew Young would train protesters. Young would lead negotiations with the white business community. King; his brother, A.D.; Fred Shuttlesworth; and Ralph Abernathy would lead the rallies and mass meetings. The key to this campaign, King said, would be economics, and it would take time for the impact to be felt. Black shoppers were going to boycott businesses until the city met its four demands: the desegregation of downtown stores; fair hiring at those stores; the dismissal of charges against those previously arrested for protesting; and the creation of a biracial committee to continue discussions on integration.

They were determined to be better prepared than they had been in Albany.

———— • ————

"God took all the fear out of me," said Calvin Woods, who joined a group of eight Black activists sitting in at a whites-only Woolworth's lunch counter as the Birmingham Movement began, at last, on the morning of April 3, 1963. Calvin's brother, the Reverend Abraham Woods Jr., led another group at the Britling Cafeteria. Before noon, thirteen protesters had been arrested and four lunch counters had been shut down. Bull Connor responded as expected: if the protests continued, he said, "I will fill that jail full."

King and Abernathy arrived later that day. Though Shuttlesworth greeted them at the airport, the Reverend J. L. Ware, the city's most prestigious Black preacher, did not. King took that as a bad sign. Ware's support for the Birmingham Movement should have been secured in advance.

King, Abernathy, and Shuttlesworth drove to the Gaston Motel, a modest, two-story, redbrick building owned by A. G. Gaston, often referred to as "Alabama's wealthiest Negro." They checked into the motel's best suite, where the rotary phone started ringing right away, though not as much as they would have liked. "Both Martin and I were beginning to wonder just how much support Fred and the others could really deliver," Abernathy said. Shuttlesworth was a hero in Birmingham among the Black community. He had been with King in Montgomery for the bus boycott; he'd been with him in Atlanta for the birth of the SCLC; and he'd been with him in Albany to face Laurie Pritchett. All that time Shuttlesworth had pressured King to come to Birmingham.

Shuttlesworth was bombastic. He was fearless. He was the survivor of a blast that had blown him out of bed and, miraculously, flipped his mattress over in time to shield him from the collapsing roof of his house. Shuttlesworth was also a divisive figure—too aggressive for some, too folksy for others. Though his oratory style was unlike King's, he possessed similar power to move an audience. He began one of his speeches with an anecdote:

> You know the story about the little boy who asked his daddy, "Daddy, what makes the lightnin' bug light?" Naturally, the man didn't want to admit to this boy that he didn't know what made the lightnin' bug light, because the father ought to know everything in the eyes of his son. Like these segregationists think they know *all* about us . . . But anyhow . . . the daddy tried to talk about somethin' else, to git off the subject . . . But this boy kept on callin' him to the point . . . "But, Daddy, I want to know— what makes a lightnin' bug light?" So he reached up in his head, where there was supposed to be a handful of hair—he was gettin' bald—and he said, "Well, I'll tell you the truth, boy." He said, "The stuff is just in him, that's all." And for the spirit that these Negroes be free, well, the stuff is just in 'em.

The crowd that greeted the preachers at St. James Baptist Church was big, about four hundred people, but not as big as King and Abernathy had hoped. The gathering the next day in downtown Birmingham for their first public protest proved even more disappointing. Four of the five targeted lunch counters closed for the day rather than face protesters; the fifth hired burly guards to block the entrance to Black customers. Reporters who had come to town expecting big things wondered why the mass movement lacked both mass and movement. King said he wasn't worried. It would take time. It would require a conflict, too, but King yet again reminded anyone who would listen that his approach to conflict was rooted in Christian theology. "Now we say in this nonviolent movement that you've got to love the white man," he said. "And God knows, he needs our love . . . And let me say that I'm not talking about emotional bosh when I talk about love." He meant, he said, "you love those who love you. You love those that you don't like. You love those whose ways are distasteful to you. You love every man because God loves him."

With *agape*, with a spirit of unconditional love derived from God, he told a cheering crowd at one rally, the people of Birmingham would show the nation how to end racial discrimination. They wouldn't stop, he promised, until the segregationists of Birmingham saw the error of their ways, until "Pharaoh lets God's people go."

Privately, however, King expressed frustration. He scheduled more meetings with pastors and business leaders. He spoke at one mass meeting after another, trying to generate support, but the initial protests still remained small and without enough friction to spark a fire. The selective-buying campaign, intended to hurt white merchants, "was proving unsuccessful," according to the city's Black newspaper, the *Birmingham World*. Emory O. Jackson, the editor of that paper, said King's efforts were being sapped by moderate members of the Black community who preferred not to be connected with the SCLC or any other group. On April 6, *The New York Times* reported that "promised mass demonstrations have not been held . . .

and there appeared to be a possibility that the campaign might be temporarily abandoned."

But everything changed the next day. And it was not King but his brother, A.D., who led the way. A. D. King was the pastor at Birmingham's First Baptist Church. He and his wife, Naomi, and their five children, had relocated to Birmingham's Ensley neighborhood in 1962. Though he had been arrested with his brother during the Atlanta sit-ins in 1960, A.D. had kept a low profile in the early years of the civil rights movement. In 1961, he had been arrested near Fayetteville, Georgia, on charges of driving under the influence of alcohol. Martin Luther King Jr. told one confidant that his father's rage and demanding personality had "destroyed" his brother. A family friend later said that A.D. tried to imitate Martin's calm demeanor, but "couldn't get past the anger that engulfed him."

On Palm Sunday, April 7, A.D. led a small group of protesters in a march on city hall. Police and city officials, including Bull Connor, waited for them.

"These people are nothing but Communist agitators," the outgoing mayor, Arthur Hanes, told a reporter at the scene. "They are turning peaceful citizens into raw savages."

When the protesters reached a roadblock they bent in prayer. Police arrested about two dozen of them and used police dogs to scatter what remained of the crowd. "Look at that dog go," Connor told a reporter. "That's what we train them for—to enforce the law—just like we train our officers."

The Birmingham News offered this account of what happened next: "A 19-year-old Negro . . . turned to fight a K-9 dog with a small piece of clay pipe. The dog downed the youth and the crowd started surging forward . . . Another Negro pulled a knife and about 15 policemen, joined by police dogs, moved in and forced the crowd back." Twenty-six people were arrested, including the teenager who was bitten by the dog. SNCC leader James Forman, who attended the protest, had a different version of events, saying a Black man who drew his knife did so only after the dogs attacked him. Newspapers all over the country ran a photo of a police dog tugging its leash and moving in the direction of a prone unidentified Black man, while a uniformed police officer stood over the Black man and prodded him with a stick. The clash made front-page news around the country, largely because of the shocking photographs of the dogs.

Later, back at the Gaston Motel, Forman found Wyatt Tee Walker and Dorothy Cotton in high spirits, "jumping up and down, elated." Forman later wrote: "They said over and over again, 'We've got a movement. We've got a movement. We had some police brutality. They brought out the dogs. We've got a movement.'"

Forman was disgusted, seeing no reason to celebrate police brutality, even if it did generate valuable news coverage.

The day after the protest, Martin Luther King Jr. met with two hundred of the city's Black ministers, imploring them to get more involved. Only a "dry-as-dust" religion permitted ministers to praise the glories of heaven while neglecting conditions on earth, he said.

"There are some preachers in Birmingham who are not with this movement," he shouted from the pulpit of his brother's church on April 11. "I'm tired of preachers riding around in big cars, living in fine homes, but not willing to take part in the fight. He is the freest man in the community. The white man can't cut off his check. If you can't stand up with your people, you are not fit to be a leader."

The audience shouted its approval. King and Abernathy led them in singing "I'm on My Way to Freedomland," accompanied by the deep tones of the church organ. They asked how many people would join them in jail on Good Friday. About fifty people stood.

"I've never been to jail in my life," said a gray-haired woman, rising from her seat, "but I'm going, too."

At the same time King and Abernathy were rallying their followers, however, city attorneys asked an Alabama Circuit Court judge to issue an injunction that would ban marches and protests. The judge quickly granted the request. King vowed to defy the order.

Police arrested 12 more protesters on Thursday, bringing the total to 160 since the start of the campaign. That night, Daddy King spoke at a mass meeting, beseeching listeners to put their bodies on the line. Meanwhile, his son was back at the Gaston Motel, making phone calls, worrying what would happen to the people in jail if the SCLC didn't raise more bail money. King spoke to Harry Belafonte and the lawyer Clarence Jones about finding additional funds. It was suggested that King might be wise to leave Birmingham and head north on a fundraising mission. King felt torn. He had promised the people of Birmingham that he would go to jail with them, and he didn't want to appear weak.

At 8:30 the next morning, April 12, about two dozen people, including Daddy King, Dorothy Cotton, and Ralph Abernathy, crowded into room 30 of the Gaston Motel. King sat at the head of his bed, smoking a cigarette, listening to various opinions about what to do next.

"I sat there," he wrote later, "conscious of twenty-four pairs of eyes. I thought about the people in jail. I thought about the Birmingham Negroes already lining the streets of the city, waiting to see me put into practice what I so passionately preached. How could my failure now to submit to arrest be explained to the local community? What would be the verdict of the country about a man who had encouraged hundreds of people to make a stunning sacrifice and then excused himself?" Yet he had never before violated a court order. "I sat," he wrote, "in the midst of the deepest silence I have ever felt . . . I was alone in that crowded room."

King got quiet. He looked, Andrew Young thought, "as if he were far away from the stuffy room." Through the open window, the men heard singing coming from the nearby Sixteenth Street Baptist Church, where SCLC staff members were training volunteers who would soon be marching and facing arrest.

King rose from the bed and walked to the next room, where he stood alone in the center of the floor.

"I think I was standing also at the center of all my life had brought me to be . . . I thought of the Birmingham Negro community, waiting," he wrote in recalling that moment. "Then my mind leaped beyond the Gaston Motel, past the city jail, past city lines and state lines, and I thought of twenty million black people who dreamed that someday they might be able to cross the Red Sea of injustice and find their way to the promised land of integration and freedom. There was no more room for doubt."

He changed into a pair of blue denim pants and a gray cotton work shirt, the kind of clothes his father and grandfather had worn when they had picked cotton in Georgia, except these were new and clean. He buttoned the gray work shirt over his crisp white dress shirt, tucked them both in his pants, and fastened his belt. When he stepped back into the other room, the people gathered there surmised that he had made up his mind.

Once again, though, he faced the reprobation of his father. Daddy King urged his son to be cautious.

M.L. rejected the advice.

Abernathy changed into blue jeans, too. He, too, buttoned on a gray work shirt over his white dress shirt. Though King encouraged his friend to avoid arrest so he could return to Atlanta and be in the pulpit for Easter, Abernathy said no; if King was going to jail, Abernathy was going with him.

"I don't remember any of the words Dr. King uttered at this moment, but he must have said something," Dorothy Cotton wrote. "I know we sang quietly and prayerfully our anthem of the moment, 'We Shall Overcome.' By this time I had tears in my eyes. I think others also cried . . . Dr. King did not cry . . . I gave him a big hug, as others in the room also did. As he headed out the door we were all behind him."

They made for a strange sight, these two small, well-groomed men in work clothes that looked fresh out of the box, their jaws locked, their eyes downcast, their expressions stern. King and Abernathy strode from the Gaston Motel to the Sixteenth Street Baptist Church. When they reached the church, entering from the back door, the crowd inside roared with excitement. Everyone understood the meaning of their unusual attire. These men of the cloth were dressed for jail.

Hundreds of people followed King and Abernathy out to the street. The crowd grew larger and louder and more excited with every step as the they marched toward city hall. Within blocks, however, they ran into police barricades.

"Stop them," Connor shouted. "Don't let them go any farther."

There were no dogs this time. A police officer on a motorcycle rolled up and blocked their path. King and Abernathy knelt to pray. A police officer yanked King by the elbow and pulled him to his feet and then did the same to Abernathy. The officer grabbed the seat of King's pants and shoved him into a paddy wagon. Abernathy was tossed in the wagon, too.

"Keep the movement going," King said before the paddy wagon doors closed.

King and Abernathy sat together in the dark, the wagon idling. Eventually, they heard the voice of Bull Connor telling one of his men to take the prisoners to jail.

"Put them in solitary," he said.

25

Birmingham Jail

DENIED HIS REQUEST to make a phone call, King vanished into solitary confinement. Guards removed the mattress from the cell, leaving a cold metal slab for a bed. A sliver of sunlight slanted from a small window in the concrete wall.

"Those were the longest, most frustrating and bewildering hours I have lived," he later wrote. "You will never know the meaning of utter darkness until you have lain in such a dungeon, knowing that sunlight is streaming overhead and still seeing only darkness below. You might have thought I was in the grip of a fantasy brought on by worry. I did worry."

To ease his mind, he began to compose a letter.

On the day of King's arrest, a group of eight white clergymen in Birmingham had issued a statement calling on Black citizens to "withdraw support from these demonstrations, and to unite locally in working peacefully for a better Birmingham." The statement continued: "We recognize the natural impatience of people who feel their hopes are slow in being realized. But we are convinced that these demonstrations are unwise and untimely." Earlier in the year, most of the same white clergymen had written a statement encouraging white people in Birmingham to obey integration orders, declaring "no person's freedom is safe unless every person's freedom is equally protected." The new statement appeared on page 2 of the April 13 edition of the *Birmingham News*, on the same page as a photo of King and Abernathy being shoved toward the paddy wagon.

The clergymen considered their message a plea for cooperation, moderation, and reason. But King, who read the statement under the weak glare of his jail cell's lightbulb, became disturbed. Why did everyone keep telling Black people to wait? The Kennedys said wait. Birmingham's mayor said wait. The reverend Billy Graham said wait. The Black professional class in Birmingham said wait. Editorial writers for *The New York Times* said wait. Give the government time to act, they all said; keep the peace, and trust the process. But for King and the people he felt called to lead, waiting signaled acceptance of an unjust plight. Waiting represented complicity. As King's mind spun, he set to work. He wrote on the margins of the newspaper, and, when he ran out of room in the newspaper margins, he scribbled on napkins and toilet paper. Sometimes he used the paper in which his sandwiches had been wrapped.

On Sunday, April 14, A. D. King led another protest. Once again, it ended in violence, as police blocked the marchers and spectators hurled rocks at police. The next day, the lawyer Clarence Jones visited King and brought the good news that Harry Belafonte had raised $50,000 in bail money for jailed protesters. At the same time, Robert Kennedy coordinated with leaders of the United Auto Workers to send an additional $160,000. King told Jones about his response to the clergymen and handed him the scraps of paper on which he'd been writing. Jones sneaked them out of jail and gave them to Wyatt Tee Walker, who gave them to his secretary, Willie Pearl Mackey King, who typed King's words on her IBM Selectric.

"The writing on the greasy sandwich wrappers was hard to make out," she recalled. The scraps were not always in order. "It was like a jigsaw puzzle. It was the worst thing I ever had to work on in my life."

Walker helped piece the letter together. Once she was sure she had correctly deciphered King's scribbles, Willie Pearl Mackey King tossed the scribbled originals in the garbage.

Martin Luther King Jr. soon received proper sheets of paper, and the typist's job got easier. But it went on for days. Typed pages went into the jail and came back with the prisoner's revisions, to be typed again. The letter stretched, eventually, to twenty double-spaced pages. As the first person to read it, and as someone who knew King, Willie Pearl Mackey King said she could sense the author's emotion. "He wasn't angry," she said. "He was hurt. He was deeply hurt that men of the cloth could not understand what he was dealing with."

Wrote King:

My Dear Fellow Clergymen,

While confined here in the Birmingham city jail I came across your recent statement calling my present activities "unwise and untimely." Seldom do I pause to answer criticism of my work and ideas. If I sought to answer all the criticisms that cross my desk, my secretaries would have time for little besides such correspondence in the course of the day, and I would have no time for constructive work. But since I feel you are men of genuine good will and that your criticisms are sincerely set forth, I want to try to answer your statement in what I hope will be patient and reasonable terms.

The cordial introduction gave way to a searing attack. Few things angered King more than racism in the church. His letter, written at a decisive moment in his leadership, written without access to his bookshelf and without the help of his frequent collaborators, would become his most passionate and lasting prose. He called upon the masterpieces of philosophy and theology he had learned at Crozer and Boston University. He called upon the works of Harry Emerson Fosdick, Harris Wofford, and his Morehouse mentor George Kelsey that had been quilted into his sermons and essays for years and that he had loosely memorized. He called upon the Apostle Paul, who had written his own letters from jail, and the Hebrew prophets such as Jeremiah and Amos. Perhaps most of all he called upon his predecessors in the Black church, including his grandfather, his father, and Vernon Johns, who combined protest and prophecy. Going to jail inspired King to preach and to protest, to write with a fervor that seldom appeared in his prose, and, in the process, to redefine American religious leadership.

King addressed his letter to the eight Birmingham clergymen, but he meant it for a wider audience. The *New York Post* published passages from the letter in May. At the same time, King submitted the letter to *The Christian Century*, where it underwent editing before running in the magazine's June 12 edition. The editor Harold E. Fey asked King to consider deleting the names of the eight clergymen "to broaden the impact of your remarks as much as possible since we are convinced they apply to all of us to a considerable degree." King agreed. With *The Christian Century*, he knew his message would reach much of the nation's Protestant leadership. He soon after circulated it to additional publications. Individual churches distributed it among members, as it became almost instantly famous.

King's letter from jail was a love letter in the broadest sense: it spoke of the need to be "extremists for love." It was a letter of thanks to God and the Black church: "I am grateful to God that, through the Negro church, the dimension of nonviolence entered our struggle." It offered a metaphor: It said America was a prison for Black people. "Injustice anywhere is a threat to justice everywhere," he wrote. It proffered patriotism: Those protesters who "sat down at lunch counters . . . were in reality standing up for the best in the American dream" and "bringing our nation back to those great wells of democracy which were dug deep by the founding fathers in their formulation of the Constitution and the Declaration of Independence." It called to the consciences of moderates and liberals: "I have almost reached the regrettable conclusion that the Negro's greatest stumbling block is not the White Citizens' Counciler or the Ku Klux Klanner, but the white moderate, who is more devoted to 'order' than to justice." It held a warning: The question, he said, "is not whether we will be extremists, but what kind of extremists we will be," while reminding these ministers of the extremism of people like the prophet Amos, Jesus, Jefferson, and Lincoln. "I would agree with St. Augustine," he wrote, "that 'an unjust law is no law at all.'"

The letter would become part of American history, a blistering, beautiful treatise on the moral obligation to fight oppression, a document that captured the spirit of the civil rights movement and the fierce brilliance of its leader. The letter showed the power King had discovered by leading a mass movement of Black Americans to join the mainstream of American life, and, at the same time, to reshape mainstream American life. It captured the essence of his beliefs and aspirations.

But it had no immediate impact in Birmingham.

On April 15, King's fourth day in jail, President Kennedy phoned Coretta King to express concern for her husband. Thirty minutes later, King received permission to phone his wife from jail. He chatted briefly with Yoki and Marty, and asked Coretta about the baby. He also asked her if the Birmingham protests were getting good coverage in the press.

"Is your spirit all right?" Coretta asked.

"Yes. I've been alone, you know."

"Yes, I know that."

She told him the president had called, and King urged her to make sure the news media knew about it. He hoped the call from Kennedy would generate more media coverage and prod the Justice Department to get involved in protecting protesters.

On April 20, after more than a week in jail, King and Abernathy were freed, their beards unkempt, their grassroots movement still in danger of collapse. King, in his first press conference, continued to complain of disunity in the Black community. A week later, when the movement led a rally for the twenty-fifth consecutive night, it was clear that audiences were diminishing in size. The city's strategy—filling the jails, sapping the movement with injunctions, and avoiding big headlines—seemed to drain the energy from King's followers.

"You know, we've got to get something going," he said privately. "The press is leaving."

Many adults in the Black community, and even some of the preachers, were eager to see the movement come to an end and see King depart, said Dorothy Cotton. "If you hear them talk now," she recalled, "they all loved

Martin Luther King. But they didn't all love Martin Luther King, and . . . they wished that he would get out of town with his mess."

James Bevel of the SCLC and Isaac Reynolds of CORE, who had been training young protesters, urged King to enlist high school students to restore the flagging size and vitality of the demonstrations. Bevel always seemed to be pushing King, and King appreciated the younger man's passion, courage, and intelligence, leaving it to Andrew Young to rein Bevel in when he became too aggressive. King wanted Bevel's ideas and his energy. Bevel was sometimes referred to as "the Prophet." "He'd never stop talking," even to racists, Young said of Bevel. "He'd go into a grocery and buy a Coke and Moon Pie and start a conversation," knowing that half the time the grocer was going to call the police as soon as he left the store. He wore a Jewish skullcap on his shaved head to honor Old Testament prophets and because he considered himself part Jewish. Bevel argued that while the adult Black community in Birmingham remained hopelessly fragmented, the children could be united in action. He and others—including James Orange, a recently graduated high school football star from Birmingham—visited high schools and found the students eager to participate.

Hundreds of them skipped school to gather on Thursday afternoon, May 2, at the Sixteenth Street Baptist Church. At the same time, however, in his suite at the Gaston Motel, King met with members of the Black middle class who were outraged that their children might be used as pawns in a violent game of chess with Bull Connor.

At noon, groups of students marched from the church toward downtown. High school students composed the majority, but much younger children marched, too. Some of them looked like they were no more than ten years old, gap-toothed and spindly-armed. They sang freedom songs, laughed, and clapped. Some groups marched toward city hall, others toward the downtown shopping district.

"Sing, children, sing!" called a spectator as one group of students joined in "We Shall Overcome."

Some of the students ran at the sight of police. Others submitted peacefully to arrest. Bull Connor ordered firefighters to block the marchers, and, although they rolled out their high-pressure hoses, they did not turn on the water. Police dogs were not used, either. By the end of the day, hundreds of juveniles had been arrested, bringing the total number of arrests to more than a thousand. Connor, keeping his promise to fill the jails, grew angry at the media's portrayal of King and the protesters. "Poor King, poor King, the biggest racketeer that ever hit America," he told one reporter. "Shakedown artist. Going up here preaching nonviolence and the only violence been here is his crowd throwing rocks."

That night, protesters packed the Sixth Avenue Baptist Church to hear King speak. "I have been inspired and moved today," he said. "I have never seen anything like it."

Bevel raised the temperature in the room, declaring: "There ain't gonna be no meeting Monday night because every Negro is going to be in jail by Sunday night."

Abernathy taunted Bull Connor, saying he knew law enforcement officers were spying on the meeting, and he didn't care.

"That got me," said James Orange, referring to Abernathy's speech. "I never seen anybody talk back like that to white folk."

The meeting ended in singing, stomping, and screaming. The students, it seemed, had reinvigorated a stagnating movement. But they had also generated scorn—from Albert Boutwell, Robert Kennedy, and even Malcolm X, who said, "Real men don't put their children on the firing line." At a press conference, King responded to the criticism: "We are ready to negotiate. But we intend to negotiate from strength."

The next day, Friday, May 3, Connor deployed his men at the eastern edge of Kelly Ingram Park. Firemen in dun-colored knee-length coats stood ready at key intersections, their hoses unfurled and configured in such a way as to make them potent weapons.

Inside the church, two thousand students listened as King gave them final instructions: "If you take part in the marches today you are going to jail, but for a good cause," he said. The crowd sang freedom songs. They stomped their feet and clapped their hands. At one in the afternoon, the church doors swung open, and the students poured out across the street toward the park. Connor took off his porkpie hat and waved, signaling his men to advance.

"Let 'em have it," he said.

The park became a battleground. Police grabbed protesters and shoved them into paddy wagons. But there were too many people to arrest. Water from high-pressure fire hoses boomed, thudding against pavement, against cars, against trees, against bodies. A slender girl dressed all in white braced herself, certain she could withstand the water, and then fell to the dirt. Protesters clung to one another. The water peeled back their shirts. It spun them around. It sent them skittering and scraping across the street. It lifted lighter children off the ground. People ran in confusion and fear, sometimes slipping out of the arms of police officers. Dogs whined and snarled. Spectators screamed and hurled bricks and bottles at the protesters.

"Freedom!" shouted one teenager as he flailed under the force of the water.

In the midst of the chaos, a fifteen-year-old boy named Walter Gadsden stepped across the street at the corner of Sixteenth Street and Sixth Avenue North, in front of the Jockey Boy Restaurant. He was a high school student who had come to watch the demonstration, not to participate. But as he crossed the street, a police dog lunged at him. Gadsden was not afraid of big dogs—his family owned one, in fact. Instinctively, he raised his left knee in self-defense, connecting with the dog's chest, but he appeared to remain calm, hands at his side. At the same moment, three more things happened: the white police officer who held the dog's leash grabbed the front of Gadsden's cardigan sweater with his right hand; Gadsden's left hand clasped the police officer's right wrist; and, perhaps most important, an Associated Press photographer named Bill Hudson snapped a picture.

Bull Connor had used the dogs for about thirty minutes, and they had inflicted little damage. Even the fire hoses had caused more havoc than injury. In the century since slavery's end, Black people in America had endured far worse, but most of it had happened without white witnesses in the news media, without widespread photographic evidence. It was the image of this single encounter—a young Black man under attack by a police dog—that appeared the next day on the front page of *The New York Times* and in other newspapers across the country. The photo shook the world and crystallized the message King and others had been trying for years to express.

In the simplest way, the photo captured the moral balance of the civil rights movement in black and white: the courage of peaceful protesters versus the savage brutality of the enforcers of white supremacy. For white people in the North—including President Kennedy—the photograph helped assert the humanity of a group of people who had long been denied that stature by their oppressors. But the image may have also offered some viewers a comfortable contrast between North and South. A single frame of film, for many white people in the North, became, quite literally, the picture of American racism—*their* issue, not ours.

A Black observer might have looked at the same image differently, especially if that Black observer had been involved in the fight for civil rights. Gadsden, after all, was not one of the nonviolent protesters; he was a bystander. He not only thrust his knee into the dog's chest but also had the temerity to grab a white police officer by the wrist. Whatever its implications, the photo brought home and nationalized the Black fight for equality in a way that the sit-ins, the Freedom Rides, and the Albany Movement had not. It sparked outrage and action like nothing before. It sent more newspaper and television reporters pouring into Birmingham. It also gave proof to something Bayard Rustin once said about King: "Martin was not really an organizer . . . The organizers were Bull Connor, the dogs, the fire hoses."

Rustin didn't mention the children, but they changed the moral equation, too.

On the same day that the photo of Gadsden and the dog appeared in newspapers, the Kennedy administration sent Burke Marshall, head of the Justice Department's Civil Rights Division, to Birmingham to mediate the dispute. Marshall was a small, quiet man. He was a white New Jersey–born graduate of Phillips Exeter Academy and Yale, a bow-tied and bespectacled father of three, and an avid bridge player. His best qualification for the job was his mastery of the art of persuasion. But when he arrived in Birmingham, he found white community leaders had made little effort to learn what the protesters wanted—they only knew they were against it.

While Marshall met with moderate white leaders in the city on Saturday, James Bevel led more marchers into action. Bull Connor didn't use dogs this time, but when someone threw a brick that landed near his feet, he did order firemen to blast their hoses and push back the crowd. As Wyatt Tee Walker later put it: "Bull Connor had something in his mind about not letting these niggers get to City Hall. I prayed that he'd keep trying to stop us ... Birmingham would have been lost if Bull had let us go down to the City Hall and pray ... There would be no movement, no publicity."

King rallied followers on May 5. "Never in the history of this nation have so many people been arrested for the cause of freedom and human dignity," he told a crowded church. "You know that approximately 2,500 people are in jail right now. Now let me say this: the thing that we are challenged to do is to keep this movement moving ... As long as we keep moving like we are moving, the power structure of Birmingham will have to give in ... And don't worry about your children. They're going to be alright. Don't hold them back if they want to go to jail, for they are doing a job for not only themselves but for all of America and for all mankind." The audience grew quiet when King talked about the plight of their children, but they came back to life and cheered and echoed him when he turned to the Bible. "Remember," he said, his voice growing louder, "there was another little child, just twelve years old, and he got involved in a discussion back in Jerusalem ... He said, 'I must be about my Father's business.' These young people are about their Father's business. And they are carving a tunnel of hope through the great mountain of despair."

Two days later, police, firefighters, and tanks clashed with thousands of people in downtown Birmingham. Protesters hurled bricks and rocks. A fire hose knocked Fred Shuttlesworth into the wall of a church.

"I waited a week to see Shuttlesworth get hit by a hose," Connor said after the preacher was carried off in an ambulance. "I wish they'd carried him away in a hearse."

On May 10, 1963, King and Shuttlesworth reached an agreement with city officials for a phased program of desegregation and the release of jailed demonstrators. "The city of Birmingham," King and Shuttlesworth announced in a joint statement, "has come to an accord with its conscience."

In reaction to the settlement, one white man told a radio reporter: "It upset me pretty highly, to give you my honest viewpoint of it. I didn't take to the idea too much, because, myself, I just can't hardly see a Negro using the same restroom that I use, not that I think that I'm the Almighty or better than he is, it's not that, it's just that, it's just a little matter of the cleanliness and the morals and everything else."

Bull Connor and Arthur J. Hanes, still clinging to power after having been voted out, blasted the attempt at compromise. "We got that agitating, Communistically-tinged King on the run," Hanes told reporters. "It breaks my heart to see some Quisling whites negotiating with him when we've got him whipped."

King flew home to spend Mother's Day in Atlanta. The next day, a radio reporter in Birmingham asked Robert Shelton, the so-called Imperial Wizard of the Ku Klux Klan, if he expected violence to erupt in reaction to the Birmingham protests. Shelton maintained that no one had done more than the KKK to preserve the peace in Birmingham. But, he added, "the people of Birmingham and the people of Alabama have been pushed just as far as they're going to be pushed. And it's going to have to stop some way."

Thirty minutes after Shelton spoke, bombs exploded at the Gaston Motel and the home of King's brother. Three people were injured at the motel. A. D. King's house was badly damaged, but he and his family were not hurt. In response to the bombings, thousands of Black men and women filled the streets, smashing windows, burning cars, and throwing rocks and bricks. State troopers swept in, striking with billy clubs and rifle butts. A.D. drove around town with a megaphone, trying to calm the crowds, urging everyone to go home. His brother rushed back to Birmingham. President Kennedy put federal troops on alert, announcing that he would not let extremists shatter the agreement reached between the protesters and the city.

King spoke the next day at the Sixth Avenue Baptist Church, where he emphasized nonviolence. "I'm convinced we're going to see an integrated Birmingham in the next few weeks," he said. "All of the white people in

Birmingham are not bad people. All of the white people in Birmingham are not against what we are fighting for. I'm sorry, but I will never teach any of you to hate white people." His voice rose higher and higher. "I'm teaching you to love those who hate us and love those who love us. Love *everybody*, because God said love!"

After the Birmingham conflict, a *Newsweek* magazine poll showed 95 percent of Black leaders and 88 percent of all Black respondents considered King their best spokesman. Jackie Robinson ranked second. Malcolm X didn't make the list. In a Gallup poll that surveyed a broader pool of Americans, King failed to rank among the ten most admired men in the world for 1963. That list included only white men.

King saw in Birmingham that widespread disorder and publicity had been more effective than economic boycotts. In plotting his next move, he considered turning the SCLC into a national membership organization. Such a strategy would have put the SCLC in direct competition with the NAACP and further chilled King's relationship with Roy Wilkins. But it also would have created a more stable base of income for the organization, perhaps allowing King to cut back on his travel. In 1963, the SCLC had a staff of forty and a budget of $450,000—up from $60,000 in 1960 but still tiny for an advocacy organization seeking to make a national impact. King raised about $100,000 of that with personal appearances. The NAACP's budget, by comparison, was almost three times that of the SCLC. But King was focused on more than fiscal matters. As a national membership organization, he said, the SCLC would be able to broaden its scope and attack racial discrimination in other regions of the country. "I will have to face the decision soon on whether I should be limiting myself to the South," he said. "In the North there are brothers and sisters who are suffering discrimination that is even more agonizing, in a sense, than in the South . . . In the South, at least the Negro can see progress, whereas in the North all he sees is retrogression."

King's letter from the Birmingham jail had included a searing attack on white moderates. He knew that many of the northern liberals who funded his work in the South resisted change in their own lives, businesses, and communities. He also knew that political leaders, including President Kennedy, found it expedient to treat racism as a purely southern phenomenon. When third-world nations and the Soviet Union criticized America for its treatment of Black citizens, Kennedy could blame the moral failure on racist diehards in the South while bragging about his admiration and support for Martin Luther King Jr.

Meantime, many Black people in the North, watching the action in Birmingham, in Mississippi, and elsewhere, took up the fight. In Detroit, thousands marched to mark the twentieth anniversary of a wartime race riot that took thirty-four lives. In Philadelphia, the Congress of Racial Equality staged sit-ins at the mayor's office to protest discrimination in hiring. In Brooklyn, CORE organized a rent strike to fight slumlords who collected rent from Black tenants but failed to provide adequate living conditions.

King went on tour, speaking to crowds of twenty-five thousand in Los Angeles and ten thousand in Chicago. As he made his way across the country, Lerone Bennett Jr. wrote, "the fire he had lighted in Birmingham leaped from ghetto to ghetto, igniting charges of social energy and welding Negroes of all ranks into a mass of indignation. With a despair born of one hundred years of oppression, with new hope born in Birmingham, Negroes exploded in the streets of America, sprawling in front of cars and bulldozers, standing-in, sitting-in, marching, singing, shouting: 'Freedom Now!'"

King had stirred the nation's conscience. With help from Bull Connor and George Wallace, he had made it impossible for white people to ignore the plight of Black people in the South. "A revolutionary condition exists," wrote the venerable syndicated newspaper columnist Walter Lippmann. "The cause of desegregation must cease to be a Negro movement, blessed by white politicians from the Northern states. It must become a national movement to enforce national laws, led and directed by the National Government." When the Negro people believe that the American government is fighting for their equality, Lippmann wrote, the nation might move peacefully toward genuine unity.

On May 24, Robert Kennedy, at the prompting of James Baldwin, met with a group of Black artists and writers at the Kennedy family's apartment at 24

Central Park South in Manhattan. Those in attendance included Harry Belafonte, Lena Horne, Lorraine Hansberry, Clarence Jones, Kenneth B. Clark,
Edwin C. Berry of the Union League, and Jerome Smith, a Freedom Rider
and CORE field-worker. After Smith described what he had experienced and
complained that he didn't know how much longer he could remain nonviolent, the meeting became antagonistic. The attorney general took it personally. He said he had come seeking ideas, not attacks. But the dialogue went
on three hours, stopping suddenly "out of sheer exhaustion," as the historian
and Kennedy confidant Arthur M. Schlesinger Jr. put it.

"Bobby . . . didn't understand our urgency," Baldwin said later, adding
that Kennedy didn't understand the depth of the problem, and "our appre-
hension of his misunderstanding made it very tense and finally very ugly. If
we couldn't make the Attorney General of the United States, who was a fairly
young and intelligent man, understand the urgency of the Black situation,
then there wasn't any hope at all!"

Though Kennedy resented the way he was treated, Schlesinger said, the
group's message got through to him. "He began, I believe, to grasp as from
the inside the nature of black anguish," Schlesinger wrote.

Less than a week later, on May 30, King sent a telegram to the White House,
asking to meet with the president and the attorney general. He was told they
were too busy.

When King phoned Stanley Levison the next day to discuss strategy, the
FBI monitored the call and notified Robert Kennedy, who asked the bureau
to share the account of the conversation with his brother. Soon afterward,
in another discussion monitored by the FBI, King told Levison that the announcement of a massive march on Washington might help put pressure on
the president. Bayard Rustin and A. Philip Randolph had been discussing
such a march for months, and Rustin had been longing for one for decades.
Levison asked King if a series of Birmingham-style protests might be more
effective.

But King had more than marches and protests at his disposal as he pushed for change. On June 9, 1963, he appeared on national television, in an interview with David Susskind, and used the opportunity to apply pressure on the president, saying Kennedy "has not yet given the leadership that the enormity of the problem demands." He also pushed at white moderates in the North, who criticized racism in the South while ignoring it and enjoying the advantages of it in their own communities.

"There is a great deal of hypocrisy in the North, and the southern white man is more honest in coming right out and saying openly what he feels about the Negro," he told Susskind. "The North must be eternally vigilant. It must not become complacent, because if this happens many of the subtle types of discrimination will continue to grow and develop and . . . the *de facto* segregation of the North will become as great as the legal segregation of the South."

King said he had never seen Black people more aroused, more determined. He warned that for the Negro everywhere, not only in the South, "there will be no stopping point short of justice and freedom."

Two days later, on June 11, Governor Wallace barred the door of the administration building at the University of Alabama to prevent two Black students from enrolling. Wallace stood aside later in the day after President Kennedy federalized the Alabama National Guard. Robert and John Kennedy spent the whole day receiving updates and talking about the situation in Alabama. It was at this moment, according to Harris Wofford, that Kennedy committed to "go all-out" in an effort to pass strong new civil rights legislation and lead a sweeping push for racial justice. Every one of the president's aides opposed it, fearing it would damage his chances for reelection, said Wofford. Only Bobby Kennedy offered encouragement.

That evening, President Kennedy made a televised speech in which he called on Congress to enact legislation that would end all segregation in public facilities. Kennedy ad-libbed the last four minutes of his speech, in which he said:

We have a right to expect that the Negro community will be responsible, will uphold the law, but they have a right to expect that the law will be fair, that the Constitution will be color blind, as Justice Harlan said at the turn of the century. This is what we are talking about and this is a matter which concerns this country and what it stands for, and in meeting it I ask the support of all our citizens.

It was the kind of address King had hoped to hear. Kennedy had not only put racial justice high on the national agenda but also committed his government to the cause. The job of ending racial discrimination would not be done with token gestures. It would be done with meaningful action by local, state, and federal authorities, Kennedy said. It would be done by citizens everywhere in their everyday lives. "Those who do nothing are inviting shame as well as violence," he said. "Those who act boldly are recognizing right as well as reality."

King called Kennedy's speech "the most eloquent, passionate, and unequivocal plea for civil rights, for justice toward the Negro ever made by any president."

Hours after the president's address, Medgar Evers, the NAACP's Mississippi field secretary, was gunned down as he walked from his car to his house in Jackson. "The sniper's bullet," wrote Claude Sitton in *The New York Times*, "struck him just below the right shoulder blade. The slug crashed through a front window of the home, penetrated an interior wall, ricocheted off a refrigerator and struck a coffee pot . . . Evers staggered to the doorway, his keys in his hand, and collapsed near the steps. His wife, Myrlie, and their three children rushed to the door . . . The screaming of the children, 'Daddy! Daddy! Daddy!' awoke a neighbor."

A week later, Kennedy proposed a sweeping civil rights bill. It wasn't that he had suddenly awakened to the plight of the Black community, his brother Robert said; it was that, for the first time, much of the nation had. For the first time, a powerful civil rights law had a chance.

In an interview one year later, King said:

Well, I think Birmingham did it . . . Birmingham created such a crisis in race relations that it . . . could no longer be ignored. And I'm

sure that, as the president faced . . . the terrible brutality and inhumanity of a Bull Connor and all that went along with him, he came
to see in a way that he had probably never seen—and in a way that
many other people finally came to see—that segregation was morally wrong and it did something to the souls of both the segregator
and the segregated.

PART III

26

The Dream, Part One

A NEW SENSE of hope and a new determination filled King after Birmingham.

The summer of 1963 marked the start of a nationwide revolution, when, as *Newsweek* magazine put it, "19 million U.S. Negroes demanded payment of the century-old promissory note called the Emancipation Proclamation," and King remained their most respected leader.

"We the Negro people are now not afraid," said Carrie Allen, a grocery store worker in Union Springs, Alabama. "We have woke up."

Protests erupted in hundreds of cities and towns. Protesters sat in at lunch counters and lined up at courthouses to register to vote, risking their lives and livelihoods every time. The white news organizations in the North not only covered the action but also reported on the conditions underlying the protests, helping many Americans to better comprehend the roots of racism, a lesson most had never received at home or in school. "The wellsprings of the river of Negro protest lie in a world as remote and as unfamiliar to most white Americans as the far side of the moon—the dark side," reported *Newsweek*. "Who are these revolutionaries? What do they want?"

Now King had the dual job of inspiring the protesters and explaining them to white America. "Undeniably," he wrote, "the Negro had been an object of sympathy and wore the scars of deep grievances, but the nation had come to count on him as a creature who would quietly endure, silently suffer and patiently wait. He was well trained in service and, whatever the provocation, he neither pushed back nor spoke back." But no more. "Just as lightning makes no sound before it strikes, the Negro revolution generated quickly . . . And the virtues so long regarded as the exclusive property of the white South—gallantry, loyalty and pride—had passed to the Negro demonstrators."

Gallantry, loyalty, and pride were on display everywhere as new assaults against segregation arose almost every day. Meanwhile, President Kennedy met with governors, business officials, labor leaders, and Republicans in Congress to build support for a civil rights bill that would, among other things, open all public accommodations to all people. Big businesses responded. The F. W. Woolworth Company told reporters it had integrated lunch counters in 150 cities since the sit-ins began in 1960. In the suburbs of Washington, D.C., a chain of movie theaters removed its WHITES ONLY signs. After a meeting with Robert Kennedy, the owner of the Austin, Texas–based Night Hawk restaurant chain agreed to integrate all his dining establishments. More than a dozen other restaurants in Austin followed Night Hawk's lead. The Howard Johnson Company, a frequent target of demonstrators, agreed to desegregate all its company-owned restaurants, except for four in Alabama. With his new song, "Blowin' in the Wind," Bob Dylan expressed what many were feeling, suggesting that change is as unavoidable as the air that swirls around us.

King saw it himself. He saw it in Jackson, Mississippi, where he attended the funeral for Medgar Evers and where five hundred demonstrators sang, clapped, and taunted police officers by shouting, "Shoot, shoot, shoot." The police didn't shoot, but they did use fire hoses and dogs to break up the crowd and make twenty-seven arrests—and even that didn't stop the protests. He saw it in Chicago, where a coalition of civil rights groups protested the city's segregated and unequal schools.

"We are on the threshold of a significant breakthrough," King told Stanley Levison in a phone call recorded by the FBI on June 4, "and the greatest weapon is mass demonstration."

Was he right, King asked Levison, to think the time had come?

"The time is now," Levison said.

By the summer of 1963, King may have been at the peak of his powers as a prophet and a political operative. Anything was possible, and yet everything was uncertain.

As a student, back when he and Coretta were dating, he had promised that he would one day kill Jim Crow. If Kennedy delivered a strong civil rights bill and businesses across the country continued to desegregate, King might claim he had delivered on that promise. Racism would not vanish in that instant, but his children might grow up in a country without legalized segregation. What then? Once, King had expressed the desire to teach, following in the footsteps of W. E. B. Du Bois and Benjamin Mays. But now, even in his private conversations with Levison, King made no suggestion of pulling back. The influence of Gandhi seemed to grow stronger. Like Gandhi, King wrote, the Negro "was willing to risk martyrdom in order to move and stir the conscience of his community and the nation. Instead of submitting to surreptitious cruelty in thousands of dark jail cells and on countless shadowed street corners, he would force his oppressor to commit his brutality openly . . . with the rest of the world looking on."

King possessed the ability to move through uncertainty, going in with a plan but also knowing that the plan would change in response to countless unknown twists of fate, guided by faith in God and confidence in himself. Now he believed a tipping point might be at hand. With groups like SNCC and CORE organizing in the South, with support from the Justice Department and new legislation from Congress, with the NAACP litigating, and with increased Black voter registration, the system of Jim Crow–style oppression might collapse. At the same time, King faced challenges beyond dealing with a cautious president. He faced a violent reaction from white segregationists who saw their own definition of patriotism and their vision of American society under attack. He faced pressure from a growing radical wing of the civil rights movement, personified by but not limited to Malcolm X, who didn't trust the white people in power to ever share that power. He faced a suspicious FBI director and an increasingly anxious attorney general. The harder King pushed, the harder those opposing forces might push back. Nevertheless, he pushed.

On July 11, King traveled to Danville, Virginia, the last capital of the Confederacy, to support a demonstration. When reporters pointed out that an injunction barred the demonstration, King replied: "I have so many injunctions that I don't even look at them anymore. I was enjoined January 15, 1929, when I was born in the United States a Negro."

John F. Kennedy may have been at the peak of his powers, too.

Though the youngest president ever to take office declared in his inaugural address that the torch had been passed to a new generation, much of his time in office had been consumed by the old struggle of the Western powers versus communism and a determination to win over nations that had not chosen a side. Eight months earlier—on Monday, October 22, 1962—Kennedy had gone on television and radio to alert the nation to an existential crisis. The Soviet Union had moved previously undetected nuclear weapons into communist Cuba. Their missiles sat less than fifteen minutes by air from Washington, D.C., putting the world closer to annihilation than ever before or since. Kennedy stressed patience.

He considered Khrushchev's point of view. "If anybody is around to write after this," he told his brother at the time of the missile crisis, "they are going to understand that we made every effort to find peace and every effort to give our adversary room to move." The president lined up international support, placed U.S. forces on nuclear alert, and prepared for a possible invasion of Cuba. He announced a military blockade to keep more missiles from reaching the island. For forty-eight hours, Americans waited in terror as Soviet ships approached the blockade. Kennedy's deliberation gave the Soviets time to make their missiles combat ready. But, in the end, catastrophe was avoided. The Soviet Union agreed to pull its missiles from Cuba in exchange for the secret removal of American missiles in Turkey.

Kennedy had not planned to make civil rights the focus of the second half of his first term, and he worried about the prospect. The president was concerned that the civil rights issue "was going to be his political swan song," his brother Robert said. "We used to discuss whether what had been done was the right thing to do, just the fact that I'd gotten him into so much difficulty. We used to talk about it every three days, because there was so much attention focused on it at that time in an unpleasant way." If the civil rights legislation failed, while other legislation was delayed, Kennedy might lose his bid for reelection in 1964 over an issue that he could have avoided.

"Burke—this is not getting any better," Robert Kennedy jotted in a memo to Burke Marshall, head of the Justice Department's Civil Rights Division. The reference was to King's ongoing ties with Levison and the SCLC's Jack O'Dell. The FBI had found nothing to indicate that Levison had ongoing communist ties, but the agency nonetheless continued to eavesdrop and file reports to Robert Kennedy, eager to perpetuate the narrative that the Reds were using King to "destabilize American society," as the FBI's Deke DeLoach put it. Paranoia about communism ran so high that some people believed fluoridation of the water was a plot; in such an environment, it was easy to convince Americans, especially in the South, that the civil rights movement might also be a scheme to undermine democracy.

Robert Kennedy did not share J. Edgar Hoover's obsession with the influence of communists in the civil rights movement. If anything, Kennedy had a vested interest in supporting King. He had learned from his agonizing meeting in New York with James Baldwin and others that the movement was "going away from Martin Luther King to some of these younger people, who had no belief or confidence in the system of government," Kennedy said. Still, the attorney general continued to worry that if King's relationship with Levison became public, "not only would it damage [King], but it would also . . . damage any possible chance of the passage of legislation."

On June 15, 1963, more than three thousand people, most of them Black, marched down the sidewalks along Pennsylvania Avenue in Washington. When they massed in front of the Justice Department, Robert Kennedy stepped outside, to the cheers of the marchers. With a typed set of notes in his left hand and a bullhorn in his right, he addressed the crowd. The federal government was working hard to deliver equal justice for Negroes, he said, "but we still have a long way to go."

Two days later, Robert Kennedy phoned J. Edgar Hoover and proposed

that Burke Marshall give King more information about his associates' communist connections. Hoover agreed to the proposal, but the bureau still offered no concrete information showing communist influence within King's
organization, and the proposed talk never took place. If the nation had been
less gripped by fear of the communist menace and if top law enforcement
officials had not been conditioned to view Black people as a threat, King's
ties to Levison might have been disregarded. The Kennedys might have recognized that Levison's true loyalty, whatever his past, was to King and his
cause. The Kennedys might also have recognized the danger inherent in the
FBI's growing obsession with King. But they didn't. After failing to provide
Marshall evidence of Levison's communist ties, the FBI raised the stakes,
claiming falsely that Levison was more than a secret member of the Communist Party, that he was a key figure in the Soviet intelligence apparatus. As
the Kennedy administration pressed for its civil rights bill, the FBI increased
its scrutiny and filed more reports on King.

Beginning in early June, President Kennedy met with business leaders, educators, labor leaders, religious leaders, and governors—more than
a thousand people in all—pushing them to integrate. "Bob Kennedy—that
was all his idea," said Burke Marshall, who noted that the attorney general
was spending almost all his time on civil rights matters. "He organized it
personally . . . did the groundwork on them, did the follow-up . . . And what
he wanted to accomplish was to create . . . political pressure from the top of
society as well as from the bottom for this legislation." The Kennedys now
believed integration was the moral thing to do. They also wanted to stop the
racial turmoil sweeping the country, which reflected poorly on the nation
and gave the Soviet Union cause to criticize American democracy.

Malcolm X turned up the pressure, announcing plans to split his time
between New York and Washington, boasting that by 1970, "ninety percent
of the Negroes will be converted to Islam." Birmingham, he continued,
proved that white people in power would not compromise:

Birmingham is an example of what can happen when the Negroes
rely on the whites to solve their problems for them. The whites will
never open the doors to the Negroes, who must learn to stand on

their own feet, rely on themselves to improve their human condition . . . We don't preach hatred and violence. But we believe that if a four-legged or two-legged dog attacks a Negro he should be killed . . . We are only telling the truth about how the white man treats the Black man.

King was not directly involved in shaping the civil rights bill; most of that work was done by men such as Whitney Young of the Urban League and Clarence Mitchell and Roy Wilkins of the NAACP. Instead, King announced plans for a massive August march on Washington intended, in large part, to pressure Congress. A. Philip Randolph had been pushing for a march on Washington since 1941. When King announced his support for Randolph's march, SNCC, CORE, the Urban League, and the NAACP all agreed to participate. In a televised interview, King warned that if the federal government failed to respond to the demands of peaceful protesters, "it may open the door for the more extremist groups." He added: "It can develop into a very explosive situation. I mean explosive in terms of violence."

The Reverend George Lawrence, a Brooklyn pastor and SCLC regional representative, vowed at a press conference in New York that if the civil rights bill got held up by filibuster or weakened in compromise, the result would be "massive acts of civil disobedience all over the nation," with sit-ins at bus depots and train tracks and "bodies prostrate on runways of airports." Lawrence made his message clear: "We have a powder keg situation in America." The same sentiment came up often when journalists interviewed Black Americans in the summer of 1963. "Them white folks get scared when a Negro gets mad," said a St. Louis housewife who gave her name to a reporter as Mrs. Clyde Durham, "and we gonna have to get good and mad and let them know we mean business."

King, in private, expressed concern about that powder keg: "The Negro is shedding himself of his fear," he said, "and my real worry is how we will keep this fearlessness from rising to violent proportions."

King and others had little optimism about civil rights legislation. They weren't sure Kennedy's promised bill would pass, and, if it did pass, they weren't sure it would be effective. They planned for more marches. President

Kennedy worried the strategy might backfire—continued protests might anger moderates in Congress. On June 22, both Kennedy brothers were at the White House to confer with a group of twenty-nine civil rights leaders. King attended, of course, along with Roy Wilkins, James Farmer of CORE, A. Philip Randolph, and others. Malcolm X was not invited. Kennedy used the occasion to announce steps to curtail discrimination in hiring for government-funded construction projects and on military bases. The activists promised to help build support for Kennedy's civil rights legislation, but they rejected his suggestion that they pause their protests. In fact, King told Kennedy he planned to bring additional protests to Washington if opponents of the civil rights bill tried to use a filibuster to stop the law's passage.

"We want success in Congress," the president told the Black leaders, "not just a big show at the Capitol. Some of these people are looking for an excuse to be against us. I don't want to give any of them a chance to say, 'yes, I'm for the bill but I'm damned if I will vote for it at the point of a gun." Kennedy called the proposed march on Washington "a great mistake."

King disagreed. The march, he said, would channel the grievances of an oppressed population. It would demonstrate their unity and passion. It would dramatize the issue of American racism and build support for reform in regions of the country that had not yet seen demonstrations. "It may seem ill-timed," he told the president. "Frankly, I have never engaged in any direct-action movement which did not seem ill-timed. Some people thought Birmingham ill-timed."

"Including the Attorney General," President Kennedy said.

The president closed the discussion with a quip: "I don't think you should all be totally harsh on Bull Connor. After all, he has done more for civil rights than almost anybody else."

After the meeting, Kennedy asked King to join him for a private conversation in the Rose Garden. The president warned King he was under surveillance and urged him not to let loyalty to friends damage his cause. "They're communists," Kennedy said, referring to Levison and O'Dell. "You've got to get rid of them. If they [the opponents of civil rights] shoot you down, they'll shoot us down too—so we're asking you to be careful." Burke Marshall had pulled King aside earlier that day to tell him the same.

King soon suspended O'Dell, but he held his ground on Levison, telling Kennedy and others that he knew and trusted his longtime friend and adviser. Later, King joked that Kennedy had probably invited him to walk in the Rose Garden because J. Edgar Hoover had bugged the Oval Office.

———— • ————

The next day, June 23, King traveled to Detroit to lead an event that Black journalists described as the greatest organized demonstration of Black pride in American history. More than 125,000 people filled the city's downtown streets, singing, waving American flags, and raising signs that read "Stop Jim Crow," "Evers Died for You," and "No More Waiting."

White politicians supported the marchers, with Michigan's Republican governor, George Romney, proclaiming it "Freedom March Day," and Detroit's Democratic mayor, Jerome Cavanagh, joining the rally. When the participants reached the city's convention center, Cobo Hall, twelve thousand of them squeezed into the arena and tens of thousands more massed outside, listening through loudspeakers as Rosa Parks spoke and the Four Tops sang. The Four Tops had recently joined the roster of the fast-growing record company Motown, a Black-owned business that topped the music charts with songs that beckoned optimistically toward the future and attracted big audiences of Black and white fans. Motown's founder, Berry Gordy, had plans to record King's speech that day, marking the label's first foray into spoken-word recordings.

King arrived late, as was his habit. In this case, it may have been because he stopped at the home of his aunt, Cleo Louise King Hill, Daddy King's younger sister, who served him a slice of her homemade peach pie. He nevertheless arrived in time to present the keynote address. Dressed in a black suit, as was also his habit, King stepped atop a footstool and paused as he looked out at the sea of expectant faces, a scene that might have reminded him of his first big speech in Montgomery seven and a half years earlier, when he could see the faces of only a fraction of his audience but knew his words would carry beyond the walls.

"Now is the time to make real the promise of democracy," he said, making use of a phrase President Kennedy had used in his recent television address. It was an adaptation of a speech he'd given in North Carolina in 1962, one in which he had borrowed phrases and cadences from a Langston Hughes poem called "I Dream a World," as the scholar W. Jason Miller has written. King mixed poetry, prayer, and patriotism. For another speaker, the result might have been ponderous, but King used these religious and poetic forces to inspire all America to seize this moment of opportunity; to bring peace, love, and equality to those who had so long been denied; and to fulfill, at last, the promise of the American dream.

"I go back to believing the new day is coming," King continued. "And, so, this afternoon, I have a dream. It is a dream deeply rooted in the American dream." He settled into a rocking rhythm familiar to anyone who had heard him in church, the audience urging him along.

In this dream, he said, all over the South, the children of slaveholders and the children of those they enslaved lived together as brothers. In this dream, Black and white children held hands in harmony. In this dream, his own children would be judged "on the content of their character not on the color of their skin."

He repeated, "I have a dream," again and again, as he built, slowly, to his conclusion:

> I have a dream this afternoon that the brotherhood of man will become a reality in *this* day. And with *this* faith I will go out and carve a tunnel of hope through the mountain of despair . . . With *this* faith, *we* will be able to achieve this new day when *all* of God's children . . . join hands and sing with the Negroes in the spiritual of old: Free at last, free at last, thank God almighty we are free at last.

The crowd roared and sang out in praise.

A week later, back in New York, the Reverend George Lawrence drove King from Brooklyn to Harlem, where King was set to speak at Salem Church. The night before, Malcolm X had urged his followers to "go up there tomorrow and let Uncle Tom know that we are against him and do not believe what he preaches." Late in the afternoon of June 30, hundreds of people lined the street and gazed from open windows, waiting for King. About twenty policemen stood by. King and Lawrence pulled up to the curb at Seventh Avenue and 129th Street in Lawrence's Ford Thunderbird. As King got out of the car, a small number of Black people in the crowd began to boo. Half a dozen or so eggs were thrown, some of them striking the car but not King. Cheering from the crowd soon drowned the booing. Even so, King was dismayed.

"I can't understand what my colored brothers have against me," he told the crowd inside the church. "I have become accustomed to white mobs in Mississippi and Alabama, but I have not yet adjusted myself to what I just experienced in Harlem."

Quickly, he said, he stopped "feeling rejected," and focused instead on the poverty, isolation, and frustration "that cause individuals to respond like this."

The March on Washington for Jobs and Freedom had originally been scheduled for October 1963, but planners moved it up to August 28, seeking to build on the momentum generated by the protests in Birmingham and hoping to pressure Congress to pass strong civil rights legislation. A. Philip Randolph asked Bayard Rustin to handle the logistics. Working from a four-story tenement building in Harlem, Rustin and his team mailed thousands of manuals, leaflets, and flyers to everyone they could think of who might be sympathetic to the cause, including religious leaders and union organizers. Organizers of the march not only helped charter buses and planes but also trained a team of two thousand leaders with instructions on maintaining order. Posters and handbills said the marchers would demand meaningful civil rights laws, massive federal works programs, full employment, decent housing, the right to vote, and integrated schools. Rustin told reporters he expected a crowd of about 100,000. Privately, he told colleagues he had no idea how many people would turn out.

Ten speakers were slated, one from each of the groups sponsoring the march. King was awarded the final spot on the program, in part because no one wanted to follow him. SNCC leaders, meanwhile, grew increasingly concerned that organizers were too focused on civility, that the government had succeeded in taking the militancy out of the march. "The Kennedy administration seemed to be trying to silence us in a way, to cool us off," John Lewis later wrote.

King spent little time preparing his remarks for the march. In the weeks leading up to the Washington demonstration, he enjoyed a rare vacation with his wife and children, spending ten days at the home of the lawyer Clarence Jones in the Riverdale section of the Bronx. Martin and Coretta took the children to the top of the Empire State Building and for a ride on the Staten Island Ferry. But King did not completely clear his calendar of work. He snuck in a brief trip to Chicago, where he made a speech and stopped by the Cook County Jail to see his friend Dick Gregory, the comedian, who had been arrested in a protest against school segregation. Activists in the city had been complaining for years that Chicago's schools were overwhelmingly segregated, and that many predominantly Black schools suffered overcrowding. City officials responded by purchasing trailers to house the overflow of students rather than reassigning them to schools in white neighborhoods. As the schools grew even more segregated, year by year, the protests grew larger, attracting King's attention but not his participation—at least not yet.

While in New York with his family, King spent part of each day working on a new book, one that grew from the seed of his "Letter from Birmingham Jail." Levison negotiated a deal for King with the publishing company Harper & Row. King would call the book *Why We Can't Wait*, the title a response to the many white politicians and religious leaders who complained that Negroes sought too much too soon. He would open the book with a sharp warning that he intended to carry his crusade beyond the American South, addressing issues that might make some of his northern backers skittish:

It is the beginning of the year of our Lord 1963. I see a young Negro boy. He is sitting on the stoop of a vermin-infested apartment house in Harlem. The stench of garbage is in the halls. The drunks, the jobless, the junkies are shadow figures in his everyday world. The boy goes to a school attended mostly by Negro students with a scattering of Puerto Ricans. His father is one of the jobless. His mother is a sleep-in domestic, working for a family on Long Island.

He had an August 31 deadline for the book but would need more time.

While staying with Clarence Jones, King was monitored by the FBI, the bureau having tapped the lawyer's phone on the premise that Jones had once shown interest in communism. A memo dated August 13, marked confidential, said that King used Jones's phone on August 8 to talk to Dorothy Cotton in a "conversation of a personal nature in which King asked if she had been a good girl and she replied that she had to be good inasmuch as he was not with her." The memo continued: "She stated she missed King and asked whether his wife had been able to hear any of this conversation. He assured her that his wife was not able to hear the conversation."

Later that evening, King phoned a woman named Dorothy L. Newborn of suburban Mt. Vernon, New York. Newborn was a former model, the ex-wife of the jazz pianist Phineas Newborn Jr., and a mother of two. According to the same FBI memo, King told Dorothy Newborn that "he loved her madly." Newborn asked if King had reserved a hotel room in Washington. King said he had not. "I will tell you one thing . . . ," Newborn reportedly said, "I am getting tired of playing second fiddle." King was said to answer: "Speak, my darling." King told Newborn he would work on making a hotel reservation, and concluded the call, according to the FBI, saying, "OK baby . . . I love you."

On August 23, the FBI listened and made notes as King spoke to Wyatt Tee Walker about the program for the March on Washington, which was five days away. King said he was worried there would not be enough time for all the speakers and recommended extending the length of the program. He also suggested reducing the number of women on the program from four to one.

Later the same day, King made personal phone calls to two more women.

The first woman, identified as Martha, a resident of Washington, D.C., complained that it had been three months since she'd heard from King. She said she was beginning to doubt his affections, according to the bureau's transcript of the recorded conversation. King said he'd tried calling, but Martha hadn't been home. When Martha expressed disbelief, King changed the subject. "You gonna march with us next week?" he asked. When Martha asked if she could see King the day of the march, he told her no, that he would be too busy, but that he would try to see her before that, on August 25, when he visited Washington to appear on *Meet the Press*.

When King hung up the phone with Martha, at about 5:00 p.m., he quickly placed a call to another woman, identified as Dolores Evans in the FBI records, the wife of a dentist in Los Angeles. King called her "Dodi."

"Oh, I've missed you so much," he said. "You shouldn't do this to me."

King and Evans had been photographed together in late May at an SCLC fundraising event in Los Angeles. The photo appeared in the May 30 edition of the *Los Angeles Sentinel*.

"Please don't talk that way," Evans said. "You make me feel like I'm doing something horrible and I already have a complex, a guilt complex."

"Well, I'm saying this in all of the friendliness and all of the joy that one can say something negative with," King said.

"Yes, I know," she said. "But when you say it, it makes me feel worse, and I suffered, really, from a terrible, terrible complex . . . in the past few days."

"Well, don't," King said.

Later, Evans said: "I'm so afraid that I, in some way, will be connected with you."

"But that could be avoided, the connection," King said.

King promised to phone her again the next day.

"I just love to hear you," he said in signing off.

Clarence Jones didn't know his home phone was tapped in the summer of 1963, when the Kings were his guests. Later, when he got suspicious and raised the subject, King dismissed his concerns, gently mocking his friend for "believing there was an FBI agent in every home."

On July 23, less than a month before King's trip to New York, J. Edgar

Martin Luther King Jr., Montgomery, 1956 (Photograph by Dan Weiner / © John Broderick)

ABOVE: Martin Luther King Sr. and Alberta King at Ebenezer Baptist Church in Atlanta, 1970 (Associated Press)

RIGHT: King graduating from Morehouse College at age nineteen, 1948 (Courtesy of Morehouse College)

Martin and Coretta Scott King with their daughter Yolanda, Dexter Avenue Baptist Church, 1956 (Photograph by Dan Weiner / © John Broderick)

King arrested by Montgomery police, 1958 (Charles Moore / *Montgomery Advertiser*)

Coretta greets Martin as he leaves the Montgomery courthouse, 1956. (Associated Press)

King and Ralph Abernathy ride in a front seat after a yearlong campaign to integrate Montgomery's buses. (Dr. Ernest C. Withers Sr. / Courtesy of the Withers Family Trust)

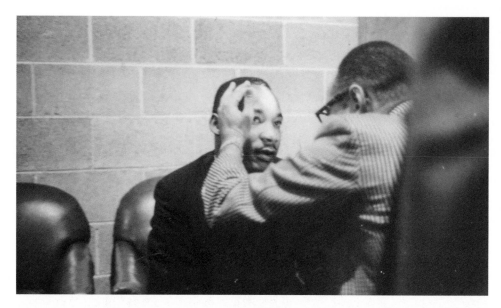

King is examined by a doctor after being punched in the head by Roy James, a member of the American Nazi Party. (James Karales for *Look* magazine / Library of Congress)

King meets with Roy James and declines to press charges. "We have to pray for him," he said. (James Karales for *Look* magazine / Library of Congress)

King at home with family, 563 Johnson Avenue, Atlanta, fall 1962 (James Karales for *Look* magazine / Library of Congress)

Abernathy and King arrested by Birmingham police, April 1963 (Associated Press)

As King delivers his "I Have a Dream" speech, Bayard Rustin (in glasses) stands behind, Gordon "Gunny" Gundrum (park ranger) eyes the crowd, and Mahalia Jackson (hat and back of head visible) stands and shouts. (© Bob Adelman)

King and President Lyndon B. Johnson in the Cabinet Room of the White House, 1966
(LBJ Library photo by Yoichi Okamoto)

King and Abernathy sing at an SCLC retreat, with Dorothy Cotton seated behind King.
(Bob Fitch Photography Archive, Department of Special Collections, Stanford University Library)

King and Andrew Young at the Montgomery airport, 1966 (Bob Fitch Photography Archive, Department of Special Collections, Stanford University Library)

White youths taunt marchers on Chicago's Southwest Side, August 1966. (Associated Press)

Floyd McKissick, King, and Stokely Carmichael lead the Meredith March, Mississippi, June 1966. (Bob Fitch Photography Archive, Department of Special Collections, Stanford University Library)

The final march, Memphis, 1968
(Dr. Ernest C. Withers Sr. / Courtesy
of the Withers Family Trust)

Coretta Scott King holds her youngest daughter, Bernice, during the funeral for her husband, April 1968. (Photograph © Flip Schulke / CORBIS / via Getty Images)

Hoover had sent a memo to Robert Kennedy, again making the case that communist forces were using Levison to influence and control King. Nothing in the hundreds of pages of memos produced by agents suggested that Levison was conducting business with communists or trying to manipulate King for the benefit of the Communist Party. Levison and King spent most of their time on the phone discussing how to make democracy work for all its citizens, talking about the courts, Congress, the media, and the powers of the presidency.

But the FBI clung to its suspicion. The bureau's Atlanta office had been ordered to report on the feasibility of tapping King's home and SCLC office. Though agents reported that the wiretaps could be safely installed in King's home and office, the plan was dropped. Given King's busy travel schedule, Kennedy decided, the wiretaps would not generate enough information to justify the risk involved.

But that would not be the final word.

27

The Dream, Part Two

FRANCINE YEAGER WAS just a blue-jeaned teenager from the South Side of Chicago, with a toothbrush, two bottles of Pepsi, and a change of underwear in her backpack, but she was part of a growing crowd of people, Black and white, arriving by buses and trains, walking, singing, laughing, people from great cities and tiny towns, carrying signs, carrying suitcases, bearing their own private wounds and dreams, everyone walking in the same direction, to the March on Washington for Jobs and Freedom, Wednesday, August 28, 1963.

People had the power to change the world. That's why she was there. She walked under clear skies. The weather was warm, with temperatures inching up to the low eighties, but extremely pleasant for a summer day in Washington, D.C.

Francine was nineteen. She had never before traveled without her parents. But her mother and father hadn't tried to stop her. They sensed her determination, and they knew she was not a kid who got in trouble. Maybe they even admired her bravery. As she watched the events of the civil rights movement on television, Francine had grown steadily more outraged. Bull Connor's dogs in Birmingham had finally compelled her to get involved. How could she live in a world with such hatred and not respond? Anyway, she told her parents, it would be like church, with nice people coming together in a community full of love and hope to make a better world. Her best friend, Florestine, would travel with her. And she would get to hear Martin Luther King Jr.

Special trains from Chicago carried passengers to the march. In almost every major American city, churches and NAACP chapters hired buses and organized car caravans. The SCLC and other organizations covered travel costs for people in need. Francine, a student at Southeast Junior College and a part-time grocery-store cashier, paid her own way. As she got off the train and began walking in the direction of the Lincoln Memorial, she saw young people toting luggage for old people, daddies with their daughters on their shoulders, and mothers pushing babies in strollers. White people called Black people "sir" and "ma'am" and said "Good morning" and "How are you?" Everywhere, it seemed, guitars were strumming.

"Florestine," Francine said, "this is what heaven's gonna be like when we get there."

That feeling of heaven, or racial utopia, is what King, Bayard Rustin, and other organizers of the march had wished and worked for. An assembly line of volunteers used five tons of American cheese to make eighty thousand free sandwiches in what one sandwich-maker called "an act of love." Organizers had hoped for a crowd of 100,000, but by the time the speeches started at two o'clock that afternoon, there were at least 200,000 people, maybe 250,000, gazing in the direction of Abraham Lincoln's statue, crowding along the edges of the long reflecting pool, and spreading out under the surrounding trees. It was televised theater, covered live, presenting Black and white viewers with a message of dignity and pride that the Black press had been trumpeting and the white press had tended to ignore for years.

Knowing that the world would be watching and that many white people expected the march to turn into a riot, organizers reminded participants to behave responsibly. They put out word that they would only permit placards bearing messages on preapproved themes such as voting rights and integration. Police assured them that a small counterprotest by the American Nazi Party would be isolated and closely monitored. City officials ordered bars and liquor stores closed. The Washington Senators postponed two baseball games. Federal offices shut for the day. Workers installed hundreds of portable toilets and drinking fountains.

Ninety-one percent of Americans had television sets in their homes.

All summer long, they had been watching civil rights protests in southern states on the evening news, protests marked by fire hoses, police dogs, and handcuffs. Now, for one day, at least, the nation's three television networks gave live coverage to a protest that transformed the image of the civil rights struggle—transformed the image of people of color—like nothing before or since.

Roger Mudd, the thirty-five-year-old news anchor for CBS, had been so nervous about how he would fill a whole day of live coverage that, upon reaching his position at the Lincoln Memorial, he had vomited. If violence erupted or if the speakers grew too inflammatory, Mudd was told, the Justice Department would flip a cutoff switch on the sound system. But for Mudd and other reporters, the story proved easy to cover. There were no surprises, no calls for violence, no fights. Though three-fourths of the marchers were Black, TV viewers might have thought the racial mix was closer to fifty-fifty, as the camera crews went out of their way to find white faces in the crowd and directors lingered on them, conveying a message of harmony. The day "had all the combined elements of a political rally, a revival meeting, and a 4th of July picnic," commentator Eric Sevareid told viewers on CBS. It was "the biggest gathering of American Negroes in their three hundred years in this country," and evidence, he said, "that the Negro cause is becoming a general and universal cause."

Francine and her friend Florestine paid little attention to the television cameras. They walked and sang and talked to strangers until they got as close as they could to Abe Lincoln. They settled onto a grassy spot to the right of the stage, about halfway down the length of the reflecting pool. Cicadas buzzed in the trees. People around them took off their shoes and lay down in the grass. They dangled their feet in the reflecting pool but did not wade in it. The young women from Chicago would be too far away to see Martin Luther King, but they would hear him just fine.

Bob Dylan, Mahalia Jackson, and others sang. No women had been offered speaking slots, despite pressure from Dorothy Height, president of the National Council of Negro Women. In an attempt at appeasement, it was decided that A. Philip Randolph would ask six women, including Rosa Parks and Myrlie Evers, the widow of Medgar Evers, to stand and be recognized. Parks managed to get in a few words, saying, "Hello, friends of freedom, it's a wonderful day."

John Lewis gave one of the most forceful speeches of the day, complaining that President Kennedy's civil rights bill didn't go far enough, even after Washington's Archbishop Patrick O'Boyle had attempted to censor the speech.

Finally, Randolph introduced King, calling him "the moral leader of our nation."

King stepped up, smiled slightly, and spread the pages of his speech before him. He faced east, looking out over the biggest mass of people he had ever seen, their faces shining in the late-afternoon sun. He wore a black suit, a black tie, a white shirt, and a white pocket square with three triangular peaks. His wristwatch, cufflinks, and wedding band, all gold, threw small sparks of light. Coretta, seated nearby, wore a black-and-white print dress. Rustin, his tie loosened, hustled around the stage, sweating, muttering, puffing cigarettes, scrambling to get people where they belonged. A white National Park Service ranger stood by King's left shoulder, the final line of defense in case someone tried to come at the preacher with a knife or fired a shot from the crowd. Gordon Gundrum was the ranger's name, but everyone called him "Gunny."

He's short. That was the first thing Gunny noticed about King. Though it wasn't his job, the park ranger stepped in front of the famous preacher and lowered the microphones. He wanted to make sure King's voice came through loud and clear and the microphones didn't obstruct anyone's view of King's face. With that done, he turned his focus to the crowd, looking for suspicious behavior. Gunny was twenty-five years old, the fourth of fifteen kids, a sixth-grade dropout, a mountain kid, as he put it, from a small town near Albany, New York. He had never thought of himself as prejudiced, but then again, he couldn't recall ever meeting a Black person as a child. Now, looking out on a sea of faces darker than his own, he recalled a moment as a little boy when he had picked up a penny and put it in his mouth and his grandmother had told him to spit it out because "some nigger might've had that penny in his mouth." That had only confused him. When he joined the U.S. Marine Corps, he and his Black bunkmate couldn't go to the same restaurants around Parris Island in Beaufort, South Carolina. That's when Gunny realized there were big pieces of American life and history he had never considered. It was like learning you had an uncle and a set of cousins you had never met. He thought about that as he scanned the faces in the crowd. What else had he missed? The Black people marching on the Mall had reason to be angry, and yet they were singing and laughing and linking arms with white people.

Gunny stood six feet tall but looked even bigger thanks to his large, tan, broad-brimmed hat. He had been on duty since six in the morning. All day, he had feared an eruption of the kind of violence he'd seen on TV from Birmingham. He hadn't given any thought to who might start the violence, or why. When his boss said to treat the marchers as nicely as possible to avoid sparking an incident, that only heightened his anxiety. At one point, earlier in the afternoon, when the crowd had been riled up by a speaker, Gunny had raised his hand, attempting to restore calm. *Well,* he had thought, *that didn't work.*

At another point, he had spotted a suspicious character, a short, slender Black man with a beard, making his way toward the stage, avoiding eye contact. Gunny had intercepted him.

"Where are you going?"

"I want to go up."

"Where's your pass?" Gunny put his body between the little man and the stage.

"I left it in the hotel room." The little man looked around. "You don't know who I am, do you?"

"No."

"I'm Sammy Davis."

Embarrassed that he had not recognized one of America's best-known entertainers, whom he'd seen many times on television, Gunny escorted him to the stage, where Davis took his seat with the other celebrities who had made the trip, including Josephine Baker, Charlton Heston, Paul Newman, Marlon Brando, Rita Moreno, Harry Belafonte, James Baldwin, Ruby Dee, Tony Curtis, Sidney Poitier, and Steve McQueen.

King gazed at the crowd, "the living, breathing heart" of the movement he had somehow been called to lead. He spoke slowly, his voice solid, strong, calm, but trembling slightly. He was happy to be here, he said, for a day that would be remembered as the greatest public demonstration for freedom in American history.

His face glistened with sweat. He grasped the edges of the lectern and rocked slightly from side to side. No effort had been made to create an aesthetically pleasing backdrop for the afternoon's speakers. Behind King stood rows of sweaty police officers and firefighters working security and wearing folded white hats in tribute to Gandhi. Little if any thought had been given to the appearance of the lectern, where wires and microphones tangled and sprouted like an overrun garden. To the TV producers, the crowd was more interesting than the speakers, whose remarks were mostly political.

Gunny did not dare reach in front of King now, but the microphones still seemed high.

"Five score years ago," King boomed, when Abraham Lincoln signed the Emancipation Proclamation, he offered hope to millions of men and women who'd only known slavery, suffering, and injustice. Our president offered the people a bright and brilliant daybreak after their long night of misery. But one hundred years later, King said, "the Negro is still not free."

"My Lord!" someone in the crowd shouted.

King went on. After one hundred years, Black Americans are still shackled by segregation and discrimination, still isolated by poverty, still made to feel like exiles in their own country.

"Yes, yes!" came a cry. This time it was Mahalia Jackson, seated in front of King and to his left.

"And so, we've come here today to dramatize a shameful condition," King told the crowd.

He had stuck to the script, almost word for word, to that point. He arrived at his hotel in Washington at ten o'clock the night before without having started work on his speech. It took him about two hours to make an outline and another ninety minutes to turn the outline into a finished draft. It was sometime between three and three-thirty when he finished. The other speakers had each been given only eight minutes, and though King had been told he could take ten, he was nevertheless unaccustomed to such brevity. Early in the morning, a final version of the speech was typed, mimeographed, and distributed to the press.

President Kennedy watched on television from the Oval Office. He had never heard or seen King address a crowd.

"He's damn good," the president said.

King continued, still working from his script, still keeping his hands on the lectern. He beseeched this enormous congregation of believers to maintain their courage and pride, to rise above their enemies, to overcome their anger, to avoid the temptation to distrust all white people, to answer the threat of violence with the promise of love. Our white friends here with us today, he said, proved that the destinies of Black and white Americans were inseverable, that there could never be true freedom for anyone until there was freedom for all.

Gunny couldn't take it anymore. He reached out with his left hand and shoved the microphones down, several inches lower, giving Americans watching on TV a quick view of his shirtsleeve and wristwatch and making sure, finally, that viewers would have an unobstructed vision of King's face for the rest of the speech. King didn't seem to notice.

King's stage presence, his poses and gestures, which he had practiced most of his life, radiated through the crowd. The audience yelled and clapped in response to his remark about their shared destiny. Here they were, at least for one afternoon, united.

King continued: There was no turning back now, he said. We must go forward together. We cannot stop, not ever, not so long as Black people are the victims of police brutality; not so long as they remain barred from so many of the nation's hotels and motels; not so long as their housing and schools remain segregated and second-rate; not so long as they are denied the vote.

No, he said, "We cannot turn back!"

He was approaching the ten-minute mark. It was going well, although not as well as Detroit.

Francine Yeager looked around and noticed that a few of the people standing nearby had departed, to beat the traffic. But King's words riveted her. This was why she had come, to hear King give his answer to Bull Connor's dogs, to make sense of what she'd seen on TV, to find faith.

King spoke for them all. We will not be satisfied, he said, "until justice rolls down like waters, and righteousness like a mighty stream."

He shifted his weight side to side now, swaying gently with the rhythm of his own words, using his whole body to say *no, no, no:* We will no longer accept the world as we find it today. We will no longer allow our children to be robbed of their self-worth by signs that read WHITES ONLY.

As King paused and pursed his lips, Francine flashed to a memory from her childhood. She had never seen a WHITES ONLY sign in Chicago, but she vividly recalled the precise moment when she had first felt stripped of her self-worth. It had happened when she had been in the first or second grade at St. Raphael, a Catholic school in Chicago's Englewood neighborhood. The school was about 20 percent Black, 80 percent white, although it was changing quickly as white families moved in droves to the suburbs. Francine's best friend at St. Raphael was a white girl named Geraldine. Geraldine lived across the street from school and went home every day for lunch, returning for recess. One spring day, when Geraldine went home and showed her parents her new class photo, she returned to the playground without her usual smile. The girls were dressed identically in the school uniform of blue jumpers, white blouses, long white socks, and black patent-leather shoes.

"Can I ask you something, Francine?" Geraldine's face blushed.

"Of course!" Francine answered. "You can ask me anything!"

Geraldine paused and stared at her feet. "Are you white or are you nigger?"

Francine did not know what to say. Her thoughts went to her family and how they looked, some darker than others. Francine knew she was fair, with coarse or what some people called "nappy" hair. She thought about Geraldine's question and decided that whatever this "nigger" word meant, she did not like it. The only terms she had ever heard that described her ethnicity were "colored" or "Negro." Having settled that in her own mind, finally, she responded, "I'm colored."

Geraldine walked away. The girls never again played together. Now, as King spoke, Francine felt the pain all over. She wondered, for the first time in years, what had happened to Geraldine.

King's voice seemed to expand in Francine's head. It grew not just louder but bigger. It rippled across the pool and blew through the trees and crowded out her other thoughts. It crowded out Geraldine.

He was nearing the end of his written speech.

Go home, he told the people. Go home to Mississippi, to Louisiana, to Georgia. Go home to Alabama. Go home to your impoverished cities in the North, go home with the knowledge that change will come. Do not give up. No, never give up.

"Let us not wallow in the valley of despair."

Yes, King had started slowly and softly so that he could gradually build power—Gunny was sure of it now. The park ranger found himself caught up in the emotion, distracted from his job. The words came out of King like a song, or a hymn. It was magic, Gunny thought. The people stretched out around and in front of King were no longer listeners. They were singing along with him.

"Yes! Yes!"

"Tell them how it is!"

"Amen! Amen!"

Many journalists assumed he was done. TV networks began to cut away. Silence engulfed the mall; 250,000 people waited. Three months later, King told an interviewer he didn't know why he "turned aside" from his prepared speech, quit it completely, looked up from his typewritten pages, and said: "And so even though we face the difficulties of today and tomorrow . . ." And then he began one of the most famous orations in American history.

"I still have a dream."

He shook his head side to side and then glanced quickly up to the sky. He leaned back the same way he often did in the pulpit when he wanted to engage more intimately with his audience, when he used the language he had absorbed from his father, his grandfather, and other preachers he had heard all his life.

The crowd urged him on.

"It is a dream deeply rooted in the *American* dream," he said.

As he looked down, quickly, a smile brightened his brown eyes.

He had a dream, he said, that America would one day live up to its foundational promise: "We hold these truths to be self-evident, that all men are created equal."

He had a dream, he said, that the children of slave owners and the children of those they'd enslaved would sit together "at the table of brotherhood"; that the state of Mississippi would become a land of justice and equality; that his four children would be judged by the content of their character, not the color of their skin.

"I have a *dream* today!"

He hurried that last sentence, tying it to the previous one like a kite tail, making the words soar higher and faster on a wind that carried everyone along.

"I have a dream," he continued, that even in Alabama, a state ruled by racists and riddled with hate, yes, even in Alabama, little Black children and little white children will "join hands . . . as sisters and brothers."

"I have a dream!" A man's voice echoed King's from the audience.

"Tell 'em about the dream," Mahalia Jackson shouted, her voice drowned out as King began to speak again.

"I have a dream," he said, "that one day every valley shall be exalted, and every hill and mountain shall be made low. The rough places will be made plain . . ."

King flung his right hand up into the air as the words rang out.

Oh, Francine thought, we're *really* going to church now! The spirit had captured the preacher, and what a blessing it was to be here with him. What a blessing to receive words that shone like a beacon, words that came out of the night and lit the darkness and showed you the way forward. Francine felt like King was in conversation with her now, with everyone. He was revealing the path to the future as he dug into the quarries of memory. King reminded listeners that his people had suffered, that their trust had been violated, that they had fought and died in the struggle for freedom, and yet they had never quit. They never *would* quit. His voice was so big, so strong. But this audience was big, too. This audience was strong. We are his witnesses, Francine thought, and we will take his words and make them part of our own hearts. We will carry these words and they will carry us.

King continued, climbing higher. He would leave here today and return home to the South with faith, he said, with faith that America would soon be a true land of brotherhood, that people would go forth from this beautiful gathering and work and pray and struggle and protest with the knowledge that they would soon be free, that all Americans would soon sing out with a new truth: "My country, 'tis of thee, sweet land of liberty, of thee I sing. Land where my fathers died, land of the pilgrim's pride, from every mountainside, let freedom ring."

Let freedom ring.

All over this land.

Let freedom ring.

From New Hampshire, from New York, from California, from Colorado, from Georgia, from Tennessee, from "every hill and molehill of Mississippi."

From every mountainside.

Let freedom ring.

He raised his arm above his head. Then, during his closing words, he stretched out both arms, clenched his fists, and rose onto the balls of his feet:

And . . . when we allow freedom to ring . . . we will . . . speed up that day when all of God's children . . . will . . . join hands and sing in the words of the old Negro spiritual: Free at last! Free at last! Thank God Almighty, we are free at last!

As King stepped back and turned from the crowd, Gunny felt the people's response. As he recalled it years later, waves of energy surged through the air, through the people, and through him, too, and so he quickly stepped in front of King, because he understood that this was a great man who deserved to be protected, and Gunny made his body a shield.

People *do* have the power to change the world, Francine thought. This is how it happens. *This is history.*

People hugged and cried and vowed to carry on the fight for freedom and cleaned up their trash and promised to keep in touch. Years later, after she herself had become a pastor in the American Baptist ministry and after she had had children and grandchildren and retired with her husband to Merrillville, Indiana, Francine would remember three things from the train ride home that night: the steel mills of Pittsburgh lighting the night sky in shades of orange, purple, and red; the joyous songs of her fellow passengers; and the oath she took with Florestine that they would work and sacrifice and carry King's dream of justice with them forever.

28

"The Most Dangerous Negro"

KING WENT DIRECTLY from the March on Washington to the White House.

"I'd like to go," said Coretta, who had spoken to President Kennedy on the phone but had never met him.

"Oh, you can't go," King told his wife.

"Well, I don't see why I can't go."

He blamed it on protocol. Coretta wasn't on the list of approved visitors.

"Well, alright then," she said.

———

"I have a dream," John F. Kennedy said as he shook King's hand.

It was five in the afternoon. Kennedy had spent all morning in a secret meeting about strategy in Vietnam, and he would convene another meeting on the same subject that evening, but not before conferring for an hour with King and nine other leaders of the march. Upon learning the men had not eaten lunch, Kennedy ordered ham, cheese, and turkey sandwiches.

Roy Wilkins, Walter Reuther, and A. Philip Randolph did most of the talking, stressing that they wanted Kennedy's civil rights legislation to include provisions to end discriminatory hiring. Kennedy was delighted that the big event had come off smoothly. The men laughed and largely agreed on issues, although Vice President Lyndon Johnson warned that the vote on civil rights legislation faced uncertain prospects. The president, Johnson said with his Texas drawl, "can plead and lead and persuade and even threaten Congress, but he can't run the Congress."

Kennedy urged the leaders to tell the press they fully expected Republican members of Congress to vote for the bill, in order to "make it more difficult for them to say no." He also encouraged them to think beyond the law, to think about how Black people could help themselves, to take inspiration from the rapid economic rise of the American Jewish community, and "get the Negro community to regard the education of their children as the best way out." When Kennedy mentioned for a second time the importance of persuading Black children to work diligently in school, as Jewish families did, Wilkins politely interrupted the president to say Black parents were doing their best to educate their children and would do so more easily if the parents and children didn't face "built-in discrimination."

King asked whether pressure could be brought to bear on former president Eisenhower to support Kennedy's rights legislation, but otherwise he remained largely silent, as was his habit when in meetings attended by Randolph and Wilkins.

After the meeting, King and the other march leaders were driven to a nearby television studio, where they taped an interview with a moderator named Jay Richard Kennedy, a novelist, screenwriter, and activist who had once served as a business manager to Harry Belafonte. Unbeknownst to King or anyone else in the civil rights arena, Jay Kennedy now served as the Central Intelligence Agency's top informant on civil rights activity.

The March on Washington offered a glimpse of King's beloved community—Black and white people literally singing in harmony; mobilized teenagers mingling with middle-aged union workers; all of them committed to fighting racism, raising consciousness, and pressing the federal government to act.

King's popularity soared after his speech, but not everyone was moved in the way he intended. Malcolm X referred to the giant demonstration as "The Farce on Washington," and he accused King and other leaders of the event of toning down their militancy to appease their white financial backers and the Kennedy administration. That's why planners of the march agreed to avoid disrupting the city and government, Malcolm claimed. That's why James Baldwin wasn't allowed to speak, Malcolm said, "because they know

Baldwin is liable to say anything ... It was a circus, a performance that beat anything Hollywood could ever do."

But if the march had been too tame for Malcolm X, it was still too militant for J. Edgar Hoover and others at the FBI. A week before the march, the bureau's domestic intelligence division had produced a sixty-eight-page report stating that the Communist Party of America—a tiny organization with only about four thousand members by that time—exerted little or no influence on the civil rights movement. Hoover did not take it well. "This memo reminds me vividly of those I received when Castro took over Cuba," the director scrawled on the report's cover letter. "You contended then that Castro & his cohorts were not Communists & not influenced by Communists ... I for one can't ignore the memos re King, O'Dell, Levison ... et al as having only infinitesimal effect on the efforts to exploit the American Negro by the Communists."

Two days after the March on Washington, the FBI's head of intelligence operations, William C. Sullivan, produced a memo that reversed the report he had helped produce a week earlier:

The Director is correct. We were completely wrong about believing the evidence was not sufficient to determine some years ago that Fidel Castro was not a communist or under communist influence. On investigating and writing about communism and the American Negro, we had better remember that and profit by the lesson it should teach us.

... Personally, I believe in the light of King's powerful demagogic speech yesterday he stands head and shoulders over all other Negro leaders put together when it comes to influencing great masses of Negroes. We must mark him now, if we have not done so before, as the most dangerous Negro of the future in this Nation from the standpoint of communism, the Negro and national security.

Sullivan's memo may have been intended primarily to appease his angry boss, who hated to see King gain greater fame as a moral leader, but it also served as a reminder, as the historian David J. Garrow has written, that the FBI was guided by both paternalism and racism in its assumption that Black Americans were especially vulnerable to communist manipulation. Hoover and the FBI did not treat Roy Wilkins, Whitney Young, or A. Philip Randolph the way they treated King. Among the leading civil rights activists, King, with his ties to Stanley Levison and his ability to move masses of people, was perceived as the biggest threat. Given the level of risk King posed, Sullivan wrote, the FBI might find it necessary to go beyond the kind of "conclusive evidence . . . that would stand up in testimony or court" in building its case against King. Never mind the law, in other words; King had to be stopped.

Oddly, and inexplicably, the FBI failed to emphasize to the Kennedys one of the strongest pieces of evidence it held to tie King to a so-called secret member of the Communist Party of the United States of America (CPUSA), a political party with ties to the Soviet Union. In 1957 and 1958, Levison had arranged for King to receive a total of $10,000 in cash gifts from himself and a close friend. At the same time, and into the early 1960s, Levison continued to make substantial donations to the CPUSA, according to recently released FBI documents: $25,000 in 1957, $12,000 in 1958, $13,000 in 1959, $12,000 in 1960, $12,000 in 1961, and at least $2,500 in 1962. At the time, by way of comparison, the median family home in America cost about $12,000. If the FBI's claims are true, why would Levison continue to make donations when he had otherwise seemingly cut ties with the CPUSA? One theory, put forth by Garrow, is that Levison had invested the party's money in American businesses decades earlier and felt duty-bound to share the returns. Andrew Levison, Stanley's son, offers another explanation. Stanley remained friends with and business adviser to former Communist Party supporters who made contributions out of "habit and sentiment," as he put it, even as their activity in the party diminished. The FBI may have attributed all those contributions to Stanley. Regardless of the money's source, the bureau knew about Levison's donations at the time, but by 1963, as Garrow writes, executives at the FBI may have failed to make their best case against King because they had become preoccupied with his private life.

In the view of Hoover's men, the Jones wiretaps revealed King's immorality as well as his ongoing contact with Levison. Another FBI memo, dated September 16, 1963, said King's alleged ties to communists proved that the American Negro had become the Communist Party's "favorite target" as it worked to undermine democracy. But Hoover and his men feared more than the communists; they also feared change. King, Sullivan wrote, was "the most dangerous and effective Negro leader in the country," adding that "we are right now in this nation engaged in a form of social revolution."

No matter how strongly King stressed the American values of his movement, no matter how often he quoted from the Constitution, the Bible, and patriotic songs, he was still perceived and treated as a threat. No one within the FBI or the Kennedy administration suggested that law enforcement ought to be protecting leaders of the civil rights movement rather than investigating and undermining them.

In interviews in the summer of 1963, King addressed the rumors of communist influence on the civil rights movement, rumors that had been spread by FBI leaks to the press. In one television interview, he said:

> SCLC is so firmly established as a Christian nonviolent movement that it would be impossible to be influenced in any way by the method or philosophy of communism . . . It is our firm conviction that communism is based on an ethical relativism, a metaphysical materialism, a crippling totalitarianism and a denial of human freedom that we can never accept . . . The means we use must be as pure as the end we seek.

Those who feared communist influence on the civil rights movement, he said, ought to recognize that equal justice was a democratic ideal:

> I think the conditions which brought the street demonstrations into being do much more to aid the communist cause than the determined struggle to get rid of these conditions. The fact is, as long as you have segregation and discrimination alive in this nation, the communists will have a convenient propaganda weapon.

Robert Kennedy, unconvinced, struggled to understand why King didn't take the communist threat more seriously. At the very least, King's ties to Levison damaged King's reputation in Washington, where such things mattered. On October 7, the FBI formally requested permission to install wiretap coverage on King's home and office in Atlanta. Three days later, Robert Kennedy signed the authorization. He also approved an FBI request for a wiretap on Bayard Rustin.

Years later, Robert Kennedy's associates would argue that the attorney general had permitted the wiretaps because Hoover had pressured him to do so. In a series of 1964 interviews that would remain sealed until after his death, Kennedy said he believed that Levison was a communist and that King had fallen under Levison's influence. "Their goals were identical, really, I suppose," Kennedy said of Levison and King. But in those same interviews, the attorney general offered additional context for his capitulation. Hoover, he said, claimed he had dirt on the Kennedys, too, including a report about a liaison with "a group of girls on the twelfth floor . . . of the LaSalle Hotel." Robert Kennedy said the liaison never happened, but he offered it as evidence of Hoover's methods.

The interviewer asked: "Did you think, or do you now think that Mr. Hoover is a dangerous person . . . or just nasty?"

"No," Kennedy said, "I think he's dangerous."

Kennedy went on to say that he and President Kennedy had viewed Hoover as "a danger that we could control."

But, at times, it appeared that Hoover was the one more fully in control. Agents installed taps on the phones in King's home on Johnson Avenue in Atlanta, as well as in his SCLC office, at 330 Auburn Avenue, NE. The FBI rented a one-bedroom unit on the twentieth floor of the Peachtree Towers apartment building, where agents would monitor and record King's calls. On Friday, November 8, 1963, federal agents began listening to every phone call placed to or from King's home and office. Robert Kennedy, as attorney general, was supposed to review the wiretaps after thirty days and decide, based on the content of the calls, if they were warranted. But it would appear that he never did. By the end of November

1963, other events would arise to overwhelm not just Robert Kennedy but the entire world.

——— • ———

"No expression one-tenth so radical has ever been heard by so many Americans," wrote Murray Kempton in *The New Republic*, describing King's "I Have a Dream" speech. Norman Mailer, writing in *Esquire*, said the American Negro, the group with the greatest potential for violence in America, showed they "also possessed the finest capacity for order and discipline in the nation." Their act of "revolutionary genius" on the Mall in Washington, he wrote, "created the second leg of the movement."

In the wake of the March on Washington, the nationwide protest movement grew, as King had hoped it would. In Birmingham, more than 3,600 Black people registered to vote in a two-month period, an unprecedented number. In St. Augustine, Florida, the Reverend C. T. Vivian, an SCLC staff member, began making plans to challenge that city's segregationist customs and laws in much the same way they'd been challenged in Birmingham. "Here was Martin King becoming bigger and bigger and bigger, right? And it's just exactly what I wanted," Vivian recalled years later.

Even within homes, within relationships, people acted in bold new ways after the March on Washington. Walter Stovall, a white man from Georgia, decided to be more open with his work colleagues about his marriage to a Black woman named Charlayne Hunter. "I can now wear my wedding ring all the time," Stovall wrote at the time. "I used to just wear it on weekends." In California, a white real estate dealer, Richard S. Hallmark, quit his job because his company wouldn't rent or sell to Negroes. "I'm not a martyr or a crusader, but this made me ashamed," he said. "The colored people are here to stay, so we might as well get used to it."

King's popularity had never been greater, but he did not exult in celebration after the March on Washington. As Dorothy Cotton recalled: "What I noticed often happened with Dr. King is, when he got great and positive feedback, as he did after that speech, he could become very subdued, because that, too, laid an extra burden on him."

At a staff retreat, King and other SCLC leaders considered towns that might make good targets for the next big protest. "More and more, I have come to feel that our next attack will have to be more than just getting a lunch counter integrated or a department store to take down discriminatory signs," King said. "I feel we will have to assault the whole system of segregation in a community." Yet again, however, the integration movement faced opposition, in part from radical Black activists, including Malcolm X, who said King had been co-opted and defanged by the Kennedys. Malcolm said he was impressed with the March on Washington "the same way I would be with the Rose Bowl Game." King's speech was moving, but "while King was having a dream, the rest of us Negroes are having a nightmare." An even more virulent response, however, came from angry white people, mostly in the South, who heard King use words like "attack" and "assault" and made up their minds to fight back.

On September 4, seven days after the March on Washington, a white man named Robert Chambliss drove from Birmingham to nearby Daisy City to buy dynamite. He said he needed a whole case—140 sticks—to clear land the KKK had just bought.

"If you are going to blow up some niggers," said the man selling Chambliss the dynamite, "I will throw in a few extra sticks."

Chambliss, known to some as "Dynamite Bob" for his skill with explosives, put the sticks in the trunk of his blue Ford Falcon and drove back to Birmingham.

For Alabama's segregationists—"the segs," as northern white reporters called them—the attacks on their preferred way of life kept coming. Governor George Wallace vowed to use the Alabama National Guard to keep schools from integrating, while President Kennedy threatened to federalize those same troops to protect Black students. The same night that Robert Chambliss bought his dynamite, a blast ripped apart the Birmingham home of Arthur Shores, a Black attorney.

A riot followed in Birmingham's Smithfield section, injuring twenty-one people, including four policemen. A twenty-one-year-old Black man named John Coley, an army veteran, was shot and killed during the melee, perhaps because he bore a resemblance to Fred Shuttlesworth, who was also at the scene. Initially, police said Coley had been shot after he had burst from a house firing a gun. When investigators determined that Coley had been an unarmed spectator, police changed their story and said he had been the accidental victim of stray shotgun pellets fired over the rioters' heads. Motorcades rolled through the city, with white protesters waving Confederate flags.

On September 13, after a fiery speech by a segregationist, more than a hundred white student protesters stormed city hall. One student stood on Albert Boutwell's desk, waving a Confederate flag, while others dropped burning cigarettes on the carpet. A police officer asked one of the students to read City Ordinance 63–17, covering demonstrations and disorders, but no one was arrested. The mayor told the students they had his support. "The whole question of integration is distasteful to me," Boutwell said. "I believe the good Lord had good reasons for a difference in the races. I believe they will be preserved."

First came the ticking, then the blast.

Doors burst open, walls shook, stained-glass windows shattered. Fire blazed from the roof. Sobs and screams filled the air, followed by sirens.

It was September 15, 1963, Youth Day at Sixteenth Street Baptist Church in Birmingham, the same church where young men and women had gathered months earlier, praying and singing, before crossing the street to face police dogs and water cannons. Now fifteen sticks of dynamite had blown out the east side of the redbrick church. When rescuers reached the basement, they found four dead children buried under debris. Killed were eleven-year-old Denise McNair and fourteen-year-olds Addie Mae Collins, Cynthia Wesley, and Carole Robertson. Twenty more people were injured, including Addie Mae Collins's twelve-year-old sister, Sarah, who was blinded in one eye. It would take fourteen years for officials to convict Chambliss for his role in the bombing. It would take thirty years for two other participants, Thomas Edwin Blanton Jr. and Bobby Frank Cherry, to be convicted.

King got the news as he prepared to step up to the pulpit at Ebenezer. "Dear God, why?" he asked himself. He flew to Birmingham the same day, but not before sending two telegrams. The first went to President Kennedy, warning that the "worst racial holocaust this nation has ever seen" would occur if the federal government did not do something. His second telegram, to Governor Wallace, read: "The blood of our little children is on your hands."

Feelings of grief and bitterness flooded him. He thought about the fact that the face of Jesus Christ had been, literally, blown from a stained-glass window and wondered if it was a sign that evil had shattered the message of Christ. He asked himself, he said, "if men were this bestial, was it all worth it? Was there any hope? Was there any way out?"

No city officials attended the funeral service for the victims of the bombing. Governor Wallace said the blast could have been the work of communists or publicity-seeking civil rights workers. But, at the same time, fifty-three white Birmingham lawyers released a public statement calling for support of integration laws. One white lawyer, Charles Morgan, speaking to the Young Men's Business Club, declared: "Who did it? The answer should be we all did it . . . Every person in this community who has, in any way, contributed to the popularity of hatred is at least as guilty, or more so, than the demented fool who threw that bomb."

King eulogized the girls at a crowded church in Birmingham, calling them "heroines of a holy crusade for freedom and human dignity." He went on to answer his own questions about whether there was any hope, any way out. The children "did not die in vain," he said. "Good still has a way of growing out of evil. The blood of these little girls must serve as a revitalizing force to bring light to this dark city."

But the words were not enough for everyone. "As I watched the ineffectual moral outrage of the Black southern preachers, the cold coverage of the white media and the posturing of the John F. Kennedy White House, my whole world view fell into place," recalled Kareem Abdul-Jabbar, a sixteen-year-old high school basketball star still going by the name Lew Alcindor at the time. "My faith was exploded . . . I would gladly have killed whoever killed those girls."

Sixty-eight days after the murders in Birmingham, a sniper shot President Kennedy in Dallas. King was at home in Atlanta. When he heard the news on TV, he called out to Coretta. Together, they prayed for Kennedy's survival. When he learned Kennedy was dead, King sat in silence for a long time.

"This is what is going to happen to me also," he finally said.

Coretta held her husband's hand. She wanted to say something that would comfort him but couldn't find words.

"I could not say, 'It won't happen to you,'" she recalled. "I felt he was right."

29

Man of the Year

IT WAS 9:20 p.m., November 25, 1963, three days after Kennedy's assassination, and President Lyndon B. Johnson's voice twanged through the telephone.

> JOHNSON: I want to tell you . . . how worthy I'm going to try to be of all your hopes . . .
> KING: You know you have our support and backing. We know what a difficult period this is.
> JOHNSON: It's just an impossible period.

Johnson went on to talk about his legislative goals, which included passing a major civil rights bill. King said Johnson's stance was "mighty fine."

> KING: I think one of the great tributes we can pay in memory of President Kennedy is to try to enact some of the great progressive policies that he sought to initiate.
> JOHNSON: Well, I'm gonna support 'em all and you can count on that . . . and I'll have to have y'all's help, and I never needed it more than I do now.
> KING: Well, you know you have it, and just feel free to call on us for anything.
> JOHNSON: Thank you so much, Martin . . . Any suggestions you got, bring 'em in.

A week later, King met for forty-five minutes with Johnson and the presidential civil rights adviser Lee White. The president made no mention of the FBI's spying or its concerns about King's alleged links to purported Communist Party members. King emerged from the meeting to say he was impressed with the president's dedication to issues affecting the American Negro.

Johnson used his first major address as president to declare his commitment to Kennedy's civil rights bill. Though his relationship with Robert Kennedy was a tense one, Johnson would attempt to work with the attorney general on the most urgent domestic issue of their time. In an interview years later, however, Johnson would criticize Robert Kennedy for the decision to spy on King. "I thought I was dealing with a child. I never did understand Bobby," Johnson said. "I never did understand how the press built him into the great figure that he was. He came into public life as [Senator Joseph] McCarthy's counsel and then he was [Senator John] McClellan's counsel and then he tapped Martin Luther King's telephone wire . . . Martin Luther King's activity was financed by Kennedy." Johnson may have been referring to Robert Kennedy's work in helping to raise bond money for protesters in Birmingham. "He tapped the phone with his right hand and gave him one-hundred-dollar bills with the left," Johnson said.

Johnson's reflections did not acknowledge the aggressive role the attorney general had played in the fight against racial discrimination and in shaping civil rights legislation, but they did make clear the extreme level of animosity between the president and his attorney general.

As King spent Christmas in Atlanta, Hoover's men listened to the family's every phone call. They heard nothing about communism. But, within days of the start of the wiretaps, agents reported on King's conversations with three women identified by agents as "girlfriends."

Hoover's goal, now, was to ruin the "burrhead," as he called King. Was it because King was a leftist? Because he had ties to alleged communists? Because he had publicly criticized white southern FBI agents' conduct in civil rights cases? Because he was Black? Because he posed a threat to the status quo? Regardless, Hoover had spotted a weakness in King and sought to exploit it.

As Burke Marshall of the Justice Department put it, "I think the FBI and Mr. Hoover deliberately set out to get Martin King."

———— • ————

On December 29, 1963, *Time* named King its Man of the Year, the first Black person ever selected for the honor. But the reporter who visited and interviewed King over a period of eight days found a man who did not seem to be enjoying his prominence, and a man who no longer radiated the warmth and optimism he had manifested most of his life. The magazine's story described him as an "unimposing figure" with a "funereal" wardrobe (five of his six suits were black) and "very little sense of humor." King, according to the magazine, spent little time at home, slept but four hours a night, and lived under the constant threat of assassination. Even the portrait commissioned for the cover of the magazine—and approved by its subject—made the Man of the Year appear more worried than triumphant, with his shoulders slanted forward and his eyes cast down and to the magazine reader's right.

"The quality, not the longevity, of one's life is what is important," King told the reporter. "If you are cut down in a movement that is designed to save the soul of a nation, then no other death could be more redemptive."

The following week, as the magazine arrived by mail at American homes and received prominent display on newsstands, King traveled to Washington to listen to oral arguments in a Supreme Court case, *New York Times Co. v. Sullivan,* that had begun years earlier when Montgomery's police commissioner had accused Ralph Abernathy and others of publishing a defamatory advertisement in *The New York Times.* Before his arrival, FBI agents had installed listening devices in two lamps and had housekeepers place the lamps in rooms reserved for King and his associates at the Willard Hotel. In two other nearby rooms, agents installed radio receivers and tape recorders to monitor King's activity.

On January 5, the surveillance recorded a group of people in a room occupied by King's friend Logan Kearse, the pastor of Baltimore's Cornerstone Baptist Church, according to a recently released summary from the files of William C. Sullivan, the assistant director leading the King investigation. The complete transcripts and audio recordings of this and other King encounters are not scheduled for release until 2027, under a judge's order. As of 2022, only a report characterizing the recording was available. The report claimed that Kearse had "brought to Washington several women 'parishioners' of his church" and invited King and others to meet them. "The group met in his room and discussed which women among the parishioners would be suitable for natural and unnatural sex acts," according to the bureau's report. "When one of the women protested that she did not approve of this, the Baptist minister immediately and forcibly raped her." Someone edited the document with a pen and added a shocking and unsupported claim: "King looked on, laughed and offered advice." The next night, according to the same report, King and about a dozen others "participated in a sex orgy" involving consumption of alcohol, "the vilest language imaginable," and "acts of degeneracy and depravity."

Should the report be trusted, given what is now known about Hoover's obsession and the FBI's deliberate program to disrupt and discredit King?

"I think it's questionable evidence," said Stanley Pottinger, a former assistant attorney general in the Justice Department, who listened to some of the FBI's tapes of King, including a portion of the Willard Hotel recordings. The voices on the recordings were difficult to discern, Pottinger said, especially when there were large numbers of people in a room. When the voices were clear, the FBI transcriptions were accurate, Pottinger said. But reports like the one from the Willard Hotel did not include transcriptions, only summaries made by agents. It will remain difficult to draw conclusions, he said, at least until the tapes and transcripts are released.

In 1976, Justice Department officials reviewed fifteen reels of audiotape from the Willard Hotel, as well as a composite tape containing selections from the fifteen reels. The composite tape "appeared to consist of little more than episodes of private conversations and activities which the Bureau chose to extract from the original recordings," according to the Justice Department. Although the report did not say whether investigators listened to every minute of every recording, the report, published in 1977, contained no mention of an orgy or an alleged rape.

"We do not contemplate dissemination of this information at this time but will utilise [*sic*] it, together with results of additional future coverage, in our plan to expose King for what he is," an FBI official wrote on January 11, 1964. In a memo two days later, Sullivan wrote: "It is highly important that we do develop further information of this type in order that we may completely discredit King as the leader of the Negro people."

After the Willard Hotel surveillance, agents scrambled to install bugs in more hotel rooms. They also circulated transcripts and shared recordings with White House officials and reporters, trying to undermine King's credibility. Years later, when it presented no risk to his career, Sullivan blamed Hoover for the tactics. "Many of us," Sullivan wrote, "myself included, sent Hoover memos that would echo his attitude toward King just to get him off our backs."

Within twenty-four hours of his return from Washington, according to the FBI, King arranged to meet Dorothy Cotton at the apartment on Delmar Lane in Atlanta that King often used as a retreat. The FBI continued stalking King in February when he traveled to Hawaii and Los Angeles with Dolores Evans, according to the Bureau.

In mid-April, Hoover sent a memo to one of the president's top aides reporting that King had been telling friends he would engage in a hunger strike if a filibuster stalled the civil rights bill. "I'm getting ready to die," King was reported to have said several times. "Don't water it down. Or let me die."

Less than two weeks later, on April 26, 1964, King traveled to Las Vegas for a speech to the local NAACP chapter and, according to a state agent, took part in a sexual encounter with the gospel singer Clara Ward and a female dancer whom Ward had paid $100. The agent interviewed the dancer three weeks after the encounter and filed a report. "She said that she was actually afraid to indicate that she wanted to leave but finally was so disgusted with the activity that she did," read the report. King was accompanied in Las Vegas by a "paramour" from Los Angeles who spent time in King's suite that night but did not participate in the sex with Ward and the dancer, according to the FBI.

Over a span of seventeen months, according to Sullivan, the FBI made recordings of King in fifteen hotel rooms, "and Hoover listened to all of them." Hoover also instructed agents to make the tapes available to "some members of the press, to some select congressmen, and to President Johnson." When the recording devices picked up King making a highly distasteful joke about John F. Kennedy's sex life, Hoover made certain Kennedy's brother, the attorney general, heard about it. Jackie Kennedy, the president's widow, heard about it from Robert Kennedy and said later, in an oral history, "I just can't see a picture of Martin Luther King without thinking, you know, that man's terrible."

Coretta King knew about her husband's infidelities, the bureau reported, and, "outwardly, at least, adopted a cynical attitude toward them, indicating that she is content to be Mrs. Martin Luther King. Periodically, however, she berates King for not fulfilling his marital 'responsibilities.'" At that point someone, possibly Sullivan, added another handwritten sentence to the document: "He told her she should go out and have some sexual affairs of her own. This bureau has no knowledge to show that Mrs. Martin L. King is other than an honorable woman of good character."

The FBI soon began attempting to use the information it gathered to undermine King's work. Bureau officials talked about planting news stories that would drive a wedge between King and Roy Wilkins. They talked about encouraging additional news stories about King's travel expenses. When FBI agents learned that two colleges planned to offer King honorary degrees, they moved to block the awards by sharing some of the information gathered on the civil rights leader with school leaders. Agents also discussed the possibility of elevating another Black man to replace King as the leader of the movement after the bureau wrecked King's reputation. They considered a New York attorney named Samuel R. Pierce Jr., who would go on to serve as secretary of Housing and Urban Development under President Ronald Reagan. "When this is done, and it can and will be done," Sullivan wrote in a memo, "obviously much confusion will reign . . . The Negroes will be left without a national leader of sufficiently compelling personality to steer them in the proper direction. This is what could happen, but need not happen if the right kind of a national Negro leader could at this time be gradually developed so as to overshadow Dr. King."

When Hoover told a congressional committee that communists influenced the civil rights movement, King fired back. Given how badly Black people were treated in America, he said, it was remarkable that the communists had failed to win more hearts and minds. He said he found it "difficult to accept the word of the FBI on communistic infiltration in the civil rights movement when it has been so completely ineffectual in protecting the Negro from brutality in the South." King went on to say he wished Hoover would apply the same diligence in seeking church bombers that he did in hunting for communists in the civil rights movement. In one wiretapped phone conversation, King revealed his anger and perhaps a sense of helplessness, saying in regard to Hoover: "I want to hit him hard."

It was a bewildering time for King, his friend Harry Belafonte said. When King visited Belafonte's Manhattan apartment, the men would ordinarily take off their shoes, place a record on the turntable, and sing along with Lead Belly, Odetta, or the folk trio Peter, Paul, and Mary. But such moments of relaxation were rare. "Martin had a lot to sort out," Belafonte said. "The more he got into it, the more he appreciated that the role he was to play would be at a severe cost." Even at the peak of his fame, Belafonte said, King remained unconvinced that he deserved the recognition and power he'd accrued. He seemed, to Belafonte, to be a genuinely modest man, a man who enjoyed an audience but had little interest in the trappings of fame. Though King accepted his renown as the price of effective leadership, he was riddled with doubt about his own worthiness.

The person who helped him most during moments of self-criticism, ironically, was Stanley Levison, who was the reason for much of the FBI scrutiny facing King. It was Levison, said Belafonte, who reminded King that a man didn't have to be perfect to be the perfect leader at a moment of opportunity. But King had been trying to limit his interactions with Levison to appease Robert Kennedy. The separation added to King's distress.

At one point, Belafonte noticed that King had developed a nervous tic, like a small hiccup located at the back of his throat, so subtle you had to be in a quiet room to hear it. Belafonte interpreted it as a sign of anxiety. When it finally vanished, he asked King if he'd been aware of the tic.

"Yeah," he said.

"Well, how did you get rid of it?" Belafonte asked.

"I made peace."

"With what?"

"With death."

* * *

On January 8, 1964, in just the second major speech of his presidency, and just seven weeks after John Kennedy's assassination, Lyndon Johnson used his State of the Union address to announce a crusade to transform American society. "Unfortunately," he said, "many Americans live on the outskirts of hope—some because of their poverty, and some because of their color, and all too many because of both. Our task is to replace their despair with opportunity. This administration today, here and now, declares unconditional war on poverty in America." The weapons in the war would be "better schools, and better health, and better homes, and better training, and better job opportunities." The goals were not only to relieve poverty but also to cure and prevent it, to right the nation's vast wrongs.

Six days after the State of the Union speech, the FBI showed President Johnson a transcript of the salacious recordings made during King's stay at the Willard Hotel. Four days after that, Johnson hosted King, Roy Wilkins, James Farmer, and Whitney Young for a meeting at the White House, where the president predicted success for his civil rights bill. After the session, King told reporters, "We are not prepared to compromise in any form," and said he was pleased with Johnson's commitment to the issue.

At the time, King was revising his book on the Birmingham Movement. Toward the end of the manuscript, he had included a proposal for a program of national reparations for slavery and segregation. After his meeting with Johnson, he discussed with his advisers whether to rewrite the section to focus on poverty, not race, considering that the civil rights bill seemed more likely to pass quickly and Johnson would soon be pivoting toward a broader campaign. In the end, King compromised. The "Negro Bill of Rights" became the "Bill of Rights for the Disadvantaged," calling for the eradication of poverty, guaranteed full employment, and an unconditional income paid to everyone as a right of citizenship. King did not forget about race, though. His Bill of Rights emphasized redress for the historical exploitation and victimization of the descendants of enslaved people, as well as for their ongoing mistreatment. Prejudice and economic injustice, he wrote, were "two evils" in "malignant kinship." It was no accident, he continued, that wages were lower in the South than in the North, that Black people had lower levels of education than white, and that the automation of jobs affected Black people in disproportion to white.

King wrote:

> Few people consider the fact that, in addition to being enslaved for two centuries, the Negro was, during all those years, robbed of the wages of his toil. No amount of gold could provide an adequate compensation for the exploitation and humiliation of the Negro in America down through the centuries . . . Yet a price can be placed on unpaid wages. The ancient common law has always provided a remedy for the appropriation of the labor of one human being by another. This law should be made to apply for American Negroes. The payment should be in the form of a massive program by the government of special, compensatory measures which could be regarded as a settlement in accordance with the accepted practice of common law. Such measures would certainly be less expensive than any computation based on two centuries of unpaid wages and accumulated interest.

King saw Black reparations as a form of social atonement, a way to heal, to restore bonds shattered by slavery and racism. That's why he focused on "the forgotten white poor" as well as the mistreated Black. That's why he refused to make a choice between ending poverty and compensating Black people for the injustices they suffered. America had a responsibility to do both, he insisted.

"Democracy, in its finest sense," he wrote, "is payment."

It had been nearly ten years since the Supreme Court's decision in *Brown v. Board of Education.* In those ten years, *The New York Times* observed, "the stereotype of the apathetic, satisfied Negro" had been obliterated; the federal government had joined the fight against racial segregation; and people of all races and political views had come to agree that race would be "the great domestic issue facing this country" for years to come. After a decade, however, only 1 percent of white children in the South went to school with Negro children. Negro men were still twice as likely as white men to be unemployed, and the median income for Negro families remained stuck at about half that of white families. Many schools in the North had grown *more* segregated as white families over the course of the decade migrated from cities to suburbs, in part to escape the growing urban Negro population. In New York City, a majority of white people surveyed by *The New York Times* said the civil rights movement had gone too far. The white people surveyed "spoke of Negroes' receiving 'everything on a silver platter' and of 'reverse discrimination' against whites," the *Times* reported. More than half of those surveyed said the movement was going "too fast," and nearly half said picketing hurt the Negro cause more than it helped. The *Times* referred to the phenomenon as a "white backlash," a new term for the newspaper in 1964.

The movement in America, so far, had been something rare—an attempt by rebels to join, not overthrow, a society. The respectful nature of the protests had a great deal to do with King's Christianity-based leadership. But how long could it last? How far would it go? Would the revolution be contained, asked the *Times*, in a manner "acceptable to enlightened white opinion?" Did it have to? By 1964, some white writers suggested, as the southern author Robert Penn Warren put it, that King's style of leadership had "somehow given a sense of a soft line, a rapprochement, that flatters the white man's sense of security."

As violent assaults took innocent Black lives, as Kennedy's assassination left many to wonder if the promise of federal support for equal rights would fade, as Alabama governor George Wallace received impressive support in the Democratic presidential primaries, and as Republicans rallied around conservative senator Barry M. Goldwater of Arizona as their candidate in the 1964 general election, the tone of the freedom struggle changed. Some of the protesters who had viewed nonviolence as a useful tactic grew angry at the slow pace of change. Even some of the white people most sympathetic to the cause began to fear, as one southern correspondent for a northern newspaper wrote, "that black demands for 'Freedom now! Freedom now!' were about to pull the pillars of society crashing down." At the same time, Wallace and other segregationists fanned the flames of racism, creating an environment in which white violence against Black activists became an increasing threat. The peaceful spirit of the March on Washington seemed like a dream slipping out of reach.

"Martin Luther King, God bless his heart, can't stop the trouble today," the comedian and activist Dick Gregory said. "In the South, the whites consider him a radical, a communist. But in the North the Negro considers him a conservative . . . Out of 22 million Negroes only one million are with Malcolm X. But a lot of them are saying, 'I'm tired of King. I'm tired of the NAACP. I'm ready to fight the white folks.' They are saying 'Get your goddamn shotgun and move over with Malcolm X.' So, Malcolm X is getting to be about the only man who can stop a race riot. Martin Luther King can't stop one."

King challenged those who called him soft. Putting the "love ethic" at the heart of the struggle hardly represented weakness, he argued, adding that "many of these arguments come from those who have gotten so caught up in bitterness that they cannot see the deep moral issues involved." When asked how America ought to prevent race riots, King gave a simple reply: Integrate faster. If violence erupted, it would be the fault of the white people in power who failed to solve the problem, not the Black people who demanded change.

"I'm not saying that you sit down and patiently accept injustice," he said. "I'm talking about a very strong force, where you stand up with all your might against an evil system."

King tried to keep the SCLC young and energetic, even though it was run mostly by Baptist preachers in their thirties and forties. "We need people who are confrontational," he told Andrew Young when they hired Hosea Williams, a hotheaded activist and World War II veteran. "Hosea was always trying to get himself killed," said Young, "and we'd say, 'Hosea, take your time.'" King was wise enough to know he needed mad geniuses such as Williams and James Bevel, although sometimes he got more madness than he could handle. Bevel, said Young, "was probably clinically insane."

As the SCLC planned its work for 1964, Bevel lobbied for a return to Birmingham, where two major department stores had yet to integrate, no Black policemen had been hired, and voter registration lagged. Wyatt Tee Walker nominated Atlanta for the SCLC's next target, while Hosea Williams, Bernard Lee, and others pushed for St. Augustine, Florida. Others, eager to put maximum pressure on Congress, argued for a series of protests in Washington, D.C. Internal tensions grew. Walker demanded that King fire the difficult-to-control Bevel. When King refused, Walker announced plans to quit. King considered replacing Walker with Bayard Rustin, whose reputation as an organizer had been enhanced by his work for the March on Washington, but some of the Baptist ministers in the SCLC opposed Rustin because of his homosexuality while others opposed him for his imperious personality.

The demands of the job kept King on the move, scrambling to generate publicity and revenue. He told audiences he planned to organize a statewide voter drive in Alabama. At the same time, the SCLC launched Operation Breadbasket to compel government and businesses to boost Black employment. Beginning in Atlanta, Operation Breadbasket promoted a new form of political protest, demanding more and better jobs for Black people, backed by the threat of boycotts. King believed similar pressure might be applied to improve housing conditions in poor communities. The SCLC also joined other organizations to form a new group, the Council of Federated Organizations (COFO), to coordinate efforts in fighting Jim Crow and registering voters in Mississippi. But it still wasn't clear if King or anyone else had a coherent long-term strategy.

"The truth of the matter is that SCLC is broke," Wyatt Tee Walker wrote to Roy Wilkins, explaining why the SCLC had failed to pay its $500 annual membership fee to the NAACP. "We seem to be in a slump that shows no immediate sign of changing." For the fiscal year ending August 31, 1964, the organization would declare expenses of $677,381, which was $50,000 more than it had in income.

In a letter to King marked "confidential," the attorney Clarence B. Jones described "a total collapse of effective civil rights leadership." After the March on Washington, Jones wrote, civil rights groups of every orientation, led by King, should have united and carried out a sweeping plan of action. Instead, they were doing little more than reacting to each crisis and waiting for the federal government to act. At the same time, Jones said, "a counter-revolutionary alliance of forces" went to work, allowing George Wallace and Barry Goldwater to gain influence as defenders of the segregated status quo.

Years later, Hosea Williams would say that King and the SCLC struggled "mainly because of Martin's middle-class makeup," which prevented him from seeing rank-and-file volunteers as potential leaders, capable of organizing their own campaigns. By the mid-1960s, Williams said, the Black masses began to lose interest in leadership by the Black middle and upper classes. When that happened, King didn't adapt, and other, more militant leaders, including Malcolm X, filled the void.

Vincent Harding, a history professor who protested with King in Albany and elsewhere, had a similar view of the challenges King faced in 1964. King's strategy was to get on national TV, appeal to the conscience of white America, and hope that those white Americans would pressure the government to end discrimination. But that strategy left many Black Americans feeling unempowered and dubious of the government's commitment to change. "I remember Martin constantly being amazed at . . . the coldness of the analysis that was coming out of the White House," Harding said. "Very often he talked about how *unfeeling* they seemed to be . . . and how hesitant they were to move." King wanted to believe, Harding added, that politicians would be guided by the same moral imperatives that guided him. He wanted to believe that the people in power shared his sense of responsibility for the welfare of others. But to some, that made him appear naïve.

After the U.S. House of Representatives approved President Johnson's civil rights bill, southern Democrats in the Senate attempted to kill it by filibustering, as King had feared. Critics of the bill complained that it infringed on property rights and personal autonomy. Mississippi's governor, Ross Barnett, said Black protesters had taken to the streets to "blackmail this Congress." Opponents attacked the bill on constitutional grounds, too, arguing that it was illegal for the federal government to tell private businesses whom to serve. On March 26, 1964, King visited the Capitol, hoping his presence would focus media attention and put pressure on reluctant elected officials to permit the bill to come to a vote. On his way out of the building, followed by a gaggle of reporters and photographers, King crossed paths with Malcolm X, who had also come to Washington to put pressure on Congress. It was the first time the men had met.

"Well, Malcolm, good to see you," said King.

"Good to see you," said Malcolm.

"Hold it!" called the photographers standing nearby, as they moved in to take pictures.

The men shook hands. Given more time to talk, they might have discovered much in common, including frequent death threats, FBI surveillance, and the belief that the civil rights bill would not be enough to deliver justice or calm the growing unrest among Black Americans. Like King, Malcolm had become not merely a voice for change but a famous man. A month earlier, he had been in Miami with Cassius Clay, cheering and offering spiritual guidance as the young boxer defeated the heavyweight champion Sonny Liston. When Clay announced his decision to join the Nation of Islam, Malcolm X won not only a prominent convert but also a massive public relations coup.

But Malcolm's life was chaotic. He had been suspended from the Nation of Islam after he discovered that his mentor, Elijah Muhammad, had been carrying on affairs with his young secretaries, getting some of them pregnant. Increasingly wary of the group's ways, he announced his departure on March 8. Facing death threats from the Nation of Islam because of his challenge to Elijah Muhammad's authority, Malcolm confronted an uncertain future. Though he acknowledged the possibility of an "honest white-black brotherhood" and showed growing interest in political affairs, he continued to view most white people as thoroughly racist, Christianity as hopelessly stained by its ties to slavery, and Martin Luther King Jr. as out of touch. "No more turning the other cheek," he had said at a Harlem rally two days before his encounter with King. "No more jive like that. There will be nonviolence only with those who are not violent with us."

Now the men smiled as cameras flashed. King was thirty-four, four years younger than Malcolm. King was the insider, Malcolm the outsider. King was college-educated, Malcolm was jail-educated. Each man found it useful to cast the other in the role of rival. King made clear that people in power had better pay attention to him if they didn't want to deal with his more antagonistic contemporary, while Malcolm moved audiences with the reminder that their anger was justified, that their self-restraint need not be eternal, that not everyone had to maintain the kind of patience practiced by King.

30

A Law Observance Problem

"I AND MY friends have come to have lunch," King told the white man barring his entry to the Monson Motor Lodge.

It was just past noon on June 11, 1964, a searingly hot day in St. Augustine, Florida, the nation's oldest continuously inhabited, European-established city. It was also one of the first American arrival points for enslaved Black Africans. Nearly four hundred years after its founding, St. Augustine had a population of fifteen thousand, about three-fourths of them white. The city's economy relied on white northern tourists, who visited the segregated beaches, stayed in segregated hotels, and posed for photos in the old Slave Market at the entrance of the Plaza de la Constitución.

Those tourists also dined at the Monson Motor Lodge's popular restaurant, where a sign on the door read MASTER HOSTS, and where King stood uncomfortably at the entrance, unable to get in. The sun beat down.

"We can't serve you," said James Brock, a balding man with horn-rimmed glasses who was also president of the Florida Hotel and Motel Association. "We are not integrated."

A burly white man, impatient for his lunch, shoved King aside to enter the restaurant.

On the previous night, Brock had been spotted on a downtown street carrying a shotgun, a billy club, a pistol, and a flashlight; he had been designated a special deputy to the sheriff, assigned to maintain law and order in the face of civil rights protests. Now, as Brock confronted the nation's best-known civil rights leader, white customers inside the restaurant rose from their tables and gathered by the windows to watch. TV camera crews, reporters, and a handful of activists crowded around.

"We feel you should serve us." King spoke calmly, but his eyes flitted nervously from side to side. He had received a death threat prior to his arrival in St. Augustine, and he had already been shoved by a man he had not seen coming. As the crowd shifted and grew, Ralph Abernathy took up a position close to his friend.

"Reverend King," Brock said, "I'd like to prevail on you on behalf of my wife and my family, my two young daughters and myself, who are trying to operate a business here, prevail upon you to encourage your, uh, nonviolent army to peacefully solicit some other property other than mine. As you know, I've unfortunately had to arrest eighty-four people here since Easter."

That number grew as police arrived and took King and Abernathy to jail, charging them as "unwanted guests."

The writer Louis Lomax once called King the "foremost interpreter of the Negro's tiredness." King had proved it true many times, beginning with his first big speech in Montgomery, when he had said, "There comes a time when people get tired of being trampled over by the iron feet of oppression... when people get tired of being plunged into the abyss of humiliation." But not only did King interpret the weariness of his people; he also transformed it. He told people that if they endured, they would see better days. He sounded weary himself, at times, but never hopeless. He told a St. Augustine audience:

> You know, they threaten us occasionally with more than beatings... They threaten us with actual physical death. They think that this will stop the movement. I got word way out in California that a plan was underway to take my life in St. Augustine, Florida. Well, if physical death is the price that I must pay to free my white brother and all of my brothers and sisters from a permanent death of the spirit, then nothing can be more redemptive.

The most recent spurt of violence in St. Augustine had begun prior to King's arrival. When local officials had begun arrangements to commemorate the city's quadricentennial, Black activists had tried to block federal funding for the celebration, saying federal money should not go to such a thoroughly segregated city. Young Black protesters had been arrested for distributing pamphlets and sentenced to indefinite terms in a state reformatory. White antagonists had hurled homemade bombs and fired guns at Black-owned homes. A white man had been shot to death while riding through a Black neighborhood with a shotgun. Four Black men had been severely beaten after spying on a Klan meeting. Rifles had been fired into the home of Dr. R. B. Hayling, one of the protest leaders, while he and his wife and their two daughters had been sleeping. The family's boxer dog had been struck and killed. "Daddy, they just didn't understand about our dog," one of Hayling's daughters had said after the attack. "He looked real mean, but he wouldn't hurt anybody. They shouldn't have killed him."

J. B. Stoner, a white supremacist and anti-Semite, had come to town to speak at Klan rallies and to lead armed marches through Black neighborhoods. "People in other parts of the country like to think of niggers as human beings because they have hands and feet," Stoner said to a cheering crowd at one rally. "So do apes and gorillas have hands and feet. If a nigger has a soul I never read about it in the Bible. The only good nigger is a dead nigger . . . The nigger is a willing tool of the communist Jews and is being used to destroy America. They want to pump the blood of Africa into our white veins."

A few days prior to King's arrival, white thugs armed with bicycle chains and iron pipes had attacked peaceful marchers. Andrew Young had been knocked unconscious and kicked as he lay in the street. White city leaders accused the protesters of stirring trouble. Business owners feared that King's arrival and the heightened tension would force them into an even greater conflict. "You need to survive. You don't argue," said one white restaurant owner who had initially tried to integrate his dining room but had given up. Growing up in Europe during the Nazi occupation, he had never felt fear, the restaurant owner told one reporter. "But now I come to this peaceful, pretty little place in the United States of America, and I find, walking down the street, for the first time in my life, that I am afraid." And, still, white people such as this European immigrant failed to speak out against the city's segregation rules.

The fear of change went beyond St. Augustine. Barry Goldwater, in his bid for the presidency, appealed to many white Americans who yearned for a return to what they considered simpler times. Goldwater vowed that as president he would leave civil rights issues to the states, a threat so profound that it moved King to abandon his policy of electoral neutrality, calling Goldwater a threat to the "health, morality, and survival of our nation."

In St. Augustine, however, Sheriff L. O. Davis said it was King who posed the real threat to America, reminding newspaper reporters and readers that the FBI had identified the civil rights activist as a "communist and communist leader." King and other protesters, Davis said, were making life more difficult for the people they claimed to support. While he had never thought much about integration prior to the demonstrations, the sheriff said, recent events had made him an impassioned segregationist. The sheriff offered a prediction as to how the clash would end: "You know when King's usefulness is over, he'll be made into a martyr."

King spent a night in solitary confinement, in a "very lonely, dark and desolate cell." Guards examined his array of diet pills with suspicion, even though such pills were popular at the time with people who struggled to control their weight. He told a Black jail employee that, after fifteen times behind bars, this was the first time he'd been "treated like a hog."

While King sat in a cell the southern filibuster of the civil rights bill failed, thanks in part to Senate Minority Leader Everett Dirksen, who rallied enough Republicans to overcome the southern Democrat segregationists, all but guaranteeing passage of the law promised by President Kennedy and pushed by President Johnson.

After two days, King was free. He departed from St. Augustine, briefly, to deliver two college commencement addresses. The protests in St. Augustine had already served a purpose, putting pressure on federal officials, but the local conflict raged on. A group of white men led an "anti-civil rights march" through the city's downtown. One of the town's Black leaders, a high school band director named Robert Braden, had his home blasted with shotgun pellets. Eleven rifle shots struck the empty cottage where King and other SCLC leaders had been staying. Someone fired a shotgun from a passing car at a white SCLC official and his son. Black people trying to integrate a whites-only beach were attacked and beaten. Seventy protesters arrived at the Monson Motel, including sixteen rabbis from northern cities. When they refused to leave, James Brock tried to force them aside as a group of white businessmen cheered. At the same time, a small group of Black men and women jumped into the motel swimming pool, prompting Brock to dump two containers of muriatic acid, a cleaning supply, into the water. Police arrested forty-one people.

On the night of June 25, hundreds of robed Klansmen, many of them carrying clubs, marched through the city, attacking Black people, tearing the clothes from a thirteen-year-old girl, and beating a journalist who helped the girl escape. Thirty people, most of them Black, were hospitalized. Sheriff Davis said his officers were unable to arrest white assailants because "everybody was fighting so hard."

Jackie Robinson joined the protesters. King also invited a group of Boston University professors, including his dissertation adviser, L. Harold DeWolf, to come to St. Augustine and negotiate with city officials. Upon arriving, DeWolf was surprised that King had brought his son Marty to St. Augustine. King explained that he wanted to spend more time with the seven-year-old, and while St. Augustine might seem like a dangerous place, every place King went at the time was dangerous.

As Klan leaders provoked and threatened, King, Robinson, Abernathy, and others urged restraint. All the while, King sought a way to leave St. Augustine with dignity. He found it when Florida governor C. Farris Bryant created a four-man, biracial "peace committee" to negotiate an end to the conflict. With the committee in place, King called off the protests and went back to Atlanta. Asked later if anything had been accomplished in St. Augustine, Robert Hayling, the local activist, said the violence had probably helped President Johnson push the civil rights bill through the Senate. But the people of St. Augustine, he said, could not point to any "tangible gains."

King had another good reason to get out of St. Augustine: the center of the civil rights storm had moved quickly and dramatically to Mississippi, where three young activists had disappeared after having been stopped by police for speeding in Neshoba County. The missing men were James E. Chaney, twenty-one years old, a plasterer from Meridian, Mississippi; Michael "Mickey" Schwerner, a twenty-four-year-old member of CORE from Brooklyn; and Andrew Goodman, a twenty-year-old Queens College student from New York. Schwerner and Goodman were white. They had volunteered to work on the Freedom Summer voter registration drive. After the bombing of the Sixteenth Street Baptist Church, the flagrant and unpunished violence of Klansmen in St. Augustine, and now the disappearance of Chaney, Schwerner, and Goodman, the White House issued a statement expressing concern with a "law observance problem."

———— · ————

Twenty years earlier, on his first trip to the American North, a teenage Martin Luther King Jr. had been forced to sit behind a curtain while in the dining car of a train as he traveled from Atlanta to Connecticut for a summer job on a tobacco farm. When the train had reached Washington, D.C., he had been permitted to step through the curtain, like an actor emerging onstage with a new identity. Now, at age thirty-five, King returned to Washington, D.C., to watch President Johnson sign the Civil Rights Act of 1964, considered one of most important pieces of legislation passed by Congress in the twentieth century. The law banned segregation in public accommodations and outlawed discrimination based on race, sex, religion, or national origin in the workplace. It gave the attorney general power to sue school districts that failed to integrate, and it barred federal funds from going to state and local programs that discriminated. In that moment, the balance of power changed in the American South; the federal government took a side—clearly and openly—in support of integration.

In his nationally televised remarks, Johnson said:

We believe that all men are created equal, yet many are denied equal treatment. We believe that all men have certain unalienable rights, yet many Americans do not enjoy these rights. We believe that all men are entitled to the blessings of liberty, yet millions are being deprived of these blessings, not because of their own failures but because of the color of their skin ...

My fellow citizens, we have come to a time of testing. We must not fail.

Journalists noted that Johnson was the first southerner to serve as president since Woodrow Wilson, and that the Civil Rights Act might prove to be one of Johnson's pinnacle achievements. After signing the bill, the president presented King with one of his pens, which King said he would treasure. But within weeks of receiving the pen, as he vowed to continue the struggle for equal rights, and as surveys revealed that white Americans considered the Black community ungrateful, King spoke not with gratitude but with increasing anger.

Echoing the questions he'd been hearing of late, he asked:

What more will the Negro want? What will it take to make these demonstrations end? Well, I would like to reply with another rhetorical question: Why do white people seem to find it so difficult to understand that the Negro is sick and tired of having reluctantly parceled out to him those rights and privileges which all others receive upon birth or entry in America?

Why, he asked, did white society get to decide how much freedom it doled out to the Negro? He continued:

What the Negro wants—and will not stop until he gets—is absolute and unqualified freedom and equality here in this land of his birth, and not in Africa or in some imaginary state. The Negro no longer will be tolerant of anything less than his due right and heritage. He is pursuing only that which he knows is honorably his. He knows that he is right ... Few white people, even today, will face the clear fact that the very future and destiny of this country are tied up in what answer will be given to the Negro. And that answer must be given soon.

On July 20, 1964, King flew from Atlanta to Jackson, Mississippi, accompanied by Dorothy Cotton, Andrew Young, Bernard Lee, and C. T. Vivian, the men wearing lapel pins that read "S.C.L.C. Freedom Now." As the plane lifted off, King read *The New York Times* headline "Violence Flares Again in Harlem." Young scribbled notes on a yellow legal pad. Lee read *The Souls of Black Folk* by W. E. B. Du Bois while Cotton read V. O. Key's *Southern Politics*, which she turned to only when she wasn't chatting with King.

A young white man with a conservative haircut and a thick southern accent sat across the aisle from King. He leaned over and asked, "Excuse me . . . Are you Martin Luther King?"

"Yes, I am."

"I wonder if I could ask you two questions."

King's traveling companions leaned forward to listen, as did a nearby magazine writer, Calvin Trillin, who scribbled notes, which he later turned into an article in *The New Yorker*:

"I wonder," the young passenger asked, "do you feel you're teaching Christian love?"

"Yes, that's my basic approach," King said.

"Do you think the people you preach to have a feeling of love?"

"Well, I'm not talking about weak love," King said. "I'm talking about love with justice . . . I'm talking about the love that is strong, so that you love your fellow-men enough to lead them to justice."

"Do you think that's the same love Jesus taught?" the young man asked.

"Yes, I do."

"Even though you incite one man against another?"

"You have to remember that Christ was crucified by people who were against him," said King, politely. "Do you think there's love in the South now? Do you think white people in the South love Negroes?"

"There hasn't always been love," the young man answered. "I admit we've made some mistakes."

"Uh-huh. Well, let me tell you some of the things that have happened to us. We were slaves for two hundred and fifty years. We endured one hundred years of segregation. We have been brutalized and lynched. Can't you understand that the Negro is bound to have some resentment? But I preach that, despite this resentment, we should organize militantly but non-violently . . . I don't think you'd be talking to me now if we hadn't had some success in making people face the issue."

"I happen to be a Christian," the man said.

"Do you think segregation is Christian?" King asked.

"I was anticipating that," he said. "I don't have any flat answer. I'm questioning your methods as causing more harm than good."

"Uh-huh. Well, what do you suggest we need?"

"I think we need respect and good will."

"How do you propose to get that?" King asked.

"I don't know. I just don't agree that it does any good to incite people. I know there's resentment, and you're able to capitalize on this resentment and create friction and incite discord. And you know this."

"I don't think we're inciting discord but exposing discord," King said.

"I think much more progress was made between the two races before the last few years, when you and other people started inciting trouble between the two races."

"What is this progress?" asked King. "Where was the lunch-counter desegregation? Where was the civil-rights law?"

"Well, I just wanted to ask those questions," said the young man.

"Uh-huh," said King. "Well, I'd like to be loved by everyone, but we can't always wait for love. Maybe you ought to read my writings. I've done quite a bit of writing on non-violence."

"Well, I think you are causing violence," the young man said.

"Uh-huh. Well, I'm sorry you don't think I'm a Christian."

"I didn't say that."

"Well, I'm sorry that you don't think that what I preach is Christian, and I'm sorry you don't think segregation is un-Christian."

King went back to his newspaper.

When the plane stopped in Montgomery, the young man moved to another seat for the second leg of the trip.

King drove that afternoon from Jackson, past cotton, corn, and cattle farms, and into the predominantly Black section of Greenwood, Mississippi, where weathered shacks had tar paper nailed in varying shapes to the roofs, where front porches sagged, and work clothes hung from wash lines. A heat wave baked the state, with temperatures in the high nineties, broken only by the occasional thunderstorm. The sun reflected off the chrome bumpers of King's car. He opened the door and stepped outside into the oppressive heat, dressed in his usual black suit.

After making his first stop at a pool hall, where he spoke to the patrons, he removed his suit jacket and walked door to door among the clapboard shacks, smiling and laughing with barefoot children who scampered around him. As wooden screen doors swung open and increasing numbers of people stepped outside, King stood on a wooden bench to make a speech. "You must not allow anybody to make you feel you are not significant," he said. "Every Negro has worth and dignity. Mississippi has treated the Negro as if he is a thing instead of a person." Later that night, when he spoke again, this time to a crowd of about a thousand people, a small plane flew overhead and dropped leaflets warning that any disorder incited by King or other Negroes would make it the "right duty and moral obligation of the white man in Leflore County to restore law and order."

Mississippi had long been one of the most dangerous places in America to be Black. Since 1882, no state in the nation had recorded more lynchings. The dark, fertile soil grew some of the nation's best cotton crops, producing riches for the white people who owned most of it. Mississippi also produced some of the nation's best blues music, with songs such as Charley Patton's "Mississippi Boweavil Blues" that reflected the grim lives and deep-rooted dignity of those living on the land. By 1964, Mississippi remained the only state in the union where no Black children attended school with white children. King and the SCLC had largely avoided the state, even as SNCC and other members of the Council of Federated Organizations organized volunteers there. They were not the only ones afraid of Mississippi, as the writer Willie Morris once observed. "If modern industrialism and the national urge to homogeneity came to Mississippi later than to other areas of the United States," Morris wrote, "if the traditional federal authority had to reach more than halfway to meet what finally became the better instincts of the place, then this had to do with the direness of its immemorial past."

Robert Moses, a Black, Harvard-educated New Yorker, had been working on voter registration in Mississippi for three years, taking a different approach from King's, wearing work pants and T-shirts, avoiding confrontations at lunch counters, and focusing on political organization. Rather than seeking acceptance in Mississippi society, Moses and others in SNCC sought to change the dynamic. Moses wrote in one memo: "All direct-action campaigns for integration have had their backs broken ... The only attack worth making is an attack aimed at the overthrow of the existing political structures of the state."

To attempt such an overthrow, he and others recruited college students from around the country, most of them white northerners. Moses agreed with King in one respect, saying change would come only if white people understood what Black people endured. He and his northern volunteers set up Freedom Schools in the hopes of registering enough Black voters to challenge the all-white Mississippi delegation at the Democratic presidential convention taking place in August in Atlantic City, New Jersey, and replace them with delegates from the biracial Mississippi Freedom Democratic Party (MFDP). Volunteers set out to register Black Mississippians for the MFDP, even as they continued trying to get voters registered for the official Democratic Party as well. But many Black Mississippians remained hesitant, afraid of retribution from white officials.

"We're on a voter registration drive, and we'd like to have you join us," said one white volunteer when he stopped at a home where men had just returned from working the fields and the women had just returned from cleaning white people's homes. No one said a word. Finally, one of the farmers spoke. "Well," he said. "I don't know about that."

SNCC's Freedom Summer project would go on to recruit eighty thousand people to cast ballots in mock elections designed to disprove claims that Black people in the South lacked the ambition to vote. In Mississippi and elsewhere throughout the South, SNCC had united young volunteers in the kind of grassroots work that had largely eluded King and the SCLC. "We were the beloved community," said Casey Hayden, a SNCC worker from Texas, "harassed and happy, just like we'd died and gone to heaven and it was integrated there."

SNCC not only attracted young volunteers from the North but also energized Black people from the South, including Fannie Lou Hamer, the youngest of twenty children born into an impoverished sharecropping family. Hamer was already active in her Mississippi branch of the NAACP, but it took a SNCC voting rights meeting to light her fire. SNCC's focus on the local—and its rejection of top-down leadership—led Hamer and others to organize grassroots campaigns.

James Chaney, Andrew Goodman, and Michael Schwerner had been part of Mississippi's Freedom Summer. Now federal agents swarmed the state, searching for the young men's bodies, the flutter of helicopters and the buzz of reconnaissance jets reminding King that organizers here faced even graver danger than they did in Birmingham or St. Augustine. Indeed, Robert Kennedy was worried enough about King's safety in Mississippi that he phoned President Johnson on July 21, complaining that state officials had refused to provide adequate protection. "It's a ticklish problem," Kennedy said nervously, in a conversation recorded by the president, "because, if he gets killed, it could create some kind of problems, just being, being dead, but also a lot of other kinds of problems."

When Johnson told Kennedy he should ask the FBI to protect King, the attorney general admitted that his relationship with J. Edgar Hoover was shattered beyond repair, and that he wasn't comfortable asking Hoover for help. Johnson knew that already, but he seemed to enjoy making Kennedy squirm. Johnson, as vice president, had felt humiliated by John and Bobby Kennedy. Now Johnson had the upper hand. Both men knew it.

"I understand," Kennedy said, "that he sends all kinds of reports over to you about me . . . about me plotting the overthrow of the government by force of violence, leading a coup . . . It's a very difficult situation."

Johnson assured Kennedy that he had seen no such reports from the FBI director.

A few minutes after hanging up with Kennedy, Johnson phoned Hoover and suggested the FBI keep King safe in Mississippi.

As he arrived on July 24 in Philadelphia, Mississippi, where Chaney, Goodman, and Schwerner had last been seen, King had plenty of protection. FBI agents, newspaper reporters, and other activists accompanied King's black Oldsmobile in a caravan of thirteen cars.

After visiting a pool hall and losing a game of eight-ball to a teenager, King went to work.

"Three young men came here to help set you free," he told a crowd in a community center. "They probably lost their lives. I know what you have suffered in this state, the lynchings and the murders. But things are going to get better. Walk together, children, don't you get weary."

"I just want to touch you," said an elderly woman, approaching King.

Thunder clapped and raindrops pattered on the gravel road as King went back to his car and drove away. The next day, a Saturday, after a cup of coffee at a recently integrated restaurant in the town of Meridian's tiny airport, King flew home to Atlanta.

On July 26, as King contemplated a trip to Harlem, he spoke by phone with Bayard Rustin: "I have been trying to think a great deal about the violence that has been erupting not only in Harlem and Brooklyn but now in Rochester and maybe other places, and what I could do, or what my role is as a leader in the nonviolent revolution and as one the people look to as moral guidance. And I frankly haven't . . . come up with an answer." The riots in Harlem had broken out after a white police officer had shot a fifteen-year-old Black boy; police had said the teen threatened the officer with a knife, but witnesses insisted the teen was unarmed.

New York City mayor Robert F. Wagner Jr. had asked King to come to the city to discuss the riots, and perhaps help stop them, but King told Rustin he was worried he would look "kind of like a Tom" if he helped the mayor. King remained the most popular leader in the nation among Black people, according to a *New York Times* survey taken in the summer of 1964, but he worried that he was often perceived as part of the establishment. "I have set up a sort of tentative meeting with him for tomorrow night," King said, referring to Wagner, "but I'm still not sure it's the best thing to do."

Rustin urged caution. King should tell the mayor, Rustin said, that the best way to end rioting would be to address fundamental inequalities in housing, employment, and education. Anything else would be perceived as weakness on King's part. The mayor, King said, had proposed an off-the-record meeting.

"No," Rustin said. "Don't do that, Martin. No, sir. You have to be free . . . to make a statement to the press in which you urge the mayor to get on with more housing, to integrate those schools, and to find jobs for the unemployed. Without that, you're in a box. You mustn't be used that way."

But Rustin wasn't being completely frank with King. In a phone call two days earlier with another New York activist, Rustin had stated much more forcefully his opinion that King should steer clear of New York, that he would only aggravate an already dangerous situation, that he would become a target of the community's anger. "I would not want Martin [in New York]," Rustin had said. "It's alright for me to be booed in Harlem. But you can't take the symbol of our movement and have it booed."

Nevertheless, King did meet with Wagner, he did tour the scenes of the riots in Harlem, and he did face criticism from local activists. His friends Ossie Davis and Ruby Dee wrote King to say they were "amazed and disappointed" to see King being used by the mayor. "We implore that you will move at once to reassure the people and the leadership of the Harlem Community that their dilemma at this painful hour is much more important to you than the Mayor's," they wrote.

Soon after, King joined Roy Wilkins and other leaders in calling for a moratorium on marches and demonstrations until after the November 3 presidential election. James Farmer of CORE and John Lewis of SNCC opposed the moratorium and asked King to reconsider his position. Malcolm X, interviewed in Cairo, Egypt, accused King and Wilkins of selling out, saying that the old-guard civil rights leaders were more concerned with President Johnson's reelection than with the plight of America's Black community. "I don't think Negroes should restrain themselves from showing dis-enchantment over America's failure to provide what they should have had by right since birth," Malcolm said. "I'd die before I'd tell Negroes to restrain themselves."

But King saw strength in restraint. With their restraint, he said, Black people disproved the essence of white supremacist ideology, because no in-ferior people could possibly commit and maintain a commitment to nonvio-lence in the face of such assault.

At the same time, additional violence erupted across the country. In Dixmoor, Illinois, a Chicago suburb, the trouble started when a white liquor store manager physically attacked a Black woman after accusing her of theft. A peaceful demonstration at the store turned ugly, leaving dozens injured. In Philadelphia, an uprising began after an argument between a Black woman and two white police officers. In Jersey City, violence broke out after police ar-rested a Black man for disorderly conduct and public drunkenness. The biog-rapher David Levering Lewis wrote, "It was entirely possible to admire Martin King for his exemplary goodness while cheering the arsonists and looters."

On August 4, the FBI found the buried bodies of Chaney, Goodman, and Schwerner on a farm owned by a KKK member in Mississippi's Neshoba County. The next day, King returned to St. Augustine, where the Monson Motor Lodge's restaurant had been integrated and almost immediately hit with two firebombs, and where the biracial committee on desegregation had fallen apart. By the end of the summer of 1964, according to one tally, there had been thirty-five shootings, eighty beatings, and more than one thou-sand arrests of civil rights protesters nationwide, in a four-month period. Though King reminded his followers that unearned suffering redeemed the soul, their patience was not eternal. A kind of war was underway. Everyone was involved, at least emotionally. It engulfed the nation.

King traveled on August 9 to New York, where he told a capacity audi-ence of 4,100 at Riverside Church that the threat of violence would not fade so long as "the Negro feels himself on a lonely island in a vast sea of prosper-ity." From there, he and Ralph Abernathy flew to the Netherlands and West Germany for three days of lectures. King forgot his passport when crossing into communist East Berlin on September 13, but the police at Checkpoint Charlie recognized him and let him through. Speaking to an overflow church crowd, King said that "Christian love will overcome all man-made barriers," an obvious reference to the communist-built wall that divided the city.

From Berlin, King and Abernathy flew to Rome for a meeting with Pope Paul VI. "I think new days have come when a Pope meets a fellow who happens to have the name Martin Luther," King said. While praising the pope for making it "palpably clear ... that he is committed to the cause of civil rights in the United States," King urged the Catholic leader to do more. The Catholic Church had enormous influence in America's northern cities, where Negroes faced discrimination in housing and employment, he said, "and a reaffirmation of its position would mean much."

After a few days of relaxation in Madrid, King returned to the United States, where he went back on the road to urge his followers to vote in the November election and defeat Barry Goldwater. In Atlantic City, SNCC workers remained optimistic that the Mississippi Freedom Democratic Party might replace the regular Mississippi delegation at the Democratic National Convention. Given that the established Democratic organization in Mississippi had excluded Black participants, the MFDP delegation argued that they were the people's true representatives. They also pointed out that many white Democratic leaders in Mississippi had pledged their support for the candidacy of Republican senator Barry Goldwater. Even so, President Johnson wanted the regular delegation to remain in place. He feared that the acceptance of the MFDP would damage his support among white voters in the South. Organizers of the MFDP hoped that King might persuade the president to support the seating of both Mississippi delegations.

As the Democratic National Convention began with a hearing of the Credentials Committee, SNCC organizer Fannie Lou Hamer riveted television audiences with her harrowing account of trying to register to vote. "Is this America," she asked, her face glowing with sweat, "the land of the free and the home of the brave, where we have to sleep with our telephones off the hooks because our lives be threatened daily, because we want to live as decent human beings, in America?"

President Johnson offered a compromise, saying the MFDP would be permitted to participate in the convention but not to vote. When the MFDP's leaders rejected the offer, Johnson tried again, offering to give two MFDP members at-large seats at the convention and welcoming the other delegates as guests. He also promised that the 1968 convention would bar state delegates who discriminated against Black people. King and Rustin favored the compromise, but the MFDP delegates rejected it. They went on to support Johnson in the election, but they remained bitter and skeptical about how much could be gained by trying to work with the federal government. Many of the young activists also came away more frustrated than ever with King, saying that he had done President Johnson's bidding. The Democratic Party made clear it had no intention of adjusting the balance of power between Black and white in Mississippi. King came away looking to many in the MFDP like part of the establishment.

King grew wearier than ever.

"He felt compelled to try to give the equivalent of his 'I Have a Dream' speech every night in every city," Andrew Young said, and to attend dinners after the speeches, and to thank all the cooks and busboys in the kitchen, and to sign autographs and pose for photographs. Too excited after dinner to sleep, he would pace his hotel room, tell jokes, sip wine or gin, and, as Young put it, "try to shed the mantle of being Dr. Martin Luther King." With Young and others, King would deliver mock eulogies, teasing them about their flaws, cracking them up and simultaneously reminding them their work was dangerous. He continued his habit of seldom sleeping for more than a few hours a night.

Activists unhappy with his seemingly moderate approach savaged him, equating his moderation with passivity. Death threats arrived almost daily, and, as Ralph Abernathy noted, the people making these threats were hardly "just big talkers." They were the same people responsible for the deaths of Medgar Evers, for four little girls in Birmingham, and for Chaney, Goodman, and Schwerner in Mississippi. At times, Abernathy said, King was "terrified." That sense of terror "manifested itself in a melancholy moodiness," Abernathy explained. King would lose himself in thought "for long periods of time, and when he talked about the future he would be pessimistic and even apocalyptic." At age thirty-five, he spoke of retirement, of allowing someone else to lead the movement. King wondered what would happen, Abernathy said, if he backed away and violence erupted.

Sometimes, according to Abernathy, King sought refuge in a hospital. "This happened not once but a number of times," he said. Coretta confirmed as much in her memoir and in unpublished interviews conducted during the writing of that memoir, saying Martin had moments "when he felt depressed." Many times, she said, he contemplated taking a year off or choosing a new career path. When Martin's mood darkened, Coretta said, she would remind him, "You have a lot for which to be thankful. God has allowed you to see so much of your dream come true. You still have a lot left that you would like to see done, but you have been able to see much progress come about."

King hid his emotions in most interviews, but, at the end of the summer of 1964, he offered a glimpse of his feelings to the writer Robert Penn Warren:

> I guess you go through these moments when you think about what you're going through, and the sacrifices and the suffering you face, that your own people don't have an understanding—not even an appreciation . . . You know, they've heard these things about my being soft, my talking about love, and they transfer their bitterness toward the white man to me.

King said he didn't want pity. His plight, his feelings weren't important. He was focused, he said, on the redemption of the society that made people treat him the way they did.

One night when King was out of town, Coretta and Yoki watched a television program that discussed the Harlem riots. Before Coretta knew what was happening, people on the TV screen were criticizing her husband and the weakness of his nonviolent strategy. Yoki became upset. "Mommy, do you think they're going to kill all the Negro leaders and make the other Negroes agree to segregation?" she asked.

"What leaders?" Coretta asked.

"You know, the Negro leaders."

She wouldn't say "Daddy," but Coretta knew. It was at about this time that Yoki learned from her schoolmates that her own home had been bombed when she'd been an infant and that her father had once been stabbed in the chest.

"No," Coretta said. "They can't kill all the Negro leaders. Don't you worry about that."

31

The Prize

UTTERLY EXHAUSTED YET unable to sleep, King, on October 13, 1964, checked into St. Joseph's Infirmary in Atlanta, where he swallowed a sleeping pill and, finally, fell into slumber. Coretta called the next morning to tell him he'd won the Nobel Peace Prize.

"I thought I was still asleep," King told reporters from his hospital bed, where he allowed photographers to snap pictures as a nurse checked his temperature. "For a moment I thought it was all a dream."

When Coretta and a few of his closest aides—Andrew Young, Dora McDonald, and Bernard Lee—joined him in the hospital room, he asked them to join him in prayer and pointed out that the Nobel would require them all to work harder than ever. He soon dressed and used the hospital's auditorium for a press conference, explaining to reporters that he'd been hospitalized for fatigue and a lingering virus. Doctors had also told him he was twenty pounds overweight and suffering high blood pressure.

"I do not consider this merely an honor to me personally, but a tribute to the discipline, wise restraint, and majestic courage of the millions of gallant Negroes and white persons of good will who have followed a rule of love," he said, adding that he intended to donate "every penny" of the $54,000 award to the civil rights movement. At age thirty-five, he was the youngest person ever to receive the Nobel Peace Prize, the first American southerner, and the second African American. Ralph Bunche, as a United Nations emissary, had won the Nobel in 1950 for negotiating a peace accord between Israel and Egypt.

Even in the moments after receiving the news, King already seemed to realize that the award would make it all but impossible for him to retire to a quiet pastorship or professorship. "History has thrust me into this position," he said. "It would be both immoral and a sign of ingratitude if I did not face my moral responsibility to do what I can in this struggle."

Not everyone offered congratulations. "They're scraping the bottom of the barrel," said Bull Connor in Birmingham. "He's caused more strife and trouble in this country than anyone I can think of."

"I consider it one of the biggest jokes of the year," said Virgil Stuart, chief of police in St. Augustine.

"King could well qualify for the 'top alley cat' prize," J. Edgar Hoover wrote on one of the Nobel news stories that crossed his desk.

State officials in Georgia had no reaction, according to *The Atlanta Constitution*. Neither did President Johnson, who didn't want to risk offending white southern voters two weeks before the election. Robert Kennedy, running for the U.S. Senate from New York, called the honor "richly deserved." The Reverend Martin Luther King Sr. reacted as both a preacher and a proud parent. "God had surely looked down into Georgia," he wrote. "And He must have said, Well, here are people I will give a mission and see how well they can carry it out . . . A people had been led by a young man who could have found comfort elsewhere, yet stayed when he was needed, bearing witness."

Coretta experienced conflicting feelings, including frustration. FBI wiretaps captured her on the phone with her husband, telling him he'd received a congratulatory telegram from President Johnson. Coretta laughed and said Johnson had probably been pressed by an adviser to do it. Later, reflecting on the wider meaning of the Nobel, she wrote: "It was a great tribute, but an even more awesome burden. I felt pride and joy, and pain too, when I thought of the added responsibilities my husband must bear; and it was my burden too."

After a week of rest, King went back on the road, encouraging Black people to vote in the presidential election. He began in Chicago, then visited Cleveland and Los Angeles before returning to Chicago, where he stood atop flatbed trucks and led sixteen street-corner rallies in one day. In essence, King was campaigning for Johnson, even if he didn't say as much, and when Johnson defeated Goldwater in a landslide, Johnson phoned King the next day to thank him. "I thought I'd call a half dozen or so folks," said the president, "and tell them how much I appreciated their confidence, and what a *good* job I thought they'd done."

Despite winning handily, Johnson had lost Louisiana, Mississippi, Alabama, Georgia, and South Carolina, states that had been longtime Democratic bastions. Nevertheless, King celebrated. The election marked a victory for the movement, he said, and he intended to capitalize on it, pushing for an expansion of voting rights and an improvement in conditions for Black northerners, who faced widespread discrimination in jobs, housing, and education. To truly deliver on civil rights, King said, "the physical ghetto itself must be eliminated."

The week after the election, King and his staff gathered for a retreat at the Gaston Motel in Birmingham, to plot SCLC strategy. King talked about his desire to do more work in the North and West. But voting rights in the Deep South continued to dominate discussions. The approach now, King said, must be to attack the places where voting rights were obstructed and push for federal intervention. The Civil Rights Act had not gone far enough in assuring Black people the right to vote, King and others agreed, and it was the ballot, more than anything, that would open the door to full citizenship.

Amelia Boynton, one of the leaders of the Dallas County Voters League, spoke at the SCLC retreat and tried to convince King to help the faltering campaign for voting rights in her hometown of Selma, Alabama. Jim Bevel lobbied for a broader campaign covering all of Alabama, while Ralph Abernathy and others also lobbied for Selma, where the state judge James Hare had recently issued an injunction that banned the gathering of civil rights activists and where the bellicose sheriff Jim Clark might serve as a useful foil. King and Abernathy saw Boynton's presence at the retreat as a powerful sign: the Black people of Selma were dedicated, organized, and eager to join the struggle.

While King made plans, including for his trip to Oslo to accept the Nobel Prize, a new wave of FBI reports flowed from J. Edgar Hoover's office to that of the acting attorney general, Nicholas Katzenbach, and others in the Johnson administration, many of them focused on King's private conduct. Katzenbach had replaced Robert Kennedy, the latter having been elected to the U.S. Senate from New York. While Katzenbach shared Kennedy's commitment to civil rights, King lost a powerful ally in the Justice Department when Kennedy resigned.

"Now, what am I going to do about Martin Luther King with all these reports that are coming in on him all the time?" Johnson asked Katzenbach in a November 11 phone call.

"Lord," Katzenbach said with a chuckle. "Looks like he's too far gone on a lot of this . . . Maybe getting the Nobel Prize will make him more careful? Of course, Hoover loves that because they don't like King."

Johnson said he was being pressed to attend a dinner in honor of King. "I can't do that, can I?" he asked.

"I would think you could, but I wouldn't advise you to," said Katzenbach.

A week later, King was on vacation, staying at Adam Clayton Powell Jr.'s retreat in Bimini, the westernmost part of the Bahamas, when news reporters tracked him down to get his comment on a breaking story. Hoover, who seldom conducted press conferences, had met with a group of women journalists and labeled King as America's "most notorious liar." Dorothy Cotton, who was one of three people with King in Bimini, said it was the first time she had seen him cry. King, she said, perceived Hoover's remarks as an attack on his whole life's work. "I know that he was wounded by that," she said.

In a telegram to Hoover, King said he was "appalled and surprised" at the director's comments. And he doubled down on the criticism that helped put him in Hoover's crosshairs in the first place, reiterating that white FBI agents in the South were too cozy with local law enforcement officials. King also reminded Hoover that the bureau had yet to make arrests in the Birmingham church bombing that had killed four girls. In addition to the telegram, King issued a statement to the press:

> I cannot conceive of Mr. Hoover making a statement like this without being under extreme pressure. He has apparently faltered under the awesome burden, complexities and responsibilities of his office.

Therefore, I cannot engage in a public debate with him. I have nothing but sympathy for this man who has served his country so well.

Civil rights activists called for Hoover's resignation, but the FBI director, approaching his seventieth birthday, said he had no intention of stepping aside. In talks with William C. Sullivan, the FBI's chief of domestic
intelligence, Hoover expressed his frustration that the American news media
would not report on King's sexual activities. The bureau had been peddling
the stories to news reporters, to no avail. But after the public clash between
Hoover and King, Sullivan got more aggressive: he ordered the FBI's laboratory to create a composite tape containing some of the most explicit moments recorded in King's hotel rooms. On Saturday, November 21, Sullivan
ordered an agent to fly to Miami and mail the tape in an unmarked package
to King's office in Atlanta. He enclosed an anonymous letter on unwater-
marked paper, typewritten, tightly spaced, peppered with intentional typos
and misspellings, composed to suggest that its author was a disaffected Black
man. Its opening sentence echoed Hoover, who made a point of saying he
would never put the word "reverend" or "doctor" before the man's name. The
letter read:

KING,

In view of your low grade, abnormal personal behavior I will not
dignify your name with either a Mr. or a Reverend or a Dr. And,
your last name calls to mind only the type of King such as King
Henry the VIII and his countless acts of adultery and immoral
conduct lower than that of a beast.

    King, look into your heart. You know you are a complete fraud
and a great liability to all of us Negroes. White people have enough
frauds of their own but I am sure they don't have one at this time
that is any where near your equal. You are no clergyman and you
know it. I repeat you are a colossal fraud and an evil, vicious one at
that. You could not believe in God and act as you do. Clearly you
don't believe in any personal moral principles.

King, like all frauds your end is approaching . . . Your "honorary" degrees, your Nobel Prize (what a grim farce) and other awards will not save you. King, I repeat you are done.

No person can overcome facts . . . Lend your sexually psychotic ear to the enclosure. You will find yourself and in all your dirt, filth, evil and moronic talk exposed on the record for all time . . . Listen to yourself you filthy, abnormal animal. You are on the record . . . all your adulterous acts, your sexual orgies . . . you are on the record. King you are done . . .

King, there is only one thing left for you to do. You know what it is. You have just 34 days . . . You are done. There is but one way out for you. You better take it before your filthy, abnormal fraudulent self is bared to the nation.

The letter was written and sent thirty-four days before Christmas, perhaps implying that King should take his own life before that date or risk exposure. But the package sat for weeks in King's office, unopened, while King traveled and arrangements were made for King and Hoover to discuss their differences, and while the FBI continued to tempt reporters with dirt on King. On November 30, the FBI assistant director Deke DeLoach told a wire-service columnist named Robert S. Allen that King was a "pervert" and "completely subject to communist discipline." DeLoach showed the reporter a photo of King with one of his mistresses and said the bureau had obtained recordings of the civil rights leader's "most sordid . . . sex perversions and excesses." DeLoach also offered a typed, single-spaced, two-page list of questions that should be put to King—all of which Allen chose to ignore.

The next day, King arrived thirty minutes late for a meeting with Hoover at the director's FBI office. King spoke first, saying he was eager to clear up any misunderstandings and maintain a good relationship with the FBI. In all likelihood, he did not yet know that his home phone was tapped and his hotel rooms were bugged, and he certainly did not know that an FBI-produced sex tape and a threatening FBI-produced letter were sitting in an unopened package at SCLC headquarters in Atlanta. After King's initial statement,

Hoover spoke almost without interruption for an hour, explaining the nuances of the FBI's work in the South and defending his agency against King's allegations of bias.

"Hoover talked *at* us," Andrew Young recalled later, "not to us . . . and never brought up anything about communism or rumors of sex." Years later, DeLoach, who was in the room, would call the meeting "a love feast [*sic*] . . . a very amicable meeting, a pleasant meeting," with Hoover warning King that his work was too important to be damaged by questions concerning his character. When it was over, King used the same word as DeLoach, "amicable," to describe the conference. He added: "I sincerely hope we can forget the confusions of the past and get on with the job . . . of providing freedom and justice for all citizens of this nation."

But the conflict was far from over. In fact, while King and Hoover met that day, a *Chicago Daily News* reporter waiting outside the office was offered documents similar to the one DeLoach had offered Allen. In the weeks to come, the FBI would share information on King with prominent religious leaders and potential donors to the SCLC, as well as journalists. When James Farmer of CORE heard about the tape from Ted Poston of the *New York Post*, Farmer phoned King and said it was urgent for King to meet with him. The next night, as the men sat on a couch in an airport lounge in New York, Farmer asked King if he knew that the FBI had been leaking stories about him.

"About what?" King asked.

Farmer suspected that King knew exactly what the stories were about.

As the FBI continued to peddle the story, Hoover and his agents waited to see how King would respond to the package that had been mailed to his office.

32

The Director

ALL HIS LIFE, King had sought to avoid personal conflict—with his father, for starters, but also with Coretta, with Roy Wilkins, and even at times with city officials in Montgomery, Atlanta, Albany, and Birmingham. It might seem odd to say that one of the world's leading dissidents preferred to steer clear of dissidence, but it was true. King tangled with rivals when it became imperative in the fight for justice, as he did in Montgomery after his initial attempts at compromise failed and as he did again in Birmingham after it became clear that aggravating Bull Connor would generate nationwide support for desegregation. But when it came to J. Edgar Hoover, his most dangerous nemesis, King reverted to conflict avoidance and paid a price for it.

The Kennedy brothers had feared, coddled, and cajoled Hoover. Lyndon Johnson had flattered him. "Well, it's probably better to have him inside the tent pissing out, than outside the tent pissing in," Johnson supposedly said of the FBI director. But King was a pastor, not a politician, and he failed to comprehend Hoover's ire.

Hoover was one of the most trusted and admired men in America. The director had built his career by insisting America needed protection—from gangsters, communists, and a wide assortment of so-called deviants—and the public, for the most part, expressed gratitude for his vigilance. In one 1954 survey, 78 percent of Americans indicated a favorable opinion of Hoover, while only 2 percent reported an unfavorable opinion. Nearly two-thirds of those surveyed said they felt "pretty sure" the FBI had "most of the American communists under its eye." By 1965, 85 percent of Americans had a favorable view of the FBI, and 75 percent said they would be pleased if they had a son who became an FBI agent. Hoover had built the best-equipped and most admired national police force in the world. He marketed his work brilliantly, too, seeing to it that newspapers, magazines, and even television shows and movies portrayed him and his agents as heroes.

Hoover's twin obsessions—safeguarding America and safeguarding his own position of power—may have grown from his own feelings of insecurity. But the American people didn't care about that. They only wanted to feel safe.

John Edgar Hoover was born in 1895 and raised in a white, Protestant, middle-class neighborhood called Seward Square in Washington, D.C., three blocks behind the Capitol. The neighborhood, known locally as Pipetown, was occupied mostly by government clerks and their families. Edgar, as friends and family called him, grew up under the tight surveillance and strict discipline of his mother, Anna Marie Hoover, with whom he would live until her death in 1938. His father, Dickerson Hoover, worked as a map printer for the federal government, suffered severe depression, and died in 1921 at age sixty-four. Edgar overcame a childhood stutter by speaking in an unstoppably rapid torrent, which would become his lifelong habit. In high school, after the football coach took one look and rejected him as too small, Hoover joined the school's cadet corps. He wore his cadet uniform when he sang in the choir and taught Sunday school classes at the Church of the Covenant, which later merged with another church to become the National Presbyterian Church.

At the time, Hoover gave serious thought to becoming a minister. He not only believed in God but also liked the way people listened to him when he spoke in church, and he thought he would enjoy leading and promoting social activities. Ultimately, though, he concluded that his religious faith was not deep enough. As a teenager, Hoover appears not to have dated girls. Friends said the cadet corps was his true love—just as friends would say, years later, he was married to the FBI. After graduation from an all-white high school, Hoover enrolled at the all-white George Washington University, where he joined the Kappa Alpha fraternity, which, according to Hoover's biographer Beverly Gage, celebrated the defeated slaveholding culture of the South.

At age eighteen, he took an entry-level job at the Library of Congress, half a mile from his home, continuing a family tradition of civil service work, and at twenty-two he went to work at the Justice Department, where he helped lead an investigation that resulted in the conviction and deportation of Marcus Garvey, the Pan-Africanist. In 1924, Hoover was promoted to the job of acting director of the Bureau of Investigation, as the FBI was known at the time. That was five years before Martin Luther King Jr. was born.

Hoover revolutionized American law enforcement. Prohibition fueled an era of brazen criminality, and local police officials and business executives turned to the federal government for help. Hoover's agents got involved in the biggest criminal cases in the country and scored the biggest headlines when they apprehended or killed brash outlaws such as John Dillinger, Machine Gun Kelly, and Babyface Nelson. The FBI, which collected the fingerprints of millions of convicted criminals, became indispensable, especially in pursuit of criminals who traversed state lines. Hoover made the bureau thoroughly modern and efficient. His G-men, as they were called, became icons. They were depicted in the media as courteous, brave, and patriotic, the same as their boss. Americans who couldn't name the vice president or a single Supreme Court justice knew and instantly recognized J. Edgar Hoover. He was a stocky man with small black eyes, a spatula nose, and crooked teeth, and yet, despite his uninspiring appearance, he became the proud symbol of American crime fighting, "the unceasing defender of the nation against cultural rot and degeneracy," as one of his assistants put it, "a living symbol of all those things that so many Americans wanted their nation to be—tough, strong, brave, honest, decent."

Hoover created an FBI training school for local police officers, ensuring that his approach to law enforcement would spread. He protected his friends, punished his enemies, and kept files on those who were not yet friends or enemies, in case the need ever arose to protect or punish them. Hoover inherited a scandal-plagued agency and moved quickly to instill discipline. Morals mattered. Agents dressed and behaved conservatively, as per the boss's orders. Special scrutiny was devoted to radicalism and obscenity. The bureau issued annual summaries of crime statistics. Hoover developed a system to monitor and harass political dissidents, and he asked citizens to volunteer information on the political activities of radical activists in their communities.

Hoover made himself indispensable to presidents by monitoring their critics and rivals. In 1932, when thousands of World War I veterans converged on Washington to lobby Congress for swifter payment of bonuses they'd been promised, Hoover's agents infiltrated the march and sent reports to the White House designed to discredit the protesters. As the Great Depression spawned more and larger radical activist groups, Hoover grabbed more power by promising that the FBI would investigate anti-American activity. That work expanded during World War II, as fear spread among American leaders that radicals in America might collaborate with Nazi Germany and the Soviet Union to subvert American interests. After the war, the Soviet Union became a hostile adversary rather than an ally. American policymakers feared that Soviet leaders, in their quest for world domination, were out to stoke discontent, riling up radicals everywhere, including the bitterly divided, explosive South.

All these things, to Hoover, threatened America and its Christian foundations. He expected ministers to help the FBI "preserve the dignity of man as the image of God and to mold the individual to be a worthy citizen in a democracy." But King, in Hoover's view, represented a threat to the nation's spiritual and political well-being.

The FBI's interest in King began in response to his association with Stanley Levison. "To Hoover," wrote Paul Letersky, Hoover's young office assistant, "Communism wasn't simply a competing ideology; it was pure, unadulterated evil, a disease of the human spirit, and anyone who wittingly or unwittingly advanced its cause was the enemy." Hoover believed that communists exerted influence on King. When King criticized the FBI as racist, Hoover took the remark personally, as he took most criticism. And the director became even more compulsive about the King investigation when wiretaps revealed the nature of the civil rights leader's personal life.

The director did not act alone. Much of the bureau worked to undermine King, some agents driven by loyalty to Hoover and others driven by their own animus. Among the latter was William C. Sullivan, director of the domestic intelligence division, also known as Division Five. Sullivan— sometimes referred to as "Crazy Billy" within the bureau—appears to have been genuinely offended by King's behavior. Sullivan was a short, neatly dressed man with a New England accent. He rose through the ranks of the FBI, from special agent to supervisor, unit chief, section chief, inspector, chief inspector, assistant director in charge of domestic intelligence and foreign operations, and, finally, assistant to the director in charge of all investigations. It was Sullivan who became outraged by King's success at the March on Washington and who made the initial decision to bug King's hotel room at the Willard Hotel. It was Sullivan who pitched the idea of promoting Samuel R. Pierce to supplant King as a civil rights leader. It was Sullivan who directed the FBI laboratory to make a tape with highlights of the scenes captured from microphone coverage of King's hotel rooms. And it was Sullivan who wrote the threatening letter that went along with the tape.

By 1964, Sullivan and the men of Division Five were deeply devoted to documenting King's sexual activity. That same year, the bureau planted its first human informant in the SCLC's Atlanta office: James A. Harrison, an accountant from Stockton, California, who became a valuable source of information on SCLC finances, planned demonstrations, and office gossip.

On November 30, 1964, Hoover wrote to the president about a meeting between Roy Wilkins of the NAACP and FBI assistant director Deke De-Loach in which Wilkins reportedly said "that personally he would not mind seeing King ruined, but that he felt that while King was no good, the ruin-ation of King would spell the downfall of the entire civil rights movement." The memo went on: "Wilkins indicated that while the sexual degenerate and communist allegations against King are true, many of his Negro associates would rise to his defense." The NAACP director went on to say that he and other Black leaders had tried to persuade King to take a job as a college presi-dent or a full-time pastor, according to Hoover's letter.

A few days later, Hoover wrote to Johnson again, informing the president that King had asked four men with histories of communist affiliations—Stanley Levison, attorney Clarence Jones, Bayard Rustin, and Harry Wachtel (a student radical turned World War II veteran turned corporate lawyer)—to help him write his Nobel Prize acceptance speech. A week after that, on December 9, Hoover informed the president that King had been asked to join a group of activists calling for the withdrawal of American troops in Vietnam.

The FBI's harassment of King continued, too. In Atlanta one day, agents called in a fire alarm at one of King's hideaways, not only to disturb him, apparently, but also to let him know he could not escape their surveillance. Occasionally, a reporter would approach King and discuss the information leaked by the FBI. Sometimes reporters were exploring the possibility of writing a story, and sometimes they were simply letting King know about the FBI's tactics. But King would not address the charges, the FBI would not make formal accusations, and journalists refused to publish the story.

King was saved by journalists who upheld standards of fairness and decency, at a time when even mild swear words never appeared in print or on the air. "We don't print that kind of stuff," said Louis Harris, editor of *The Augusta Chronicle*, in a conversation with the editor Eugene Patterson of *The Atlanta Constitution*, when they realized they'd both been offered the same salacious story on King. "If you print it about him, you can print it about any man." But the same journalists who chose to protect King's privacy failed to take on the more important story: the FBI's secret operation to destroy the nation's leading civil rights leader.

Late in 1964, when the *Newsweek* reporter Ben Bradlee told Nicholas Katzenbach, the new attorney general, that Hoover was leaking the King sex story to the media, Katzenbach flew to Lyndon Johnson's ranch in Texas to tell the president.

Johnson shook his head.

"Terrible, terrible," he said. "I've never heard of it."

Katzenbach was assured that the FBI would stop pitching such stories to the press, but the leaks kept coming. In fact, DeLoach said the president was torn—he wanted the dirt on King, but he didn't want others in the White House to know he was getting it. That's why he had Hoover's letters sent to his personal secretary, Mildred Stegall, who stored them in the president's private safe. Johnson's keen interest in the memos, DeLoach said, contributed to the president's "aloofness" with King.

There is no way to measure the impact of the bureau's campaign on

King's organizational efforts, his fundraising abilities, or his psychological health. But the surveillance clearly damaged King's relationship with the president.

Johnson and Hoover had been neighbors before Johnson moved into the White House. Johnson's children thought of Hoover as an uncle. When the Johnsons' pet beagle died, Hoover gave them another. Johnson named the dog J. Edgar. If Johnson and Hoover had not been friends, would the president have been more inclined to heed the warning of his attorney general and rein in Hoover? Would Johnson and King have built a stronger relationship? If Hoover hadn't smeared King, would King have been less vulnerable to violent attacks by those who believed him a danger to democracy?

"The only thing unique about Dr. King," said Katzenbach in congressional testimony years later, "was the intensity of the feeling and the apparent extremes to which the Bureau went in seeking to destroy the critic . . . Nobody in the Department of Justice connected with civil rights could possibly have been unaware of the intensity of Mr. Hoover's feelings. Nobody could have been unaware of the potential for disaster which those feelings embodied."

Throughout his career, Hoover worked, heroically in his mind, to put down perceived threats to the American way of life. The enemies targeted by Hoover and the FBI were, for the most part, the same enemies identified in the American media and in much of American society. That explains why so many of the people who knew Hoover said he was motivated most by fear of change. King checked all of Hoover's boxes: He had ties to former communists. He was a Negro. He was a Washington outsider. He sought to end systemic racism and patterns of inequality that were embedded in America's history and traditions. And he flagrantly violated the standards of culturally accepted sexual behavior. Hoover was a lifelong bachelor who had a dependent relationship with his mother. His closest friend was FBI associate director Clyde Tolson, with whom he lunched almost daily, dined many evenings, and vacationed frequently. "They were," writes the biographer Beverly Gage, "in essence a couple."

By 1964, Hoover was a sixty-nine-year-old man who had devoted his life to maintaining a carefully constructed sense of order. He saw King as the ultimate disrupter of societal norms. In a way, Hoover read King correctly at a time when few others did. While Malcolm X and others criticized King for being too conservative, and high-ranking officials in the Justice Department saw King as a reasonable reformer, Hoover recognized King for the radical he was and the radicalism he would inspire, especially when he began to work beyond the American South and take on issues bigger and broader in scope than integration.

While King dreamed of and worked for a more inclusive and equitable democracy, Hoover, perhaps more effectively than anyone, tried to stop it.

In a phone call on November 20, 1964, Lyndon Johnson told Deke De-Loach he worried about Hoover's animosity toward King.

JOHNSON: How's the boss feel?

DELOACH: He *was* outraged at the criticism by Martin Luther King.

JOHNSON: Well, that's right, but he knows Martin Luther King.

DELOACH: Yes, sir.

JOHNSON [laughing]: I mean, he knows him better than anybody in the country. And there's no reason why he ought to get in a fight . . . with him.

But the fight was already well underway, and Johnson knew it.

33

A New Sense of
"Some-bodiness"

KING SAID HE didn't want to arrive in Oslo for the Nobel Prize ceremony looking like Sugar Ray Robinson, the legendary boxer famed for traveling with a massive entourage. In the end, about two dozen people accompanied him, including his parents, his brother and sister, Ralph and Juanita Abernathy, Bayard Rustin, Wyatt Walker, Harry Wachtel, L. D. Reddick, and Dorothy Cotton. Martin and Coretta, as was their habit, flew on separate planes. They did not bring their children.

On the flight, King told Wachtel he was worried about the FBI's campaign to expose King's personal transgressions. Wachtel, a Jewish shopkeeper's son, had made a fortune as a Wall Street lawyer and sought now to put his skills to use in more idealistic pursuits. Admitting to Wachtel that he had made mistakes, King vowed to do better. On the same flight, Wachtel and Rustin discussed King's FBI problem. Wachtel said he thought King should "bell the cat," in other words, develop a plan to at least neutralize if not discredit Hoover.

But King was ill-equipped for such a battle.

"He just couldn't face up to it," Wachtel said years later. "One of the reasons that he couldn't stand up and fight was that he had his own guilt."

In an interview years later, Levison would describe King as a deeply guilt-ridden man, overwhelmed by a sense of responsibility and depressed by feelings of inadequacy.

Those closest to him commented often on his emotional health. "Only Martin's family and close staff members knew how depressed he was during the entire Nobel trip," Coretta said. "It was a time when he ought to have been happy... But he was worried that the rumors might hurt the movement and he was worried about what black people would think. He was always worried about that... We had to work with him to help him out of his depression... and the public never knew what he was going through."

Decades later, the psychiatrist Nassir Ghaemi would write that King probably suffered severe depression, a psychiatric illness that can enhance "realism in the assessment of one's circumstances" as well as empathy toward others. The psychologist James Beshai, who studied with King at Crozer Theological Seminary and remained a friend for the rest of King's life, put it differently. If King suffered emotional distress, Beshai said, it was because "he was a man with a determination to stand up for his thinking and also to live a good Christian life" and often felt he came up short. "I didn't see depression," he said. "I saw a man carrying on his mission with dignity and courage."

En route to Norway, the Kings stopped in London, where Martin preached at St. Paul's Cathedral and called on all nations to participate in a "massive economic boycott" of South Africa's apartheid state. He and Coretta arrived in Oslo on December 8 and met privately the next day with the Norwegian king, Olav V, at the Royal Palace. King would make two speeches: a short one at the medal ceremony, followed by a longer lecture the next day.

King wore striped tuxedo pants, a gray tailcoat, and a striped ascot for his first speech, as he addressed a question that he said had puzzled him: Why present an award for a movement that had not achieved the "peace and brotherhood which is the essence of the Nobel Prize"? Why celebrate when the children of Birmingham, only yesterday, had marched for justice and been met with snapping dogs and pummeling fire hoses? The answer, he concluded, was to recognize that nonviolent protest offered a solution to the most pressing moral and political challenge of the moment—"the need for man to overcome oppression and violence without resorting to violence and oppression." He accepted the award, he said, despite the work yet to be done, on behalf of a movement determined to spread freedom and justice, no matter the risk.

At a reception later that night, Daddy King, who never drank alcohol, offered a toast to God. "I always wanted to make a contribution," said the former sharecropper and country preacher. "And all you got to do if you want to contribute, you got to ask the Lord, and let Him know, and the Lord heard me and in some kind of way I don't even know He came down through Georgia and He laid his hand on me and my wife and He gave us Martin Luther King... and when my head is cold and my bones are bleached the King family will go down not only in American history but in world history as well because Martin King is a Nobel Prize winner."

For his formal lecture the next day at Oslo University, King signaled his growing ambition to build a movement that would work to end not only racial discrimination but poverty and warfare, too. At a moment when he might have felt fatigued, besieged, and tempted to retreat, when he might have accepted his Nobel Prize as a reward for a job well done, he chose instead to commit more determinedly than ever to his work, to describe his vision for a better, more ethical world, and to express his resolve to do the work required to make it a reality. He closed with words of optimism:

> Old systems of exploitation and oppression are passing away . . .
> Doors of opportunity are gradually being opened to those at the
> bottom of society. The shirtless and barefoot people of the land are
> developing a new sense of "some-bodiness" and carving a tunnel of
> hope through the dark mountain of despair. . . In a dark, confused
> world, the kingdom of God may yet reign in the hearts of men.

> Coretta felt so proud, as she noted later, she thought she "might burst."

The Kings and a few others traveled from Oslo to Stockholm and then Paris.

"By then Martin was completely exhausted," Coretta said.

Coretta, Dora McDonald, Christine King Farris (Martin's sister), and

Alberta King made plans for a "night on the town" to end their trip in Paris, but when Martin saw the burgundy velvet dress Coretta intended to wear—one of the few fancy dresses she owned, and one she wore when she performed concerts—he insisted she change into "something more appropriate, by which I'm sure he meant more 'matronly,'" Coretta recalled. "Choosing not to argue, though, I offered to change clothes and stay at home with him. I realized later that it was a good thing I did. Martin was exhausted; he took a sedative and went to sleep."

The next day, the Kings returned to the United States. Despite FBI efforts to discourage celebration of the Nobel Prize, they received a hero's welcome in New York City, with fireboats shooting streams of water over the Hudson River, a luncheon hosted by New York governor Nelson Rockefeller, a rally in Harlem, and a medal presented by New York City mayor Robert Wagner. From New York, King's core group went to the White House, where President Johnson greeted Martin, Coretta, and Martin's parents. In Atlanta, hesitation over honoring King was overcome only when the mayor, Ivan Allen, organized a closed-door meeting of business leaders and Coca-Cola president J. Paul Austin urged his peers to hold an integrated banquet for 1,500, an event that would have been unimaginable five years earlier.

King made good on his promise to donate every cent of the Nobel Prize money. However, he kept the gold Rolex watch that went along with the honor and wore it almost every day thereafter.

34

Crowbar

FROM THEIR APARTMENT in Peachtree Towers in Atlanta, FBI agents listened and took notes as Coretta used her home phone. In separate conversations, Coretta told Andrew Young and Dora McDonald about concerns with Martin's emotional state. He seemed to ramble when he spoke; in London, he had quarreled with Ralph Abernathy; and he continued to feel anxiety over his feud with J. Edgar Hoover.

One of the FBI agents wrote in a memo: "The above information is being furnished . . . to acquaint the Bureau with how shaken Dr. King has become as a result of recent events and as a further indication of an area where he may be vulnerable to further pressures."

Hoover tightened the screws. He sent a memo to Bill Moyers, then a special assistant to Lyndon Johnson, saying he thought the president should know about new information showing that King "has the reputation among many Negro leaders of being a heavy consumer of alcoholic beverages and is known . . . to be extremely loose in his moral behavior."

On January 5, 1965, King phoned Abernathy at his West Hunter Street Baptist Church office and asked him to come right away to the SCLC's headquarters. "As soon as I heard his voice," Abernathy said, "I knew he was deeply disturbed." When Abernathy arrived, King showed him the anonymous letter and audiotape that had arrived in a package from Miami and, after sitting for weeks, had just been discovered. King hit *play* on his tape recorder. Abernathy heard muffled voices, whispers, and sighs. He recognized King's voice and his own. King watched Abernathy's face for his reaction.

"It was at the Willard Hotel in Washington, D.C.," King said. "I've listened to it three times."

The tape covered several nights and several locations, not just the Willard, he concluded. Though he expressed anger at the invasion of his privacy, King never questioned whether the voice on the tape was his own, according to Abernathy. The men agreed that the letter and the recording were the obvious work of the FBI. Suddenly, King and Abernathy gained fuller awareness of the extent of the bureau's surveillance and the degree of Hoover's rage. In Abernathy's view, the arrival of the tape signaled the opening of a "second front" in the fight for civil rights: "For the FBI had become our enemy just as surely as the Ku Klux Klan and other racist organizations that were waiting for us in Selma."

Abernathy wondered if Coretta had heard the recording, but he didn't ask. In a book published posthumously in 2017, Coretta wrote that she had been the first to read the letter and listen to the tape, her husband's office mail having been brought to the house. Even before they were married, Coretta had known about Martin's infidelities. Now she chose to remain loyal. Nothing she heard on the tape, she said, convinced her that Martin had been cheating on her.

Years later, as she recounted the story of the FBI tape in her memoir, she took the opportunity to address "the question everyone wants to know: Do I believe my husband was unfaithful?" She'd been dealing with the question of Martin's loyalty almost from the day she met him. She had been making sacrifices for him, because, as she said, he loved her and needed her. But she avoided a straight answer to her own question. "I don't have any evidence," she wrote, "and I never had a gut feeling that told me he had strayed. I never experienced any feelings of being rejected. I believe that women know if their husbands are unfaithful. They feel it. I understand that men can become very indifferent and cold, but I never sensed anything of that sort from Martin. I'm not saying that Martin was a saint. I never said he was perfect. Nobody is perfect. But as far as I'm concerned, our marriage was a very good marriage, and it was like that all the way to the end."

Her husband, meanwhile, offered a clear-eyed appraisal of the FBI's tactics: "They are out to get me, harass me, break my spirit," he told a friend in a phone call recorded by the FBI. Years later, Coretta said she had "no question" the FBI was trying to push Martin to suicide.

King asked his advisers whether he should extend the hand of peace and conciliation to Hoover, or "dare him to do his damnedest," as one of those advisers, the psychologist Kenneth Clark, recalled. Clark urged King to stand up to Hoover, to dare the director to release the tapes. "God damn it, you may be Christ-like, but you're not Christ," Clark said. That remark brought laughter, but it neither amused nor persuaded King.

A week after his discovery of the tapes, King sent Abernathy and Andrew Young to meet with the FBI's Deke DeLoach. The conversation, by all accounts, accomplished nothing. When King traveled to New York, FBI agents watched him deplane at the newly renamed John F. Kennedy Airport and bugged his hotel room again. The surveillance picked up little of interest, except for more evidence of King's anxiety.

Meanwhile, Hoover's obsession with King escalated after the Nobel Prize. "It reminded me of some older relatives that I've had," said Ramsey Clark, a Justice Department official at the time who later became attorney general. "As you get on in years . . . you tend to want to talk about things or relive things, and [Hoover] would tell the same thing a number of times. In fact, it was hard for me to talk to him for thirty minutes without him bringing up Dr. King . . . and it would be derogatory."

Hoover's efforts took a toll. King was hounded and threatened by his own government, labeled a fraud by the nation's most trusted lawman, living under almost constant surveillance, uncertain about whom to trust, living with the fear that he might wake up any morning to a newspaper article describing his moral failings, and knowing that the FBI's assault on his reputation would only embolden those who wanted him dead. "As the years unfolded," Coretta recalled, "we always recognized the possibility of something . . . which could mar his reputation."

In Mobile, Alabama, the local White Citizens' Council set up a telephone line for people who wanted to dial in to hear a prerecorded attack on King: "If Martin Luther 'Riot' King and Dick Gregory want to do something for their people," said the message, "they ought to go to the Congo and try to civilize them . . . Riot King has brought more violence to the South than anyone else in the past 110 years." When King announced plans to lead a January voter registration drive in Selma, the local newspaper reminded readers that J. Edgar Hoover had branded King "the most notorious liar in the country" and urged local citizens to pay no attention to the "controversial darkie."

King still didn't know his home and office phones were tapped. He may have suspected that Stanley Levison's phones were tapped, but he appeared to be unaware that the phones of Bayard Rustin and Clarence Jones were also being monitored. He went on with his work, allowing the public to see none of his distress. If anything, his public pronouncements grew bolder, impelled by his Nobel Prize and by the example of Christ's redemptive suffering.

Above all else, King liked to remind audiences, he remained a preacher. It was in the pulpit he seemed most comfortable, almost carefree.

On January 14, 1965, he arrived in Selma and strode, head held high, into Brown Chapel. The audience sang and swayed and then hushed as he began to speak. The Dallas County Sheriff's Department, eager to learn King's plans, had installed a microphone to record his words. While the mic picked up little useful intelligence, it captured King's assuredness as he carried an audience with him, moving them from conversation to collective action, toward redemption:

Maybe I ought to tell you why I'm here.

"Preach it now . . . go ahead and tell us."

I'm here because I was *invited* here.

"That's right . . . glad you're here!"

And I have organizational connections here. The Dallas County
Voters' League is an affiliate of the Southern Christian Leadership
Conference, so I *belong* here.

He put an extra syllable in "belong" and almost sang it, as the audience
applauded.

I am here because injustice is here.

"That's right!"

I cannot stand idly by when any community finds itself caught in the
shackles of man's inhumanity to man, because injustice anywhere is
a threat to justice everywhere. Just as the eighth-century prophets
left their little towns and villages captured by "thus saith the Lord,"
just as the Apostle Paul left his little village of Tarsus, and decided
to hotfoot it all around the Greco-Roman world and carry the gospel of Jesus Christ, I am compelled to carry the gospel of freedom
everywhere men are oppressed.

"All right!"

He went on to explain what he hoped to achieve and how he hoped
to achieve it. He urged his audience to believe that, together, they could
change Selma and the South, beginning on Monday, when they would
march:

If we will march by the hundreds, our success will enter the conscience of this nation and after a while the forces in power in Alabama will have to say, "You can't stop people like this" . . . We will
appeal to the conscience of Selma. This is Selma's opportunity to
repent!

"It's time!"

This is Selma's opportunity to say to the nation, "We've gone down the wrong path like the Prodigal of old. We've strayed to the far country of brutality" . . . Monday can be a day when Selma will . . . move back to the Father's house.

He concluded with soaring words that sounded like a poem and a prayer, the audience's pitch rising to pandemonium:

Somehow we can say, America, for your security, we have sailed the bloody seas of two world wars. For your security America, our sons died in the trenches of France, in the foxholes of Germany, in the islands of Japan. And now we are saying, America, we just want to be *free*!

"Doctor! Doctor!"

We cannot be our full selves unless we have freedom . . . We will sing again as we did earlier:
"Before I'll be a slave
I'll be buried in my grave
And go home to my Father
And be saved."

The following day, on his thirty-sixth birthday, January 15, 1965, King received a phone call from President Johnson, who was at his ranch in Texas.

JOHNSON: Hello.
KING: Hello?
JOHNSON: This Lyndon Johnson. I had a call from you and I tried to reply to it a couple of times, Savannah, and different places, and they said you were traveling and I got to traveling last night. Just got down here to meet the Prime Minister of Canada this morning and I had a moment, I thought maybe we better try to—I better try to reply to your call.

KING: Well, I certainly appreciate your returning the call and I don't want to take but up to a minute or so of your time. First, I want to thank you for that great State of the Union message. It was really a marvelous presentation. I think we are on the way now toward the Great Society.

Johnson did not discuss details of his legislative agenda, only his excitement about getting it quickly through Congress. With massive spending to attack poverty and with a bill to ease voter registration, he said, "seventy percent of your problems" would be solved.

"That's right," King said.

Johnson said he wanted to eliminate the tests and taxes blocking Black people from voting. And he wanted voting to take place at post offices, where local government officials would be less likely to interfere. When Johnson stopped talking, King explained the purpose of his original call: urging the president to appoint a Negro to his Cabinet. Johnson said he planned to create a new department to oversee issues of "housing and urban and city problems—which is the number-one problem in America, as I see it." He said he was considering the Black economist Robert Weaver to head the new department.

JOHNSON: There's not going to be anything, though, Doctor, as effective as all of 'em voting.

KING: That's right.

When Johnson had first taken office, he had addressed King as "Martin" in phone calls; now it was "Doctor." Ramsey Clark explained the dynamic years later, saying, "The President had been poisoned away from Dr. King . . . thought King was a bad person."

Johnson went on to tell King that he didn't want to portray voting rights as a racial issue. Instead, he wanted to remind Americans that everyone had a right to vote. He urged King to join his publicity campaign:

JOHNSON: And if you can find the worst condition that you run into in Alabama, Mississippi, or Louisiana, or South Carolina . . . if you just take that one illustration and get it on radio, and get it on television, and get it . . . in the pulpits, get it in the meetings, get it everyplace you can, pretty soon the fellow that didn't do anything but . . . drive a tractor, he'll say, "Well, that's not right. That's not fair."

KING: Yes.

JOHNSON: And then that will help us on what we're going to shove through in the end.

KING: Yes. You're exactly right about that.

JOHNSON: And if we do that, we'll break through as—it'll be the greatest breakthrough of anything, not even excepting this '64 act. I think the greatest achievement of my administration . . . was the passage of the 1964 Civil Rights Act. But I think this'll be bigger, because it'll do things that even that '64 act couldn't do.

KING: That's right. That's right.

A month earlier, Johnson had told King that he couldn't possibly push through a voting rights bill, given all the other ambitious legislation on his agenda. Now, he said, not only was he going to propose a voting rights bill, but he believed its passage could turn out to be his greatest accomplishment.

Johnson and King shared the vision of a political coalition that would help build a new American South free from segregation and government-sanctioned discrimination. The vision included federal examiners with the power to register voters, a ban on literacy tests, and a mandate that any changes in voting practices receive preapproval from Washington. Johnson had personal and political motivations, of course. Such a coalition would help prevent Republicans from gaining a political stronghold in the Deep South. But the president said he needed King's help—in the fight for the voting rights bill and his other proposed legislation. Johnson, who understood ambition and power as well as any American politician, didn't care at the time about FBI accounts of King's private life. He wanted King's help in passing these bills. If King had been more selfish, he might have asked the president for a favor in return. He might have asked Johnson to get Hoover off his back. But he didn't.

JOHNSON: "You get in there and help us."

KING: "Well, I certainly will."

———— • ————

Jimmy George Robinson drove from Texas to Alabama to get close to Martin Luther King. Robinson was a tall, slender man with a face like an ax, all angles and edges. He was a founding member of the National States Rights Party, a group composed largely of Klan members, former Klan members, and anti-Semites. In 1963, he'd been arrested for assault on his wife. In 1964, police charged him with carrying a rifle and a Confederate flag to a civil rights march in Dallas.

On January 19, 1965, Robinson watched from across the lobby as Martin Luther King Jr. checked into the Hotel Albert in downtown Selma. Until recently, Black people had not been permitted to stay at the Albert, an elegant four-story hotel built in part by enslaved Alabamans and modeled after the iconic Doge's Palace in Venice. Some reports said King would be the hotel's first Black guest, along with his traveling companions, Ralph Abernathy and Dorothy Cotton. The three SCLC leaders wore long, heavy coats as they stepped up to the registration desk. When their backs were turned, Robinson moved across the room.

The first punch hit King in the temple. King's hat went flying and his head bounced off the counter.

"Get him! Get him!" a white woman in a leather jacket called to the attacker, rooting him on.

Robinson threw another punch and kicked King in the legs and groin. Robinson was tackled and arrested.

Soon after, Dorothy Cotton found King in his hotel room, seated in a chair, wearing nothing but his shorts and undershirt, nursing his wound. He was smoking a cigarette, drinking beer from a can, and sweating profusely.

"Did it hurt?" she asked.

"Oh," King said, smiling, "he packs a pretty good wallop."

King then put on his white shirt and his pressed black suit and headed for a mass meeting.

Robinson's attack may have been sudden, but it was hardly a surprise, and it indicated the rising anger King faced from southern white racists, who made him a symbol of everything they opposed, feared, and reviled. Selma was the birthplace of Bull Connor; the city that the historian J. Mills Thornton III called "the single most inflexibly and fervently segregationist" in Alabama; a city of twenty-eight thousand in which Black people made up slightly more than 50 percent of the population but only about 1 percent of the voters. Selma and the surrounding Dallas County were changing fast. Older residents remembered a time when more than a third of Black people were illiterate and thousands worked as tenant farmers for white families. Now the lines between the races had begun to move, slightly but significantly.

Many Black people had moved from the country into town. They were sending their children to school and keeping them enrolled in greater numbers. With the help of the federal government, they were notching political and legal victories that threatened to change long-standing customs and conditions. They were registering to vote in growing numbers, even if those numbers remained small. The election of the new mayor, the moderate Joe Smitherman, offered some hope. Selma's library had integrated. Signs on city hall and courthouse water fountains proclaiming WHITES ONLY had come down. A growing number of restaurants had agreed to serve Black customers, albeit grudgingly. "We seek your indulgence and understanding of the unpleasant situation into which we have been forced," read one of the handbills presented to white restaurant customers.

Selma's leading white citizens argued that the Negro community should have been pleased with the rate of change and with the respectful response of the authorities to their appeals for reform. Why push for more?

In preparation for King's arrival, Bernard Lafayette Jr., a longtime SNCC staff member, had studied the community. His conclusion: The White Citizens' Council was laden with law enforcement officers, "and they wanted to preserve the existing law, which was segregation, because that was best for white people," Lafayette said. Even in the Black community, some people were wary of King's arrival. "If you tried to fight the system," Lafayette said, "your mother-in-law would lose her job and then your family would get after you."

Many of Lafayette's colleagues within SNCC remained skeptical of

King, viewing him as too old-fashioned, or too accommodating, or too far removed from the people he led. The young radicals in SNCC complained that King and the SCLC were "hoggin' all the publicity and all the money and doing very little to deserve it," as Julian Bond, one of SNCC's founders, put it. For certain members of SNCC, Hosea Williams said, the "number one goal in their life was to embarrass Martin Luther King Jr."

Lafayette felt differently. A native of Tampa, Florida, Lafayette was eleven years younger than King and had been reading about the civil rights leader since the Montgomery bus boycott. Nonviolent protest, he said, contradicted everything he'd been taught as a young man. Joe Louis, the "Brown Bomber," had been his hero. Lafayette knew what the Bible said about peace and love, but he didn't see how he could make that part of his life, not when white people treated him the way they did—until he had heard King. "It was not coming from Scripture," Lafayette said. "It was coming from his soul." As a participant in the Nashville sit-ins, Lafayette had tried to make nonviolence part of his own soul.

But it wasn't until he met King a few years later that he understood the man's power. "I was surprised that he was not taller than he was," he said. "But his voice was a giant." And his courage was even greater than his voice. By the time King came to Selma, Lafayette had seen him up close many times, in church meetings and in private strategy sessions. He had been King's driver on late-night journeys through Georgia and Alabama when King could have napped but didn't, sitting in the passenger seat and telling jokes and humorously mimicking famous preachers and activists, making sure Lafayette didn't fall asleep at the wheel. King also struck Lafayette as remarkably modest, a man who listened more than he talked. Lafayette believed that King would easily win over the Black community in Selma. But the next step would be difficult and possibly ugly, provoking a reaction that would either generate sympathy and support for the cause or get a lot of people killed.

"The point of the movement," he said, "was to take a crowbar and stick it into the cracks of the system." To Lafayette, King was the strongest crowbar America ever made.

King came to Selma with President Johnson's words fresh in mind: "Get it on radio. Get it on television. Get it in the pulpits." He came to put on a show—but it was a more dangerous show than Johnson appreciated. King assigned Hosea Williams, James Bevel, and Andrew Young to organize the campaign in Selma. All three of them possessed enormous egos. Williams and Bevel were particularly antagonistic with each other. Bevel thought Williams was too militant. Williams thought Bevel lacked courage. If Bevel and Williams agreed on anything, though, it was their annoyance with Young, who "only wants to pray and do nothing," as Williams put it. King seemed to encourage his lieutenants' squabbling. He liked to let Bevel and Williams frighten the white establishment before he sent in Young to negotiate. In Selma, conflict would be key. King was counting on his colleagues to rally the Black community and antagonize Sheriff Jim Clark.

King made no secret of his strategy, which was the same one he had settled on in talking to President Johnson: to dramatize the moral issue and arouse the federal government. "We must be willing to go to jail by the thousands," he announced on his first day in Selma. "We are not asking, we are demanding the ballot."

Jim Clark stood on the courthouse steps—a button reading "NEVER" on his lapel, a gun on his hip, a billy club in his hand. He was forty-three years old, a World War II veteran, and a cattle farmer. Clark's commitment to segregation was total. Selma treated its Negro community perfectly well, he said, and the Negro community had been perfectly content until Martin Luther King and other "agitators" stirred them up. "They had lived there peaceably for a hundred to a hundred fifty years, the Blacks and whites did," he said, "and there was no discontent on the part of either one as far as we could tell." Now Clark was determined to prove that the moderates recently elected to local office had it all wrong, that Black protesters had to be squashed, not coddled.

On January 22, more than one hundred schoolteachers walked to the Selma courthouse, only to be turned around by Clark and his deputies, who prodded the teachers with clubs but made no arrests. The teachers not only risked their jobs; they risked their personal safety.

The teachers' willingness to join the campaign galvanized the community. At the same time, lawyers for the movement won a battle in court when a federal judge issued a temporary restraining order that barred local officials from hindering voter registration. On Monday, January 25, King led a group of 250 marchers to the courthouse. This time, Clark lost his temper and began to shove the marchers with his nightstick.

One of them, Annie Lee Cooper, hit back. The right hook buckled Jim Clark's knees. Three deputies pounced on Cooper, and Clark retaliated with his club as newspaper photographers and television cameras captured the struggle.

Cooper, fifty-three years old, was the night receptionist at the Tower Motel. She'd been trying to register to vote since moving from Kentucky to Alabama, but she had failed the registration test every time. "Once I stood in line from 7 a.m. to 4 p.m., but never got in to register," she said. In 1963, when her boss had seen her at a voting rights rally, she'd been fired from her job. She had come to this rally in the hopes, yet again, that she might register.

"I try to be nonviolent," Cooper said later. But when Clark manhandled her, she said, "I jerked loose, pushed him back and told him not to twist my arm. He hit me. Then I lit into him."

King traveled to Chicago on January 27, where he delivered four speeches. During one speech, he spotted five white men in the front row, including Jimmy George Robinson, the man who had slugged him in Selma. When he finished, King, who continued to travel without a bodyguard, noticed Robinson moving forward. When King called out to him, Robinson turned and walked away.

King faced growing hostility. In Alabama, one writer called him "the prophet from Oslo," adding that the prophet was more interested in winning headlines than winning reform. Hadn't Selma integrated its restaurants? Hadn't the city followed the federal judge's order by extending the hours for voter registration? When the history of Selma is presented in fifty or one hundred years, wrote Don W. Wasson, managing editor of *The Mont-*

gomery Advertiser, it might read: "In one city in Alabama, Selma in Dallas County, the white people tried to meet the demands of the times as dictated by the federal courts with reasonableness, but it was not allowed by the racial agitators."

At the same time, the publisher of *The Selma Times-Journal* urged President Johnson to appoint a committee to investigate "the actual conditions existing in Selma." Such a committee, wrote the publisher Roswell Falkenberry, would find that outside agitators had stymied Selma officials in their genuine effort to observe state and federal laws on integration.

Meanwhile, every day, hundreds of Black people lined up to register to vote in Selma, and, every day, they were turned away. On February 1, King and Abernathy marched at the head of a column from Brown Chapel toward the courthouse, intent on being arrested. Thirty miles to the northwest, in Coretta Scott King's hometown of Marion, about three hundred marchers demanded the right to vote. There were no arrests in Marion. In Selma, however, King and more than 250 others were jailed, most of them charged with parading without a permit. In earlier marches, protesters had split into small clusters to avoid violating the parade-permit rule, but this time they had marched as a group, knowing it would likely lead to arrests.

Thunderous applause from the inmates erupted as a gate clanged and King and Abernathy walked into a holding cell. King greeted the inmates and listened to their stories of being beaten by guards, not knowing the charges filed against them, and waiting months for trials. King and Abernathy refused to post bond. Before long, they were moved to an eight-foot cell, away from the crowd. Using Waldorf-Astoria Hotel stationery that he had in his pocket, King jotted instructions, urging Andrew Young to organize more marches. Get a congressional delegation to visit Selma. Push President Johnson and the Justice Department to act. Keep Selma in the news every day.

"These fellows respond better when I am in jail," he said.

⸺ • ⸺

Malcolm X, who also understood the importance of drama, left New York early on the morning of February 3, flew to Montgomery, and then drove to

Tuskegee, where he spoke to a crowd of three thousand Tuskegee Institute students. The battle was wearing on Malcolm. Nation of Islam enforcers continued to track him. If the enforcers wanted to kill him, Malcolm said, he was confident they would succeed. "I taught them myself," he said.

He told the students that 1965 would be "the longest and hottest and bloodiest year in the history of the race revolution." He also read from a telegram that he said he had sent to George Lincoln Rockwell, saying that if Rockwell and his American Nazi Party continued their campaign of terror, they would be met with "maximum physical retaliation by those of us who are not handcuffed by a policy of nonviolence." That was a change from 1961, when Malcolm and Rockwell had appeared together at a rally in Washington, united in their opposition to integration.

Now one student asked Malcolm about his rift with Elijah Muhammad, a rift that had been relished by the FBI. Malcolm managed a diplomatic reply: "Elijah believes that God is going to come and straighten things out . . . I'm not willing to sit and wait on God to come . . . I believe in religion, but a religion that includes political, economic, and social action designed to eliminate some of these things, and make a paradise here on earth while we're waiting for the other." With that statement, he didn't sound so different from King, which might explain why some of the students attending the lecture asked Malcolm to join them in making the hundred-mile drive to Selma, where another eight hundred protesters had been arrested that day. Malcolm accepted the invitation.

Malcolm had gradually moved away from the Nation of Islam's beliefs on race and religion, and toward what the theologian James H. Cone called a universal perspective on humanity "centered on his commitment to the black liberation struggle in America." Malcolm admitted he was a man in transition, "in outer limbo," as he put it, which might explain why he felt drawn to King. While King never said publicly that he was trying to avoid Malcolm, he did say that he found Malcolm's call for people to arm themselves "very unfortunate." If Black people take up arms, King said, it will only give certain white Americans "an excuse to kill up a lot of us."

The day after his speech at Tuskegee, with King still in jail, Malcolm sat beside Coretta Scott King in Brown Chapel Church. "Mrs. King," he said, "will you tell Dr. King that I'm sorry I won't get to see him?" He continued: "I want him to know that I didn't come to make his job more difficult. I thought that if the white people understood what the alternative was they would be willing to listen to Dr. King."

When his turn came to speak, Malcolm issued a warning, saying white people should thank Dr. King for holding Black people in check, because not everyone believed in restraint.

Later the same day, February 4, at a White House press conference, President Johnson said all Americans should be "indignant" when one American is denied the right to vote. Though Johnson still didn't mention a voting rights bill, King was thrilled. The president had taken a stand on the side of the Selma protesters and voting rights. At the same time, the federal district judge Daniel Thomas issued an order banning lengthy registration tests for would-be voters and requiring local officials to clear the backlog of applications.

The news was so good that SCLC officials called off their scheduled protest, prompting a sharp response from King. "Please don't be too soft," he wrote from jail to Young. "We have the offensive. It was a mistake not to march today. In a crisis we must have a sense of drama . . . We may accept the restraining order as a partial victory, but we cannot stop."

King spent four days in jail. He left on February 5, dressed in a suit and tie, his face unshaven. A female admirer approached and kissed his cheek, leaving a lipstick smear. Speaking to reporters, King said he had no intention of calling off the campaign. Other leaders, he said, planned to expand their voting rights protests across the state of Alabama, particularly in Marion and nearby Lowndes County, where Black people made up 80 percent of the population and not one Black person was registered to vote. He also called on President Johnson and Congress to pass a law tough enough to overcome the opposition of segregationists.

The next day, the White House press secretary, George E. Reedy, announced that President Johnson would ask Congress for just such a law.

Still, King said, the campaign would go on.

"What do they want?" asked an elderly white man in Selma, incredulously. Selma had followed a judge's order to open voter registration. The city's restaurants had integrated. The president had heard their cry. What more did they want?

But forces had been unleashed that King couldn't stop even if he wanted to. Little Black children who once might have played cowboys and Indians were now playing "Jim Clark and Negro," a game that went like this, according to a northern newspaper reporter: "I'll be Jim Clark, you be the Negro. I'll hit you on the head, you fall down."

All over the country, and perhaps most vividly in Selma, a new level of ambition and audacity took hold among the Black community.

"Let's see how that white water tastes," Bruce Dozier and his friends would say, laughing, when they saw whites-only fountains in downtown Selma. The twelve-year-old would sneak a sip and run away. But for all the excitement about King and the protests and the visible cracks in the wall of segregation, Dozier would recall years later, schools and neighborhoods in Selma remained strictly segregated, white men still ran the town, and the white restaurant owners who claimed they'd desegregated were "like George Wallace standing in the schoolhouse doors—oh, no, I wasn't going in." People had the sense, Dozier said, that the revolution had barely begun, and it still wasn't clear if or when the white power structure would relent to Black demands.

The New York Times offered a biblical analogy to explain the state of the civil rights movement: Jim Clark was the Pharaoh, but all he wanted to do was stop the plagues. King was Moses, but the Promised Land remained out of sight. Even if King felt confident President Johnson would deliver a voting rights law, and even if that law gave all Americans equal access to the ballot, and even if newly elected officials responded to the demands of a newly powerful voting bloc, it would take years to achieve something approaching true equality in American society.

After his release from jail, King flew to New York, back to Atlanta, and then to Washington, where he met with Attorney General Katzenbach and Vice President Hubert Humphrey. He also met for fifteen minutes with President Johnson—a meeting in which the president affirmed his commitment to new voting rights legislation. Afterward, King praised the president's "deep commitment" to guaranteeing the right to vote for all Americans.

King returned to Selma, traveled to Michigan for a speaking engagement, and then went home to Atlanta, where he was hospitalized again for exhaustion. Ralph Abernathy said his friend "collapsed under the pressure and had to be hospitalized with the same mysterious ailment that always plagued him during these rugged campaigns." He went back to Selma, but he still felt unwell, even as he led more marches and strategy sessions. Abernathy phoned Bayard Rustin on February 17 to say King was "sick . . . and terribly run down," and to ask if Rustin could get Harry Wachtel or someone else to pay for King to go on a vacation.

The next day, King was in Atlanta again, resting, as C. T. Vivian led an evening march on the jail in Marion, Alabama, protesting the arrest earlier that day of the SCLC's James Orange. The marchers moved only half a block before the chief of police ordered them to disperse. The group stopped. Some knelt to pray. When troopers began prodding marchers with nightsticks, some of them fled. The troopers gave chase, swinging their nightsticks. Some of the protesters took refuge in a nearby café. When the troopers entered the café and clubbed a woman named Viola Jackson, her twenty-six-year-old son, Jimmie Lee Jackson, tried to fight them off. One trooper shoved Jimmie Lee against a cigarette machine while another pulled his pistol and shot Jimmie Lee twice in the stomach. The wounds were fatal.

Three days later, in Harlem, gunmen from the Nation of Islam assassinated Malcolm X.

In a telegram to Malcolm's wife, Betty Shabazz, King wrote:

I was certainly saddened by the shocking and tragic assassination of
your husband. While we did not always see eye to eye on methods
to solve the race problem, I always had deep affection for Malcolm
and felt that he had the great ability to put his finger on the existence
and root of the problem . . . Always consider me a friend and if I can
do anything to ease the heavy load that you are forced to carry at
this time, please feel free to call on me.

King and Malcolm X were often portrayed as antagonists, in part
because of Malcolm's vitriol and because of comments attributed to King in
a 1965 *Playboy* magazine interview conducted by Alex Haley. But the recent
discovery of Haley's unedited interview transcript shows that King was not
as critical as *Playboy* made him sound.

The magazine quoted King saying of Malcolm: "He is very articulate,
as you say, but I totally disagree with many of his political and philosophical views . . . I have often wished that he would talk less of violence, because
violence is not going to solve our problem. And in his litany of articulating
the despair of the Negro without offering any positive, creative alternative, I
feel that Malcolm has done himself and our people a great disservice. Fiery
demagogic oratory in the black ghettoes, urging Negroes to arm themselves
and prepare to engage in violence, as he has done, can reap nothing but grief."
Here's what King actually said.

PLAYBOY: Dr. King, what is your opinion of Negro extremists who advocate armed violence and sabotage?
DR. KING: Fiery, demagogic oratory in the black ghettoes, urging Negroes to arm themselves and prepare to engage in violence can achieve
nothing but negative results. Those who are fired up in the audiences go
home and face the same unchanged conditions; what is left but for them
to become bitter, disillusioned and cynical. The extremist leaders who
offer a call to arms are invariably unwilling to lead what they themselves

know would certainly end in bloody, chaotic total failure. The struggle of the Negro in America, to be successful, must be waged with positive efforts that are kept strictly within the framework of our democratic society. This means reaching and moving the large groups of people necessary—of both races—to activate sufficiently the conscience of a nation. It is this effort that the S.C.L.C. attempts to achieve through the program which we call creative non-violent direct-action.

PLAYBOY: Dr. King, would you care to comment upon the articulate former Black Muslim, Malcolm X?

DR. KING: I have met Malcolm X, but circumstances didn't enable me to talk with him for more than a minute. I totally disagree with many of his political and philosophical views, as I understand them. He is very articulate, as you say. I don't want to seem to sound as if I feel so self-righteous, or absolutist, that I think I have the only truth, the only way. Maybe he does have some of the answer. But I know that I have so often felt that I wished that he would talk less of violence, because I don't think that violence can solve our problem. And in his litany of expressing the despair of the Negro, without offering a positive, creative approach, I think that he falls into a rut sometimes.

In 1965, King was much more humble and uncertain about Malcolm than the magazine made it appear. He remained critical of the Nation of Islam, but more open-minded with regard to Malcolm X. King and Malcolm had discovered common ground in their attacks on racism and inequality. In death, Malcolm would become a "cultural folk hero," as the historian Peniel E. Joseph put it, a symbol of defiance. "But his greatest impact," Joseph writes, "may have been on Martin Luther King Jr."

When King returned to Selma, he received a phone call from Katzenbach, saying the Justice Department had learned about a failed attempt on King's life. Katzenbach urged King to be careful. King was accustomed to death threats, but lately, "he had been receiving an excessive number," as Abernathy put it. Close confidants urged him to avoid unnecessary risk.

Less than twenty-four hours after the murder of Malcolm X, King stepped to the pulpit at Brown Chapel and addressed another huge crowd, vowing to ignore a ban on night marches issued by Governor Wallace and announcing plans for a march on the state capitol in Montgomery. "We will be going there to tell Governor Wallace that we aren't going to take it any-more," he said.

After a four-day fundraising trip, King flew home to Atlanta. He quickly departed again for Washington, where he expressed his opposition to the war in Vietnam in a speech to students at Howard University, a controver-sial position even on a college campus. At the time, public opinion surveys showed that only 19 percent of Americans favored withdrawal of American troops from Vietnam, while 23 percent favored escalating the battle. With little sleep, King returned to Selma.

On March 3, he presided at Jimmie Lee Jackson's funeral, where he announced that the fifty-mile march to Montgomery would begin four days later. Jackson's death and the refusal of state officials to meet the protesters' demands, King said, required dramatic action. He said:

[Jimmie Lee Jackson] was murdered by every white minister of the gospel who has remained silent behind the safe security of his stained-glass windows. He was murdered by the irresponsibility of every politician . . . who has fed his constituents the stale bread of hatred and the spoiled meat of racism. He was murdered by the ti-midity of a federal government that is willing to spend millions of dollars a day to defend freedom in Vietnam but cannot protect the rights of its citizens at home. He was murdered by every sheriff who practices lawlessness in the name of law. He was murdered by the cowardice of every Negro who passively accepts the evils of segrega-tion and stands on the sidelines in the struggle for justice.

Two days later, on Friday, March 5, King and Jackie Robinson traveled to Frankfort, Kentucky, to lead a demonstration on behalf of a state bill to remove racial barriers in public accommodations. While there, King met Georgia Davis Powers, one of the march organizers. "My heart quickened as

I saw him move toward us," Powers wrote, recalling their meeting. "His skin was a mahogany-bronze… His dark brown eyes looked straight into those of whomever he was addressing." They discussed public policy as they rode together in the back seat of the car taking them to the march and conferred again when the day's events were over. Davis would go on to become the first Black woman elected to the Kentucky state senate. She would also become King's lover, according to her 1995 memoir, *I Shared the Dream*. "Guilt not-withstanding, I would come whenever he called and go wherever he wanted," she wrote. She added: "There were times I knew we were under surveillance by the FBI when we were together."

From Kentucky, King flew to Washington, D.C., for his third meeting with President Johnson in as many months. He arrived at 6:22 p.m., his flight delayed by bad weather. Johnson told King that Senate Minority Leader Everett Dirksen had pledged to support a strong voting rights bill. Johnson asked King to work with Nick Katzenbach to shape the legislation.

After the meeting, reporters asked King if he planned to go ahead with Sunday's march in Selma.

King said he had told the president that "Negroes had to continue their demonstrations to dramatize their plight."

In truth, though, as he flew home to Atlanta, King was gripped with doubt about the wisdom—and safety—of Sunday's scheduled march.

35

Selma

MORE THAN SIX hundred people marched through Selma on March 7, 1965. They walked down streets they had walked all their lives, from Sylvan to Water to Broad, where they turned left and made their way up the western ramp of the Edmund Pettus Bridge.

Martin Luther King was not among them.

"It was suggested," King said, "that I remain in Atlanta for my Sunday church responsibilities and mobilize national support for a larger thrust forward."

King had initially ordered the men not to march that day. He had changed his mind only reluctantly, giving in to pressure from James Bevel and Hosea Williams. From its start, the procession had a solemn feel, recalled John Lewis. They proceeded quietly, "not even singing songs." The day was cold and windy. When the marchers reached the top of the bridge, Lewis said, "we saw a sea of blue, Alabama State Troopers, and behind the state troopers we saw Sheriff Clark and his posse. They had made an announcement that all white men over the age of twenty-one to come down to the courthouse and be deputized the night before, to become part of the posse, to stop the march."

SNCC leaders had decided not to have the organization participate in the march. The group's leaders were angry that King had swooped in and stolen the attention after their years of work in Selma. Many within SNCC called for more aggressive forms of protest than those favored by King. But Lewis decided to join the march as an individual, not in his role as SNCC's chairman.

Major John Cloud, speaking through a bullhorn, ordered the marchers to disperse. When the demonstrators halted but held their ground, Cloud gave the order: "Troopers, advance! Drive them back!"

Horse hooves pounded the pavement and canisters of tear gas burst. The marchers screamed and fell to their knees, gagging and gasping for air.

"You saw these men putting on their gas masks," Lewis said. "They came toward us, beating us with nightsticks, trampling us with horses, releasing the tear gas. I was the first one to be hit. I was hit in the head, my legs. My knees went from under me and I fell to the ground. I thought I saw death. I thought I was going to die. And apparently a group of young men picked me up and carried me someway and somehow back to the Brown Chapel Church."

Philip Henry Pitts watched the same scene from the other side of the bridge. Just two years out of the University of Alabama law school, Pitts, a white man, represented the fourth generation to join the family office of Pitts and Pitts in downtown Selma. His father, W. McLean Pitts, served as Selma's city attorney. Now the younger Pitts sat in a sheriff's car parked beside the Glass House Drive Inn restaurant, watching as peaceful protesters met unprovoked violence. As marchers fled, posse members spurred their horses in pursuit. Troopers cracked their nightsticks against marchers' skulls. Tear gas filled the air. White spectators cheered from the side of the road. Some of the spectators joined the attack.

"So much happened at that time," recalled Pitts, decades later, as he drove his car over the bridge and parked in the same spot he'd parked that day, gazing up at the steel span. "Some of it you want to remember and some of it you don't. I sat in a car by the Edmund Pettus Bridge and watched. *My God, what is this happening?* Of course, I didn't voice any objection to it. Of course, I knew it was wrong. I *knew* it was wrong. I never voiced any objection. I didn't even tell my daddy I knew it was wrong. It was really inhuman. Jim Clark had deputies riding on horses, hitting them on the back of the head. I knew it was wrong and somebody should have stopped it. But who was going to stop it? Sometimes I regret not voicing my objections, but, hell, they wouldn't have listened to me."

The troopers and police pushed the protesters back toward Brown Chapel, back into Selma's predominantly Black neighborhood. Bottles and bricks flew. More than seventy people were hospitalized. That night, ABC interrupted its broadcast of the movie *Judgment at Nuremberg* to show television viewers what racial hatred looked like in America. All over the country, people responded with spontaneous protests. Two days later, Detroit mayor Jerome Cavanagh and Michigan governor George Romney led ten thousand people in a demonstration of solidarity with the Selma marchers. In Chicago, demonstrators shut down the Loop during rush hour.

Meanwhile, in Atlanta, King made plans to return to Alabama and lead another attempted march on Tuesday from Selma to Montgomery. Lawyers, he said, would seek a temporary restraining order forbidding Alabama and Dallas County officials from interfering this time. King and other leaders called on the White House and the Justice Department to supply protection. He also sent a telegram to religious leaders around the country, asking them to join him in Selma. "In the vicious maltreatment of defenseless citizens of Selma," he wrote, "where old women and young children were gassed and clubbed at random, we have witnessed an eruption of the disease of racism which seeks to destroy all America. No American is without responsibility."

The day after the bloody attack in Selma, President Johnson phoned his friend J. Lister Hill, Alabama's senior senator, for advice. Johnson said he didn't want to see more bloodshed, didn't know how to communicate with George Wallace, and didn't want to lend his support to the SCLC's request for a restraining order because, as he said, it would look like "I might be advocating the goddamn march."

"It's a hell of a dilemma," Hill said. "It sure is."

Johnson said he faced dilemmas "all day here, all day long," including a recent decision about whether to send two battalions of marines to South Vietnam to protect an American air base near Danang. College students and a few U.S. senators had begun to protest America's military presence in Vietnam. Johnson feared he was stepping deeper into a morass, one that might sink his ambitious domestic agenda. Stress over Vietnam disturbed Johnson's sleep and corroded his personality, leaving him depressed, making his family's life "pure hell," as Lady Bird Johnson put it.

King returned to Selma, conflicted about whether to go through with Tuesday's planned march. Bevel and Williams wanted action. So did SNCC organizers. Some of them chided King for having sat out the last push across the Edmund Pettus Bridge, the conflict now referred to as Bloody Sunday. Hundreds of religious leaders poured into Selma in response to King's appeal, some of them driving through the night to arrive in time for the Tuesday protest, coming without so much as a change of clothes. But White House officials wanted King to call it off. When SCLC attorneys petitioned Judge Frank M. Johnson Jr. of the federal district court for an order barring state obstruction of the demonstration, Johnson said he would only consider it after a full hearing later in the week. The judge wanted the march postponed and said he would issue an order to stop the procession if organizers didn't comply with his wishes.

It was late Monday night, almost midnight, when King spoke to a crowd of hundreds at Brown Chapel. His demeanor, one witness said, "gave the distinct impression that he was involved in some kind of profound struggle with his conscience." At first, he told his associates he intended to postpone the march. Then he said it was on again.

"Dr. King, you promised you would not march," Katzenbach said in a phone call.

"Mr. Attorney General," said King, "you have not been a Black man in America for the past three hundred years."

Still, King remained conflicted. He opened a conference call with advisers saying: "Gentlemen, I'm at one of the most difficult moments of my life. I have to make a terribly difficult decision . . . I know I've got to make this decision alone." One adviser, Harry Wachtel, suggested a compromise. King might walk to the bridge and stop there. But King feared that such a move would look like a victory for the state and local police. On the other hand, he didn't want to violate a federal court order or lead his followers to slaughter. "These people are crazy down here," he said on the conference call, referring to white opponents of the march. "They have had it. They have five hundred state troopers out there right now."

The advisers told King he should march and expect to be arrested.

"I lean towards that . . . ," he said, "that I will appear in the church at the moment that we are getting ready to march, make a brief statement, and go on."

"This is an historic moment for Martin," said Bayard Rustin, one of the men on the call. "This is a moral question. He has no choice before God but to move."

At 5:00 a.m., King called Katzenbach to say the march would proceed. But after a few hours' sleep, King, still in his pajamas, discussed a compromise with two officials sent by Katzenbach from Washington. If King would agree to an abbreviated march—turning his forces around when they reached the bridge—the Justice Department would ensure that state troopers would leave the marchers alone. King agreed to the deal.

He arrived at Brown Chapel at 2:55 p.m., where an interracial crowd of more than three thousand waited for him. King made no mention of his negotiations with the Justice Department, but the absence of knapsacks and camping gear indicated to at least some marchers they were probably not going all the way to Montgomery. "I have got to march," King told the audience at Brown Chapel. "I don't know what lies ahead of us. There may be beatings, jailings, tear gas. But I would rather die on the highways of Alabama than make a butchery of my soul."

The weather was clear and cold. The pack moved, slowly, down Sylvan Street, King and his brother, A.D., at the front, along with Jim Bevel, James Farmer, James Forman, and others. Marchers sang "We Shall Overcome" and "Ain't Gonna Let Nobody Turn Me Around." As the group neared the Edmund Pettus Bridge, Katzenbach's emissaries walked beside King and spoke in his ear, saying Jim Clark and Al Lingo, commander of the state troopers, had agreed to back off if King and his followers stopped at the bridge. Marchers eyed Selma's rooftops, looking for Klan snipers they feared might be lurking.

King and his fellow marchers saw ahead of them a blockade of a hundred grim-faced, helmeted troopers, arms folded, feet apart. There were no horses or gas masks this time, but dozens of unofficial "posse men" lined the sides of the road, in addition to the uniformed officers, toting an assortment of weapons.

"I am asking you to stop where you are," Major John Cloud shouted through a microphone.

King shouted back. They were going to Montgomery to present a petition to the governor, he said. But a strong wind from the south muffled his words.

"This march will not continue," said Cloud. "You can have your prayer and then return to your church."

Ralph Abernathy led a prayer as hundreds knelt: "We come to present our bodies as a living sacrifice," he said. "We don't have much to offer, but we do have our bodies, and we lay them on the altar today."

Cloud turned to the troopers and gave an unexpected command: "Clear the road completely—move out!"

The wall of state troopers parted. Highway 80 stood open, the path to Montgomery clear.

"Everybody felt a miracle had occurred and the Red Sea had opened and we were going to march to Montgomery," said Harris Wofford, one of the marchers.

But King turned around.

Back at Brown Chapel, he offered a weak explanation: "At least we had to get to the point where the brutality took place. And we made it clear when we got there that we were going to have some form of protest and worship. I can assure you that something happened in Alabama that's never happened before. When Negroes and whites can stand on Highway 80 and have a mass meeting, things aren't that bad."

Governor Wallace had a different view: "Law and order prevailed," he said.

King could have announced his intentions before the march. He could have made clear that his goal that day was not a march to Montgomery but a show of brotherhood, with Black and white ministers walking arm in arm to the bridge and back, in support of voting rights. Instead, his fudging brought more criticism. Clergymen who had traveled to Selma from distant cities complained that their efforts had been wasted.

"What in the world happened?" Wofford asked. "I don't know when the 'Martin Loser King' became one of the slogans, but it was the first time I had seen the growth of that kind of . . . anti-King movement."

Militant activists said King had blown an opportunity to put pressure on Governor Wallace. To James Forman of SNCC, it was worse than that. In his view, King had formed a de facto partnership with the federal government, serving as a "safety valve for the American system by taking the pressure off"—the same pressure that SNCC and others were trying to create.

After the aborted march, three white ministers who had come to town to join the protest were beaten by white vigilantes. One of them, James Reeb, a Presbyterian minister who lived and worked in Boston's Roxbury neighborhood, would die from the resulting injuries. King's rift with SNCC widened when he admitted he had negotiated a compromise with authorities on the march that would become known as Turnaround Tuesday. The rift widened further when King announced a suspension of protests while waiting for Judge Johnson to rule on the Selma-to-Montgomery march.

A few days later, King flew to Chicago, where he spoke to more than five thousand people at a Sunday-morning service at Liberty Baptist Church. "I get so tired and weary," he said. "I wonder if all my work is in vain. But I thank God for the power and strength of all the millions of people who are in the struggle with me. The cross-country demonstrations and contributions have given me strength to march forward nonviolently with God on my side."

King had a second appearance scheduled that day in Chicago but canceled it, according to news reports, because he had a bad case of hiccups. Meanwhile, in Washington, fifteen thousand people massed in front of the White House to protest police brutality and violence in Alabama, while ten thousand marched through Harlem, with a group of Roman Catholic nuns leading the way. Countless thousands more demonstrated, from Portland, Maine, to Casper, Wyoming, most of the protests led by religious leaders, often with the participation of local government officials. St. Augustine, Florida, witnessed its first big protest since King had launched his series of demonstrations there in 1964.

That evening, King received a call from Lyndon Johnson. The president planned to discuss voting rights before a joint session of Congress, televised live to the nation on Monday night, March 15, and he wanted King to be there, seated next to Lady Bird Johnson. King accepted but called back later to say he couldn't make it. He needed to be in Selma to preach at James Reeb's memorial service.

* * *

Throughout the Selma campaign, King stayed in a guest bedroom at the home of his friends Sullivan and Jean Jackson. He was comfortable enough with the Jacksons to stroll the house in his navy-blue pajamas, but at 9:00 p.m. on March 15 he was still dressed in his shirt and tie as he settled into an easy chair to watch Johnson's address from the U.S. Capitol. Across the country, seventy million viewers tuned in to hear the president. After a brief introduction, Johnson said:

> At times history and fate meet in a single place to shape a turning point in man's unending search for freedom. So it was at Lexington and Concord. So it was a century ago at Appomattox. So it was last week in Selma, Alabama.
>
> There, long-suffering men and women peacefully protested the denial of their rights as Americans. Many were brutally assaulted. One good man, a man of God, was killed.
>
> There is no cause for pride in what has happened in Selma. There is no cause for self-satisfaction in the long denial of equal rights to millions of Americans.

The chamber was silent.

> Rarely, in any time, does an issue lay bare the heart of America itself.
> Rarely are we met with a challenge, not to our growth or abundance,

our welfare or security, but rather to the values and the purposes and meaning of our beloved Nation.

The audience of legislators applauded.

This was the first nation in the history of the world to be founded with a purpose. The great phrases of that purpose still sound in every American heart ... "All men are created equal" ... "government by the consent of the governed."

Using language that may have been inspired by King, Johnson went on to describe the ways in which state and local officials in the South denied millions of Black people the right to vote and to participate in democracy. Previous civil rights laws had failed to solve the problem, but a bill he planned to send to Congress on Wednesday would make it all but impossible to refuse to register Black voters. Johnson continued:

The real hero of this struggle is the American Negro. His actions and protests, his courage to risk safety and even to risk his life, have awakened the conscience of this Nation ...

He has called upon us to make good the promise of America. And who among us can say that we would have made the same progress were it not for his persistent bravery, and his faith in American democracy.

The president, his expression stern, barreled to his conclusion:

What happened in Selma is part of a far larger movement which reaches into every city and state in America. It is the effort of American Negroes to secure for themselves the full blessings of American life.

Their cause must be our cause too. Because it is not just Negroes, but really it is all of us, who must overcome the crippling legacy of bigotry and injustice.

He paused and delivered each of his next four words deliberately: "And . . . we . . . *shall* . . . overcome!"

Members of the audience jumped to their feet, applauding.

In Selma, Jean Jackson looked over at King.

He was crying.

On March 21 in Birmingham, police found four powerful homemade time bombs in Black neighborhoods—at a church, a high school, a funeral home, and a private home. Army demolition experts dismantled them before they could explode.

As the bombs were discovered, King launched another march in Selma, ninety miles away, this time with judicial approval, with Alabama National Guard members assigned by the federal government to provide protection, and with enough supplies to sustain a four-day trek to Montgomery. The day was sunny and cool. The people linked arms and began to walk, departing from Brown Chapel at 12:48 p.m.

The Montgomery Advertiser reported: "They were many types and descriptions—white-collared clergymen, beatniks with beards, college students in denims and sweaters, and old men and women, teen-agers and babies."

King compared his followers to the Israelite slaves who left Egypt, but with an important difference: his followers didn't have to travel to find the land of milk and honey; they were already there. "We know we can work within the framework of our democracy to bring about a brighter day," he said. "We will turn the Heart of Dixie into a state with a heart of brotherhood and freedom . . . Alabama will be a new Alabama. Its children will finally enter the Promised Land."

King wore a lei around his neck, a gift from a delegation of marchers from Hawaii. Near the Edmund Pettus Bridge, a white man in a record shop set up a loudspeaker to blast the song "Dixie," followed by "Bye, Bye, Black-bird," at the marchers. A black Volkswagen drove past the marchers with signs on its doors and fenders reading MARTIN LUTHER KINK; WALK, COON; and COONSVILLE, U.S.A. White children at the roadside chanted "Nigger lover!" and "Half-breed!" A man stood in front of a diner and thumbed his nose for a full twenty minutes as the procession moved past him.

The marchers responded with a song of their own: "We Shall Overcome." They walked out of Selma across the bridge with the sun at their backs on a flat stretch of highway cut through moss-covered trees. They traveled seven miles to arrive at their first campsite, where three hundred, including King, would spend the night. King slept in a small pink-and-white trailer while others tucked themselves into sleeping bags under large tents. Soldiers guarded the camp. Those not sleeping at the campsite returned by bus, truck, and train to Selma for the night. On Monday morning, the campers woke in a frost-covered cow pasture, rolled up their sleeping bags, and started walking again. Bothered by blisters, King put on a second pair of socks. Coretta walked by his side. "My feet don't feel so good either," she said. When the marchers approached a service station, the white owner barricaded his driveway and closed the station. A small plane dropped leaflets urging white business owners to fire Black employees. Former president Harry S. Truman, interviewed in Independence, Missouri, called the march "silly," adding, "They can't accomplish a darned thing."

King returned to Selma for a staff meeting and then traveled to Cleveland, Ohio, for a fundraiser, as the march moved on without him for a day. In Cleveland, he issued a warning, saying the demonstrations taking place in the South would surely spread "unless there is imaginative leadership in the North." In fact, demonstrations in Cleveland had already begun, with Black laborers complaining about unions that accepted only white members.

On Wednesday, he and Coretta rejoined the marchers for the final leg of the journey to Montgomery. The marchers were entertained that night by a lineup of entertainers that included Harry Belafonte, Tony Bennett, Nina Simone, Leonard Bernstein, Billy Eckstein, Pete Seeger, and Sammy Davis Jr.

The next day, March 25, 1965, thousands of people from Montgomery joined the procession, including many of the same people who had sustained the city's bus boycott less than a decade earlier. Abernathy estimated the crowd at fifty thousand. The police said it was twenty-five thousand. Either way, it was the biggest parade Montgomery had ever seen, with a seemingly endless river of people, most of them Black, coursing through the city's downtown streets. "There were nuns in flowing black habits arm in arm with jowly labor leaders who discriminate in their unions," wrote the journalist Jack Newfield. "There were rabbis, junkies, schoolboys, actors, sharecroppers, intellectuals, maids, novelists, folk-singers, and politicians—10,000 motives and 40,000 people." Jim Letherer, a white man from Michigan, made the entire walk on crutches, having lost his right leg to cancer as a child. An elderly man, cane between his legs, sat on his front porch and wept. "Walking through the Negro section made me feel like I was walking through Paris again with the liberation army," said Edward Koch, a Democratic Party leader from New York City who would later become a U.S. congressman and New York mayor. As the marchers reached downtown and passed the Whitley Hotel, Black porters stared out the windows on one side of the building and white customers stared out the windows on the other.

The crowd stopped and gathered in front of the state capitol, where a podium had been set up on a flatbed truck. An Alabama state flag and a flag of the Confederacy flew atop the capitol's white dome. Inside, Governor Wallace sat in the cafeteria eating roast beef smothered in ketchup. As King stepped to the podium, he gazed out at the crowded streets. Patchy clouds moved across a gray sky. People climbed the stairs of King's old church, Dexter Avenue Baptist, to get a better view. A helicopter circled overhead and two dozen police in green helmets guarded the capitol building's steps.

King spoke slowly and calmly. His face had softened since his time in the pulpit at the church down the block. His skin no longer stretched so tightly over his strong cheekbones. His eyes wandered across the crowd as he summarized the suffering of the people who stood before him, describing their sunburns, soaked clothes, and sore feet. He reminded them of something an elderly woman had said during the Montgomery bus boycotts, almost a decade ago, when asked one day if she wanted a ride to work. "No," the woman said. "My feets is tired, but my soul is rested."

King went on to enumerate the many reasons why these marchers and Black Americans in general might be tired—tired of the church bombings, the murders, denial of the right to vote, substandard schools, police brutality, and much more. But for all their anger, for all their pain, King insisted, once again, that suffering was part of the process of redemption. And once again, he placed the modern movement in historical context. The Israelites had to suffer to be free. Christ had to be crucified to rise again. The cruelties of racism would, by necessity, lead to the rebirth of America. "There never was a moment in American history," he said, "more honorable and more inspiring" than the moment that brought these men and women of every race and faith together in Selma to march with the city's tormented citizens.

King directed his words at both Black and white Americans, reminding them of all they had in common. He cited the historian C. Vann Woodward's 1955 book, *The Strange Career of Jim Crow*, saying segregation in the South had been employed not merely to express and maintain white supremacy but also as a "political stratagem" to hold down the wages of Black *and* white workers. The white elite used race to keep workers from uniting in an interracial populist movement. But today's march offered hope, he said, that such division might come to an end. Let us come together, he said, to march against segregated housing, against poverty, against restrictive voting laws.

"Our aim," he said, "must never be to defeat or humiliate the white man but to win his friendship and understanding." The goal was the creation of a working, healthy community. "That will be the day of man as man."

How long would it take? His voice thundered as he asked and answered the question and concluded his speech:

> It will not be long, because truth crushed to earth will rise again.
>
> How long? Not long, because no lie can live forever.
>
> How long? Not long, because you shall reap what you sow . . .
>
> How long? Not long, because the arc of the moral universe is long, but it bends toward justice.
>
> How long? Not long, because mine eyes have seen the glory of the coming of the Lord;
>
> He is trampling out the vintage where the grapes of wrath are stored;
>
> He has loosed the fateful lightning of his terrible swift sword;
>
> His truth is marching on.

36

"The True Meaning of My Work"

TWENTY-SIX SHUTTLE BUSES had been hired to move marchers out of Montgomery, but twenty-one of the drivers called in sick. By dusk, hundreds of people remained stranded downtown. At Dannelly Field Airport, many outgoing flights were delayed for hours. Long lines formed for the bathrooms and phones. King looked around at the bedlam at the airport and saw beauty: "white and Negro, nuns and priests, ministers and rabbis, labor organizers, lawyers, doctors, housemaids and shopworkers . . . a microcosm of the mankind of the future in this moment of luminous and genuine brotherhood."

But in the chaos, A. Philip Randolph collapsed.

"It's my fault," said Bayard Rustin, who blamed himself for pushing the seventy-five-year-old dean of the civil rights movement to march that day. Police suggested taking Randolph to a hospital, but Rustin refused. Union leaders formed a barricade around their leader as news photographers snapped pictures. Just then, King arrived. He quietly parted the crowd and told Rustin to put Randolph on Dick Gregory's private plane.

"It was Martin Luther King at his best," said Rachelle Horowitz, who flew with Rustin, Randolph, and C. T. Vivian on the four-seat plane that night. "At the height of all the chaos, he was calm, and he was absolutely determined to take care of Mr. Randolph."

That same night, March 25, Viola Liuzzo drove back to Selma, her 1963 Oldsmobile crammed with marchers. Liuzzo was thirty-nine years old, married, a mother of five from Detroit. A white woman, Liuzzo challenged her children to consider their racial prejudices. How would they feel, she asked them, if all the Santas at the mall were Black? What if fashion magazines put only Black girls on the cover? When Liuzzo told her family she was going to Selma in response to Martin Luther King's call for volunteers, her husband, a Teamsters Union business agent, balked.

It wasn't her fight, he said.

"It's everybody's fight," she answered.

After dropping off a carload of marchers in Selma, Liuzzo and another SCLC volunteer headed back to Montgomery to fetch more people. On a quiet stretch of highway in rural Lowndes County, four Klansmen in another car spotted Liuzzo and her companion. Outraged, apparently, at the sight of a white woman with a Black male passenger, the Klansmen shot at the Oldsmobile. Liuzzo was killed. Her passenger survived.

The next morning, J. Edgar Hoover phoned President Johnson to say the FBI had identified and would soon arrest Liuzzo's killers. One of the four Klansmen, Hoover said, had been an FBI informant.

JOHNSON: You hire someone and they join the Klan?

HOOVER: No, we go to someone who is in the Klan and persuade him to work for the government. We pay him for it. Sometimes they demand a pretty high price . . . Now, this man that we have now, this informant, he's not a regular agent of the Bureau. But he's one of these people that we put in, just like we do into the Communist party, so they'll keep us informed. And fortunately, he happened to be in on this thing last night. Otherwise we would be looking for a needle in a haystack.

King sent Hoover a telegram, congratulating him on the arrests. Later, the bureau's informant, Gary Thomas Rowe Jr., would admit that he had taken part in an assault on Freedom Riders in Birmingham in 1961. He would also confess to the fatal shooting of a Black man in 1963. Rowe would go on to testify in three trials of the men accused of shooting Liuzzo. The first trial ended in a hung jury, the second in acquittal. Only in the third trial, a federal civil rights case, were the defendants found guilty and sentenced to ten years in prison. Liuzzo's family filed an unsuccessful suit against the FBI, saying the bureau bore responsibility for the death because of the negligent way that Rowe had been trained and deployed.

On the Sunday after the murder, King appeared on *Meet the Press* and told the television audience that he and the SCLC intended to organize a nationwide economic boycott of Alabama. Federal law and federal pressure were not enough. He called upon unions to refuse to transport goods from Alabama, for consumers to change their buying habits, and for the government to halt funding for federal programs in the state. The first boycott would last ten days, King said, but it would likely be extended if the state refused to take serious steps toward integration. The announcement was greeted with criticism, even among those who usually supported King, including Whitney Young of the Urban League and Bayard Rustin.

SCLC leaders gathered on March 31 at the Lord Baltimore Hotel in Maryland to discuss the organization's future. Randolph Blackwell and Harry Boyte pushed for a program of small, interracial discussion groups in communities throughout the South. Hosea Williams proposed a bolder plan: recruiting hundreds of northern volunteers to help with voter registration in more than a hundred rural counties and ten southeastern cities. King talked about the fight against poverty, saying he'd been giving the subject more thought since winning the Nobel Prize. "I realize," he said, "I must more and more extend my work beyond the borders of the South . . . and become involved to a much greater extent with the problems of the urban North."

Meanwhile, King fretted about his friend Abernathy, who complained that he felt unappreciated at times. Abernathy took pride in standing by King's side, by accompanying him to jail cells, by warming up crowds for the speaker everyone came to hear. These were acts of both friendship and struggle, but they took a toll on Abernathy, who received little acclamation for his work. After the Nobel ceremony in Oslo, when King had been presented a Rolex as part of his prize, he bought a gold Bulova watch for Abernathy as a token of appreciation. Abernathy would wear the watch every day for the rest of his life, but his feelings remained bruised. Even at the hotel in Baltimore, Abernathy grew angry when he learned he had been assigned an ordinary room while King had been given a suite, according to L. D. Reddick's notes. In "deep despair," according to Reddick, Abernathy skipped several meetings. SCLC board members, seeking to appease him, agreed that Abernathy should be assigned more independent travel so that he might earn greater recognition for his work. But King went a step further, asking the SCLC board to commit to a succession plan in case of his death, one that would make Abernathy his replacement.

The next day, as the Baltimore meetings continued, an FBI-approved protest took place outside the hotel. An African American minister named Lightfoot Solomon Michaux led about a hundred of his Church of God parishioners, who dressed in potato sacks, carried signs reading "God Save America," and sang "Happy Am I." Michaux said King's proposed boycott would put thousands of Black Alabamans out of work. "We're being led into a dangerous new revolution by Martin Luther King," he said, "and I'm against it." Michaux was the first minister in the country, Black or white, with his own television show. The scholar Lerone A. Martin has described Michaux as a "Bureau Clergyman," one of the clergy who had an open and cooperative relationship with the FBI, using his status to attack King and celebrate the bureau as a champion of Christianity.

White journalists from the North observed, as John Herbers of *The New York Times* wrote, that "the movement seems to have taken on a new militancy that was not apparent in previous campaigns led by Dr. King." King had always been confrontational, and he was certainly not becoming more violent. But he and other activists were becoming more ambitious, talking about expanding their work to the North and attacking economic inequality.

Stanley Levison urged caution. In many ways, he said, Selma had been King's greatest triumph. "Selma and Montgomery made you one of the most powerful figures in the country—a leader not merely of Negroes, but millions of whites," Levison wrote in a letter to King on April 7, 1965. King had done it without the help of a political party, a labor union, or a wealthy benefactor. He was the rarest of leaders—one who had retained his independence, one whose power sprang from morality, from his commitment to improving democracy rather than overthrowing it. But there was a downside to success. The coalition King had built, Levison said, "is basically a coalition for moderate change, for gradual improvements which are to be attained without excessive upheavals." If King pushed for change in the North, if he continued to attack poverty in addition to race, he might lose followers and financial support. "The American people are not inclined to change their society in order to free the Negro," Levison wrote. "They are ready to undertake some, and perhaps major, reforms, but not to make a revolution."

In early April, King canceled his public engagements and went home to rest again. From Atlanta, he flew with Coretta to Miami and then to Nassau, in the Bahamas, for more rest. On April 17, in a phone call recorded by the FBI, Bayard Rustin told one of his associates that he had discussed his concerns about King's mental health with an expert. The expert said King suffered from fatigue, "but he's distressed with the whole sexual angle, that's more important than anything else," Rustin said. "He said it's an extreme form of neuroticism which only occurs during periods of intense fatigue."

Four days later, Rustin and Andrew Young discussed the same thing, while the FBI recorded the call.

YOUNG: I think Martin is doing much better.

RUSTIN: Good.

YOUNG: It really just is that he is mentally fatigued and that this leads to depression and the problem is that he can't take a rest around here anyway because he always feels that he should be in a movement. He feels like going to Nassau is like a vacation . . .

RUSTIN: Yep.

YOUNG: And some of us were thinking that if there could be some kind of official state invitation from one of the African countries or something for a visit.

RUSTIN: There could be but, God, if he goes that way he will get even less rest . . .

YOUNG: Well, it's got to be an invitation for him to do something specific or he will feel guilty . . . I contend that he is really not needed in Alabama and, frankly, with all this Klan stirring it up and these folks getting desperate, I think there is no sense for him being around Alabama all the time.

RUSTIN: Right.

YOUNG: So I was trying to tell him to leave the program to me and Ralph and someone and maybe you and him and maybe someone else just take off and go some place for two weeks . . . Is there any university that in two weeks you could arrange two speaking engagements that we could convince him on?

In another phone call, Rustin and Harry Wachtel discussed whether King needed more than rest and whether he would be receptive to psychiatric treatment. They did not resolve the question.

———— • ————

When Coretta and Martin returned from the Bahamas to Atlanta on April 17, it was not to the rented house on Johnson Avenue in which they had lived since 1960, but to a new home. Coretta had finally persuaded her husband to move. At the time, King's annual church salary was $6,000. They chose a modest four-bedroom home at 234 Sunset Avenue in the Vine City neighborhood, a predominantly Black, working-class section of southwest Atlanta. They paid $10,000, or the equivalent of about $96,000 in 2022, and hired a member of Ebenezer church as a contractor to get the place in shape. But even with such a modestly priced home, and even with Coretta's conservative taste in furnishings, Martin expressed a sense of guilt, saying the place was too extravagant, that he worried he would be criticized for materialism. He acceded to Coretta's wish for carpeting, but only in their bedroom, where guests would not see it. They covered their living room sofa and chairs in plastic and kept a bust of Franklin Delano Roosevelt and a small statue of a seated Gandhi on the coffee table in front of the sofa. The house had a two-car garage, a fenced yard, and a modern kitchen. It also had an untapped telephone line, the FBI having elected not to install another wire.

King didn't have time to get comfortable in the new house, however. He traveled to New York and Boston, where he raised more money and hinted at the SCLC's ambitions to attack discrimination in the North. When asked in Boston if he had any memories of the city from his time as a student, he said yes, he remembered the difficulty he faced in finding an apartment. "I went into place after place where there were signs that rooms were for rent," he said. "They were for rent until they found out I was a Negro and suddenly they had just been rented."

He remained on the move, almost without pause, throughout May and into June, including a stop in Louisville, Kentucky, where his brother, A.D., was now pastor of the city's biggest Black church, Zion Baptist, his third new pulpit in four years. Among friends, Martin expressed concern about his brother's heavy drinking. But some of those same friends remained concerned about Martin. The economic boycott of Alabama had gained no traction. Local activists in Selma complained that their cause had been abandoned when King and the TV cameras had moved on. Bickering continued between the SCLC and SNCC. Quarrels continued within the SCLC, too, over whether to focus time and money in the North or the South, among other things. King juggled the competing interests, trying to keep everyone happy.

In mid-June, he vacationed again, in Jamaica, this time staying a week. He talked to Andrew Young and others about taking a sabbatical, perhaps for as long as a year. By the time he returned, however, he seemed to have given up on the idea of an extended leave.

On July 2, at an SCLC rally in Petersburg, Virginia, he declared that "the war in Vietnam must be stopped." His remarks attracted attention from the press—and from J. Edgar Hoover, who interpreted King's objection to the war as further evidence of his disloyalty. Four days later, King flew to Chicago, where local activists had invited the SCLC to fight discrimination in housing, schools, jobs, health care, and criminal justice. King had been saying for years that racism in Chicago and other northern cities, while often more subtle, was just as pernicious as the southern variety, "a new form of slavery covered up with certain niceties," as he put it. Now the activists in Chicago challenged King to do something about it—to build a movement in Chicago as he had in Birmingham and Selma.

King might have said no. He might have listened to the advice of aides such as Andrew Young, who said the SCLC lacked the necessary funding and manpower for a campaign in the North. He might have justified a sabbatical. After a decade of activism, he had earned a break. He had inspired Black southerners to stand up and fight against staggering odds, and he had led them to victories. The Civil Rights Act of 1964 and the soon-to-be-passed Voting Rights Act of 1965 marked historic achievements, validation of what he had been telling people since the first day of the Montgomery boycott: that God and the Constitution were on their side, that the long arc of history bent toward justice.

When he had begun preaching in Montgomery, King recalled in one interview, he thought he would lead his church for a few years and then become a college professor. He still thought about it. "I dream of the day," he told the interviewer Alex Haley, "when the demands presently cast upon me will be greatly diminished." But he didn't see that happening anytime soon—at least not for five years. For now, he said, he subjected himself to "endless self-analysis . . . to be as certain as I can that I am fulfilling the true meaning of my work, that I am maintaining my sense of purpose, that I am holding fast to my ideals, that I am guiding my people in the right direction. But whatever my doubts, however heavy the burden, I feel that I must accept the task of helping to make this nation and this world a better place to live in—for *all* men, Black and white alike." He was still an optimist, he said—enough so to believe that America might yet find "the high road to the fulfillment of the Founding Fathers' dream, when they wrote, 'We hold these truths to be self-evident . . .'"

But it wouldn't happen if he confined his activity to the South, he had come to believe. He would have to root out racism in all its "hidden and subtle and covert disguises," he said, beginning with Chicago.

37

"A Shining Moment"

HE FORGOT CORETTA's birthday that year, but she said she didn't mind. "In the light of my own involvement and commitments," she wrote, "it is not too difficult for me to understand and forgive little things like this which do occur, sometimes."

She was thirty-eight years old, the mother of four children, ages two, four, seven, and nine. In 1965, she spent more time than ever out of the house, working for the movement, beginning in March with a series of Freedom Concerts on the West Coast. In April, she traveled to Detroit for a dinner honoring and raising money for Rosa Parks, who had struggled to find work, first in Montgomery and later in Detroit, and who had suffered deteriorating health. Parks had spent a decade in "deep economic insecurity," as the scholar Jeanne Theoharis writes, in part because others in the movement had resented the attention showered on her. Coretta's presence in Detroit may have been an attempt at making amends.

In May, Coretta King spoke at a gathering of the Women's International League for Peace and Freedom in Chicago. And on June 8, she was the only woman to speak at an anti–Vietnam War rally attended by more than fifteen thousand people at Madison Square Garden in New York City. Earlier that year, at an SCLC retreat, Martin had asked Coretta to speak about Vietnam and whether the organization had a responsibility to take a stand against the war. "I talked about how it would continue to drain resources from education, housing, health, and other badly needed social programs," she recalled. "I said, 'Why do you think we got the Nobel Prize? It was not just for civil rights . . . Peace and justice are indivisible.'"

A month later, King raised the issue of Vietnam in a phone call with President Johnson. King got the impression that Johnson knew he had "made a mistake in Vietnam but does not know how to get out of it," as the SCLC leader said in a call recorded by the FBI. King told his secretary, Dora McDonald, that he had "hit" the president hard on Vietnam.

Coretta saw herself as a partner in her husband's work, on civil rights and in opposition to the war. She wanted to do even more, but she felt constrained. "My husband feels it important that one parent remain at home to give them [the children] security," she told a reporter in Seattle. "But I would like to make a more complete witness by marching, and, if necessary, going to jail."

Martin, on the other hand, almost never spent time home alone with the children when Coretta traveled. Instead, the Kings relied on friends and family to watch Yoki, Martin, Dexter, and Bernice. In a memoir written years later, Coretta recalled a conversation in which she told Martin she wanted to take a more active role in the movement:

During one exchange, he told me, "You see, I am called [by God], and you aren't."

I responded, "I have always felt that I have a call on my life, too. "I've been called by God, too, to do something [. . .]"

Still not convinced, Martin turned to me and said, "Well, somebody has to take care of the kids."

"No problem," I said. "I will do that."

Looking a bit crushed, he asked, "You aren't totally happy being my wife and the mother of my children, are you?"

"I love being your wife and the mother of your children," I said. "But if that's all I am to do, I'll go crazy."

During a 1965 television interview conducted at his home, King was asked if he had educated his wife on matters of activism. "Well, it may have been the other way around," he said. "I think at many points she educated me. When I met her, she was very concerned about all the things we are trying to do now. I never will forget the first discussion we had when we met was the whole question of racial inequality and economic inequality and the question of peace . . . I wish I could say to satisfy my masculine ego that I led her down this path, but I must say we went down together, because she was as actively involved when we met as she is now."

The Feminine Mystique, written by Betty Friedan, had been published in 1963 and remained enormously popular in 1965, describing the widespread dissatisfaction among American women, and encouraging them to declare: "I want something more than my husband and my children and my home." At one point in 1965, Coretta began working on an essay for the first issue of a magazine called *New Lady*, a publication that billed itself as "the Negro woman's guide to a new way of life." By the time she finished, the article ran to thirteen pages of text and photos. Coretta must have been proud of it, because she mailed a copy to Rosa Parks. "Women have been the backbone of the whole civil rights movement," Coretta wrote in the article. "Women have . . . made it possible for the movement to be a mass movement." It was a simple fact, but nevertheless an overlooked one.

In Montgomery, Parks had sparked the bus boycott and Jo Ann Robinson and the Women's Political Council had launched it. Aurelia Browder, Claudette Colvin, Susie McDonald, and Mary Louise Smith had served as plaintiffs in the federal lawsuit that led to the Supreme Court decision that desegregated the city's buses. Ella Baker had long served as one of the movement's best organizers. Diane Nash had helped initiate the Freedom Rides and cofounded SNCC. Septima Clark and Fannie Lou Hamer had led the push for voter registration in much of the Deep South. In Maryland, Gloria Richardson had fought for integration and economic rights. And then there were countless women such as Coretta Scott King and Juanita Abernathy who endured many of the same perils as their husbands while receiving little credit for their work—work that included not only marching and organizing but also taking care of children, filling in for their husbands, and advising their spouses on matters of strategy, leadership, and politics. In addition to the other challenges, Coretta Scott King ran her household on a modest budget, because her husband insisted that most of the income from his speeches and writings go to the SCLC.

The headline on her essay for *New Lady* read "The World of Coretta

King: Family to Rear, Husband to Love, Home to Manage—and a Cause to Serve." In the article, Coretta offered her clearest explanation of how she navigated a path that left many ambitious women of the 1960s feeling lost and angry. Over and over, she returned to the themes of compromise and perseverance. She began: "While my husband was being prepared for the job that he is doing, I feel that I was being prepared also to be the helpmate ... I feel very strongly that it was meant to be this way."

At Antioch College, as she recalled in the article, she had insisted on doing her student teaching in the Yellow Springs Public Schools, along with her white classmates. But the Yellow Springs schools were segregated, and Antioch officials wanted her to travel nine miles to an integrated school in Xenia, Ohio. She "felt like crying" when her teachers and classmates refused to support her. "Then I thought, 'I am a Negro and I am going to be a Negro the rest of my life. I just can't let this kind of thing get me down ... I'll have to accept this' ... So I made the compromise," she wrote. She accepted even worse, according to Hosea Williams, who said that he witnessed King's cruel treatment of Coretta on more than one occasion. "'Shut up and go ahead in the back room!'" Williams said he heard Martin yell at Coretta. "She would get up quietly and go on back. Martin had told her many times."

Williams was a frequent critic of Coretta. But if the men in the SCLC dismissed King's wife, the women admired her. They saw a woman fighting to balance her dedication to her family and her causes. Xernona Clayton, an SCLC staff member from Atlanta who traveled at times with Coretta, said she was always impressed by Coretta's calm determination. For Coretta to leave Atlanta and perform a concert, she not only had to rehearse, arrange her travel, and promote her appearances but also had to make sure the children would be cared for in her absence. Before leaving, she would type a list of meals for the week, including desserts. Even when she was on the road, without consulting notes or a calendar, Coretta knew when the children had doctors' appointments, piano lessons, and haircuts, Clayton said, and Coretta checked in frequently to make sure nothing was forgotten.

"Coretta Scott King was a disciplinarian," wrote her son Dexter, "took no guff from hers or any others. Froze you with a look."

Carole Hoover, another SCLC staff member, said it was clear that Dr. King respected and relied on his wife's opinion when it came to high-level questions of strategy. "She was very much engaged with those things that were important to him," Hoover said. "He genuinely valued her thinking."

People in the office heard rumors about King's infidelity, and specifically about his relationship with Dorothy Cotton. "That rumor floated several times," Hoover said. "I don't think Coretta ever bought into that."

But others in the SCLC did buy into it. When King returned to Atlanta from one of his frequent trips, he usually went to Cotton's home before going to his own house, said Stoney Cooks, an SCLC staff member. It was understood within the organization that the relationship had been going on for years. "Only the people who were very close to him even knew about it," Cooks said, and Cotton "didn't flaunt it."

Nevertheless, the women of the SCLC saw Coretta and Dr. King as powerful partners, said Edwina Smith Moss. "They didn't profess to be perfect, and Coretta was such an asset to Dr. King," Moss recalled. "She was strong, and she came out of the South . . . If Dr. King ever wanted to quit, she wouldn't have let him. She was not fearful. If she had been, it would've shown . . . She understood the FBI wanted to break them up . . . Coretta had steel. Coretta had a sense of the movement. You couldn't have done that without a real sense of the movement. She was the power behind the throne . . . She was not the person to break. If she was going to have a battle, it was going to be with Dr. King, and it was not going to be in public . . . They may have had all kinds of battles in the house, but thank God it stayed in the house."

"It is a great temptation," Coretta wrote, "to demand more of my husband's attention. We women are like that. But I have had to realize that he belongs to the world and therefore cannot be the same kind of husband and father that he would like to be." Doing her part for the cause of freedom, she said, included explaining to the children why their father went to jail and why he wasn't home as much as other fathers and why, sometimes, he didn't come home when the family expected him.

"I have considered my own role very important from the beginning," she wrote.

The assassination of President Kennedy frightened her, Coretta wrote. The assassination of Malcolm X frightened her more. She felt stuck, "weak and depressed," after Malcolm's death.

She reminded herself, she wrote, that she and her husband and all humans were coworkers with God, building a world of peace and love. As she concluded in her article: "When you decide to give yourself to a great cause, you must arrive at the point where no sacrifice is too great. This is the first demand that is made of us in our great struggle for civil rights. I shall stand with Martin Luther King, Jr., my husband, as he faces them."

"Racism is genocide," King said at his first press conference in Chicago, on July 23, 1965. "When a man cannot get a good job and good wages, he is a slave. When he cannot get good, substantial housing, he is a slave. When a man cannot get integrated education, he is a slave. Before I'll be a slave, I'll be buried in my grave. We are eternally through with racial segregation."

King met with a group of fifty Chicago activists on his first night in town. The next day, he hustled from one Chicago neighborhood to another, running late at every stop, speaking to crowds of three hundred here, five hundred there, making twenty-four stops over the course of the weekend, visiting churches and public housing projects, primarily, as he drummed up support for a big downtown march scheduled for Monday, July 26.

Ralph Abernathy, Andrew Young, James Bevel, and C. T. Vivian accompanied King. Coretta remained in Atlanta. Al Raby, a Chicago schoolteacher and protest leader, guided the out-of-towners. The march would climax six weeks of protests by local activists seeking the dismissal of the school superintendent, Benjamin C. Willis, whose policies they blamed for the city's segregated education system. Willis had the support of city leaders and claimed that his policies were colorblind, but Black schools were far more crowded than white, and almost all the new schools built since 1955 had been segregated. As Black schools became overcrowded, the administration put students in mobile classrooms—referred to derisively as "Willis Wagons."

But protests went nowhere. As King could plainly see, even in his first extended tour of the city, Chicago wasn't Birmingham, and neither Willis nor Mayor Richard J. Daley was Bull Connor. But racism permeated Chicago life. In the years following World War I, as Black families migrated from the South and a growing number of Black families moved into white neighborhoods, twenty-six Black homes were bombed. In 1919, a race riot left thirty-eight people dead, twenty-five of them Black. Rioters burned the homes of more than one thousand Black people. In response, city officials committed more deeply to segregation. Realtors used contracts that forbade property owners from selling or renting their properties to Black people, as they did in other cities. Chicago and other city governments marked Black neighborhoods as areas of an impending decline in property value—redlining those parts of town, as the process became known, and making it difficult for families there to qualify for bank mortgages. When Black families did move into white neighborhoods, white families often moved out.

At the age of seventeen, Richard Daley had been a member of the Hamburg Athletic Club, one of the gangs that had started the 1919 race riot. A few years after the riot, he was elected club president. Now, as mayor, he courted and received much of the city's Black vote. Daley didn't demand or enforce segregated schools in Chicago. He didn't have to. The schools were segregated because the city's neighborhoods were segregated. People called it de facto segregation, meaning that it was a fact, a given, a natural outcome of private individuals' choices, in contrast to de jure segregation, which was required by law. But the distinction was misleading. Segregation in the North was both de jure and de facto; it was a function of law, public policy, and discriminatory business practices, for starters. Chicagoans commuting to and from work on the new Dan Ryan Expressway saw it for themselves. The original design for the highway had been shifted several blocks to create a firewall of sorts between Black and white neighborhoods. There was nothing accidental or natural about it.

According to the Chicago Urban League, 89.2 percent of Black elementary school students attended schools that were populated entirely or almost entirely by Black children in 1965, up from 87.8 percent the year before. Though about half of Chicago's school students were Black, Black people held only about a quarter of all faculty and administrative jobs.

Bevel, Bernard Lafayette, and other leaders hoped King would make this the first of many visits to Chicago and that he might soon turn his attention from the city's segregated schools to its segregated housing. If King managed to make the Chicago school protests into a broader attack on institutional racism, wrote *The Wall Street Journal*, he might establish "patterns which will be followed by civil rights leaders in a number of other major Northern urban areas."

But he faced a set of unfamiliar challenges. One prominent local minister, the Reverend J. H. Jackson—longtime leader of the National Baptist Convention—urged other Black clergymen to shun the civil rights leader. "Chicago doesn't need any outsiders coming in to solve their problems," said Jackson, who had clashed with King before. Some of the white northern reporters covering King in Chicago said he would soon learn that racial politics were more complicated in the North than in the South. With 100,000 Black people on the city, state, and county payrolls, and with thousands more living in government-subsidized housing, King might find it difficult to attract protesters. Many Black Chicagoans, the journalists wrote, would be reluctant to anger the city's all-powerful mayor. Given Daley's tight control of the city, one Chicago official predicted, King would have trouble getting two hundred people to march on city hall.

Skeptics deemed King naïve. They said he didn't understand urban poverty or northern politics. But the issue was not new to him. He'd been traveling all over the country, learning and speaking out about conditions in the North since the 1950s, as the historian Jeanne Theoharis has documented. But King's comments on northern racism were either dismissed or overlooked by white reporters and readers in the North. "In my travels in the North," King wrote in 1965, "I have become increasingly disillusioned with the power structures there . . . [that] welcomed me to their cities and showered praise on the heroism of southern Negroes. Yet when the issues were joined concerning local conditions, only the language was polite; the rejection was firm and unequivocal."

King wasn't coming north because he'd suddenly discovered the issues of urban poverty, police brutality, and slum housing. He was coming north because he had been saying all along that the North, that the whole country, had a problem. As he wrote in *Why We Can't Wait,* "the depth of racism in American life" had been underestimated for too long. Only mass action would dissolve the stereotype of the inferior Black man. Only a reckoning with racism would kill it. Only the "noble crusade" of protest would force white Americans to liberate themselves from the "tangled web of prejudice" and accept Black people as true partners in a democratic society.

Having won a great victory with the Voting Rights Act, King chose yet again not to step aside but to step forward, into the breach. *Brown v. Board of Education* hadn't integrated northern schools. The Civil Rights Act of 1964 hadn't integrated neighborhoods or eliminated slum housing. Protests hadn't stopped police brutality. But King was undeterred. If northern racism was more subtle, if the political landscape was more complicated, and if the solutions were less obvious, those were not reasons to abandon hope. By confronting the problem and generating a sense of crisis, he wrote, protesters would force the establishment to negotiate.

King still believed in the power of nonviolent protest, in the example of Jesus, in love. He still believed, as he said upon his arrival in Chicago, that white parents, when they overcame their fears and looked in their hearts, would realize that Black children deserved the same safe neighborhoods and the same good school their own children did. To be more specific, on the subject of fair housing, King believed that protesters would compel the federal government to guarantee equal access to the market for private homes. After World War II, subsidies and loan guarantees had made owning a home seem like a core part of the American dream, but Black families faced systemic obstacles.

In a 1962 speech, "The Ethical Demands for Integration," King said that desegregation had the power to break down legal barriers, but it was not enough: "Something must touch the hearts and souls of men so that they will come together spiritually because it is natural and right." He had concrete demands for reform in Chicago, but he was after something more, something bigger, something transformative of American society.

Before the march on July 26, King required medical attention. Notes made by the doctor who treated him in Chicago, Jasper F. Williams, indicated that the patient suffered "1. Fatigue 2. Bronchitis. 3. Mild hypertension. 4. Gastrointestinal increased motility, associated with nervous tension." King received a vitamin B injection—essentially a placebo—and arrived an hour late for the march from Buckingham Fountain to city hall. "The doctors tell me I can't get by on two or three hours of sleep a night," he told reporters. "I try to do it, and I learn I just can't." After the march, he would see the doctor a third time and postpone his flight out of town.

A massive crowd greeted him at Buckingham Fountain on the city's lakefront. *The Chicago Defender* estimated a throng of fifty thousand marchers. Police put the number at ten thousand. The slow-moving mass shut down rush-hour traffic. Aides held an umbrella over King's head to shield him from the sun. At 5:12 p.m., at the corner of State and Madison, often referred to at the time as the world's busiest intersection, King stopped. There were people as far as he could see, stretching for blocks, past department stores and diners, under the Van Buren Street elevated train tracks at the southern edge of the Loop, across Congress Parkway, and all the way back toward Buckingham Fountain and Lake Michigan, where the march had begun. No cars or buses moved. The people had occupied the city. Spectators lined the sidewalks, three and four deep, cheering and waving. King looked out across the crowd, smiled, and began to sing: "We shall overcome . . ."

After Chicago, still sick, still exhausted, he arrived late to Cleveland, where he made a series of speeches. Cities in the North "were not acting right about the Negro," he said. After ignoring the problems of the South for years, northerners had "inherited the problems of the South." Now, he said, America needed to create a "Bill of Rights for the Disadvantaged," as he had outlined in his 1964 book, *Why We Can't Wait*, to offer the same kind of housing and tuition benefits contained in the GI Bill. Only with that, and with increased voter registration among urban Black people, would the North solve its problems.

Covering King's visit, Cleveland's Black newspaper, the *Call and Post*, warned that people expected too much from King, that the civil rights movement had begun to look like a one-man show. King wouldn't have to hustle from street corner to street corner drumming up support for his marches if leaders in the North did their part, the newspaper declared. "Dr. King should not be in Cleveland begging Negroes to register, when to do so, only requires the time to go down to the Board of Elections." The headline on the piece read: "Dr. Martin Luther King Is Not a Superman."

But King continued hustling from speech to speech, interview to interview, city to city, until he arrived in Washington, D.C., to meet with President Johnson and witness Johnson's signature of the Voting Rights Act on August 6, 1965. Joining King were Roy Wilkins, James Farmer, and Rosa Parks, among others. Coretta King watched the ceremony on television. She was home taking care of Marty and Dexter, who had both had their tonsils removed. Martin had been so busy that Coretta had never found time to tell him about the scheduled surgeries. It was one of the few occasions, she wrote years later, when she felt sorry for herself. "I felt very supportive of his being there," she wrote, "but I also had this feeling of being alone, of being entirely by myself."

Later that day, outside the White House, five hundred people protested U.S. policies in Vietnam. King made no public comment on the demonstration. His focus, as he prepared to fly home to Atlanta, was on the newly signed law, which, he said, would "go a long way toward removing all the obstacles to the right to vote."

It was, he added, "a shining moment."

38

Burning

"THERE IS NO more civil rights movement," James Bevel said as the SCLC gathered for its annual convention in Birmingham.

King didn't go that far in his statements, but he did say that massive demonstrations might no longer be necessary in the South if people complied with the new law.

Journalists in the South predicted rapid and sweeping political and cultural change. Black people would register to vote in huge numbers. Staunch segregationists would be shoved out of office. In cities and counties where Black voters outnumbered white, Black politicians would win office and wield power. Black citizens would get a fair share of government services, including new schools and paved streets. As schools integrated, achievement levels and income levels would rise until Black and white Americans, eventually, achieved parity. Neighborhoods and workplaces would integrate, voluntarily. Police and judges would deliver equal justice. It might take a few generations, but the political and cultural changes would begin, and life would improve for all.

"The voting rights law holds out promise of eventually not only restoring peace to the South," wrote Jack Nelson from the Atlanta bureau of the *Los Angeles Times*, "but of creating a new area of better relations between the races . . . As the Rev. Dr. Martin Luther King Jr. once predicted, it may be that . . . even big Jim Clark, the sheriff at Selma, will take off his 'NEVER' button."

Such optimism seemed reasonable as federal officials moved to sue jurisdictions that enforced poll taxes. In Alabama, Black voters began registering in unprecedented numbers—numbers so impressive that Jim Clark not only removed his "NEVER" button but also hosted a barbeque for Black voters in his campaign for reelection. The voters were not fooled, however; they put him out of office.

At its convention in Birmingham, the SCLC discussed plans to shift its work to the North. Details, however, remained scarce. The organization remained disorganized. The people hired to bring a sense of order, one after another, had failed. Andrew Young had taken over as executive director, but he had no experience running a big organization. "Andy described his style of organization as sort of a jazz musician," said Stoney Cooks, who joined the SCLC in 1965 as a project director. "Anybody could take the lead." Officials at the annual convention talked about how best to call attention to the issue of poverty. They also discussed whether the SCLC's board should issue a statement in support of King's call for a negotiated settlement of the hostilities in Vietnam. The organization agreed to a resolution, but it fell short of an endorsement, saying board members "recognize that [King's] conscience compels him to express his concern . . . and commend him" for his courageous stance. The resolution went on to say that the SCLC's primary purpose was to fight for full citizenship for Negroes and the organization would not get involved in the peace movement or foreign affairs.

While the SCLC would remain focused on civil rights, King told reporters that he, individually, would speak out more aggressively in opposition to the war. He said he planned to write to Lyndon Johnson and the leaders of North Vietnam, South Vietnam, China, and the Soviet Union, pleading for them to sit down together and find a way to end the fighting.

When reporters asked King why he had waited so long to join the antiwar movement, he pointed out that Coretta had already been active in the cause but that he felt it had been "physically impossible to go all out on the peace question and all out on the Civil Rights question." He might have added that his advisers had been warning him that he risked alienating President Johnson and damaging the civil rights movement. King had been saying for years that he believed in nonviolence, and that his belief applied to international affairs. After winning the Nobel Peace Prize, he felt greater responsibility to oppose the war. He had held back, King said, "until it got to the point that I felt I had to speak out. The time is so potentially destructive and dangerous that the whole survival of humanity is at stake."

President Johnson had just announced that 50,000 more American soldiers would deploy to Vietnam, bringing the total to 125,000, the first phase of an ongoing buildup. The majority of Americans supported the American presence in Vietnam. Johnson warned the public not to expect a rapid solution. "I would not want to prophesy or predict whether it would be a matter of months or years or decades," he said. "We will stand in Vietnam."

After the SCLC convention, King flew to Puerto Rico for a vacation. But his rest was disturbed by news reports from Los Angeles on August 11, 1965.

"It was unusually hot that day," Marquette Frye recalled. "All that August it was hot." Frye, a twenty-one-year-old Black man, was driving through the Watts section of Los Angeles, about a block from his home, when two white California Highway Patrol officers stopped him on suspicion of drunk driving. It was just after 7:00 p.m.

As Frye took a sobriety test, a crowd of about two hundred Black people gathered around the corner of 116th Street and Avalon Boulevard. Frye's mother, Rena Price, arrived, screaming at her son and the police. The police arrested them both. When Frye refused to get in the police car, the crowd grew bigger and hotter, the heat generated in part, as the *Los Angeles Times* reported, by "a long-smoldering hatred in many of the onlookers who felt— rightly or wrongly—that police had been guilty of brutality to Negroes." More officers arrived. Soon, thousands of Black people took to the streets. They fired shots and threw rocks and bricks at police, who cordoned off an eight-block area but failed to control the unrest.

"I have lived in this city for seventeen years . . . but I have never heard policemen talk like they did last night," a forty-year-old Black woman who witnessed the incident told a reporter. "My husband and I saw ten cops beating one man. My husband told the officers, 'You've got him handcuffed.' One of the officers answered, 'Get out of here, nigger. Get out of here, all you niggers.'"

Another witness, an eighteen-year-old girl, told a reporter: "I threw bricks and rocks and anything I could get my hands on . . . to hurt them. We were throwing at anybody white. Why not do it to you guys? You're doing it to us."

The next day was worse. "Burn, baby, burn!" people shouted as they threw homemade bombs, set buildings ablaze, and looted stores. The fires burned through the night, with the crowds driving away firefighting crews. Police failed to retake the neighborhood. The governor sent in the National Guard.

The novelist Walter Mosley, who was thirteen years old and living in Watts at the time, would later write, in the voice of his fictional character Easy Rawlins:

> But if you come from down in Watts or Fifth Ward or Harlem, every soul you come upon has been threatened and beaten and jailed. If you have kids they will be beaten. And no matter how far back you remember, there's a beatin' there waiting for you. And you see some man stopped by cops and some poor mother cryin' for his release it speaks to you. You don't know that woman, you don't know if the man bein' arrested has done something wrong. But it doesn't matter. Because you been there before. And it's hot, and you're broke, and people have been doin' this to you because of your skin for more years than your mother's mother can remember.

L.A.'s mayor, Samuel W. Yorty, and other city officials didn't get it. Four years earlier, a group of Black ministers had sought the removal of the city's police chief, William H. Parker. Now Parker refused to meet with representatives of the Black community. "These rioters do not have any leaders," Parker said. He told reporters at a news conference that the unrest had begun "when one person threw a rock and then, like monkeys in a zoo, others started throwing rocks."

The uprising stretched on for days. When the activist Dick Gregory tried to settle one out-of-control crowd, he was shot in the leg, apparently by one of the protesters. In five days, the riots would leave thirty-four people dead, including twenty-three killed by police or National Guard troops. A thousand more people were injured. About 3,500 people were arrested, mainly for violating the strict curfew put in place in Watts and other Black neighborhoods in the city. At least six hundred buildings were damaged, reducing much of Watts to rubble and ashes. By August 16, the curfew and the mass arrests had worked to largely end the uprising.

Several SCLC colleagues warned King to avoid Los Angeles—saying that there was nothing to organize, nothing to lead, that nonviolence was no longer an option. He ignored the warnings. In Watts on August 18, he addressed a crowd of about five hundred people who packed into the second-floor meeting space of the Westminster Neighborhood Association and overflowed down the stairs and into the street.

"All over America," he said, "the Negroes must join hands—"

"And burn!" interrupted a man in the crowd.

"—and work together in a creative way."

Another heckler shouted at King.

A woman shouted at the heckler: "You're talking to Dr. Martin Luther King. Get out, psycho!"

"With respect to Dr. King," a man said, "we need people like Parker and Yorty down here—not Dr. King. They're the ones responsible for what's going on here."

King said he would do his best to get the police chief and the mayor to come to Watts.

"They're not going to come down here," a woman shouted at King. "You're going to have to go to them."

The crowd hushed as King began to speak with emotion: "I'm here," he said, "because at bottom we are brothers and sisters and whatever pains you pains me. When you suffer I suffer. When you're happy I'm happy . . . We are not free in the South and you are not free in the cities of the North." (King's use of the word "North" in such instances included the West as well.)

He urged people not to succumb to hatred of white people. "Don't forget," he said, "that when we marched from Selma to Montgomery, it was a white woman who died. Whites and Blacks together—we shall overcome."

King told reporters after the meeting that he and other civil rights leaders shared blame for the riots. Over the years, he said, he had seen the conditions in the nation's big cities that had built toward this violence but had not addressed them: "We as Negro leaders . . . have failed to take the civil rights movement to the masses of the people."

The next day, King met Mayor Yorty in his office. Yorty was a World War II veteran, a Democrat who, at fifty-five, had grown more conservative with age. His head was rectangular, his gray hair combed straight back in a wave, his smile charming. Like a lot of white people that week in Los Angeles, he wasn't used to having Black people stand up to him. King told the mayor that the city needed a citizen review panel to investigate police brutality. Yorty said King should worry about the looting and burning committed by the city's Negro citizens, not unfounded charges of police brutality.

The meeting lasted two hours and forty-five minutes. Bayard Rustin, who often complained about King's disdain for confrontation, said he had never seen King so eager to engage in conflict as he was that day in the mayor's office. Yorty "denounced Martin to his face," Rustin recalled, saying the civil rights leader wasn't wanted, wasn't needed, and didn't belong in Los Angeles. King told Yorty that justice was more important than politics, that he had come because he had been called. "It was just beautiful," Rustin said. "In fact it was one of the finest speeches Martin made, and it was done under absolute tension."

At a press conference after the meeting, as King politely criticized city officials, Mayor Yorty stood in the wings and covered his face with his hand, as if he couldn't bear to watch what was happening.

King was "absolutely undone" by the devastating poverty and the sense of hopelessness he observed in Los Angeles, Rustin said. While King didn't have an organization that he could put to work on the problems faced by Black people in large cities in general or Los Angeles in particular, he did have a phone number. He was one of the few Black Americans who could call the White House and have his call answered or at least quickly returned. And that's what he did, speaking to Lyndon Johnson late in the day on August 20.

> KING: Hello?
>
> JOHNSON: Yes, Dr. King.
>
> KING: Yes, Mr. President. How are you today?
>
> JOHNSON: Well, I'm doing pretty good . . . I thought you made a mighty good statement yesterday . . .
>
> KING: Yes, well, we have been in a difficult situation here.
>
> JOHNSON: Well, it's difficult all over the country.

The president told King about progress on his latest anti-poverty legislation and asked King for his views on the situation in Los Angeles.

> KING: I'm not optimistic at this point about the possible outcome . . .
>
> JOHNSON: By the way . . . I took your statement you made the other day . . . I said what we've got to do is . . . find a cure and go and correct these conditions where the housing and the ghettos and the rats are eating the children and the schools and the hunger and the unemployment and so forth.
>
> KING: Yes.
>
> JOHNSON: They're all God's children and we better get at it.
>
> KING: Yes, yes.
>
> JOHNSON: But I wanted you to know I said that. Pardon me for interrupting. Go ahead.
>
> KING: That's all right. But in my meeting with Police Chief Parker and Mr. Yorty—Mayor Yorty—I just felt that they are absolutely insensitive to the problem and to the needs, to really cure the situation . . . I'm fearful that if something isn't done to give a new sense of hope to the people in that area—and they are poverty-stricken—that a full-scale race war can develop here. And I'm concerned about it, naturally, because I know that violence . . . doesn't help.
>
> JOHNSON: That's right. Now, what should we do about it? What's your recommendation?

KING: If they could get, in the next few days, this poverty program going in Los Angeles, I believe that it would help a great deal.

Johnson said he would have the White House civil rights adviser, Lee White, call King the next day to talk about poverty-fighting programs for Los Angeles. He also told King "you better get your thinking cap on" to help promote the upcoming White House conference on civil rights and the president's antipoverty agenda.

JOHNSON: I've been seeing you on television every night. You make a reasonable, fair, just thing. I think you ought to say that the president recognized this thing months ago and talked to me about it . . . We can't wait. And we've got to have some of these housing programs. We've got to get rid of these ghettos. And we've got to get these children out from where the rats eat on 'em at night and we've got to get 'em some jobs.

Johnson said he was worried that his four years of work on civil rights would be overshadowed by the riots, or by the war in Vietnam, or by both. His political rivals, he told King, were calling him weak. "I haven't got the crowd supporting me anymore," the president said.

JOHNSON: They all got the impression, too, that you're against me in Vietnam. You don't leave that impression. I want peace as much as you do and more so because I'm the fellow that had to wake up this morning with fifty Marines killed. But these folks will not come to the conference table and I'm—

King interrupted—something he seldom did in conversation with Johnson.

KING: I have said this, Mr. President. I am concerned about peace, and I have made it clear . . . that at the present time . . . two things, first, that it is just unreasonable to talk about the United States having a unilateral

withdrawal. On the other hand, you have called fourteen or fifteen times for unconditional talks, and it's Hanoi . . .
JOHNSON: That's right . . . that's the perfect position.

Johnson said he wanted King to meet with the U.S. ambassador to the United Nations, Arthur Goldberg, to learn more about what the ambassador was "trying to do behind the scenes" to end the conflict in Vietnam.

JOHNSON: Let's don't let this country get divided.

King said he would talk to Goldberg next week, and Johnson said he would have Lee White call King the next day to talk about relief for the people of Los Angeles.

JOHNSON: Now, is there any other suggestion you got?
KING: Well, that's really the main one.
JOHNSON: I appreciate your doing this. That's really the way to function. You did a good service going out there and trying to give some leadership, and then call in to report if you got any suggestions or recommendation, why, I'm just as close as a telephone if you got enough money to pay it and if you haven't, why, call collect.

King laughed, and the men said goodbye.

39

Beware the Day

Ten years earlier, during the Montgomery bus boycott, King had hoped and believed that Black Americans had the opportunity to "become instruments of a great idea," to spread nonviolent social change across the country and around the world. Now King sounded much more pessimistic, as if the moment had passed.

In an essay for the *Saturday Review*, a magazine that appealed to economically comfortable, upper-middlebrow readers, King wrote: "The flames of Watts illuminated more than the western sky; they cast light on the imperfections in the civil rights movement and the tragic shallowness of white racial policy in the explosive ghettos." By some reports, President Johnson's so-called War on Poverty was getting results, such as reducing hunger and getting more children enrolled in early education programs. Johnson's agenda seemed like a response to King's long-running demands. But now it didn't look like enough. Many Black leaders worried that Johnson's commitment to racial justice was fading. King had a growing awareness, as the historian Sylvie Laurent writes, that even liberal lawmakers "would not spontaneously tackle the structural roots of racial inequality and class exploitation."

While the South had made progress in the decade gone by, King wrote, conditions for Black people in the North had stagnated or deteriorated. Poverty-stricken northern neighborhoods, generally, had grown more impoverished and isolated. Schools in big cities had become more racially and economically segregated. Police brutality went on, "rationalized, tolerated, and usually denied."

King wrote that while he had been treated respectfully by most big-city mayors in the North, he had nonetheless come away convinced that their "blindness, obtuseness, and rigidity" toward the rights of the Negro people "would only be altered by a dynamic movement." He was prepared to lead that movement, he wrote, but added: "The critical task will be to convince Negroes driven to cynicism that nonviolence can win."

King's essay in the *Saturday Review* reflected his concern about the conditions and potential for violence in the North. "But for the sober council of Martin Luther King," wrote *The Chicago Defender*, "the streets of American big cities would be flowing with blood." It was not a new concern for King. As a student at Crozer Theological Seminary, when he studied the writings of the theologian Walter Rauschenbusch, he had written: "I must be concerned about unemployment, slumms [sic], and economic insecurity." He had used his Nobel speech to say that ending poverty and war was just as urgent as ending racial injustice. He was returning to one of the basic lessons instilled in him as a child attending Sunday school at Ebenezer Baptist Church, said the historian and civil rights activist Timuel Black: "The story of Dr. King is a human story. His mother and father inspired the feeling in him through their religious commitment that people like him had an obligation to make this a better world." No matter how grim the outlook, King returned to his belief in the morality of the universe. Even if the cause seemed hopeless at the time, he felt compelled to act, to love. "You feel that sense of obligation," Black said, "when you're around a man like that."

———— ◦ ————

On August 30, 1965, as a new school year began, thousands of Black children in Georgia enrolled for the first time at schools that had long been exclusively white. Among those Black children were Yolanda King, Martin Luther King III, Juandalynn Abernathy, Donzaleigh Abernathy, and Ralph Abernathy III, all of whom enrolled in Atlanta's Spring Street School. There were no violent outbreaks and no significant protests across the state, according to *The Atlanta Constitution*, which reported that the schools in Georgia, by integrating, assured the continuation of $55 million in federal funding and qualified for more than $40 million in new funds. "Everything is rosy," said B. B. Harris, superintendent of schools in Gwinnett County, Georgia, where fifty-eight Black children attended previously all-white schools that day.

But even as the Kings and Abernathys witnessed firsthand some of the progress their movement had helped to make, SCLC leaders had no detailed plan of action to expand the scope of their work. Morale within the SCLC was low. Donations were down. Hosea Williams's voter registration project was floundering and facing accusations of mismanagement. The organization's program director, Randolph Blackwell, and its affiliates director, C. T. Vivian, threatened to quit. King told the staff he was eager to begin work in Chicago, but Andrew Young, among others, worried that the organization lacked the cash and manpower to launch a major initiative on new turf. The best way to help in the North, Young said, was to register Black voters in the South and change the balance of national politics. "We had been successful in Alabama because we knew everybody," he wrote. But in Chicago they hardly knew anyone.

"It was my impression," wrote Dorothy Cotton, "that our Chicago host group was not ready for the kind of movement we traditionally launched in the South." Even Bayard Rustin, who lived in New York, argued that King and the SCLC should stick to voter registration in the South, "and leave the northern urban areas to other groups."

King overruled them all, saying the crisis was too great to ignore and that support for the campaign in Chicago would grow as the work got underway. "The present mood dictates that we cannot wait," he said. "We must . . . commit ourselves to the whole long-range program."

The members of his team seldom argued once King had made up his mind, Cotton recalled. "When the team got quiet after Dr. King spoke," she wrote, "it was because he was convincing—coming from a place inside himself that we couldn't counter, nor did we want to." But even after he had made up his mind and won over his associates, King could have chosen to begin his work in Chicago with a more precise target in mind. He might have built on three years of work already done by Al Raby and other local activists and focused on discrimination in the city's public schools. In Birmingham and

Selma, the SCLC had learned to simplify its goals, in part to make it easier for the public and the press to understand the protesters' demands. But he didn't do that for Chicago, and the decision was intentional. James Bevel had been arguing that problems in Chicago—and throughout the North—had to be defined broadly. Economic exploitation was at the root of every issue, as King argued with increasing frequency, including inferior education, discriminatory employment practices, and segregated housing. "We're going to create a new city," Bevel bragged. "Nobody will stop us."

While the staff made plans, King went to New York for a meeting, on September 10, with Arthur Goldberg, the U.S. ambassador to the United Nations. King told Goldberg he spoke as a "minister concerned with bringing Christian ethics to bear on the social evils of today." The men met for more than an hour. Goldberg told King that the United States was seeking an honorable end to the conflict in Vietnam but would not be "forced out." King said he was "deeply distressed" about the war. He also told the ambassador he thought the United States should welcome the People's Republic of China to the United Nations.

King's comments brought sharp criticism from Senator Thomas J. Dodd, a Democrat from Connecticut, a member of the Senate Foreign Relations Committee, and a close friend of President Johnson. Dodd said King had "absolutely no competence to speak about complex matters of foreign policy" and was guilty of "nothing short of arrogance" in trying to undermine the president and the United States. The senator said he had always defended King against allegations that he was "under communist influence," but now King was inviting more criticism. Dodd mentioned, threateningly, that federal law made it illegal for private citizens to engage in freelance foreign policy work. It didn't help that King brought Bayard Rustin along on his meeting with Goldberg. South Carolina senator Strom Thurmond, who had switched his party affiliation from Democratic to Republican the year before, called Goldberg's decision to meet with King and Rustin "a disgrace to the country."

The Black press, for the most part, applauded King's stance. "Dr. Martin Luther King, sometimes called De Lawd even by some of his ardent admirers, has been on the receiving end of a batch of brickbats recently," wrote

Poppy Cannon White in the *New York Amsterdam News*. "Seems he has been meddling with questions that should not concern him at all. Like the fate of the whole human race!" She continued: "He could, if he would, rest on his laurels. Instead he has raised his voice. He has spoken out loud against our national insanity in Vietnam and asked for an opportunity to use the prestige of the Nobel Peace Prize as it should be used—in the interests of peace." Jackie Robinson, while not endorsing King's stand on Vietnam, attacked Dodd, as well as the Black leaders who failed to rally around King.

But the criticism in the white media upset King. On Sunday night, September 12, he joined a conference call with some of his key advisers: Levison, Young, Wachtel, Clarence Jones, and the Black activist Cleveland Robinson. King told the group he was convinced that Lyndon Johnson had orchestrated Dodd's attack and that it suggested that King and Johnson were headed for an ugly confrontation.

"I have already gotten unkind editorials on what I said," King said during the conference call. "The criticism that affects me more is the one that says that I am power drunk and that I feel I can do anything because I got the Nobel Prize and it went to my head, and the true motive of my statements are never revealed . . . No, I really don't have the strength to fight this issue and keep my civil rights fight going . . . The other thing is the deeper you get involved the deeper you have to go and take stands and make speeches and appearances and I'm already overloaded and almost emotionally fatigued."

Most of the advisers urged King to limit his comments on Vietnam, at least in the short term, to avoid being pulled into more controversy. Only Robinson, a Jamaican-born labor organizer, disagreed. "I wouldn't be afraid of that," he told King and the others on the call, which was recorded by the FBI. "What Martin said is right all down the line, and it may start a movement among the people, and nothing could be better."

The men spoke again the next day, this time adding Bayard Rustin and Walter Fauntroy of the SCLC's Washington, D.C., office to the group call.

King said, "My star is waning . . . I want to put the issue behind me temporarily because the central issue for me is civil rights . . . but under no conditions will I bring to an end my speaking out on the question on peace when

I deem it timely and necessary." The purpose of the call, for King, was to get his advisers to help him combat the negative press. He wanted to spread the message, he said, "that I'm not a kook out here," that he was entitled to make his views heard on Vietnam, and that he would not compromise his work on civil rights to speak out on the war.

Robinson, again, urged King to fight: "For the first time a Black man of mighty stature is speaking up on this question . . . This is the key to the whole problem."

But not all King's advisers were so supportive. In a call later the same day with Wachtel, Rustin criticized King for his statements on Vietnam and China.

"Rank and file Negro sentiment is against Martin," Rustin said, "because they are saying, 'China is not our problem. We ain't got no freedom here. What the fuck is wrong with King. He better get off this China shit and help us solve our problems . . .' Martin is only concerned about the press. He has gone mad about the press."

Wachtel talked about getting "back on track" by focusing on Chicago instead of Vietnam. But Rustin said King didn't belong in Chicago, either. He needed to concentrate on the South.

"Then let's get a campaign in the South going," Wachtel said.

In another conference call, on September 28, King said he was scheduled to speak at the fiftieth anniversary of the Women's International League for Peace and Freedom, an organization Coretta had been involved with for years. "I don't see how, on that platform, I could avoid talking about peace and Vietnam," he said. He told the men on the call that he was scheduled to appear on the same program as Staughton Lynd—a conscientious objector, radical historian, and peace activist—and that Lynd's participation might attract negative press.

"You have a big problem . . . and I say you should not be there," Rustin said.

"Well, I don't want to get in bad with Lynd," King said. "He is a friend of mine."

Wachtel asked if someone else might read King's speech on his behalf.

"Well, Coretta could read the speech," King said.

"I think Martin should remain basically a civil rights leader and not a peace leader," Levison said.

The men agreed that King might safely appear at the event if he spoke about his moral opposition to the war without getting into specifics. But, once again, in a follow-up call, Rustin complained to Wachtel: "One of these days this guy is going to fall flat on his head because he doesn't have the moral courage to disagree with anybody except his advisers. He said Staughton Lynd is his friend and that he doesn't want to get in trouble with him. Who the fuck is Staughton Lynd?"

In the early days of the Montgomery bus boycott, when King had found himself thrust unexpectedly into a position of leadership, Rustin had pressed King to think beyond Montgomery's buses and consider the potential for a sweeping national movement. Now, as King expanded his role to address issues of poverty, militarism, and northern racism, Rustin tried to pull him back. Rustin may have felt it was the practical course. The SCLC was a study in organizational chaos, and it was about to undertake a mission in a new city where its leader had no experience and no particular plan. This mission would pit King against a political opponent in Mayor Daley, who was far more shrewd and far more powerful than Bull Connor or Jim Clark. The outlook was dim. But Rustin's frustration with King may have also stemmed from a prejudice of Rustin's own: he could not relate to King's faith in God, even though King kept explaining it.

"First and foremost," King wrote in a newspaper column soon after his conference calls with advisers, "I am a minister of the Gospel. As a clergyman, in the prophetic Judeo-Christian tradition, I would be less than honest if I did not say, with all the force at my command, and at every opportunity which presents itself, that I believe war is wrong . . . As a minister, I cannot advocate racial peace and non-violence for black men alone, nor white men alone, nor for yellow men alone . . . If a man of God fails to see this; if he fails to seek to help bring about peace on earth as well as good will among mankind, he isn't much of a spokesman for the Christ who predicted, centuries ago, that he who lives by the sword shall perish by the sword."

Others understood and appreciated King's beliefs. From South Vietnam, a Buddhist monk and antiwar activist named Thich Nhat Hanh published an open letter to King, one that applauded the American preacher's ecumenical approach to social action. "I am sure that since you have been engaged in one of the hardest struggles for equality and human rights, you are among those who understand fully . . . the indescribable suffering of the Vietnamese people," Thich Nhat Hanh wrote. The monk went on to cite the writings of Paul Tillich, Reinhold Niebuhr, and other favorites of King. "The world's greatest humanists would not remain silent. You can not remain silent . . . You can not be silent since you have already been in action and you are in action because, to you, God is in action, too."

For Thanksgiving that year, the Kings served turkey and stuffing, with pies and cakes for dessert. In addition to Martin and Coretta and their four children, there were five invited guests: SCLC board member Marian Logan and her husband, Dr. Arthur Logan, who were visiting from New York, and three young SCLC workers. Stoney Cooks, one of the invited staffers, was struck by the modesty of King's home. It was not what he had expected. King sat at the head of the table and offered a short prayer before the meal. Coretta sat in the middle, between the adults and children. There were no maids or servants. Coretta served the food while Martin and the guests talked.

Vietnam dominated the conversation. Cooks said he got the impression he and the other young guests had been invited because King wanted to hear how they felt about the war. The Logans stated strongly that they thought it was a mistake for King to publicly oppose the war, because it would distract from his important civil rights work. The three young men at the table, Cooks said, were cautious not to speak too boldly, but they told King they were hearing a great deal of concern among their friends about the escalating conflict in Vietnam.

"Dr. King brought it up," Cooks said. "It was like it was a burden on him."

40

Chicago

THE REEK OF urine hit them as they walked in the door of their new part-time home.

The Chicago apartment was "dingy . . . no lights in the hall, one dim bulb at the head of the stairs," as Coretta put it years later. The stench, she learned, was attributable to the fact that the building's front door never closed, "and the drunks came in off the street to use the hallway as a toilet."

She and Martin arrived at the apartment—at 1550 South Hamlin Avenue, in the North Lawndale neighborhood—on a cold Wednesday afternoon, January 26, 1966. The temperature inside felt little different from the temperature outside. Reporters who had come to meet them noted that Mrs. King, in her "Persian lamb coat with mink-trimmed collar," as the *Chicago Tribune* described it, did not seem to belong in this dump, with its dirty windows, cracked floor tiles, and stained bathtub.

"I have to be right here with the people," King said. "I can learn more about the situation by being here with those who live and suffer here." He and his close associate Bernard Lee planned to spend three days a week in the apartment, King said, while Coretta would visit as often as her schedule permitted. Rent was high given the quality and location of the place: $90 a month, or about $830 in 2022. SCLC organizers purchased secondhand furniture for the apartment.

King had been warned about the dangers of Chicago. But it wasn't the rats or the street gangs or the dilapidated housing that concerned his friends and allies; it was the social and political landscape they feared. Chicago's

Black population had grown rapidly in the first half of the twentieth century, as the so-called Great Migration brought families from the South. But the city had proven less than great for many of the migrants. Black families clustered in the near South Side, carving out their own domain, as they did in Harlem, in large part because they were shunned in other parts of the city.

In the 1960s, about a quarter of Chicago's 3.5 million population was Black, up from about 14 percent in 1950—an increase of more than 300,000 people looking for decent housing, jobs, and schools. As the Black population grew and spread, white homeowners fled. As racist real estate practices made it difficult for Black families to move elsewhere, Bronzeville, as the heart of the Black community was known, became crowded and blighted. Many of Bronzeville's handsomest blocks were demolished and replaced by massive public housing complexes, which made the neighborhood even more crowded and blighted. Segregated housing reinforced and worsened patterns of segregated schools.

Timuel Black was eager to help King organize in Chicago. But he had his doubts about the minister's chances for success. As an educator and activist, Black had watched with pride as King had broken down barriers to equality in the South. He wondered if King understood Chicago's dynamics. Did he understand that South Side Black people looked down on West Side Black people? Did he understand that many Black people felt beholden to Mayor Daley, directly or indirectly, for their jobs? That even many of the city's Black ministers were part of Daley's Democratic machine? Did he understand how difficult it would be to convince Chicagoans to pledge nonviolence? "I said to myself," Black recalled, "if one of those motherfuckers hits me, the nonviolent movement is over." Still, there was cause for hope, Black said, because King was King. The man had an almost miraculous ability to bring together a community—with his rhetoric, his courage, his self-sacrifice. And if anyone could get the northern press to reconsider its bias and look at northern racism with some of the same liberal sense it brought to the South, he said, King was the man.

On his first night in Chicago, King held an open house, inviting neighbors to visit. He talked for a long time with six members of a local gang, the

Vice Lords, about Gandhi and the concept of peaceful protest. Everyone, including King, sat on the floor. "We would say, 'We respect what you're saying, but if someone hits me, I'm going to hit him back,'" recalled Lawrence Johnson, one of the Vice Lords. King argued that the gang members would never win that way. The police would always have more power. "Hearing this, seeing him, being young, living in a depressive life in America, you couldn't help but to fall in love with him," Johnson said.

Despite the admonishment, the Vice Lords believed there was at least one thing they *could* do better than the police: protect Dr. King.

"I think he thought that, too," said Johnson.

King also met with Chicago's police superintendent, O. W. Wilson, a former academic at the University of California at Berkeley who had a reputation as a reformer. King promised to keep city officials informed of his plans—plans, he said, that would likely include acts of civil disobedience. But the Chicago Freedom Movement showed few signs of life at that point. King seemed more like a tourist than a resident, as he continued to crisscross the country, responding to crises, raising money for the SCLC, and preaching Sundays at Ebenezer. At times, his Ebenezer sermons reflected his personal feelings, including his sense of responsibility to speak out on Vietnam. He told his congregation on February 6 that "it's just as evil to kill Vietnamese as it is to kill Americans." More generally, he went on to say, people had a moral responsibility to confront difficult issues. "God's unbroken hold on us," he said, "is something that will never permit us to feel right when we do wrong, or to feel natural when we do the unnatural. God has planted within us certain eternal principles, and the more we try to get away from them the more frustrated we will be."

Back in Chicago on February 9, King and Abernathy led reporters on a tour of a slum building. To put an end to conditions like these would require the SCLC's biggest campaign to date, King said, one that worked across neighborhoods and united an array of organizations. Rent strikes might be required to pressure landlords to improve conditions. In addition to the community organizing, the SCLC began operating a Chicago chapter of Operation Breadbasket, the Atlanta program that pushed for economic opportunities and fair hiring practices. King said that the SCLC and other groups in Chicago would boycott local industries that failed to hire Black men and women for "bigger and better jobs." It might require a year and a half of pressure, he estimated, before improvement became evident.

At the same time, Mayor Daley announced a plan—as lacking in detail as King's—to clean up the city's slums by the end of 1967. Though Daley was angry about King's presence in the city, he struck a conciliatory pose in public. "Elimination of slums is the No. 1 program of this administration," the mayor said shortly before King's arrival. "All of us, like Dr. King, are trying to end slums."

On February 23, King improvised a sit-in, taking over a three-story apartment building at 1321 South Homan Avenue and saying that his coalition would collect the rent from tenants and make repairs until the building's owner took responsibility for the shameful condition of his property. When reporters asked if King had a legal right to occupy the apartment building, he said the moral issues were more important than the legal ones. Coretta swept piles of uncollected garbage on the building's back porch while King and Al Raby carried trash cans to the curb. King took a quick liking to Raby, as did most people. Raby was a thin, balding man who could easily be overlooked. He once described himself as a "terrible speaker," totally lacking in charisma. He had dropped out of school, served in the U.S. Army, enrolled in night school, and got a job teaching seventh grade at an all-Black school in Chicago. Despite his lack of charisma, Raby had an uncanny ability to unite people in action. He had helped make the city's Coordinating Council of Community Organizations one of the strongest civil rights groups in the North. Now King and Raby hoped to make 1321 South Homan Avenue a focal point of media attention and the start of a broader campaign.

King said his organization would pay three unemployed men who lived in the building $2 an hour to serve as janitors. The activists would hold the building in an unofficial "trusteeship" until living conditions improved, he vowed. The owner of the building objected to King's attempt to collect rent and promised to sue. The owner also said he would be willing to give his building to King and his organization if they took over his mortgage payments.

Later that day, King met for an hour with Elijah Muhammad at the Nation of Islam leader's South Side mansion. King joked that he and Muhammad had something in common as a couple of "Georgia boys." While the men and their organizations had differences, King told reporters after the meeting that "there now appear to be some areas—slums and areas other than slums—in which our two movements can cooperate." Bennett Johnson, a local activist who helped broker the meeting, said King and Muhammad agreed that the white power structure in Chicago would be intimidated by the appearance of an alliance between the two men.

On the same day that King and Muhammad met, President Johnson gave a speech in New York in response to growing protest over the conflict in Vietnam, calling on Americans to show the world that the nation had not given up its fight for freedom. He said he appreciated the importance of open debate but added that "no foe anywhere should mistake our arguments or indecision or our debates for weakness." Johnson added: "If the aggressor persists in Vietnam, the struggle may well be long." Outside the hotel where Johnson spoke, nearly four thousand people protested, many of them waving Viet Cong flags.

Though King had limited his comments concerning Vietnam as he began his work in Chicago, his opposition to the war was well-known, and he continued to face criticism for it in the press. Russell Kirk, an influential conservative theorist and newspaper columnist, wrote that King's recent moves suggested that the civil rights leader had become "somewhat intoxicated by his own publicity." By taking over private property in Chicago, by associating with Elijah Muhammad, and by interfering in matters of foreign policy, King showed poor judgment, Kirk wrote. "American public opinion shifts in great waves. When Dr. King commenced his crusades, most Americans believed him to be in the right. But most Americans do not relish the odd notion that 'civil rights' are above the law, or that Christian reformers should league themselves with frantic pseudo-Moslem fanatics. And if he discards his mantle of probity and sense, Martin Luther King is nothing." A national public opinion poll had recently found that 41 percent of respondents would be less inclined to support civil rights organizations if those organizations opposed the war in Vietnam.

King responded in his own syndicated newspaper column, which ran in multiple Black papers, writing that a lot of white people were wondering when he would stop demonstrating and boycotting; when he would stop speaking out against war, poverty, and racism; when things in America could go back to normal. His answer was simple, he said. So long as war, poverty, and racism remain part of "normal" America, he wrote, "then I prefer to be maladjusted."

Dorothy Cotton wrote that King was "surprised and dismayed" by the number of allies and friends who criticized his position on Vietnam. "In one staff meeting," Cotton wrote, "Dr. King grew weary of the debate about the issue; he left the meeting and drove to my house. When he arrived there he was sort of giggly about the fact that he'd just left, not telling the team where he was going or why. But they knew. He was tired of the team's loud argument—mostly advising him what supporters would say if he spoke out against the war. He did not come to my house to discuss the issue. His manner was almost childish. 'They don't know where I am,' he laughingly said to me. My sense is that the more his leadership was criticized, the stronger he seemed to hold his view that war was not the way."

King spent the spring shuttling between Chicago and Atlanta, with additional trips to Hartford, Detroit, Dallas, New York, Washington, Paris, and Stockholm. In one of his European speeches, he explained succinctly the importance of his campaign to eradicate poverty in Chicago:

> The history of our time is one of revolution against political domination, and no nation is devoid of a caste system of some sort. Therefore, the grand experiment which we now conduct in America is of tremendous relevance to the rest of the world.

King never called for the end to capitalist regimes. He was not a socialist. "Though he called for a fairer distribution of wealth, he didn't criticize private ownership of productive assets and natural resources as inherently unjust," the scholar Tommie Shelby writes. King extolled Marx as a champion of the poor but criticized communism for its inattention to individual rights.

He condemned capitalism for generating massive economic inequality while arguing that the system could be reformed. He called for higher worker wages and strong unions, but he did not insist on equal pay for all workers regardless of skill or for nonprofit worker cooperatives. "King is therefore best described as a liberal egalitarian or a social democrat," writes Shelby. "His vision embraced the best elements from capitalism and socialism."

In April, King was in Miami for the SCLC's semiannual board meeting, where he faced more discussion of the organization's disorganization. The Vietnam question arose again. An article in *The Christian Century* by Charles Fager, a former SCLC staff member who chose to publish his piece in that magazine in part because he knew King read it, had called King's recent statements on the war "almost tame." King had built his movement on morality, on Christianity, wrote Fager. The Nobel Prize winner seemed to be walking a "tortuous middle path," opposing the war but not opposing it so loudly as to damage SCLC fundraising efforts. It seemed unlikely, Fager wrote, that King could remain so cautious "without seriously compromising his acknowledged role as a man of principle." At the meeting in Miami, King asked the board to approve a strongly worded declaration of the organization's opposition to American policy in Vietnam. The board agreed, but its statement of support for King's stance only generated more criticism in the press among those who believed King should stick to civil rights.

While in Miami for the board meeting, King met with the movie producer Abby Mann, whose screenplay for the 1961 drama *Judgment at Nuremberg* had won an Academy Award. Mann wanted to make a film based on King's life story. At dinner one night, with Abernathy, Young, and Mann, King pushed his plate away. "No, no," he said. "It's all no good if we can't say what we feel about Vietnam."

The men had not been talking about Vietnam at the time.

In another conversation, King and Mann were discussing the broad outline of their potential movie on King's life. Mann asked, somewhat in jest, how the movie should end.

"It ends with me getting killed," King said.

"He smiled," Mann later recalled, "but he wasn't joking."

———

Hoping to invigorate his movement in Chicago, King announced plans for a summer rally at Soldier Field. He vowed that 100,000 people would gather at the stadium and march to city hall, where they would present a detailed set of demands on jobs, housing, education, welfare, and health care. If Mayor Daley would not receive their list of demands, King said, he would present them anyway, even if had to tack them to the door, just as his namesake, Martin Luther, had purportedly done at the door of the Wittenberg Castle church centuries ago.

A few days later, Martin and Coretta flew to Washington for President Johnson's White House Conference on Civil Rights. King was almost invisible at the two-day conference, sidelined, most likely, because he had angered Johnson with his statements on Vietnam. Coretta, however, enjoyed a rare moment in the spotlight when she sang the national anthem at a dinner attended by 2,500 delegates before the opening of the conference. And it was Coretta, not Martin, who was quoted the next day in *The Washington Post*. "When you feel what you are doing is right," she said, "you are ready for the tough times when they come, and you face them and accept them. You learn, too, that the bad times do not last forever, and you know that they are part of the price you must pay for the privilege of standing by your convictions."

The purpose of the conference, according to the white journalists who covered it, was to build support among white Americans for the Johnson administration's plans to improve housing, education, and employment for Black people. "Yet there is rising concern within the government and the civil rights movement itself," reported *The Washington Post*, that white sympathy "with the Negro cause is wearing thin in the wake of Watts and strident Negro protest." Johnson had proposed the conference a year earlier. In the intervening period, protests had grown louder and angrier. Riots had erupted. King and others had spoken out on Vietnam. "A small and disproportionately noisy section of the civil rights movement would rather deny many realities of Negro life today . . . and escape into black nationalism and other fantasies," wrote *The New York Times* in an editorial. The challenges in achieving genuine equality for the Negro, the newspaper said, remain "grim and towering."

The white media was correct in reporting that the civil rights movement had splintered and that some activists had grown more aggressive. If anyone needed proof, James Meredith provided it. While the mainstream leaders were meeting in Washington, Meredith announced that he intended to undertake a sixteen-day, 220-mile "walk against fear," from Memphis to the Mississippi state capitol in Jackson. Meredith had gained fame as the University of Mississippi's first Black student. He admired King, but he had never believed in nonviolence. He had become disillusioned with the mainstream civil rights movement.

"Very few people understand what I really did," Meredith recalled, referring to his "walk against fear." The fear he opposed was not just the fear of registering to vote in Mississippi, or even the fear of violence; it was also the fear of stepping out of the civil rights movement's mainstream. "Blacks stayed in line because they were scared to get out of line," Meredith said years later. "That's still the problem. I set out to redirect it . . . Just like I set out to break the system of white supremacy at Ole Miss, I set out to redirect the so-called Black Movement in America."

On the second day of his walk, Meredith wore gray trousers, a brown-and-red-checkered shirt, and a pith helmet. He carried an ivory-handled African walking stick. Late in the afternoon, he was walking on the side of Highway 51, two miles south of Hernando, Mississippi, when he heard a voice coming from a thicket of water lilies and honeysuckle vines.

"Jaaa-mes . . ."

He turned in time to see a chubby white man in a white shirt and sunglasses pointing a 16-gauge automatic Remington shotgun.

The man, an unemployed hardware clerk named Aubrey James Norvell, closed in.

Meredith dived. Norvell shot and missed.

The gunman moved closer and shot again twice, spraying Meredith with pellets in the head, neck, back, and legs.

"They reported I was dead," Meredith said, "but I ain't never agreed to that."

With Meredith hospitalized, King and other activists agreed to meet in Memphis and continue what would quickly come to be referred to as the Meredith March. The next day, King was joined by Roy Wilkins and Charles Evers of the NAACP; Whitney Young of the Urban League; Floyd Mc-Kissick, the new director of the Congress of Racial Equality; the Reverend James Lawson, pastor of Centenary Methodist Church in Memphis; and Stokely Carmichael, the new chairman of SNCC.

King was one of the first to visit Meredith in his Memphis hospital room.

"How are you feeling?" he asked.

"I'm stiff," Meredith said, "but otherwise I'm as well as I've ever been."

As Meredith would write years later about that moment, not entirely exaggerating: "Martin Luther King and I were about to unleash a chain of events that would transform my one-man walk against fear into the biggest and last great march of the civil rights era in the South—and an event that catalyzed the disintegration of the civil rights movement itself."

41

Black Power

THEY WALKED SOUTH on U.S. Highway 51 in Mississippi, in sweltering heat.

It was June 7, 1966.

From the start, King said, this march felt different. It was small, with no more than twenty people, and it didn't begin in a packed church with songs and reminders of the beautiful power of nonviolence and faith in God. The marchers were angry, in no mood for appeals to interracial harmony.

From his hospital bed that day, James Meredith told reporters he would never again make the mistake of walking through Mississippi unarmed, that he was sorry he hadn't been able to fire back at the man who'd shot him. His attitude carried over to some of the men replacing him on the march.

"If one of these damn white Mississippi crackers touches me," King heard one of the men say, "I'm gonna knock the hell out of him."

They spoke of permitting only Black marchers, saying they didn't need "white phonies and liberals invading our movement." When they sang "We Shall Overcome," a few of the marchers dropped the stanza that referred to "black and white together." When King asked why, the men said they didn't believe goodwill among the races was possible.

King wore dark sunglasses and a white short-sleeved shirt. At the top of a small hill, not far from where Meredith had been shot, a group of Mississippi highway patrolmen stopped the marchers and ordered them to move to the side of the road.

"We marched on the pavement from Selma to Montgomery," King told one of the troopers.

"I don't care if you march to China as long as you march on the side of the road," he said.

"No," King said, "we're just going to Jackson."

The men locked arms.

One of the white troopers shoved SNCC's Cleveland Sellers to the ground. King stumbled over his fallen colleague. Stokely Carmichael lunged at the trooper, but King grabbed his arm and held him back.

The marchers gathered themselves and huddled beside an ice-cream stand to discuss their options. King argued that the group would make a greater impact marching on the side of the road than not marching at all, and the others agreed. After covering about six miles, they returned to Memphis for a meeting with newly arrived activists, including Roy Wilkins and Whitney Young, leaders of the nation's two most venerable Black organizations.

Wilkins and Young were not often engaged in marches, but they saw an opportunity to use the crisis in Mississippi to press the case for the proposed Civil Rights Bill of 1966. Wilkins, who had undermined King and the SCLC, was scornful of SNCC, too, complaining that the organization's tilt toward Black separatism would have disastrous consequences for the movement. Since the defeat of the Mississippi Freedom Democratic Party, SNCC had become a training ground for young activists who would go on to seed the feminist and antiwar movements, "but SNCC workers themselves had become more uncertain about the values guiding their work," writes the historian Clayborne Carson. Carmichael wanted the march to serve as a shout, not a plea or a negotiation. He sought to cast Lyndon Johnson as the enemy. Carmichael accused Wilkins and Young of acting as puppets for white politicians. Black people, Carmichael said, were no longer willing to take orders from white authorities. "I have never rejected violence," Carmichael warned.

Carmichael was born on June 29, 1941, in Trinidad, in the West Indies, which was under British control from 1802 until it became independent in

1962. His father, a carpenter, moved to Harlem when Stokely was two years old; he lived with his grandmother in Trinidad until he joined his parents in New York when he was almost eleven. Stokely graduated from the highly selective Bronx High School of Science and then from Howard University, where he earned a degree in philosophy. The idea of Black independence, planted by his father, grew inside him, he said, "ready to take an American form later on."

Carmichael was tall, slender, charming—and razor sharp. He laughed often and spoke his mind freely and excitedly. At twenty-five, Carmichael had already served time in jail as a veteran Freedom Rider in Mississippi, and had helped build an independent Black political party in Lowndes County, Alabama. In May 1966, he had replaced John Lewis as SNCC chairman, signaling a move toward greater militancy for the group, Carson writes, but failing to find a set of ideas that would unify the Black community. When Carmichael met Wilkins and Young in Memphis, he wasn't trying to make friends. In fact, as he later told the journalist Milton Viorst, Carmichael wanted to frighten the older men. "So I started acting crazy, cursing real bad," he said. "I said, 'You sellin' out the people, and don't think we don't know it. We gonna getcha' . . . We wanted to let them know it would be impossible to work with us."

But King knew Carmichael wasn't crazy.

"Wilkins couldn't believe it," Carmichael recalled. "He went to Dr. King, and Dr. King . . . didn't say a word. King was just beautiful. Young and Wilkins fell completely into the trap and stormed out of there."

Carmichael hoped to drive away the others, but he believed he could work with King—and pull him to the left. The more miles the men trekked that week, the more King began using the word "Black," SNCC's preferred term, rather than "Negro." King admired, respected, and enjoyed debating Carmichael. But King never swayed from his commitment to integration and nonviolence. A television reporter walked with them at one point. After King reminded the reporter that their march was a nonviolent one, the reporter turned to Carmichael to ask if he shared King's philosophy. "I just don't see it as a way of life," Carmichael said. "I never have. I also realize that no one in this country is asking the white community in the South to be nonviolent, and in that sense is giving them a free license to shoot us at will."

Carmichael had been experimenting with a new slogan at the time, describing himself as an advocate of "Black power." Richard Wright had used the term as the title of his 1954 book, which told the story of the author's trip to Africa's Gold Coast, before Ghana gained its independence from Britain in 1957. But Carmichael employed the phrase in a new way, to suggest that integration was not enough, that Black people needed and demanded political and economic autonomy. When he tested "Black power" on the Meredith March, audiences went wild, he said. On June 16 in Greenwood, Mississippi, a city of twenty-two thousand where SNCC had a strong presence, Carmichael was arrested for pitching a tent on the grounds of Stone Street Negro Elementary School. A newspaper photographer captured the image of a white police officer wielding a club at Carmichael, who had his back turned to the officer. After posting bail, Carmichael rushed to a meeting of about a thousand supporters, who cheered him as he climbed atop a platform to speak.

"We want Black power!" he shouted. "All we've been doing is begging the federal government. The only thing we can do is take over." He went on to say "every county courthouse in Mississippi should be burned tomorrow to get rid of the filth in them."

"We want Black power!" he shouted, and the crowd took up the chant: "We want Black power! We want Black power!"

Newspaper headlines nationwide heralded Carmichael's demand, some of them using capital letters for the phrase as it entered the mainstream: "Black Power!"

King, who had been in Memphis that night for a television interview, rejoined the march the next day and heard the new phrase bandied about. "Immediately," he wrote, "I had reservations." He worried that the call for Black power and its implicit threat of violence would widen the gaps between SNCC and other civil rights groups, not to mention that it might disenfranchise white allies of the movement who took comfort in King's calls for nonviolence. King and Carmichael met that day for five hours, along with members of their staffs, at a small Catholic parish house in Yazoo City. King explained his concerns about "Black power." Carmichael dismissed them. "Black power" didn't mean violence, he said; it meant strength, self-determination.

"Why not use the slogan 'black consciousness' or 'black equality'?" King asked.

Those expressions were soft, Carmichael said. They didn't inspire action or courage. Carmichael admitted that he was pleased to see King struggling with the new slogan. If King hadn't been on the march and hadn't been forced to take a stand on the controversial catchphrase, "Black power" never would have attracted so much attention.

King laughed at that.

"I've been used before," he said. "One more time won't hurt."

Carmichael may have entered the march with the view that King was someone he could manipulate, but as the men marched for miles and spoke for hours, day after day, about "every blessed thing under the sun," Carmichael developed new affection for the man he respectfully addressed as "Dr. King." Carmichael had seen King in meetings and at rallies. In those settings, he said, King had always seemed "strained, under pressure, vaguely distracted" and "certainly not happy." But as he marched through Mississippi, Carmichael wrote, King looked "more relaxed than I'd ever seen him," as if the Meredith March offered him welcome relief from his routine. To see the way King interacted with people, Carmichael wrote, was "amazing, incredible, inspiring."

Sometimes, when they crossed through a small settlement or the outskirts of a plantation, they would spot a cluster of rural Mississippians far off in the distance, like a mirage. How long had they been out in the blistering summer sun, waiting? When they spotted King, the men and women would stampede, in one instance knocking Carmichael off his feet. King would smile and shake hands and offer words of inspiration: "A new day's coming . . . We ain't what we want to be, and we ain't what we gonna be."

The message was anything but rote, Carmichael said. King said it with passion.

"For most of them," Carmichael wrote, "especially those off the plantations for whom just standing there defiantly where their bosses could see them waiting for Dr. King, this was their first real act of self-affirmation. For me, it was moving, the evident love of the people for Dr. King. And he for them. And I could see in his face and his eyes how deeply touched he was."

The group of marchers swelled to more than six hundred the day after Carmichael's first "Black power" speech. Byron De La Beckwith, the presumed killer of Medgar Evers, drove his truck back and forth past the marchers. The day after that, on June 21, King led a small group of protesters to Philadelphia, Mississippi, where he intended to hold a memorial service for the murdered civil rights workers James Chaney, Michael Schwerner, and Andrew Goodman. When a group of white men attacked the marchers, police made no attempt to intervene until a few of the marchers retaliated. But even after the police stepped in, whites pushed forward, throwing rocks and bottles at the marchers. Cars and trucks, kicking up red dust, buzzed the marchers.

When the protesters reached the county jail, King and Abernathy led a prayer service. A young white man turned a water hose on the group. The mob of white men surrounded the marchers. King was visibly shaken—"his lips trembled and his eyes kept darting toward the group of whites," *The Chicago Defender* reported—as he began to speak.

"We are no longer afraid," he said.

"Come over here . . . and I'll give you reason to be!" one of the white onlookers shouted.

When firecrackers exploded, King began to chant, "The Lord is our shepherd . . . the Lord is our shepherd."

The crowd of hecklers swelled to about three hundred. Roy Reed, covering the speech for *The New York Times*, thought he might soon be reporting on an assassination.

King continued.

"In this county Andrew Goodman, James Chaney, and Mickey Schwerner were brutally murdered," he said. "I believe in my heart that the murderers are somewhere around me at this moment."

"You're damn right," said Deputy Sheriff Cecil Price, one of sixteen people who'd been ordered to stand trial in connection with the murder. He said it loud enough for King to hear.

King continued: "They ought to search their hearts. I want them to know that we are not afraid. If they kill three of us, they will have to kill all of us."

The whites hooted.

"I am not afraid of any man," King said.

"Hey, Luther . . . ," someone shouted, "come up here alone and prove it."

After the speech, a mob of about twenty-five white men attacked the rear of the column of marchers. King stood about a hundred yards away. Bottles and rocks flew. One white man swung a club, another wielded a hoe. That night, after King had left, white men sprayed Philadelphia's Black community with gunfire and, on at least two occasions, Black people returned fire.

The same night, at a mass meeting in Yazoo City, King expressed his unhappiness with the growing violence and, once again, with the violent connotations of "Black power."

"I'm not interested in power for power's sake," he said, "but I'm interested in power that is moral, that is right, and that is good." Black people comprised 10 percent of the nation's population, not enough to stand or fight alone. "There's going to have to be a coalition of conscience, and we aren't going to be free here in Mississippi and anywhere else in the United States until there is a committed empathy on the part of the white man." He also reminded his audience that white people such as Viola Liuzzo, Michael Schwerner, and Andrew Goodman had sacrificed their lives in the struggle for civil rights, that he would never cast white people as the enemy. Black people were going to win their rights, win their freedom, he said—but not through violence and not through hate.

Two days later, as marchers attempted to set up tents at a Black school in Canton, highway patrolmen ordered them to leave. King stood atop a flatbed truck, urging his followers not to move and not to fight with the officers.

His words echoed Carmichael's when he said, "This demonstrates to us this evening that things still must be dealt with firmly and with power here in the state of Mississippi."

The troopers hurled tear gas canisters and swung the stocks of their shotguns at demonstrators. One of the canisters struck Carmichael in the chest. King jumped down from the truck and covered his face as others fell to the ground, vomiting, gasping for air.

"I'll put him with his God," a trooper barked as he shoved and swung his shotgun stock to hit a white Catholic priest who was wearing a clerical collar.

"You niggers want your freedom, well, here's your freedom!" shouted another officer as he kicked a Black woman.

At a nearby gymnasium that night, Carmichael fired up the crowd. "When they touch one Black man, we've got to let them know we're gonna disrupt the whole country," he said. "While our Black brothers are fighting in Vietnam, we're getting gassed for trying to vote in Canton, Mississippi."

King saw the hatred up close in Mississippi. As he recalled later: "I just gave up. I wouldn't say I was so afraid as that I had yielded to the real possibility of the inevitability of death . . . Brother, they were some *days!*"

One day when King was marching in Mississippi, three white men in Natchez, Mississippi, shot and killed Ben Chester White, a sixty-five-year-old Black man. White was shot seventeen times with a rifle and once with a shotgun, his body dumped in Pretty Creek. Despite testimony from FBI agents who said that one of the accused killers had confessed and implicated his two accomplices, no one was convicted for Ben White's murder. One of the white men told FBI agents that they had chosen their victim at random, hoping to lure King to Natchez and assassinate the civil rights leader. The entire incident, apparently, escaped King's attention.

As the March Against Fear, as it became known, neared its conclusion, leaders continued to squabble over the use of the "Black power" slogan, without resolution in sight. Finally, they compromised and agreed to stop trying to shout one another down. On Sunday, June 26, King led marchers on an eight-mile trek in ninety-degree heat from Tougaloo to the state capitol in Jackson. SNCC workers slyly stuck BLACK POWER bumper stickers on police cars while James Orange led chants of "Freedom Now!" A crowd of about twenty-five thousand, by some estimates, gathered on the capitol steps, the largest civil rights demonstration the state had ever seen. King's Boston University theology professor L. Harold DeWolf joined the last leg of the march, as did Stanley Levison and Harry Wachtel. Hundreds of white people jeered the speakers. About fifty Klansmen stood by "to make sure these niggers don't cause any trouble," one of the Klansmen told a reporter.

King, soaked with sweat, spoke bluntly, saying that in only three years since his famous speech in Washington, D.C., he had already seen his dream "turned into a nightmare." He had seen too many Black people suffering from poverty, from the racist enforcement of the law.

But, still, he said, this long, hot march gave him hope "that even here in Mississippi justice will come to all of God's children."

This march, he said, proved Black people were no longer afraid.

———— • ————

What did the people want? Freedom? Power? Better jobs? Better housing? An end to racist policing? Better education for their children? To the white reporters and white supporters of the movement with only a superficial view, it seemed as if Black Americans were getting these things. That's why so many in the media reacted harshly to Carmichael, to cries of "Black power," and even to King as he navigated this militant turn in the civil rights movement and conceded that he was watching his dream of American harmony fade.

After riots and police attacks on innocent Black people in Harlem, Watts, and Mississippi, Mike Wallace told CBS viewers that "the most serious casualty of all was the relationship between the Black man and the white man," which must have come as an insult to those who had been beaten and teargassed. Even in the North, Wallace continued, white people were "fed up with racial turmoil" and taking to the streets to stage counterprotests. Wallace asked King in an interview if he realized that a growing number of Black people were being urged to take up arms in the cause for justice. King replied:

There's no doubt about that. I will agree that there is a group in the
Negro community advocating for violence now. I happen to feel
that this group represents a numerical minority . . . I don't think this
vocal group will be able to make a real dent in the Negro community . . . I contend that the cry of "Black power" is at bottom a reaction to the reluctance of white power to make the kind of changes
necessary to make justice a reality for the Negro. I think we've got
to see that a riot is the language of the unheard. And what is it that
America has failed to hear? It has failed to hear that the economic
plight of the Negro has worsened over the last few years.

In fact, the economic signals were mixed. The unemployment rate for
Black men and women fell to 7.3 percent in the fall of 1966, part of a slow,
steady improvement, but the rate among white people was less than half
that. That gap, as well as the heightened expectations of Black Americans,
continued to fuel discontent.

Time magazine called Carmichael's brand of activism "The New Racism."
Along Mississippi's highways, the magazine reported, marchers had been
heard crying "We gonna get white blood!" In Watts, "embittered Negroes
want to disincorporate the entire area and re-establish it as 'Freedom City,'
with its own officials and police." Black power, the magazine said, might sig-
nal the collapse of King's nonviolent movement.

The Black press was not so horrified and not so worried. *The Chicago
Defender*, in an editorial, said the "Black power" cry appealed to those who
could not count on their state or federal government for protection, leaving
them no choice but to protect themselves "with as much vigor as is required
by the occasion." Pacifism no longer suited the "awakening black masses,"
The *Defender* editorial continued. "Power, black power has become the battle
cry of the Black Revolution. This resolve . . . is not inconsistent with the logic
and objectives of the civil rights struggle."

Privately, King complained that Carmichael and SNCC had damaged
the Meredith March. He came home from Mississippi dejected. "Don't worry
about that," Coretta told him. "Nonviolence will be here when Black power

and all the rest is gone. What you represent is permanent and lasting." She told a reporter: "He comes home depressed just like anyone else when things are not going right. And I console him and remind him of the good things that have happened."

King wasn't happy with Carmichael's new rallying cry, or with the heightened fury behind it, but he didn't dismiss it out of hand. In fact, he seemed to reject the motto more than the philosophy. Wasn't his push into Chicago a push for Black power? Wasn't Operation Breadbasket an attempt to help launch and support more Black-owned businesses? Even if he avoided the words "Black power," King spoke more affirmatively and more often on the same subjects that Malcolm X had emphasized during his life, and Carmichael invoked now. The push for integration had defined much of King's life. He'd been raised in a Black middle-class neighborhood, attended one of the best Black colleges in the nation, studied at integrated schools in the North, and risen to fame and power by preaching about the sins of segregation.

But he also knew, as the theologian James H. Cone wrote, that much of his power derived from the Black church, which had been an independent Black institution since the eighteenth century. That might explain why King moved philosophically toward a version of Black power after marching with Carmichael, after being booed by younger Black activists, and after seeing the slums of Chicago and Los Angeles. Though he remained firmly committed to nonviolence, and though he had to be careful not to disenfranchise liberal white supporters, King began to sound some of the same themes that had resonated for Malcolm X.

King wrote: "Unfortunately, when hope diminishes, the hate is often turned most bitterly toward those who originally built up the hope." He recalled being booed one night in Chicago by supporters of the Black power movement. "I went home that night with an ugly feeling," he said. "Selfishly I thought of my sufferings and sacrifices over the last twelve years. Why would they boo one so close to them? But as I lay awake thinking, I finally came to myself, and I could not for the life of me have less than patience and understanding for those young people."

For twelve years, he had held out "radiant promises of progress." He had urged followers to maintain faith in the white community, in democracy. He had raised their hopes—and crushed them.

"They were now hostile," he wrote, "because they were watching the dream that they had so readily accepted turn into a nightmare."

42

"I Hope King Gets It"

It was 3:15 p.m. on July 10, 1966, the hottest day Chicago had experienced in years. Thunderclouds that promised to break the heat never did. The temperature approached one hundred degrees. As his car rolled into Soldier Field, King gazed out the window and saw a sea of empty seats. Organizers had hoped for a crowd of 100,000 people for their rally; they got about 30,000.

Cries of "Black power" rang out from the stands. One spectator carried a sign bearing a black fist gripping a rifle.

"Who dropped the ball?" King asked Al Raby, who had helped organize the event. King didn't raise his voice, but he was visibly upset.

King stepped to the podium to speak, offering a message that reflected the evolving mood of Black America. "We must appreciate our great heritage," he said. "We must be proud of our race . . . We must believe with all of our hearts that black is as beautiful as any other color." But, he continued, Negroes need the support of the white majority. White people had fought and died in support of the movement, too. "The Negro needs the white man to free him from his fears," he said. "The white man needs the Negro to free him from his guilt. Any approach that overlooks this need for a coalition of conscience is unwise and misguided. A doctrine of Black supremacy is as evil as a doctrine of white supremacy."

After the rally, his mood lifted by the crowd, King led a march to city hall, where he taped a scroll containing more than forty demands to the door. The demands included an end to discrimination in housing and hiring, improved education, and the creation of a citizens' police review board.

When King left, someone removed his list of demands and replaced it with a sign that read: "Support your local police."

———————

The next day, King and eleven colleagues met for three hours with Mayor Daley. King restated his group's demands. After the session, Daley told reporters he was frustrated. Every city had slums. Every city had unemployment. Chicago was trying to solve its problems, he said, but it would take time. "We asked them, 'What would you do that we haven't done?'" Daley said. "They had no answers. I asked for their help and suggestions, and they frankly said the answers were difficult." King told reporters he was disappointed by Daley's response and promised to launch an immediate direct-action campaign.

On Tuesday night, Martin and Coretta had dinner at Mahalia Jackson's home. After the meal, Mahalia offered to drive them to a mass meeting on the West Side. The Kings had brought their children with them to Chicago on this trip, but the kids were spending the night with friends of the family. On their way to the mass meeting, King heard gunshots and wailing police sirens. He saw Black men running through the streets. He and Coretta and Mahalia stopped at a church to ask what was happening. They learned that six youths had been arrested in a scuffle after police had shut off a fire hydrant people had been using for relief from the summer heat. Prior to the incident, Black people in the neighborhood had already been upset that white Chicagoans had access to more swimming pools than Black Chicagoans. Police seldom shut off fire hydrants in nearby white neighborhoods. All over the West Side that night, police clashed with citizens. Buildings were burned and stores looted. At the corner of Lake and Wood Streets, snipers in a high-rise building exchanged gunfire with more than a hundred officers. Six policemen, as well "an uncounted number of civilians," were shot, according to the *Chicago Tribune*. More than a hundred were arrested.

The next night, more buildings burned. Police made more arrests. The Kings, including the children, spent the night with Mahalia Jackson. On

Thursday night, Coretta took the children with her to a meeting, trying to keep them calm and quiet as they sat with her on the platform, even though it was long past bedtime for their youngest, Bernice. Later, when Coretta and the children got back to their West Side apartment, "the riot was going full swing," she wrote. "There was a lot of broken glass on the streets, and . . . we could hear shooting."

When she got upstairs, Coretta found two reporters waiting for her in the apartment. She tried to get the children to sleep, but they wanted to look out the window at the action below. After the three little ones went to bed, Coretta and Yoki watched from a rear window as looters emptied a small grocery store. The sound of gunfire continued through the night. Martin phoned several times to tell her he was safe, that he was among the rioters, trying to keep people calm, and unable to get home. "I finally went to sleep around four o'clock," Coretta wrote. "Martin must have come in some time after that, but I didn't hear him."

The violence lasted three nights.

"You can't charge it directly to Martin Luther King," Daley told reporters, "but surely some of the people that came in here and have been talking for the last year on violence and . . . instructing people in how to conduct violence. They are on his staff and they are responsible in a great measure . . . Certain elements that were in our city were in here for no other purpose than to bring disorder on the streets of Chicago."

Coretta and the children returned to Atlanta, but King remained in Chicago, where he met with community leaders and organized a meeting in which a local police commander listened to the complaints of West Side residents. Late Friday night, July 15, he met at his apartment with leaders of Chicago's major gangs, encouraging them to embrace nonviolent protest and implore their followers to avoid conflict with police, hoping he might stop the riots. Roger Wilkins, an assistant attorney general in the Justice Department, showed up at about one in the morning and found dozens of people crowded into King's apartment. With no air conditioner, and not even a fan, the room was oppressively hot. King sat on the floor, "trying to convince these kids that rioting was destructive," Wilkins recalled. "For hours this went on; and there were no photographers there, no newspaper men. There was no glory in it."

King kept the assistant attorney general waiting until about four in the morning, when the gang members finally left.

Roger Wilkins, a nephew of Roy Wilkins, had long considered King to be "kind of a showboat." But that night, Wilkins started to see King in a new light. "He was a great man," Wilkins said, "a great man!"

When King was in Mississippi, the FBI discontinued its electronic surveillance of SCLC headquarters in Atlanta. The move came in response to an order by Attorney General Katzenbach requiring his reapproval for all telephone surveillances every six months. After that, the flow of information from Hoover to President Johnson slowed somewhat, as the bureau's in-house SCLC informant, the accountant Jim Harrison, became a more important source of information.

On July 19, the president discussed the crisis in Chicago in a phone call with Daley. King was being unreasonable, Daley complained, saying the civil rights leader's demands were beyond the city's capacity to meet. Meanwhile, in Chicago and in cities all over the country, Daley said, Black gang members were buying guns, radical Black activists were being trained for violent rebellion, and King, whether he intended to or not, was giving them cover to carry out criminal acts.

"The King rally . . . was 50 percent Johnson—Johnson the killer, Johnson the destroyer of human life, Johnson the killer in Vietnam," Daley said.

Daley said the same people were protesting racial discrimination and Vietnam. The system of law and order was under attack by people who sought "constant agitation," Daley went on, and King was at the center of the unrest: "He's not your friend. He's against you in Vietnam. He's a goddamn faker . . . I don't know how the hell we approach it. It's the most dangerous thing we have facing our country."

On July 29, King's men led a demonstration outside the office of a real estate company accused of refusing to work with Black customers. But angry white hecklers outnumbered protesters, and the demonstrators were forced to retreat. The next day, with King out of town, community organizer Al Raby, Andrew Young, Jesse Jackson, and others led five hundred people in a march from New Friendship Baptist Church to the real estate office in the Gage Park neighborhood, about eight miles southwest of downtown Chicago. The *New York Times* noted that the surrounding neighborhoods were populated by about 100,000 people—99,993 of them white. Some of those white residents armed themselves with rocks, bricks, and bottles as they awaited the marchers. One man carried a sign that read WHITE POWER! Twenty-five people were hurt and eighteen arrested as the rocks, bricks, and bottles flew. The mob overturned cars and set them aflame. Protesters tried again on Sunday, and once again came under attack.

King joined the marchers on Friday afternoon, August 5. He arrived at Marquette Park by car at about five in the afternoon, two hours late. Even before the march began, young white men threw rocks and sticks at the demonstrators. Members of the American Nazi Party distributed literature. The Gage Park neighborhood was populated largely by Polish and Lithuanian families of low and moderate incomes. Those families believed they would have no choice but to sell their homes if Black people moved to the neighborhood, said Bernard Lafayette, one of the protest organizers.

"I hope King gets it," said a young white man carrying a Confederate flag.

"I'll go to school with 'em and I'll work with 'em," another young man said, referring to Black students, "but I won't live with 'em. I seen what they did to other neighborhoods and I don't want 'em doing it here." One white man carried a sign that read "King would look good with a knife in his back." Cries of "white power!" rang out. Men waved Confederate flags and signs emblazoned with swastikas. THE ZOO WANTS YOU, read another painted sign.

The civil rights marchers moved slowly, singing songs of hope and faith, as they passed rows of freshly painted porches and neatly trimmed shrubs. Young white men pounded the sidewalk with baseball bats.

"Kill coon King!" a group of elderly white men chanted.

The tormentors threw rocks, bottles, bricks, and cherry bombs. As King walked, a Black man shadowed him. The man held his hands above King's head, doing his best to serve as a last line of defense against flying objects. When a cherry bomb exploded, King flinched. A white priest was struck with a brick. A knife thrown at King hit a student instead. The white rioters roared as police carried the wounded student away.

At the corner of California Avenue and West 63rd Street, a pack of teenagers charged at King's bodyguards. Police tackled and handcuffed them.

King, dressed in a gray suit with a blue shirt and no tie, moved hesitantly forward. Whenever the marchers came to a stop, those marching by their leader's side closed in around him and held up their picket signs to shield him. But they couldn't protect him completely. A rock hit King squarely between the shoulder blades, just below his neck. He closed his eyes and fell to his knees.

"He waited for the impact of the bullet," wrote one reporter at the scene, but when he realized there had been no bullet, only a rock, he rose slowly, brushed off the back of his neck, and announced he was okay.

Another cherry bomb exploded. Again, King flinched. White rioters overturned cars and mauled an effigy of King.

"You nigger-loving S.O.B.s!" a middle-aged white man in a suit shouted at the police.

The battle raged through the night, long after the peaceful Black protesters had departed. Dozens were arrested. About forty marchers were injured. King said he was proud of the young Black gang members who had marched and helped protect other marchers without retaliating. He had been teargassed and threatened with death in Mississippi just a few weeks earlier; he had been manhandled by police in Alabama; and he had been stabbed years ago in Harlem; but nothing, he said, prepared him for Chicago's violent racism.

"I've never seen anything like it in my life," he said. "I think the people of Mississippi ought to come to Chicago to learn how to hate."

The scenes of white rage in Chicago did not have the effect on the nation that Bull Connor and his dogs had had in Birmingham. King had once again used conflict to bring American racism into the open, but this time it brought no great reckoning. President Johnson's latest civil rights bill—intended to end racial discrimination in jury selection and the sale and rental of homes, among other things—drew tepid support from congressional leaders, as real estate brokers lobbied to kill or water it down.

King came under attack from all sides.

"These 'rights' leaders and the foggy clergymen who abet them are not heroes," wrote the conservative *Chicago Tribune* in an editorial. "For all their pious protestations of nonviolence, they are working hand in glove with the criminal element to create confusion and turbulence and to compound danger to Chicagoans. They can no longer even pretend to be ignorant of this link . . . If the marchers keep to their sabotage, it will be time to indict the whole lot of them."

Roy Wilkins offered his own critical assessment of the Chicago protest, saying, "Nothing has come of it except a hardening of attitudes."

But King's critics at the time didn't understand one important thing, according to Jesse Jackson. They didn't understand that King was not merely fighting for desegregation; he was fighting for integration in the broadest sense, which meant the voluntary and intentional sharing of power. Full integration, said Jackson, means an opening of hearts and minds, an awakening to the true meaning of equality. It was the logical conclusion of a lifetime of work. If humans are made in God's image, all humans ought to come together, regardless of race of nationality.

"This is the moment of truth for the civil rights movement," said CORE's Floyd McKissick. "Black Power is really going to define what a liberal is. If he doesn't go for it, he's not a friend."

McKissick, who had recently visited Southeast Asia, expressed frustration that Black people, who comprised only 10 percent of the American population, comprised roughly 20 percent of the casualty lists in the Vietnam War. Like King, McKissick said he saw no reason to confine his activism to issues of racial segregation. "Our basic theory is that people must be treated as human beings," he said. "We can't be too narrow and selfish. The fight at home is the fight over there. They're one and the same."

By moving into the North and speaking with increasing force on issues such as peace and poverty, by seeking integration in the fullest terms, King helped the civil rights movement pivot into a wider political movement. He helped invigorate the antiwar movement. And he helped compel new actors, including an ad hoc group of clergy called the National Committee of Negro Churchmen, which took out an advertisement in the July 31, 1966, edition of *The New York Times* embracing SNCC's demands for Black power. The clergymen wrote: "What we see shining through the variety of rhetoric is not anything new but the same old problem of power and race which has faced our beloved country since 1619," when the first enslaved Africans arrived in the English colonies that would become the United States. The call for Black power did not have to mean separation or domination, the clergymen wrote; it meant Black people sought to end the imbalance of power that made white people feel they were justified in getting what they wanted through their accumulated power and while tying "a white noose of suburbia around the necks" of Black people, leaving them all too often poor and unprotected or even persecuted by the unequal application of the law. The letter helped encourage what the theologian James H. Cone called Black liberation theology, a theology "inspired by Martin Luther King and Malcolm X," as Cone put it, a theology that empowered people to "fight for justice as King said and love ourselves as Malcolm said . . . teaching us how to be both unapologetically Black and Christian at the same time."

Once again, King found himself swimming amid the waves of change, compelled by his own determined action as much as by forces working against him. The riots in Chicago made front-page national news, as he had hoped, yet his demands remained unclear. The Black men and women marching with him were not interested in moving into Gage Park anytime soon, but they demanded and risked their lives for the right to do so.

On August 19, Mayor Daley secured a temporary injunction in Cook County Circuit Court that limited King's operations to one march of five hundred people per day. King countered with an announcement of a march on August 28 in the nearby suburb of Cicero, another all-white stronghold. Two days before the scheduled Cicero march, King and Daley met in the Monroe Room at the Palmer House Hotel, along with seventy-seven civic, business, and religious leaders, including the head of the Chicago Real Estate Board, as well as activists and community organizers. They emerged with a deal: King agreed to halt his demonstrations after Daley and the other leaders agreed to a ten-point program designed to end discrimination in housing. The agreement, if taken seriously by city officials, would strengthen enforcement of the city's housing ordinance; compel the Real Estate Board to endorse integration; move the city to build smaller, scattered units of public housing rather than clusters of high-rise units; and bring an end to the discriminatory patterns of housing assignments for families on public welfare. King called it "the most significant program ever conceived to make open housing a reality in the metropolitan area." It would, he said, make possible the "total eradication of housing discrimination."

It would make those things possible, but only with commitment from the city, private businesses, and the federal government. Meanwhile, in Washington, D.C., Senator Everett Dirksen of Illinois all but crushed hopes of passing the fair-housing provision of the president's new civil rights bill, telling a group of religious leaders from Chicago that he deemed a ban on racial discrimination in housing unconstitutional because it interfered with the rights of property owners. "You wouldn't want me to throw my conscience in the Potomac River, would you?" Dirksen asked.

To Chester Robinson of Chicago's West Side Organization, it looked like the city's poor Black people had won nothing but empty promises. He vowed to lead his own march in Cicero.

While Black editorial writers blamed President Johnson for caving in to the real estate lobby and failing to fight for his fair-housing legislation, some white journalists criticized King, saying he had little to show for his Chicago campaign. But if King didn't change Chicago, or Los Angeles for that matter, Chicago and Los Angeles changed King. He began to strike more anti-capitalist themes, saying that America, despite its great wealth, still struggled with poverty and still muddled through endless wars. He sounded more like

Malcolm X, in some ways, calling America a morally sick society. Eliminating Jim Crow was no longer enough, he said, not so long as some people lived in "unbelievable affluence" while others, blocks away, lived in poverty, with "wall to wall rats and roaches" and little hope of escape.

Back at Ebenezer in Atlanta on Sunday, King said the events of the summer had at times left him discouraged. The agreement in Chicago was "a first step in a thousand-mile journey." But it was a journey he had been called by God to make, he said, subtly referring to the night that he had been alone in his kitchen in Montgomery, more than a decade earlier, and heard the voice of God. "I choose to identify with the underprivileged," he said. "I choose to identify with the poor," he said. "I choose to give my life for the hungry . . . This is the way I am going. If it means suffering a little bit, I'm going that way. If it means sacrificing, I'm going that way. If it means dying for them, I'm going that way, because I heard a voice saying, 'Do something for others.'"

43

"Not an Easy Time for Me"

In 1964, in a Gallup public opinion survey, Americans had named King the fourth most admired man in the world, behind Lyndon Johnson, Winston Churchill, and Dwight Eisenhower, and ahead of Robert Kennedy, Billy Graham, and Pope Paul VI. In 1965, he had slipped to sixth place out of ten, and in 1966 he fell off the list entirely. Among the respondents, 63 percent said they viewed King negatively.

At the same time, the popularity of the name Martin, after rising steadily for a decade, took a sharp fall. In 1963, 6,072 American babies had been named Martin. By 1966, the number had fallen by more than 30 percent, to 4,208.

On September 19, the Civil Rights Act of 1966 failed in the U.S. Senate, as reporters had been predicting for weeks. The legislation never came close to securing the votes needed for passage. Afterward, Lyndon Johnson's advisers concluded that the American public would no longer support "big and bold" programs for the benefit of the Black community.

"Don't you find," the journalist Mike Wallace asked King in a television interview, "that the American people are getting a little tired, truly, of the whole civil rights struggle?"

King did not find that to be the case. But he did show signs of his own fatigue. His staff was demoralized. Some of the ministers he usually counted on for support were finding it difficult to back his stance against the war in Vietnam. "They couldn't protest the war *and* do funeral services for soldiers," said Bernard Lafayette Jr. Outbreaks of violence spread around the country, even to the normally tranquil city of Atlanta. King found it more difficult than ever to raise money for SCLC work.

In Grenada, Mississippi, white mobs, angry about school integration, attacked Black children. King traveled there to support the protesters, but the national media gave the story only modest attention. At the same time, *The New York Times* printed a front-page news analysis that said the civil rights movement was in disarray, white liberals were preoccupied with Vietnam, and white moderates were becoming apathetic or hostile to the plight of their Black countrymen. Conservative politicians, including Ronald Reagan, the Republican gubernatorial candidate in California, sought to politicize the white backlash, the *Times* reported, making "riots-in-the-streets" a fear-inducing catchphrase in their campaigns. Conservative politicians accused protesters like King of disrespecting law and order, contributing to waves of crime. Alabama governor George Wallace was said to be planning a new run for the presidency in 1968.

"It is not so much a backlash," said Thomas F. Pettigrew, a social psychologist at Harvard, as an "out from under the rock phenomenon." The hatred, he said, had always been there.

The Yale historian C. Vann Woodward wrote in *Harper's Magazine* that the civil rights movement seemed to be following the same course as Reconstruction: "a rising tide of indignation against an ancient wrong, the slow crumbling of stubborn resistance, the sudden rush and elation of victory—and then . . . the onset of reaction and the fading of high hopes."

The movement spiraled downward. King, in speaking out against Vietnam, may have contributed to a shift in white liberal activism, as increasing numbers of young protesters joined the antiwar movement. President Johnson's preoccupation with the war, too, undercut his commitment and reduced the funding available for his domestic agenda. J. Edgar Hoover's vicious smear campaign raised questions as to whether King could be trusted, while many northern liberals became disenchanted or embittered as protests hit close to home. Many white supporters of the civil rights crusade were repelled by the new, more militant tone of leaders such as Stokely Carmichael. All that "hate whitey talk," as one white activist told the *Times*, was bound to affect white people's attitudes.

King had promised that the nonviolent movement would give rise to a new America. Increasingly, though, Americans doubted that the new America would be a better one. Young people inclined to rebellion turned to the speeches of Malcolm X, the books of Frantz Fanon, and the music of the Rolling Stones. "Violence is a cleansing force," wrote Fanon, a Black psychiatrist who was born in Martinique and participated in the Algerian National Liberation Front's struggle against the French before dying in 1961. "It frees the native from his inferiority complex and from his despair and inaction." His last book, *The Wretched of the Earth*, became essential reading for young radicals.

The number of American deaths in Vietnam tripled in 1966. College students protested in growing numbers. They burned their draft cards and talked of fleeing to Canada. "Make love, not war" became the slogan of the day, a statement against Vietnam as well as a declaration of universal brotherhood. It was a declaration not unlike King's call for a beloved community—except that this one focused less explicitly on racial injustice and did not revolve around the Bible. The new ethos involved sex without fear of procreation. It celebrated cohabitation without need of marriage. It encouraged disdain for authority, especially the authority that fostered war. And it offered escape from the world's earthly woes through mind-altering drugs. For those who were not participating, it often looked like the disintegration of society into hedonism. Suddenly, it wasn't just the Black community in revolt; it was the unwashed, long-haired flower children, too, striving to get beyond the world of white supremacy, materialism, and militarism. "There were tensions galore," wrote the New Left veteran and scholar Todd Gitlin, "between the radical idea of political strategy—with discipline, organization, commitment to results *out there* at a distance—and the countercultural idea of living life to the fullest, *right here*, for oneself . . . and the rest of the world be damned (which it already was)."

That explains, in part, why King and the SCLC found it difficult to raise money from their usual constituents in the North, why King faced growing skepticism in the press, and why he found it increasingly difficult to appeal to the public's sense of morality. This was a time for scorn, a time for distrust, a time when faith seemed old-fashioned, or even naïve. The shifting attitudes had enormous consequences for the civil rights movement, warned one of the SCLC's biggest supporters, Leslie Dunbar, director of the nonprofit Field Foundation. Ongoing cynicism might lead many white people in the North to conclude that the problems of the American Negro were best handled by the police. "That way," Dunbar said, "whites would be able to sleep peacefully in the suburbs and let Negroes riot among themselves."

"This is not an easy time for me," King said in a candid speech to about three hundred radio and television directors in Chicago. "It is not a pleasant or noble time for the civil rights movement. We stand in one of those valley moments now, not on the peak of achievement of a more democratic society."

Having forgotten his prepared remarks, he spoke extemporaneously for twenty-eight minutes. In the past few years, despite important victories in Congress, conditions for the American Negro had deteriorated, he said. Given the situation, he continued, it was no wonder many spoke of the need for Black power. Black people did need power, especially political and economic power, he explained, "for the ghetto is built to contain the Negro in weakness." They needed pride, too, he said, because the "Negro has too long been ashamed of his color, of his hair, of his biological structure." But if "Black power" meant using violence or advocating for separatism, he stood firmly against it, because "God is interested in the freedom of the whole human race, not just one part of it."

At the speech that launched his career in activism, on December 5, 1955, at Holt Street Baptist Church in Montgomery, King had told his audience that the pursuit of justice would not be enough to deliver true freedom to all of God's people, that it would take Christian love to do that. Eleven years later, he said much the same thing, but this time with perspective from his own experiences. "This period did not accomplish everything," he said in the fall of 1966 at the SCLC's retreat in Frogmore, South Carolina, reflecting on the work of the past decade. Legislative and judicial victories, he continued, "did very little" to help poor Black people in the North. New laws and court decisions failed to destroy the roots of American racism, he said, adding that "our society is still structured on the basis of racism."

Most Americans had not been asked to sacrifice for equality. They had not been asked to make reparations for slavery and Jim Crow. They had not addressed or attempted to cure the nation's vast inequalities of wealth and opportunity. The new federal laws had cost most Americans nothing. That would have to change, King said, even if it meant pulling America toward a system of democratic socialism like those found in European countries. But it was no longer clear how many people would join with him on such a path to equality. On Election Day, November 8, 1966, Republicans tilted the balance of political power in Congress, gaining forty-seven seats in the House and three in the Senate, performing especially well in the South. In California, Ronald Reagan won the governorship in a landslide. Former vice president Richard Nixon, positioning for a presidential run in 1968, called the election results "the sharpest rebuff of a president in a generation."

The day after the election, President Johnson phoned his vice president, Hubert Humphrey, to discuss the results. Johnson said he wasn't too discouraged, because Democrats still had solid majorities in the House and Senate. But in listing the reasons why moderate voters seemed to be swinging toward the Republican Party, the president blamed liberals, labor leaders, and "Martin Luther King in Chicago."

On December 14, 1966, *The New York Times* reported that the FBI had been tapping King's phones and listening to his conversations. "Was this done for reasons of national security? Who authorized the taps? We don't know," wrote the columnist James Reston, who broke the story. "What we do know is that information gathered in this manner was discussed with newspaper reporters by high officials of this Government." King told reporters he and his colleagues had assumed for years that their phones were tapped, but he said he didn't know who had tapped them or why.

President Johnson worried that a scandal would erupt if the public learned about the extent of the surveillance, especially the surveillance of King. In a phone call with his adviser Clark Clifford after the news broke in the *Times*, Johnson blamed John Kennedy and Robert Kennedy for the taps, especially Robert. "They got his signature on a tap on Martin Luther King,"

Johnson said, referring to the former attorney general. "It's been going on two, three, four years . . . And the Martin Luther King [material], it'll make a better book than Manchester's if you read the taps." Johnson was referring to William Manchester's *The Death of a President*, a highly anticipated book about the assassination of John F. Kennedy. "And I would think it would really rock a good many people." Johnson said he opposed FBI wiretaps, unless they were vital to national security. In the case of King, he said: "It's pretty hard to tie him in with the security of the nation."

Johnson was being disingenuous, covering himself in case of scandal. Clearly, both he and Hoover had enjoyed the fruits of the King surveillance, and Johnson had continued to receive frequent memos on King from Hoover and the FBI's Deke DeLoach. Though the reports never documented that King posed any threat to national security, as Johnson acknowledged, they nonetheless treated King like a criminal. King felt the effects. He lived under constant scrutiny and threat of exposure for his personal conduct; saw his reputation tarnished as more reporters received tips about his private life; and had his relationship with the president tainted, perhaps damaging his effectiveness as an activist. If, as he claimed, Johnson "never wanted it done," he had done a poor job conveying his wishes.

The day after news of the taps appeared in the *Times*, King testified before a U.S. Senate subcommittee. He made no mention of the surveillance. Instead, he accused the government of "squandering" money on war and manned space flight while spending minuscule amounts to fight poverty and racism. King read a forty-four-page statement in which he repeatedly linked Vietnam to civil rights. "The security we profess to seek in foreign adventures," he said, "we will lose in our decaying cities. The bombs in Vietnam explode at home; they destroy the hopes and possibilities for a decent America."

The vast majority of poor people still had hope, he said, but that hope would disappear and violence would fill the void if conditions did not improve. "I am now convinced," he said, "that the simplest approach will prove to be the most revolutionary—the solution to poverty is to abolish it directly by a . . . guaranteed annual income." The idea was not so radical. In fact, three years later, President Richard Nixon would come close to enacting a plan to give every family of four a guaranteed annual income of $1,600, a move that had the support of more than a thousand American economists. Why hadn't it yet been done? King faulted racism. Most of white society cared more for tranquility than for justice. It was easier to ignore the plight of Black Americans than to deal with it. "The attainment of security and equality for Negroes has not yet become a serious and irrevocable national purpose," he said. "I doubt there ever was a sincere and unshakable commitment to this end."

The civil rights movement, he said, in conclusion, had not done enough. Too often, he and others in the movement had focused on the middle class, neglecting the poor, particularly in the North. In the process, the nation had raised people's hopes without fulfilling them, leaving "deep frustration and the deep sense of alienation." For all the work and all the gains of the past decade, he said, "America as a nation has never yet committed itself to solving the problems of its Negro citizens." And the nation never would make that commitment, he said, unless leaders in Washington concluded that "no lesser alternative is possible."

For Christmas, the King and Abernathy children staged a performance of the fairy tale "Sleeping Beauty" for their parents. A week later, King flew to Los Angeles, where he hoped to rest and begin work on a new book. But he faced frequent interruptions. Antiwar activists phoned to ask him to deliver a major speech on Vietnam. Others appealed to him to launch a third-party bid for president in 1968. SCLC budget and personnel issues continued to nag at him.

Less than two weeks later, on January 14, his suitcases loaded with books, King departed for Ocho Rios in Jamaica, where he would stay in a villa with no phone. Bernard Lee accompanied him. At the airport, King bought a copy of the left-wing magazine *Ramparts*, the cover bearing an image of Christ's body on the cross in what appeared to be a battlefield in Vietnam. The magazine contained a special section of photographs of hungry, abandoned, and wounded Vietnamese children. "Torn flesh, splintered bones, screaming agony are bad enough," read one photo caption. "But perhaps most heart-rending of all are the tiny faces and bodies scorched and seared by fire."

A few days later, King and Lee were joined in Jamaica by King's secretary, Dora McDonald. King hoped to use his Jamaican respite to write three thousand words a day for the new book, one he would call *Where Do We Go from Here: Chaos or Community?* McDonald would type her boss's handwritten pages and send them to Levison in New York for review. Coretta joined her husband for the final week of the three-week working vacation. At one point during that final week, a reporter and photographer for *Ebony* visited, producing a seven-page spread with photos of King swimming in the pool, walking on the beach in dress shoes and slacks, and eating breakfast with Coretta. The *Ebony* reporter assured readers that Ralph Abernathy and Andrew Young were maintaining SCLC operations in King's absence and noted that "nobody deserved a vacation more than MLK."

When he returned to Atlanta, King told advisers he was determined to oppose the Vietnam War more forcefully, even if it ruptured his relationship with President Johnson and cost the SCLC support. He didn't intend to abandon the cause of civil rights, he said. In fact, he hoped that his antiwar activity might unite peace activists and civil rights activists in a larger movement that pressed the government to end racism, poverty, and war. At the very least, he would be true to his principles. All along, he'd been saying that nonviolence was more than a strategy to him, that it was a guiding principle, a core belief rooted in his religious faith. Had his friends and advisers not believed him? Had they not understood the depth of his commitment? "I don't see getting out of the civil rights," he said in a telephone conference call with advisers, "but we could be much more successful if we could get the peace people to do it, to cooperate, to have a march on Washington around the cutbacks to the poverty programs. All the communities are mad because they have been cut back. You still have a civil rights issue there. The break with the administration is the difference and that is the point we have to come to."

He had no plan yet for how to unite the loose strands of American activists. Meanwhile, *The New York Times* published yet another front-page story, in February 1967, saying the civil rights movement had "collapsed" and found itself in a "last-ditch battle for survival in its few remaining spheres of influence." Offices had been abandoned. Street protests had dried up. Civil rights workers in the South had become an endangered species. Andrew Young told the *Times* reporter that SCLC donations were off 40 percent from a year earlier, in part because many donors lost interest when the SCLC became active in the North. When Young went to the Ford Foundation in search of grant money to make up for those lost donations, a foundation official replied harshly in a letter: "What you would like to accomplish is laudatory, but I was left with a small degree of skepticism, doubtless resulting from my past observations of somewhat related projects where the impact was relatively insignificant for the costs involved." What the foundation wanted to see, the executive wrote, was a five-year plan and an overall strategy with measurable targets that would represent "SCLC's full thrust."

King understood that his focus on Vietnam exacerbated the SCLC's problems. In the history of the United States, no protest leader had enjoyed as much access to the president of the United States as King had to Johnson. But King and Johnson hadn't met in almost a year. King had passed on two invitations, perhaps because of his disdain for confrontation, but also perhaps because his conscience would not allow him to cooperate with an advocate and purveyor of war.

On February 25, making his first public appearance in two months, King spoke at a conference in Los Angeles sponsored by *The Nation*, the liberal magazine. "When I see our country today intervening in what is basically a civil war, destroying hundreds of thousands of Vietnamese children with napalm, leaving broken bodies in countless fields and sending home half-men, mutilated, mentally and physically; when I see the recalcitrant unwillingness of our government to create the atmosphere for a negotiated settlement of this awful conflict . . . I tremble for our world."

In March, King and the noted pediatrician Benjamin Spock led an antiwar march through Chicago. King's advisers continued to discourage his Vietnam protests, saying he had already damaged his effectiveness as a champion of civil rights. In a March 25 phone call, Levison told King that Norman Cousins, editor of the *Saturday Review,* had decided he would no longer publish King's work. Cousins called the peace movement a "Hate America" movement, according to Levison, and went on to predict that "King and the SCLC would be mud within six months" if they persisted in opposing the war. King said he didn't care.

"I was telling Andy [Young] tonight that at times you do things to satisfy your conscience and they may be altogether unrealistic or wrong tactically, but you feel better," King told Levison. "I just know, on the war in Vietnam, I will get a lot of criticism and I know I can hurt SCLC. But I feel better, and I think that is the most important thing." If he didn't feel good about himself, he told Levison, he would be no good to the SCLC or any other cause. His whole identity was wrapped up in his work and in his beliefs. There could be no moral compromises. "I feel so deep in my heart that we are so wrong in this country," he explained, "and the time has come for a real prophecy, and I am willing to go that road."

When King told his advisers that he planned to speak out against the war at a big event on April 15 in New York organized by James Bevel and a group called the Spring Mobilization Committee, the advisers expressed concern. Some of the other speakers were more radical than King; he might not wish to be associated with them. The advisers discussed having King speak first and leave immediately after his remarks. Then they hit on another idea: for King to be the sole speaker at an event on April 4 at Riverside Church sponsored by a group called Clergy and Laymen Concerned About Vietnam. The move was a gamble: King might receive even more attention in the press than he would have at the April 15 rally, but he would have a better chance to clearly convey his message and control the tone of the event. King's speech would be followed by a panel discussion with the rabbi Abraham Joshua Heschel; the Reverend John C. Bennett, president of the Union Theological Seminary; and the historian Henry Steele Commager.

King continued to do civil rights work, but he received less attention for it, and the FBI continued to undermine his efforts, focusing more on his antiwar activity than his sexual encounters in a steady stream of memos to the White House. On March 8, an internal FBI memo reported that King wanted to "direct his entire efforts in opposition to the war in Vietnam." The FBI report said King had grown "very sensitive" about his failure in Chicago and his loss of "appeal to the ghetto Negro." The agent writing the memo suggested King's confidence could be further undermined by planting questions with a bureau-friendly reporter who would publish an article explaining that King's views closely paralleled those of the Communist Party.

On March 29, King traveled to Louisville, Kentucky, where he helped lead a march in support of fairness in housing and met for ninety minutes with Muhammad Ali, who was, at the time, engaged in a struggle to avoid the draft. "My prayers, my sacrifices, my life and my death are all for Allah," Ali told reporters. "If I thought reporting and joining the war and possibly dying would help bring freedom, justice, and equality to 22 million so-called Negroes here, you would not have to draft me. I would join tomorrow." King, who seldom cracked a smile when speaking to reporters, loosened up with Ali. When a reporter asked the men what they had discussed in their private meeting, Ali jumped in before King could answer: "Nothing," he said. "We're just friends, just like Khrushchev and Kennedy . . . whatever went [on] back here is our business."

King laughed. Asked if he agreed, he said, "Oh, yes, yes, we had a very good discussion."

Though Ali and the Nation of Islam called for separation of the races, not integration, Ali added: "We're all Black brothers. We use different approaches to our everyday problems, but the same dog that bit him bit me. When we go out, they don't ask [if] you're a Christian, a Catholic, a Baptist, or a Muslim. They just start whupping Black heads."

At the SCLC's board meeting that week in Louisville, King asked the organization to issue a strong, formal statement of opposition to Johnson's war policies. The board declined. But King pressed on, preparing for his speech at Riverside Church. King often relied on friends and colleagues to compose first drafts of his speeches. For this one, he turned to Vincent Harding, a history professor working at Spelman College. Harding attended church services at Ebenezer, where King's sermons made it clear he opposed the war "from a deeply Christian perspective," and had opposed it since the earliest days of American involvement in Vietnam, Harding recalled. In the summer of 1965, Harding began studying the history of Vietnam. Later the same year, he had written notes on the conflict to help King prepare for his meeting with U.S. ambassador Arthur Goldberg at the United Nations. He had also written King's earlier antiwar speech, delivered in Los Angeles. Even before he conferred with King about the Riverside speech, Harding said he understood how the civil rights and antiwar movements were united in King's vision. He contemplated what he called King's fundamental identity: "What does it mean to be a follower of Jesus, the peacemaker, who called others to be peacemakers . . . ? What does it mean to take seriously this whole idea that our national identity . . . is secondary to our spiritual identity?" Muhammad Ali had raised the same kind of questions when he had declared that "no Viet Cong ever called me nigger." Harding had heard King ask the question many times: "Children of God, where do you stand? Where do you stand in relation to your own country? Where do you stand in relation to sufferings and oppressions of the world? And where do you stand in relationship to our country's contribution to those sufferings?"

Harding produced most of the speech. King's friend John David Maguire, a professor of religion at Wesleyan University, contributed a section. King gave them an outline but appears to have done little if any of the writing.

Days before the Riverside Church speech, American newspapers published the latest casualty reports from the war. An average of 160 American soldiers were dying each week, according to the Pentagon, compared to 1,800 enemy soldiers per week, although American journalists covering the war cast doubt on the reliability of those numbers. Meanwhile, a new report from the National Advisory Commission on Selective Service concluded that Black men were far more likely than white men to be drafted, placed in combat units, and killed. A story in *The Washington Post* reported that Black men serving in Vietnam had been emboldened by their experiences in the war to demand equal rights when they got back home. "I better not be turned down for anything because of race . . . not after this crap," said one wounded soldier, a Black man named Curtis Leathers, as he lay in a battlefield surgical hospital. "If I'm qualified, I better get it."

Arriving in New York, King spoke first at a press conference. "Twice as many Negroes as whites are in combat" relative to their proportion of the American population, he told the reporters, adding that the numbers were "a reflection of the Negro's position in America." He urged "all white people of good will" who were eligible for the draft to boycott the war by becoming conscientious objectors. He also encouraged clergymen of draft age to give up their ministerial exemptions and become conscientious objectors. He called for a nationwide campaign of teach-ins and preach-ins to educate Americans about the evils of the Vietnam War. He was not just giving his opinion on the war anymore; he was suggesting a course of rebellion; he was engaging in a political protest that was certain to make headlines and further anger President Johnson.

After the press conference, King had dinner at Union Seminary with Andrew Young, Rabbi Heschel, Reverend Bennett, and about twenty others. While he ate, King removed a copy of his speech from his breast pocket, read through it, and made notes in the margins. Richard Fernandez, executive secretary of the group that sponsored the speech, looked on in awe. Fernandez had made the arrangements with Young to get advance copies of the speech for the press, knew when and how it had been completed, and felt certain that King was seeing the completed work for the first time. After less than fifteen minutes of reading and revising, King put the speech back in his pocket and continued eating.

More than three thousand people packed the church, which was modeled after the thirteenth-century Chartres Cathedral in France, its twenty-story tower rising over the Hudson River as "a beacon to the world." Many people stood outside, unable to get in. The crowd greeted King with a standing ovation.

"I come to this magnificent house of worship tonight because my conscience leaves me no other choice," he said. He read without breaking from his script, without dramatic gestures, without his usual range of dynamics and tone. He read with a sense of deliberateness, one that suggested that he had come not to lift members of his audience but to push them.

For two years, he said, he had struggled to overcome the betrayal of his own silence on Vietnam. Many people asked him why he chose to speak out against the war. Wasn't he damaging the civil rights campaign? He understood the question, he said, but he nevertheless felt dismayed that his friends and allies didn't really know him, didn't understand the depth of his dedication, the sincerity of his religious calling, didn't truly understand the world in which they lived.

He explained how the path from Dexter Avenue Baptist Church in Montgomery led him to this place. He explained how recent scenes of violence in Los Angeles and Chicago had tortured him, because, as he spoke to angry young Black men in those cities and pleaded with them to remain nonviolent, they challenged him with a difficult question: "What about Vietnam?" If America can use violence to solve its problems, they asked, why shouldn't we?

> Their questions hit home, and I knew that I could never again raise my voice against the violence of the oppressed in the ghettos without having first spoken clearly to the greatest purveyor of violence in the world today—my own government. For the sake of those boys, for the sake of this government, for the sake of the hundreds of thousands trembling under our violence, I cannot be silent.

He talked about the disproportionate casualties borne by Black soldiers. He talked about the money that might have been spent on Johnson's Great Society programs rather than on bombs. But he went further—further than he had gone in any of his other antiwar speeches, tying together themes he had been exploring much of his life, themes that suffused his work as a minister, as a boycott leader, as an advocate of nonviolent resistance. He asked his audience to consider the perspective of a peasant in Vietnam, and to recognize that the peasant's life held as much meaning and value as their own.

He came this day, he said, to speak for those peasants, for the voiceless, for those who had lost their families, their villages, their land, their hopes. *We* have done this, he said. *We* have corrupted and killed our brothers and sisters in Vietnam.

Americans like to frame their wars in simple terms, he continued: us against them, capitalism against communism, democracy against totalitarianism. But America once stood as a world symbol of revolution and freedom. Now, the nation found itself in the business of squashing revolution and crushing freedom. He urged his listeners to broaden their view of moral solidarity, to consider the other's point of view, to see and accept our own weaknesses and errors.

King presented another dream, a bigger dream, a more challenging one than he had offered to the masses in 1963 before the Lincoln Memorial in Washington, D.C. It was a dream he had been exploring since his days as a seminarian at Crozer Theological Seminary, when Nietzsche had made him doubt whether Christian love could change the world and when Gandhi had helped him overcome those doubts, when he had become convinced that God intended human beings to achieve solidarity, to love one another, to take responsibility for one another. He had said it in 1963, when he praised the white people who had participated in the March on Washington. "They have come to realize that their freedom is inextricably bound to our freedom," he had said that glorious summer day.

He said it again now, in even grander terms, as he reached the conclusion of his latest speech. To think beyond race, class, and nation meant giving unconditional love to all mankind, he said. This is what God calls on us to do. This is what God expects of us. Should we give up? Should we say it's too hard? That it is not realistic? He continued:

> Or will there be another message—of longing, of hope, of solidarity . . . whatever the cost? The choice is ours.

44

A Revolution of Values

ALMOST OVERNIGHT, KING became the nation's most famous opponent of a war that had the approval of an overwhelming majority of Americans. Newspaper editorials questioned not only his patriotism but even his commitment to civil rights.

The New York Times wrote that it was "both wasteful and self-defeating" for King to focus on Vietnam. *The Washington Post* warned that many of those who respected King "will never again accord him the same confidence." *Life* magazine called his speech "a demagogic slander that sounded like a script for Radio Hanoi." Even *The Pittsburgh Courier*, a reliable supporter through the years, warned that King "does not speak for all Negro America and besides he is tragically misleading them." Leaders of the NAACP warned that King's statement would be interpreted by many Black Americans as an attempted fusion of the civil rights and peace movements, and that such an interpretation would accelerate what already appeared to be declining interest in the fight for racial equality. Barry Goldwater said King's conduct came close to treason.

Even Stanley Levison expressed disappointment, although he seemed to place the blame in part on King's speechwriters.

"I am troubled by this speech of yours," Levison told King in a call recorded by the FBI, "because I thought you were trying to bring together too many complex ideas . . . The speech was not balanced. This speech did not typify your expression on this subject. I do not think it was a good expression of you, but apparently you think it was."

"Well," King answered, "it was probably politically unwise, but I will not agree that I was morally unwise. I figure I was politically unwise but morally wise. I think I have a role to play which may be unpopular . . . I don't know if careful thinking would have made me revise the speech."

"I feel that the whole speech was not a typical analysis that you would make," Levison said.

King admitted that not all the words were his own. "But I spent the whole afternoon thinking about this speech," he said, "and I thought I had to say something."

In the days ahead, pounded by waves of criticism, King told his advisers he felt misunderstood and unfairly attacked. He suggested arranging a meeting with some of his critics, including Roy Wilkins, Ralph Bunche, and Whitney Young. King worried, as he said in a recorded phone call with Levison and Harry Wachtel, that his critics would "take this opportunity to say that I failed in Chicago." Answered Wachtel: "They may even pull J. Edgar Hoover's old stuff out of the bottom of the bag."

Hoover did seize on the opportunity, writing falsely in a letter to Johnson that Levison, the so-called communist, had written King's speech. Hoover compared King's Vietnam policy to the "propaganda line which the Communist Party USA" pushed.

Johnson reacted in "cold anger," as his press secretary George Christian put it. The president, said Christian, had grown "coldly contemptuous of Martin Luther King."

Johnson struck back at King, sending word to the Black syndicated columnist Carl Rowan that Rowan should publish an article stating that King's antiwar speech had hurt the civil rights movement. Rowan did just that, writing an article that appeared in *Reader's Digest*, one of the nation's top-selling magazines. "Why did King reject the advice of his old civil-rights colleagues?" the article asked. "Some say it was a matter of ego—that he was convinced that since he was the most influential Negro in the United States, President Johnson would *have* to listen to him . . . Others revived a more sinister speculation . . . talk of communists influencing the actions and words of the young minister." Rowan went on to say that King had given Americans Black and white reason to question his loyalty and that he had permanently damaged his ability to lead. "By urging Negroes not to respond to the draft or to fight in Vietnam," Rowan wrote, "he has taken a tack that many Americans of all races consider utterly irresponsible."

King would not back down. On April 15, he helped lead the Spring Mobilization Committee's massive march in New York City, one of the biggest antiwar protests the nation had seen. King said the crowd that day looked even bigger than the one assembled for the 1963 March on Washington. He walked at the front of the throng, along with Harry Belafonte, Dr. Benjamin Spock, Floyd McKissick, Stokely Carmichael, and others. Marchers chanted "Hell no, we won't go!" and "Hey, hey, LBJ, how many kids did you kill today?" Demonstrators burned their draft cards. Others carried daffodils and chanted "Flower Power!" Protesters waved signs reading "Stop the Bombing" and "No Vietnamese Ever Called Me Nigger." Standing in front of the United Nations building, King said: "I would like to urge students from colleges all over the nation to use this summer and coming summers educating and organizing communities across the nation against war."

While Martin spoke in New York, Coretta addressed a crowd of about fifty thousand at an antiwar rally in San Francisco, where *The New York Times* noted that many of the young people in attendance wore "West Coast 'hippie' hair styles . . . bell-bottom trousers and turtleneck sweaters." In her speech, Coretta King called Lyndon Johnson an "uncertain president." She aimed her remarks at the president when she pleaded: "For God's sake, stop the bombing."

The week after the huge march in New York, King told Levison he had been in the hospital briefly for a series of tests. Doctors said he was fine, but King said he had been hoping they might order him to rest for a few weeks.

There was no rest in sight. King took to the road again in late April, visiting Cleveland, Berkeley, and Cambridge, Massachusetts. The journalist David Halberstam tagged along for ten days, conducting interviews for a profile in *Harper's Magazine*. He found his subject "elusive, formal, gracious, distant." Halberstam witnessed at least one tender moment, however. One day in Atlanta, when King took his children swimming at a friend's house, Bernice fell and scraped her knee. King grabbed a piece of chicken as he tried to comfort her. "Let's put some fried chicken on that," he said playfully. "Yes, a little piece of chicken, that's always the best thing for a cut."

But, for the most part, Halberstam described a fraught and anxious man. "Being with him," the journalist wrote, "is like being with a Presidential candidate after a long campaign; he has been through it all . . . King on the inside seems the same as King on the outside—always solemn, always confident, convinced that there is a right way and that he is following it; always those dark, interchangeable suits; the serious shirt and responsible tie."

Halberstam asked if King had moved closer to the philosophy of Malcolm X. Though King said he would never embrace Black separatism, he acknowledged that his approach had changed. "For years, I labored with the idea of reforming the existing institutions of the society, a little change here, a little change there," he said. "Now I feel quite differently. I think you've got to have a reconstruction of the entire society, a revolution of values." Specifically, King said, that might mean the nationalization of certain industries, a massive campaign of urban economic revitalization, and a guaranteed income.

King also said his view of white Americans had changed. After his experience in Chicago, after seeing how white people in the North resisted appeals to integrate their schools and neighborhoods, he had concluded that only a small part of white America supported racial justice.

"Most Americans," he said, "are unconscious racists."

If King seemed more radical now than he had in the past, he still didn't seem radical enough for many. "He's got one foot in the cotton field and one in the White House," an anonymous SNCC worker told a *Newsweek* reporter.

King predicted the summer of 1967 would bring more riots if changes weren't made, but the trouble began sooner than he thought. On May 2, 1967, about thirty young Black men and women carried rifles into the California state capitol building in Sacramento to protest a proposed bill to ban carrying loaded weapons in public. The protesters were members of the Black Panther Party for Self-Defense, a group founded to patrol the streets of Oakland. Its founders, Huey Newton and Bobby Seale, said white police departments were not protecting Black people so much as containing, oppressing, and brutalizing them, which is why Black people needed the right to carry weapons.

"Political power comes through the barrel of a gun," said Newton, who described himself to reporters as an admirer of Malcolm X, W. E. B. Du Bois, Stokely Carmichael, and the slave rebellion leader Nat Turner. "We do not believe in passive and nonviolent tactics," he said. "They haven't worked for us Black people. They are bankrupt."

Violence erupted that summer in Buffalo, Newark, Minneapolis, Detroit, Cincinnati, Milwaukee, Boston, Washington, D.C., and other cities. Dozens were killed, hundreds jailed. Arsonists torched hundreds of buildings in predominantly poor Black neighborhoods. A congressional investigation reported that there had been seventy-six riots in the first nine months of the year. Between 1965 and 1967, the report said, 118 civilians and 12 law enforcement officers had been killed in the unrest, while almost 29,000 people, the vast majority of them Black men, had been arrested.

H. Rap Brown, the new chairman of SNCC, urged Black people to "wage guerilla war on the honkie white man." The controversial U.S. representative Adam Clayton Powell Jr. called violence "a cleansing force" and "a necessary phase of the black revolution." In Detroit, the federal government sent troops to patrol the streets. In Newark, participants in the Conference on Black Power adopted a resolution to initiate a national dialogue on "the desirability of partitioning the U.S. into two separate and independent nations, one to be a homeland for white and the other to be a homeland for black Americans." The authors of the resolution concluded that Black and white Americans had lost hope in the possibility of a successful union, that the future promised only more suffering, that the best option now was separation. The measure passed to thundering applause. Wrote Robert S. Browne, one of the initiative's supporters: "There is an excellent chance that, following partition, neither nation would be overtly racist. The basis for the present racial animosity would be largely removed by the very act of separation. Reciprocal tourism might very well become a leading industry for both nations."

King's new book bore the perfect title for these days of rage: *Where Do We Go from Here: Chaos or Community?* Unfortunately, many book critics concluded that King no longer possessed the answer to his question. "Martin Luther King once had the ability to talk to people, the power to change them by evoking images of revolution," wrote Andrew Kopkind in *The New York Review of Books.* "But the duty of a revolutionary is to make revolutions (say those who have done it), and King made none. By his own admission, things are worse in the U.S. today—for white people and black—than when he began the bus boycott in Montgomery eleven years ago . . . The fault is no more King's than it is ours, though no less, either. He has been outstripped by his times, overtaken by the events which he may have obliquely helped to produce but could not predict. He is not likely to regain command."

Kopkind's brutish review reflected a trend in the left-wing press toward nihilism and sanctimony. To Kopkind, who embraced a kind of revolutionary anarchy, it seemed as if King had lost the support of white liberals and now found himself wandering here and there, right, left, and further left, scoring victories nowhere, failing to read the mood of his audience, failing to appreciate that his invocations of Christianity struck many as passé or weak. *Where Do We Go from Here*, Kopkind wrote, sounded as if it were meant to be "read aloud in suburban synagogues." That was meant as the ultimate insult. King's career in civil rights had been predicated on the assumption that America would eventually absorb its underclass and its alienated people and grant them first-class citizenship. Now it was clear that America would do no such thing, not at that time, maybe not ever. The civil rights movement was dead. Liberalism was dead, too. "There are few mourners," Kopkind wrote.

But King did not share the growing cynicism that captured many left-wing book critics, and he *did* mourn. He expressed his sadness in calls with his friends and supporters. He said he had seen up close the frustration among poor Black people, especially in the cities, and he was pained but not surprised by the explosion of their anger. "There were dark days before, but this is the darkest," he told Wachtel. His calls for nonviolence were clearly not resonating as they once had.

Yet he continued to grasp for solutions. "I've been trying to think of a way to make a major statement about riots and where our country is going," he told Levison in a recorded call on July 19. "It may be done at a press conference, but it must be done in a dramatic kind of way. I haven't decided how but it can't be merely condemning the riots. It's got to be condemning the intolerable conditions leading to them, and the fact that not enough is being done."

On July 25, King sent a telegram to Johnson, saying the violence coursing through the nation's cities represented "a blind revolt against the revolting conditions which you so courageously set out to remedy." King called it an emergency and urged Johnson to promote legislation to guarantee jobs. But the president ignored him. In fact, on the same day that King sent his telegram, J. Edgar Hoover spoke to the president to present more evidence of what he deemed to be King's dangerously conspiratorial behavior.

"Mr. President," Hoover said in a recorded call, "I just got word that Martin Luther King will give a press conference at 11 this morning in Atlanta. Now, the statement King is going to make will differ very greatly from what Roy Wilkins and what Whitney Young has said and will, in a sense, condone the national result from the inhuman conditions that the Negroes are forced to exist in the country. King . . . was told by Levison, who is his principal adviser and who's a secret communist, that he has more to gain nationally by agreeing with the violence . . . , as the president is afraid at this time and is willing to make concessions for it."

Hoover suggested that King condoned rioting. The FBI director also told the president that King had inside information about a plan to set fires in Chicago's Loop.

"King said that the worst has not yet happened in this country in such places as Cleveland, Oakland, and Philadelphia," Hoover said.

Johnson thanked the FBI director and told him to keep watching the troublemakers.

In private conversations, Johnson made it clear that he no longer saw

King as an ally. "I think we're in more danger from these left-wing influences now than we've ever been in the thirty-seven years I've been here," he told former president Dwight Eisenhower.

The war in Vietnam had come to dominate Johnson's presidency. He defended his decision that summer to send more troops to Vietnam, soon bringing the total to 525,000. More than 12,000 American soldiers had already been killed and about 75,000 wounded. The United States was spending about $2 billion a month on the war. "And yet," reported *The New York Times* from Vietnam that summer, "in the opinion of most disinterested observers, the war is not going well. Victory is not close at hand. It is clearly unlikely in the next year or even the next two years. American officers talk somberly about fighting here for decades."

King repeatedly made the connection between the war in Vietnam and the riots in America. But he increasingly felt as if no one was listening to him. In an August 22 phone call, he told Levison he refused to pay attention to those who told him he should return to what he had done best, which was fighting segregation in the South. His new idea, King said, was to launch a major "dramatization of the poverty problem," perhaps in Washington, D.C., a campaign that would pressure the Johnson administration to deliver legislation to eliminate slums and provide jobs and health care for all. If President Johnson would fight a war on poverty *instead* of a war in Vietnam, countless thousands of lives would be saved.

Soon after that conversation, King told his staff that these troubled times called for a new kind of civil disobedience. He proposed a direct confrontation with the federal government, a massive occupation of Washington, one that would "cripple the operations of an oppressive society." It was a radical, militant plan, but it was also a plan that broke from the confines of Black versus white, Black power versus Freedom Now. It was a plan that reflected King's refusal to accept limits in his quest for community. But he offered no details on how such a protest might work. In the meantime, Coretta said, his moods grew darker than ever. A series of fundraising concerts flopped, despite appearances by Harry Belafonte, Joan Baez, and Sammy Davis Jr. The Supreme Court denied King a new hearing on a 1963 contempt charge from

Birmingham, which meant he would soon have to spend another five days in jail.

"He felt that, somehow, he had to have . . . a solution," Coretta said. "He knew that people would be turning to him for solutions and answers, and this bothered him because he had not come up with a creative solution . . . I remember during that summer, it must have been in August . . . , he got very depressed and in a state of depression [that] was greater than I had ever seen it before over the riots. He said people expect me to have answers and I don't have any answers. He said I don't feel like talking to people. I don't have anything to tell them."

One day, when he missed a flight, he told Coretta he had missed it because, deep down, he didn't want to make the trip.

"I get tired of going and not having any answers," he said.

"He had begun to take this very personally," Coretta recalled.

She tried to boost his spirits. "You mustn't believe that people are losing faith in you," she said. "There are millions of people who have faith in you and believe in you and feel that you are our best hope." She added: "I believe in you, if that means anything."

"Yes," he said. "That means a great deal."

"Somehow, you've got to pull yourself out of this and go on," she said.

"I don't have any answers," he said.

"Well," she said, "somehow the answers will come. I'm sure they will."

45

Please Come to Memphis

Two aspiring politicians in Memphis were desperate for King's help. Both were Black and running for office against white incumbents after a summer of violence that required three thousand members of the Tennessee National Guard to quell. They sent a telegram to King:

1 OCTOBER 1967

DR ML KING

234 SUNSET AVE ATL

DEAR MARTIN

WILL COUNT IT URGENT THAT YOU COME TO MEMPHIS TO HELP
US PUT OVER OUR CRUSADE ... PLEASE COME. WE DARE NOT
TAKE NO FOR AN ANSWER.

King did not make the trip. A. W. Willis and the Reverend James Lawson lost their bids for local offices by wide margins.

In five months, Lawson would again summon King to Memphis, and this time King would come.

Unknown to King, or Lawson, the FBI was drafting a long letter to all its field offices, laying out the long-term goals of the bureau's counterintelligence operation for "Black Nationalist Hate Groups." Among the bureau's stated goals, according to the letter: "Prevent the rise of a 'messiah' who could unify, and electrify, the militant black nationalist movement. Malcolm X might have been such a 'messiah'; he is the martyr of the movement today. Martin Luther King, Stokely Carmichael and Elijah Muhammad all aspire to this position. Elijah Muhammad is less of a threat because of his age. King could be a very real contender for this position should he abandon his supposed 'obedience' to 'white, liberal doctrines' (nonviolence) and embrace black nationalism."

Field offices would be instructed to exploit conflicts between Black groups, gather information on the "unsavory backgrounds" of leaders, and use the news media to discredit those leaders. King, the FBI letter said, should be considered one of the operation's "primary targets."

Ten days after King declined Lawson's first request to come to Memphis, a television crew arrived at King's house on Sunset Avenue in Atlanta, hoping to document his domestic life. The interviewer asked King why he had no security for his family, considering that a bomb or a bullet could come through his window at any moment.

King answered calmly, without hesitation. "We don't have any fences around for protective purposes," he said. "I don't have any armed bodyguards. I guess it grows out of a philosophy that I have. I'm absolutely committed to this struggle for racial justice and for brotherhood. I guess every day I live under the threat of death, and I had to come to the conclusion that something *could* happen, but I couldn't allow this possibility to immobilize me. And I think ultimately freedom *does* mean fearlessness."

It was a Wednesday, probably late in the afternoon since the children were not in school. King wore his usual uniform: black suit, white shirt, black tie. Coretta wore a bright orange dress. Yolanda, Marty, Dexter, and Bernice were all dressed neatly and behaving nervously for the camera. After being interviewed in the living room, King and the children moved to the backyard, where Dexter and Bernice played on a swing set and Marty and Yolanda shot a basketball.

When the television interviewer asked Yolanda what she wanted to be when she grew up, she giggled, stuck out her tongue, and said she might like to be a Broadway actress.

When Marty was asked the same question, he answered quickly: "A preacher!"

"Just like your father?" the interviewer asked the boy, who was almost ten.

"Yes."

"You think you'll carry on the same kind of work that he's doing?"

"Yes."

Marty handed his father the basketball. King looked toward the hoop, bent his knees, and hoisted an awkward underhand shot that rattled off the rim.

"I *almost* made it," he said with a chuckle.

For six weeks, King's missed shots reverberated. The civil rights movement remained stalled, if not broken down—broken down by racism that was hardly unique to the South. King had been saying it all along, saying that American democracy remained an unkept promise. The movement had forced the nation to address some of its inequities and merely exposed others. The same liberals who helped fight Jim Crow in the South declined to address issues of job discrimination, housing segregation, and police assaults on Black communities in the North. These conditions would not change, the arc of justice would not bend toward freedom, without continuous pressure, "without a radical reconstruction of society itself." So far, King said, America had not changed because so many Americans thought it did not need to change, that Black Americans would retreat from their fight for full equality. This, King said, "is the illusion of the damned."

King continued to preach through the fall of 1967, continued to speak out strongly, continued to pray, until, finally, he saw the way forward: he would help foment a confrontation too big and too volatile to be ignored.

On December 4, 1967, King held a press conference at Ebenezer church. Outside, Auburn Avenue's once-bustling business district now offered run-down restaurants, boarded-up shops, and vacant lots. The floors of the old church King's grandfather built were worn. The painted white walls had taken on a grayish tinge. King stepped to a bank of microphones and announced his plan: Four months from today, in the spring of 1968, the SCLC would lead a nonviolent army of poor people to Washington, D.C. It would become known as the Poor People's Campaign. Protesters would build a shantytown on public land, within sight of the White House and Capitol, and they would engage in acts of civil disobedience to disrupt the operation of the city and the federal government. The shantytown army would recruit, welcome, and train poor people from around the country to join the protest. And those people—all of them—would stay in Washington as long as necessary to compel the federal government to address the issues afflicting America's poor and weak, until the nation agreed to a radical redistribution of wealth.

King called this mobilization a "last non-violent approach to give the nation a chance to respond." He added: "God only knows what will happen if there is no response."

Privately, King seemed torn about how much emphasis to place on Vietnam that day. In his prepared remarks for the media, he mentioned the war twice, but he omitted those references as he read his statement.

When reporters asked, he said he planned to attack both poverty and the "unjust war." Though the protest in Washington would focus primarily on addressing the concerns of the poor, antiwar demonstrators would be welcome to participate, as would Black power advocates, so long as they remained nonviolent. He hoped to make this demonstration diverse, he said, with poor people from every racial group and every region of the country, as well as the "swelling masses of young people" who had grown disenchanted with American materialism and militarism. This was a chance to expand the struggle, to create something new, and perhaps to change the basic fabric of American life.

King knew it was risky. The SCLC was short on money and manpower. It had never organized anything so complicated. The effort would prove a personal test for King, too. Though he still had the respect of the vast majority of Black Americans, it was not clear whether he maintained the power to move a significant portion of white people. If the new campaign failed, he would take the blame. His influence would be further diminished. "If this means scorn or ridicule, we embrace it, for that is what America's poor now receive," he said. "If it means jail, we accept it willingly, for the millions of poor already are imprisoned by exploitation and discrimination."

Within days of King's announcement, the FBI requested permission to reestablish wiretaps on SCLC phone lines in Atlanta. The request read:

> Since SCLC's President, Martin Luther King, Jr., has urged massive civil disobedience throughout the country in an effort to spur Congress into action to help the plight of the Negro, it is felt that we need this installation to obtain racial intelligence information concerning their plans. King has warned that these massive demonstrations may result in riots. Because of this, we should be in a position to obtain intelligence so that appropriate countermeasures can be taken to protect the internal security of the United States.

The attorney general, Ramsey Clark, rejected the request. Undaunted, Hoover and the bureau continued working to undercut King. The bureau increased its flow of reports to the White House, supplying information not only on the Poor People's Campaign but also on King's criticism of the war, his ties to communists, and his sex life.

"We have permitted the Stokely Carmichaels, the Rap Browns, and the Martin Luther Kings to cloak themselves in an aura of respectability to which they are not entitled," one Johnson aide wrote in a memo to the president, adding that King's so-called civil disobedience was, in truth, "criminal disobedience."

The FBI agreed, warning that the Poor People's Campaign had the potential to incite another summer of riots, in Washington and beyond. In fact, the bureau noted in one report, violence might be the real goal of the campaign—not just for the Black nationalists who would use King's protest as a pretense to strike but also for Stanley Levison, King's "shrewd and dedicated Communist" adviser.

———— • ————

King returned to Atlanta to spend Christmas with his family and to preach from the pulpit at Ebenezer. In his sermon that day, he said he felt like "the victim of deferred dreams, of blasted hopes." But he had not given up, he declared. He recalled his most famous speech, less than five years earlier, on the National Mall in Washington, D.C. "Toward the end of that afternoon," he said, "I tried to talk to the nation about a dream that I had had, and I must confess to you today that not long after talking about that dream I started seeing it turn into a nightmare."

The nightmare began two weeks later when four innocent girls were killed by a bomb in a Birmingham church, and it continued as cities such as Los Angeles and Detroit erupted in flames, and went on still as he faced a barrage of bricks and rocks in Chicago. The nightmare grew darker as white people in the North turned their backs on their Black brothers and sisters, and it grew darker yet again, he said, as the president of the United States sent 500,000 American men to fight in Vietnam, spending countless billions that could have gone toward improving schools, feeding the hungry, healing the sick, and aiding the poor.

But King said he was not quitting:

I still have a dream, because, you know, you can't give up in life . . . I have a dream that one day men will rise up and come to see that they are made to live together as brothers. I still have a dream this morning that one day every Negro in this country, every colored person in the world, will be judged on the basis of the content of his character rather than the color of his skin . . . I still have a dream that one day the idle industries of Appalachia will be revitalized, and the empty stomachs of Mississippi will be filled, and brotherhood will be more than a few words at the end of a prayer . . . I still have a dream today that one day justice will roll down like water, and righteousness like a mighty stream . . . I still have a dream today.

On January 15, 1968, King celebrated his birthday with members of the SCLC staff who had gathered in Atlanta to discuss the Poor People's Campaign. A plan took shape. The SCLC would send dozens of workers across the country to recruit volunteers to join the protest. King himself would travel the country raising money and awareness.

But even among those he could usually rely upon for support, King faced doubt. Bayard Rustin, who had handled many of the logistics for the 1963 March on Washington, declined to get involved this time. Rustin now led the A. Philip Randolph Institute, which coordinated the AFL-CIO's work on civil rights and economic justice, and he opposed the Washington campaign, saying it would likely harden resistance to King's cause. Rustin added in a memo to King: "Personally, I cannot imagine a situation more flammable."

Roy Wilkins and Whitney Young condemned King's plan, too. Even Marian Logan, a trusted member of the SCLC's board, criticized King in a memo to her fellow board members. Logan said she was troubled by how "inadequately" the event was being planned. Did King have a specific set of policy changes he wanted Congress to enact? If he did have demands, were they realistic? Had he contemplated how much damage he might do to the cause if the protesters rioted? In many ways, Logan was right in noting that King had few specific demands and only a vague plan. He was relying, yet again, on his ability to improvise, to throw himself into a protest and see what happened. Andrew Young called it a "faith venture."

But faith in King was fading, and he noticed it.

"We weren't convinced that the Poor People's Campaign could be controlled," said Stoney Cooks, an SCLC staffer who attended the meeting on King's birthday. As doubt crept in about King's leadership, others in the organization pushed their own agendas.

James Bevel and Jesse Jackson acted as if they hoped to break away or perhaps even supplant King, said Cooks. At one point on the morning of his birthday, King became so frustrated by his team's negativity and disorganization that he walked out of the meeting in anger, complaining of a migraine headache.

In those early days of 1968, Coretta described her husband as "terribly distressed." She wrote: "I had not seen him like this before." When she tried to lift his spirits, she added, her "words took root only for a moment."

Friends and colleagues said King grew despondent at times. "I certainly saw the exhaustion," said Dorothy Cotton, describing King as "*emotionally weary, as well as physically tired.*" She continued: "I felt his weariness, just weariness of the struggle, that he had done all that he could do."

To Andrew Young, King seemed more depressed than ever: "He talked about death all the time . . . Martin was keeping a hell of a pace. He was speaking a lot. He was preaching every Sunday at church. He hadn't been on a vacation. He was staying up late at night arguing all the time . . . He didn't want to sleep. We used to say he not only had a war on poverty, he had a war on sleep, 'cause he'd want to stay up and talk until three, four in the morning, and then he'd go to sleep and be back up at seven . . . He was just in an extremely hyper, social period."

Ralph Abernathy worried about King, too, saying his friend seemed "worried . . . nervous, and very, very jittery."

He recalled finding King on the balcony of a hotel at three o'clock one morning in 1968, staring at nothing. When Abernathy asked what he was doing, King pointed to a rock and began to sing the popular old hymn "Rock of Ages," which is often sung at funerals, given the last verse:

> *While I draw this fleeting breath,*
> *when mine eyes shall close in death,*
> *when I soar to worlds unknown,*
> *see thee on thy judgment throne,*
> *Rock of Ages, cleft for me,*
> *let me hide myself in thee.*

On February 4 at Ebenezer, King preached to the congregation about the virtues of service and the shallow meaning of personal greatness. He adapted his sermon from a 1949 homily by a white Methodist minister named James Wallace Hamilton. The sermon drew from a passage in the Gospel of Mark (10:35–45) in which the brothers James and John ask to sit beside Jesus in heaven, one on the left and one on the right. Jesus tells the brothers such a privilege is not his to grant, and that "whoever wishes to become great among you must be your servant." King, following Hamilton's example, called this selfish desire a "drum-major instinct," after the figure who marches at the front of a parade.

King's "drum-major sermon" was aimed not at a national audience but at his regular Sunday worshippers. When he preached at Ebenezer, he sounded more like his father than he did elsewhere, shouting at some moments, laughing at others, and engaging in give-and-take with the faithful.

He began slowly, stating the title of his sermon and reading from the Bible. Gradually, he gained speed and strength. When a baby cried, he worked the baby into his sermon. "Our first cry as a baby was a bid for attention," he said. Even infants, innately, possess the drum-major instinct. Adults have it, too. "We like to do something good and, you know, we like to be praised for it," he said. He talked about people who spend huge sums of money to impress their neighbors and others who brag about their college degrees. The hunger for attention can be dangerous, he said. It drives people to lie. It compels people to insist on the superiority of one race to another. It makes corporations greedy. It propels nations to war.

As King preached, his father shouted out repeatedly: "Make it plain! Make it plain!"

King made it plain. There's nothing wrong with the pursuit of greatness, he said, if you seek greatness in serving others:

> Everyone can be great because everyone can serve. You don't have to have a college degree to serve. You don't have to make your subject and verb agree to serve . . . You only need a heart full of grace, a soul generated by love, and you can be that servant.

Every now and then, King said, he thought about his own death, and what people would say at his funeral, and whether he would be judged worthy to sit by Jesus's side. He didn't want a long funeral, he said. He didn't want his eulogist to talk about his Nobel Peace Prize or his college degrees. "I'd like someone to mention *that* day that Martin Luther King Jr. *tried* to give his life serving others," he said, his voice loud, strong and quavering, the word "tried" full of grit and gravel. The congregation was rapt. His father was silent.

I'd like for someone to say *that* day that Martin Luther King Jr. tried to *love* somebody! I want you to say that day that I tried to be *right* on the war question! I want you to be able to say that day that I *did* try to feed the hungry . . . I want you to say that I tried to *love* and *serve* humanity!

Yes, if you want to say that day that I was a drum major, say that I was a drum major for justice. Say that I was a drum major for *peace*, that I was a drum major for righteousness, and all of the other shallow things will not matter . . . I just want to leave a committed life behind.

A week later, on February 11, at another staff meeting in Atlanta, King told the SCLC's leaders that the Poor People's Campaign faced serious trouble. "We have not gotten off the ground," he said. He wanted to bring three thousand people to Washington, he said, and, so far, not even twenty had been recruited. Meanwhile, President Johnson was telling reporters that King should call off the campaign and lobby Congress for civil rights legislation.

King said he wasn't worried about angering Johnson, but he was worried about failing to assemble a strong movement. "If we cannot do it," he said, "I would rather pull out now—the embarrassment and criticism would be much less now."

He took to the road to help recruit volunteers and raise money for the Poor People's Campaign, traveling through Georgia, Mississippi, and Alabama. For one stretch of his trip, he took his boys, Marty and Dexter, along. When a newspaper editor in Albany, Georgia, criticized him for traveling without bodyguards, King said he couldn't live that way: "I'd feel like a bird in a cage ... There's no way in the world you can keep somebody from killing you if they really want to kill you."

⁕

While King fought to save the Poor People's Campaign, James Lawson phoned with another request for King's presence in Memphis. This time it was even more urgent, he said. Two sanitation workers had been killed, crushed by the compactor on their garbage truck. Now all the city's sanitation men were on strike, demanding better pay, safer working conditions, and the right to organize. Almost all the sanitation workers were Black men. They wanted to be recognized as working professionals, Lawson said, not lackeys. They wanted to be treated like men. But the mayor, Henry Loeb III, refused to negotiate.

Lawson still believed in King. He believed King's nonviolent strategy still had the power to knock down segregation and unravel racism. It would take more time, of course, but it was happening, despite recent setbacks. In Memphis, King would apply more pressure. He would have a platform to talk about poverty, race, and his Poor People's Campaign. But that wasn't the most important reason to come to Memphis. The most important reason, Lawson argued, was that the sanitation workers needed King's help.

"I knew he would come," Lawson said.

⁕

On March 4, the FBI sent the "messiah" directive to all its field offices, naming King as a "primary target" and ordering all agents to move into action within thirty days. In northern cities, bureau operators recruited "ghetto informants" to penetrate the SCLC and disrupt plans for the Poor People's Campaign.

Years later, Andrew Young would say he and others close to King failed to appreciate the panic federal officials felt over the upcoming campaign in Washington. "There was a determination to stop us that we didn't realize," he said.

Despite the escalating tension, King hadn't spoken to President Johnson in months. On March 16, twelve days after the "messiah" directive, King ended any hope of a reconciliation when he announced to reporters that he would not support the president's bid for reelection. Though he remained proud of the work he and Johnson had done together to help deliver passage of the Civil Rights Act of 1964 and the Voting Rights Act of 1965, it all came down to Vietnam now, King said.

"I must say I'm very disappointed, and I think a change is absolutely necessary," he told reporters. "We must end the war in Vietnam. President Johnson is too emotionally involved, and face-saving is more important to him than peace."

Six weeks earlier, North Vietnam had launched a series of surprise attacks across South Vietnam, hitting behind American lines, even striking at the U.S. embassy in Saigon. The stunning assault coincided with Tet, the Vietnamese new year, and became known as the Tet Offensive. It gave Americans more reason to feel the nation's military was sinking deeper and deeper into a quagmire. As the president's popularity plummeted in public opinion polls, Senators Robert F. Kennedy and Eugene J. McCarthy announced plans to challenge Johnson for the Democratic Party's nomination. King had never formally endorsed a candidate for elected office, but he said he might soon break from that pattern. In privately recorded phone calls, President Johnson said he expected King to throw his support behind Kennedy.

"The thing I feared from the first day of my presidency was actually coming true," Johnson said in an interview years later. Robert Kennedy had set out to "reclaim the throne in the memory of his brother . . . The whole situation was unbearable for me."

On the day that King denounced Johnson, four Black teenage boys were arrested for firebombing a building in downtown Memphis. Protests spread to the suburbs. The city's biggest newspaper, *The Commercial Appeal*, carried a front-page story on March 17 saying Martin Luther King would be in town the next day to lead a protest rally. A white city councilman warned that if Memphis wasn't careful, "black power people from Chicago" might follow King, and "we'll have more people than we can deal with."

The next day, King entered Mason Temple in Memphis at 9:07 p.m., coming in through a side door. Every seat was filled, and the doorways and aisles were jammed. He was more than ninety minutes late, but his delay only energized the crowd of ten thousand. He smiled and raised his arms in the air as he made his way to the stage.

The sanitation workers' strike was in its sixth week. City officials had reluctantly agreed to meet some of the strikers' demands, but the two sides remained divided on important issues.

King escalated the pressure, urging all Black people in Memphis to stop working if the city refused to agree to the strikers' demands. "Along with wages and other securities, you're struggling for the right to organize," he said. "This is the way to gain power. Don't go back to work until all your demands are met."

King then asked the protesters to help him make Memphis the start of his national campaign to end poverty, and he promised to return for a massive march through the center of the city. After that, he flew to New York.

The sanitation workers' strike, noted *The Commercial Appeal*, had suddenly become something bigger and more dangerous: it had become a racial protest.

—— · ——

King spent three days in New York and New Jersey beating the drum for the Poor People's Campaign. On March 25, he addressed an assembly of rabbis, where his friend Abraham Joshua Heschel pronounced that "the whole future of America will depend on the impact and influence of Dr. King."

After his conference with the rabbis, King met with Black radicals he feared might incite violence in the months ahead, including the writer LeRoi Jones (later known as Amiri Baraka). King returned from those meetings to Harry Belafonte's Manhattan apartment "bitterly disappointed," saying he didn't think he'd gotten through to Jones or anyone else.

"Having failed that," Belafonte said, Martin "went into a place of melancholy."

———·———

Worried and tired, King returned to Memphis for his march on behalf of the striking sanitation workers. He arrived two hours late. A local funeral home sent one of its Cadillacs to pick him up at the airport. By the time King reached Clayborn Temple African Methodist Episcopal Church, a huge crowd awaited. People pressed their noses to the glass of his car's windows and refused to back away. For a moment, King and his colleagues were trapped inside. The swarm was wilder and more dangerous than expected.

Finally, Lawson arrived and helped to part the crowd. King exited the funeral car, linked arms with his fellow marchers, and led them down Hernando Street. Many of the striking sanitation workers carried placards with bold capital letters that declared "I AM A MAN."

The procession turned left on Beale Street. Behind King, members of the Invaders street gang used the placards to shatter windows. Stores were looted. Police shot and killed a sixteen-year-old Black male. More than two hundred people were arrested. Scores were injured. Police ushered King away from the melee. In the aftermath of the violence, the white media blamed King. It was the riot white city leaders and the FBI had predicted.

"We are in serious trouble," King told Stanley Levison in a phone call the next day. Recruiting for the Poor People's Campaign would be all but impossible with the heightened fear of violence hanging over it. His critics would pounce, saying, "'Martin Luther King is dead, he's finished, his nonviolence is nothing, no one is listening to it.'"

Levison said King was overreacting, that he couldn't expect everyone to follow his path of nonviolence, that occasional outbursts were inevitable. But King would not be consoled. "Let's face it," he said, "we do have a great public-relations setback where my image and leadership are concerned . . . It will put many Negroes in the position of saying, 'Well . . . Martin Luther King is at the end of his rope' . . . You watch your newspapers. Watch *The New York Times* editorials . . . I think it will be the most negative thing about Martin Luther King that you have ever seen."

He was right. Newspapers all over the country, including the *Times*, questioned King's ability to maintain nonviolence. *The Commercial Appeal* said he had "wrecked his reputation as a leader."

King asked Levison and others from his leadership team to meet him the next day at his office in Atlanta.

The movement might not recover, he said, "unless I do something now."

That evening, back in Atlanta, Martin and Coretta had dinner at the home of Ralph and Juanita Abernathy. Martin bought the catfish and Juanita cooked it.

"Martin was real depressed that night," Juanita recalled.

After dinner, King moved to the living room and settled into a love seat. "Can't y'all afford a whole sofa?" he asked.

He quickly nodded off and slept there through the night.

King assembled his executive team two days later, on Saturday, March 30.

"He was wrestling with depression," said Jesse Jackson, who attended the meeting. King talked about a hunger strike and wondered if the divided leaders of the civil rights struggle would come together around his deathbed. He announced that he would go back to Memphis as soon as possible, lead another march, and remain in Memphis until city officials met all the demands of the striking sanitation workers. Even if he had to postpone the Poor People's Campaign, he said, he was determined.

When staff members reacted coolly to the idea, King erupted with a force that stunned those in the room. "He really opened up and let everyone know how he was feeling," Andrew Young said. "It was a kind of feeling on his part that everyone was betraying him . . . He just unloaded, unburdened himself." King, who seldom lost his temper, came down with surprising force on James Bevel and Jesse Jackson, accusing them of selfishness.

And then he walked out.

Abernathy followed him.

"What's wrong, Martin?"

"I'll be all right," King answered.

Left alone, King's executive team worked out a compromise. Bevel, Jackson, Hosea Williams, and James Orange would leave immediately for Memphis to orchestrate another march. The remaining staff would accelerate the Poor People's Campaign.

———————

At seven o'clock Wednesday morning, April 3, King kissed Coretta goodbye and promised to call her that night from Memphis. He and Abernathy drove directly to the Atlanta airport.

"There was nothing special about the goodbye," she said later. "It was an ordinary goodbye." The children were still sleeping.

At the airport, authorities informed King and Abernathy that their Eastern Airlines flight might have a bomb aboard. After a careful inspection, the plane was deemed bomb-free. The passengers were cleared to go to Memphis, and King chose to proceed. "Well, looks like they won't kill me this flight," he told Abernathy.

———————

After the riot, police had escorted King to the white-owned Holiday Inn Rivermont in Memphis, and the FBI had alerted friendly reporters to the fact that King had spent two nights there, as if to suggest he had abandoned the Black community. Now, as he arrived again in Memphis, King returned to his usual choice of lodging: the Lorraine Motel. Television and newspaper reporters not only identified his motel but also gave the exact room. It was room 306, located on the second floor, with a sweeping view of the motel's grease-stained parking lot and empty swimming pool.

After lunch, King and members of his staff met at Lawson's church, where they learned that the City of Memphis had obtained a federal injunction barring them from holding any demonstrations for ten days. One reason for the injunction, according to an attorney for the city, was that King's life might be in danger.

King was not persuaded by the argument. A team of six Memphis lawyers agreed to fight the court order. When one of the lawyers asked King how much this march mattered to him, King answered: "My whole future depends on it."

That night, King met with leaders of the Invaders street gang, pleading with them to refrain from violence. He phoned Coretta to say things were going well. He told her about the injunction and said he planned to march whether it was lifted or not.

Though he was supposed to speak that evening at Mason Temple, King asked Abernathy to fill in, saying he felt sick and needed to rest. King was in his pajamas when Abernathy called and asked him to come to the church. "The people who are here want you, not me," Abernathy said.

A thunderstorm raged outside. On the last night of his life, King wore a long black raincoat over his suit and tie. People reached out to touch him as he stepped in the door and down the aisle to the pulpit.

Thunder echoed. Wind rattled the windowpanes. Shutters banged. Abernathy made the introduction. King spoke without notes.

"Something is happening in Memphis," he said. "Something is happening in our world."

He then took his listeners on a "mental flight" through human history. He talked about the Israelites' escape from slavery in Egypt, about Greece, where he imagined Plato, Aristotle, Socrates, Euripides, and Aristophanes discussing "the great and eternal issues of reality." He talked about the Roman Empire and the Renaissance. He talked about the man for whom he was named, Martin Luther. He talked about Abraham Lincoln. Those men lived in fascinating times, King said. But if God had given him the choice to live in any time, even if only for a short time, King said, he would have chosen *this* moment—even though the world was "all messed up"—because "the masses of people" were crying out for freedom.

The crowd encouraged him with cries of "Amen!" and "Tell it!" The thunder and lightning gave way to a steady patter of rain on the roof.

King reminded his audience that the sanitation workers and Black people around the country were only asking to be treated like men, like people, like God's children. He called on his audience to show a greater determination to work with him, unselfishly, to make America live up to its foundational promises.

Toward the end of his speech, King reminisced about the woman in Harlem who had stabbed him with a letter opener years ago and the doctor who had told him that he might have died if he had sneezed. He recalled receiving a letter "from a little girl, a young girl . . . a student at the White Plains High School," as he put it, who had written to say she was happy that King hadn't sneezed.

"I am happy that I didn't sneeze," he said, because he would have missed the student lunch counter sit-ins of 1960, the citizen uprising in Albany, the thrilling protests in Birmingham that led to the Civil Rights Bill, the beautiful gathering in Washington in 1963 when he told America about his dream, and the courageous journey of the masses from Selma to Montgomery.

"I'm so happy that I didn't sneeze," he said. "And they were telling me . . ."

He didn't finish the sentence. His mind flashed to an incident from earlier in the day, and he talked about the bomb threat on his plane that morning. He said he had been warned recently of additional death threats from "some of our sick white brothers."

Sweat covered his brow. His voice grew louder, echoing in the rafters:

Well, I don't know what will happen now. We've got some difficult days ahead. But it really doesn't matter with me now, because I've been to the mountaintop. And I don't mind. Like anybody, I would like to live a long life . . . But I'm not concerned about that now. I just want to do God's will. And He's allowed me to go up to the mountain. And I've looked over. And I've *seen* the Promised Land.

His eyes scanned down and then to the left and then back up at his audience.

I may not get there with you. But I want you to know tonight, that we, as a people, will get to the Promised Land!

The audience roared, and King roared back.

So I'm happy tonight! I'm not worried about *anything*! I'm not fearing *any* man! Mine eyes have seen the glory—

This time, as the audience roared, a tiny smile flashed across King's face. It disappeared as fast as it came, and he took a breath.

—of the coming of the Lord!

He knifed the air with his left hand and turned away as the audience erupted in euphoric applause.

Abernathy rose from his seat and threw both arms around King's waist. Abernathy looked in his best friend's eyes and saw tears.

———

Twelve hours later, Andrew Young and SCLC's lawyers were in federal court fighting the injunction that barred them from marching. Dorothy Cotton told King she had to go back to Atlanta to lead a workshop. King asked her to stay, "rather pleadingly," as she recalled, but Cotton insisted she had to go.

King phoned his office in Atlanta to give them the title for his Sunday sermon at Ebenezer. He said it would be called "Why America May Go to Hell."

His brother, A.D., had come to see him in Memphis. Together, they phoned their mother, who didn't know both her boys were in Memphis, and played a little prank on her. Martin started the call and handed the phone to his brother to pick up the conversation in the middle of a sentence, to see if Alberta would notice. She did. Martin took the phone back from his brother and spoke to Alberta for more than forty minutes. He said he would be home Saturday night and asked his mother to cook him a big dinner.

At about five o'clock, Young returned from court with good news: the judge had agreed to modify the injunction and permit a demonstration if it followed certain safety rules.

The march was set for April 8, five days away.

———

King stood before the bathroom mirror dressed in his suit pants and a white undershirt. He mixed white shaving powder in a cup of warm water as he chatted with Abernathy about what they would be having for dinner that night at the home of their friend the Reverend Billy Kyles. Abernathy got on the phone and called Gwen Kyles, the minister's wife, and got the answer. He relayed to King that they were having roast beef, candied yams, pig's feet, neck bones, chitlins, turnip greens, and corn pone.

King patted his face dry, slapped on cologne, buttoned his shirt, and tied his tie.

Shortly before six, he stepped out on the motel's balcony, alone.

The air outside was cool and crisp, the sky cloudy.

King leaned on the railing and gazed out over the parking lot and the worn brick buildings of the city's industrial district, including a run-down rooming house at 422½ Main Street.

It had windows at the rear facing the Lorraine Motel. Rooms at the boardinghouse went for $8.50 a week, and one of them—room 5B—had just been rented that afternoon by a slender white man in a crisp dark suit and tie.

"You comin', Ralph?" King asked as he went back in the room to get his jacket.

In his pockets King had a Cross pen, a packet of Salem menthol cigarettes, and scribbled notes for an upcoming speech.

He stepped back outside. He looked down at the parking lot, where some of his colleagues had assembled.

"Our leader!" called Jesse Jackson when he spotted King, alone on the balcony.

"Jesse!" King leaned over the railing. "I want you to come to dinner with me tonight!"

"Doc, Jesse took care of that before you did," said Billy Kyles. "He got himself invited!"

The men laughed.

Solomon Jones, King's driver that day, warmed up the Cadillac.

Andrew Young and James Orange shadowboxed playfully in the parking lot.

Jackson, still shouting up to the balcony, introduced King to Ben Branch, a saxophonist and bandleader, who planned to perform that night at Mason Temple in support of the sanitation workers.

"Ben, I want you to sing for me tonight at the meeting," King said. "I want you to do that song, 'Take My Hand, Precious Lord' . . . Sing it real pretty."

Jones, the driver, told King it was getting cold. "Why don't you put on your topcoat," he said.

King stood up straight. He answered, "OK, I will," and moved away from the railing.

A single shot rang out.

The bullet struck King in the face, ripped through his neck, and knocked him backward onto the balcony floor.

The men in the parking lot charged up the steps to the balcony, all of them in the line of fire. Abernathy reached King first. King's eyes were open, arms spread wide, his blood pooling on the cold concrete. "Martin, can you hear me?"

Abernathy was an easy target, but no second shot was fired.

A white man, a stranger, brought a towel from his room and wrapped it around King's face.

The men on the balcony pointed to the boardinghouse across the parking lot, where they thought the gunman might have been positioned. Sirens wailed.

A lone ambulance arrived.

The ambulance crew carried King down the steps, surrounded by his friends.

Police cordoned off the streets and searched for a white man in a white Mustang seen fleeing the area.

"I hope the son of a bitch doesn't die," J. Edgar Hoover said when he got the news. "If he does, they'll make a martyr out of him." At 6:16, eleven minutes after he was shot, King was wheeled into the emergency room at St. Joseph's Hospital. His eyes were closed.

He died there at 7:05 p.m. on April 4, 1968.

Martin Luther King Jr. was thirty-nine years old.

His death lit the nation on fire—that night and for years to come. Memphis burned. Detroit burned. Washington, D.C., burned. More than a hundred cities went up in flames. Dozens of Black men died. More than ten thousand were arrested.

"Every racist in the country has killed Dr. King," the activist James Farmer told a reporter. "Evil societies always destroy their consciences."

Epilogue

MARTIN LUTHER KING's children received the news when a special bulletin interrupted one of their favorite television shows. The CBS anchorman Walter Cronkite told them and the nation: "Dr. Martin Luther King, the apostle of nonviolence in the civil rights movement, has been shot to death in Memphis, Tennessee."

Seven-year-old Dexter, ten-year-old Martin, and twelve-year-old Yolanda ran to their mother. Coretta Scott King was on the phone. She raised a finger, signaling for the children to be quiet.

"I understand," she said.

The children waited.

"I understand," she said again.

Finally, she hung up.

"Your father," she said calmly. "There's been an accident."

Cities across the country erupted in violence. The next day, April 5, Coretta Scott King flew to Memphis to retrieve her husband's body. On April 8, she stood before a gathering of forty thousand in the city where her husband had just been assassinated, and led the marchers downtown in support of the city's still striking sanitation workers.

The day after the march, more than 1,300 mourners jammed into Ebenezer Baptist Church. Loudspeakers carried the funeral service to tens of thousands standing outside in the sun. After the ceremony, King's casket was loaded on a mule-drawn wagon and carried through the streets of Atlanta to Morehouse College, for another memorial service. Rosa Parks, Stokely Carmichael,

Mahalia Jackson, James Baldwin, Robert F. Kennedy, and Richard Nixon were among those in attendance.

Two days later, President Johnson, who did not attend the funeral, signed one of the last important legislative achievements of the civil rights era—the Civil Rights Act of 1968, also known as the Fair Housing Act. "Fair housing for all . . . is now a part of the American way of life," he proclaimed.

On Mother's Day, thirty-eight days after her husband's assassination, Coretta marched with three thousand supporters through the rubble and the burnt buildings of Washington, D.C., to launch the Poor People's Campaign. As more supporters arrived, they pitched tents near the Lincoln Memorial and called their encampment Resurrection City.

It rained for eleven of the next nineteen days, turning Resurrection City into a quagmire.

The rain finally stopped.

On June 5, Senator Robert F. Kennedy won the California presidential primary.

He was assassinated that evening.

The prime suspect in *King's* assassination, James Earl Ray, was arrested in London three days later as he attempted to board a flight to Brussels, Belgium. Though Ray confessed to the crime, Coretta Scott King and other friends and family members never accepted the government's conclusion that the killer had acted alone.

On June 19, at the Lincoln Memorial, Coretta spoke to the residents of Resurrection City and thousands of others. She described an America so blinded by racism that it failed to see how violent its culture had become. "Starving a child is violence. Suppressing a culture is violence. Punishing a mother and her family is violence . . . Ghetto housing is violence. Ignoring medical needs is violence. Contempt for poverty is violence."

The time had come, she said, to form "a solid block of woman power" to demand change. "Love is the only force that can destroy hate," she said, paraphrasing her husband. The national news media portrayed the campaign as a disorganized failure—a gaggle of hippies and drifters with a mishmash of vague and conflicting goals. Five days later, on June 24, police tore down Resurrection City.

Later that year, Coretta helped establish the King Center for Nonviolent Social Change, a memorial dedicated to the advancement of her husband's legacy. Some civil rights activists criticized the new center, saying it competed for funds with and drew attention away from the SCLC. Coretta also began working for the establishment of a national holiday in her husband's honor.

In 1969, Martin Luther King's brother, A.D., was found floating in his swimming pool, dead, at the age of thirty-eight. Five years later, King's mother, Alberta, was shot and killed by a deranged man during a service at Ebenezer Baptist Church.

Throughout the 1970s, Black politicians began winning elections, especially in mayoralties, in unprecedented numbers. Andrew Young, in 1972, became the first Black person elected to Congress from Georgia since Reconstruction. Less than a decade later, Young was elected mayor of Atlanta.

In 1983, President Ronald Reagan signed a bill marking the third Monday of each January as Martin Luther King Jr. Day. Reagan, whose policies were disastrous for many Black Americans, had long opposed the move. "On the national holiday you mentioned, I have the reservations you have," he wrote to one elected official at the time, "but here the perception of too many people is based on image, not reality."

Asked by reporters if he believed King had been a communist sympathizer, Reagan answered, "We'll know in thirty-five years, won't we?"

Thirty-five years later, when the FBI released thousands of pages from its secret files on King, no evidence emerged to suggest that communist operatives controlled or manipulated King. The documents did offer new details on his extramarital affairs, as well as on the emotional strain he endured. The biggest revelation contained in the FBI reports, however, may have been the extent and determination of the bureau's campaign to thwart King—and the degree to which the campaign was fueled by the personal obsessions of J. Edgar Hoover and President Johnson. Complete FBI transcripts and surviving recordings are scheduled for release in 2027.

Coretta Scott King continued to speak out and march on behalf of countless causes, including women's rights, gay rights, religious freedom,

AIDS awareness, nuclear disarmament, and the anti-apartheid movement in South Africa. She remained in the family home in Vine City for decades, preserving it almost as if it were a museum, with her husband's side of the bed empty, his suits still in the closet, his car still in the garage, windows dusty, tires deflated. In a locked glass case in the basement, she kept a bouquet of artificial red flowers that Martin had purchased for her on March 12, 1968. He had never previously bought artificial flowers, Coretta said, "and they weren't very attractive, but maybe he knew, maybe he wanted me to have something that would last."

Coretta Scott King died in 2006 at age seventy-eight. The intimate letters from her husband that she kept in a blue suitcase under her bed have never been made public.

Today, almost a thousand cities and towns in the United States have streets named in honor of Martin Luther King Jr. More than one hundred public schools bear his name. In Washington, D.C., a King memorial stands within sight of the Lincoln and Jefferson memorials along the National Mall's Tidal Basin. Cut out of white stone, King stands thirty feet tall, arms folded across his chest, gaze focused to the southeast. It is the only national monument in Washington dedicated to a person of color.

"Out of a mountain of despair, a stone of hope," reads the quotation that greets visitors to the memorial.

But in hallowing King we have hollowed him.

From Montgomery to Chicago, along those streets named Martin Luther King Jr. Drive and Martin Luther King Jr. Avenue and Martin Luther King Jr. Highway and Martin Luther King Jr. Boulevard, poverty and segregation rates remain much higher than local and national averages, according to recent studies.

In those schools named for King, and in almost every school in America, King's life and lessons are often smoothed and polished beyond recognition. Young people hear his dream of brotherhood and his wish for children to be judged by the content of their character, but not his call for fundamental change in the nation's character, not his cry for an end to the triple evils of materialism, militarism, and racism. As King's friend Harry Belafonte told me, "In none of the history books of this country do you read about radical heroes."

On my most recent visit to the Martin Luther King Jr. Memorial in Washington, D.C., in the spring of 2022, I found none of King's books for sale in the gift shop.

Our simplified celebration of King comes at a cost. It saps the strength of his philosophical and intellectual contributions. It undercuts his power to inspire change. Even after Americans elected a Black man as president and after that president, Barack Obama, placed a bust of King in the Oval Office, the nation remains racked with racism, ethno-nationalism, cultural division, residential and educational segregation, economic inequality, violence, and a fading sense of hope that government, or anyone, will ever fix those problems.

Where do we go from here? In spite of the way America treated him, King still had faith when he asked that question. Today, his words might help us make our way through these troubled times, but only if we actually read them; only if we embrace the complicated King, the flawed King, the human King, the radical King; only if we see and hear him clearly again, as America saw and heard him once before.

"Our very survival," he wrote, "depends on our ability to stay awake, to adjust to new ideas, to remain vigilant and to face the challenge of change."

Amen.

Notes

Prologue

3 *360 lynchings*: "Lynching in America," Equal Justice Initiative, https://lynchinginamerica.eji.org/explore/alabama, accessed January 4, 2022.

3 *crowd of five thousand*: Joe Azbell, "5,000 at Meeting Outline Boycott; Bullet Clips Bus," *Montgomery Advertiser*, December 6, 1955.

3 *"We are here this evening"*: *King: A Filmed Record . . . Montgomery to Memphis*, The Martin Luther King Film Project, 1970, Kino Classics DVD, 2013.

5 *chewed his fingernails*: Juandalynn Abernathy, interview with author, November 1, 2018.

5 *shouted at the TV*: L. D. Reddick, *Crusader Without Violence: A Biography of Martin Luther King, Jr.* (New York: Harper & Bros., 1959), 4.

5 *Topsy*: Juandalynn Abernathy, interview with author.

5 *napped well*: Reddick, *Crusader Without Violence*, 2.

5 *depression*: Numerous people who knew King well, including Coretta Scott King, Andrew Young, and Clarence Jones, used the word "depression" to describe King's psychological state at times, and Dr. Nassir Ghaemi, professor of psychiatry at Tufts University Medical Center, has written extensively about evidence suggesting King's "episodic depression."

1. The Kings of Stockbridge

9 *bucket of milk*: All details of the scene with the mill owner, including dialogue and expressions of feelings, come from two sources, the first being an unpublished, unfinished manuscript called "The Autobiography of Daddy King as Told to Edward A. Jones," written in August 1973, copies of which were recently discovered at the Martin Luther King, Jr., Research and Education Institute at Stanford University (hereafter referred to as the Stanford King Institute) and the King Center archives in Atlanta. The manuscript includes more than 150 pages of transcripts from taped interviews with Martin Luther King Sr. The second source is Martin Luther King Sr., *Daddy King: An Autobiography*, with Clayton Riley (New York: William Morrow, 1980), 32–36.

9 *bright summer day*: Martin Luther King Sr., *Daddy King*, 32–36.

10 *voice low and tight*: Ibid.

11 *"I just wondered"*: Ibid.

11 *"a radical experiment"*: Eric Foner, *A Short History of Reconstruction*, updated ed. (New York: Harper Perennial, 2015), xx.

11 *"The slave went free"*: W. E. B. Du Bois, *Black Reconstruction in America* (1935; repr. Oxford: Oxford University Press, 2007), 30.

12 *checkers, dominos*: Ruth Barefield Pendleton, comp., *Minutes: Central Committee 1963* (Birmingham, Ala.: Birmingham Historical Society, 2013), 79.

12 *"the centre of the Negro problem"*: W. E. B. Du Bois, *The Souls of Black Folk* (1903; repr. New York: Signet Classics, 1969), 141.

13 *"a look of very quiet"*: Ibid., 25.

13 *August 20, 1895*: Marriage records, Henry County, Georgia, Ancestry.com.

13 *Ellenwood*: 1900 U.S. Census, Ancestry.com.

13 *accident in the quarry*: "The Autobiography of Daddy King," 14.

13 *"while our backs shivered"*: Ibid., 3.

14 *carrying their shoes*: Ibid., 53.

14 *alternated between Methodist and Baptist*: Ibid., 59.

14 *"He didn't care anything about church"*: Ibid., 22.

14 *Black Baptists outnumbered white*: Paul Harvey, *Redeeming the South: Religious Cultures and Racial Identities Among Southern Baptists, 1865–1925* (Chapel Hill: University of North Carolina Press, 1997), 46.

14 *Hog-killing time*: "The Autobiography of Daddy King," 47.

15 *"So many things"*: Martin Luther King Jr., "Overcoming an Inferiority Complex," sermon, Dexter Avenue Baptist Church, Montgomery, Ala., July 14, 1957, Stanford King Institute, kinginstitute.stanford.edu/king-papers/documents/overcoming -inferiority-complex-sermon-delivered-dexter-avenue-baptist-church, accessed September 14, 2020.

15 *In the first census*: Nathan King's parents (Martin Luther King Jr.'s likely great-grandparents) are listed in the same census report as Jacob and Diannah Branham, ages sixty-five and sixty, respectively. King's ancestors may have been enslaved by the white Branham family of Putnam County, Ga. Joel Branham enslaved twelve Black people in 1850, and Henry Branham enslaved twenty-nine. Both men were physicians. It would appear that the African American Branhams changed their names to King between 1870 and 1880, although it's not clear why. Had they been previously owned by Elisha L. King and his wife, Elizabeth Ann King, of Putnam County? Did they take the name King to reconnect with family members who had remained on Elisha King's plantation?

15 *"My mother was way over"*: "The Autobiography of Daddy King," 48.

16 *"two-eyed kitchen stove"*: Ibid., 56.

16 *"two or three months a year"*: Ibid., 18.

16 *"full of whiskey"*: Martin Luther King Sr., *Daddy King*, 45–46.

16 *walked barefoot*: Alveda King, interview with author, May 10, 2022.

2. Martin Luther

17 *couldn't write*: U.S. Census, 1920, Ancestry.com.

17 *"assuring survivors"*: "The Autobiography of Daddy King as Told to Edward A. Jones" (unpublished manuscript, August 1973), 10–11.

17 *"as if they were dogs"*: Ibid., 77.

17 *describing himself as a farmer*: Michael King draft registration card, September 12, 1918, Ancestry.com.

18 *Floyd Chapel*: The road running just east of the church and through the heart of Stockbridge is now called the Martin Luther King Senior Heritage Trail.

18 *334,000 Black Baptists*: Paul Harvey, *Redeeming the South: Religious Cultures and Racial Identities Among Southern Baptists, 1865–1925* (Chapel Hill: University of North Carolina Press, 1997), 46.

18 *"carrying a coat-pocket full"*: Peter Gorner, "Daddy King: 'There's No Hate in My Heart,'" *Chicago Tribune*, December 23, 1980.

19 *preacher* and *an enslaved person*: Christine King Farris, *Through It All: Reflections on My Life, My Family, and My Faith* (New York: Atria Books, 2009), 4.

19 *"I have give"*: Martin Luther King Sr., *Daddy King: An Autobiography*, with Clayton Riley (New York: William Morrow, 1980), 90.

20 *tired of seeing racial slurs*: Ibid., 86.

20 *only one who survived*: Bernita D. Bennette, "A. D. Williams," Manuscript Department, Moorland-Spingarn Research Center, Howard University, Washington, D.C., David J. Garrow personal collection, 6.

20 *"As he talked about this only daughter"*: "The Autobiography of Daddy King," 10–11.

20 *"early entanglements"*: Martin Luther King Sr., *Daddy King*, 44.

21 *"I may smell"*: Ibid., 38.

21 *Jennie Williams objected*: Gorner, "Daddy King: 'There's No Hate in My Heart.'"

21 *"Wife, this King"*: Ibid.

22 *failed freshman English twice*: Martin Luther King Sr., *Daddy King*, 87.

22 *professional aspiration*: June Dobbs Butts, interview with author, August 1, 2018.

23 *"Was I worth it?"*: L. D. Reddick, *Crusader Without Violence: A Biography of Martin Luther King, Jr.* (New York: Harper & Brothers, 1959), 50.

23 *of course he was worth it*: Ibid.

24 *"He really related to Martin Luther"*: Isaac Farris, interview with author, January 7, 2022.

24 *"Both father and I"*: "Attack on the Conscience," *Time*, February 18, 1957.

3. Sweet Auburn

25 *"the richest Negro street in the world"*: Emmet John Hughes, "The Negro's New Economic Life," *Forbes*, September 1956.

25 *"that neither immigrants"*: Gary Pomerantz, *Where Peachtree Meets Sweet Auburn: A Saga of Race and Family* (New York: Penguin Books, 1997), 98.

26 *"shook the house"*: Christine King Farris, interview with Julieanna L. Richardson, July 11, 2010, The HistoryMakers Digital Archive.

26 *uniformed waiters*: "Newly Elected Pastor and Wife Are Honored Guests at Elaborate Installation Banquet," *Atlanta Daily World*, April 6, 1932.

26 *It didn't take long*: "The Autobiography of Daddy King as Told to Edward A. Jones" (unpublished manuscript, August 1973), 90.

26 *"a leader, a politician"*: W. E. B. Du Bois, *The Souls of Black Folk* (1903; repr. New York: Signet Classics, 1969), 211.

27 *A small grocery store*: Census records and city directories show a grocery store across the street from the King home.

27 *"Every black child"*: James Farmer, *Lay Bare the Heart: An Autobiography of the Civil Rights Movement* (Fort Worth: Texas Christian University Press, 1998), 37.

28 *"You just wait and see"*: Ted Poston, "42nd Spingarn Medalist: Martin Luther King Jr.; The Preacher Who Fights," *Baltimore Afro-American*, June 8, 1957.

28 *to master an impressive vocabulary*: Alberta King, interview with Lavelle Dyett, WBZ-TV Boston, "Sixteen '74," 1974, Peabody Awards Collection Archives, kaltura .uga.edu/media/t/1_cli0lpos/86446941, accessed June 25, 2020.

28 *"run around the community"*: Martin Luther King Jr., "Propagandizing Christianity," sermon at Dexter Avenue Baptist Church, September 12, 1954, King Papers, Stanford University.

28 *always did the preaching*: Carolyn Marvin, "Church Remembers King," *Atlanta Constitution*, April 4, 1970.

29 *"five big candles on it"*: Christine King Farris, *Through It All: Reflections on My Life, My Family, and My Faith* (New York: Atria Books, 2009), 27.

29 *dominate the board and bankrupt his rivals*: June Dobbs Butts, interview with author, November 27, 2018.

29 *expected home for dinner*: Christine King Farris, "The Young Martin," *Ebony*, January 1986.

29 *"My father always had"*: Alberta King, interview with Dyett.

30 *Several times a year*: James H. Miller, interview with author, Stockbridge, Ga., April 22, 2021.

30 *pokeweed*: Isaac Newton Farris Jr., interview with author, February 12, 2022.

30 *He took the family to Floyd Chapel*: Ibid.

30 *"Hatred makes nothin' but more hatred"*: "The Autobiography of Daddy King," 74.

30 *Daddy King sat at the head*: Christine King Farris, interview with Richardson.

30 *"He was very interested"*: Alberta King, interview with Barbara Walters, NBC TV, April 2, 1970, NBC News archives.

31 *"My prayer"*: Quoted in James Baldwin, "A Highroad to Destiny," in *Martin Luther King, Jr: A Profile*, ed. C. Eric Lincoln, rev. ed. (New York: Hill & Wang, 1984), 100.

31 *ordered the children to spank*: L. D. Reddick, *Crusader Without Violence: A Biography of Martin Luther King, Jr.* (New York: Harper & Brothers, 1959), 60.

31 *"so strong and hard driving"*: Louis E. Lomax, *To Kill a Black Man: The Shocking Parallel Lives of Malcolm X and Martin Luther King Jr.* (Los Angeles: Holloway House, 1968), 48.

31 *"I think Martin"*: Bayard Rustin and Harry Wachtel in conversation with Walter Naegle, October 31, 1985, transcript, David J. Garrow personal collection.

31 *"You've killed him!"*: Reddick, *Crusader Without Violence*, 59.

32 *Half of all Black Americans*: Sidney Lens, *Radicalism in America* (New York: Thomas Y. Crowell, 1966), 309.

32 *The number of Black craftsmen*: Ibid.

32 *"We tried to instill"*: Alberta King, interview with Walters.

32 *dog named Mickey*: Christine King Farris, interview with Richardson.

33 *"sweetness in religion"*: Walter McCall, interview with Herbert Holmes, n.d., transcript,

Martin Luther King Oral History Collection, Martin Luther King Jr. Collection, King Center, Atlanta, 18–19.

33 *"you don't have to fight"*: Lewis V. Baldwin, *There Is a Balm in Gilead: The Cultural Roots of Martin Luther King, Jr.* (Minneapolis: Fortress Press, 1991), 123.

33 *"Bring some unsaved person"*: "Revival Begins at Ebenezer," *Atlanta Daily World*, April 14, 1936.

33 *The Reverend H. H. Coleman led the revival*: "Revival Spirit at Ebenezer Nightly," *Atlanta Daily World*, April 22, 1936.

33 *"Men must get hungry"*: Ibid.

34 *On the basketball court*: Ted Poston, "Martin Luther King Jr.: He Never Liked to Fight!," *Baltimore Afro-American*, June 15, 1957.

34 *"If you were running"*: Emmett Proctor, interview, April 15, 1970, transcript, Taylor Branch Papers, folder 701, scan 45, Southern Historical Collection, Wilson Library, University of North Carolina Library, Chapel Hill.

34 *"Let's go to the grass"*: Quoted in Lerone Bennett Jr., *What Manner of Man: A Biography of Martin Luther King, Jr.* (Chicago: Johnson Publishing, 1964), 21.

34 *"The boys would tease him"*: June Dobbs Butts, interview with author, August 1, 2018.

35 *He grew up hearing shouted sermons and soaring songs*: Reddick, *Crusader Without Violence*, 85.

35 *"behind the scenes setting forth"*: Martin Luther King Jr., "An Autobiography of Religious Development," November 20, 1950, in *The Papers of Martin Luther King, Jr.*, vol. 1: *Called to Serve, January 1929–June 1951*, ed. Clayborne Carson (Berkeley: University of California Press, 1992), 368.

36 *"Children are less likely"*: Kenneth B. Clark, *Prejudice and Your Child* (Boston: Beacon Press, 1955), 86.

36 *swim in any of the city's public pools*: Martin Luther King Jr., interview with John Freeman, *Face to Face*, BBC, aired October 29, 1961.

36 *could recall seeing Black people physically attacked*: Ibid.

36 *a letter that also appears*: Martin Luther King Jr., "M. L. King, Jr., Writes," *Atlanta Daily World*, May 2, 1937.

36 *"The man said he didn't owe"*: Quoted in Trezzvant W. Anderson, "My Son Martin! A Father Lays Bare His Heart, His Faith, His Fears," *Pittsburgh Courier*, June 29, 1957.

37 *"I can see how it went from me to him"*: Ibid.

37 *"that nigger that stepped"*: King, interview with Freeman.

37 *"We're comfortable in these seats"*: "The Autobiography of Daddy King," 35.

37 *"I was going to be fighting"*: Martin Luther King Sr., *Daddy King: An Autobiography*, with Clayton Riley (New York: William Morrow, 1980), 108–109.

38 *"It wasn't that she was compromising"*: Alveda King, interview with author, May 10, 2022.

38 *"If our white ministers"*: "Wet, Dry Forces Gird for Drive," *Atlanta Constitution*, May 11, 1935.

38 *At the time, the average salary for*: "Why Not Equal Pay for Equal Work," *Atlanta Daily World*, December 1, 1941.

38 *"To serve God"*: "The Autobiography of Daddy King," 29.

38 *"there was a sense of somebodiness within us"*: Martin Luther King Jr., interview with Studs Terkel, WFMT, October 22, 1964, studsterkel.wfmt.com/programs/dr-martin -luther-king-jr-discusses-civil-rights-regards-his-i-have-dream-speech.

39 *"300 or more colored ushers"*: "Atlanta Excited as GWTW Festival Begins," *Atlanta Daily World*, December 14, 1939.

39 *"a social-economic regime"*: G. Glenwood Clark, review of *Gone with the Wind*, by Margaret Mitchell, *William and Mary College Quarterly Historical Magazine*, 2nd ser., 17, no. 1 (January 1937): 131.

39 *DC-3*: Warren G. Harris, *Clark Gable: A Biography* (New York: Three Rivers Press, 2002), 211.

40 *Packard convertible*: Ibid.

40 *"Reverend King was beseeched"*: June Dobbs Butts, interview with author, November 27, 2018.

40 *Confederate flags fluttered in the breeze*: "Ebenezer Choir Scores at Gala 'GWTW' Ball," *Atlanta Daily World*, December 15, 1939.

4. "Black America Still Wears Chains"

42 *"ditties"*: Naomi Ruth Barber King, *A.D. and M.L. King: Two Brothers Who Dared to Dream* (Bloomington, Ind.: Author House, 2014), 3.

43 *When a church member's phone rang*: Coretta Scott King, interview with Charlotte Mayerson, July 16, 1968, audio recording, Smathers Library, University of Florida, Gainesville.

43 *"almost imperturbable, rarely registering"*: Donald Hugh Smith, "Martin Luther King Jr.: Rhetorician of Revolt" (PhD diss., University of Wisconsin, 1964).

43 *She was not a classically trained musician*: Ibid.

43 *"the most obsequious, quiet woman"*: June Dobbs Butts, interview with author, November 27, 2018.

44 *persuaded her husband*: Martin Luther King Sr., *Daddy King: An Autobiography*, with Clayton Riley (New York: William Morrow, 1980), 131.

44 *"He loved that suit"*: Christine King Farris, *Through It All: Reflections on My Life, My Family, and My Faith* (New York: Atria Books, 2009), 27.

44 *"lovely, dry sense of humor"*: Alveda King, interview with author, May 10, 2022.

44 *"Let's see, now"*: Quoted in Coretta Scott King, *My Life with Martin Luther King, Jr.*, rev. ed. (New York: Henry Holt, 1993), 77.

44 *"Bunch was very gifted with children"*: Martin Luther King Sr., *Daddy King*, 130.

44 *"She knew each of her children"*: Ibid., 131.

44 *"She never did have hate in her heart"*: Martin Luther King Sr., interview with John Craig Flournoy, July 30, 1983, in John Craig Flournoy, "Young Martin: The First Nineteen Years in the Life of Martin Luther King Jr." (master's thesis, Southern Methodist University, 1986).

45 *encyclopedia*: Ibid.

45 *"woman of health and spirits"*: L. D. Reddick, *Crusader Without Violence: A Biography of Martin Luther King, Jr.* (New York: Harper & Bros., 1959), 51.

45 *"She was very dear to us"*: Ibid.

46 *"in need of major repairs"*: Joseph K. Oppermann, *Three Double-Shotgun Houses:*

493ABC Auburn Avenue, Martin Luther King, Jr. National Historic Site (Atlanta: National Park Service, 2017), www.npshistory.com/publications/malu/hsr-double-shotgun-houses.pdf.

46 *cheese, eggs, and bacon*: Christine King Farris, interview with Julieanna L. Richardson, July 11, 2010, The HistoryMakers Digital Archive.

46 *"Have some cake"*: June Dobbs Butts, interview with author.

47 *"We'll get colored policemen"*: Gary Pomerantz, *Where Peachtree Meets Sweet Auburn: A Saga of Race and Family* (New York: Penguin Books, 1997), 147.

47 *King would continue to support*: "Dobbs, King Debate Issues at Mass Meet," *Atlanta Daily World*, May 8, 1953.

47 *"The racial condition"*: Jessie O. Thomas, "Urban League Bulletin," *Atlanta Constitution*, May 4, 1941.

48 *"gave me all he had"*: "Beaten in Georgia, Says Roland Hayes," *New York Times*, July 17, 1942.

48 *might be alerted to their plight*: I. P. Reynolds, "King Deplores Injustices in Sunday Sermon," *Atlanta Daily World*, August 3, 1942.

49 *She was the founder of the nation's first*: "Educational, Civic Leader to Be Interred at 3 Today," *Atlanta Daily World*, November 25, 1953.

49 *M.L. attended David T. Howard*: "BTWHS Students Heard by DTH Graduates," *Atlanta Daily World*, June 3, 1937.

49 *An obstreperous child*: Farris, *Through It All*, 22–23.

50 *Brother and sister competed to learn*: Carolyn Marvin, "Church Remembers King," *Atlanta Constitution*, April 4, 1970.

50 *interrupting*: Ted Poston, "He Never Liked to Fight!," *Baltimore Afro-American*, June 15, 1957.

50 *In one Sunday-school session*: "Attack on the Conscience," *Time*, February 18, 1957.

50 *Later, he told his parents*: Ibid.

50 *"the shouting and the stamping"*: William Peters, "Our Weapon Is Love," *Redbook*, August 1956.

51 *"My heart throbs anew"*: King's speech was later published in Booker T. Washington High School's yearbook, *The Cornellian*, May 1944.

51 *King would brag*: Martin Luther King Jr., interview with Alex Haley, unedited transcript of *Playboy* interview, Rubenstein Library, Duke University, October 23, 1964.

51 *judges gave first prize*: "Savannah Girl Is Winner of Elks Oratorical Meet," *Atlanta Daily World*, April 22, 1944.

51 *formerly enslaved parents*: "Cornell's Champion Orator," *The Cornellian*, March 14, 1910.

51 *Cornell College*: "Coleman Won Oratorical," *Cedar Rapids Gazette*, March 5, 1910.

51 *His speech had been reprinted*: Winston H. Ashley, compiler, *Fifty Orations That Have Won Prizes in Speaking Contests, Including the Orations That Have Won Prizes in the Interstate Oratorical Association and Other Intercollegiate Prize Speaking Contests* (New York: Noble and Noble, 1928), 158–66.

52 *"That night will never"*: King, interview with Haley.

5. The Open Curtain

53 *"He came through it all"*: James Baldwin, "The Dangerous Road Before Martin Luther King," *Harper's Magazine*, February 1961.

53 *King seemed to love people*: Ibid.

53 *"single-minded determination"*: Christine King Farris, "The Young Martin," *Ebony*, January 1986, 57.

54 *"The first time that I was seated"*: Martin Luther King Jr., "Pilgrimage to Nonviolence," *Christian Century*, April 13, 1960, www.christiancentury.org/article/pilgrimage-nonviolence.

55 *"Tweedie and I"*: Emmett Proctor, interview, April 15, 1970, transcript, Taylor Branch Papers, folder 701, scan 45, Southern Historical Collection, Wilson Library, University of North Carolina, Chapel Hill.

55 *Polish immigrants*: "Blacks Recall Connecticut Tobacco Farms," *Journal Inquirer* (Manchester, Conn.), July 17, 1989.

56 *"It was a bitter feeling going back"*: Ted Poston, "Fighting Pastor: Martin Luther King," *New York Post*, April 10, 1957.

56 *"do not by far"*: Gunnar Myrdal, *An American Dilemma: The Negro Problem and American Democracy* (New York: Harper & Brothers, 1944), li.

57 *"The American Negro problem"*: Ibid., xlvii.

57 *"seemed changed"*: Lerone Bennett Jr., *What Manner of Man: A Biography of Martin Luther King, Jr.* (Chicago: Johnson Publishing, 1964), 26.

57 *"playing a part"*: Ibid.

57 *"We called him 'Runt'"*: Patrick Parr, "Reverend Samuel McKinney Remembers His Friend Dr. King," *Seattle*, January 15, 2015, www.seattlemag.com/article/reverend-samuel-mckinney-remembers-his-friend-dr-king.

58 *Enrollment at the college averaged 350*: Gary Dorrien, *Breaking White Supremacy* (New Haven, Conn.: Yale University Press, 2018), 154.

58 *Though he could blend in*: Robert Williams, interview with Taylor Branch, April 3, 1984, Taylor Branch Papers, no. 5047, Southern Historical Collection, Wilson Library, University of North Carolina, Chapel Hill.

58 *seldom attended dances*: Herman Bostick, interview with Herbert Holmes, March 30, 1970, Taylor Branch Papers, Southern Historical Collection, Wilson Library, University of North Carolina, Chapel Hill.

58 *"Well, we just won't go"*: Alberta King, interview with Lavelle Dyett, WBZ-TV Boston, "Sixteen '74," 1974, Peabody Awards Collection Archives, kaltura.uga.edu/media/t/1_cli0lpos/86446941, accessed June 25, 2020.

58 *He owned one suit*: June Dobbs Butts, interview with author, August 1, 2018.

59 *research on lynchings*: John J. Ansbro, *Martin Luther King, Jr.: The Making of a Mind* (Maryknoll, N.Y.: Orbis Books, 1982), 76.

59 *Black church . . . shaped King's intellectual views*: James Cone, "Martin Luther King: The Source for His Courage to Face Death," *Concilium*, March 1983, 74–79.

59 *"to learn their plight"*: Bennett, *What Manner of Man*, 28.

59 *"We used to sit up"*: Walter McCall, interview with Herbert Holmes, King Center, Atlanta.

59 *2 percent of Black men and women*: Nancy MacLean, *Freedom Is Not Enough: The Opening of the American Workplace* (New York: Russell Sage Foundation, 2006), 28.

60 *"The Negro is on a special errand"*: Benjamin E. Mays, *The Negro's God: As Reflected in His Literature* (New York: Atheneum, 1968), 250.

60 *"However learned"*: Randal Maurice Jelks, *Benjamin Elijah Mays, Schoolmaster of the Movement: A Biography* (Chapel Hill: University of North Carolina Press, 2012), 148.

60 *"Whatever the system was"*: Benjamin Mays, interview with Coleman Brown, March 4, 1970, in Coleman Brown, "Grounds for American Loyalty in a Prophetic Christian Social Ethic—with Special Attention to Martin Luther King Jr." (PhD diss., Union Theological Seminary, 1979).

60 *"During my student days"*: Martin Luther King Jr., *Stride Toward Freedom: The Montgomery Story* (1958; repr. Boston: Beacon Press, 2010), 78.

61 *"King came to the conclusion"*: Walter McCall, interview with Herbert Holmes, King Center, Atlanta.

61 *made his debut as a journalist*: Martin Luther King Jr., "N.C. Educator Gives Inspiring Youth Talk," *Atlanta Daily World*, March 7, 1947.

62 *"We must remember"*: Martin Luther King Jr., "The Purpose of Education," *Maroon Tiger*, January–February 1947, in *The Papers of Martin Luther King, Jr.*, vol. 1: *Called to Serve, January 1929–June 1951*, ed. Clayborne Carson (Berkeley: University of California Press, 1992), 123–24.

62 *pioneering study*: Kenneth L. Smith and Ira G. Zepp Jr., *Search for the Beloved Community: The Thinking of Martin Luther King Jr.* (Valley Forge, Pa.: Judson Press, 1974).

62 *"All week long"*: Quoted in William Peters, "Our Weapon Is Love," *Redbook*, August 1956.

63 *"It is obvious that prophets address themselves"*: Martin Luther King Jr., blue book, exam, March 26, 1946, Robert H. Woodruff Library of the Atlanta University Center, Morehouse College Martin Luther King Jr. Collection: Series 5: Educational Materials.

63 *"Right in there"*: John Craig Flournoy, "Young Martin: The First Nineteen Years in the Life of Martin Luther King, Jr." (master's thesis, Southern Methodist University, 1986), 49.

64 *"I thought I could help them choose"*: "The Autobiography of Daddy King as Told to Edward A. Jones" (unpublished manuscript, August 1973), 85.

64 *"I know that"*: Ibid., 86.

64 *"I came to see that God had placed"*: Martin Luther King Jr., "My Call to the Ministry," statement written for the American Baptist Convention, Montgomery, Ala., August, 9, 1959, Stanford King Institute, kinginstitute.stanford.edu/king-papers/documents/my-call-ministry.

64 *"King became a minister"*: Quoted in Donald Hugh Smith, "Martin Luther King Jr.: Rhetorician of Revolt" (PhD diss., University of Wisconsin, 1964).

6. "A Sense of Responsibility"

65 *"Can't hold 'em!"*: Larry Williams, interview with Taylor Branch, December 27, 1983, in Taylor Branch Papers, no. 5047, Southern Historical Collection, Wilson Library, University of North Carolina, Chapel Hill.

65 *fall of 1947*: The precise date of King's first sermon at Ebenezer is unknown, but the

Atlanta Daily World reported that he was scheduled to preach the 11:00 a.m. service on November 16, 1947.

65 *main chapel was filled*: "The Autobiography of Daddy King as Told to Edward A. Jones" (unpublished manuscript, August 1973), 87.

65 *"Never before had we seen"*: Ibid.

67 *"He was a good thinker"*: June Dobbs Butts, interview with author, August 1, 2018.

67 *connected quickly*: Ibid.

67 *"Life Is What You Make It"*: Taylor Branch, *Parting the Waters: America in the King Years, 1954–63* (New York: Touchstone, 1989), 66; David J. Garrow, *Bearing the Cross: Martin Luther King, Jr., and the Southern Christian Leadership Conference* (New York: William Morrow, 1986), 38.

67 *life was theirs to shape*: The remainder of this paragraph is paraphrased from Harry Emerson Fosdick, "Life Is What We Make It," typed sermon for NBC broadcast, May 4, 1941, Harry Emerson Fosdick Papers, Burke Library at Union Theological Seminary, Columbia University, New York.

68 *King would continue using Fosdick's sermons*: "Rev. M. L. King Jr. at Liberty Sunday," *Atlanta Daily World*, April 24, 1948.

68 *"words are shared assets"*: Keith D. Miller, "Composing Martin Luther King, Jr.," *PMLA* 105, no. 1 (January 1990): 70–82.

68 *did not tell his son*: John Craig Flournoy, "Young Martin: The First Nineteen Years in the Life of Martin Luther King Jr." (master's thesis, Southern Methodist University, 1986), 51.

69 *offering lines from Edgar Allan Poe*: David Levering Lewis, *King: A Critical Biography* (New York: Praeger, 1970), 22.

69 *"Robinson and Stevens, the Wreckers"*: Garrow, *Bearing the Cross*, 36.

69 *After Spelman*: "Juanita S. Stone, 89," *Atlanta Journal-Constitution*, June 8, 2018.

70 *"You don't need to risk"*: Martin Luther King Sr., *Daddy King: An Autobiography*, with Clayton Riley (New York: William Morrow, 1980), 142.

71 *"a comparatively weak"*: Brailsford R. Brazeal to Charles E. Batten, March 23, 1948, Stanford King Institute, kinginstitute.stanford.edu/king-papers/documents /brailsford-r-brazeal-charles-e-batten.

71 *"My call to the ministry was quite different"*: Martin Luther King Jr., "My Call to the Ministry," statement written for the American Baptist Convention, Montgomery, Ala., August 9, 1959, Stanford King Institute, kinginstitute.stanford.edu/king-papers /documents/my-call-ministry.

71 *"If you can do one single thing"*: Marion E. Jackson, "Work for Just Peace, M'house Grads Told," *Atlanta Daily World*, June 9, 1948.

71 *"for both M.L. and myself"*: June Dobbs Butts, interview with author, August 1, 2018.

72 *On the day Dobbs and King heard him*: June Dobbs Butts to author, November 21, 2018.

72 *Daddy King was a frequent womanizer*: Butts, interview with author. Stanley Levison also discussed Daddy King's womanizing in an interview with the historian Arthur M. Schlesinger Jr., August 3, 1976. Schlesinger's undated memo on the conversation is in the David J. Garrow personal collection.

72 *"It obsessed him"*: June Dobbs Butts, interview with author.

72 *M.L. argued that the act of dancing*: Margaret L. Randolph, "Attacks Way Problems of Dancing Is Met," letter to the editor, *Atlanta Daily World*, June 24, 1948.

7. The Seminarian

74 *scar on the back of his left hand*: Selective Service registration card, September 4, 1948, National Archives.

74 *A wounded Confederate soldier*: Patrick Parr, *The Seminarian: Martin Luther King Jr. Comes of Age* (Chicago: Lawrence Hill Books, 2018), 19.

75 *King expressed guilt*: Marcus Wood, interview with Taylor Branch, October 4, 1983, in Taylor Branch Papers, no. 5047, Southern Historical Collection, Wilson Library, University of North Carolina, Chapel Hill.

75 *"He once asked"*: James Beshai, interview with author, May 6, 2022.

75 *"He was a very honest man"*: James Beshai, interview with author, May 7, 2022.

76 *He later hired King to babysit*: James B. Pritchard, interview with Taylor Branch, June 25, 1984, in Taylor Branch Papers, no. 5047, Southern Historical Collection, Wilson Library, University of North Carolina, Chapel Hill.

77 *"I am a profound advocator"*: Martin Luther King Jr., "Preaching Ministry," outline, September–November 1948, Stanford King Institute, kinginstitute.stanford.edu/king -papers/documents/preaching-ministry.

77 *"I was well aware of the typical white stereotype"*: Lerone Bennett Jr., *What Manner of Man: A Biography of Martin Luther King, Jr.* (Chicago: Johnson Publishing, 1964), 34.

77 *"He could eat more than any little man"*: David Levering Lewis, *King: A Critical Biography* (New York: Praeger, 1970), 28.

78 *a regular column*: Parr, *The Seminarian*, 41.

78 *"Just a matter of arithmetic"*: J. Pius Barbour, "Meditations on Rev. M. L. King, Jr., of Montgomery, Ala.," *National Baptist Voice*, March 1956.

78 *"I guess it must have been a gift from God"*: Alberta King, interview with Lavelle Dyett, WBZ-TV Boston, "Sixteen '74," 1974, Peabody Awards Collection Archives, kaltura .uga.edu/media/t/1_cli0lpos/86446941, accessed June 25, 2020.

78 *"This I could never accept"*: Martin Luther King Jr., *Stride Toward Freedom: The Montgomery Story* (1958; repr. Boston: Beacon Press, 2010), 78.

79 *a crisis of confidence*: Ibid., 83.

79 *drew a .45*: Walter McCall, interview by Herbert Holmes, King Center, Atlanta.

80 *In a front-page story*: "N.J. Inn Keeper Held After Four Charge Refusal," *Philadelphia Tribune*, June 20, 1950.

80 *His father had always made him feel*: Zinobia Jordan Austin, interview with Taylor Branch, February 3, 1984, in Taylor Branch Papers, no. 5047, Southern Historical Collection, Wilson Library, University of North Carolina, Chapel Hill.

80 *The bartender was found guilty*: Walter McCall, interview with Herbert Holmes, King Center, Atlanta. Additional research on Maple Shade by Patrick Duff.

80 *"They refused to serve us"*: Charles Layne, "Rev. King Lauds City on Strides to Integration," *Philadelphia Tribune*, October 28, 1961.

80 *"first civil rights struggle"*: Ibid.

8. "Madly, Madly in Love"

81 *Amelia Elizabeth Moitz*: Patrick Joyce, interview with author by email, October 17, 2021.

81 *"King was extremely fond of her"*: Marcus Garvey Wood, *And Grace Will Lead Me Home . . . The Ministry of Rev. Marcus Garvey Wood: Covering Fifty Years, 1945–1995* (Baltimore: Gateway Press, 1998), 50.

82 *"Already he was a scholar"*: Ralph David Abernathy, *And the Walls Came Tumbling Down: An Autobiography* (New York: Harper & Row, 1989), 89.

82 *"Well, hello, Mr. Abernathy"*: Ibid., 90.

82 *King worked hard*: Kenneth Smith, interview with Taylor Branch, November 3, 1983, in Taylor Branch Papers, no. 5047, Southern Historical Collection, Wilson Library, University of North Carolina, Chapel Hill.

82 *"desire to give himself to a greater cause"*: Patrick Parr, *The Seminarian: Martin Luther King Jr. Comes of Age* (Chicago: Lawrence Hill Books, 2018), 210.

82 *"Exceptional intellectual ability"*: George Davis, "Confidential Evaluation of Martin Luther King Jr.," November 15, 1950, in *The Papers of Martin Luther King, Jr.*, vol. 1: *Called to Serve, January 1929–June 1951*, ed. Clayborne Carson (Berkeley: University of California Press, 1992), 334.

83 *"It is hopeless for the Negro"*: Reinhold Niebuhr, *Moral Man and Immoral Society: A Study in Ethics and Policy* (Louisville, Ky.: Westminster John Knox Press, 2013), 252.

84 *One Crozer classmate recalled*: Parr, *The Seminarian*, 193.

84 *November 19, 1950*: King mentions the lecture in Martin Luther King Jr., *Stride Toward Freedom: The Montgomery Story* (1958; repr. Boston: Beacon Press, 2010); the author and activist Patrick Duff identified the date by checking church calendars.

84 *"His message was so profound"*: King, *Stride Toward Freedom*, 84.

84 *"When we love on the* agape *level"*: Martin Luther King Jr., "Nonviolence and Racial Justice," *Christian Century*, February 6, 1957.

85 *"I listened"*: Parr, *The Seminarian*, 95.

85 *"We were madly, madly in love"*: Ibid.

86 *"He wanted to marry her"*: James Beshai, interview with author, May 6, 2022.

86 *"She liked me and I found myself liking her"*: Lerone Bennett Jr., *What Manner of Man: A Biography of Martin Luther King, Jr.* (Chicago: Johnson Publishing, 1964), 40.

86 *On the morning of his graduation*: David Levering Lewis, *King: A Critical Biography* (New York: Praeger, 1970), 32.

86 *"a man of a broken heart"*: David J. Garrow, *Bearing the Cross: Martin Luther King, Jr., and the Southern Christian Leadership Conference* (New York: William Morrow, 1986), 41.

86 *had been King's "true love"*: Harry Belafonte, interview with author, April 4, 2017.

87 *Betty went on to become an interior decorator*: Patrick Joyce, email message to author, October 17, 2019.

87 *"I wouldn't say he was broken-hearted"*: Quoted in "Martin Luther King Jr.: The Man and the Dream," *Biography*, season 7, episode 8, aired January 19, 1998, on A&E Home Video, DVD.

9. The Match

88 *"For a number of years"*: Martin Luther King Jr., Fragment of Application to Boston University, December 1950, Stanford King Institute, kinginstitute.stanford.edu/king -papers/documents/fragment-application-boston-university.

89 *"because personhood"*: Kenneth L. Smith and Ira G. Zepp Jr., *Search for the Beloved Community: The Thinking of Martin Luther King Jr.* (Lanham, Md.: University Press of America, 1986), 107.

89 *"He said God talked with him"*: June Dobbs Butts, interview with author, August 1, 2018.

90 *"try to make sure he could win the girlfriend of the tallest"*: "Martin Luther King Jr.: The Man and the Dream," presented by Peter Graves.

90 *"You're not eating your beets"*: LaVerne Eagleson (née Weston), interview with author, July 16, 2019.

91 *Morehouse pennants*: Coretta Scott King, *My Life, My Love, My Legacy*, as told to Barbara Reynolds (New York: Henry Holt, 2017), photo insert.

91 *phone calls home*: Taylor Branch, *Parting the Waters: America in the King Years, 1954–63* (New York: Touchstone, 1989), 94.

91 *"Martin was the guru"*: Sybil Morial, interview with author, November 28, 2018.

92 *"spiritually located in the South"*: Lewis V. Baldwin, *There Is a Balm in Gilead: The Cultural Roots of Martin Luther King, Jr.* (Minneapolis: Fortress Press, 1991), 41.

92 *"I am going back"*: Quoted ibid.

92 *Mary said she knew two women Martin might like*: Coretta Scott King transcripts, University of Florida, Alden and Allene G. Hatch Papers (hereafter referred to as Hatch Papers), box 22, folder 4, 3/40. Coretta remembered her name as Lavern Western.

92 *"I said, 'You better give me the telephone number'"*: Martin Luther King Jr., interview with F. Lee Bailey, late 1967, *Good Company*, ABC-TV.

92 *on a Thursday night in February*: L. D. Reddick, *Crusader Without Violence: A Biography of Martin Luther King, Jr.* (New York: Harper & Bros., 1959), 105.

92 *"He was a typical man"*: Coretta Scott King transcripts, Hatch Papers, box 22, folder 4, 3/41.

93 *He arrived right on time*: Reddick, *Crusader Without Violence*, 105.

93 *She got in the car, and King drove them*: Cara Feinberg, "Mrs. King and I, on When She Met Martin," *Boston Globe*, February 5, 2006.

93 *But the more he talked, the better he looked*: Coretta Scott King transcripts, Hatch Papers, box 22, folder 4, tape 3.

93 *"You have some* great *hair"*: Reddick, *Crusader Without Violence*, 105.

93 *she would have the edge*: Coretta Scott King, interview with Donald H. Smith, December 7, 1963, audiotape, Smith collection, University of Wisconsin, Madison.

93 *At one of Coretta's comments*: Bennett, *What Manner of Man*, 47.

93 *"Oh, you can think, too"*: Feinberg, "Mrs. King and I, on When She Met Martin."

93 *"just radiated so much charm"*: Coretta Scott King transcripts, Hatch Papers, folder 4, tape 3.

93 *"because he had come from"*: Coretta Scott King, "The World of Coretta King," *New Lady*, January 1966.

94 *They named their second girl*: Edythe Scott Bagley with Joe Hilley, *Desert Rose: The Life and Legacy of Coretta Scott King* (Tuscaloosa: University of Alabama Press, 2012), 53.

94 *twenty-five children*: Ibid., 8.

94 *never smoked or drank*: Coretta Scott King, "The World of Coretta King."

94 *sixth grade*: Ibid.

94 *fourth-grade education*: Ibid.

94 *"She ain't nothin' but breath and britches"*: Lynn Cothren, interview with author, September 13, 2018.

95 *she became the first Black woman*: Bagley, *Desert Rose*, 18.

95 *"She was a hardy youngster"*: Ibid., 54.

95 *Corrie, as friends called her*: Coretta Scott King, interview with Charlotte Mayerson, July 16, 1968, audio recording, Smathers Library, University of Florida, Gainesville.

95 *Coretta walked five miles to attend*: L. D. Reddick, "Crusader Without Violence," typed manuscript, L. D. Reddick Papers, Schomburg Center for Research in Black Culture, New York Public Library (hereafter referred to as Schomburg Center).

95 *"This was one thing that stands out"*: Coretta Scott King, interview with Arnold Michaelis, December 1, 1965, outtakes from "Martin Luther King Jr.: A Personal Portrait," Brown Media Archives, University of Georgia, Athens.

95 *The faculty at the Lincoln School*: Coretta Scott King, interview with Donald H. Smith, December 7, 1963, Wisconsin Historical Society.

95 *violin, piano, and trumpet*: Coretta Scott King, "The World of Coretta King."

96 *"This factor"*: Bagley, *Desert Rose*, 26–27.

96 *"This kind of humiliation, constantly"*: Coretta Scott King, interview with Michaelis.

96 *"really no one cared about what happened"*: Coretta Scott King, *My Life with Martin Luther King, Jr.*, rev. ed. (New York: Henry Holt, 1993), 36.

96 *A second sister*: Coretta Scott King transcripts, Hatch Papers, box 22, folder 5.

96 *"So that meant I had to spend a lot of time"*: Coretta Scott King transcripts, Hatch Papers, folder 9, tape 30.

96 *"We went to the Twelfth Street Grill"*: Walter Rybeck, interview with author, June 2, 2020.

97 *bused tables*: Coretta Scott King, "Why I Came to College," *Opportunity: Journal of Negro Life* 26, no. 2 (April–June 1948).

98 *Juilliard and New York City intimidated her*: Coretta Scott King, "The World of Coretta King."

98 *Jim Crow Scholarship*: Emory O. Jackson, "Alabama Bars 129 from Studies Offered in Its Institutions," *Alabama Tribune*, July 23, 1954.

98 *"I saw myself as a concert singer"*: Coretta Scott King, *My Life, My Love, My Legacy*, 33.

98 *"I can worship in my room"*: Ibid., 51.

99 *his use of Shakespearean sonnets*: Martin Luther King Jr., speech, Bowdoin College, May 6, 1964, audio recording, www.bowdoin.edu/mlk/mlks-visit-to-bowdoin.html.

99 *"he was always trying to convince me"*: Cara Feinberg, "For Coretta, Finding Her Direction," *Boston Globe*, January 19, 2003.

99 *"I thought he was a very nice young man"*: Jeanne Martin Brayboy, author interview, November 23, 2018.

10. The Dynamic Force

101 *"Of course he asked me"*: Coretta Scott King, interview with Donald Smith, December 7, 1963, transcript of audiotape, Taylor Branch Papers, University of North Carolina, Chapel Hill.

101 *deliberate person*: Ibid.

101 *"I had a kind of warmth"*: Coretta Scott King, interview with Charlotte Mayerson, July 16, 1968, audio recording, Smathers Library, University of Florida, Gainesville.

102 *Samsonite suitcase*: Lynn Cothren, interview with author, February 24, 2021.

102 *"Your letter was sweet"*: Martin Luther King Jr. to Coretta Scott, July 18, 1952, Stanford King Institute, kinginstitute.stanford.edu/king-papers/documents/coretta-scott.

103 *he was considering marrying*: Coretta Scott King, interview with Mayerson.

103 *He deemed it inappropriate*: Martin Luther King Sr., *Daddy King: An Autobiography*, with Clayton Riley (New York: William Morrow, 1980), 149.

103 *Martin picked up Coretta from the train*: Coretta Scott King, interview with Mayerson.

103 *"The next morning I woke up and I was just so unhappy"*: Ibid.

104 *"He would always tell me"*: Coretta Scott King transcripts, Hatch Papers, box 22, folder 4, 5/57.

104 *in Martin's apartment*: Coretta Scott King, *My Life with Martin Luther King Jr.*, rev. ed. (New York: Henry Holt, 1993), 65.

104 *"Coretta, do you take my son seriously?"*: Ibid.

104 *"Unless you know my son better than I do"*: Coretta Scott King, interview with Mayerson.

104 *"Not a word, just like a little child"*: Ibid.

104 *"He was so displeased with me"*: Ibid.

105 *"I went to school, I would say, with a mission"*: Coretta Scott King, interview with Donald H. Smith, University of Wisconsin, Madison, 1963.

105 *Martin was "very definite"*: Coretta Scott King, *My Life with Martin Luther King Jr.*, 60.

105 *"when a mother has to work"*: Martin Luther King Jr., *Stride Toward Freedom: The Montgomery Story* (1958; repr. Boston: Beacon Press, 2010), 223.

105 *"the most important decision I would make"*: Coretta Scott King, interview with Mayerson.

105 *ambitious, intelligent, and exciting*: Edythe Scott Bagley, *Desert Rose: The Life and Legacy of Coretta Scott King* (Tuscaloosa: University of Alabama Press, 2012), 98.

105 *"I suppose it's because"*: Quoted ibid., 99.

105 *"They are industrious"*: Betty Washington, "The Woman Beside Martin Luther King," *Chicago Defender*, August 26, 1965.

105 *"nothing transcendent"*: Harry Belafonte, interview with author, April 4, 2017.

106 *"stepped into her space"*: Ibid.

106 *" She was a quintessential"*: Maya Angelou, eulogy for Coretta Scott King, February 7, 2006, www.americanrhetoric.com/speeches/mayaangeloueulogyforcorettaking.htm.

11. Plagiarism and Poetry

107 *She called him Martin*: Coretta Scott King transcripts, Hatch Papers, box 22, folder 6, 30/10.

107 *"Negro tenant on the J.C. Moore place"*: "First Cotton Blooms," *Marion Times-Standard*, June 18, 1953.

107 *Coretta fretted*: Coretta Scott King transcripts, Hatch Papers, box 22, folder 4, 6/40.

107 *a strand of pearls*: "Rev. Martin L. King, Jr. Weds Charming Alabaman," *Atlanta Daily World*, July 12, 1953.

107 *Though the guest list grew*: Coretta Scott King transcripts, Hatch Papers, box 22, folder 4, 6/32.

107 *Before the ceremony, the elder Reverend King*: Coretta Scott King transcripts, Hatch Papers, box 22, folder 4, 6/40.

108 *"Coretta, I wouldn't marry M.L."*: Coretta Scott King, interview with Charlotte Mayerson, July 16, 1968, audio recording, Smathers Library, University of Florida Library, Gainesville.

108 *More than 350 guests greeted them*: "Rev. and Mrs. M. L. King, Jr., Honored with Reception," *Atlanta Daily World*, June 28, 1953.

108 *"They were very concerned"*: Coretta Scott King, interview with Mayerson.

108 *The newlyweds returned to Boston*: L. D. Reddick, *Crusader Without Violence: A Biography of Martin Luther King, Jr.* (New York: Harper & Bros., 1959), 106.

108 *His specialties included pork chops*: Coretta Scott King transcripts, Hatch Papers, box 22, folder 4, 7/43.

109 *But that didn't mean it was a partnership*: Coretta Scott King transcripts, Hatch Papers, box 22, folder 4, 6/35.

109 *he wanted eight children*: Coretta Scott King, *My Life with Martin Luther King Jr.*, rev. ed. (New York: Henry Holt, 1993), 98.

109 *"Martin had, all through his life"*: Ibid., 57–58.

109 *"That was an adjustment I had to make"*: Ibid., 88.

110 *"There is but one refuge"*: Howard Thurman, "Supportive Order Inherent in Life (1963–05–17); For Love's Sake (1958–05–30)," Pitts Theology Library, Emory University, The Howard Thurman Digital Archive, thurman.pitts.emory.edu/items/show/1241, accessed October 16, 2021.

110 *King watched Jackie Robinson*: Howard Thurman, *With Head and Heart: The Autobiography of Howard Thurman* (San Diego: Harvest Books, 1979), 254.

111 *"Was the King"*: David J. Garrow, "King's Plagiarism: Imitation, Insecurity, and Transformation," *Journal of American History* 78, no. 1 (1991): 86–92.

111 *"convincing mastery"*: L. Harold DeWolf, first reader's report, February 26, 1955, Stanford King Institute, kinginstitute.stanford.edu/king-papers/documents/first-readers-report-l-harold-dewolf.

111 *"But doubt is not the opposite"*: Paul Tillich, *Systematic Theology*, Vol. 2, *Existence and the Christ* (Chicago: University of Chicago Press, 1975), 116.

112 *took enough from Tillich*: Lewis V. Baldwin, *There Is a Balm in Gilead: The Cultural Roots of Martin Luther King, Jr.* (Minneapolis: Fortress Press, 1991), 170.

112 *"Being-Itself"*: Martin Luther King Jr., "The Three Dimensions of a Complete Life," sermon delivered April 9, 1967.

12. Gideon's Army

113 *furious calls to social action*: In 1949, after a white police officer shot and killed a Black man, Johns preached a sermon called "It Is Safe to Murder Negroes." He advertised the title of the sermon on the board outside the church, which sat down the block from the state capitol and across the street from the Alabama Department of Public Safety. With white police officers listening outside the building, Johns told his congregation: "I'll tell you why it's safe to murder Negroes. Because Negroes stand by and let it happen."

114 *"Despite its shortcomings, we loved it"*: Martin Luther King Jr., *Stride Toward Freedom: The Montgomery Story* (1958; repr. Boston: Beacon Press, 2010), 21–22.

114 *Coretta preferred to remain in the North*: Coretta Scott King, interview with Donald H. Smith, University of Wisconsin, 1963.

114 *"I asked God if he would follow me"*: Patrick Parr, "Reverend Samuel McKinney Remembers His Friend Dr. King," *Seattle*, January 15, 2015, www.seattlemag.com /article/reverend-samuel-mckinney-remembers-his-friend-dr-king.

115 *"You just let 'em know"*: Carl T. Rowan, "The Cradle (of the Confederacy) Rocks," in Jon Meacham, ed., *Voices in Our Blood: America's Best on the Civil Rights Movement* (New York: Random House, 2003), 130.

115 *The Tuskegee Institute announced*: "Tuskegee Omits 'Lynching Letter': Southern Institute Proposes a New Annual Report on Racial Relations," *New York Times*, December 31, 1953.

115 *The local Black newspaper*: *Alabama Tribune*, January 22, 1954.

115 *Among the city's 120,000 residents in 1955*: J. Mills Thornton III, *Dividing Lines: Municipal Politics and the Struggle for Civil Rights in Montgomery, Birmingham, and Selma* (Tuscaloosa: University of Alabama Press, 2002), 23.

116 *"Babies wuz snatched"*: Quoted in "Image 135 of Federal Writers' Project: Slave Narrative Project, Vol. 1, Alabama, Aarons-Young," Library of Congress, www.loc.gov /resource/mesn.010/?sp=135.

117 *"Treading the tight-rope"*: Rosa Parks notes, n.d., 1956–58, Rosa Parks Collection, Library of Congress, box 18, folder 1.

118 *"That certainly does smell good"*: Ralph David Abernathy, *And the Walls Came Tumbling Down: An Autobiography* (New York: Harper & Row, 1989), 125.

118 *"I immediately fell in love with him"*: Ralph Abernathy interview with Taylor Branch, March 5, 1984, transcript, Taylor Branch Papers, University of North Carolina, Chapel Hill.

118 *"My husband always said"*: Juanita Abernathy, interview with author, August 2, 2018.

119 *"There was not a docile or scared bone in him"*: Ibid.

120 *"When I discovered King"*: Liam T. A. Ford, "Dexter Avenue Pastor," *Montgomery Advertiser*, January 17, 1993.

120 *He was offered the job*: Joseph C. Parker Sr., to Martin Luther King Jr., March 10, 1954, Stanford King Institute, kinginstitute.stanford.edu/king-papers/documents/joseph-c -parker-sr.

120 *he wrote to the chairman*: Martin Luther King Jr. to R. D. Nesbitt, April 14, 1954, in *The Papers of Martin Luther King, Jr.*, vol. 2: *Rediscovering Precious Values, July 1951–November 1955*, ed. Clayborne Carson (Berkeley: University of California Press, 1994), 260.

120 *"I will make myself happy in Montgomery"*: Coretta Scott King, *My Life, My Love, My Legacy*, as told to Barbara Reynolds (New York: Henry Holt, 2017), 33.

120 *Coretta traveled to Chicago*: "Social Swirl," *Atlanta Daily World*, April 4, 1954.

121 *"Education cannot thrive"*: Robert J. Donovan, "School Segregation Outlawed," *Boston Globe*, May 18, 1954.

121 *virtually silent*: Martin Luther King Jr., interview with David Susskind, June 9, 1963, video recording, search.alexanderstreet.com/view/work/bibliographic _entity%7Cvideo_work%7C4247869/tanf-susskind-archive-interview-dr-martin -luther-king-jr, accessed March 10, 2021.

122 *"To get publicity is of the highest"*: Gunnar Myrdal, *An American Dilemma: The Negro Problem and American Democracy* (New York: Harper & Brothers, 1944), 48.

13. "A Precipitating Factor"

123   *"The South isn't ready for it"*: Jack Freeman, "Students at Lanier Shocked by Supreme Court Decision," *Montgomery Advertiser*, May 18, 1954.

123   *"the Negro section of town"*: Martin Luther King Jr., *Stride Toward Freedom: The Montgomery Story* (1958; repr. Boston: Beacon Press, 2010), 10.

123   *Their neighbors were working-class men and women*: 1955 Montgomery City Directory, Ancestry.com, www.ancestry.com/interactive/2469/12007216?backurl=&ssrc=&backlabel=Return#?imageId=11993452, accessed December 11, 2019.

124   *1136 East Grove Street*: L. D. Reddick, *Crusader Without Violence: A Biography of Martin Luther King, Jr.* (New York: Harper & Bros., 1959), 109.

124   *new sinks*: Inventory of repairs, Martin Luther King Jr. Collection, Morehouse College, Atlanta.

124   *Daddy King delivered a sermon*: "Rev. M. L. King, Jr. to Be Installed Sunday," *Atlanta Daily World*, October 30, 1954.

124   *Malden worked fast but carefully*: Nelson Malden, interview with author, May 23, 2019.

125   *"When a minister is called"*: Martin Luther King Jr., "Recommendations to the Dexter Avenue Baptist Church for the Fiscal Year 1954–1955," in *The Papers of Martin Luther King, Jr.*, vol. 2: *Rediscovering Precious Values, July 1951–November 1955*, ed. Clayborne Carson (Berkeley: University of California Press, 1994), 287–94.

126   *twenty-three Black children*: "Negroes Seek Entry in City White School," *Alabama Tribune*, September 2, 1954.

126   *"Nobody ever said anything"*: Martin Luther King Jr., interview with Donald H. Smith, November 29, 1963, Wisconsin Historical Society.

127   *"shameful and deplorable one-sidedness"*: "Negro Civic Groups Seek Better Recreational Areas," *Montgomery Advertiser*, September 15, 1954.

127   *In 1951, St. Jude's opened*: J. Mills Thornton III, *Dividing Lines: Municipal Politics and the Struggle for Civil Rights in Montgomery, Birmingham, and Selma* (Tuscaloosa: University of Alabama Press, 2002), 37.

127   *"Montgomery is fast taking the lead"*: "Baseball Democracy in Montgomery," *Alabama Tribune*, December 11, 1953.

128   *"Montgomery was an easygoing town"*: King, *Stride Toward Freedom*, 26–27.

128   *"just niggers doing"*: J. Mills Thornton III, "Challenge and Response in the Montgomery Bus Boycott of 1955–1956," *Alabama Review* 33 (July 1980): 163–235.

128   *"Only a few days would elapse"*: "Mr. Rufus Lewis," in Wally G. Vaughn and Richard W. Wills, eds., *Reflections on Our Pastor: Dr. Martin Luther King, Jr., at Dexter Avenue Baptist Church, 1954–1960* (Dover, Mass.: Majority Press, 1999), 17.

128   *"mayor of the Black underbelly"*: Joe Azbell, interview with Blackside, Inc., October 31, 1985, for *Eyes on the Prize: America's Civil Rights Years (1954–1965)*, Washington University Libraries, Film and Media Archive, Henry Hampton Collection, repository .wustl.edu/downloads/n296x1037.

130   *"Hurting feet"*: Jo Ann Gibson Robinson, *The Montgomery Bus Boycott and the Women Who Started It* (Knoxville: University of Tennessee Press, 1987), 36.

130   *Black people had boycotted*: Randall Kennedy, "Martin Luther King's Constitution: A

Legal History of the Montgomery Bus Boycott," *Yale Law Journal* 98, no. 6 (April 1989); and August Meier and Elliott Rudwick, "The Boycott Movement Against Jim Crow Streetcars in the South, 1900–1906," *Journal of American History* 55, no. 4 (March 1969): 756–75.

130 *If they were to boycott*: Robinson, *The Montgomery Bus Boycott and the Women Who Started It*, xii.

131 *"I made a commitment"*: Fred Gray, interview with author, January 3, 2020.

131 *"her appearance and what was within"*: Rufus Lewis, interview with Blackside, Inc., October 31, 1985, for *Eyes on the Prize: America's Civil Rights Years (1954–1965)*, Washington University Libraries, Film and Media Archive, Henry Hampton Collection, repository.wustl.edu/downloads/ww72bd25r.

132 *"It takes the right type of person"*: Gray, interview with author.

132 *he spent three additional hours*: Robert Williams, interview with Taylor Branch, 1984, University of North Carolina, Chapel Hill.

132 *Coretta typed the dissertation*: Octavia Vivian, *Coretta: The Story of Coretta Scott King* (Minneapolis: Fortress Press, 2006), 44.

132 *preached forty-six sermons*: King, "Annual Report, Dexter Avenue Baptist Church," 1954–55, in Carson, *The Papers of Martin Luther King, Jr.*, vol. 2, 578–83.

132 *Before long, his church*: "Dr. Ralph Brison," in Vaughn and Wills, *Reflections on Our Pastor*, 73.

132 *"a bourgeois leader"*: Reddick, *Crusader Without Violence*, 223.

132 *"Pastor King's preaching has a freshness"*: "Mrs. Thelma Austin Rice," in Vaughn and Wills, *Reflections on Our Pastor*, 25–26.

133 *"Every way I turned"*: Martin Luther King Sr. to Martin Luther King Jr., December 2, 1954, King Papers, Boston University.

133 *"Everybody loved him"*: "Mr. Robert D. Nesbitt, Jr.," in Vaughn and Wills, *Reflections on Our Pastor*, 38.

133 *"I didn't have the feeling"*: Coretta Scott King transcripts, Hatch Papers, box 22, folder 8, 1968.

133 *"intensive campaign"*: "Mass Meetings Strengthen NAACP in Capitol City," *Huntsville Mirror*, June 25, 1955.

134 *"There is no time to pause"*: Ibid.

134 *Dent wanted King*: Albert W. Dent to Martin Luther King Jr., July 25, 1955, in Carson, *The Papers of Martin Luther King, Jr.*, vol. 2, 567.

134 *"It was always there"*: "Mrs. Dorothy Calhoun," in Vaughn and Wills, *Reflections on Our Pastor*, 148–49.

135 *"Long repressed feelings"*: King, *Stride Toward Freedom*, 29.

135 *"Mississippi Shame Story"*: "Howard, Civil Rights Man, Slated for Address at Montgomery Soon," *Atlanta Daily World*, November 25, 1955.

135 *In the audience that night*: David T. Beito and Linda Royster Beito, *Black Maverick: T. R. M. Howard's Fight for Civil Rights and Economic Power* (Urbana: University of Illinois Press, 2009), 155.

137 *"goat head"*: Rosa Parks, unpublished draft, circa 1956–58, Rosa Parks Collection, Library of Congress, box 18, folder 1.

138 *"Well, Fred"*: Gray, interview with author.

14. "My Soul Is Free"

139 *third person*: Howell Raines, *My Soul Is Rested: Movement Days in the Deep South Remembered* (1977; repr. New York: Penguin, 1983), 45.

139 *"Brother Nixon"*: Ibid.

139 *"Another Negro woman has been arrested"*: Jo Ann Gibson Robinson, *The Montgomery Bus Boycott and the Women Who Started It* (Knoxville: University of Tennessee Press, 1987), 45–46.

140 *Juanita Abernathy typed*: Juanita Abernathy, interview with author, August 2, 2018.

140 *On Saturday night*: Ralph Abernathy interview with Donald H. Smith, December 3, 1963, Smith Collection, University of Wisconsin, Madison.

140 *"The Montgomery City Lines"*: Joe Azbell, "Negro Groups Ready Boycott of City Lines," *Montgomery Advertiser*, December 4, 1955.

140 *He reflected*: Martin Luther King Jr., *Stride Toward Freedom: The Montgomery Story* (1958; repr. Boston: Beacon Press, 2010), 39.

141 *"Remember we are Fighting"*: "Negro Boycott Poster," *Montgomery Advertiser*, December 6, 1955.

141 *"Martin, Martin, come quickly"*: King, *Stride Toward Freedom*, 41.

141 *"I jumped in my car"*: Ibid., 42.

141 *"Well, my body may be a bit tired"*: Robinson, *The Montgomery Bus Boycott and the Women Who Started It*, 60.

142 *"And as I watched them"*: King, *Stride Toward Freedom*, 42.

142 *hit on an idea*: Edgar French to L. D. Reddick, June 19, 1959, L. D. Reddick Papers, Schomburg Center.

142 *"In that meetin'"*: Quoted in Raines, *My Soul Is Rested*, 49.

143 *"was a neutral man"*: Rufus Lewis, interview with Blackside, Inc., October 31, 1985, for *Eyes on the Prize: America's Civil Rights Years (1954–1965)*, Washington University Libraries, Film and Media Archive, Henry Hampton Collection, repository.wustl.edu /downloads/ww72bd25r.

143 *modest demands*: King, *Stride Toward Freedom*, 98–99.

143 *"You know that whatever"*: Ibid., 47.

144 *"most decisive"*: Ibid.

144 *"alerted for duty"*: "Police Alerted in Alabama Bus Segregation Dispute," *Fort Worth Star-Telegram*, December 5, 1955.

144 *"a state of anxiety"*: King, *Stride Toward Freedom*, 48.

144 *cool, crisp air*: Joe Azbell, "5,000 at Meeting Outline Boycott; Bullet Clips Bus," *Montgomery Advertiser*, December 6, 1955.

144 *Workers hurried to set up*: Donald Hugh Smith, "Martin Luther King Jr.: Rhetorician of Revolt" (PhD diss., University of Wisconsin, 1964).

144 *"By now my doubts"*: King, *Stride Toward Freedom*, 49.

145 *"They were on fire"*: Joe Azbell, interview with Blackside, Inc., October 31, 1985, for *Eyes on the Prize: America's Civil Rights Years (1954–1965)*, Washington University Libraries, Film and Media Archive, Henry Hampton Collection, repository.wustl.edu/downloads /n296x1037.

145 *without notes*: King, *Stride Toward Freedom*, 50.

145 *"I was in the street"*: Willodean Malden (née Mitchell), interview with author, May 23, 2019.

146 *"The fear left"*: Ralph Abernathy, interview with Blackside, Inc., November 6, 1985, for *Eyes on the Prize: America's Civil Rights Years (1954–1965)*, Washington University Libraries, Film and Media Archive, Henry Hampton Collection, repository.wustl.edu /downloads/vx021g754.

146 *"It was like a revival starting"*: Quoted in Henry Hampton and Steve Fayer, *Voices of Freedom: An Oral History of the Civil Rights Movement from the 1950s Through the 1980s* (New York: Bantam Books, 1991), 24.

147 *"That first speech"*: Rufus Lewis, interview with Norman Lumkin, June 25, 1973, Statewide Oral History Project, Trenholm State Community College Library, Montgomery, Ala.

15. "We Ain't Rabbit No More"

148 *"Open your mouth"*: Martin Luther King Jr., *Stride Toward Freedom: The Montgomery Story* (1958; repr. Boston: Beacon Press, 2010), 52.

148 *climbed a mountain*: Ibid., 56.

148 *"inadvertently radicalized"*: Randall Kennedy, "Martin Luther King's Constitution: A Legal History of the Montgomery Bus Boycott," *Yale Law Journal* 98, no. 6 (April 1989): 999–1067.

149 *"there is some animosity"*: "Some Observations on the Bus Boycott," *Montgomery Advertiser*, December 8, 1955.

149 *"I can see no conflict"*: King, *Stride Toward Freedom*, 106.

150 *"History has a way"*: Emory O. Jackson, "The Tip-Off," *Atlanta Daily World*, December 23, 1955.

150 *"Negroes were born walking"*: Ibid.

151 *After King finished meeting*: Samuel DeWitt Proctor, *The Substance of Things Hoped For: A Memoir of African-American Faith* (Valley Forge, Pa.: Judson Press, 1999), 74. Proctor was a speaker at Dexter Avenue church in July 1956.

152 *"And everyone would go home"*: Quoted in Henry Hampton and Steve Fayer, *Voices of Freedom: An Oral History of the Civil Rights Movement from the 1950s Through the 1980s* (New York: Bantam Books, 1991), 30.

152 *"I tried to discourage"*: Alberta King, interview with Lavelle Dyett, WBZ-TV Boston, "Sixteen '74," 1974, Peabody Awards Collection Archives, tanfor.uga.edu/media/t/1 _cli0lpos/86446941, accessed June 25, 2020.

152 *"I'm tired"*: Dealy Cooksey, interview with Willie M. Lee, January 24, 1956, Valien Papers, Amistad Research Center, Tulane University, New Orleans, La.

153 *"What you're seeing here"*: Ted Poston, "This Is Montgomery: No Longer Afraid," *Baltimore Afro-American*, September 1, 1956.

154 *"A woman in my church"*: Mrs. Earl R. Johnson, interview with Anna Holden, January 31, 1956, Valien Papers, Amistad Research Center, Tulane University, New Orleans, La. Note: The Fisk researchers, in transcribing interviews, often favored the spelling "Nigras." Given the absence of audio recordings and factoring for southern accents, it's likely that many of the interviewees were using the word "Negro" and that the Fisk researchers, who often transcribed words phonetically, were spelling it "Nigra."

154 *The FBI's office in Mobile*: David J. Garrow, *The FBI and Martin Luther King, Jr.: From "Solo" to Memphis* (New York: Penguin Books, 1983), 22.

154 *"The bus boycott made us"*: Ted Poston, "This Is Montgomery: The White Citizens Councils," *Baltimore Afro-American*, August 18, 1956.

154 *"Elect Billy Tucker"*: Ibid.

155 *"do not care whether"*: Quoted in Joe Azbell, "Mayor Stops Boycott Talk," *Montgomery Advertiser*, January 24, 1956.

155 *During a public meeting*: NAACP memo, untitled, January 31, 1956, David J. Garrow personal collection.

155 *"I found myself trembling"*: William Peters, "The Man Who Fights Hate with Love," *Redbook*, September 1961.

155 *"Fellows"*: King, *Stride Toward Freedom*, 119.

156 *"He sleeps well"*: L. D. Reddick, "Crusader Without Violence," manuscript, New York Public Library.

156 *"Our house was always full"*: Coretta Scott King, interview with Donald H. Smith, University of Wisconsin, 1963.

156 *"I could not be there"*: Coretta Scott King, interview with Blackside, Inc., December 20, 1985, for *Eyes on the Prize: America's Civil Rights Years (1954–1965)*, Washington University Libraries, Film and Media Archive, Henry Hampton Collection, repository .wustl.edu/downloads/hq37vq29v.

156 *The death threats*: "Attack on the Conscience," *Time*, February 18, 1957.

156 *"Nigger, we are tired of you"*: L. D. Reddick, *Crusader Without Violence: A Biography of Martin Luther King, Jr.* (New York: Harper & Bros., 1959), 166.

157 *"Rationality left me"*: "King Says Vision Told Him to Lead Integration Forces," *Montgomery Advertiser*, January 28, 1957.

157 *"That was my case"*: James Lawson, interview with author, November 26, 2018.

157 *"a little sensitive"*: L. D. Reddick, "Vision and Voices" (unpublished manuscript, June 9, 1957), L. D. Reddick Papers.

158 *"was amazed and depressed"*: Ibid.

158 *The first twenty-five years*: Martin Luther King Jr., "Why Jesus Called a Man a Fool," sermon, Mount Pisgah Missionary Baptist Church, Chicago, Ill., August 27, 1967, Stanford King Institute, kinginstitute.stanford.edu/king-papers/documents/why -jesus-called-man-fool-sermon-delivered-mount-pisgah-missionary-baptist.

16. A Warning

159 *At the little house*: Tonya Jameson, "King 'Was a Part of Us,'" *Montgomery Advertiser*, January 17, 1993.

159 *didn't want the baby to be cold*: Ibid.

159 *The explosion*: Joe Azbell, "Blast Rocks Residence of Bus Boycott Leader," *Montgomery Advertiser*, January 31, 1956.

159 *Hundreds of Black neighbors*: Coretta Scott King, interview with Arnold Michaelis, December 1, 1965, outtakes from "Martin Luther King Jr.: A Personal Portrait," Brown Media Archives, University of Georgia, Athens.

159 *he spoke to Coretta first*: Joe Azbell, "Blast Rocks Residence of Boycott Leader."

160 *"We believe in law and order"*: Ibid.

160 *"they waited too late"*: Eugene Ligon, interview with Norman Lumpkin, June 25, 1973, Statewide Oral History Project, Trenholm State Technical College Library, Montgomery, Ala.

161 *"I don't know what I would've done"*: Coretta Scott King, interview with Michaelis, reel 6.

161 *"I realized then"*: Ibid.

161 *"Lord, I've done all that I can do"*: Edythe Scott Bagley with Joe Hilley, *Desert Rose: The Life and Legacy of Coretta Scott King* (Tuscaloosa: University of Alabama Press, 2012), 132.

161 *"He functioned better"*: Coretta Scott King, *My Life with Martin Luther King, Jr.*, rev. ed. (New York: Henry Holt, 1993), 165.

162 *"During the bus boycott"*: Barbara Reynolds, "Coretta Scott King, Martin Luther King's Other Half," *Washington Post*, October 21, 2011.

162 *Gray remembered*: Fred Gray, interview with author, January 3, 2020.

162 *"the largest political crowd"*: Joe Azbell, "Coliseum Crowd Overflows to Hear 'Dixie Defender," *Montgomery Advertiser*, February 11, 1956.

162 *"If any Negro wants desegregation"*: Bob Ingram, "Throngs Pack Coliseum for Eastland's Address," *Montgomery Advertiser*, February 11, 1956. As Isabel Wilkerson wrote in *The Warmth of Other Suns: The Epic Story of America's Great Migration* (New York: Random House, 2010), Black people faced violence even after fleeing to the North.

163 *but now he was classified 1-A*: "42,000 Walk in Rain as Montgomery Police Arrest 87," *Cleveland Call and Post*, March 3, 1956.

163 *Thurgood Marshall of the NAACP*: "Deputies Beginning Roundup for 115 Charged in Boycott," *Montgomery Advertiser*, February 22, 1956.

163 *"In the last three weeks"*: Joe Azbell, "City Limits," *Montgomery Advertiser*, February 6, 1956.

163 *FBI agents clipped newspaper articles*: FBI memo, Mobile office to director, April 6, 1978.

163 *"Whether we want to be or not"*: Quoted in David J. Garrow, *Bearing the Cross: Martin Luther King, Jr., and the Southern Christian Leadership Conference* (New York: William Morrow, 1986), 71.

164 *"Little did any of us know"*: L. Harold DeWolf to Martin Luther King Jr., March 16, 1956, L. D. Reddick Papers, Schomburg Center.

164 *"Prayer has been used"*: Martin Luther King Jr. to L. Harold DeWolf, June 1, 1956, L. D. Reddick Papers, Schomburg Center.

164 *"the strain under which I am working"*: Quoted in Garrow, *Bearing the Cross*, 79.

164 *"DO NOT BACK DOWN"*: Walter R. McCall to Martin Luther King Jr., February 1, 1956, Stanford King Institute, kinginstitute.stanford.edu/king-papers/documents/walter-r-mccall-6.

164 *the biggest group of people ever indicted*: "Deputies Beginning Roundup for 115 Charged in Boycott."

165 *"the moment of umbilical severance"*: Louis E. Lomax, *To Kill a Black Man: The Shocking Parallel Lives of Malcolm X and Martin Luther King Jr.* (Los Angeles: Holloway House, 1968), 49.

165 *Rufus Lewis volunteered*: Joe Azbell, "75 Nabbed by Deputies on Boycott Indictments," *Montgomery Advertiser*, February 23, 1956.

165 *"Well, here comes my preacher"*: Ibid.

165 *King was making history*: In Detroit, a forklift driver named Will Hairston read about King in the newspaper. As a side job, Hairston wrote and recorded songs, selling the 45 rpm records for a dollar each from the back of his green station wagon. Calling himself "Brother Will," Hairston drove through Detroit's neighborhoods with a loudspeaker attached to the roof of the wagon, offering tunes that entertained, informed, and sang out

for justice, with a newsy song on each A-side and a gospel song on each B-side. Inspired by King's leadership of the boycott, Hairston composed a song called "Alabama Bus":

Lord, there come a bus, don't have no load
You know, they tell me that a human being stepped on board
You know, they tell me that the man sat on the bus
You know, they tell me that the driver began to fuss
He said: "look here, man, you're from the Negro race,
And don't you know you're sitting in the wrong place?"
The driver told the man: "I know you paid your dime
But if you don't move you gonna have to pay a fine."
The man told the driver: "My feets are hurtin'"
The driver told the man to move behind the curtain

Stop that Alabama bus, I don't wanna ride
Stop that Alabama bus, I don't wanna ride
Stop that Alabama bus, I don't wanna ride
Lord, an Alabama boycott, I don't wanna ride

I wanna tell you 'bout the Reverend Martin Luther King
You know, they tell me that the people began to sing
You know, the man God sent out in the world
You know, they tell me that the man had the mighty nerve
You know, the poor man didn't have a bus to rent
You know, they tell me, great God, he had the mighty strength
And he reminded me of Moses in Israel land
He said: "A man ain't nothing but a man."
He said: "Look here, Alabama. Don't you see?"
He says: "All of my people gonna follow me."
You know, they tell me Reverend King was very hurt
He says: "All of my people gonna walk to work"

They said: "Look here, boy, you hadn't took a thought
'Cause don't you know you broke the anti-boycott law?"
They tell me Reverend King said: "Treat us right."
You know, in the Second World War my father lost his sight
You know, they tell me Abraham signed the pledge one night
He said that all of these men should have their equal rights . . .

Stop that Alabama bus, I don't wanna ride
Lord, an Alabama boycott, I don't wanna ride

You know, they tell me Reverend King was a Bible inspired
When all the buses was passin', nobody would ride
You know, they tell me that the Negroes was ready to go

They had-a-walked along the streets until their feet were sore
You know, they tell me Reverend King had spreaded the word
At an Alabama bus stop, so l heard
You know, they sent a lot of money, saying: "King go on,"
You know, in nineteen and twenty-nine that man was born
You know, the five hundred dollar fine was very heavy
You know, the poor man was born the fifteenth of January

Stop that Alabama bus, I don't wanna ride

166   *he was pleased to discover*: Coretta Scott King, *My Life, My Love, My Legacy*, as told to
        Barbara Reynolds (New York: Henry Holt, 2017), 78.
166   *Coretta played a key role*: Ralph Abernathy, interview with Taylor Branch, November
        19, 1984, handwritten notes from interview, Taylor Branch Papers, University of
        North Carolina, Chapel Hill.
166   *"very long, philosophical"*: Bayard Rustin, interview with David J. Garrow, audiotape,
        April 22, 1982, David J. Garrow personal collection.
166   *"The experience in Montgomery"*: Martin Luther King Jr., "Pilgrimage to Nonviolence,"
        Christian Century, April 13, 1960, www.christiancentury.org/article/pilgrimage
        -nonviolence.
166   *"The man is a genuine"*: Ted Poston, "This Is Montgomery: No Hat in Hand," *Baltimore
        Afro-American*, August 25, 1956.
167   *"We shall all stand together"*: Bayard Rustin to Arthur Brown, February 23, 1956, in *I
        Must Resist: Bayard Rustin's Life in Letters*, ed. Michael G. Long (San Francisco: City
        Lights Books, 2012), 166.
167   *"Gandhi-like methods"*: Bayard Rustin to Arthur Brown and Ralph DiGia, February 25,
        1967, in Long, *I Must Resist*, 172.
167   *"I am convinced"*: Ibid., 170–71.
167   *The headline the next day*: "'Not Worried' Says Alabama's Gandhi," *Baltimore
        Afro-American*, March 3, 1956.
168   *The judge was an ardent segregationist*: "Montgomery Boycott: New Phase," *The Nation*,
        February 25, 1956.
168   *"We will continue to protest"*: Quoted in Garrow, *Bearing the Cross*, 74–75.
168   *"What Dr. King delivered to Blacks there"*: Howell Raines, *My Soul Is Rested: Movement
        Days in the Deep South Remembered* (1977; repr. New York: Penguin, 1983), 56.
168   *"Strange—whites are getting scared"*: Glenn E. Smiley to John Swomley, 1956, David J.
        Garrow personal collection.
168   *"I believe that God has called"*: Glenn E. Smiley to Heil Bolinger, February 29, 1956,
        David J. Garrow personal collection.
169   *"The Negro has to be a superb diplomat"*: Quoted in "Roy Wilkins, 50-Year Veteran of
        Civil Rights Fight, Is Dead," *New York Times*, September 9, 1981.
169   *"the law needs help"*: Martin Luther King Jr., *Stride Toward Freedom: The Montgomery
        Story* (1958; repr. Boston: Beacon Press, 2010), 211.
169   *"the great decent majority"*: Ibid.
169   *"very uncomfortable with people"*: Bayard Rustin, Ed Edwin, and Walter Naegle, *The*

Reminiscences of Bayard Rustin (New York: Oral History Research Office, Columbia University, 1988), 205.

169 *"You don't know me"*: Harry Belafonte, *My Song: A Memoir* (New York: Knopf, 2011), 148.

170 *"He seemed a little bit anxious"*: Harry Belafonte, interview with author, April 4, 2017.

170 *"much interested in what"*: Eleanor Roosevelt to Martin Luther King Jr., October 17, 1956, telegram, L. D. Reddick Papers, Schomburg Center.

170 *"some of my better ones"*: Earline Browning to Martin Luther King Jr., March 6, 1956, Stanford King Institute, kinginstitute.stanford.edu/king-papers/documents/earline -browning.

170 *"a fact that never ceased"*: Ralph David Abernathy, *And the Walls Came Tumbling Down: An Autobiography* (New York: Harper & Row, 1989), 170.

170 *"It was as if Martin"*: Louis Lomax, *To Kill a Black Man* (1968; repr. Los Angeles: Holloway House, 1987), 44.

171 *"King has been working on"*: "Attack on the Conscience."

171 *"Unfortunately, her voice lacked"*: Theodore Chas. Stone, "Distinguished Crowd Hears Mrs. M. L. King," *Chicago Defender*, October 22, 1956.

171 *"warmth, sincerity"*: Bob Queen, "Meet Mrs. Martin Luther King," *Pittsburgh Courier*, March 30, 1957.

172 *Gayle and other segregationists*: "Who Exploded That Bomb?," *Opelika (Ala.) Daily News*, August 29, 1956.

172 *"Oh, my God"*: Rustin, Edwin, and Naegle, *The Reminiscences of Bayard Rustin*, 92.

173 *"placed a headstone"*: Luther A. Huston, "High Court Rules Bus Segregation Unconstitutional," *New York Times*, November 14, 1956.

173 *sideshow*: Juan Williams, "The Case for Thurgood Marshall," *Washington Post*, February 14, 1999.

173 *"our twelve months of glorious dignity"*: King, *Stride Toward Freedom*, 162.

173 *about forty carloads*: "Klan Stages Parade Here," *Montgomery Advertiser*, November 14, 1956.

173 *"as though they were watching"*: King, *Stride Toward Freedom*, 151.

174 *"one of the most remarkable"*: Eleanor Roosevelt, quoted in "Salute to Montgomery," *Liberation*, December 1956.

174 *"one of the most significant"*: Harry Emerson Fosdick, quoted in "Salute to Montgomery."

174 *The men stepped outside*: Forest Castleberry, "Boycott Leaders Take Desegregated Bus Ride," *Alabama Journal*, December 21, 1956.

174 *King, Abernathy, and Smiley*: Jim Bishop, *The Days of Martin Luther King, Jr.* (New York: Barnes & Noble, 1971), 186–87.

174 *"Is this the reverend?"*: Castleberry, "Boycott Leaders Take Desegregated Bus Ride."

174 *"a mighty good ride"*: Ibid.

17. Alabama's Moses

177 *a brick thrown through*: Henry Hampton and Steve Fayer, *Voices of Freedom: An Oral History of the Civil Rights Movement from the 1950s Through the 1980s* (New York: Bantam Books, 1991), 31.

177 *"Maybe we'd like"*: Trezzvant W. Anderson, "My Son Martin! A Father Lays Bare His Heart, His Faith, His Fears," *Pittsburgh Courier*, June 29, 1957.

178   *"self-protection"*: Kenneth Clark, interview with Arthur M. Schlesinger Jr., September 9, 1976, Schlesinger Papers, New York Public Library.

178   *"meek and submissive"*: Stanley Levison, interview with Arthur M. Schlesinger Jr., August 3, 1976, David J. Garrow personal collection.

178   *Only Coretta had the courage*: Andrew Young, interview with Tom Dent, May 31, 1981, audio recording, Amistad Research Center, Tulane University, New Orleans, La.

178   *spearhead a mass movement*: Ella Baker, interview with Eugene Walker, September 4, 1974, Southern Oral History Program, Southern Historical Collection, University of North Carolina Library, Chapel Hill.

178   *accusations of communist influence*: Ibid.

179   *Coretta filled in*: Coretta Scott King, University of North Carolina tapes.

179   *"LOOK OUT!"*: L. D. Reddick, *Crusader Without Violence: A Biography of Martin Luther King, Jr.* (New York: Harper & Bros., 1959), 173.

180   *"collapsed at the rostrum"*: Martin Luther King Jr., *Stride Toward Freedom: The Montgomery Story* (1958; repr. Boston: Beacon Press, 2010), 87.

180   *a bomb made from twelve*: Ibid., 170.

180   *hearts, minds, laws*: J. Mills Thornton III, *Dividing Lines: Municipal Politics and the Struggle for Civil Rights in Montgomery, Birmingham, and Selma* (Tuscaloosa: University of Alabama Press, 2002), 87–88.

181   *"a people with a common resolve"*: C. Vann Woodward, *The Strange Career of Jim Crow* (London: Oxford University Press, 1966), 8.

181   *a high-fidelity record player*: Bob Queen, "Meet Mrs. Martin L. King," *Pittsburgh Courier*, April 6, 1957.

181   *"At this point"*: Martin Luther King Jr. to L. Harold DeWolf, January 4, 1957.

181   *"a person with a new sense of dignity"*: Martin Luther King Jr., interview with Richard D. Heffner for "The Open Mind," NBC, February 10, 1957, Stanford King Institute, king institute.stanford.edu/king-papers/documents/interview-richard-d-heffner-open-mind.

182   *"risen from nowhere"*: "Attack on the Conscience," *Time*, February 18, 1957.

183   *"You're Dr. King"*: Quoted in Coretta Scott King, *My Life with Martin Luther King, Jr.*, rev. ed. (New York: Henry Holt, 1993), 143–44.

183   *a postcard for Rosa Parks*: Martin Luther King Jr. to Rosa Parks, March 22, 1957, Rosa Parks Collection, Library of Congress.

183   *Paris-based correspondent*: Ollie Stewart, "Ralph Barry, Detroit, Marries French Girl," *Baltimore Afro-American*, April 6, 1957.

184   *"wiser at twenty-eight"*: Freddie Colson Jr., "Dr. Benjamin E. Mays: His Impact as Spiritual and Intellectual Mentor of Martin Luther King Jr.," in *Walking Integrity: Benjamin Elijah Mays, Mentor to Generations*, ed. Lawrence E. Carter (Atlanta: Scholars Press, 1996), 226–27.

184   *"Martin, in a sense"*: Bayard Rustin, Ed Edwin, and Walter Naegle, *The Reminiscences of Bayard Rustin* (New York: Oral History Research Office, Columbia University, 1988), 462.

184   *But the men disagreed*: Taylor Branch, *Parting the Waters: America in the King Years, 1954–63* (New York: Touchstone, 1989), 217.

185   *"Give us the ballot"*: Martin Luther King Jr., "Give Us the Ballot," speech, Washington, D.C., May 17, 1957, Stanford King Institute, kinginstitute.stanford.edu/king-papers /documents/give-us-ballot-address-delivered-prayer-pilgrimage-freedom.

186 *"as the number one leader"*: James L. Hicks, "King Emerges as the Top Negro Leader," *New York Amsterdam News*, June 1, 1957.

186 *Gathered around the table*: Guest book, 2419 Massachusetts Avenue, Washington, D.C., courtesy of J. Blanton Belk.

186 *"the total commitment"*: J. Blanton Belk, interview with author, March 12, 2017.

187 *"We had a miraculous day today"*: Quoted ibid.

187 *"traveling toward the promised land"*: Quoted in "Negro Gains Cited," *New York Times*, June 3, 1957.

187 *published an article*: David J. Garrow, *Bearing the Cross: Martin Luther King, Jr., and the Southern Christian Leadership Conference* (New York: William Morrow, 1986), 73.

187 *"It is hardly a moral act"*: Martin Luther King Jr., "Our Struggle," *Liberation*, April 1956.

187 *"You could go into"*: Jesse Jackson, interview with author, March 7, 2018.

188 *"The Montgomery bus boycott"*: James Lawson, interview with author, September 18, 2018.

188 *"Frankly, I worry"*: Quoted in Reddick, *Crusader Without Violence*, 177.

188 *"inferiority and self-hatred"*: Martin Luther King Jr., "Advice for Living," *Ebony*, September 1957, Stanford King Institute, kinginstitute.stanford.edu/king-papers /documents/advice-living-0.

189 *Coretta helped him compose*: Coretta Scott King, "The World of Coretta King," *New Lady*, January 1966.

189 *"caused him some real pain"*: Garrow, *Bearing the Cross*, 99.

190 *One minister complained*: Erna Dungee, interview with L. D. Reddick, February 27, 1957, L. D. Reddick Papers, Schomburg Center.

190 *"he was taking too many bows"*: Reddick, *Crusader Without Violence*, 179.

190 *"prominent minister"*: Robert M. Ratcliffe, "Could Be a Scandal," *Pittsburgh Courier*, June 29, 1957.

190 *King's romantic affairs*: Garrow, *Bearing the Cross*, 96.

190 *In the fall . . . Jeffrey Hayden visited*: Jeffrey Hayden letter to Maude Ballou, September 16, 1957, L. D. Reddick Papers, Schomburg Center.

190 *"It's getting almost so bad"*: David Margolick, "The Day Louis Armstrong Made Noise," *New York Times*, September 23, 2007, www.nytimes.com/2007/09/23/opinion /23margolick.html.

191 *popularity among Black and white*: Gerald Early, "Martin Luther King and the Middle Way," *Christian Century*, August 28–September 4, 1996.

191 *He confessed his frustration*: Annual Report, Dexter Avenue Baptist Church, 1957.

191 *third time in three*: Martin Luther King Jr., "Loving Your Enemies," sermon, Dexter Avenue Baptist Church, Atlanta, Ga., November 17, 1957, Stanford King Institute, kinginstitute.stanford.edu/king-papers/documents/loving-your-enemies.

191 *"Frankly, I'm worried"*: Lerone Bennett Jr., *What Manner of Man: A Biography of Martin Luther King, Jr.* (Chicago: Johnson Publishing, 1964), 81.

191 *Late in the afternoon*: Judy Wagnon, "Negro to Appeal Oak Park Fine," *Montgomery Advertiser*, October 15, 1957.

191 *Oak Park was the jewel*: Ted Poston, "This Is Montgomery: Separate and Unequal," *Baltimore Afro-American*, September 15, 1956.

192 *"making Montgomery"*: Wagnon, "Negro to Appeal Oak Park Fine."

192 *180 state parks for white people*: Rebecca Retzlaff, "Desegregation of City Parks and the Civil Rights Movement: The Case of Oak Park in Montgomery, Alabama," *Journal of Urban History* 47, no. 4 (October 2019).

193 *sold its zoo animals*: Heather McGhee, *The Sum of Us: What Racism Costs Everyone and How We Can Prosper Together* (New York: One World, 2021), discusses the many ways in which racism has economic costs for white people as well as people of color and challenges the notion that progress for one group must come at the expense of others.

193 *would serve as a warning*: "Idle Oak Park," editorial, *Alabama Journal*, June 21, 1960.

193 *the swimming pools remained closed*: Retzlaff, "Desegregation of City Parks and the Civil Rights Movement."

194 *leader promised "bloodshed"*: "Klan Head Sees Bloodshed If Rev. King Hits Schools," *Chicago Defender*, January 17, 1959.

194 *"Our maid has worked"*: Clyde Bear, interview with Anna Holden, March 27, 1956, Amistad Research Center, Tulane University, New Orleans, La.

18. "I'm Glad You Didn't Sneeze"

195 *"I had no abnormal fears"*: "The Woman Behind Martin Luther King," *Ebony*, January 1959.

195 *"was always stronger"*: Coretta Scott King, interview with Martin Agronsky for "Look Here," NBC, October 27, 1957, Stanford King Institute, kinginstitute.stanford.edu /king-papers/documents/interview-martin-agronsky-look-here.

195 *traveled 780,000 miles*: "Man on the Go," *Jet*, July 17, 1958.

197 *"The white race and their poison Bible"*: Elijah Muhammad, "Islamic World," *New York Amsterdam News*, February 8, 1958.

197 *"You have my prayers"*: Martin Luther King Jr. to Elijah Muhammad, April 9, 1958, Stanford King Institute, kinginstitute.stanford.edu/king-papers/documents/elijah -muhammad.

197 *"Dear Martin"*: Maude Ballou to Martin Luther King Jr., August 25, 1958, L. D. Reddick Papers, Schomburg Center.

198 *"Ella had all the qualities"*: John Lewis, *Walking with the Wind: A Memoir of the Movement*, with Michael D'Orso (New York: Simon & Schuster, 1998), 214.

198 *"Martin wasn't well trained"*: Ella Baker, interview with David J. Garrow, audiotape, September 27, 1984, David J. Garrow personal collection.

198 *"These were young Baptist preachers"*: Andrew Young, *An Easy Burden: The Civil Rights Movement and the Transformation of America* (Waco, Tex.: Baylor University Press, 2008), 137.

198 *Rustin and Levison had to prevail*: Barbara Ransby, *Ella Baker and the Black Freedom Movement* (Chapel Hill: University of North Carolina Press, 2003), 180.

198 *mistreated because of her gender*: Coretta Scott King, *My Life with Martin Luther King, Jr.*, rev. ed. (New York: Henry Holt, 1993), 142.

199 *"much of the tension"*: Martin Luther King Jr., to Earl Mazo, September 2, 1958, Stanford King Institute, kinginstitute.stanford.edu/king-papers/documents/earl -mazo.

199 *"The Negro leaders"*: Rocco Siciliano to Dwight D. Eisenhower, June 25, 1958,

Eisenhower Presidential Library, www.eisenhowerlibrary.gov/sites/default/files /research/online-documents/civil-rights-eisenhower-administration/1958-06-25 -siciliano-to-dde.pdf.

199　*"The joy which filled"*: James Baldwin, "The Dangerous Road Before Martin Luther King," *Harper's Magazine*, February 1961.

200　*Yiddish-speaking Russian immigrants*: U.S. Census, 1920.

200　*"wittiest boy"*: "Far Rockaway Seniors Pick Class Notables," *Brooklyn Daily Eagle*, May 21, 1930.

200　*wiretap his home phone*: David J. Garrow, "The FBI and Martin Luther King, Jr.," *The Atlantic*, July/August 2002.

200　*"Stan, as a strategist"*: Harry Belafonte, interview with author, April 4, 2017.

201　*"And he said"*: Stanley Levison, interview with James M. Mosby Jr., February 14, 1970, Moorland-Spingarn Research Center, Howard University, Washington, D.C.

202　*"Dear Martin: Your last chapter"*: Stanley Levison to Martin Luther King Jr., April 1, 1958, Martin Luther King Papers, Boston University archive.

202　*"If it is true"*: Ibid.

203　*"a document of far-reaching"*: Abel Plenn, "The Cradle Was Rocked," *New York Times*, October 12, 1958.

203　*"races trample over races"*: C. Eric Lincoln, ed., *Martin Luther King, Jr.: A Profile* (New York: Hill & Wang, 1970), 52.

203　*"Boy, if you don't get"*: Quoted in L. D. Reddick, *Crusader Without Violence: A Biography of Martin Luther King, Jr.* (New York: Harper & Bros., 1959), 226.

203　*"Gal, you just nod"*: Montgomery Improvement Association 1, no. 10 (September 27, 1958), L. D. Reddick Papers, Schomburg Center.

204　*"tried to break my arm"*: Dick Hines, "King Charges Police Brutal After Arrest," *Montgomery Advertiser*, September 4, 1958.

204　*"publicity stunt"*: "Police Head Balks King Jail Term," *Montgomery Advertiser*, September 6, 1958.

204　*"You are a 'marked man'"*: J. Raymond Henderson to Martin Luther King Jr., September 17, 1958, quoted in David J. Garrow, *Bearing the Cross: Martin Luther King, Jr., and the Southern Christian Leadership Conference* (New York: William Morrow, 1986), 109.

204　*focused its coverage*: "President Scored over Integration," *New York Times*, September 20, 1958.

204　*the Black press took a different view*: "7,000 Attend Rally for 'Mixed' Schools, Jack's Name Booed," *New York Age*, September 27, 1958.

205　*"Are you Martin Luther King?"*: "King Escaped Death by Hair," *Chicago Defender*, September 22, 1958.

205　*seven-inch*: Joseph Endler and Richard C. Wald, "Harlem Woman Stabs Rev. Martin Luther King," *New York Herald Tribune*, September 21, 1958.

205　*King didn't move*: Ibid.

205　*"Long live King!"*: "Leslie Matthews Unlimited," *New York Age*, September 27, 1958.

205　*"That was probably the fifth stabbing"*: Andrew Young, interview with author, January 19, 2019.

205　*"My husband was"*: Coretta Scott King, *My Life with Martin Luther King, Jr.*, 158.

206 *"as a constructive member"*: Martin Luther King Jr., "Dr. King Bears No Ill-Will," *Atlanta Daily World*, October 1, 1958.

206 *"rest his body and mind"*: Howard Thurman, *With Head and Heart: The Autobiography of Howard Thurman* (San Diego: Harvest Books, 1979), 255.

206 *"From the moment you came"*: Martin Luther King Jr. to A. Philip Randolph, November 8, 1958, Stanford King Institute, kinginstitute.stanford.edu/king-papers /documents/philip-randolph-6.

207 *"I am now convinced"*: Martin Luther King Jr., "Dr. King Bears No Ill-Will."

19. The Pilgrimage

208 *"I ask my husband"*: Anonymous to Martin Luther King Jr., January 1, 1959, in *The Papers of Martin Luther King, Jr.*, vol. 5: *Threshold of a New Decade, January 1959–December 1960*, ed. Clayborne Carson (Berkeley: University of California Press, 2005), 100.

208 *Four out of five southern ministers*: "4 of Every 5 Dixie Ministers Answering Poll Back Integration," *Atlanta Constitution*, October 20, 1958.

208 *"What it comes to"*: James Baldwin, *Nobody Knows My Name: More Notes of a Native Son* (New York: Dial Press, 1961), 116.

209 *smear him as a communist*: Lawrence Reddick, *Pilgrimage: The Story of Martin Luther King in India*, unpublished, n.d., Reddick Papers, Schomburg Center.

209 *"To become the instruments"*: Martin Luther King Jr., "Address at the Thirty-sixth Annual Dinner of the War Resisters League," speech, New York, February 2, 1959, Stanford King Institute, kinginstitute.stanford.edu/king-papers/documents/address -thirty-sixth-annual-dinner-war-resisters-league.

209 *"two scorpions in a bottle"*: Hanson W. Baldwin, "Danger Era Seen for U.S., Though Not General War," *New York Times*, February 4, 1959.

209 *"Christianity in action"*: David Levering Lewis, *King: A Critical Biography* (New York: Praeger, 1970), 98.

209 *"colored people"*: King, "Address at the Thirty-sixth Annual Dinner of the War Resisters League."

210 *served warm meals*: L. D. Reddick notes on meeting with Richard Wright, undated, L. D. Reddick Papers, Schomburg Center.

210 *size-nine shoes*: L. D. Reddick, "Crusader Without Violence," manuscript, New York Public Library.

210 *"looking like a chubby college professor"*: L. D. Reddick, notes on meeting with Richard Wright, n.d., L. D. Reddick Papers, Schomburg Center.

210 *brief shopping trip*: Ibid.

210 *rue Monsieur le Prince*: Hazel Rowley, *Richard Wright: The Life and Times* (Chicago: University of Chicago Press, 2008), 496.

210 *show his daughter the red scar*: Ibid., 497.

210 *"This is what happens"*: Ibid.

210 *"To other countries"*: "Leader in Fight on Segregation in South Visits India," *St. Louis Post-Dispatch*, February 11, 1959.

211 *supporter of the Soviet Union*: Ibid.

211 *not to give money to beggars*: Martin Luther King Jr., "My Trip to the Land of Gandhi,"

Ebony, July 1959, Stanford King Institute, kinginstitute.stanford.edu/king-papers
/documents/my-trip-land-gandhi.

211   *wore a rose:* Carson, *The Papers of Martin Luther King, Jr.,* vol. 5, 81.

211   *"But isn't that discrimination?":* Martin Luther King Jr., *Why We Can't Wait* (New
York: Harper & Row, 1964), 148.

211   *"broad-based and gigantic":* Ibid., 151.

212   *"drained terribly nervously":* James E. Bristol to Dorothy Bristol, February 25, 1959,
Stanford King Institute, kinginstitute.stanford.edu/king-papers/documents/james-e
-bristol-corinne-b-johnson.

212   *"We had hundreds of invitations":* King, "My Trip to the Land of Gandhi."

212   *"Unlike his Indian models":* L. D. Reddick, *Pilgrimage,* unpublished manuscript on India
trip, n.d., Schomburg Center.

213   *"for committing the crime":* Michelle Norris, "Martin Luther King Recording Found in
India," *All Things Considered,* NPR, January 16, 2009, www.npr.org/templates/story
/story.php?storyId=99480326.

213   *"those little narrow streets":* Martin Luther King Jr., "A Walk Through the Holy Land,"
March 29, 1959, Stanford King Institute, kinginstitute.stanford.edu/king-papers
/documents/walk-through-holy-land-easter-Sunday-sermon-delivered-dexter-avenue
-baptist.

215   *"I know he will never":* L. D. Reddick, notes on SCLC Administrative Committee
meetings, April 2 and 3, 1959, Stanford King Institute, kinginstitute.stanford.edu
/king-papers/documents/notes-lawrence-dunbar-reddick-sclc-administrative
-committee-meetings-2-april.

215   *"The personality that had to be played up":* Ella Baker, interview with Eugene Walker,
1974, University of North Carolina Library, Chapel Hill.

215   *"It will galvanize":* "The Mack Parker Tragedy," *Chicago Defender,* May 4, 1959.

216   *"The tragic truth":* Martin Luther King Jr., "Address at the Religious Leaders
Conference," Washington, D.C., May 11, 1959, Stanford King Institute, kinginstitute
.stanford.edu/king-papers/documents/address-religious-leaders-conference-11-may
-1959.

20. Leaving Montgomery

217   *"When an airplane takes off":* "Why Rev. M. L. King Is Leaving Montgomery," *Jet,*
December 17, 1959.

217   *"scarred by the struggle":* Martin Luther King Sr., *Daddy King: An Autobiography,* with
Clayton Riley (New York: William Morrow, 1980), 172.

218   *"What I have been doing":* "Why Rev. M. L. King Is Leaving Montgomery."

218   *"For almost four years":* "Martin Luther King's Secretary to Auction Historic Trove of
Papers," *Los Angeles Daily News,* September 18, 2013.

219   *He wept:* Ibid.

219   *"Alabama's Gain":* "Alabama's Gain, Georgia's Loss," *Dothan Eagle,* December 7, 1959.

219   *"toughest city in the South":* Emory O. Jackson, "King Says South Out to Kill 1954
Supreme Court Decision," *Atlanta Daily World,* December 11, 1959.

219   *"speedier breakdown of segregation":* Ibid.

219   *"they could be bigger":* Howell Raines, *My Soul Is Rested: Movement Days in the Deep
South Remembered* (1977; repr. New York: Penguin Books, 1983), 56.

220 *had just read the comic-book account*: David Levering Lewis, *King: A Critical Biography* (New York: Praeger, 1970), 113.

221 *"relative apathy"*: Stanley Levison to Martin Luther King Jr., November 3, 1958, Stanford King Institute, kinginstitute.stanford.edu/king-papers/documents/stanley -d-levison-2.

221 *"That's why the SCLC"*: James Lawson, interview with author, August 19, 2018.

221 *"We got arrested a bunch of times"*: Robert Avery, interview with author, August 2, 2020.

221 *"Let us not fear"*: "Negro Leader Urges Students to Continue Segregation Protest," *News and Observer* (Raleigh, N.C.), February 17, 1960.

222 *"I came not to bring inspiration"*: Bernard Lafayette Jr., interview with author, March 21, 2018.

222 *"We believed in Martin Luther King"*: John Lewis, interview with author and David McMahon, August 6, 2019.

222 *"wrestling match"*: James Lawson, interview with author, September 18, 2018.

223 *"to harass me"*: "'Another Attempt by the State of Alabama to Harass Me,' Says Rev. King, Jr., of Indictment," *Atlanta Daily World*, February 18, 1960.

223 *"people will believe that I took money"*: Quoted in James Baldwin, "The Dangerous Road Before Martin Luther King," *Harper's Magazine*, February 1961.

223 *"I called the airport"*: Quoted ibid.

223 *"thoroughgoing liberal"*: Martin Luther King Jr., "Pilgrimage to Nonviolence," *Christian Century*, April 13, 1960.

224 *"I have learned now"*: Martin Luther King Jr., "Suffering and Faith," *Christian Century*, April 27, 1960.

225 *burglar bars*: "Busy, Busy, Busy Describes Action Around Dr. King's Home," *Baltimore Afro-American*, October 24, 1964; "Martin Luther King Says: 'I'd Do It All Again,'" *Sepia*, December 1961.

225 *$110 a month*: David J. Garrow, *Bearing the Cross: Martin Luther King, Jr., and the Southern Christian Leadership Conference* (New York: William Morrow, 1986), 137.

225 *hung a calendar*: Bob Adelman and Charles R. Johnson, *King: The Photobiography of Martin Luther King, Jr.* (New York: Viking Studio, 2000), 66.

225 *"caused the children in the schools"*: Coretta Scott King transcripts, Hatch Papers, 17/14.

225 *43,934 miles on it*: Southern Chevrolet Inc., receipt, Boston University archive.

225 *"I think the sit-ins serve"*: Martin Luther King Jr., on *Meet the Press*, NBC, April 17, 1960, transcript, L. D. Reddick Papers, Schomburg Center.

226 *borrowed $800*: Clayborne Carson, *In Struggle: SNCC and the Black Awakening of the 1960s* (Cambridge, Mass.: Harvard University Press, 1981), 20.

226 *contributed to the strong turnout*: Ibid., 22.

226 *"bitter terms"*: Loudon Wainright, "Martyr of the Sit-Ins," *Life*, November 7, 1960.

226 *"for leadership of this group"*: Raines, *My Soul Is Rested*, 102.

227 *"I recognized"*: James Lawson, interview with author, August 9, 2018.

227 *"This inclination"*: Ella Baker, "Bigger Than a Hamburger," *Southern Patriot*, May 1960, www.crmvet.org/docs/sncc2.htm.

227 *"We seek the same goals"*: Roy Wilkins to Martin Luther King Jr., April 27, 1960, NAACP Papers, Manuscript Division, Library of Congress.

227 *"The pressure of all this"*: Wainright, "Martyr of the Sit-Ins."

228 *"The phone rang"*: Edward Kosner, interview with author, January 22, 2019.

228 *about two thousand people*: "Speaker Backs Sit-Down Strikes," *Black Dispatch* (Oklahoma City), August 5, 1960.

228 *"It was the most impressive thing"*: James Meredith, interview with author, July 23, 2020.

229 *"The Negro wants his freedom"*: "Speaker Backs Sit-Down Strikes."

229 *"I thought he needed my advice"*: James Meredith, interview with author, July 24, 2020.

229 *"As we sat talking"*: William Peters, "The Man Who Fights Hate with Love," *Redbook*, September 1961.

230 *"I decided that the best thing"*: Quoted in Garrow, *Bearing the Cross*, 140.

230 *Rich's department store*: "Students Seek Entry to Atlanta Lunch Counters," *Atlanta Daily World*, March 9, 1960.

230 *Two weeks later*: "Downtown Pickets Are Discouraged," *Atlanta Daily World*, March 27, 1960.

231 *army veteran and linotypist*: "Engagement of Miss King and Mr. Farris Announced," *Atlanta Daily World*, February 7, 1960.

231 *purchased her wedding dress from Rich's*: Alveda King, interview with author, May 10, 2022.

231 *"What happened in Little Rock"*: George B. Leonard Jr., "The Second Battle of Atlanta," *Look*, April 25, 1961.

231 *"Racial peace will make it possible"*: Ibid.

231 *"I am optimistic"*: Ibid.

232 *"they didn't want that undermined"*: Charles Black, interview with author, May 5, 2022.

232 *refused the food*: "Jailed Sit-Downers Denied Text Books," *Baltimore Afro-American*, October 29, 1960.

232 *"It was such a minor case"*: Martin Luther King Jr., interview with Berl I. Bernhard, transcript, March 9, 1964, Oral History Collection, John F. Kennedy Presidential Library and Museum, Boston (hereafter referred to as JFK Library).

232 *worried Martin would still be in custody*: Coretta Scott King, *My Life with Martin Luther King Jr.*, rev. ed. (New York: Henry Holt, 1993), 178.

232 *"You have to be strong for me"*: Ibid.

232 *four in the morning*: Martin Luther King Jr. to Coretta Scott King, probably October 26, 1960, King Papers Project, Stanford University.

233 *When he complained*: Peters, "The Man Who Fights Hate with Love."

21. "Kennedy to the Rescue!"

234 *"I did not feel at that time"*: David J. Garrow, *Bearing the Cross: Martin Luther King, Jr., and the Southern Christian Leadership Conference* (New York: William Morrow, 1986), 142.

235 *"running high"*: "Many Ministers Endorse the Republican Candidates," *Atlanta Daily World*, October 11, 1960.

235 *"A long view"*: Stanley Levison to Martin Luther King Jr., October 13, 1960,

Stanford King Institute, kinginstitute.stanford.edu/king-papers/documents/stanley-d-levison-3.

235 *tears in his eyes*: William Safire, "View from the Grandstand," *New York Times*, April 13, 1987.

235 *"Nixon doesn't deserve to win"*: Ibid.

235 *"He said . . . he was much concerned"*: Frank Reeves, interview with John F. Stewart, March 29, 1967, Oral History Collection, JFK Library.

236 *"a phone call to the house"*: "Vandiver Criticizes Kennedy on Dr. King," *New York Times*, November 1, 1960.

236 *"not welcome in Georgia"*: "Vandiver Says Negro Pastor Not Welcome," *Alabama Journal*, December 1, 1959.

236 *"He asked the assistance"*: S. Ernest Vandiver, interview with John F. Stewart, May 22, 1967, Oral History Collection, JFK Library.

236 *a historian disclosed it*: Clifford M. Kuhn, "'There's a Footnote to History!' Memory and the History of Martin Luther King's October 1960 Arrest and Its Aftermath," *Journal of American History* 84, no. 2 (September 1997): 583–95.

237 *"I think I received a new understanding"*: Garrow, *Bearing the Cross*, 149.

237 *"Kennedy to the Rescue!"*: "Kennedy to the Rescue," *Philadelphia Tribune*, October 25, 1960.

238 *"So this is why"*: Martin Luther King Jr., interview with Berl I. Bernhard, transcript, March 9, 1964, Oral History Collection, JFK Library.

238 *"the best-known leader of Negro opinion"*: Ralph McGill, "An Essay on Dr. M. L. King," *Atlanta Constitution*, November 5, 1960.

239 *"They are never honest enough"*: Martin Luther King Jr., "The Rising Tide of Racial Consciousness," address at the Golden Anniversary of the National Urban League, September 6, 1960.

239 *"Why did Daddy go to jail?"*: Coretta Scott King, *My Life with Martin Luther King, Jr.*, rev. ed. (New York: Henry Holt, 1993), 175.

240 *"Well . . . of course when"*: James Farmer, interview with Taylor Branch, November 18, 1983, Taylor Branch Papers, folder 611, Southern Historical Collection, Wilson Library, University of North Carolina, Chapel Hill.

241 *"When we were walking around the table"*: Dorothy Cotton, interview with Roland S. Martin, January 2018, accessed August 31, 2022, https://youtu.be/r8NhRwkX74c.

241 *"We ended up singing"*: Dorothy Cotton, interview with W. Jason Miller, July 28, 2017, courtesy of Miller.

241 *"I felt kind of a connection"*: Cotton, interview with Martin.

241 *was a tobacco and cotton farmer*: Dorothy Cotton, interview with Joseph Mosnier, July 25, 2011, Southern Oral History Program, Smithsonian Institution, National Museum of African American History & Culture, Washington, D.C.

241 *recalled her childhood*: Dorothy Cotton, interview with Horace Huntley, April 22, 1999, Birmingham Civil Rights Institute.

241 *"I recall nothing nurturing"*: Dorothy F. Cotton, *If Your Back's Not Bent: The Role of the Citizenship Education Program in the Civil Rights Movement* (New York: Atria Books, 2012), 28.

241 *"a bubbly, nice lady"*: Theresa Ann Walker, interview with author, July 8, 2020.

241 *"Dorothy can be washing the dishes"*: Cotton, *If Your Back's Not Bent*, 21.

242 *drove her to Atlanta*: Ibid., 90.

242 *"The movement became my life"*: Markus Schmidt,"King's Trip Took Away a City Leader," *Petersburg Progress-Index*, February 17, 2009.

242 *soothing the big egos*: Andrew Young, interview with Tom Dent, transcript, n.d., Amistad Research Center, Tulane University, New Orleans, La.

242 *"He loved his wife"*: Cotton, interview with Miller.

242 *"did everything but call herself"*: Juanita Abernathy, interview with author, August 2, 2018.

244 *jazz and blues*: Andrew Young, interview with Robert Penn Warren, March 17, 1964, Vanderbilt University, Special Collections and University Archives, whospeaks.library .vanderbilt.edu/interview/andrew-young.

244 *"Women can maintain"*: Ibid.

244 *"a nice young lady"*: Martin Luther King Jr. Papers, Boston University archives, 1961.

245 *"just nibbling sweet grass"*: Martin Luther King Jr., "The Seeking God," sermon, Ebenezer Baptist Church, October 2, 1960, in *The Papers of Martin Luther King Jr.*, vol. 6: *Advocate of the Social Gospel, September 1948–March 1963*, ed. Clayborne Carson (Berkeley: University of California Press, 2007), 408–10.

245 *"Put us in jail"*: Martin Luther King Jr., "Loving Your Enemies," sermon, Detroit Council of Churches, March 7, 1961, in Carson, *The Papers of Martin Luther King Jr.*, vol. 6, 421–29.

245 *expecting it to happen*: "Increasing Number in South See Integration as Inevitable," *Miami Herald*, February 12, 1961.

246 *"Devout, reverent"*: "General Program, 1960–61," SCLC memo, L. D. Reddick Papers, Schomburg Center.

246 *"From reports of"*: "Out-of-Town Groups Blamed in Birmingham," *Alabama Journal*, May 15, 1961.

247 *Robert F. Kennedy . . . phoned*: King, interview with Bernhard.

247 *Seigenthaler's limp body*: "Bus Station Riots Leave 20 Injured," *Montgomery Advertiser*, May 21, 1961.

248 *exceeding the number of homes*: Gene Roberts and Hank Klibanoff, *The Race Beat: The Press, the Civil Rights Struggle and the Awakening of a Nation* (New York: Vintage Books, 2007), 156.

248 *"I guess he called me"*: King, interview with Bernhard.

248 *"Dr. King was very upset"*: Burke Marshall, interview with Louis F. Oberdorfer, May 29, 1964, Oral History Collection, JFK Library.

248 *"Troops are on the way"*: Martin Luther King Jr., WSB-TV footage, May 21, 1961, dp.la /exhibitions/activism/civil-rights-actions/freedom-rides.

249 *remained in frequent contact*: King, interview with Bernhard.

249 *Adults stretched out*: John F. Murphy, "Dr. King, Besieged, Voices Confidence," *New York Times*, May 22, 1961.

249 *"The law may not be able"*: Martin Luther King Jr., "Address at Freedom Riders Rally at First Baptist Church," in *The Papers of Martin Luther King, Jr.*, vol. 7: *To Save the Soul of America, January 1961–August 1962*, ed. Clayborne Carson (Oakland: University of California Press, 2014), 230–31.

249 *Thousands of white people*: "Angry Mob Quits Church Before Cloud of Tear Gas," *Montgomery Advertiser*, May 22, 1961.

249 *"We were expecting"*: Bernard Lafayette Jr., interview with author, May 22, 2019.

249 *"All the kids knew"*: David Halberstam, "Negro Girl a Force in Campaign; Encouraged Bus to Keep Rolling," *New York Times*, May 23, 1961.

249 *"Several of us wanted"*: John Lewis, interview with author and David McMahon, August 6, 2019.

249 *"The cause of human decency"*: David Levering Lewis, *King: A Critical Biography* (New York: Praeger, 1970), 134.

250 *"universities of nonviolence"*: James Lawson, interview with author, August 9, 2018.

250 *"They questioned his reticence"*: Ella Baker, interview with John H. Britton, July 19, 1969, transcript, Taylor Branch Papers, folder 528b, University of North Carolina Library, Chapel Hill.

250 *"nothing less than a moral revolution"*: James Baldwin, "The Dangerous Road Before Martin Luther King," *Harper's Magazine*, February 1961.

22. The New Emancipation Proclamation

252 *"He was so short"*: Tyrone Brooks, interview with author, August 3, 2018.

252 *"It has its advantages"*: "The Mike Wallace Interviews," WNTA-TV, February 7–8, 1961, in *The Papers of Martin Luther King, Jr.*, vol. 7: *To Save the Soul of America, January 1961–August 1962*, ed. Clayborne Carson (Oakland: University of California Press, 2014), 156–66.

253 *"He pays less"*: William Peters, "The Man Who Fights Hate with Love," *Redbook*, September 1961.

253 *"He is more serious"*: Ibid.

253 *"First, of course"*: Ibid.

254 *"Yolanda, the eldest"*: Ibid.

254 *"What he has done"*: Ibid.

254 *"I marveled at his patience"*: James Lawson, interview with author, September 18, 2018.

255 *"issue a formal executive order"*: Martin Luther King Jr., press release, June 5, 1961, in Carson, *The Papers of Martin Luther King, Jr.*, vol. 7, 244.

255 *"Kennedy felt uncomfortable"*: Harris Wofford oral history, February 3, 1969, Larry J. Hackman, JFK Library.

256 *"Here was a family"*: Mahalia Jackson, *Movin' On Up*, with Evan McLeod Wylie (New York: Hawthorn Books, 1966), 180.

256 *Martin excused himself*: Ibid.

256 *flag at city hall*: Robert E. Baker, "Albany's Anti-Negro Tack May Set South's Course," *Washington Post*, August 5, 1962.

257 *set up an office*: Howard Zinn, *SNCC: The New Abolitionists* (1964; repr. Chicago: Haymarket Books, 2017), 126.

257 *"They were rebuffed"*: Dr. William G. Anderson, interview with author, October 26, 2020.

257 *"We will not stand"*: "Five Atlantans Arrested in Albany Station," *Atlanta Daily World*, December 12, 1961.

257 *police escort*: Bruce Galphin, "Albany Balks at Truce Price; Rev. King Rallies Negroes," *Atlanta Constitution*, December 16, 1961.

257 *"the Negro's burden"*: Ibid.

257 *wanted Black jurors*: Albany Movement minutes, November 17, 1961, David J. Garrow personal collection.

258 *"This was a mass movement"*: William Anderson, interview with author, October 26, 2020.

258 *dropped the argument*: James Forman, *The Making of Black Revolutionaries* (1972; repr. Seattle: University of Washington Press, 2000), 255.

258 *cold, gray, drizzly*: "'Total Victory!' Battle Cry at Albany," *Baltimore Afro-American*, December 30, 1961.

258 *led the procession*: "Albany Police Arrest Dr. King, 266 Others," *Atlanta Journal-Constitution*, December 17, 1961.

258 *120 police officers*: David Miller, "Dr. King in Mass Jailing," *New York Herald Tribune*, December 17, 1961.

258 *The marchers sang*: James Gillespy, "King, Marchers to Courthouse Steps, Jailed," *Atlanta Daily World*, December 17, 1961.

258 *neared city hall*: David Miller, "Dr. King in Mass Jailing."

259 *"We are simply going"*: Ibid.

259 *stood six feet tall*: David Miller, "Non-Violence: Police Chief and Minister," *New York Herald Tribune*, December 18, 1961.

259 *"like his head, neck, and shoulders"*: Chris Vail, interview with author, November 1, 2020.

259 *"I researched Dr. King"*: Howell Raines, *My Soul Is Rested: Movement Days in the Deep South Remembered* (1977; repr. New York: Penguin, 1983), 361.

259 *He vowed to fire*: Vail, interview with author.

259 *didn't employ them*: "Things Normal Again, Albany Whites Say," *Atlanta Journal and Constitution*, December 24, 1961.

259 *raised a megaphone*: David Miller, "Non-Violence: Police Chief and Minister."

259 *"They have no respect for humans"*: Gillespy, "King, Marchers to Courthouse Steps, Jailed."

259 *"If convicted I will refuse"*: David Miller, "Inside the Jail," *New York Herald Tribune*, December 18, 1961.

259 *"enough personal glory"*: Ibid.

260 *"I'll tell you"*: Allen Secher, interview with author, May 4, 2021.

260 *"the vigor of the Negro"*: Robert E. Baker, "Albany's Anti-Negro Tack May Set South's Course."

260 *"This small city"*: Tom Lankford, "Integration Techniques at Stake as Albany Program Bogs Down," *Birmingham News*, July 29, 1962.

261 *"I had the sense"*: Charles Black, interview with author, May 5, 2022.

261 *"very, very persuasive"*: Beverly Gage, *G-Man: J. Edgar Hoover and the Making of the American Century* (New York: Viking, 2022), 530.

262 *"someone with Levison's secret"*: David J. Garrow, "The FBI and Martin Luther King," *The Atlantic*, July/August 2002.

262 *"We know that freedom"*: Martin Luther King Jr., proposal for Second Emancipation Proclamation, Berl I. Bernhard Personal Papers, JFK Library.

263 *rising steel prices*: Ernest Dunbar, "A Visit with Martin Luther King," *Look*, February 12, 1963.

264 *"The time has now come"*: "A Message from Jail," *New York Amsterdam News*, July 21, 1962.

264 *"very unhappy about the subtle"*: Bill Shipp, "Freed by Mystery Fine Donor, Rev. King Meets Police Chief," *Atlanta Constitution*, July 13, 1962.

264 *"Dr. King, what do you cats"*: James Bevel, interview with Katherine Shannon, July 6, 1968, Civil Rights Documentation Project, transcript from David J. Garrow personal collection.

264 *he welcomed their criticism*: David Levering Lewis, *King: A Critical Biography* (New York: Praeger, 1970), 164.

264 *"Nothing can hurt us more"*: WSB-TV, July 25, 1962, Brown Media Archives, University of Georgia, Athens.

265 *"were not nice Christian people"*: Coretta Scott King, interview with Arnold Michaelis, December 1, 1965, outtakes from "Martin Luther King Jr.: A Personal Portrait," Brown Media Archives, University of Georgia, Athens.

265 *"until he fixes it"*: Hedrick Smith, "Dr. King's 3 Children Visit Him; He Is Allowed Out of Jail Cell," *New York Times*, August 6, 1962.

265 *called off a series*: Hedrick Smith, "Dr. King Set Free After Conviction," *New York Times*, August 11, 1962.

265 *"We killed them with kindness"*: Lewis, *King*, 151.

265 *"The mistake I made there"*: Martin Luther King Jr., interview with Alex Haley, *Playboy*, January 1965.

266 *"The change started"*: William Anderson, interview with author, October 26, 2020.

266 *"Even in the short term"*: Vail, interview with author.

267 *"A non-violent campaign"*: Martin Luther King Jr. to Israel Dresner, October 9, 1962, Dresner family private collection.

268 *"Dr. King dropped his hands"*: Septima Clark, interview with Jacquelyn Hall, July 25, 1976, Southern Oral History Program Collection, University of North Carolina Library, Chapel Hill.

268 *"Don't touch him"*: Jacquelyn Dowd Hall, Eugene P. Walker, Katherine Mellen Charron, and David P. Cline, "Septima Clark and Women in the Civil Rights Movement," *Southern Cultures* 16, no. 2 (Summer 2010), www.southerncultures.org/article/i-train-the-people-to-do-their-own-talking-septima-clark-and-women-in-the-civil-rights-movement/, accessed December 11, 2020.

268 *Rosa Parks ran to a nearby store*: Septima Clark, interview with Eugene Walker, July 30, 1976, Southern Oral History Program Collection, University of North Carolina Library, Chapel Hill.

268 *he blamed the "evil forces"*: Robert Brank Fulton, "To Whom It May Concern," letter, September 29, 1962, Swarthmore College Peace Collection.

268 *declined to press charges*: Lou Isaacson, "City Acts Fast to Jail Man Who Hit King," *Birmingham News*, September 28, 1962.

268 *"Well . . . when I saw him throwing"*: Clark, interview with Walker.

268 *"Every man should"*: Dunbar, "A Visit with Martin Luther King."

269 *"Suppose he had a knife or gun?"*: Ibid.

23. Temptation and Surveillance

270 *nine consecutive days in Atlanta*: King's work schedule, November 1962, SCLC records, David J. Garrow personal collection.

270 *3006 Delmar Lane NW*: David J. Garrow, "The Troubling Legacy of Martin Luther King," *Standpoint*, June 2019, 32.

270 *When he fell asleep on the sofa*: Donzaleigh Abernathy, interview with author, November 2, 2018.

270 *four and a half hours*: Ernest Dunbar, "A Visit with Martin Luther King," *Look*, February 12, 1963.

270 *he felt "depressed"*: Andrew Young, *An Easy Burden: The Civil Rights Movement and the Transformation of America* (Waco, Tex.: Baylor University Press, 2008), 181.

271 *"had a particularly difficult time"*: Ralph David Abernathy, *And the Walls Came Tumbling Down: An Autobiography* (New York: Harper & Row, 1989), 471–72.

272 *"cool it down"*: Ibid., 474–75.

272 *"Martin really believed in love"*: Kenneth Clark, interview with Arthur M. Schlesinger Jr., September 9, 1976, Schlesinger Papers, New York Public Library.

272 *"Both had powerful fathers"*: Stanley Levison, interview with Arthur M. Schlesinger Jr., August 3, 1976, interview notes from David J. Garrow personal collection.

272 *"There is a privacy"*: Martin Luther King Jr., sermon, n.d. (probably between 1954 and 1960), audio recording, Stanford King Institute, kinginstitute.stanford.edu/king -papers/documents/mans-sin-and-gods-grace#ftnref2. On the recording, King changes the second line to the present tense, as if suggesting that grace continues to save him.

273 *spoke almost daily*: L. D. Reddick, unpublished biography of Ralph Abernathy, 2, L. D. Reddick Papers, Schomburg Center.

273 *"My husband was trustworthy"*: Juanita Abernathy, interview with author, August 2, 2018.

273 *"to Martin and the movement"*: Abernathy, *And the Walls Came Tumbling Down*, 198.

273 *easy conversation often eluded him*: Andrew Young, interview with Tom Dent, February 1, 1984, Amistad Research Center, Tulane University, New Orleans, La.

273 *"I tried to provide"*: Abernathy to L. D. Reddick, Reddick notes for unpublished Abernathy biography, L. D. Reddick Papers, Schomburg Center.

274 *"Abernathy was always making sure"*: C. T. Vivian, interview with author, July 6, 2018.

274 *same brand of shoes*: Tom Houck, interview with author, July 6, 2018.

274 *Aramis*: Juandalynn Abernathy, interview with author, November 1, 2018.

274 *"Ralph, you look like a bulldog"*: Houck, interview with author.

274 *"Martin, you're a moneyed Negro"*: Ibid.

274 *"the light and bright"*: Ibid.

274 *never letting them win*: Donzaleigh Abernathy, interview with author, November 2, 2018.

275 *"I mean, he always spent holidays"*: Coretta Scott King transcripts, Hatch Papers, box 22, folder 9.

275 *"burgundy-colored"*: Dexter Scott King, *Growing Up King: An Intimate Memoir*, with Ralph Wiley (New York: Warner Books, 2003), 21–22.

275 *"Just being the person"*: Coretta Scott King, interview with Arnold Michaelis, December 1, 1965, outtakes from "Martin Luther King Jr.: A Personal Portrait," Brown Media Archives, University of Georgia, Athens.

276 *"Coretta was the smartest"*: Edwina Moss, interview with author, June 4, 2018.

276 *"One of the greatest problems we face"*: "Dr. King Says F.B.I. in Albany, Ga., Favors Segregationists," *New York Times*, November 19, 1962.

276 *"The FBI men, ever lurking"*: Pat Watters, *Down to Now: Reflections on the Southern Civil Rights Movement* (New York: Pantheon Books, 1971), 225.

276 *"the dread fact"*: Ibid., 228.

277 *"Where were they living?"*: James Baldwin, interview, February 2, 1970, Jean Stein Personal Papers, JSTPP-001–012, JFK Library.

277 *Hoover had sent a letter*: FBI memo, August 11, 1962.

277 *stalked him months later*: David J. Garrow, *Bearing the Cross: Martin Luther King, Jr., and the Southern Christian Leadership Conference* (New York: William Morrow, 1986), 232.

277 *"I still think"*: Berl I. Bernhard, interview with John F. Stewart, July 25, 1968, Oral History Collection, JFK Library.

277 *"It would appear obvious"*: Cartha D. "Deke" DeLoach to John Mohr, memo, January 15, 1963, FBI archives.

277 *"an instance of his insincerity"*: J. Edgar Hoover to Berl I. Bernhard, memo, January 18, 1963, FBI archives.

278 *Two days after King's critical remarks*: David J. Garrow, *The FBI and Martin Luther King, Jr: From "Solo" to Memphis* (New York: Penguin Books, 1983), 57.

24. "The Stuff Is Just in 'Em"

279 *"not advisable"*: James R. McDowell, "Letter from Lovett to Mrs. King," *The Church Awakens: African Americans and the Struggle for Justice*, episcopalarchives.org/church -awakens/items/show/146, accessed January 16, 2021.

279 *"the best possible secondary education"*: Frank Wells, "Episcopal Schools Open, King Told," *Atlanta Constitution*, March 16, 1963.

279 *"It only proves again"*: "Son of Martin Luther King Is Rejected," *Hanford Sentinel*, March 16, 1963.

280 *"If they rough us up"*: "Fear Violence at Oscar Awards over Race Issue," *Chicago Daily Defender*, March 16, 1963.

280 *"repeated mayhem"*: "Miss. Cops, Dog Scatter 100 in Voting March," *Chicago Daily Defender*, March 28, 1963.

281 *"You show me a black man"*: Malcolm X as told to Alex Haley, *The Autobiography of Malcolm X* (New York: Ballantine Books, 1964), 454.

281 *"From birth to death"*: Lerone Bennett Jr., *The Negro Mood and Other Essays* (New York: Ballantine Books, 1964), 29–30.

281 *"they have been persuaded"*: Martin Luther King Jr., "Bold Design for a New South," *The Nation*, March 30, 1963.

282 *"which creates a* de facto *segregation"*: Ernest Dunbar, "A Visit with Martin Luther King," *Look*, February 12, 1963.

282 *"made Martin decide"*: James Lawson, interview with author, February 1, 2019.

282 *"segregation now"*: "Wallace Makes Federal Government His Target in Speech," *Birmingham Post-Herald*, January 15, 1963.

283 *"I'm just a good old country boy"*: James Saxon Childers, "Just a Good Old Country Boy,'" *Birmingham News*, October 18, 1931.

283 *"absolutely genuine"*: Ibid.

284 *"the South's toughest city"*: Andrew M. Manis, *A Fire You Can't Put Out: The Civil Rights Life of Birmingham's Reverend Fred Shuttlesworth* (Tuscaloosa: University of Alabama Press, 1999), 203.

284 *Unionists were among*: Glenn T. Eskew, *But for Birmingham: The Local and National Movements in the Civil Rights Struggle* (Chapel Hill: University of North Carolina Press, 1997), 108.

284 *Project C*: Ibid., 210.

284 *inadequate fireproofing*: Lee E. Bains Jr., "Birmingham, 1963: Confrontation over Civil Rights" (BA honors essay, Harvard University), in *Birmingham, Alabama, 1956–1963: The Black Struggle for Civil Rights*, ed. David J. Garrow (Brooklyn, N.Y.: Carlson Publishing, 1989), 170.

285 *In Albany, it had been a mistake*: Martin Luther King Jr., interview with Donald H. Smith, November 29, 1963, Wisconsin Historical Society.

285 *aloof*: David Halberstam, notes and draft of speech, Halberstam Collection, Boston University Library.

285 *"God took all the fear out of me"*: Calvin Woods, interview with author, January 4, 2020.

285 *"I will fill that jail full"*: "Connor Warns He'll Fill Jail in Mix Effort," *Alabama Journal*, April 4, 1963.

286 *Ware's support*: Ralph David Abernathy, *And the Walls Came Tumbling Down: An Autobiography* (New York: Harper & Row, 1989), 238.

286 *"Both Martin and I"*: Ibid., 240.

286 *"You know the story"*: Quoted in Pat Watters, *Down to Now: Reflections on the Southern Civil Rights Movement* (New York: Pantheon Books, 1971), 234–35.

287 *four hundred people*: "Birmingham Given Pivot Status in Drive for Mix," *Selma Times-Journal*, April 4, 1963.

287 *"Now we say"*: Quoted in James H. Cone, *Martin & Malcolm & America: A Dream or a Nightmare* (Maryknoll, N.Y.: Orbis Books, 2020), 130.

287 *a spirit of unconditional love*: "King Tells Integration Demands in Birmingham," *Chicago Defender*, April 6, 1963.

287 *"Pharaoh lets God's people go"*: Quoted in Harvard Sitkoff, *The Struggle for Black Equality*, 25th anniversary ed. (New York: Hill & Wang, 2008), 121.

287 *"was proving unsuccessful"*: "6 New Arrests," *Birmingham World*, April 17, 1963.

287 *King's efforts were being sapped*: "Current of Compromise Flows Through Tension Here," *Birmingham World*, April 14, 1963.

287 *"promised mass demonstrations"*: Foster Hailey, "10 More Negroes Seized in Birmingham Sit-Ins," *New York Times*, April 6, 1963.

288 *relocated to Birmingham . . . in 1962*: "Brother of Dr. M. L. King Accepts Ensley Pastorate," *Birmingham Mirror*, January 20, 1962.

288 *driving under the influence*: "Fayette Grand Jury Indicts Rev. A. D. King," *Atlanta Daily World*, March 10, 1961.

288 *told one confidant*: Andrew Young, interview with Tom Dent, February 1, 1984, Amistad Research Center, Tulane University, New Orleans, La.

288 *"couldn't get past the anger"*: June Dobbs Butts, author interview, October 3, 2018.

288 *"These people are nothing but"*: "Dogs Snap, Negroes Cry, Parade Crushed in Ala.," *Boston Globe*, April 8, 1963.

288 *"Look at that dog go"*: Ibid.

288 *"A 19-year-old Negro"*: "26 Negro Marchers Arrested Here," *Birmingham News*, April 8, 1963.

288 *had a different version*: James Forman, *The Making of Black Revolutionaries* (1972; repr. Seattle: University of Washington Press, 2000), 311.

289 *"dry-as-dust"*: Martin Luther King Jr., *Why We Can't Wait* (New York: Harper & Row, 1964), 67.

289 *"There are some preachers"*: George Barner, "King and Abernathy: Trumpets of Gospel," *New York Amsterdam News*, April 13, 1963.

289 *"I'm on My Way to Freedomland"*: Ibid.

289 *"I've never been to jail"*: Ibid.

290 *"I sat there"*: King, *Why We Can't Wait*, 70–71.

290 *"as if he were far away"*: Andrew Young, *An Easy Burden: The Civil Rights Movement and the Transformation of America* (Waco, Tex.: Baylor University Press, 2008), 214.

290 *"I think I was standing"*: King, *Why We Can't Wait*, 71.

291 *gray cotton work shirt*: "King Jailed as Officers Halt March," *Montgomery Advertiser*, April 13, 1963.

291 *"I don't remember any of the words"*: Dorothy Cotton, *If Your Back's Not Bent: The Role of the Citizenship Education Program in the Civil Rights Movement* (New York: Atria Books, 2012), 213.

291 *no dogs this time*: "King Jailed as Officers Halt March."

292 *yanked King by the elbow*: Boston TV News digital library, bostonlocaltv.org/catalog /V_QGC70WT8X3Y3JZS, accessed June 9, 2021.

292 *"Keep the movement going"*: UPI news reports, multiple newspapers, April 13, 1963.

292 *"Put them in solitary"*: Abernathy, *And the Walls Came Tumbling Down*, 252.

25. Birmingham Jail

293 *solitary confinement*: Martin Luther King Jr., *Why We Can't Wait* (New York: Harper & Row, 1964), 74.

293 *"Those were the longest"*: King, *Why We Can't Wait*, 73.

293 *"withdraw support from these demonstrations"*: "White Clergymen Urge Local Negroes to Withdraw from Demonstrations," *Birmingham News*, April 13, 1963.

293 *"no person's freedom is safe"*: "Ala. Ministers Urge Peace and Calm in Integration," *Alabama Citizen*, February 2, 1963.

294 *napkins and toilet paper*: Willie Mackey King, interview with author, November 8, 2021.

294 *"The writing on the greasy"*: Willie Mackey King, interview with author, July 8, 2020.

295 *"He wasn't angry"*: Willie Mackey King, interview with author, November 8, 2021.

295 *"My Dear Fellow Clergymen"*: The earliest known version of the letter, with Willie Mackey's initials, found in the archives of *The Christian Century* magazine, differs slightly from later versions, including the version published by *The Christian Century*. Copyediting marks on the document show small changes. For example, "Maybe

again, I have been too optimistic" became "Perhaps I have once again been too optimistic." King would continue to revise the letter as it went on to be published elsewhere.

296 *"to broaden the impact"*: Harold S. Fey to King, May 22, 1963, *Christian Century* archives, Chicago.

297 *"Is your spirit all right?"*: Wiretap transcript, April 15, 1963, Birmingham Police Department, David J. Garrow personal collection.

297 *"You know, we've got to"*: Quoted in David J. Garrow, *Bearing the Cross: Martin Luther King, Jr., and the Southern Christian Leadership Conference* (New York: William Morrow, 1986), 247.

297 *"If you hear them talk now"*: Dorothy Cotton, interview with Horace Huntley, April 22, 1999, Birmingham Civil Rights Institute.

298 *"He'd never stop talking"*: Andrew Young, interview with author, January 23, 2019.

299 *"Poor King"*: WRVR, *The Birmingham Story*, radio documentary audio recordings, American Archive of Public Broadcasting, americanarchive.org/catalog/cpb-aacip -500-xd0qwv5h?term=MARTIN&#at_1306.45_s.

299 *"That got me"*: James Orange, interview, July 15, 2003, Voices of Labor Oral History Project, Georgia State University Library, Atlanta.

299 *"Let 'em have it"*: Reese Cleghorn, "Martin Luther King Jr.: Apostle of Crisis," *Saturday Evening Post*, June 15, 1963.

300 *"Freedom!"*: Ibid.

301 *"Martin was not really an organizer"*: Bayard Rustin and Harry Wachtel, transcript of audiotaped conversation, October 31, 1985, courtesy of Walter Naegle.

301 *to learn what the protesters wanted*: Ibid.

302 *"Bull Connor had something in his mind"*: Quoted in Garrow, *Bearing the Cross*, 251.

302 *"Never in the history"*: Martin Luther King Jr., "Keep On Moving," speech, May 5, 1963, "Sing for Freedom," Smithsonian Folkways records.

302 *"I waited a week"*: Claude Sitton, "Rioting Negroes Routed by Police at Birmingham," *New York Times*, May 8, 1963.

303 *"The city of Birmingham"*: "Negroes End Desegregation Campaign," *Birmingham News*, May 10, 1963.

303 *"It upset me"*: "Birmingham: Testament of Nonviolence, 1; A Happy Day in Birmingham, May 10, 1963," WRVR, audio recording, American Archive of Public Broadcasting, americanarchive.org/catalog/cpb-aacip-500-r785p02p?term =MARTIN&#at_5.69_s.

303 *"We got that agitating"*: "Negroes Cut Back Terms for Ending Birmingham Crisis," *New York Times*, May 10, 1963.

303 *"the people of Birmingham"*: "Birmingham: Testament of Nonviolence, 2; The Klan Two Bombs and a Riot," WRVR, audio recording, American Archive of Public Broadcasting, americanarchive.org/catalog/cpb-aacip-500-xd0qwv5h?term =MARTIN&#at_1306.45_s.

303 *Three people were injured*: "Blasts Rock Home of King's Brothers and Gaston Motel," *Birmingham News*, May 12, 1963.

303 *A.D. drove around town*: "Birmingham: Testament of Nonviolence, 2."

303 *"I'm convinced we're going to see"*: Ibid.

304 *In a Gallup poll*: "Gallup Poll: LBJ, Ike and 'Winnie,'" *Rapid City Journal*, December 27, 1963.

304 *The NAACP's budget*: NAACP Budget Committee, memo, December 18, 1963, Library of Congress.

304 *"I will have to face the decision"*: Reese Cleghorn, "Martin Luther King Jr., Apostle of Crisis," *Saturday Evening Post*, June 15, 1963.

305 *"the fire he had lighted"*: Lerone Bennett Jr., *What Manner of Man: A Biography of Martin Luther King, Jr.* (Chicago: Johnson Publishing, 1964), 156.

305 *"A revolutionary condition"*: Walter Lippman, "The Negroes and the Nation," *Washington Post*, May 28, 1963.

306 *took it personally*: Arthur M. Schlesinger Jr., *Robert Kennedy and His Times* (Boston: Mariner Books, 2002), 334.

306 *"Bobby . . . didn't understand"*: James Baldwin, interview, February 2, 1970, Jean Stein Personal Papers, JSTPP-001–012, JFK Library.

306 *"He began, I believe, to grasp"*: Schlesinger, *Robert Kennedy and His Times*, 335.

307 *"has not yet given the leadership"*: Martin Luther King Jr., interview with David Susskind, "Open End," WNTA-TV, aired June 9, 1963.

307 *"There is a great deal of hypocrisy"*: Ibid.

307 *spent the whole day*: Edwin O. Guthman and Jeffrey Shulman, eds., *Robert Kennedy, in His Own Words: The Unpublished Recollections of the Kennedy Years* (New York: Bantam Books, 1988), 199.

307 *"go all-out"*: Harris Wofford, *Of Kennedys and Kings: Making Sense of the Sixties* (New York: Farrar, Straus & Giroux, 1980), 172.

307 *"We have a right to expect"*: John F. Kennedy, "Address to the American People on Civil Rights," June 11, 1963, JFK Library.

308 *"the most eloquent"*: Martin Luther King Jr., interview with Berl I. Bernhard, March 9, 1964, transcript, JFK Library.

308 *"The sniper's bullet"*: Claude Sitton, "N.A.A.C.P. Leader Slain in Jackson; Protests Mount," *New York Times*, June 13, 1963.

308 *It wasn't that he had suddenly awakened*: Guthman and Shulman, *Robert Kennedy in His Own Words*, 210–11.

308 *"Well, I think Birmingham"*: Martin Luther King Jr., interview with Bernhard.

26. The Dream, Part One

313 *"19 million U.S. Negroes"*: "The Negro in America," *Newsweek*, July 29, 1963.

313 *"We the Negro"*: Ibid.

313 *"Undeniably"*: Martin Luther King Jr., *Why We Can't Wait* (New York: Harper & Row, 1964), 16.

313 *"Just as lightning"*: Ibid.

314 *Night Hawk restaurant chain*: "City Restaurants Sign Integrate Pact," *Austin American-Statesman*, June 6, 1963.

314 *"We are on the threshold"*: "Martin Luther King Racial Matters," FBI memo, June 4, 1963.

315 *"was willing to risk"*: King, *Why We Can't Wait*, 37.

316   *"I have so many injunctions"*: "After King Talks and Negroes Walk," *Danville Register*,
       July 12, 1963.

316   *"was going to be"*: Edwin O. Guthman and Jeffrey Shulman, eds., *Robert Kennedy, in His
       Own Words: The Unpublished Recollections of the Kennedy Years* (New York: Bantam
       Books, 1988), 176.

317   *"Burke—this is not getting any better"*: David J. Garrow, *The FBI and Martin Luther King
       Jr.* (New York: Penguin Books, 1981), 58.

317   *"destabilize American society"*: Cartha D. "Deke" DeLoach, *Hoover's FBI: The Inside
       Story by Hoover's Trusted Lieutenant* (Washington, D.C.: Regnery History, 1995), 202.

317   *"going away from"*: Guthman and Shulman, *Robert Kennedy, in His Own Words*, 198.

317   *"not only would it damage"*: Robert Kennedy, interview with Anthony Lewis, December
       4, 1964, JFK Library.

317   *"but we still have a long way to go"*: Phil Casey, "3000 in Peaceful Rights March Here,"
       Washington Post, June 15, 1963.

318   *"Bob Kennedy"*: Burke Marshall, interview, October 6, 1968, Jean Stein Personal
       Papers, JFK Library.

318   *"ninety percent of the Negroes"*: M. S. Handler, "Malcolm X Starting Drive in Washington,"
       New York Times, May 10, 1963.

319   *"it may open the door"*: Martin Luther King Jr., interview with David Susskind, June 9,
       1963, video recording, search.alexanderstreet.com/view/work/bibliographic
       _entity%7Cvideo_work%7C4247869/david-susskind-archive-interview-dr-martin
       -luther-king-jr, accessed March 10, 2021.

319   *"massive acts of civil disobedience"*: "Massive Protest in Capital Seen If Congress Fails to
       Aid Negroes," *New York Times*, June 12, 1963.

319   *"Them white folks"*: "The Future: Not How Much—but When," *Newsweek*, July 29, 1963.

319   *"The Negro is shedding"*: Quoted in David J. Garrow, *Bearing the Cross: Martin Luther
       King, Jr., and the Southern Christian Leadership Conference* (New York: William
       Morrow, 1986), 273–74.

320   *"We want success in Congress"*: Quoted in Arthur M. Schlesinger Jr., *Robert Kennedy and
       His Times*, 40th anniversary ed. (Boston: Mariner Books, 2018), 349.

320   *"It may seem ill-timed"*: Quoted ibid., 350.

320   *"They're communists"*: Quoted ibid., 357.

321   *"Freedom March Day"*: "Cavanagh, King to Head March Down Woodward," *Detroit
       Free Press*, June 23, 1963.

321   peach pie: "Cleo Louis King Hill, Aunt of Martin Luther King Jr.," *Detroit News*,
       November 10, 1998.

321   black suit: Robert Pearson, "Negroes 'on the Threshold of a Breakthrough'—King,"
       Detroit Free Press, June 24, 1963.

321   *"Now is the time to make real"*: Martin Luther King Jr., "I Have a Dream," speech at the
       Walk to Freedom, June 23, 1963, Detroit, Motown recording. This is also the source
       for all subsequent quotes from this speech.

322   *"I Dream a World"*: W. Jason Miller, *Origins of the Dream: Hughes's Poetry and King's
       Rhetoric* (Gainesville: University Press of Florida, 2015), 142–43.

322   from Brooklyn to Harlem: "Dr. King Is Target of Eggs in Harlem," *New York Times*, July
       1, 1963.

322 *"go up there tomorrow"*: "Eggs Hit King's Car in Harlem," *Atlanta Constitution*, July 1, 1963.

323 *Thunderbird*: Photograph, Schomburg Center.

323 *"I can't understand"*: "King Jeered," *Christian Science Monitor*, July 2, 1963.

323 *" feeling rejected"*: Stephen Drury Smith and Catherine Ellis, eds., *Free All Along: The Robert Penn Warren Civil Rights Interviews* (New York: The New Press, 2019), 182.

324 *"The Kennedy administration"*: John Lewis, *Walking with the Wind: A Memoir of the Movement*, with Michael D'Orso (New York: Simon & Schuster, 1998), 215.

324 *stopped by the Cook County Jail*: "King Visits Gregory in Jail," *Chicago Daily Defender*, August 19, 1963.

324 *"It is the beginning of the year"*: King, *Why We Can't Wait*, ix.

326 *photographed together*: "Pledge Show Profits to King," *Los Angeles Sentinel*, May 30, 1963.

326 *"believing there was an FBI agent"*: Clarence Jones, email interview with author, March 19, 2021.

27. The Dream, Part Two

328 *blue-jeaned teenager*: Francine White (née Yeager), interviews with author, February 26 and April 2, 2021. All details, quotes, thoughts, and feelings attributed to White come from these interviews and were confirmed in follow-up interviews.

329 *five tons of American cheese*: Anna Petersen, "80,000 Lunches Made Here by Volunteers for Washington Marchers," *New York Times*, August 28, 1983.

329 *The Washington Senators postponed*: "Nats Call Off Two Games, August 27–28," *Washington Post*, August 17, 1963.

329 *hundreds of portable toilets*: Martin Arnold, "Road Facilities to Aid Caravans," *New York Times*, August 28, 1963.

330 *vomited*: Roger Mudd, *The Place to Be: Washington, CBS, and the Glory Days of Television News* (New York: PublicAffairs, 2008), 118.

330 *cutoff switch*: Ibid.

330 *"had all the combined elements"*: Quoted in Aniko Bodroghkozy, *Equal Time: Television and the Civil Rights Movement* (Urbana: University of Illinois Press, 2012), 105.

331 *smiled slightly*: All physical descriptions of King and the reaction of the crowd are from *The March: The Story of the Greatest March in American History*, PBS, Smoking Dog Films, 2013, as well as YouTube videos, including this one: https://www.youtube.com /watch?v=vlaSZ7jhWWk. All quotes from King's "I Have a Dream" speech delivered at the March on Washington for Jobs and Freedom, August 28, 1963, are from the Motown recording of that event.

331 *black-and-white print dress*: Louise Oettinger, "The Sunny Day Shone," *Washington Post*, August 29, 1963.

331 *He's short*: Gordon Gundrum, interview with author, July 10, 2018. All subsequent quotes, observations, and thoughts attributed to Gundrum come from this interview.

333 *"the living, breathing heart"*: Martin Luther King Jr., *Why We Can't Wait* (New York: Harper & Row, 1964), 134.

333 *He arrived at his hotel*: Martin Luther King Jr., interview with Donald H. Smith, November 29, 1963, Wisconsin Historical Society.

333 *It took him about two hours*: Ibid.

334 *"He's damn good"*: Taylor Branch, *Parting the Waters: America in the King Years, 1954–63* (New York: Touchstone, 1989), 883.

335 *"Can I ask you something"*: Francine White (née Yeager), interview with author, June 18, 2021. All dialogue and details based on the interview with White were submitted for fact-checking and approval by the author.

336 *What a wonderful response*: Three months after the March on Washington, King told an interviewer: "I started out reading the speech and I read it down to a point and just all of a sudden I decided. The audience response was wonderful that day, you know. And all of a sudden this thing came to me that I have used, I'd used it many times before, the thing about 'I have a dream,' and I just felt that I wanted to use it here. I don't know why. I mean, I hadn't thought about it before the speech and . . . I just turned aside from the manuscript . . . and I never did go back." Martin Luther King Jr., interview with Donald H. Smith, November 29, 1963, Wisconsin Historical Society.

337 *"Tell 'em about the dream"*: For years to come, historians would debate whether Mahalia Jackson inspired King, spontaneously, to talk about the dream. But a newly discovered, pristine recording of the speech kept for years in the archives of Motown Records seems to end the speculation. This recording makes clear that King had already begun talking about his dream when Mahalia offered her approval and her encouragement, joining him in a duet of sorts. As Mahalia shouted, King continued, his voice covering hers. A *Washington Post* reporter who attended the March on Washington and filed a story that day reported hearing the shout, but the reporter didn't say who had shouted or when. In interviews and in her autobiography, Mahalia Jackson made no claims to having inspired King's speech. In *Movin' On Up*, with Evan McLeod Wylie (New York: Hawthorn Books, 1966), Jackson wrote that King was a "quiet-spoken man who can preach a whole sermon without getting his collar wet. But on this wonderful afternoon the pride and joy he felt about the great march and the spectacle of that multitude of people with all the hopes they cherished for their children carried him away, too." *Movin' On Up*, 192–205.

28. "The Most Dangerous Negro"

340 *"I'd like to go"*: Coretta Scott King, interview with Charlotte Mayerson, July 16, 1968, audio recording, Smathers Library, University of Florida, Gainesville.

340 *"I have a dream"*: Taylor Branch, *Parting the Waters: America in the King Years, 1954–63* (New York: Touchstone, 1989), 883.

340 *ham, cheese, and turkey*: "Big Day—End and a Beginning," *Newsweek*, September 9, 1963.

340 *"can plead and lead"*: White House sound recording, Tape 108/A43, August 28, 1963, JFK Library.

341 *"make it more difficult"*: Ibid.

341 *"get the Negro community"*: Ibid.

341 *"The Farce on Washington"*: Manning Marable and Garrett Felber, eds., *The Portable Malcolm X Reader* (New York: Penguin Books, 2013), 263.

341 *"because they know Baldwin"*: Ibid., 273.

342 *little or no influence*: "Communist Party USA—Negro Question," memo, August 23, 1963, FBI archives.

342 *"This memo reminds me"*: Ibid.

342 *"The Director is correct"*: William C. Sullivan to Alan H. Belmont, memo, August 30, 1963, FBI archives.

343 *Levison had invested the party's money*: David J. Garrow, interview with author, April 22, 2022.

343 *Levison's donations*: David J. Garrow, "The Troubling Legacy of Martin Luther King," *Standpoint*, June 2019.

344 *"SCLC is so firmly"*: Martin Luther King Jr., interview, WSB-TV, July 26, 1963, Brown Media Archives, University of Georgia, Athens.

345 *Robert Kennedy signed the authorization*: "Martin Luther King Jr., Security Matter—Communist," memo, October 10, 1963, FBI archives.

345 *"Their goals"*: Edwin O. Guthman and Jeffrey Shulman, eds., *Robert Kennedy, in His Own Words: The Unpublished Recollections of the Kennedy Years* (New York: Bantam Books, 1988), 146.

345 *"a group of girls"*: Robert F. Kennedy, interview with Anthony Lewis, December 4, 1964, JFK Library.

345 *"Did you think"*: Ibid.

345 *twentieth floor*: Peachtree Towers Apartment Lease, October 23, 1963, FBI archives.

346 *"No expression one-tenth so radical"*: Murray Kempton, "The March on Washington," *The New Republic*, September 4, 1963.

346 *"also possessed the finest capacity"*: Norman Mailer, "The Big Bite," *Esquire*, December 1963.

346 *3,600 Black people*: David Levering Lewis, *King: A Critical Biography* (New York: Praeger, 1970), 231.

346 *"Here was Martin King"*: C. T. Vivian, interview with author, July 6, 2018.

346 *"I can now wear my wedding ring"*: "Quote and Unquote," *SCLC Newsletter*, September 1963.

346 *"I'm not a martyr"*: "America's Gandhi," *Time*, January 3, 1964.

346 *"What I noticed"*: Dorothy Cotton interview, in "Citizen King," dir. Orlando Bagwell and W. Noland Walker, *American Experience*, PBS Home Video, aired January 19, 2004.

347 *"More and more"*: "America's Gandhi."

347 *"the same way I would be"*: "March 'Impressed' Malcolm X," *New York Amsterdam News*, September 7, 1963.

347 *"If you are going to blow up"*: Testimony from trial transcript, State of Alabama v. Robert E. Chambliss, Alabama Tenth Judicial Circuit, October 28, 1977, 247.

348 *One student stood*: "School Mix Fight Pledged by Boutwell," *Birmingham News*, September 14, 1963.

348 *"The whole question"*: Ibid.

349 *"if men were this bestial"*: Martin Luther King Jr., interview with Alex Haley, *Playboy*, January 1965.

349 *"Who did it?"*: Quoted in John N. Herbers, *Deep South Dispatch: Memoir of a Civil Rights Journalist*, with Anne Farris Rosen (Jackson: University Press of Mississippi, 2018), 106.

349 *"heroines of a holy crusade"*: John Herbers, "Funeral Is Held for Bomb Victims," *New York Times*, September 19, 1963.

349 *"As I watched"*: Jay Caspian Kang, "What the World Got Wrong About Kareem Abdul-Jabbar," *New York Times Magazine*, September 17, 2015.

350 *"This is what is going to happen"*: Coretta Scott King, *My Life with Martin Luther King, Jr.*, rev. ed. (New York: Henry Holt, 1993), 227.

29. Man of the Year

351 *"I want to tell you"*: Telephone conversation no. 56, sound recording, LBJ Presidential Library, Austin, Tex., www.discoverlbj.org/item/tel-00056, accessed April 29, 2021.

352 *"I thought I was dealing with a child"*: Reminiscences of President Lyndon Baines Johnson, August 19, 1969, oral history transcript, LBJ Presidential Library, Austin, Tex.

353 *"I think the FBI"*: Ibid., 192.

353 *eight days*: "A Letter from the Publisher," *Time*, January 3, 1964.

353 *approved by its subject*: William Robert Miller, *Martin Luther King, Jr.: His Life, Martyrdom and Meaning for the World* (New York: Weybright and Talley, 1968), 176.

354 *"I think it's questionable evidence"*: Stanley Pottinger, interview with author, September 15, 2021.

354 *difficult to draw conclusions*: Stanley Pottinger, email interview with author, November 30, 2021.

354 *"appeared to consist of"*: "Report of the Department of Justice Task Force to Review the FBI Martin Luther King Jr., Security and Assassination Investigations," January 11, 1977.

355 *"We do not contemplate"*: S. B. Donahoe to Alan H. Belmont, memo, January 11, 1964, FBI archives.

355 *"It is highly important"*: William C. Sullivan to Alan H. Belmont, memo, January 13, 1964, FBI archives.

355 *transcripts*: Bayard Rustin once noted that, after reading the FBI's transcripts of his conversations, he was struck by their accuracy, saying, "There is not a single thing in my talks with King where they misrepresented or . . . lied."

355 *"Many of us"*: William C. Sullivan, *The Bureau: My Thirty Years in Hoover's FBI*, with Bill Brown (New York: W. W. Norton, 1979), 138.

355 *"I'm getting ready to die"*: Quoted in J. Edgar Hoover to Walter Jenkins, April 14, 1964, Mildred Stegall Papers, LBJ Presidential Library, Austin, Tex.

355 *Ward had paid $100*: FBI memo, June 1, 1964.

356 *"and Hoover listened to all of them"*: Sullivan, *The Bureau*, 141–42.

356 *a highly distasteful joke*: *Jacqueline Kennedy: Historic Conversations on Life with John F. Kennedy, Interviews with Arthur M. Schlesinger, Jr., 1964* (New York: Hyperion, 2011), 260.

356 *"I just can't see a picture"*: Ibid.

356 *"outwardly, at least"*: Undated, redrafted FBI report, likely written between December 1963 and April 1964, FBI archives.

356 *drive a wedge*: FBI memo, April 14, 1964.

356 *"When this is done"*: William C. Sullivan to Alan H. Belmont, memo, January 8, 1964, Jack Anderson Papers, box 307, folder 4, George Washington University Library, Washington, D.C.

357 *"difficult to accept the word"*: "King Says Hoover Aids 'Smear' of Civil Rights," *Wichita Beacon*, April 24, 1964.

357 *"I want to hit him hard"*: Quoted in David J. Garrow, *The FBI and Martin Luther King, Jr.: From "Solo" to Memphis* (New York: Penguin Books, 1983), 113.

357 *"Martin had a lot to sort out"*: Harry Belafonte, interview with author, April 4, 2017.

357 *if he'd been aware*: Ibid.

358 *Lyndon Johnson used*: Lyndon Baines Johnson, Annual Message to Congress on the State of the Union, January 8, 1964, LBJ Library.

358 *"We are not prepared to compromise"*: Jack Raymond, "Johnson Is Hopeful House Will Debate Rights This Month," *New York Times*, January 19, 1964.

358 *"Bill of Rights for the Disadvantaged"*: Martin Luther King Jr., *Why We Can't Wait* (New York: Harper & Row, 1964), 151.

359 *"two evils"*: Ibid., 12.

359 *"Few people consider"*: Ibid., 150–51.

359 *"Democracy, in its finest sense"*: Ibid., 20.

360 *"the stereotype of the apathetic"*: "Since the Supreme Court Spoke," *New York Times*, May 10, 1964.

360 *"spoke of Negroes' receiving"*: Fred Powledge, "Polls Show Whites in City Resent Civil Rights Protest," *New York Times*, September 21, 1964.

360 *"somehow given a sense"*: Stephen Drury Smith and Catherine Ellis, eds., *Free All Along: The Robert Penn Warren Civil Rights Interviews* (New York: The New Press, 2019), 171.

361 *"that black demands"*: John N. Herbers, *Deep South Dispatch: Memoir of a Civil Rights Journalist*, with Anne Farris Rosen (Jackson: University Press of Mississippi, 2018), 145.

361 *"Martin Luther King, God bless"*: "'Little Negro' Ready to Use His Shotgun," *Capital Times* (Madison, Wisc.), May 18, 1964.

361 *"many of these arguments"*: Smith and Ellis, *Free All Along*, 172–73.

361 *"I'm not saying"*: Ibid., 180.

361 *"Hosea was always trying"*: Andrew Young, interview with author, January 23, 2019.

362 *"was probably clinically insane"*: Rolundus R. Rice, *Hosea Williams: A Lifetime of Defiance and Protest* (Columbia: University of South Carolina Press, 2022), ix.

362 *"The truth of the matter"*: Walker letter to Wilkins, May 11, 1964, David J. Garrow personal collection.

363 *expenses of $677,381*: SCLC income statement, September 29, 1964, David J. Garrow personal collection.

363 *"a total collapse"*: Clarence B. Jones to Martin Luther King Jr., April 15, 1964.

363 *"mainly because of Martin's middle-class makeup"*: Hosea Williams, interview with John Barber, Hosea Williams Papers, Auburn Avenue Research Library on African American Culture and History, Atlanta-Fulton Public Library, Atlanta, Ga.

363 *"I remember Martin"*: Vincent Harding oral history, December 9, 1969, JFK Library.

364 *"Well, Malcolm"*: Ted Knap, "Malcolm X Crashes King Press Session," *Pittsburgh Press*, March 27, 1964.

364–65 *"No more turning"*: "Malcolm X Planning Rally to Choose 'Bullets or Ballots,'" *Baltimore Sun*, March 23, 1964.

30. A Law Observance Problem

366 *"I and my friends"*: "Negro Leader Arrested at Restaurant," *San Mateo Times*, June 11, 1964.

366 *"Master Hosts"*: "Reverend Martin Luther King Jr. Arrested in Florida," Associated Press Archive, www.youtube.com/watch?v=lYTQnjMd-58, accessed June 14, 2021.

366 *"We can't serve you"*: Ibid.

366 *A burly white man*: John N. Herbers, *Deep South Dispatch: Memoir of a Civil Rights Journalist*, with Anne Farris Rosen (Jackson: University Press of Mississippi, 2018), 151.

366 *carrying a shotgun*: John Herbers, "Martin Luther King and 17 Others Jailed Trying to Integrate St. Augustine Restaurant," *New York Times*, June 12, 1964.

367 *"Reverend King"*: "Reverend Martin Luther King Jr. Arrested in Florida."

367 *"unwanted guests"*: Herbers, "Martin Luther King and 17 Others Jailed Trying to Integrate St. Augustine Restaurant."

367 *"foremost interpreter"*: Louis Lomax, *The Negro Revolt* (New York: Signet, 1963), 102.

367 *"You know, they threaten us"*: Quoted in Pat Watters, *Down to Now: Reflections on the Southern Civil Rights Movement* (New York: Pantheon Books, 1971), 287.

368 *"Daddy, they just didn't understand"*: Quoted ibid., 280–81.

368 *"People in other parts"*: Quoted in Herbers, *Deep South Dispatch*, 159.

368 *"You need to survive"*: Quoted in Watters, *Down to Now*, 285.

369 *"health, morality"*: Martin Luther King Jr., statement on nomination of Barry Goldwater, July 16, 1964, Martin Luther King, Jr., Papers, 1950–1968, Martin Luther King, Jr., Center for Nonviolent Social Change, Inc., Atlanta, Ga.

369 *"You know when King's usefulness"*: Quoted in Watters, *Down to Now*, 286.

369 *"very lonely"*: David J. Garrow, *Bearing the Cross: Martin Luther King, Jr., and the Southern Christian Leadership Conference* (New York: William Morrow, 1986), 331.

369 *"anti-civil rights march"*: John Herbers, "200 Whites March at St. Augustine," *New York Times*, June 13, 1964.

370 *"everybody was fighting so hard"*: Homer Bigart, "St. Augustine Aides Say They Cannot Keep Peace," *New York Times*, June 27, 1964.

370 *more time with the seven-year-old*: L. Harold DeWolf, interview, Ralph J. Bunche Oral History Collection, Moorland-Spingarn Research Center, Howard University, Washington, D.C.

370 *"tangible gains"*: Robert B. Hayling, interview with John Britton, August 16, 1967, Moorland-Spingarn Research Center, Howard University, Washington, D.C.

371 *"law observance problem"*: "President Acts," *New York Times*, June 24, 1964.

371 *"We believe"*: "Johnson's Address on Civil Rights," *New York Times*, July 3, 1964.

372 *"What more will the Negro want?"*: Martin Luther King Jr., interview with Alex Haley, *Playboy*, January 1965.

373 *flew from Atlanta*: Calvin Trillin, "Plane to Mississippi: An Encounter with Martin Luther King Jr.," *New Yorker*, August 29, 1964. The details and quotes that follow are from this article.

375 *"You must not allow"*: John Herbers, "Dr. King Starts Mississippi Tour," *New York Times*, July 22, 1964.

375 *"right duty"*: "Racial Roundup," *Jackson Clarion-Ledger*, July 22, 1964.

375 *lynchings*: Lynchings by state, Tuskegee Institute archives, law2.umkc.edu/faculty/projects/ftrials/shipp/lynchingsstate.html.

375 *"If modern industrialism"*: Willie Morris, *Terrains of the Heart and Other Essays on Home* (Oxford, Miss.: Yoknapatawpha Press, 1981), 8.

376 *"All direct-action campaigns"*: Robert Moses to SNCC executive committee, memo, n.d., 1964, Freedom Summer Digital Collection, Wisconsin Historical Society, content.wisconsinhistory.org/digital/collection/p15932coll2/id/62381.

376 *"We're on a voter registration drive"*: Clayborne Carson, *In Struggle: SNCC and the Black Awakening of the 1960s* (Cambridge, Mass.: Harvard University Press, 1981), 117.

377 *"We were the beloved community"*: Casey Hayden, "Sermonette on the Movement," *Southern Changes* 9, no. 5 (1987): 28.

377 *"It's a ticklish problem"*: Lyndon B. Johnson and Robert Kennedy, telephone conversation no. 4288, July 21, 1964, sound recording, LBJ Presidential Library, Austin, Tex., www.discoverlbj.org/item/tel-04288.

377 *"I understand . . . that he"*: Ibid.

378 *Oldsmobile*: John Herbers, "Dr. King Speaks to Negro Group at Philadelphia, Miss., Rally," *New York Times*, July 25, 1964.

378 *"Three young men"*: Ibid.

378 *"I just want to touch you"*: Ibid.

378 *cup of coffee*: "Dr. King Leaves Mississippi," *New York Times*, July 26, 1964.

378 *"I have been trying to think"*: Martin Luther King Jr. and Bayard Rustin, telephone conversation, July 26, 1964, FBI transcript. This is also the source for all subsequent quotes from King and Rustin in this passage.

378 *most popular leader*: Layhmond Robinson, "Negroes' View of Plight Examined in Survey Here," *New York Times*, July 27, 1964.

379 *"I would not want Martin"*: Bayard Rustin and Henry Schwarzschild, telephone conversation, July 24, 1964, transcript, FBI archives.

379 *face criticism*: "'Don't Need You' Rev. King Told by N.Y. Negroes," *Chicago Defender*, July 29, 1964.

379 *"amazed and disappointed"*: Ossie Davis and Ruby Dee to Martin Luther King Jr., July 28, 1964, Bayard Rustin Papers, Library of Congress.

380 *"I don't think"*: "Negro Leaders Split Again," *Chicago Defender*, August 1, 1964.

380 *"it was entirely possible"*: David Levering Lewis, *King: A Biography*, 3rd ed. (Urbana: University of Illinois Press, 2013), 249.

380 *"the Negro feels himself"*: Paul L. Montgomery, "CORE to Continue Its Direct Action," *New York Times*, August 10, 1964.

381 *"I think new days"*: Paul Hofmann, "Pope and Dr. King Confer on Rights," *New York Times*, September 19, 1964.

381 *"Is this America"*: Fannie Lou Hamer, testimony before the Credentials Committee of the Democratic National Convention, Atlantic City, N.J., August 22, 1964, www .youtube.com/watch?v=RobTthUg04c, accessed October 12, 2021.

382 *"He felt compelled"*: Andrew Young, *An Easy Burden: The Civil Rights Movement and the Transformation of America* (Waco, Tex.: Baylor University Press, 2008), 311.

382 *mock eulogies*: Andrew Young, interview with author, January 19, 2019.

382 *"just big talkers"*: Ralph David Abernathy, *And the Walls Came Tumbling Down: An Autobiography* (New York: Harper & Row 1989), 490–91.

383 *"when he felt depressed"*: Coretta Scott King transcripts, Hatch Papers, 27/26.

383 *"I guess you go through"*: Robert Penn Warren, *Who Speaks for the Negro?* (New Haven, Conn.: Yale University Press, 2014), 220.

384 *"Mommy, do you think"*: Coretta Scott King, "The World of Coretta King," *New Lady*, January 1966.

384 *from her schoolmates*: Ibid.

31. The Prize

385   *"I thought I was still asleep"*: Bill Shipp, "Nobel Peace Prize Goes to Rev. King," *Atlanta Constitution*, October 15, 1964.

385   *nurse checked his temperature*: "King in Hospital; Happy over Nobel Prize Selection," *Chicago Defender*, October 15, 1964.

386   *"They're scraping"*: "Cheers and Scorn for Nobel Award," *New York Times*, October 15, 1964.

386   *"I consider it"*: Ibid.

386   *"King could well qualify"*: Quoted in David J. Garrow, *The FBI and Martin Luther King, Jr.: From "Solo" to Memphis* (New York: Penguin Books, 1983), 121.

386   *"God had surely"*: Martin Luther King Sr., *Daddy King: An Autobiography*, with Clayton Riley (New York: William Morrow, 1980), 183.

386   *Coretta laughed*: J. Edgar Hoover to Bill Moyers, October 22, 1964, Mildred Stegall Papers, LBJ Presidential Library, Austin, Tex.

386   *"It was a great tribute"*: Coretta Scott King, *My Life with Martin Luther King, Jr.*, rev. ed. (New York: Henry Holt, 1993), 3–4.

387   *"I thought I'd call"*: Lyndon B. Johnson and Martin Luther King Jr., telephone conversation, November 5, 1964, WH6411–05–6239, Presidential Recordings Digital Edition, Miller Center, University of Virginia.

388   *"Now, what am I going to do"*: Lyndon B. Johnson and Nicholas Katzenbach, telephone conversation, November 11, 1964, WH6411–16–6324–6325–6326–6327, Presidential Recordings Digital Edition, Miller Center, University of Virginia, prde.upress.virginia.edu/conversations/4005048.

388   *first time she had seen him cry*: Dorothy Cotton, interview with Nick Kotz, n.d., Kotz Papers, box 38, folder 1, Wisconsin Historical Society.

388   *"I know that he was wounded by that"*: Dorothy Cotton interview, in "Citizen King," dir. Orlando Bagwell and W. Noland Walker, *American Experience*, PBS Home Video, aired January 19, 2004.

388   *"I cannot conceive of Mr. Hoover"*: John Herbers, "Dr. King Rebuts Hoover Charges," *New York Times*, November 20, 1964.

389   *"KING, In view of your low grade"*: Anonymous letter to Martin Luther King Jr., n.d., National Archives, College Park, Md.

390   *"pervert"*: Robert Allen, diary, November 30, 1964, private collector.

390   *"most sordid"*: Ibid.

390   *thirty minutes late*: Paul Letersky, *The Director: My Years Assisting J. Edgar Hoover* (New York: Scribner, 2021), 87.

391   *"Hoover talked at us"*: Peter Ross Range, "Playboy Interview: Andrew Young," *Playboy*, July 1977.

391   *"a love feast"*: Cartha D. "Deke" DeLoach, testimony for U.S. Senate Select Committee to Study Governmental Operations, with Respect to Intelligence Activities, December 3, 1975.

391   *"amicable"*: Anthony Lewis, "Hoover and King Discuss Dispute," *New York Times*, December 2, 1964.

391   *sat on a couch*: James Farmer, interview with Nick Kotz, "early 1999," according to typed transcript, Kotz Papers, Wisconsin Historical Society.

391   *"About what?"*: Ibid.

32. The Director

392 *78 percent of Americans*: Gallup survey, May 1954, Gallup Vault, https://news.gallup
.com/vault/210107/gallup-vault-edgar-hoover-fbi-american-communists.aspx.

393 *He wore his cadet uniform*: Jack Alexander, "The Director—II," *New Yorker*, October 2,
1937.

393 *his religious faith*: Ibid.

394 *"the unceasing defender"*: Paul Letersky, *The Director: My Years Assisting J. Edgar Hoover*
(New York: Scribner, 2021), xii.

395 *"preserve the dignity"*: J. Edgar Hoover, "Wholly Loyal," *Crusader*, June 1961, 15.

395 *"To Hoover"*: Letersky, *The Director*, 85.

395 *"Crazy Billy"*: Ibid., 207.

396 *New England accent*: William C. Sullivan, *The Bureau: My Thirty Years in Hoover's FBI*,
with Bill Brown (New York: W. W. Norton, 1979), 9.

396 *"that personally he would not mind"*: J. Edgar Hoover to Lyndon Baines Johnson,
November 30, 1964, Mildred Stegall Papers, LBJ Presidential Library, Austin, Tex.

396 *asked four men*: J. Edgar Hoover letter to Bill Moyers, December 2, 1964, Mildred
Stegall Papers, LBJ Presidential Library, Austin, Tex.

397 *"We don't print"*: Gene Roberts and Hank Klibanoff, *The Race Beat: The Press, the Civil
Rights Struggle and the Awakening of a Nation* (New York: Vintage Books, 2007), 371.

397 *Johnson shook his head*: Burke Marshall, interview with Nick Kotz, April 28, 2000,
Kotz Papers, Wisconsin Historical Society.

397 *"Terrible"*: Ibid.

397 *the president was torn*: Cartha D. "Deke" DeLoach, interview with Nick Kotz, March
8–9, 2000, Kotz Papers, Wisconsin Historical Society.

398 *"The only thing unique "*: Nicholas Katzenbach, testimony before the U.S. Senate, Select
Committee to Study Governmental Operations with Respect to Intelligence
Activities, December 3, 1975.

398 *"in essence a couple"*: Beverly Gage, *G-Man: J. Edgar Hoover and the Making of the
American Century* (New York: Viking, 2022), xii.

399 *"How's the boss feel?"*: Lyndon Baines Johnson and Cartha D. "Deke" DeLoach,
telephone conversation no. 6431, November 20, 1964, sound recording, LBJ Presidential
Library, Austin, Tex., accessed August 5, 2021.

33. A New Sense of "Some-bodiness"

400 *looking like Sugar Ray Robinson*: Harry Wachtel and Bayard Rustin, telephone
conversation, November 7, 1964, FBI archives.

400 *two dozen people*: Izzy Rowe, "Izzy Rowe's Note Book," *Pittsburgh Courier*, January 9,
1965.

400 *flew on separate planes*: Coretta Scott King, *My Life with Martin Luther King, Jr.*, rev. ed.
(New York: Henry Holt, 1993), 4.

400 *"He just couldn't face"*: Bayard Rustin and Harry Wachtel in conversation with Walter
Naegle, October 31, 1985, transcript, David J. Garrow personal collection.

401 *"Only Martin's family"*: David J. Garrow, *Bearing the Cross: Martin Luther King, Jr., and
the Southern Christian Leadership Conference* (New York: William Morrow, 1986), 543.

401 *"realism in the assessment"*: Nassir Ghaemi, "Martin Luther King Jr.: Depressed and
Creatively Maladjusted," *Psychology Today*, January 16, 2012.

401   *"he was a man with a determination "*: James Beshai, author interview, May 6,
      2022.

401   *"massive economic boycott"*: "Dr. King Proposes a Rights Alliance," *New York Times*,
      December 10, 1964.

402   *"I always wanted to make a contribution"*: David Halberstam, "The Second Coming of
      Martin Luther King," *Harper's Magazine*, August 1967.

402   *"Doors of opportunity"*: Martin Luther King Jr., Nobel Lecture, December 11, 1964,
      www.nobelprize.org/prizes/peace/1964/king/lecture/.

402   *"might burst"*: Coretta Scott King, *My Life with Martin Luther King, Jr.*, 12.

402   *"By then Martin"*: Ibid., 13.

403   *"something more appropriate"*: Coretta Scott King, *My Life, My Love, My Legacy*, as told
      to Barbara Reynolds (New York: Henry Holt, 2017), 126.

34. Crowbar

404   *"The above information"*: Quoted in David J. Garrow, *The FBI and Martin Luther King,
      Jr.: From "Solo" to Memphis* (New York: Penguin Books, 1983), 133.

404   *"has the reputation"*: J. Edgar Hoover to Bill Moyers, December 21, 1964, Mildred
      Stegall Papers, LBJ Presidential Library, Austin, Tex.

404   *"As soon as I heard his voice"*: Ralph David Abernathy, *And the Walls Came Tumbling
      Down: An Autobiography* (New York: Harper & Row, 1989), 309.

405   *"It was at the Willard"*: Ibid., 310.

405   *"second front"*: Ibid.

405   *Coretta had known about Martin's infidelities*: Coretta Scott King, interview with
      Charlotte Mayerson, July 16, 1968, audio recording, Smathers Library, University of
      Florida, Gainesville.

405   *"the question everyone wants to know"*: Coretta Scott King, *My Life, My Love, My Legacy*,
      as told to Barbara Reynolds (New York: Henry Holt, 2017), 129–30.

406   *"They are out to get me"*: Garrow, *The FBI and Martin Luther King, Jr.*, 134.

406   *"no question"*: Ibid., 128.

406   *"dare him to do his damnedest"*: Kenneth Clark, interview with Arthur M. Schlesinger
      Jr., September 9, 1976, Schlesinger Papers, New York Public Library.

406   *"God damn it"*: Ibid.

406   *"It reminded me"*: Quoted in Ovid Demaris, *The Director: An Oral Biography of J. Edgar
      Hoover* (New York: Harper's Magazine Press, 1975), 227.

406   *"As the years unfolded"*: Coretta Scott King, interview, July 19, 1968, Hatch Papers.

406   *"If Martin Luther 'Riot' King"*: "Ala. Racist Group Stages 'Dial-an-Attack' on King,"
      Chicago Defender, January 4, 1965.

407   *"controversial darkie"*: "A Visitation to Be Ignored," *Selma Times-Journal*, December 30,
      1964.

407   *"Maybe I ought to tell you"*: Martin Luther King Jr., speech, January 14, 1965, audio
      recording from Dallas County, Ala., Sheriff's Department.

409   *a phone call from President Johnson*: Martin Luther King Jr. and Lyndon Baines
      Johnson, telephone conversation no. 6737, sound recording, January 15, 1965, LBJ
      Presidential Library, Austin, Tex.

410   *"The President had been poisoned"*: Ramsey Clark, interview with Nick Kotz, April 27,
      2000, Kotz Papers, Wisconsin Historical Society.

412 *carrying a rifle*: "Anti-Integration Picket Arrested by Dallas Police," *Fort Worth Star-Telegram*, August 15, 1964.

412 *Dorothy Cotton found King*: Nick Kotz, *Judgment Days: Lyndon Baines Johnson, Martin Luther King Jr., and the Laws That Changed America* (Boston: Houghton Mifflin, 2005), 257.

413 *"the single most inflexibly"*: J. Mills Thornton III, *Dividing Lines* (Tuscaloosa: University of Alabama Press, 2002), 380.

413 *1 percent of the voters*: "The Central Point," *Time*, March 19, 1965.

413 *"We seek your indulgence"*: Thornton, *Dividing Lines*, 469.

413 *"and they wanted to preserve the existing law"*: Bernard Lafayette Jr., interview with author, May 22, 2019.

414 *"hoggin' all the publicity"*: Howell Raines, *My Soul Is Rested: Movement Days in the Deep South Remembered* (1977; repr. New York: Penguin, 1983), 214.

414 *"number one goal"*: Hosea Williams, interview with Taylor Branch, October 29, 1991, Hosea L. Williams Papers, Auburn Avenue Research Library on African American Culture and History, Atlanta-Fulton Public Library System, Atlanta, Ga.

414 *"It was not coming from Scripture"*: Bernard Lafayette Jr., interview with author, March 21, 2018.

415 *"only wants to pray"*: Hosea Williams, interview with Branch.

415 *"We must be willing"*: John Herbers, "Alabama Vote Drive Opened by Dr. King," *New York Times*, January 3, 1965.

415 *"They had lived there peaceably"*: Jim Clark, interview with Blackside, Inc., February 19, 1986, for *Eyes on the Prize: America's Civil Rights Years (1954–1965)*, Washington University Libraries, Film and Media Archive, Henry Hampton Collection, repository .wustl.edu/downloads/4t64gq24.

416 *"Once I stood in line"*: "Selma Woman's Girdle a Big Factor in Fight with Sheriff," *Jet*, February 11, 1965.

416 *"I try to be nonviolent"*: Ibid.

416 *four speeches*: Ruth McCoy, "A Big Sunday for Rev. King," *Chicago Defender*, January 31, 1965.

416 *spotted five white men*: Ibid.; and Coretta Scott King, "The World of Coretta King," *New Lady*, January 1966.

417 *"In one city"*: "Selma Inscribes Note of Reason in History Text," *Montgomery Advertiser*, January 31, 1965.

417 *"the actual conditions"*: "Selma Paper Urges Probe by Congress," *Montgomery Advertiser*, February 3, 1965.

417 *a gate clanged*: Charles E. Fager, *Selma, 1965* (New York: Charles Scribner's Sons, 1974), 52–53.

417 *away from the crowd*: Ibid., 52–53.

417 *"These fellows respond better"*: David J. Garrow, *Bearing the Cross: Martin Luther King, Jr., and the Southern Christian Leadership Conference* (New York: William Morrow, 1986), 384.

418 *"I taught them myself"*: "Malcolm X Predicts Hot Racial Year," *Alabama Journal*, February 4, 1965.

418 *"centered on his commitment"*: James H. Cone, *Martin & Malcolm & America: A Dream or a Nightmare* (Maryknoll, N.Y.: Orbis Books, 1991), 211.

418 *"an excuse to kill up a lot of us"*: Ibid., 204.

419 *"Mrs. King"*: Coretta Scott King, interview with Blackside, Inc., December 20, 1985, for *Eyes on the Prize: America's Civil Rights Years (1954–1965)*, Washington University Libraries, Film and Media Archive, Henry Hampton Collection, repository.wustl.edu /downloads/hq37vq29v.

419 *"indignant"*: John D. Morris, "Johnson Pledges Alabama Action," *New York Times*, February 4, 1965.

419 *"Please don't be too soft"*: Garrow, *Bearing the Cross*, 386.

419 *a lipstick smear*: Roy Reed, "Dr. King to Seek New Voting Law," *New York Times*, February 6, 1965.

420 *"What do they want?"*: John Herbers, "Negro Goals in Selma," *New York Times*, February 6, 1965.

420 *"Jim Clark and Negro"*: Ibid.

420 *"Let's see how that white water tastes"*: Bruce Dozier, interview with author, July 23, 2021.

421 *"collapsed under the pressure"*: Abernathy, *And the Walls Came Tumbling Down*, 323.

421 *"sick . . . and terribly run down"*: Ralph Abernathy and Bayard Rustin, telephone conversation, February 17, 1965, transcript, FBI archives.

423 *"he had been receiving"*: Abernathy, *And the Walls Came Tumbling Down*, 327.

424 *"We will be going there"*: John Herbers, "Dr. King, Back in Alabama, Calls for March on Capitol to Push Voting Drive," *New York Times*, February 23, 1965.

424 *19 percent*: William L. Lunch and Peter W. Sperlich, "American Public Opinion and the War in Vietnam," *Western Political Quarterly* 32, no. 1 (1979): 21–44.

424 *"was murdered by every white minister"*: Fager, *Selma, 1965*, 85.

424 *"My heart quickened"*: Georgia Powers Davis, *I Shared the Dream* (Far Hills, N.J.: New Horizon Press, 1995), 97–98.

425 *"Guilt notwithstanding"*: Ibid., 148.

425 *"There were times I knew"*: Ibid., 3.

35. Selma

426 *"It was suggested"*: David J. Garrow, *Bearing the Cross: Martin Luther King, Jr., and the Southern Christian Leadership Conference* (New York: William Morrow, 1986), 397.

426 *"not even singing songs"*: John Lewis, interview with author and David McMahon, August 6, 2019.

427 *"Troopers, advance!"*: "Pincers of Terror in Alabama," *Newsday*, March 8, 1965.

427 *"So much happened"*: Philip Henry Pitts, interview with author, December 27, 2018.

428 *"In the vicious maltreatment"*: Garrow, *Bearing the Cross*, 399–400.

428 *"I might be advocating"*: Lyndon Baines Johnson and J. Lister Hill, March 8, 1965, Presidential Recordings Digital Edition, Miller Center, University of Virginia.

429 *"pure hell"*: Michael Beschloss, "Beschloss on Lady Bird Johnson," *Newsweek*, July 22, 2007.

429 *"gave the distinct impression"*: Garrow, *Bearing the Cross*, 401.

429 *"Dr. King, you promised"*: Jack Greenberg, *Crusaders in the Courts: How a Dedicated Band of Lawyers Fought for the Civil Rights Revolution* (New York: Basic Books, 1994), 356.

429 *"Gentlemen"*: Martin Luther King Jr., telephone conference call, March 9, 1965, transcript, FBI archives.

430 *King agreed to the deal*: Lyndon Baines Johnson and Bill Moyers, March 9, 1965, conversation WH6503–04–7045, Presidential Recordings Digital Edition, Miller Center, University of Virginia.

430 *"I have got to march"*: Roy Reed, "Dr. King Leads March at Selma; State Police End It Peaceably Under a U.S.-Arranged Accord," *New York Times*, March 10, 1965.

431 *a strong wind from the south*: Ibid.

431 *"We come to present our bodies"*: "The Central Point," *Time*, March 19, 1965.

431 *"Clear the road"*: Ibid.

431 *"Everybody felt a miracle"*: Harris Wofford, interview in "Citizen King," dir. Orlando Bagwell and W. Noland Walker, *American Experience*, PBS Home Video, aired January 19, 2004.

431 *"At least we had to get"*: Ibid.

431 *"Law and order prevailed"*: John Herbers, "U.S. Mediated Peaceful Confrontation," *New York Times*, March 10, 1965.

432 *"safety valve"*: James Forman, *The Making of Black Revolutionaries* (1972; repr. Seattle: University of Washington Press, 2000), 442.

432 *"I get so tired"*: "5,000 Hear King at Liberty Baptist Church," *Chicago Defender*, March 15, 1965.

432 *bad case of hiccups*: "Dr. King: Death Won't Stop Drive," *Boston Globe*, March 15, 1965.

432 *fifteen thousand people massed*: "Thousands All Over Nation March in Protest to Selma," *Chicago Tribune*, March 15, 1965.

433 *navy-blue pajamas:* Jawana Jackson, interview with author, August 14, 2021.

433 *"At times"*: President Lyndon Johnson, speech to Congress on voting rights, March 15, 1965, records of the U.S. Senate, National Archives.

435 *crying*: Stephen B. Oates, *Let the Trumpet Sound: The Life of Martin Luther King, Jr.* (New York: HarperCollins, 1982), 345.

435 *homemade time bombs*: "4 Time Bombs Planted in B'ham Negro Areas," *Montgomery Advertiser*, March 22, 1965.

435 *"They were many types"*: "Thousands March U.S. 80 Under Eye of Army Troops," *Montgomery Advertiser*, March 22, 1965.

435 *"We know we can work"*: Ibid.

435 *set up a loudspeaker*: Ibid.

435 *Volkswagen drove past*: Renata Adler, "Letter from Selma," *New Yorker*, April 10, 1965.

436 *The marchers responded with a song of their own*: Joseph Ellwanger, interview with author, June 25, 2019.

436 *pink-and-white trailer*: "King Allots 14 Miles Today for Marchers," *Selma Times-Journal*, March 22, 1965.

436 *a second pair of socks*: "Rain Dampens March as Third Day Begins," *Selma Times-Journal*, March 23, 1965.

436 *"They can't accomplish"*: Ibid.

436 *"unless there is imaginative"*: "Righters Face Last Full Day of Marching," *Alabama Journal*, March 23, 1965.

437 *"There were nuns"*: Jack Newfield, "Marching to Montgomery: The Cradle Did Rock," *Village Voice*, April 1, 1965.

437 *cane between his legs*: Ibid., 270.

437 *"Walking through the Negro section"*: Ibid.

437 *Black porters stared out the windows*: Adler, "Letter from Selma."

437 *roast beef smothered in ketchup*: Bob Ingram, "Marchers Might Fume to See Wallace Eat," *Montgomery Advertiser*, March 26, 1965.

437 *King spoke slowly and calmly*: Martin Luther King Jr., "Our God Is Marching On," March 25, 1965, reprinted in *A Testament of Hope: The Essential Writings of Martin Luther King Jr.*, ed. J. M. Washington, (New York: HarperOne, 1986), 227–30.

36. "The True Meaning of My Work"

439 *Twenty-six shuttle buses*: Jack Newfield, "Marching to Montgomery," *Village Voice*, April 1, 1965.

439 *"white and Negro"*: Martin Luther King Jr., *Where Do We Go from Here: Chaos or Community?* (New York: Harper & Row, 1967), 9.

439 *"It's my fault"*: Newfield, "Marching to Montgomery."

439 *"It was Martin Luther King at his best"*: Rachelle Horowitz, interview with author, March 21, 2018.

440 *challenged her children*: Donna Britt, "A White Mother Went to Alabama to Fight for Civil Rights. The Klan Killed Her for It," *Washington Post*, December 15, 2017.

440 *"It's everybody's fight"*: "Johnson and Liuzzo Agree 'Wife Did Not Die in Vain,'" *Baltimore Sun*, March 27, 1965.

440 *"You hire someone and they join the Klan?"*: Lyndon Baines Johnson and J. Edgar Hoover, telephone conversation no. 7162, March 26, 1965, sound recording, LBJ Presidential Library, Austin, Tex.

441 *"I realize"*: Quoted in David J. Garrow, *Bearing the Cross: Martin Luther King, Jr., and the Southern Christian Leadership Conference* (New York: William Morrow, 1986), 415.

441 *gold Bulova*: Kwame Abernathy, interview with author, June 22, 2021.

442 *"deep despair"*: L. D. Reddick, "Climax at Baltimore," unpublished, undated manuscript, L. D. Reddick Papers, Schomburg Center.

442 *"We're being led"*: "D.C. Negroes Picket King at Hotel," *Baltimore Sun*, April 1, 1965.

442 *"Bureau Clergyman"*: Lerone A. Martin, "Bureau Clergyman: How the FBI Colluded with an African American Televangelist to Destroy Dr. Martin Luther King, Jr.," *Religion and American Culture: A Journal of Interpretation* 28, no. 1 (January 2018): 1–51.

442 *"the movement seems"*: John Herbers, "Boycott as Rights Weapon," *New York Times*, April 4, 1965.

442 *"Selma and Montgomery made you"*: Stanley Levison to Martin Luther King Jr., April 7, 1965, David J. Garrow personal collection.

443 *"but he's distressed"*: Bayard Rustin, telephone conversation, April 17, 1965, FBI transcript, David J. Garrow personal collection.

443 *"I think Martin is doing much better"*: Bayard Rustin and Andrew Young, telephone conversation, April 21, 1965, FBI transcript, David J. Garrow personal collection.

444 *receptive to psychiatric treatment*: Bayard Rustin and Harry Wachtel, April 21, 1965, telephone conversation, FBI transcript.

444 *hired a member of Ebenezer*: Coretta Scott King, "The World of Coretta King," *New Lady*, January 1966.

444 *Coretta's wish for carpeting*: Lynn Cothren, interview with author, September 13, 2018.

444 *bust of Franklin Delano Roosevelt*: Arnold Michaelis Library of Living History, 1950–1990, Walter J. Brown Media Archives and Peabody Awards Collection, University of Georgia Libraries.

445 *"I went into place after place"*: Robert L. Levey, "Dr. King Appeals for Brotherhood," *Boston Globe*, April 23, 1965.

445 *"the war in Vietnam"*: Martin Luther King Jr., "Remaining Awake Through a Great Revolution," speech at California Western University, May 29, 1964, sandiegohistory .org/journals/cusp-american-civil-rights-revolution/.

446 *"I dream of the day"*: Martin Luther King Jr., interview with Alex Haley, *Playboy*, January 1965.

37. "A Shining Moment"

447 *"In the light of my own involvement"*: Coretta Scott King, "The World of Coretta King," *New Lady*, January 1966.

447 *"deep economic insecurity"*: Jeanne Theoharis, *The Rebellious Life of Mrs. Rosa Parks* (Boston: Beacon Press, 2013), 164.

447 *"I talked about how"*: Coretta Scott King, *My Life, My Love, My Legacy*, as told to Barbara Reynolds (New York: Henry Holt, 2017), 148.

448 *"made a mistake in Vietnam"*: J. Edgar Hoover to Marvin Watson, July 23, 1965, Mildred Stegall Papers, LBJ Presidential Library, Austin, Tex.

448 *"hit" the president hard*: Ibid.

448 *"My husband feels"*: "King's Wife Says Cause Would Go On Without Him," *Baltimore Afro-American*, March 20, 1965.

448 *"'You see, I am called'"*: Coretta Scott King, *My Life, My Love, My Legacy*, 97.

449 *"I want something more"*: Betty Friedan, *The Feminine Mystique* (New York: W. W. Norton, 1963), 32.

449 *mailed a copy to Rosa Parks*: Rosa Parks Papers, Walter P. Reuther Library, Wayne State University, Detroit, Mich.

449 *"Women have been the backbone"*: Coretta Scott King, "The World of Coretta King."

450 *"'Shut up and go ahead'"*: Hosea Williams, interview with John Barber, n.d., transcript, Hosea L. Williams Papers, Auburn Avenue Research Library on African American Culture and History, Atlanta.

450 *including desserts*: Lynn Cothren, interview with author, September 13, 2018.

450 *without consulting notes*: Xernona Clayton, interview with author, February 19, 2019.

450 *"Coretta Scott King was a disciplinarian"*: Dexter King, *Growing Up King: An Intimate Memoir*, with Ralph Wiley (New York: Warner Books, 2003), 9.

451 *"She was very much engaged"*: Carole Hoover, author interview, July 10, 2020.

451 *went to Cotton's home*: Stoney Cooks, interview with author, July 13, 2018.

451 *"Only the people who were"*: Ibid.

451 *"They didn't profess to be perfect"*: Edwina Moss, interview with author, August 7, 2018.

452 *"When you decide to give yourself"*: Coretta Scott King, "The World of Coretta King."

452 *"Racism is genocide"*: "King Shakes Up Chicago," *Chicago Defender*, July 24–30, 1965.

453 *89.2 percent*: Peter H. Prugh, "Windy City Thunder," *Wall Street Journal*, July 22, 1965.

454 *"Chicago doesn't need"*: "Confetti," *Chicago Defender*, July 27, 1965.

454 *100,000 Black people*: Howard James, "March Aimed Beyond Chicago," *Christian Science Monitor*, July 28, 1965.

454 *trouble getting two hundred people*: Prugh, "Windy City Thunder."

454 *Skeptics deemed King naïve*: Jeanne Theoharis, "'The Thin Veneer of the North's Racial Self-Righteousness': Martin Luther King Jr.'s Challenge to Northern Racism," *Journal of Civil and Human Rights* 7, no. 1 (2021): 35–70.

454 *"In my travels"*: Martin Luther King Jr., "Beyond the Los Angeles Riots: Next Step, the North," *Saturday Review*, November 13, 1965.

455 *"the depth of racism"*: Martin Luther King Jr., *Why We Can't Wait* (New York: Harper & Row, 1964), 130–31.

455 *white parents*: Ibid.

455 *"Something must touch the hearts and souls"*: James Melvin Washington, ed., *A Testament of Hope: The Essential Writings and Speeches of Martin Luther King Jr.* (New York: Harper One, 1986), 124.

456 *"1. Fatigue 2. Bronchitis"*: Medical evaluation, n.d., Williams Clinic, Chicago, Martin Luther King Jr. Collection, box 7, 24, Morehouse College, Atlanta.

456 *see the doctor a third time*: "King, Ailing, Leads 30,000 Marchers in 'Greatest Demonstration Ever Seen,'" *Chicago Defender*, July 27, 1965.

456 *At 5:12 p.m.*: Ibid.

456 *King looked out*: Ibid.

456 *"were not acting right"*: "King in Cleveland, July 27–29, 1965," Historic Films, reel F-6020, https://www.historicfilms.com/search/?q=Martin+Luther+king#p1c_cdcd0 a5cd4e7bffea260c4b46a547d2f72a49316.

457 *"Dr. King should not be in Cleveland"*: "Dr. Martin Luther King Is Not a Superman," *Call and Post*, August 7, 1965.

457 *"I felt very supportive"*: Coretta Scott King, *My Life, My Love, My Legacy*, 137.

457 *"a shining moment"*: Caroll Kilpatrick, "Voting Rights Bill Signed in Ceremony at Capitol," *Washington Post*, August 7, 1965.

38. Burning

458 *"There is no more civil rights movement"*: "Rights Forces, After Wide Legal Gains, Grope for New Ways to Bring Negro Equality," *New York Times*, August 15, 1965.

458 *demonstrations might no longer be necessary*: "Rights Drive Alliances to Be Sought," *Baltimore Sun*, August 10, 1965.

458 *"The voting rights law"*: Jack Nelson, "Political Shakeup Seen in South," *Los Angeles Times*, August 8, 1965.

459 *hosted a barbeque*: Stephen B. Oates, *Let the Trumpet Sound: The Life of Martin Luther King, Jr.* (New York: HarperCollins, 1982), 361.

459 *"Andy described his style"*: Stoney Cooks, interview with author, April 2, 2018.

459 *"physically impossible"*: Homer Bigart, "Dr. King to Send Appeal to Hanoi," *New York*

Times, August 13, 1965. The *Times* was beginning to capitalize "Civil Rights," as seen here, in a sign of the movement's stature.

460 *"I would not want to prophesy"*: "Johnson's Moves," *New York Times*, August 1, 1965.

460 *"It was unusually hot"*: Marquette Frye, interview, 1985, Fox 11, Los Angeles, vimeo .com/229325605.

460 *"a long-smoldering hatred"*: Charles Davis Jr., "Anatomy of a Riot," *Los Angeles Times*, August 15, 1965.

460 *"I have lived in this city"*: Ibid.

461 *"I threw bricks"*: Ibid.

461 *"But if you come from down in Watts"*: Walter Mosley, *Little Scarlet: An Easy Rawlins Novel* (Boston: Little, Brown, 2004), 48.

461 *"These rioters do not have"*: "Area Appears Devoid of Community Leadership," *Los Angeles Times*, August 14, 1965.

461 *"when one person threw a rock"*: "Chief of Police in Los Angeles, William H. Parker, Dies at 64," *New York Times*, July 17, 1966.

462 *shot in the leg*: Ibid.

462 *he addressed a crowd of about five hundred*: Dick West, "Dr. King Hears Watts Protest over Heckling," *Los Angeles Times*, August 19, 1965.

463 *worry about the looting*: "King Assailed by Yorty After Stormy Meeting," *Los Angeles Times*, August 20, 1965.

463 *"denounced Martin to his face"*: Bayard Rustin and Harry Wachtel, telephone conversation, October 31, 1985, transcript of audiotape, courtesy of Walter Naegle.

464 *speaking to Lyndon Johnson*: Lyndon Baines Johnson and Martin Luther King Jr., telephone conversation no. 8578, August 20, 1965, 5:10 p.m., sound recording, Recordings and Transcripts of Telephone Conversations and Meetings, LBJ Presidential Library, Austin, Tex., accessed October 20, 2021, www.discoverlbj.org /item/tel-08578.

39. Beware the Day

467 *"The flames of Watts"*: Martin Luther King Jr., "Next Stop: The North," *Saturday Review*, November 13, 1965.

467 *"would not spontaneously tackle"*: Sylvie Laurent, *King and the Other America: The Poor People's Campaign and the Quest for Economic Equality* (Oakland: University of California Press, 2018), 102.

467 *"rationalized, tolerated"*: King, "Next Stop: The North."

468 *"But for the sober council"*: "Freedom or Death," *Chicago Defender*, January 5, 1966.

468 *"I must be concerned"*: Martin Luther King Jr., *The Papers of Martin Luther King Jr.*, vol. 6: *Advocate of the Social Gospel, September 1948–March 1963*, ed. Clayborne Carson (Berkeley: University of California Press, 2007), 72.

468 *"The story of Dr. King"*: Timuel Black, interview with author, February 24, 2019.

469 *"Everything is rosy"*: "Integrate Schools in 50 Georgia Communities," *Atlanta Constitution*, August 31, 1965.

469 *"We had been successful"*: Andrew Young, *An Easy Burden: The Civil Rights Movement and the Transformation of America* (Waco, Tex.: Baylor University Press, 2008), 381.

469 *"It was my impression"*: Dorothy Cotton, *If Your Back's Not Bent: The Role of the Citizenship Education Program in the Civil Rights Movement* (New York: Atria Books, 2012), 248.

469 *"and leave the northern urban areas"*: Quoted in Young, *An Easy Burden*, 383.

469 *"The present mood"*: Quoted in David J. Garrow, *Bearing the Cross: Martin Luther King, Jr., and the Southern Christian Leadership Conference* (New York: William Morrow, 1986), 442.

469 *"When the team got quiet"*: Cotton, *If Your Back's Not Bent*, 187.

470 *"minister concerned"*: "We're Committed to Viet Peace, Goldberg's Reply to Dr. King," *New York Post*, September 11, 1965.

470 *"absolutely no competence"*: "Dodd Raps King for Peace Outline," *Atlanta Journal and Constitution*, September 12, 1965.

470 *"Dr. Martin Luther King, sometimes called De Lawd"*: Poppy Cannon White, "The Lawd Is Right," *New York Amsterdam News*, September 25, 1965.

471 *Jackie Robinson, while not endorsing*: Jackie Robinson, "Jackie Robinson Says: Learn Loyalty," *Chicago Defender*, October 2, 1965.

471 *"I have already gotten unkind editorials"*: Martin Luther King Jr., conference call, September 13, 1965, FBI transcript, David J. Garrow personal collection.

472 *"You have a big problem"*: Martin Luther King Jr., conference call, September 28, 1965, FBI transcript, David J. Garrow personal collection.

473 *"One of these days"*: Bayard Rustin and Harry Wachtel, telephone conversation, September 28, 1965, FBI transcript, David J. Garrow personal collection.

473 *"First and foremost"*: Martin Luther King Jr., "My Dream: Peace," *Chicago Defender*, January 1, 1966.

474 *"I am sure that since"*: Thich Nhat Hanh, "Do Not Kill Man, Even in Man's Name," *Gazette and Daily* (York, Pa.), October 4, 1965.

474 *"Dr. King brought it up"*: Stoney Cooks, interview with author, July 13, 2018.

40. Chicago

475 *"dingy . . . no lights"*: Coretta Scott King, *My Life with Martin Luther King, Jr.*, rev. ed. (New York: Henry Holt, 1993), 257–58.

475 *"Persian lamb coat"*: "Dr. King, Mate Live in Flat—for One Day," *Chicago Tribune*, January 27, 1966.

475 *dirty windows*: "Dr. King's Flat, Altho Painted, Is Very Dismal," *Chicago Tribune*, January 26, 1966.

475 *"I have to be right here"*: "King and Wife Move into Slum," *Chicago Defender*, January 27, 1966.

475 *$90 a month*: "King Picks 'Typical' Flat; 8 Men Repair It," *Chicago Tribune*, January 23, 1966.

476 *"I said to myself"*: Timuel Black, interview with author, February 24, 2019.

477 *sat on the floor*: Bennett Johnson, interview with author, October 26, 2018.

477 *"We would say, 'We respect'"*: Mary Lou Finley, Bernard Lafayette Jr., James R. Ralph Jr., and Pam Smith, eds., *The Chicago Freedom Movement: Martin Luther King Jr. and Civil Rights Activism in the North* (Lexington: University of Kentucky Press, 2016), 31.

477 *"it's just as evil"*: Quoted in David J. Garrow, *Bearing the Cross: Martin Luther King, Jr., and the Southern Christian Leadership Conference* (New York: William Morrow, 1986), 461.

478 *"bigger and better jobs"*: "Dr. King Tells Plan for Negro Boycott," *Chicago Tribune*, February 12, 1966.

478 *"Elimination of slums"*: "Daley Will Attend U.S. Slum Meeting," *Chicago Tribune*, February 1, 1966.

478 *moral issues were more important*: "Dr. King Takes Over Slum Building," *Chicago Tribune*, February 24, 1966.

478 *"terrible speaker"*: Robert McClory, "The Activist," *Chicago Tribune*, April 17, 1983.

479 *met for an hour*: Bennett Johnson, interview with author, October 26, 2018.

479 *"Georgia boys"*: "King, Muslims Join Forces in War on Slums," *Chicago Defender*, February 26, 1966.

479 *"there now appear to be"*: Ibid.

479 *appearance of an alliance*: Bennett Johnson, interview with author.

479 *"no foe anywhere"*: "Lyndon Won't Widen War," *Chicago Tribune*, February 24, 1966.

479 *"If the aggressor persists"*: John D. Pomfret, "Johnson Denies 'Blind Escalation' in Vietnam War," *New York Times*, February 24, 1966.

479 *"somewhat intoxicated"*: "Dr. King's Chicago Antics Suggest Publicity Intoxication," *Rock Island Argus*, March 11, 1966.

479 *41 percent*: Roy Reed, "Dr. King's Group Scores KY Junta," *New York Times*, April 14, 1966.

480 *His answer was simple*: "My Dream: Dixie's Normalcy," *Norfolk New Journal and Guide*, March 12, 1966.

480 *"In one staff meeting"*: Dorothy Cotton, *If Your Back's Not Bent: The Role of the Citizenship Education Program in the Civil Rights Movement* (New York: Atria Books, 2012), 250.

480 *"The history of our time"*: Martin Luther King Jr., speech from European tour, March 1966, David J. Garrow personal collection.

480 *"Though he called for"*: Tommie Shelby, "Prisons of the Forgotten: Ghettos and Economic Justice," in *To Shape a New World: Essays on the Political Philosophy of Martin Luther King, Jr.*, ed. Tommie Shelby and Brandon M. Terry (Cambridge, Mass.: Belknap Press of Harvard University Press, 2018), 200.

481 *he knew King read it*: Charles Fager, interview with author, July 17, 2020.

481 *"almost tame"*: Charles Fager, "Dilemma for Dr. King," *Christian Century*, March 16, 1966.

482 *"It ends with me getting killed"*: Abby Mann, "A Visit with Dr. King at the Top of the Mountain," *Los Angeles Times*, April 21, 1968.

482 *"When you feel what you are doing"*: Dorothy McCardie, "Mrs. King, D.C. Teacher Have Reunion," *Washington Post*, June 3, 1966.

482 *"Yet there is rising concern"*: Rowland Evans and Robert Novak, "Wooing the Whale," *Washington Post*, April 20, 1966.

482 *"A small and disproportionately"*: "An Embattled Conference," *New York Times*, June 2, 1966.

483 *"Very few people understand"*: James Meredith, interview with author, July 23, 2020.

483 *gray trousers*: "How Meredith Was Ambushed," *Pittsburgh Press*, June 7, 1966.

483 *water lilies and honeysuckle vines*: James Meredith, *A Mission from God: A Memoir and Challenge for America* (New York: Atria Books, 2012), 1.

484 *"How are you feeling?"*: Ibid., 197.

484 *"Martin Luther King and I"*: Ibid.

41. Black Power

485 *twenty people*: Gene Roberts, "Troopers Shove Group Meeting Resuming Meredith March," *New York Times*, June 8, 1966.

486 *"We marched on the pavement"*: "In Single File on Dixie March," *Kansas City Times*, June 8, 1966.

486 *"but SNCC workers"*: Clayborne Carson, *In Struggle: SNCC and the Black Awakening of the 1960s* (Cambridge, Mass.: Harvard University Press, 1981), 3.

486 *"I have never rejected violence"*: "The New Racism," *Time*, July 1, 1966.

487 *"So I started acting crazy"*: Quoted in Milton Viorst, *Fire in the Streets: America in the 1960s* (New York: Simon & Schuster, 1979), 372.

487 *"I just don't see it"*: Quoted in Aram Goudsouzian, *Down to the Crossroads: Civil Rights, Black Power, and the Meredith March Against Fear* (New York: Farrar, Straus & Giroux, 2014), 84.

488 *"We want Black power!"*: "Burn Every Courthouse, Marcher Asks," *The Tennessean*, June 26, 1966.

489 *"Why not use the slogan"*: Martin Luther King Jr., *Where Do We Go from Here: Chaos or Community?* (New York: Harper & Row, 1967), 32.

490 *"For most of them"*: Stokely Carmichael, *Ready for Revolution: The Life and Struggles of Stokely Carmichael* (New York: Scribner, 2003), 513.

490 *police made no attempt to intervene*: Roy Reed, "Philadelphia, Miss., Whites and Negroes Trade Shots," *New York Times*, June 22, 1966.

490 *"his lips trembled"*: "Meredith Marchers Clash with Mississippi Whites," *Chicago Defender*, June 22, 1966.

490 *Roy Reed, covering*: Roy Reed, *Beware of Limbo Dancers* (Fayetteville: University of Arkansas Press, 2012), 152.

490 *"In this county Andrew Goodman"*: Reed, "Philadelphia, Miss., Whites and Negroes Trade Shots."

491 *"I'm not interested in power"*: David J. Garrow, *Bearing the Cross* (New York: William Morrow, 1986), 484.

492 *"This demonstrates to us"*: "Citizen King," dir. Orlando Bagwell and W. Noland Walker, *American Experience*, PBS Home Video, aired January 19, 2004.

492 *"I'll put him with his God"*: Jack Nelson, "Tear Gas Terror," *Los Angeles Times*, June 24, 1966.

492 *"You niggers want your freedom"*: Ibid.

492 *"When they touch one Black man"*: Ibid.

492 *"I just gave up"*: King quoted in "Citizen King."

492 *shot seventeen times*: "Trial Begins in Natchez," *McComb Enterprise-Journal*, December 4, 1967.

492 *lure King to Natchez*: "Jurors for Trial of Ernest Avants Still to Be Chosen," *Hattiesburg American*, December 7, 1967.

493 *crowd of about twenty-five thousand*: "Jackson Rally Ends Civil Rights March," *Jackson Clarion-Ledger*, June 27, 1966.

493 *"to make sure these niggers"*: Ibid.

493 *"turned into a nightmare"*: Gene Roberts, "12,000 End Rights March to Jackson," *New York Times*, June 27, 1966.

494 *"There's no doubt about that"*: Martin Luther King, interview by Mike Wallace, September 27, 1966, "60 Minutes Rewind," CBS, https://www.youtube.com/watch?v =_K0BWXjJv5s.

494 *7.3 percent*: "Rate of Joblessness Declines to 3.9%," *New York Times*, December 14, 1967.

494 *"The New Racism"*: "The New Racism," *Time*, July 1, 1966.

494 *"with as much vigor"*: "Black Power," *Chicago Defender*, July 2, 1966.

494 *"Don't worry about that"*: "The Strength of Mrs. King," *Los Angeles Times*, August 31, 1966.

495 *"Unfortunately, when hope"*: King, *Where Do We Go from Here*, 46.

42. "I Hope King Gets It"

497 *3:15*: "30,000 Hear Dr. King at Soldier Field Rally," *Chicago Defender*, July 11, 1966.

497 *cries of "Black power"*: "Negro Rally Turnout Small for Dr. King," *Christian Science Monitor*, July 12, 1966.

497 *visibly upset*: Spencer Leak Sr., interview with author, October 21, 2020.

497 *"We must appreciate"*: "Here's What Dr. King Told Vast Thousands," *Chicago Defender*, July 11, 1966.

498 *"Support your local police"*: "35,000 Hear King at Chicago Rally," *Baltimore Afro-American*, July 23, 1966.

498 *"We asked them"*: "Daley, King, Aides, Meet on Rights," *Chicago Tribune*, July 12, 1966.

498 *dinner at Mahalia Jackson's*: Coretta Scott King, *My Life with Martin Luther King, Jr.*, rev. ed. (New York: Henry Holt, 1993), 264.

498 *"an uncounted number of civilians"*: "Six Policemen Shot on West Side," *Chicago Tribune*, July 15, 1966.

499 *"the riot was going full swing"*: Coretta Scott King, *My Life with Martin Luther King, Jr.*, 268.

499 *"You can't charge it"*: "Battleground Chicago," CBS-TV News, July 15, 1966.

499 *"trying to convince these kids"*: Merle Miller, *Lyndon: An Oral Biography* (New York: G. P. Putnam's Sons, 1980), 653.

500 *"The King rally"*: Lyndon Baines Johnson and Richard J. Daley, July 19, 1966, conversation WH6607–02–10414–10415, Presidential Recordings Digital Edition, *Lyndon B. Johnson and Civil Rights*, vol. 2, ed. Kent B. Germany (Charlottesville: University of Virginia Press, 2014–).

501 *99,993*: Gene Roberts, "Rocks Hit Dr. King as Whites Attack March in Chicago," *New York Times*, August 6, 1966.

501 *"white power"*: "Rights Hecklers Burn Cars," *Chicago Tribune*, August 1, 1966.

501 *Those families believed*: Bernard Lafayette Jr., interview with author, March 23, 2018.

501   *"I hope King gets it"*: Richard Goldstein, "King in Chicago: Has White Power Killed Love Power?," *Village Voice*, August 11, 1966.

501   *"the zoo wants you"*: *King: A Filmed Record . . . Montgomery to Memphis*, The Martin Luther King Film Project, 1970, Kino Classics DVD, 2013.

502   *"He waited for the impact of the bullet"*: Goldstein, "King in Chicago: Has White Power Killed Love Power?"

502   *"You nigger-loving S.O.B.s!"*: "Rights Hecklers Burn Cars."

502   *"I've never seen anything like it"*: Ibid.

503   *"These 'rights' leaders"*: "The Sabotage of Chicago," *Chicago Tribune*, August 18, 1966.

503   *"Nothing has come of it"*: "Wilkins Speaks: Takes Issue with King's Chicago Crusade," *Baltimore Afro-American*, August 20, 1966.

503   *King's critics at the time*: Jesse Jackson, interview with author, March 7, 2018.

503   *"This is the moment of truth"*: "Crucial Point in Civil Rights," *Boston Globe*, August 22, 1966.

504   *"What we see shining"*: "Black Power," *New York Times*, July 31, 1966.

504   *"inspired by Martin Luther King"*: James H. Cone, interview with Terry Gross, *Fresh Air*, NPR, March 31, 2008, freshairarchive.org/segments/black-liberation-theology -its-founders-words.

505   *seventy-seven others*: "Cancel Rights Marches," *Chicago Tribune*, August 27, 1966.

505   *"You wouldn't want me"*: "Dirksen Is Adamant in Stand on Housing," *New York Times*, August 30, 1966.

506   *"unbelievable affluence"*: Quoted in James H. Cone, *Martin & Malcolm & America: A Dream or a Nightmare* (Maryknoll, N.Y.: Orbis Books, 2020), 224.

506   *"a first step in a thousand-mile journey"*: Martin Luther King Jr., "The Good Samaritan," August 28, 1966, David J. Garrow personal collection.

43. "Not an Easy Time for Me"

507   *popularity of the name Martin*: Social Security Administration, www.ssa.gov/cgi-bin /popularnames.cgi.

507   *"big and bold"*: Gene Roberts, "Civil Rights: A Turning Point," *New York Times*, September 19, 1966.

507   *"Don't you find"*: "Citizen King," dir. Orlando Bagwell and W. Noland Walker, *American Experience*, PBS Home Video, aired January 19, 2004.

507   *"They couldn't protest the war"*: Bernard Lafayette Jr., interview with author, March 23, 2018.

508   *"a rising tide of indignation"*: C. Vann Woodward, "What Happened to the Civil Rights Movement?," *Harper's Magazine*, January 1967.

509   *"Violence is a cleansing force"*: Frantz Fanon, *The Wretched of the Earth* (New York: Grove Press, 1961), 51.

509   *"There were tensions galore"*: Todd Gitlin, *The Sixties: Years of Hope, Days of Rage* (New York: Bantam, 1987), 213.

510   *"That way"*: Gene Roberts, "Civil Rights: A Turning Point."

510   *"This is not an easy time"*: D. J. R. Bruckner, "Dr. King Sees 'Desolate Days' for Rights Drive," *Los Angeles Times*, October 1, 1966.

511 *"the sharpest rebuff"*: "G.O.P. Finds '68 Outlook Brighter as It Counts Election Successes," *New York Times*, November 10, 1966.

511 *"Martin Luther King in Chicago"*: Lyndon Baines Johnson and Hubert Humphrey, telephone conversation no. 11023, November 9, 1966, LBJ Presidential Library, Austin, Tex.

511 *"Was this done for reasons"*: James Reston, "Washington: The Kennedy-Hoover Controversy," *New York Times*, December 14, 1966.

511 *assumed for years*: James Reston, "Dr. King 'Assumes' Phone Is Tapped," *New York Times*, December 15, 1966.

511 *"They got his signature"*: Lyndon Baines Johnson and Clark Clifford, telephone conversation no. 11195, December 23, 1966, LBJ Presidential Library, Austin, Tex.

512 *"The security we profess to seek"*: Robert B. Semple Jr., "Dr. King Scores Poverty Budget," *New York Times*, December 16, 1966.

512 *vast majority*: Jean M. White, "King Calls for Action on Guaranteed Income," *Washington Post*, December 16, 1966.

513 *more than a thousand American economists*: "Economists Urge Assured income," *New York Times*, May 28, 1968.

513 *"no lesser alternative"*: Robert B. Semple, "Dr. King Scores Poverty Budget."

513 *King bought a copy of . . .* Ramparts: Mark Lane and Dick Gregory, *Code Name "Zorro": The Murder of Martin Luther King, Jr.* (Englewood Cliffs, N.J.: Prentice-Hall, 1977), 53–54.

514 *"Torn flesh, splintered bones"*: William F. Pepper, "The Children of Vietnam," *Ramparts*, January 1967.

514 *"I don't see getting out"*: Martin Luther King, Stanley Levison, Andrew Young, and Cleveland Robinson, telephone conversation, February 18, 1967, FBI transcript, David J. Garrow personal collection.

515 *"collapsed"*: Gene Roberts, "Rights Drive Lags in Much of South," *New York Times*, February 6, 1967.

515 *"What you would like to accomplish"*: Christopher F. Riley to Andrew Young, March 14, 1967, David J. Garrow personal collection.

515 *"When I see our country"*: "Conferees Assail Johnson's Policy on Vietnam War," *Los Angeles Times*, February 26, 1967.

516 *"Hate America"*: "Communist Infiltration of the Southern Christian Leadership Conference," report, March 29, 1967, FBI archives.

516 *"I was telling Andy"*: Martin Luther King Jr. and Stanley Levison, March 25, 1967, transcript, FBI archives.

517 *"direct his entire efforts"*: Charles Brennan to William Sullivan, memo, March 8, 1967, FBI archives.

517 *"If I thought"*: "Clay Suffers Two Setbacks," *Louisville Courier-Journal*, March 30, 1967.

517 *"We're all Black brothers"*: "Clay, Dr. King Call Talk 'Renewal of Fellowship," *Louisville Courier-Journal*, March 30, 1967.

518 *King gave them an outline*: Martin Luther King Jr. and Stanley Levison, telephone conversation, April 8, 1967, transcript, FBI archives.

518 *160 American soldiers were dying*: "Vietnam Buildup Boosts Casualties," *Daily Capital News* (Jefferson City, Mo.), April 1, 1967.

518 *"I better not be turned down for anything"*: Jesse W. Lewis Jr., "Fighting Men Become Militant on Civil Rights, Too," *Washington Post*, April 2, 1967.

519 *"I come to this magnificent house"*: Martin Luther King Jr., "Beyond Vietnam—a Time to Break Silence," speech, Riverside Church, New York City, April 4, 1967, www .americanrhetoric.com/speeches/mlkatimetobreaksilence.htm, accessed April 26, 2022.

44. A Revolution of Values

522 *"both wasteful and self-defeating"*: "Dr. King's Error," *New York Times*, April 7, 1967.

522 *"does not speak for all"*: "Dr. King's Tragic Doctrine," *Pittsburgh Courier*, April 15, 1967.

522 *"I am troubled by this speech of yours"*: Martin Luther King Jr. and Stanley Levison, April 8, 1967, transcript, FBI archives.

523 *"take this opportunity to say"*: Martin Luther King Jr., Stanley Levison, and Harry Wachtel, telephone conversation, April 12, 1967, transcript, FBI archives.

523 *"cold anger"*: Nick Kotz, *Judgment Days: Lyndon Baines Johnson, Martin Luther King Jr., and the Laws That Changed America* (Boston: Houghton Mifflin, 2005), 376.

523 *"Why did King reject"*: Carl T. Rowan, "Martin Luther King's Tragic Decision," *Reader's Digest*, September 1967.

524 *even bigger than*: Douglas Robinson, "King Warns Cities of Summer Riots," *New York Times*, April 17, 1967.

524 *"West Coast"*: Paul Hoffman, "50,000 at San Francisco Peace Rally," *New York Times*, April 16, 1967.

524 *"elusive, formal, gracious, distant"*: David Halberstam, notes, undated, manuscript fragments, Halberstam Papers, Howard Gotlieb Archival Research Center at Boston University.

525 *"Let's put some fried chicken on that"*: Ibid.

525 *"Most Americans . . . are unconscious racists"*: Quoted in David Halberstam, "The Second Coming of Martin Luther King," *Harper's Magazine*, August 1967.

525 *"He's got one foot"*: "Which Way for the Negro," *Newsweek*, May 15, 1967.

526 *"Political power comes through"*: Wallace Turner, "A Gun Is Power, Black Panther Says," *New York Times*, May 21, 1967.

526 *seventy-six riots*: "House and Senate Committees Investigate Riots," *Congressional Quarterly Almanac*, 1967, library.cqpress.com/cqalmanac/document .php?id=cqal67–1311343.

526 *"wage guerilla war"*: "Guerrilla War Won't Work in Cities," *Tallahassee Democrat*, July 29, 1967.

526 *"the desirability of partitioning"*: Robert S. Browne, "The Case for Black Separatism," *Ramparts*, December 1967.

526 *"There is an excellent chance"*: Ibid.

527 *"Martin Luther King once had the ability"*: Andrew Kopkind, "Soul Power," *New York Review of Books*, August 24, 1967.

527 *"There were dark days"*: Martin Luther King Jr. and Harry Wachtel, telephone conversation, July 24, 1967, transcript, FBI archives.

528 *"I've been trying to think"*: Martin Luther King Jr. and Stanley Levison, telephone conversation, July 19, 1967, transcript, FBI archives.

528 *"a blind revolt against the revolting conditions"*: "King Calls for Massive Job Program to Curb Rioting," *Baltimore Sun*, July 25, 1967.

528 *"Mr. President"*: Lyndon Baines Johnson and J. Edgar Hoover, July 25, 1967, conversation WH6707–01–12005, Presidential Recordings Digital Edition, Miller Center, University of Virginia.

529 *"I think we're in more danger"*: Lyndon Baines Johnson and Dwight D. Eisenhower, November 3, 1967, telephone conversation no. 12401, transcript of sound recording, LBJ Presidential Library, Austin, Tex.

529 *"And yet"*: R. W. Apple Jr., "Vietnam: The Signs of Stalemate," *New York Times*, August 7, 1967.

529 *"dramatization of the poverty problem"*: Martin Luther King Jr. and Stanley Levison, telephone conversation, August 22, 1967, transcript, FBI archives.

530 *"He felt that, somehow"*: Coretta Scott King, interview with Charlotte Mayerson, July 16, 1968, audio recording, Smathers Library, University of Florida, Gainesville.

530 *"I get tired of going"*: Ibid.

45. Please Come to Memphis

531 *three thousand members*: "National Guard Is Placed on Standby as 'Precaution,'" *Commercial Appeal*, July 28, 1967.

531 *"1 OCTOBER 1967"*: A. W. Willis and James Lawson to Martin Luther King Jr., telegram, October 1, 1967, King Papers, Morehouse College, Atlanta.

532 *"Prevent the rise of a 'messiah'"*: FBI headquarters to all SACs, March 4, 1968, memorandum, in "Intelligence Activities and the Rights of Americans," Final Report of the U.S. Senate Select Committee to Study Governmental Operations with Respect to Intelligence Activities, April 26, 1976.

532 *"We don't have any fences"*: Martin Luther King Jr., interview with F. Lee Bailey, October 11, 1967, for *Good Company*, footage courtesy of Historic Films stock footage archive.

533 *Broadway actress*: Yolanda studied at the Actors and Writers Workshop of Atlanta, which was run by the parents of the actress Julia Roberts. When Roberts was born in 1967, at a time of financial difficulty for her parents, the Kings paid the hospital bill, according to the actress. Sydney Page, "It's True, Martin Luther King Jr. Paid the Hospital Bill When Actress Julia Roberts Was Born," *Washington Post*, October 31, 2022.

533 *"without a radical reconstruction"*: Martin Luther King Jr., "A Testament of Hope," *Playboy*, January 1969.

533 *"is the illusion of the damned"*: Ibid.

534 *The floors of the old church*: Milton Viorst, "Martin Luther King Intends to Tie the City in Knots This Spring," *Washingtonian*, February 1968.

534 *"last non-violent approach"*: "King Plans Spring March on Washington for Jobs," *Atlanta Constitution*, December 5, 1967.

534 *omitted those references*: Ibid.

535 *"If this means scorn"*: "Dr. King Lays Plans for a Lengthy D.C. Live-In," *Chicago Defender*, December 5, 1967.

535 *"Since SCLC's President"*: FBI memo, Moore to Sullivan, December 29, 1967, FBI archive.

535 *"We have permitted"*: Larry E. Temple to Lyndon Johnson, February 14, 1968, LBJ Presidential Library, Austin, Tex.

536 *"the victim of deferred dreams"*: Martin Luther King Jr., *The Trumpet of Conscience* (New York: Harper & Row, 1967), 67–68.

537 *"Personally, I cannot imagine"*: Bayard Rustin, memo drafted for Marian Logan to send to Martin Luther King Jr., undated, in *I Must Resist: Bayard Rustin's Life in Letters*, ed. Michael Long (San Francisco: City Lights Books, 2012), 343–44.

537 *"faith venture"*: Quoted in David J. Garrow, *Bearing the Cross: Martin Luther King, Jr., and the Southern Christian Leadership Conference* (New York: William Morrow, 1986), 601.

537 *"We weren't convinced"*: Stoney Cooks, "Dr. King's Last Birthday," *Atlanta*, January 1984.

538 *"terribly distressed"*: Coretta Scott King, *My Life, My Love, My Legacy*, as told to Barbara Reynolds (New York: Henry Holt, 2017), 151.

538 *"I certainly saw the exhaustion"*: Quoted in Garrow, *Bearing the Cross*, 602.

538 *"He talked about death"*: Andrew Young, interview with Tom Dent, August 20–21, 1980, audio recording, Amistad Research Center, Tulane University, New Orleans, La.

538 *"worried . . . nervous"*: Ralph Abernathy testimony, August 14, 1978, U.S. House of Representatives, *Investigation of the Assassination of Martin Luther King, Jr.*, 95th Congress, 2nd session.

538 *pointed to a rock*: Ibid.

539 *"drum-major instinct"*: James M. Washington, ed., *A Testament of Hope* (New York: HarperOne, 1986), 259–67.

540 *"We have not gotten off the ground"*: Martin Luther King Jr., minutes from SCLC Action Committee meeting, February 11, 1968, David J. Garrow personal collection.

540 *"If we cannot do it"*: Ibid.

540 *took his boys*: Coretta Scott King, *My Life, My Love, My Legacy*, 156.

541 *"I'd feel like a bird in a cage"*: Garrow, *Bearing the Cross*, 607.

541 *even more urgent*: James Lawson, interview with author, October 26, 2018.

541 *Lawson still believed in King*: James Lawson, interview with author, June 12, 2018.

541 *"I knew he would come"*: Ibid.

541 *"ghetto informants"*: Garrow, *Bearing the Cross*, 607.

541 *"There was a determination to stop us"*: Young, interview with Dent.

542 *"I must say I'm very disappointed"*: Carl Greenberg, "Dr. King Asks Johnson Defeat, May Back Another Democrat," *Los Angeles Times*, March 17, 1968.

542 *"The thing I feared"*: Doris Kearns Goodwin, *Lyndon Johnson and the American Dream* (New York: St. Martin's Press, 1991), 343.

542 *four Black teenage boys*: "King to Lend Vocal Support in Strike Rally," *Commercial Appeal*, March 17, 1968.

543 *"black power people from Chicago"*: Ibid.

543 *urging all Black people*: "King Urges Work Stoppage by Negroes to Back Strike," *Commercial Appeal*, March 19, 1968.

543 *become a racial protest*: "Negro Pastors Take Reins as Garbage Strike Leaders in Switch to Racial Pitch," *Commercial Appeal*, March 12, 1968.

543 *"bitterly disappointed"*: Harry Belafonte, interview with author, April 4, 2017.

544 *A local funeral home*: Ralph David Abernathy, *And the Walls Came Tumbling Down: An Autobiography* (New York: Harper & Row, 1989), 417.

544 *the white media blamed King*: Andrew Young, interview with author, January 19, 2019.

545 *questioned King's ability*: "Mini-Riot in Memphis," *New York Times*, March 30, 1968.

545 *"wrecked his reputation"*: "King's Credibility Gap," *Commercial Appeal*, March 30, 1968.

545 *"Martin was real depressed"*: Juanita Abernathy, interview with author, August 2, 2018.

545 *"Can't y'all afford a whole sofa"*: Ibid.

545 *"He was wrestling with depression"*: Jesse Jackson, interview with author, March 7, 2018.

545 *hunger strike*: Ibid.

545 *"He really opened up"*: Young, interview with Dent.

545 *"What's wrong, Martin?"*: Abernathy, *And the Walls Came Tumbling Down*, 425.

546 *"There was nothing special"*: Coretta Scott King, interview with Charlotte Mayerson, July 16, 1968, audio recording, Smathers Library, University of Florida Library. Gainesville.

546 *"Well, looks like they won't"*: Abernathy, *And the Walls Came Tumbling Down*, 428.

547 *"My whole future depends on it"*: Marc Perrusquia, "Leading Up to 6:01," *Memphis Commercial-Appeal*, March 28, 2018.

547 *He phoned Coretta*: Coretta Scott King, *My Life with Martin Luther King, Jr.*, 290.

547 *in his pajamas*: Bernard Lafayette Jr., interview with author, March 23, 2018.

547 *"The people who are here"*: Ibid., 431.

549 *Abernathy rose from his seat*: Abernathy, *And the Walls Came Tumbling Down*, 433.

549 *"rather pleadingly"*: Dorothy Cotton, *If Your Back's Not Bent: The Role of the Citizenship Education Program in the Civil Rights Movement* (New York: Atria Books, 2012), 264.

549 *Martin started the call*: "The Autobiography of Daddy King as Told to Edward A. Jones" (unpublished manuscript, August 1973), 169.

549 *big dinner*: Ibid.

550 *King leaned over the railing*: Billy Kyles, interview with Alice Bernstein, 2016, www.youtube.com/watch?v=5Jqp8-1Au7A.

551 *"Why don't you put on your topcoat"*: "Doctors Worked Hard Trying to Save King," *Memphis Commercial Appeal*, April 5, 1968.

551 *"OK, I will"*: Ibid.

551 *A white man, a stranger*: Ibid.

551 *"I hope the son of a bitch"*: Paul Letersky, *The Director: My Years Assisting J. Edgar Hoover* (New York: Scribner, 2021), 84.

551 *His eyes were closed*: Ibid.

552 *"Every racist"*: Lawrence Van Gelder, "Dismay in Nation," *New York Times*, April 5, 1968.

Epilogue

553 *"I understand"*: Dexter Scott King, with Ralph Wiley, *Growing Up King* (New York: Warner Books, 2003), 48.

554 *"Fair housing for all"*: "President Signs Rights Bill," *Washington Post*, April 12, 1968.

554 *"Starving a child is violence"*: Judith Martin and Carolyn Lewis, "Coretta King: From His Footsteps to Her Own," *Washington Post*, June 16, 1968.

555 *"On the national holiday"*: "Reagan's Doubts on Dr. King Disclosed," *New York Times*, October 22, 1983.

556   *"and they weren't very attractive"*: Jacqueline Trescott, "The New Coretta Scott King," *Washington Post*, January 15, 1978.

556   *The intimate letters*: Brian Feagans, "King Love Letters Caught in Legal Fight," *Atlanta Journal-Constitution*, October 14, 2008.

556   *almost a thousand cities and towns*: Sweta Tiwari and Shrinidhi Ambinakudige, "Streetscapes and Stereotyping: Streets Named After Martin Luther King, Jr., and the Geographies of Racial Identity,"*GeoJournal* 87, no. 1 (April 2022): 921–34.

556   *More than one hundred public schools*: Derek H. Alderman, "School Names as Cultural Arenas: The Naming of Public Schools After Martin Luther King, Jr.," *Urban Geography* 23, no. 7 (November 2002): 601–26.

556   *poverty and segregation rates*: Tiwari and Ambinakudige, "Streetscapes and Stereotyping."

557   *philosophical and intellectual contributions*: For an examination of King's political philosophy, see *To Shape a New World: Essays on the Political Philosophy of Martin Luther King, Jr.*, ed. Tommie Shelby and Brandon M. Terry (Cambridge, Mass.: Belknap Press of Harvard University Press, 2018).

557   *"Our very survival"*: Martin Luther King Jr., *Where Do We Go from Here: Chaos or Community?* (New York: Harper & Row, 1967), 181.

Acknowledgments: Beloved Community

"What makes Martin Luther King different from Jesus?"

I thought it was a joke at first.

It was the morning of June 17, 2015, and I was eating breakfast with Dick Gregory, the legendary activist and comedian, in a Washington, D.C., hotel restaurant.

Gregory didn't wait for me to answer his question.

"What makes King different from Jesus? Jesus is hearsay. Don't mean it didn't happen, but there's *film* of King. Can't nobody change nothing. Who would ever believe? When King was shot, he was the most hated man on the planet . . . Now he's the most beloved!"

Who would ever believe?

At the time of that interview, I was at work on a biography of Muhammad Ali. King wasn't on my radar. But Gregory's comment shook me. It wasn't just that King had been captured on film. It wasn't just that King's journey really was unbelievable, one of the most unbelievable and heroic journeys in all American history. It was something else: it was the fact that Dick Gregory *knew* King and knew him well. And so did a lot of other people. People I could interview—if I hurried.

I started with the oldest and most famous: Harry Belafonte, John Lewis, C. T. Vivian, Jesse Jackson, Juanita Abernathy, Andrew Young, Harris Wofford, James Lawson.

Between 2015 and 2022, despite a global pandemic, I interviewed more than two hundred people. Reverend Lawson became a teacher to me; we spoke almost every week for months. Dr. June Dobbs Butts, one of King's close friends from childhood, became not only a teacher but a dear friend. We spoke dozens of times, over the phone and in person. King's older sister, Christine, answered questions through her son, Isaac Newton Farris Jr. King's nieces and nephews shared their memories. King's Montgomery lawyer, Fred Gray, who was still practicing law as of 2022, greeted me at his office in Tuskegee, Alabama, at the corner of Fred Gray Street and East Rosa Parks Avenue. King's Montgomery barber, Nelson Malden, offered me a haircut before sizing me up and deeming my shiny head a hopeless cause. Willie Mackey King, the woman who typed King's *Letter from a Birmingham Jail*, showed me the Rolodex she had kept on her desk at her SCLC office. The Reverend Bernard Lafayette Jr. demonstrated the various vocal techniques used by Black Baptist preachers of his generation. Juanita Abernathy and I dined at Paschal's Restaurant in Atlanta under a framed photograph of her late husband, Ralph. Oh, and Mavis Staples sang to me.

It's been a blessing, one of the greatest of my life, to learn from people who not only lived through history but also bravely shaped it.

"I think a new book is necessary . . . A good book," Reverend Lawson told me in our first conversation.

Shortly before June Dobbs Butts passed away in 2019, I shared with her the first ten chapters of my manuscript. She emailed me days later to say she had read my chapters many times. "Of course I cried at points, was surprised at times . . . but there were also times when I winced," she wrote. "You have great courage, my friend, and I think M.L. would approve of you as his scribe."

I realize that Butts, a trained therapist, may have been trying to boost my confidence. She and I discussed at length the enormous responsibility that comes with writing a biography—especially a biography of a figure as beloved and influential as King. When I approached other friends and colleagues of King for interviews, many of them challenged me: Why another book about King? What are your intentions? You knew him, I replied, we don't. We need to tell his story again. We need the real King, not the candy-coated one.

I was fortunate to begin this book before the COVID-19 pandemic and to conduct many of my interviews in person. When the pandemic hit, I was fortunate to find most of my interviewees stuck at home and eager to talk on the phone.

This book is also based on tens of thousands of pages of newly released and newly discovered archival documents. In the past four years, the FBI has made public thousands of pages of new memos on King, including transcripts of electronic surveillance of King and his closest associates. Some of the most lurid details of those transcripts have been reported in the press, but this is the first King biography to place them in the context of King's life, to show the full extent and tenacity of the FBI's campaign to destroy the nation's most influential Black activist, and to show the devastating emotional effect the FBI's tactics had on King.

This is the first King biography written with access to the remarkable and enormous collection of documents amassed by L. D. Reddick, King's unofficial archivist, who worked and traveled with King throughout much of his career. I'm grateful to the Schomburg Center for Research in Black Culture for preserving the papers and making them available, and I'm especially grateful to my friend Lori Azim for her brilliant work in exploring, organizing, and analyzing those papers. Thanks to everyone at the Schomburg, especially Mary Yearwood, Cheryl Beredo, Lauren Stark, Barrye Brown, and Alexsandra Mitchell.

This is also the first biography to make use of the audiotapes Coretta Scott King recorded months after her husband's death as she worked with an editor on her first memoir. I listened to her gentle, confident voice as she described everything from her first date with her future husband to the preparations for his funeral. It is my hope that this book presents the nuanced portrait of Coretta Scott King that has so often proved elusive. She was every bit as brave as her husband. At times, her activism led his. In addition, we must recognize the invisible labor—the childcare, the organizing, counseling, cooking, cleaning, suit-pressing, all the necessary and unacknowledged work of running and supporting a movement—that fell to her and other women.

Some of my other favorite archival finds include an unpublished autobiography of Martin Luther King Sr., along with transcripts of the taped interviews that went into composing the manuscript; an unpublished autobiography of Hosea Williams; an unpublished biography of Ralph Abernathy by L. D. Reddick; David Halberstam's notes from his travels with King; and thousands of pages of interviews compiled during the Montgomery bus boycotts by researchers from Fisk University.

I spent countless hours listening to recordings made in the White House by John F. Kennedy and Lyndon Baines Johnson. I also had access to the papers of Mildred Stegall, secretary to President Johnson, who kept copies of J. Edgar Hoover's relentless flood of King-related memos to the White House. I read and listened to hundreds of hours of oral histories by civil rights activists and politicians. I am forever grateful to the librarians, archivists, researchers, and family members who helped make these materials available. Thanks, especially, to the Martin Luther King, Jr., Research and Education Institute at Stanford University; the Morehouse College Martin Luther King Jr. Collection; the Howard Gotlieb Archival Research Center at Boston University; the National Archives and Record Administration in College Park, Maryland; the Library of Congress; the John F. Kennedy Presidential Library; the Lyndon Johnson Presidential Library; the Wisconsin Historical Society; Emory University; and the University of North Carolina at Chapel Hill.

This book has benefited more than I can describe from the wisdom of writers and historians who have chronicled King and the civil rights movement, many of whom shared their research materials, answered my many questions, and read some or all of my manuscript. David J. Garrow let me spend days in his kitchen, poring through his research materials, including his audiotaped interviews. He also answered an endless stream of questions, fact-checked my manuscript, suggested new avenues of research, and introduced me to other King scholars. Jeanne Theoharis and I talked for hours, discussing ideas, psychoanalyzing key characters, and exploring new paths of inquiry. Taylor Branch, David Levering Lewis, and the late Nick Kotz offered expert guidance and made their research materials available. The scholar Derryn Moten introduced me to key people in Montgomery and read parts of my manuscript. Lewis V. Baldwin tutored me on King's religious development and read and suggested improvements on several of my chapters. I have received coaching from many other writers and scholars, including Lauren Araiza, Timuel Black, Douglas Brinkley, Katherine Mellen Charron, Patrick Duff, Gerald Early, Glenn T. Eskew, Michael Ezra, Chuck Fager, Beverly Gage, Nassir Ghaemi, Drew D. Hansen, Paul Hendrick, Randal Maurice Jelks, Peniel Joseph, Michael Long, David Margolick, Kevin McGruder, Danielle L. McGuire, Keith D. Miller, W. Jason Miller, Patrick Parr, Marc Perrusquia, Gary Pomerantz, Dick Reavis, Barbara Reynolds, Tom Ricks, Hampton Sides, Tavis Smiley, and Milton Viorst.

I am deeply grateful to Dr. Clayborne Carson, former director of the Martin Luther King, Jr., Research and Education Institute. Thanks also to the new director of the institute, Lerone A. Martin, and his entire team, especially Tenisha Hart Armstrong. At Morehouse College, thanks to Dr. Vicki Crawford, Aileen Dodd, and Lawrence Carter. At the LBJ Presidential Library, thanks to Allen Fisher and Ian Frederick-Rothwell. In Henry County, Georgia, thanks to Cooper Keller, Jim Marshall, Gene Morris, and Alfonso Thomas. I'm grateful to Phillip Cunningham at the Amistad Research Center; Cynthia Lewis at the King Center in Atlanta; Jeff Flannery at the Library of Congress; Carl Van Ness at the University of Florida; Jim Baggett at the Birmingham Public Library; Wayne Coleman at the Birmingham Civil Rights Institute; and Taylor McNeilly at the University of Richmond library. Thanks to the journalist Steve Smith for his work in turning FBI surveillance transcripts into easily searchable documents.

Thanks to all those who read and commented on some or all of the manuscript: Laurie Abraham, Lori Azim, Dick Babcock, Marci Bailey, A. J. Baime, Lewis Baldwin, Joel Berg, Jean Marie Brown, June Dobbs Butts, Joseph Epstein, David J. Garrow, Bryan Gruley, Peniel Joseph, Tom Junod, Robert Kurson, Ethan Michaeli, Shannon Luders-Manuel, Lerone A. Martin, Joshua Prager, Bob Spitz, Gabriel Tallent, Jeanne Theoharis, and Lillian Young. No one pushed me harder, word by word, emotion by emotion, than my writer pal Charlie Newton. I'm forever grateful. Special thanks also to Dan Cattau, a wonderful friend and editor, who read and edited chapters long before they were ready for the rest of the world.

Thanks, also, to Don DeLillo, whose novella *Pafko at the Wall* inspired my approach to the chapter on King's "I Have a Dream" speech. DeLillo was kind enough to read the chapter and endorse my homage.

Thanks to Michele Soulli for heroic research on the King family's genealogy. Thanks to my fact-checkers: Amy Balmuth, Olivia Williams, and Andy Young. Thanks to Charles Whitaker, dean of my beloved Medill School at Northwestern University. Thanks to all those who helped me with archival research: Lindon Assaye, Edward Burnette, Jake Eig, Siena Ballotta Garman, Sonia Gomez, Kira Jones, Tomer Keysar, Harrison Liao, Kate Mabus, Johavy Mendoza Meza, Nirmal Mulaikal, Sophia Nelson, Leah Parson, Bonnie Rowan, Trina Ryan, Sofia Sanchez, and Frazine Taylor.

Thanks to those who helped in ways too numerous to mention but too important to forget: Seth Abraham, Jeff Aeder, Douglas Alden, Ben Allaway, Jenny Belk, Brian Berg, Rabbi Daniel Burg, Bob Bonstein, Kwame Brathwaite, Richard Cahan, Airco Caravan, Matthew Charlton, Aaron Cohen, Lynn Cothren, Will Dahlberg, Dr. Barbara Williams Emerson, Victor Eskridge, Steve Fiffer, Gabe Fuentes, Jeremy Gershfeld, Oscar Gershfeld, Linda Ginzel, Clarence Goodman, Bethel Habte, Pastor Chris Harris, Bob Herguth, Valli Herman, Karen Gray Houston, Ron Jackson, Valerie Jackson, Marshall Kaplan, Bob Kazel, John Klima, Joe Lauro, Jane Leavy, Kate Lemay, Mike Lennon, Andrew Levison, Johnny Mack, David Maraniss, Joe Mathewson, Rossy Mendez, Liz Miller-Gershfeld, Marc Morial, Derek Mosley, Abdur-Rahman Muhammad, Walter Naegle, Greg Oates, Bill O'Driscoll, Sridhar Pappu, Jeff Pearlman, Lisa Pollak, Saafir Rabb, Renee Rosensteel, Tracy Sefl, Murad Siam, Rabbi Michael Siegel, Don Terry, Eric Tidwell, Heidi Trilling, William Wachtel, Harry Weinger, Mike Williams, and Jeff Winikow.

Thanks to my friends at Florentine Films, especially Ken Burns, Sarah Burns, Stephanie Jenkins, and David McMahon.

Special thanks to Isaac Newton Farris Jr. and his mother, Christine King Farris, as well as Kwame Abernathy and the entire Abernathy family.

Thanks to my agent and friend David Black; to Susan Raihofer and Sarah Smith at the David Black Agency; to my TV and film agent, Lucy Stille; to Alexander Star, my wonderful editor at Farrar, Straus and Giroux. At FSG, thanks to Janet Renard, Stephen Weil, Ian Van Wye, Janine Barlow, and everyone else who helped bring this book to life. Thanks also to Colin Dickerman, the editor who launched the book.

My understanding of fairness and love began with lessons from my parents, Phyllis and David Eig, who continue to teach and inspire me every day. I'm eternally grateful to have such a loving and thoughtful extended family, including brother Matthew Eig and his wife, Penny; brother Lewis Eig and his wife, Judy; and Jake Eig, Ben Eig, Hayden Eig, Gail Tescher, Don Tescher, SuAnn Tescher, Jonathan Tescher, Lily Brent, and Nava Brent Tescher.

My children—Lillian Eig, Lola Eig, and Jeffery Schams—never fail to fill me with joy and hope for the future. This book is dedicated to Jeffery, one of the kindest and bravest people I know. In 1997, when a friend asked me to take over for him as a mentor to a seven-year-old in the Big Brother program, I agreed, but with more than a little reluctance. Years later, when Jeffery's mother died, he became a part of our family. Today, I couldn't be prouder to call him my son.

When Martin Luther King Jr. wrote his first book, he dedicated it to Coretta, his "beloved wife and co-worker." I like that. My beloved wife and co-worker is Jennifer Tescher. There are not enough words or pages to properly thank and praise her. Jen inspires me every day with her passion for justice, her curiosity, and her willingness to do the work of making the world a better place for all.

INTERVIEW LIST

Donzaleigh Abernathy

Juandalynn Abernathy

Juanita Abernathy

Kwame Abernathy

Aloja Airewele

Ben Alloway

William G. Anderson

Lauren Araiza

Robert Avery

Richard Azbell

Jim Baggett

Lewis V. Baldwin

Gene Barge

Reggie Barrett

Rachel Been

Harry Belafonte

Betty Belk

J. Blanton Belk

James Beshai

Charles Black

Timuel Black

Janice Rothschild Blumberg

Laura Ward Branca

Taylor Branch

Jean Martin Brayboy

David Brewington

Jane Briddell

Al Brinson

Tyrone Brooks

Amos Brown

Cecil Brown

Irene Brown

Edward M. Burke

Joyce Butler

Mitchell Butler

June Dodd Butts

Billy Carter

Sandranette Chenet

Xernona Clayton

James Clyburn

Wayne Coleman

D. Louise Cook

Stoney Cooks

Lynn Cothren

Courtland Cox

Vicki Crawford

Doris Crenshaw

David Dennis

St. John Dixon

Aileen Dodd

Bernardine Dohrn

Bruce Dozier

Avi Dresner

Eugene Duffy

LaVerne Eagleson

Gerald Early

Peter Edelman

Kirby Edmonds

Elizabeth Edmonson

Locksley Edmonson

Joseph Ellwanger

Barbara Williams Emerson

Glenn T. Eskew

Victor Eskridge

Charles Fager

Louis Farrakhan

Christine King Farris

Isaac Newton Farris Jr.

Jeff Flannery

David J. Garrow

Everett Gendler

Mary Gendler

Nassir Ghaemi

Edward "Woody" Goldberg

Jerrold Goldstein

Brenda Goodman

Clarence Goodman

Robert Graetz

Jeannie Graetz

Benjamin Graham Jr.

Ronald Graham

Fred Gray

Glencile Greenlea

Dick Gregory

Gordon "Gunny" Gundrum

Drew D. Hansen

Aljosie Harding

Charles Hardy

Darrien Harper

Autumn Harper

Michael Harris

Jared Harrison

David Heim

Susannah Heschel

Ben Himmelfarb

Richard Hirsch

Carole Hoover

Rachelle Horowitz

Tom Houck

Karen Gray Houston

Jeannette Hunt

Jawana Jackson

Jesse Jackson

Valerie Jackson

Bennett Johnson

Leroy Johnson

Clarence Jones

Stephanie Lynn Jones

Robert Jordan Jr.

Peniel Joseph

Patrick Joyce

Haig Kalbian

Cooper Keller

Randall Kennedy

Alveda King

James Albert King Jr.

Joel King Jr.

Willie Mackey King

Rick Kittles

Jane Klain

Bernard Kleina

Harcourt Klinefelter

Edward Kosner

Nick Kotz

Bernard Lafayette Jr.

James Lawson

Spencer Leak Jr.

Spencer Leak Sr.

Pierre Leval

Andrew Levison

Cynthia Lewis

David Levering Lewis

John Lewis

Theodore Life

Michael G. Long

Johnny Mack

Nelson Malden

Willodean Malden

Andrew Manis

Jim Marshall

Lerone A. Martin

Martin Marty

Sam Massell

Anthony McDade

James S. McFadden

John McKnight

Taylor McNeilly

Cameron McWhirter

Miriam Melegrito

James Meredith

Peg Michels

Heather Middleton

James H. Miller

Keith Miller

W. Jason Miller

Lawrence Montgomery

Valda Harris Montgomery

Michael Moon

Marc Morial

Sybil Morial

Gene Morris

Edwina Moss

Otis Moss Jr.

Derryn Moten

Abdur-Rahman Muhammad

Walter Naegle

Sara Paretsky

Patrick Parr

Jimmy Patterson

Phillip Henry Pitts

Janet Poppendieck

Stanley Pottinger

Alvin Poussaint

Georgia Davis Powers

Dick Reavis

Barbara Reynolds

Lowell Riley

Tim Rooney

Don Rose

Walter Rybeck

Steve Schapiro

Arlie Schardt

Markus Schmidt

Allen Secher

Hampton Sides

Jean Moore Smiley

Mavis Staples

Frank Stewart

Carol Taylor

Jeanne Theoharis

Alfonso Thomas

Althea Thomas

Mia Tramz

Chris Vail

Milton Viorst

C. T. Vivian

John Vorperian

William Wachtel

Theresa Ann Walker

Jim Wall

Fred Ward

Harry Weinger

Francine White

Baruch Whitehead

O. Lawton Wilkerson

Rosalind Withers

Harris Wofford

Calvin Woods

Andrew Young

Index

A Note About the Author

Jonathan Eig is the bestselling author of *Ali: A Life*, winner of a 2018 PEN America Literary Award and a finalist for the Mark Lynton History Prize. He also served as a senior consulting producer for the PBS series *Muhammad Ali*. His first book, *Luckiest Man: The Life and Death of Lou Gehrig*, won the Casey Award. Eig's books have been translated into more than a dozen languages and have been listed among the best of the year by *The New York Times*, *The Washington Post*, and *The Wall Street Journal*. He lives in Chicago with his wife and children.